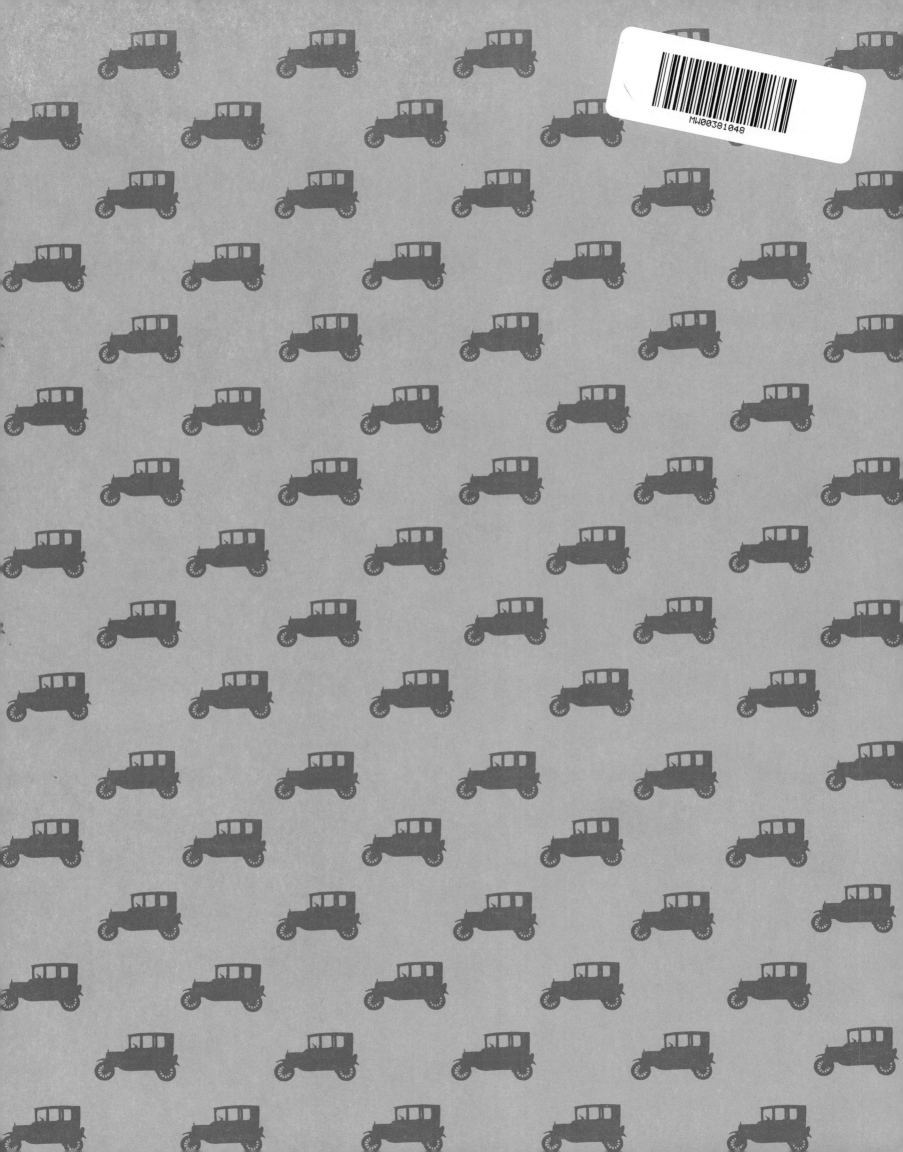

Manufactured in Yugoslavia.
10 9 8 7 6 5 4 3 2 1

ISBN: 0-88176-639-9

Library of Congress Catalog Card Number: 90-61115

CREDITS

Photography
The editors gratefully acknowledge the photographers who helped make this book possible. They are listed below, along with the page number(s) of their photos:

Les Bidrawn—46, 67 (top), 84-85. **Henry Austin Clark, Jr.**—19 (bottom), 22 (bottom), 24 (top), 27, 30, 32 (bottom), 34 (bottom), 35, 41 (top), 48, 48 (top, middle), 61-62, 67 (bottom left), 68, 70 (top), 76 (bottom), 80 (bottom), 81 (right), 89 (top), 97 (top), 107, 111 (bottom), 116 (bottom right). **Gary L. Cook**—193 (top left). **Doug Dalton**—185 (top). **Roland Flessner**—479 (upper middle), 496 (top). **Ford Motor Company, Technical Photographic Department, Charles Ordowski, Mike Golic**—6-19, 20-21, 24 (bottom), 25-26, 31 (bottom), 33 (bottom), 39 (bottom, left and right), 40 (middle), 41 (bottom), 47, 49 (bottom), 51-57, 60, 63-64, 66, 67 (bottom right), 69 (left), 70 (bottom), 71 (left), 72, 73 (right), 76 (top), 80 (top), 81 (left), 83, 86, 89 (bottom right), 93 (middle, bottom), 94 (top), 95 (bottom), 96, 97 (middle bottom), 98-102, 103 (top), 112, 115 (top, bottom), 117, 121 (upper middle right, lower middle, bottom), 122 (left), 123 (bottom left), 126 (top), 127, 129 (left), 130 (middle, bottom), 131-134, 135 (bottom), 136, 138 (bottom left), 140 (bottom), 141, 142 (middle, bottom), 143, 144 (right), 145, 146 (top, bottom left), 147-148, 149 (bottom), 151 (top), 155-156, 157 (top), 159 (top), 161, 162 (bottom), 163, 165, 167, 168 (bottom), 169, 170 (top), 171 (top), 172 (top), 173, 175-177, 180 (top), 186-189, 190 (top), 194 (top left), 194 (bottom right), 195 (top), 202 (top), 208 (bottom), 209 (top right, bottom), 211 (top), 212-213, 214 (top) 215 (middle, bottom), 216-217, 219 (bottom), 220, 211 (middle, bottom), 223 (top), 225, 227 (top), 228-229, 281 (top), 232, 233 (top), 234-237, 238 (bottom), 239-245, 247-251, 252 (bottom), 254 (bottom), 255-260, 261 (top), 263 (top), 265, 265, 269-275, 280 (top), 281-285, 287-289, 292 (middle, bottom), 293-295, 298, 299 (top, bottom right), 300-301, 307-312, 313 (top), 316-321, 325 (bottom), 326-332, 333 (bottom), 334-337, 341-432, 434-478, 479 (top, lower middle, bottom), 480-495, 496 (bottom), 497-509. **Henry Ford Museum**—115 (middle). **Thomas Glatch**—75, 80 (middle), 87 (bottom), 106 (bottom), 113 (bottom), 159 (bottom left), 207, 290, 333 (top). **Eddie Goldberger**—108 (bottom). **David Gooley**—182. **Sam Griffith**—90 (bottom), 91 (bottom), 114, 128 (bottom left), 174, 192 (middle), 302. **Jerry Heasley**—292 (top). **Bud Juneau**—36 (top), 37, 40 (top), 45, 74, 110 (bottom right), 137 (top, middle), 153 (bottom), 205 (bottom), 215 (top), 263 (bottom), 296, 306. **Milton Gene Kieft**—22 (top, center), 65, 87 (top), 192 (bottom), 199 (top), 200 (bottom), 201 (top), 222, 223 (bottom), 268. **Lloyd Koenig**—164, 166. **Dan Lyons**—38, 43, 90 (top), 91 (top), 92 (top), 94 (bottom),

95 (top), 103 (bottom), 105 (middle), 119, 135 (middle), 160, 170 (bottom), 171 (bottom), 181, 262, 264 (top). **Vince Manocchi**—29, 32 (top), 33 (top), 42, 58-59, 106 (middle), 130 (top), 158, 162 (top), 178 (bottom), 191, 192 (top), 196 (top), 197, 199 (bottom), 201 (middle), 202 (bottom), 203, 209 (top left), 210, 211 (middle, bottom), 218, 226, 227 (bottom), 230 (bottom), 231. **Jack Markley**—159 (bottom right). **Doug Mitchel**—105 (top, bottom left), 106 (top), 108 (top), 110 (bottom left), 111 (top), 113 (top), 116 (top right, bottom left), 118, 120, 121 (top, upper middle left), 125, 126 (bottom left), 128 (top, bottom right), 135 (top), 138 (top), 140 (top), 141 (top), 144 (top), 149 (top), 150, 154, 157 (bottom), 180 (bottom), 193 (top right, bottom), 194 (bottom left), 195 (bottom right), 196 (bottom), 198, 221 (top), 224, 233 (top), 238 (top), 252, 253, 254 (top), 261 (middle, bottom), 277-279, 280 (bottom). **Mike Mueller**—246. **David Patryas**—183. **Ken Ruddock**—69 (right), 71 (right), 73 (left), 105 (bottom right), 110 (top), 123 (right), 126 (bottom right), 129 (right), 137 (bottom), 139 (bottom), 144 (left), 146 (bottom right), 151 (bottom), 152, 153 (top), 172 (bottom), 180 (bottom). **Robert Sorgatz**—184 (top). **Richard Spiegelman**—31 (top), 39 (top), 93 (top), 168, 185 (bottom), 291. **David Temple**—206. **Bob Tenney**—201 (bottom), 204, 205 (top), 219 (top). **Jim Thompson**—313 (bottom). **Nicky Wright**—88, 89 (bottom left), 92 (bottom), 122 (right), 123 (middle left), 124, 138 (bottom right), 139 (top), 178 (top), 179, 194 (top right), 195 (bottom left), 200 (top), 214 (middle, bottom), 264 (bottom), 266-267, 276, 286, 299 (bottom), 305, 314-315, 322-324, 325 (top), 339-340, 433.

Owners

Special thanks to the owners of the Fords featured in this book for their enthusiastic cooperation. They are listed below, along with their automobiles and the page number(s) on which the cars appear:

Roy and Shirley Andrews—'64 Thunderbird: 261 (bottom). **Lynn Atkins**—'31 Model A: 95 (top). **Lynn Augustine**—'56 Crown Victoria: 197 (bottom); '57 Wagon: 211 (middle). **John Baker, Sr.**—'53 Pace Car: 181. **Art Banducci**—'11 Model T Touring: 37. **Samuel R. Bardone**—'46 Super DeLuxe: 135 (top). **Paul Batista**—'55 Thunderbird: 191. **Bob Baumgardner**—'59 Skyliner: 224. **Richard Bayer**—'29 Model A: 87 (bottom); '34 DeLuxe: 106 (bottom). **Tony Begley**—'67 Fairlane: 290. **Spencer Bing**—'36 Convertible: 113 (top left); '36 Fordor: 113 (top right). **Norman and Joyce Booth**—'42 DeLuxe: 130 (top). **John Breda**—'65 Thunderbird: 268. **W. Parker Brown**—'22 Model T Fire Runabout: 65. **Jerry Butak**—'66 Thunderbird: 278. **Barbra Walker Cadena**—'60 Thunderbird: 231 (bottom). **Nelson Cardadeiro**—'69 Mustang: 306. **Dean and Wanda Casey**—'66 Mustang: 276. **Jackie and Shana Cerrito**—'54 Customline: 185 (top). **Jerry**

Charter—'55 Crown Victoria: 193 (bottom). **Bill Cline**—'35 DeLuxe: 110 (bottom). **Charles and Marie Cobb**—'65 Mustang: 305. **Edward and Arlene Cobb**—'52 Convertible: 160; '53 Convertible: 170 (bottom), 171 (bottom). **D.J. Colaniro**—'37 Sedan: 116 (bottom left). **Kenneth Jay Coleman**—'62 Galaxie: 246. **Louis Crojanac**—'28 Model A: 80 (middle). **Officer R.T. Cruz, Community Service Division, Houston, Texas Police Department**—'52 Customline: 166. **Gail and John Dalmolin**—'54 Convertible: 184. **Ted Davidson and Herb Rothman**—'59 Thunderbird: 227 (bottom). **Ray and Nancy Deitke**—'56 Fairlane: 201 (top). **Terry E. Dinkel**—'53 Victoria: 178 (top), 179. **Kim Dobbins**—'09 Model T Touring: 29; '10 Model T Touring: 32-33; '34 DeLuxe: 106 (middle). **Gladys Duzell**—'64 Sunliner: 263 (bottom). **Lloyd Duzell**—'41 Sedan Coupe: 128 (top right). **Steve Engeman**—'70 Torino: 313. **Vic and Cathy Falone**—'64 Falcon: 264 (top). **Everett Faulkner**—'59 Thunderbird: 226. **Don and Sue Fenning**—'55 Club Sedan: 194 (bottom left). **Ray P. Fisher**—'73 Mustang: 339. **Tom Franks**—'55 Customline: 194 (bottom left). **Terry Freilage**—'41 DeLuxe: 126 (bottom left). **Bob Fruehe**—'13 Model T Touring: 42; '19 Model T: 58-59. **Glenn Gangestad**—'53 Convertible: 174. **Louise Gibino**—'68 Mustang: 296. **Charles Giese**—'30 Model A: 90 (bottom), 91 (bottom). **Jim Goldheimer**—'55 Convertible: 192. **Frank Gonsalves**—'26 Model T Fordor: 74. **Dick Guess**—'55 Fairlane: 193 (top left). **Gary Gumushian**—'73 Mustang: 340. **Gerald S. Hansen**—'51 Victoria: 154. **Roger Hayes**—'57 Thunderbird: 205 (bottom). **Jim Hearn**—'13 Model T Speedster: 40. **Charles Hilbert**—'58 Fairlane: 218. **George Holterman**—'60 Starliner: 233 (top). **David Horn**—'54 Skyliner: 183. **Tom Howard**—'57 Convertible: 208 (top); '57 Fairlane: 210 (middle). **Doug and Teresa Hvidston**—'71 Mustang: 324; '84 Mustang: 433. **Frank Iaccino**—'12 Model T: 38. **Fred and Diane Ives**—'55 Wagon: 194 (top right). **Jim Jeram**—'30 Model A: 90 (top). **Haward C. Jezsop**—'56 Crown Victoria: 199 (bottom). **Dick Kainer**—'64 Hardtop: 262. **Winfred and Betty Keep**—'299 (bottom). **Jonnie Keller**—'29 Model A: 87 (top). **Edward Keshen**—'56 Convertible: 198. **L. Wayne Kidd**—'34 Fire Truck: 106 (top right). **Vernon A. King, Jr.**—'30 Model A: 92 (top). **Donald Kish, Sr.**—'46 Crown Victoria: 200 (bottom). **Gilbert Kleinfeldt**—'63 Sunliner: 252 (top right). **Charles Klinger**—'58 Thunderbird: 214 (middle, bottom). **Bill Knudson**—'48 Wagon: 139 (top); '51 Country Squire: 153 (bottom). **Joe Kozmic**—'37 Standard: 114. **Vic Jacobellis**—'63 Club Victoria: 252 (top left). **Leroy Lasiter**—'70 Mustang. **Michael Laureno, Jr.**—'33 Standard: 103 (top); '34 DeLuxe: 105 (middle); '39 Convertible: 119 (top). **Tom Leroahl**—'57 Ranchero: 207. **Jerry Magayne**—'59 Skyliner: 211 (top). **Anton Malmquist, Jr.**—'56 Crown Victoria: 200 (top). **Evan and Delores Martin**—'35 Deluxe: 108 (bottom). **Gerard and Lorraine May**—'30

Model A: 91; '31 Model A: 95 (middle). **Ted Maupin**—'58 Ranchero: 215 (top). **Elgin McNall**—'52 Hardtop: 168. **Ronald E. Miller**—'65 Mustang: 267 (top left). **S. Ray Miller, Jr.**—'40 Convertible: 122 (right), 123 (middle, left). **Tina Miller**—'65 Mustang: 267 (bottom left). **Amos Minter**—'56 Wagon: 201 (bottom); '57 Thunderbird: 204, 205 (top). **Daniel Mitchel**—'64 Falcon: 264 (bottom). **Edward C. Moody**—'14 Model T Touring: 43. **G. Moyer**—'37 Sedan: 116 (top right). **Tom Mulligan**—'41 Super DeLuxe: 128 (top left). **William R. Muni**—'59 Skyliner: 222, 223 (bottom). **John L. Murry**—'52 Sunliner: 162 (top). **Leonard Nowosel**—'55 Thunderbird: 190 (bottom). **Odom's Classics**—'59 Wagon: 219 (bottom). **Larry O'Neal**—'07 Model K Roadster: 22. **Jay F. Painter**—'65 Mustang: 266 (top). **Alan C. Parker**—'55 Crestline: 192 (top). **Z.T. Parker**—'57 Club Sedan: 206. **Robert L. Parrot**—'56 Crown Victoria: 199 (top). **Donald Passardi**—'39 Woody Wagon: 119 (bottom); '46 Sportsman: 135 (middle). **Henry Patrick**—'52 Crestline Victoria: 164. **Roland Pavlak**—'55 Convertible: 192 (middle). **LLoyd W. Pettigrew**—'56 Thunderbird: 196 (top), 197 (top). **Edsel H. Pfabe**—'40 DeLuxe: 125. **Thomas and Carol Podemski**—'71 Mustang: 322-323, 325 (top). **Dixen Polderman**—'70 Mustang: 315. **Edwin Putz**—'69 SportsRoof: 302. **Dick Pyle**—'34 DeLuxe: 105 (bottom left). **Roger Randolph**—'61 Galaxie: 238 (top). **Larry Ray**—'56 Fairlane: 201 (middle). **Charles Richards**—'57 Wagon: 211 (bottom). **Gary Richards**—'57 Custom: 210 (top). **George Richards**—'57 Skyliner: 209 (top). **Carl M. Riggins**—'14 Depot Hack: 46; '23 Model T Touring: 67 (top); Model A Roadster: 84-85. **Dennis Roxworthy**—'66 Mustang: 277, 279, 280 (bottom). **Bob and Karen Sitter**—'29 Model A: 88 (top), 89 (bottom right); '30 Model A: 92 (bottom). **Ted Satler**—'35 DeLuxe: 108 (top), 110 (bottom left). **Jim and Ginger Schoenherr**—'65 Mustang: 267 (top right). **Don Simpkin**—'56 Crown Victoria: 203 (top). **Stan Sokol**—'28 Model A: 88 (bottom). **Peter H. Spear**—'36 DeLuxe: 111 (top). **Vince and Helen Springer**—'65 Mustang: 266 (bottom), 267 (bottom right). **Tom Stackhouse**—'12 Model T Speedster: 39. **Jack and Holly Stewart**—'60 Thunderbird: 230 (bottom), 231 (top). **Jim Stewart**—'41 Pickup: 128 (bottom right); '51 Pickup: 157 (bottom). **Mike and Marge Tanzer**—'64 Thunderbird: 261 (middle). **Dick and Lance Tarnutzer, Dells Auto Museum**—'26 Model T Roadster: 75; '36 DeLuxe: 113 (bottom); '51 Fordor: 159. **Frank Trummer**—'72 Mustang: 333 (top). **Gwendal Varnadore**—'34 Pickup: 106 (top left). **Thomas Venezia**—'40 Woody Wagon: 124. **Guy Viti, Jr.**—'41 Pickup: 128 (bottom left). **Ron Voyles**—'69 Torino: 304. **Alan Wendland**—'56 Thunderbird: 196 (bottom). **John White and Bill Knudson**—'46 Convertible: 137 (top, middle). **Lee Willet**—'57 Fairlane: 210 (bottom). **Jerry Windle**—'48 Coupe Sedan: 138 (bottom right). **Walter P. Wise**—'70 Mustang: 314. **Ron Wood**—'67 Mustang: 286.

CONTENTS

As the auto industry entered the '90s, competition had become intensely fierce. One way automakers tried to bring attention to their brand was with "concept cars," futuristic show cars pointing the way to the future. One of Ford's latest was the '90 ShocccWave, a two-door, performance-oriented car for the mid- to late-'90s. Ford touted the aggressive styling; driver-oriented, ergonomically driven interior, a modular dash and controls that could be individually adjusted; and a computer-controlled rear deck spoiler.

FORD:
THE COMPLETE HISTORY

Nothing of art or science is born in a vacuum. Like any human creation, cars and trucks reflect not only the spirit of their times, but also the passions and foibles of their creators. So although this book is primarily the story of Ford cars and trucks, it is also the story of Ford Motor Company and its people.

For years, Ford products and the Ford company amounted to one and the same: the legendary Model T, the simple creation of the complex man named Henry Ford who personified both. Introduced in 1908, the T was rugged, versatile, lovable—and inexpensive. Henry made it even cheaper by making it by the millions, thereby putting America on wheels. The humble T not only embodied Henry's dream of a "universal car" but was the foundation of an industrial em-

pire that has endured nearly 90 years. Henry was absolute ruler for the first 40 years, then reluctantly surrendered his power to nephew Henry Ford II in 1945. Though less visible, HF II was as much a force in company affairs until he retired in 1980. His accomplishments were necessarily less historic save one: the salvation of a company that had decayed to near ruin by 1945.

The Ford's family's personal involvement with their company makes Ford the one major U.S. automaker that may be said to have a personality. And indeed, the family has been linked with the company in the public mind for so long that the two have often seemed inseparable—perhaps because they usually were. This dynastic quality has made Ford Motor Company unique in another way. As the

late Robert W. Irvin observed in *Automotive News* in 1978, Ford "is the only auto firm which has [survived] 75 years without mergers or the like. It is [also] the only auto firm, and one of the few large corporations anywhere, still in control of the founding family." In Henry's meteoric

Henry Ford I (center), seen here in the late '30s, formed Ford Motor Company in 1903, then fathered the 1909 Model T, the '28 Model A, and the brilliant 1932 V-8. Son Edsel (right), company president beginning in 1919, took Lincoln under his wing in 1922, and inspired the '36 Zephyr, '39 Mercury, and the timeless '40 Continental—as well as most Ford styling of the era. His son, Henry II (left), took over a faltering firm in 1946, set it up as a modern corporation, and under his watchful eye okayed many product triumphs from the late '40s right on into the '80s.

rise to become one of the nation's leading industrialists, he made his family and their descendants part of the prominent elite. And indeed, Ford the folk hero was also Ford the patriarch—even "King Henry" in one cartoon critical of his opposition to organized labor.

But then, Henry Ford was nothing if not controversial, a paradox wrapped in an enigma. His early life hardly hinted of what was to come, and indeed his first car, the spindly 1896 Quadricycle, had begun as a motorized bicycle. But after two false starts, Henry established himself with Ford Motor Company. Within a decade, the Tin Lizzie had made Ford fabulously wealthy and the dominant figure in America's infant auto industry. Millions admired him as an example of what hard work and Yankee ingenuity could achieve. Yet he never lost the common touch, so he was warmly regarded despite his riches. Asked on his 50th birthday to cite the greatest handicap of the wealthy, he replied, "For me, it was when Mrs. Ford stopped cooking."

Still, this idealistic pioneer who reminded many of earlier, simpler times could also be a cynical reactionary—and he was in later life. His mercurial, chameleon-like personality baffled everyone: selfish, with a mean streak, but also generous and compassionate; narrow-minded and stubborn, yet possessed of remarkable insight, vision, and flexibility. One example: Henry said that "History as written is mostly bunk," and then built Greenfield Village as a monument to 19th Century America.

How could such a man rise to such greatness? For one thing, Ford possessed several outstanding qualities: native intelligence and common sense; an intuitive and forward-looking mind; a special engineering talent combining creativity with practicality; a remarkable memory; missionary zeal; and a lifelong capacity for hard work—especially thinking, which he called "the hardest the work there is." And, yes, good luck.

Perhaps his personal life also played a part, for Henry married a woman who understood and complemented him well. Clara Bryant, three years his junior, had also grown up on a Michigan farm and shared many of his down-home values, not the least of which was moderation. More importantly, Clara was convinced that her husband would accomplish great things. Henry called her the "believer," and she encouraged and stood by him for 59 years.

Edsel Bryant Ford, Henry and Clara's only child, was often the forgotten member of the Ford dynasty. The company loomed large in his life, but his father's shadow was always larger. Made company president in 1919, Edsel gradually gained responsibility for styling, sales, and advertising—but never labor relations, engineering, or manufacturing. Still, his achievements were many and impressive. He made Lincoln a force in the luxury field; established Ford's first in-house styling group; helped design the Tin Lizzie's Model A successor, as well as the milestone 1932 Ford V-8, and the advanced 1936 Lincoln-Zephyr; fathered the medium-price Mercury in 1939; and initiated the timeless 1940 Lincoln Continental.

Edsel died at the age of 50, a premature demise brought on in part by years of wrangling with his legendary father. It's thus doubly tragic that the name Edsel would become synonymous with "failure" under the stewardship of his son, Henry Ford II. No one was more bitter about that than Henry himself. "The disappointments are what you want to forget quickly," he told Bob Irvin in 1978, "But I do get credit for the Edsel [car].... There have been other failures, but if you are right 51 percent of the time you can make it." History proved him more than right.

Henry Ford II was the first of four children born to Edsel and Eleanor Clay Ford between 1917 and 1925, the others being Josephine, Benson, and William Clay. Benson would serve as vice-president and general manager of the Lincoln-Mercury Division from 1948-55 and as chairman of Ford's Dealer Policy Board from 1956 until his death in 1978. William Clay headed the early-Fifties Special Products Division that produced the short-lived Edsel car and served as company vice-chairman until 1989 (at this writing he remains on the board of the directors). HF II took charge as company president in 1945 and became chairman in 1960.

Like the first Henry, HF II showed few signs of eventual greatness early on. Refused graduation from Yale after turning in a paper that was someone else's work, Henry II was nonetheless modest and showed leadership at an early age—and was fated to command the family business. Not that he was really ready, though he had more formal education than his grandfather (who had never finished grade school) and had done well enough in the Navy. Still, in 1945 he hardly seemed the shining saviour the sinking company needed. After all, he was only 29. But he learned quickly, and recruited a cadre of GM professionals as well as the now-famous "Whiz Kids" to bring order and eventual success to the recovery effort.

And much more. He gets the blame for some real mistakes and mishandled managers near the end of his tenure—deadly "exploding" Pintos and "jumping" automatic transmissions, the celebrated firings of presidents Iacocca and Bunky Knudsen. But he deserves due credit for blockbusters like the Thunderbird and Mustang; historic victories in most every form of motorsports; for making Ford a public company again in 1956; and for the firm's continuing global expansion while pushing into new fields such as electronics and aerospace.

Like any Ford, "Henry the Deuce" couldn't help but be watched, and he made news on his own, as with his two highly publicized divorces or, more positively, his drive to revitalize downtown Detroit by backing the Renaissance Center in the Seventies, then the world's largest private development project. Henry Ford II was no doubt proud when in 1987, the last year of his life, Ford Motor Company earned a bigger profit than General Motors for the first time since 1924 and Ford Division outsold Chevrolet for the first time in 30 years. It was a gratifying achievement, ending yet another long, slow recovery brought on by corporate malaise in the Seventies and sharp, unexpected changes in the world economic order. But this recovery was engineered by the first non-family leaders in Ford history—which was precisely how HF II had planned it. Philip Caldwell was his hand-picked successor as chairman. Donald Petersen was another company veteran whose strong feel for product made him exactly the kind of president Ford needed.

Ford enters the Nineties with Petersen having retired, leaving Harold "Red" Poling as chairman and Philip Benton president. They inherit a Ford Motor Company that has never been stronger in product or public esteem. They also inherit enormous problems at home and abroad—and from within. Two fourth-generation Fords, Edsel II and his cousin, William Clay Ford, Jr., continue to rise through the ranks, and the board positions they secured in 1989 serves notice that they intend to play bigger roles in the future. Their ultimate contributions remain to be seen, but the saga of the Ford family vis-à-vis the Ford company is far from over.

Nor the story of Ford cars and trucks, the main subject of this book, which we happily dedicate to Ford fans everywhere. It traces the evolution of U.S. Ford cars and trucks in an easy-to-follow year-by-year format, beginning with the period leading up to the founding of Ford Motor Company. Succeeding chapters highlight each year's major new-model developments, including styling and engineering background, as well as contemporary press reaction and important corporate events. The reader should note that unless otherwise stated, production and sales figures cited are for *model* year, not calendar year.

The editors gratefully acknowledge Ford Motor Company, Ford Division, and the Henry Ford Museum for their assistance with the original factory photographs herein. We're also indebted to the many owners who made their Fords available to us for color photography, which speaks for itself. Finally, special thanks to the many Ford executives, engineers, and designers who've shared their thoughts and recollections with us over the years, for it is only through them that we can appreciate their creations in the best possible way.

The "horseless carriage" had been evolving from dream to reality for at least two centuries before Henry Ford built his first one. Most historians date the automobile (literally translated from the French as "self moving") from the three-wheeled steam-powered armaments wagon built in 1769 by French Army Captain Nicholas Cugnot—the first self-propelled vehicle created for a specific purpose. It's intriguing to note, however, that Hero of Alexandria is generally acknowledged to have built the first true steam engine in 130 B.C., and that inventor Roger Bacon had foreseen the coming of horseless carriages as early as 1250 A.D.

Despite sporadic technological advances through the 18th Century, progress toward a practical automobile didn't gain real momentum until the Industrial Revolution of the 19th Century. And once the wheels were rolling, they picked up speed fast. Steam was then the most developed source of power, and thus received the most attention from those groping toward the goal. By century's end, the essentials of the automobile as we know it today were mostly in place and even patented in some cases, however far from perfected. England took the lead on many fronts: Ackermann steering (Rudolph Ackermann, 1818), transmission (a chain-drive affair by Walter Hancock, 1827), and pneumatic tires (Robert William Thompson, 1845). But it was Germany that provided the most crucial element: the liquid-fueled internal-combustion engine. It's generally credited to Nicholas Otto, who built the first such successful four-stroke design in 1877 (hence the term "Otto Cycle," still used today), though two-strokes, electric motors, and other types of internal-combustion engines still had their proponents.

It was left to Germany's Carl Benz and Gottlieb Daimler to combine these elements into the world's first true automobiles. Though their names would later be joined in the Daimler-Benz firm, which is still with us, of course, the two men worked independently although just a few miles apart, each apparently unaware of the other's efforts. Benz's car, a delicate little three-wheeler, took to the streets first, in 1885; Daimler's more substantial four-wheeler made its initial run the following year.

The automobile fascinated Americans as much as Europeans, and a number of Yankee inventors helped speed its coming. G.B. Brayton, for example, ex-hibited a two-cycle petroleum-fueled engine at the nation's 1876 centennial exposition in Philadelphia. Three years later, one George B. Selden applied for the basic American patent on an automobile. Charles E. and J. Frank Duryea built a single-cylinder car in 1893, then formed Duryea Motor Wagon Company two years later—the first U.S. firm organized to make gas-powered automobiles. That same year, 1895, Selden was granted his patent—a development that would soon vex Henry Ford—and Frank

Duryea won America's first auto race, averaging 5.05 miles per hour over a 52.4-mile course in Chicago.

That winter, a hopeful 32-year-old mechanical engineer struggled to build his first car. Actually, Henry Ford had experimented with internal-combustion engines as early as 1888, and built his first working engine, a two-cylinder, in late December 1893. His goal was a motorized bicycle, but somehow he couldn't quite find a way to make the engine small and light enough for that purpose. It didn't matter, for Ford received some unexpected inspiration from one Charles Brady King, whose gasoline-powered car had been the first to travel the streets of Detroit, two years before.

As related by Richard Johnson in *Automotive News* in 1985, "King had befriended Ford....After making a trial run of his own car, King left for

The first gasoline engine built by Henry Ford in 1893, three years before he built his first car. The cylinder was a piece of one-inch gas pipe; practically the entire engine was made from scrap pieces and cost about a dollar.

On December 22, 1893, the engine was clamped to the sink in the kitchen of Mr. Ford's home. The painting shows how he turned the flywheel to start the engine, while Mrs. Ford fed gasoline drop by drop to the intake valve. After the engine ran for about half a minute, Mr. Ford shut it off and started to work on a larger one...for his first car.

France to study French automotive developments, and presented Ford with the parts and designs of his experimental vehicle. Shortly after arriving in France, King lost interest in automobiles and took up painting. But Ford went back to work on his own motor-driven "Quadricycle." He mounted a buggy chassis on four bicycle wheels which were fitted together with gas-pipe hubs. The vehicle's two-cylinder water-cooled engine was made of pipe, and a gasoline tank was fastened under the seat. The car had two forward speeds, of 10 and 20 miles per hour, but could not manage reverse.

"Ford planned to take to the streets in the spring of 1896. As the vehicle neared a state of readiness, he worked day and night. The future industrialist finally rolled the car out of his garage at 58 Bagley Avenue at 2 a.m. in the rain. His wife, carrying an umbrella, came out to watch her husband's contraption cough, sputter, jerk and proceed down Bagley with a kerosene lamp showing the way in the dark." Not surprisingly, this first Ford "road test" went unreported, Henry Ford neither announcing a demonstration nor making a photograph or description of his car available to any publication.

The Quadricycle, Johnson observes, "was no more mechanically advanced than previous horseless carriages. But the jubilant Ford was so inspired that he decided to commit his future to the automobile." Henry soon sold that car, then turned to building a second. The work went slowly, and was carried on pretty much in secret.

It wasn't until the November 1898 edition of *Horseless Age* that the name Henry Ford appeared in an automotive context, and then only under the heading "Minor Mention: Henry Ford, of Detroit, Mich., chief engineer of the Edison Electric Light Co. of that city, has built a number of gasoline vehicles which are said to have been successfully operated. He is reported to be financially supported by several prominent men of the city, who intend to manufacture the Ford vehicle. From Mr. Ford himself, no information can be gleaned regarding his vehicles or his plans for manufacture."

Ford's second car (*Horseless Age* had overstated Henry's production) was working by the summer of 1899, and prompted his first interview and an accompanying photo feature in the July 29 edition of the Detroit *Journal*. A week later, largely on the strength of a successful demonstration Henry gave to a wealthy Detroit lumberman, the Detroit Automobile Company was organized. Ford was given a small share of stock and was named the firm's superintendent.

In early February 1900, Ford again demonstrated his car's capabilities, this time to a reporter for the Detroit *News-Tribune*. Normally shy with strangers,

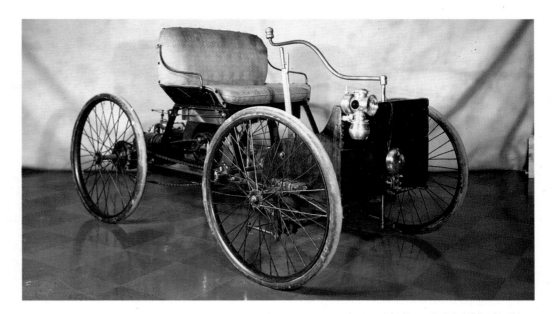

Opposite page: Henry Ford built his first gasoline engine in 1893, three years before he built his first car. The cylinder was a piece of one-inch gas pipe, and practically the entire engine was made from scrap pieces that cost about a dollar. This page: The first Ford was the "Quadricycle," which Henry first drove through the streets of Detroit on June 4, 1896. It was 2:00 a.m. and raining, so few people were aware of that historic event. This first Ford featured a buggy chassis, bicycle wheels, and a two-cylinder engine.

Henry now seemed relaxed behind the tiller and proved as loquacious as a snake-oil salesman. The rollicking three-column story that followed—headlined "Swifter Than a Race-Horse It Flew Over The Ice Streets"—provided the first inkling that Ford would one day have an easy way with reporters.

Whatever their virtues, the products of the Detroit Automobile Company did not sell. Apparently, Ford wanted to improve the model, but the company's stockholders vetoed that. As a result, the firm slowly ground to a halt in late 1900.

Ford and his assistants spent the spring and summer of 1901 building a race car, a trim, light, 26-horsepower machine. Its first test came at the Grosse Pointe race track near Detroit on October 10. Several of the nation's outstanding drivers were on hand, including Alexander Winton, a budding auto manufacturer who had built his first car the same year as Ford. In 1897, a Winton had been timed through a mile in 1 minute, 48 seconds and managed a trek from Cleveland to New York in 10 days. The following year, Winton went into business with a commercial delivery wagon.

Though Ford's machine was heavily favored at Grosse Pointe, Winton's sales manager, Charles B. Shanks, was so confident of victory that he selected a beautiful punch bowl as the trophy, something he thought would look good in the bay window of the Winton dining room. Winton and Ford were the only starters in the main event. (A third competitor, William N. Murray, a Pittsburgh millionaire who owned one of the fastest cars in the country, withdrew.)

Winton started on the inside. His deftness in rounding curves allowed him to open up an eighth-of-a-mile lead at the three-mile mark; Ford had to shut off power and run wide on each corner. But midway through the contest, Ford picked up lost ground on the straightaways, and by the sixth lap had visibly improved his position. With the crowd urging Ford on, Winton began having trouble with overheated bearings. Shanks, riding along as mechanic, as was customary in the early days, drenched the bearings with oil, but to no avail. Ford shot ahead on the eighth lap and swept across the finish line well ahead of the faltering champion. His average speed: 43.5 miles per hour.

This victory brought Henry Ford national attention and sparked his next automaking venture. A number of prominent Detroiters, including several former stockholders of the Detroit Automobile Company, had seen the triumph and were fired by the commercial possibilities of the Ford machine. Accordingly, they organized the Henry Ford Company on November 30, 1901, the name itself a tribute to Henry's newly won renown. Ford was given a one-sixth share and the post of chief en-

Opposite page: Henry Ford was involved with the Detroit Automobile Company, which in 1899 built a delivery van (top). Henry's second car was the 1898-99 Quadricycle (center)—it had a more finished appearance than the 1896 car. In 1901, Henry built his first race car (bottom)—he's at the wheel. Powered by a two-cylinder, 26-bhp engine, it averaged 43.5 miles per hour in beating out a Winton on October 10, 1901 at the Grosse Point, Michigan race track. This page: The 1901 Quadricycle (top left) featured a steering wheel rather than a tiller. The 1901 Detroit (above left) was built by the Detroit Automobile Company, of which Henry was superintendent. A Ford experimental car, circa 1901-02 (top right) boasted a two-cylinder engine. Henry gained added fame with his "999" race car. On October 25, 1902, this car beat three other contestants by covering five miles in five minutes, 28 seconds at the Grosse Point track.

gineer, but his continued preoccupation with racing quickly produced friction with other stockholders and he left after only three months, taking a $900 settlement, the uncompleted drawings for a new racing car, and the company agreed to stop using his name.

By early May of 1902, Ford had joined forces with Tom Cooper, a former champion bicycle rider who itched to race cars. With Cooper's money and Ford's know-how, the two were able to build a pair of 80-horsepower monsters which they dubbed "Arrow" and "999"—the latter after the record-breaking New York Central train. "There was only one seat," Ford would recall later. "One life to a car was enough. I tried out the cars. Cooper tried out the cars. We let them out at full speed...Going over Niagara

Falls would have been but a pastime after a ride in one of them."

Neither Ford nor Cooper had the nerve to drive these cars in competition, but Cooper said he knew a man "who lived on speed, that nothing could go too fast for him." A wire to Salt Lake City secured the services of one Barney Oldfield, another pro bicycle rider. Oldfield had never driven a car but said he'd try anything once. He learned quickly and proved fearless.

Oldfield was primed for the five-mile Manufacturers' Challenge Cup scheduled for the Grosse Pointe track on October 25, 1902. Four drivers started, Winton and Shanks among them. Oldfield opened up "999" immediately, was never headed, and defeated runner-up Shanks by a full lap. His time: 5 minutes,

28 seconds—not quite the mile-a-minute speed he said he'd aim for a year earlier, but an American record nevertheless. Again Ford's name resounded in the press, and Oldfield was launched on his career as one of America's greatest race-car drivers.

But with this came the end of Henry's preoccupation with racing. For advertising purposes he would drive "999" to a world's speed record in 1904, and his cars would race until 1912. But with his reputation firmly established, he was now able to turn to his life's work: putting a "family horse" on the market.

The foundation for this ambition was laid on August 20, 1902, when Ford and Detroit coal dealer Alexander Y. Malcomson signed an agreement to develop a commercial automobile. In November they cemented their partnership by organizing the Ford & Malcomson Company, Limited, offering shares for sale. After attracting 10 investors, the Ford Motor Company was incorporated on June 16, 1903 with $28,000 in capital. Ford, who contributed his patents, his engine, and his knowledge, was given a 25.5-percent interest in the new enterprise. A dynasty had been born.

1 9 0 3

Ford Motor Company was launched with a minimum of fanfare, making no attempt to promote itself or the car it was putting on the market. Detroit's three daily newspapers were unaware of the firm until three days after its June 13 incorporation, and they buried the news in brief stories on their back pages.

Horseless Age devoted a few lines to a rumor that the "Ford Automobile Company will build a factory at Pontiac [Michigan]," while *Motor Age* told its readers in a single paragraph that the firm would place a "Fordmobile" on the market. *Cycle and Automobile Trade Journal* ran a longer, more factual story, since by coincidence its June issue featured the automotive industry in Detroit. *Automobile* and *Automobile Topics* ignored the fledgling firm completely.

But even if it had tried to garner press attention, it likely wouldn't have received much. Ford was but one of 88 new U.S. automobile companies in 1903, 15 of them located in Michigan, and neither its capitalization nor its prospects for success were particularly noteworthy.

It's helpful to paint a brief picture of the American auto scene at the turn of the century. Interest in the newfangled contraptions was certainly strong, as suggested by the mere existence of the aforementioned publications, as well as the advent of the first National Automobile Show, staged at New York City's Madison Square Garden in 1900. But though passenger-car production was climbing rapidly, the numbers seem ludicrously small to modern eyes: a bit less than 4200 for all makes in 1900, rising to 11,235 in the year Ford opened for business.

Moreover, though "America was perhaps ready for the automobile," as Beverly Rae Kimes observed much later in *Automobile Quarterly*, "the extent of the country's preparedness remains debatable. True, automobile registrations by 1907 passed the 140,000 mark, an impressive leap from the [1900] figure of 8000. Still, an opinion poll in 1903 had indicated that a mere five percent of Americans favored the automobile, enraged non-owners...continued a vociferous dissent (one suggestion: intervention by the American Humane Society), and publications like the *North American Review* pointed out ominously in 1906 that automobiles had killed more citizens in the five months previous than had perished in Spanish-American War." (How sadly contemporary that sounds.)

Nevertheless, the horseless carriage seemed unstoppable, figuratively speaking, and its ranks were growing. Besides

Ford, the field in 1903 already included several names that are still familiar today. Oldsmobile and Pierce had been organized in 1900; while 1902 saw formation of the Thomas B. Jeffery Company (forerunner of Nash and American Motors), Packard Motor Car Company, Rapid Motor Vehicle Company (the ancestor of GMC Truck), as well as the National Association of Automobile Manufacturers and the American Automobile Association. Among other 1903 hopefuls were Overland and the firm of David Dunbar Buick.

Also new on the scene was Cadillac, formed in 1902 as an outgrowth of the old Henry Ford Company. Its first production car, the Model A, bore more than a passing resemblance to the first production Ford, which had the same designation, suggesting that Henry left a few things behind.

Ford's Model A had to its credit the great merits of simplicity, lightness, and efficiency. Its principal innovation was a two-cylinder, 100.5-cubic-inch opposed engine developing eight horsepower at just 1000 rpm from 4 × 4-inch bore-and-stroke dimensions. Riding a wheelbase of only 72 inches, the little runabout could attain speeds as high as 30 miles per hour. The transmission, often generically termed the "change-gear," was the planetary type Henry favored, with two speeds forward and one reverse. Both throttle and ignition were hand-controlled, the latter sparked from two sets of six dry-

cell batteries. The complete car weighed only 1250 pounds per Ford's insistence that weight had no relation to strength. "The car that I designed was lighter than any car that had yet been made," he later recalled. "It would have been lighter had I known how to make it so."

Like most other horseless carriages of the period, the Model A's steering wheel was on the right. (The steering wheel itself was introduced on the Ohio car built by brothers James W. and Warren D. Packard in 1900). Also typical of the age, there were no doors. Driver and passenger simply slid into their seats, their bodies in full view. There were no running boards, either, and the car stood high off the road, so occupants had to contend with a small, sharp, sometimes slippery carriage step. A detachable back seat section called a tonneau, a $100 dollar option, slipped on and off at the rear. Passengers gained access to it through a rear door.

An early advertisement billed the Model A as the "new, light touring car [that] fills the demand for an automobile between a runabout and a heavy touring car. It is positively the most perfect machine on the market, having overcome all drawbacks such as smell, noise, jolt, etc. common to all other makes of auto carriages." This pompous puffery belied a great many faults. The radiator, for example, was so inadequate that the engine, which was mounted under the seat, could get hot enough to boil its cooling water even when the car was run in high gear on level roads. Early carburetors were inefficient, and the original Model A had brake troubles. The simple splash lubrication system needed excessive amounts of oil, the circulating pump was inefficient, and spark plugs quickly fouled from oil leaking past the piston rings. Transmissions provoked complaint because their bands slipped. But every early automaker had such difficulties. Ford tinkered and replaced, and after six months the Model A was running smoothly.

The soon-to-be-famous Ford script was the new company's trademark right from the start. It was the work of one of Henry's first associates, Childe Harold Wills, who would later build the Wills Sainte Claire car. As a boy of 15 or 16,

The 1903 Model A (both pages) was the first car produced by the fledgling Ford Motor Company, which was incorporated with little fanfare on June 16, 1903. Noted for its simplicity, lightness, and efficiency, its principal innovation was a two-cylinder opposed engine that developed eight horsepower and—on good roads—was capable of speeds of up to 30 miles per hour. It rode a 72-inch wheelbase, and like most other horseless carriages the period, the steering wheel was on the right. The car had no running boards and stood high off the road. Note the detail differences between the two cars shown.

Wills had earned some money making calling cards, which he lettered in flowing script. When Ford Motor Company first grappled with advertising, nobody was satisfied with how the name "Ford" looked in print. Wills rummaged around for his old lettering set and wrote out F-O-R-D in its now-familiar style, which was adopted immediately. The signature would grace Ford vehicles through the late Forties, when it gave way to block letters. It then returned in the Sixties within an oval with a blue background, the logo that continues in worldwide use today.

From the first, Ford Motor Company stood apart from most of the other new automakers of 1903—and some established ones, too—by making money. Things were touch-and-go at first, the initial $28,000 capital kitty shrinking to just $223 within 30 days of incorporation. But on July 15, Ford sold its first car and the bank balance jumped to nearly $1000. Total calendar-year sales came to 1708—including Ford's first "export" sale, to a Canadian buyer in August— and the firm netted $36,957 within its first 3½ months. On November 21, the company paid a 10-percent dividend, the first of a steady stream that would run the next 23 years—and at a phenomenal rate in most. Reflecting its optimism and foreshadowing the future, the firm appointed New York trader Robert M. Lockwood to handle its worldwide export business in September.

But Ford Motor Company's promising start was soon overshadowed by a legal entanglement: the celebrated Selden suit, filed this year. Before it ended, the pocketbook of most everyone who made, sold, or bought an automobile in the United States would be affected.

The suit was brought by George B. Selden, a Rochester, New York, attorney, and the Electric Vehicle Company. As noted in the previous chapter, Selden had obtained the basic American patent for "road carriages" in 1895. This covered all gasoline-powered vehicles designed from that year and manufactured, sold, or used in the United States in a 17-year period ending with 1912. Selden had assigned the patent in 1899 to a concern that became the Electric Vehicle Company. By March 1903, most auto concerns had been intimidated into acknowledging the patent's validity. By summer, 26 firms had joined to form the Association of Licensed Automobile Manufacturers (ALAM) and agreed to pay the patent holders a royalty of 1.25 percent of the price of each car sold. The Association would select those manufacturers to be licensed. Others would be sued and, presumably, put out of business.

In February and again during the summer of 1903, Henry Ford and his associates approached the ALAM's acting president about obtaining a Selden license for their company. But they were rebuffed, the ALAM executive expressing a lack of confidence in Ford's ability to meet the group's "manufacturing standards" and thus be considered a credible member of the industry. Undeterred, Henry continued to build and sell cars. ALAM soon warned that Ford, its dealers, and its buyers would be prosecuted for patent infringement.

Henry responded by promising to protect his customers. Company ads echoed his defiance. One began with the false claim that "Our Mr. Ford made the first Gasoline Automobile in Detroit and the third in the United States." But it was accurate in stating that "Our Mr. Ford also built the famous '999' Gasoline

Automobile, which was driven by Barney Oldfield in New York on July 25, 1903, a mile in 55⅘ seconds on a circular track, which is the world's record. Mr. Ford, driving his own machine, beat Mr. Winton at Grosse Pointe track in 1901." It closed on a somewhat predictable note: "We have always been winners."

Though the patent holders sued Ford in 1903, it took four years to get all the evidence before the court. After that, both sides went all-out to curry public favor.

The bone of contention involved the main trial exhibits. The Seldenites presented a motor buggy to show that a car built according to patent specifications would run. Ford insisted that the vehicle would start only when facing downhill, and demonstrated his own machine with an engine resembling one patented by an Englishman in 1869 to refute Selden's claim to originality. Ford also maintained that his car would travel four times as far and four times faster over 50 miles even if the Selden car had a 45-mile head start!

It wasn't until 1909 that the New York federal district court handed down its ruling, and it was in favor of Selden. Henry appealed, calling the patent "a freak among alleged inventions," and offered a bond to each Ford buyer, backed by the $12 million assets of his firm and its bonding company. The Detroit *Free Press* echoed the sentiments of many by painting Ford's stand as heroic. "There's a man for you, a man of backbone," said an editorial called "Ford the Fighter." "Of the case behind him, the lawyers were more able to talk, but as a human figure he presents a spectacle to win the applause of all men with red blood; for this world dearly loves the fighting man, and needs him, too, if we are to go forward."

The case went to the U.S. Court of Appeals, which issued its decision on January 9, 1911. This time the victory went to Ford, and it was total. Essentially the court held that the Selden patent was valid but that Ford and other automakers were not guilty of infringement. Telegrams and letters poured into Ford offices, from opponents as well as friends. For the first time in his life, Henry Ford was front-page news in Detroit and in the automotive press, lauded on all sides as a giant-killer, a symbol of revolt against monopoly, a magnificent individualist.

Naturally, beating the Selden suit was of tremendous public relations value to Ford Motor Company. As Henry would later say, "No one factor publicized the company and its products as effectively as the company's role in liberating an industry."

This page: A 1903 Ford Model A pauses in front of the Greenfield Village general store. Opposite page: Ford turned to racing to promote his Model B cars. He announced that he would break the world's record for the timed mile, and on January 12, 1904 he did: 91.37 mph on the cinder-covered ice of Lake St. Clair.

1 9 0 4

Seeking to build on its first-year success, Ford Motor Company issued three new cars for 1904. The Model A gave way to the Model C, essentially an improved version of the little runabout, but some 100 pounds lighter despite a four-inch-longer 76-inch wheelbase. Power came from a revised version of the 100.5-cubic-inch opposed twin that developed two extra horsepower for a total of 10. Price was $800 for the two-passenger runabout "Doctor's Model," or $900 with accessory rear-seat tonneau. Top speed was claimed to be 38 mph.

Ford's other newcomers appealed to wealthier clients. One step up from the C was the new Model F, an attractive four-seat touring car priced at $1000. Striding an 84-inch wheelbase and weighing some 1300 pounds, it carried a two-cylinder engine bored out a half-inch to 127.2 cid, good for approximately 16 bhp at just 900 rpm. Topping the line was an ambitious $2000 tourer, the Model B, measuring 92 inches between wheel centers and tipping the scales at 1600 pounds. Its powerplant was a new 251.3-cid four-cylinder unit delivering 24 bhp at 1200 rpm from undersquare bore-and-stroke dimensions of 4 × 5 inches. It sat up front under a hood, the first Ford to have this feature, and drove the rear wheels via a driveshaft. Grand wood-spoke wheels mounted 32 × 3.5-inch tires, versus the C's (and A's) 28 × 3s.

Ford Motor Company was moving away from, not toward, the $500 "family horse" that Henry dreamed of, and it disturbed him. Nevertheless, these new products were clearly superior to the Model A. Their longer wheelbases meant a smoother ride, and paint jobs were more attractive. The B could even do 40 mph, boasted storage batteries instead of dry cells, and came with a 15-gallon fuel tank.

But though the Models C and F sold reasonably well, demand for the new luxury Ford was weak. As a result, calendar-year production lagged behind the first-year pace at 1695 units, a mere 7.7 percent of this year's 22,130-unit industry total. Even so, the firm was evidently confident enough about its future to form a Canadian subsidiary on August 17, Ford Motor Company of Canada, Limited.

The early part of the year saw the first Ford vehicles exhibited at auto shows, in New York, Chicago, and five other cities. From 1905 to 1910 the company exhibited under the auspices of a small group of manufacturers not licensed under the Selden patent. After winning the Selden case in 1911, Henry Ford refused to exhibit in New York under the aegis of successor associations, a policy he maintained all the way through 1940. The company did, however, participate in trade-association shows outside New York in 1911-12, then introduced new models at private gatherings in New York and other key cities.

Numerous non-automotive shows and expositions also attracted the company in its early years. Ford displayed three cars at the 1904 Louisiana Purchase Exposition in St. Louis, and cutaway chassis and engines operated by electricity were featured at industrial shows several years later. Henry Ford's personal interest in rural life was reflected in a Model T exhibit at the New York Land Show (for farmers) in 1911-12.

Before establishing branches and dealerships throughout the country, the Ford company sent out "missionary" mechanics to aid and appease complaining customers. Later, under the watchful eye of sales manager Norval Hawkins, dealers had to provide top-notch service facilities in order to obtain and hold onto their franchises (a policy not unlike the Japanese approach to the U.S. market some 70 years later). There were other requirements, too: clean, neat places of business, pleasing show windows, and attractive demonstrator cars. To satisfy the home office that these conditions were met, branch roadmen took photographs of dealerships inside and out. Snapshots were also taken of managers and salesmen to ensure a correct, businesslike appearance. Roadmen also kept constant watch over franchisees' financial condition and their standing in the community, comparing them with dealers handling other makes.

In addition, Ford agents had to keep garages and stockrooms separate from sales and display areas so that prospective consumers would not be able to see cars being ripped apart for repairs—or hear owner complaints. Chains could not be advertised or sold for fear it would suggest the possibility of breakdowns, and at least one branch ordered that malfunctioning cars be towed only after nightfall so as to reduce the impact of this "very bad advertisement." Reflecting Henry's disdain for tobacco, smoking was not permitted in a Ford dealership, even by visitors and customers. Tipping wasn't allowed, either, acceptance of a gratuity bringing instant dismissal. Fresh, clean signs—not faded or soiled ones that "invite breaking of rules"—had to be posted prominently throughout the premises. Dealers were also strongly urged to purchase standardized Ford letterhead and outdoor and window signage. Hawkins and James Couzens frequently lectured factory, branch, and dealer personnel to be on their best business behavior at all times, to answer letters promptly, and "to see callers right off."

This concern with customer relations was not only well-founded, but prophetic. Less than a decade after its incorporation, Ford Motor Company would grow a vast dealer network, which meant more of its personnel were in contact with the public than those of any other automaker or manufacturing concern. In fact, Ford likely had more sales outlets (some 7000 by the Teens) and personnel than the rest of the industry combined.

Henry Ford went racing again to promote the Model B in January of this year. As a spectacular stroke was needed to garner nationwide publicity for the new offering, Ford boldly announced that he would break the world's record for the timed mile by fitting his "Arrow" with an engine practically identical with the production Model B's. The run was set for the cinder-covered ice of Lake St. Clair northeast of Detroit.

This 1904 Ford Model C (above) sports a rear-entrance tonneau. Weighing 1250 pounds, it was powered by a two-cylinder engine rated at 10 bhp. The 1904-05 12-horsepower Model F (below) sold for $1200. Ford bragged that it climbed hills on "high speed" and that it rode "like a Yacht." It also had "the latitude of speed on the high gear of a $5,000.00 car." Another talking point was the side-entrance tonneau.

Henry made good his boast. On January 9 he unofficially covered the distance in 36 seconds, besting the record by 10 full seconds. Three days later, with official timers on hand, he did the mile in 39.4 seconds—91.87 mph. It was, said the Detroit *Tribune*, "the wildest ride in the history of the automobile.... Humped over his steering wheel, the tremendous speed throwing the machine in zigzag fashion across the 15-foot road-way, Ford was taking chances that no man, not even that specialist in averting suicide, Barney Oldfield, had dared tempt."

Ford was fully aware of the danger, but having gone that far, there was nothing else to do. "The ice seemed smooth enough," he wrote later, "so smooth that if I had called off the trial we should have secured an immense amount of the wrong kind of advertising. But instead of being smooth, that ice was seamed with fissures, which I knew were going to mean trouble the moment I got up speed. But there was nothing to do but go through with the trial, and I let the old 'Arrow' out. At every fissure the car leaped into the air. I never knew how it was coming down. When I wasn't in the air, I was skidding, but somehow I stayed top side up and on the course, making a record all over the world."

Auto people everywhere were astounded by Ford's performance, "so

sensational that even the most enthusiastic supporters of American speed machines admitted that they would like to see further proof before accepting the figures." Under the headline "Ford's Mile Raises the Dander of the Track Champion," the Detroit *Tribune* pictured a Barney Oldfield green with envy. Dominique Lamberjack, the French champion, flatly stated that the feat was impossible. After thoroughly considering the question, one Detroit paper concluded it was unlikely that any car could do a faster mile. Discounting wire reports, eastern officials of the American Automobile Association insisted on seeing affidavits signed by the six timers and two surveyors before certifying Ford's record. The group's chairman then said that if it proved authentic, it would be put in a special "made on ice" category—which brought the wrath of Detroit newspapers.

But finally, on January 20, 1904, Henry's record went into the books. Just seven days later it was eclipsed by William K. Vanderbilt in a 90-horsepower Mercedes that ran a 39-second mile (92.307 mph) on the sands of Ormond Beach, Florida.

The Model B profited little from Ford's derring-do and the ensuing controversy. The press persisted confusing the rebuilt Arrow with the "999" even though Ford personally visited the sports desk of each Detroit paper to see that the Model B received its full due.

Ford apparently didn't race again in 1904. The following year, however, he attempted to regain the mile speed record on the beach at Cape May, New Jersey. Despite a new racer, he could not break 41 seconds. The car was rebuilt, and Ford announced in 1906 that he would run a mile in 30 seconds (120 mph), but he failed to break 40 seconds in exhibitions at Ormond Beach.

Other Ford drivers had their share of success on Eastern and Midwestern tracks in 1904. A daring mechanic named Frank Kulick set light-car records for one, three, four, and five miles that would stand for more than half a dozen years. And between 1904 and 1907, Ford racers were almost invincible in their class, frequently winning against larger vehicles in open competition. Perhaps the most publicized victory was a 24-hour speed-endurance contest won by Kulick and a co-driver over eight other cars at the Michigan State Fairgrounds in mid-1907. Ford ads termed this contest "the swiftest, maddest driving ever witnessed" and claimed world records for distances covered in one, eight, and 24 hours. The company also promoted races among its test drivers and customers on a private track in Highland Park, Michigan, in 1907. These races, held on alternate Saturdays, were popular drawing cards for Detroit-area speed merchants.

Although racing enjoyed wide popularity before World War I, it came in for considerable criticism in 1905-07. Accidents had become commonplace, six drivers losing their lives in 1907 alone,

and Kulick narrowly escaped death when he went off the Michigan Fairgrounds track at full speed while testing a new race car. Henry Ford, shaken by Kulick's close call, declared that his company would forego the sport until the industry could agree on limiting the speed and power of racing vehicles. He suggested that maximum displacement be limited to 250 cubic inches so that engineers could show the superiority of their designs within sane speeds, but his call fell on deaf ears. Cars with up to 600 cid continued roaring around American tracks, and except for Barney Oldfield and the Locomobile and Thomas companies, most automakers and their leading drivers continued to race.

But Ford had another reason to quit racing: his cars had virtually no competition in their low-price, lightweight category. As *Ford Times* later noted: "After we had beaten all the one- and two-lungers and other low-priced cars, what good would victory do us?"

Nonetheless, Ford's decision was sharply criticized by dealers, who had come to rely on the racing exploits of Ford cars for their advertising. Many

The 1904 Ford Model B (above left) featured a four-cylinder engine. It was heavier and faster than the two-cylinder Models A, C, and F—and at $2000 significantly more expensive. The Model C (above right), which replaced the Model A, had a more "user friendly" price tag: $800 for the runabout, $900 with tonneau.

had even entered contests themselves since 1904, and felt they had to intensify their efforts to keep pace with rival makes. *Ford Times*, fully aware of racing's promotional value, sympathetically chronicled private Ford victories so dealers could list them in their ads. The publication also devoted considerable attention to Ford triumphs in Europe, where branches were not bound by the no-racing policy.

Henry Ford is the "madman" behind the wheel of the Arrow race car (to the left). The 91.37-mph record he set on January 12, 1904 was described by the Detroit **Tribune** *as "the wildest ride in the history of automobiling." Due to some controversy, the record wasn't made official until January 20, and it was broken just seven days later on the sands of a Florida beach.*

1 9 0 5

This was not a banner year for either Ford Motor Company or the American auto industry as a whole. Total U.S. car production rose by only some 2100 units, to 24,250, and Ford's output declined to 1599, a mere 6.6 percent share, despite some useful improvements.

They started with the top-line Model B tourer, which got a slightly different radiator and a four-cylinder engine bored out a quarter-inch to 283.6 cubic inches, though horsepower was still 24 and curb weight was up 150 pounds. The Model C was treated to a like bore increase, bringing its opposed twin to 113.4 cid, but again there was no gain in output. The C's wheelbase was also stretched to 78 inches, a gain of two inches. The Model F saw no change at all, probably because it wasn't selling well. It would be discontinued early in 1906. Prices increased about $50 across the board. In those days, buyers paid extra for "all-purpose" road equipment including windshield, headlamps, and top. In Ford's case, these items totaled about $100.

Ford historians note that the first vehicle Henry built for sale was a panel delivery truck, in 1900. Given his strong interest in mechanized workhorses for both town and country, it's not surprising that Ford Motor Company entered the commercial vehicle business this year with the Model E. Combining the Model C chassis with a special high-built panel-delivery body, it was more car than truck, and was even advertised as the "Model C with Delivery Top" (but not as the Model E). Nevertheless, the company claimed it "could carry as much as a horse-drawn wagon, at much less the cost of keeping an animal." The Model E was not all that successful, though, and Ford's first true truck wouldn't appear until 1917, when the Model T era was well underway.

Also this year, Henry Ford became the second member of the new Society of Automotive Engineers (SAE) and began experimenting with a motorized tractor that he called the "auto plow," a crude collection of car parts that was even closer to his dream of a "family horse." The first one didn't work very well, but Ford persisted with this work and in a dozen years would produce the first Fordson tractor.

But this year's biggest events involved manufacturing. First, Ford shifted production from its original plant on Mack Avenue, a converted wagon shop, to a new facility on Piquette Avenue some 10 times larger. This comprised a separate power plant, paint shop, and testing house plus a three-story main building measuring 402 by 56 feet. Piquette would remain Ford's principal manufacturing facility until superceded by the even larger Highland Park factory in 1910. It not only produced a variety of pre-T Fords but was also where the Model T was conceived and first built. Interestingly, the Michigan Historical Commission designates Highland Park as "The Home of the Model T," while the older plant has no such marker. Later the home for E-M and Studebaker production, it still stands today.

The Mack plant, located in what is now the heart of Detroit's black community, was destroyed by fire decades ago, but Henry later ordered a smaller-scale reproduction built for Greenfield Village, his monument to Americana that opened in Dearborn in 1930. A mobile replica was built by Metro Detroit Ford Dealers for the company's 75th anniversary in 1978, and appeared in many parades. Alas, there's no historical marker on the site of the original Mack plant.

This year's other manufacturing highlight was the formation of a new subsidiary, Ford Manufacturing Company, to produce engines and other powertrain components. Capitalized with $100,000, it would eventually end Ford's dependence on brothers John and Horace Dodge for transmissions. It was also part of the plan for forcing out Henry's partner, Alexander Malcomson, in 1906.

Ford's 1905 model lineup was topped by the Model B. It received a slightly different radiator, and its four-cylinder engine was bored out a quarter-inch to 283.6 cubic inches. Horsepower, however, was still 24, but the engine had to cope with a curb weight 150 pounds heavier.

This year is significant for introducing the progenitor of the hallowed Model T, the four-cylinder Model N. It was not only much better than any previous Ford, but one of the best-designed cars yet seen in the United States. With its immediate acceptance, the N put Ford on the four-cylinder path it would follow for the next 22 years.

Riding the same 78-inch wheelbase as the 1905 Model C, the N was a 1050-pound compact runabout powered by a new, oversquare 134.2-cubic-inch engine (bore and stroke: 3.63 × 3.25 inches). Packing 15 horsepower at 900 rpm, it could do 45 mph and get 20 miles per gallon of gas. And its price was right: $600 basic. If still buggy-like in the lines of its folding top, its two-passenger "boattail" body was trim and dashing. Again the engine was up front under a hood, only the hood was now nickeled. The same finish adorned a handsome pair of headlamps flanking the radiator, and there were two more on the dashboard. Wheels nestled under short, brightly polished fenders. Comparing favorably in appearance with the smarter models of its day, the Model N offered remarkable value for the money.

The N was greeted with a pre-dictable burst of enthusiasm—reflected in Ford calendar-year production that soared more than fivefold to 8729 units. Though total industry output went up, too—by a little more than a third to 33,200 units—the gain was more than enough to boost Ford's market share to a healthy 26.3 percent. No wonder *Cycle and Automobile Trade Journal* hailed the Model N as "distinctly the most important mechanical traction event of 1906."

At the same time, the Model F was dropped as Ford abandoned two-cylinder cars completely, and an improved replacement for the four-cylinder Model B arrived, the six-cylinder Model K. The

The 1906 Model N (above and below) is assured its place in the annals of Ford history—its significance being that it was the progenitor of the hallowed Model T. Although it rode the same 78-inch wheelbase as the Model C, the N was predictive by adopting a four-cylinder engine. Oversquare, with a bore and stroke of 3.63 by 3.25 inches, the 134.2 cubic inches were good for a modest 15 horsepower at a low 900 rpm, and enough to push the light 1050-pound N to a top speed of about 45 mph, reasonably impressive for 1906. The public responded enthusiastically to the Model N, as Ford production for the year shot up to 8729 units, a five-fold increase. Note the nickeled radiator shell and the step plates for easier entry and exit.

The 1906-07 Model K (above, below—with Henry at the wheel—and bottom right) proved to be a hard sell, and Henry was never enthused with it. As Ford's top-line model, it replaced the Model B, but the very idea behind it divided Henry and his chief partner, Alexander Malcomson, an advocate of high-priced luxury cars. Henry still wanted to build a $500 car for the masses. The $2500 Model K rode a wheelbase of 114/120 inches, weighed a ton, and came with a six-cylinder engine boasting 405 cubic inches and 40 bhp. Ford guaranteed that the roadster would do 60 mph. No matter—the K didn't sell. Ford thus tried to force the market by insisting new dealers order at least one and allowing discounts of up to 20 percent. At year's end, a $1000 price cut was initiated to clear out inventory.

biggest and lushest Ford yet, the K weighed 2000 pounds, rode a stately 120-inch wheelbase, and packed a large 405.4-cid engine with precisely "square" bore and stroke dimensions (4.25 × 4.25 inches) and no less than 40 bhp (developed at 1600 rpm, relatively high for the day). Price was commensurate with its specifications: a lofty $2500. Available as a touring car or roadster, Ford claimed the latter could attain 60 miles per hour.

The very concept of the Model K irked Henry Ford, who wanted a $500 car for the masses. Worse, the K was too heavy for its two-speed transmission, whose bands couldn't stand up to such a heavy car and failed often. But Alex-

ander Malcomson favored high-priced luxury cars, and this plus his sizable investment in a rival auto firm prompted a split. Thus did Henry buy out his chief partner's quarter-interest in the company in July.

That same month brought the death of the company's president, banker John S. Gray. Henry took over the office on October 22, by which point he held a controlling 58.5 percent of the company's shares. Ford and James Couzens bought out three other stockholders in 1906-07, bringing Couzens' interest to 11 percent. From here on, Henry would have the last word on every matter. Ford was now definitely *his* company.

1 9 0 7

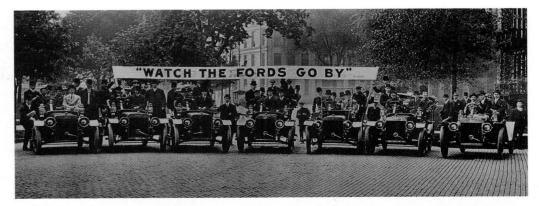

Two new light models bolstered the successful Model N this year: the costlier Model R, which Ford called "a car of more pretentious appearance," and the Model S, a less well-equipped derivative introduced late in the year and considered by some as a 1908 offering. Both were even better-looking than the N and offered a few improvements, such as footboards instead of carriage steps and a mechanical oiler instead of a force-feed affair. Runabout bodywork and 84-inch wheelbases were featured, along with a new 149-cubic-inch four-cylinder engine (bore and stroke: 3.75 × 3.38 inches) developing 15 horsepower at 1400 rpm. This engine was also adopted for the 1907 N. The S differed from the Model R in having less standard equipment and a lower price—$700 versus $750—as well as a single- rather than dual-seat accessory rear tonneau. As the final pre-T model, the S also had distinction of being the last Ford with right-hand drive.

Aside from the larger engine with three more horsepower, the winsome Model N saw no change this year save a price reduced by $100 to Henry's magic $500 figure. The Model K was also unchanged but saw a price increase, jumping $300 to $2800.

This may explain why Ford struggled unsuccessfully to sell its big car throughout 1907. In fact, the company more or less had to force it on the market. For example, new franchise applications were denied unless the applicant agreed to order at least one Model K, and discounts of up to 20 percent were allowed. The firm also tried to insist that agents accept one K for every 10 Ns. But it was all to no avail. The car simply wouldn't sell, and stocks still on hand at year's end had to be cleared at a $1000 discount.

Despite this, Ford's calendar year production took a vertical leap to 14,887 units, a near 59-percent gain over 1906. By contrast, the industry as whole rose less than 30 percent (to 43,000 units), leaving Ford with close to 35 percent of the market—remarkable for an automaker not even five years old.

Things might have been even better had Wall Street not registered a sharp drop on March 14, when the Dow Jones average fell 6.89 points—equivalent to 8.3 percent of its total value—closing at 76.23 points. It was the stock market's largest percentage drop up to that time and remains the eighth largest loss to this day. But Ford Motor Company, at least, was still in an optimistic mood, for 1907 also saw the opening of branch offices in Hamburg, Germany, and Paris.

The year also brought one of the most famous and enduring of advertising slogans, "Watch the Fords Go By," which the company would use from time to time through the early Forties. It originated with either advertising manager E. LeRoy Pelletier or traffic manager W. S. Hogue. After Pelletier's departure, *Ford Times* credited the phrase to Hogue, who was said to have shouted it at a race in which Fords were whizzing by the competition.

These words became a familiar sight on many of the "all-Ford" trains that puffed out of Detroit to all parts of the country. They were also seen on a mammoth electric sign erected atop Detroit's Temple Theater in 1908. Though other Ford slogans and the company's "winged pyramid" trademark pushed it aside within a few years, "Watch the Fords" became one of the two best-known automobile catch-phrases of all

"Watch the Fords Go By" (top) became one of Ford's most famous and enduring slogans. It emerged in 1907 and would be used off and on through the early Forties. The 1907 Model K chassis (center) shows how much room the inline six-cylinder engine needed. A slightly upmarket N, the Model R (bottom) was "a car of slightly more pretentious appearance," as Ford put it. It featured rather crude running boards in place of step plates and a mechanical engine oiler.

The 1907 Ford Model K roadster (top and center) was dashing in appearance. It sported plenty of brass, a bold radiator and big headlights, nicely integrated running boards, handsome pin striping, and a "mother-in-law" seat. The touring model (bottom) looked higher and more ponderous—and it was. The big six had a bore and stroke of 4½ by 4¼ inches, mechanical lifters, and a Holley carb.

time (the other being Packard's "Ask the Man Who Owns One").

Numerous takeoffs on this phrase have also appeared over the years. J. T. Flynn wrote an article entitled "Watch the Ford Myths Go By" for *New Republic* in 1937. Al Pearce, appearing for Ford on radio that same year, called his show "Watch the Fun Go By." A Ford-sponsored radio newscast during the World War II years was called "Watch the World Go By." A 1940 cartoon showing Henry and Edsel Ford whizzing by labor leader John L. Lewis used the original words. So did a 1944 editorial equating Henry Ford's 1942 and 1944 predictions that the war would end in a few months with his 1931 statement that "prosperity is here, but only a few realize it." *Broadcasting-Television* magazine ran a 1949 article titled "Watch the UN Go By!" concerning Ford's sponsorship of United Nations telecasts. The slogan also inspired the headline for a 1963 *Newsweek* story on Henry Ford II's luxurious new yacht, and found expression in the form of "Watch the Fords Go Back" for a 1972 *Business Week* article on automotive recalls.

1 9 0 8

Despite being a relative latecomer to the automotive field, Ford Motor Company had produced nine models—A, B, C, E, F, K, N, R, and S—by this, its sixth year in business. It had also carved out a solid place in the market, selling 6398 cars for the fiscal year ending July 31, 1908 and netting over $1.1 million for the 15 months ending December 31. Ford was now one of the "Big Four" makers and perhaps four rungs from the top of the profit ladder.

As the company prepared to introduce its tenth model, competition remained formidable and the dark cloud of the Selden suit still hung ominously on the horizon. But with the Model T, Ford would abruptly leave the pack. Over the next 18 years, it would simply dominate U.S. car sales, accounting for more than half the industry's total output in 1918-19 and 1921-25. Profits soared accordingly. In 1911-15, 1918, and again in 1921, Ford earned more money than all other automakers combined.

There was no sign of any this as the year opened, though keen observers might have noted that production at Piquette Avenue was up to 80-100 cars per day. More noteworthy, Ford was experimenting with a rope-and-pulley system by which cars were dragged along guide rails or tracks as a means of speeding assembly. This system was quickly abandoned as unworkable, however not the basic idea behind it. Then, too, Ford offered no new products through most of 1908, its 1907 R, S, K, and N continuing with absolutely no change.

Then, on March 18, Ford sent advance catalogs describing its new Model T to dealers throughout the nation, and the response was immediate and enthusiastic. "We must say it is almost too good to be true," a Detroit dealer wrote headquarters. "We have rubbed our eyes several times to make sure we were not dreaming." Said a Pennsylvania agent: "It is without doubt the greatest creation in automobiles ever placed before a people, and it means that this circular alone will flood your factory with orders." Several dealers even reported hiding the information, fearing that it would be impossible for them to sell older models on hand once word got out about the new Ford. An Illinois dealer was typical: "We have carefully hidden the sheets away and locked the drawer, throwing the key down the cold-air shaft."

As noted, Henry had been thinking about a car like the Model T for a long time, but the actual design work didn't get underway in earnest until 1907. C.J.

"Jimmy" Smith, one of several who helped give birth to the T, described how it went in Philip Van Doren Stern's 1955 book *Tin Lizzie:* "The experimental room was...about 12 by 15 feet—big enough to get a car in; also milling machines, drill presses, and lathes. In that room we did all the main parts buildup for the experimental engines. It was what you would call advanced design.

"Mr. Ford spent a lot of time in that department. He was there every day. He brought the idea to us. First he would think the thing up, then he would have them draw it up, and then we would make it up....

"Our job was to get the advanced designs—the ideas that Mr. Ford and others would bring in to us—and actually put them together and test them. We would machine them all up, even get the castings and everything, and take them and build them in a car, and take the car out and test it.

"The Model T plans were drawn up by Joe Galamb. Our section helped develop the final Model T by doing all the test work on the R, N, and S. When we had a new part, we'd put it in the car and go out and test it. Mr. Ford....would want to know how the parts worked out and all about the tests. His office was right next to the experimental room, and he would spend all his spare time working with us....Mr. Ford tested the Model T himself. He went out with us many a time. Mr. Ford wouldn't let anything go out of the shop unless he was satisfied that it was as nearly as perfect as you could make it."

Galamb was a Hungarian-born, German-trained engineer who put in many late nights at the drafting table. Other key figures included C.H. Wills, who was initially assigned to do the metallurgical work, and Charles Sorensen, foreman of Ford's pattern shop. It says something about the process and the people involved that Sorensen, as Beverly Rae Kimes recounted in *Automobile Quarterly*, "didn't even bother awaiting blueprints; simply hearing an idea from Henry was sufficient go-ahead for him to make a pattern and cast it."

Though not publicly introduced until October 1, the T is closely associated with 1908, perhaps because of those aforementioned catalogs. Still, it was obviously intended as a 1909 offering, as most manufacturers, including Ford, then started a new model year with each calendar year. Nevertheless, a few Ts were built in the final months of 1908. The generally accepted figure is 309, though company branch audits indicate that only 126 left the Piquette Avenue plant before New Year's.

Utility, not beauty, was the Model T's hallmark, yet the car's very homeliness had an appealing honesty. Its compact body was tall, narrow, and high off the road, yet that sheer ungainliness somehow gave the impression of a lithe

toughness. The inline 20-horsepower four-cylinder engine, ample fuel tank (10 gallons for the touring model), and stout wheels and springs suggested the ability to travel far and wide with utter reliability.

Because it may be unfamiliar to younger readers, let's briefly describe the car that once was as common as goggles and duster coats on the rugged, rutted roads of early 20th Century America. Weighing 1200-1500 pounds depending on body style, the Model T used a side-valve, three-main-bearing engine of undersquare bore/stroke dimensions (3.75 × 4.00 inches) and 176.7 cubic inches. Cylinders were cast *en bloc* (rather than in pairs), one of the first engines so built. With a compression ratio of just 4.5:1, it would run, as one contemporary wag put it, "on almost anything from gasoline to a good grade of kerosene." That's maybe a shade optimistic, but octane certainly didn't matter to a Tin Lizzie. Lubrication was via a combination of gravity and splash systems. Gravity also took care of delivering fuel from a gas tank mounted beneath the front seat. Cooling was by means of a thermosyphon system except on the first 2500 cars, which had water pumps.

The sturdy 100-inch-wheelbase chassis employed a beam axle and transverse leaf spring at the front—and the very same arrangement at the rear. Henry saw no need for different suspension geometry at each end of his "Universal Car."

Initial body styles comprised the usual touring and three-seat runabout (or roadster—the names were interchangeable), the latter with a one-passenger rear seat separate from the main body that was often jokingly called a "mother-in-law" seat. Respectively listed at $850 and $825, they were quite a bit upstream of the Models R, S, and N, though prices would fall in due course. Folding top and acetylene gas headlamps cost extra. Only four wheels and tires were supplied and there was no provision for carrying a spare, quite a drawback with the mostly primitive dirt roads of the day. However you did get a horn, three oil lamps, and top attachment irons.

Beginning in 1909, body choices expanded to include a closed coupe; two-door landaulet with fabric rear roof section and a taxi version of same called the "Taximeter"; a more formal sedan-like model called the Town Car, with fully enclosed rear seating; and a touring car *sans* rear doors dubbed the "Tourster" or, in some places, "Tourabout." Today, of course, the idea of multiple body styles designed for a single chassis is taken for granted, but it wasn't in 1908. As Kimes observed, the "proposition was met with considerable skepticism in the industry and the press—and had earlier been greeted with disfavor by some members of the Ford hierarchy."

The key to driving any Model T was Ford's patented planetary transmission, built in unit with the engine. Henry was quite proud of it. A ball-and-socket joint at the tail end of the transmission housing received the ball front of the driveshaft and took the driving thrust (along with radius rods) from the rear wheel bearings. Except on the first 2500 cars built, the transmission was controlled by what Kimes termed "the three most famous pedals in the world." These were marked "C", "R", and "B"—presumably to prevent novices from forgetting. Pedal "C"—clutch—worked a band inside the transmission that engaged one of the two forward speeds. Pedal "R"—reverse—connected to a similar reverse band. Pedal "B"—brake—operated a brake band that simply stopped the driveshaft from rotating and thus halted the car—more or less.

The Model T had several other attention-getting features. Its steering apparatus was on the left, a departure with far-reaching consequences given the ultimately huge production volume. Within a few years, other U.S. automakers would follow suit. The three-point engine mounting, another novelty for the day, was especially important in an era of bad roads. It avoided the distortion of the engine base common with two-point mounting, and was also soon adopted by other automakers.

Still another valuable innovation was the detachable cylinder head. Rival companies ridiculed it, asserting that it was impossible to cast a separate cylinder head that wouldn't leak. Within a half-dozen years, however, they'd be following Ford's example here, too. The arc springs afforded no luxurious ride, but freed body and chassis from the racking torsional stress suffered by most other cars. The T's improved version of the Ford planetary transmission got away from heavy stick clutches and stripped gears in a period when countless Americans did not know how to shift gears and the metal in transmissions was soft.

And there was still more. Replacing

For 1908, Ford trotted out the Models R, S, K, and N, all of them essentially unchanged. The main reason for that was that Ford was putting all its energy into the upcoming Model T, which was announced to dealers on March 18, 1908 via advance catalogs. Still, the old models would have to soldier on until the Model T went into production in the fall. The Model S roadster (above) sold for $700 in two-passenger form, or for $50 extra with a tonneau that seated two more, though they rode out in the elements. The Model N (below) was the least expensive in the line, starting at $600.

the dry cells of yore was a simple, ingenious magneto to supply current for the spark plugs. It was integral with the engine, so "every time the flywheel revolves," as ads boasted, "you get a series of sparks." The magneto required a few subsequent modifications. Sturdy vanadium steel, borrowed from the N, R, and S, was used for crankshafts, axles, gears, and springs. (Henry had discovered its superior strength in 1905, when he picked up an undamaged vanadium part from a French racing car that wrecked at Palm Beach.)

All this plus an announced $825 base price gave Ford considerable justification for claiming that "no car under $2000 offers more, and no car over $2000 offers more except in trimmings." Here truly was an Aladdin's lamp that needed only occasional rubbing to produce a long career of industrial growth, fame, and prosperity.

Still, early Model Ts had many faults. Rear axle bearings, initially made of babbitt metal, were a particularly weak point. They elongated with continued pounding on bad roads and consequently required frequent replacement. Roller bearings were substituted by 1910. Transmission bands were prone to easy burning out until a better material was adopted. Owners complained about the differently sized front and rear wheels and tires (30 × 3 and 30 × 3.5, respectively) that necessitated carrying at least one spare for each end. The touring car's rear seat was too narrow at first. Riveting improvements were needed, and later made. And cranking a Model T, especially in cold weather, caused innumerable broken arms and endless profanity. The company suggested that owners with cold garages attach an electric light to a long cord and keep it burning under the hood to keep the engine warm, a sort of primitive engine-block heater.

Then too, owners quickly learned that no two Model Ts were exactly alike. Mastering of any particular one involved a high degree of courage, skill, intuition, and luck. Despite its superior dependability and utter simplicity, the T was devastatingly eccentric. Even today it has more character than any car ever known. Buying one in 1908 was to embark on a great adventure.

So was driving. After checking fuel level (peer into the tank), you fired up with a few healthy cranks on the starter handle. (An optional electric starter would be offered in 1919.) When the engine was chugging, you adjusted the spark by means of the "mule ear" lever on the left of the steering column. Dyed-in-the-wool T-drivers still take pride in knowing precisely where to set the spark and throttle levers before starting and how to adjust the choke just so. "We all had to know the hand-cranking procedure, with the choke wire by the radiator," said a longtime aficionado. "Your

The Model T Ford debuted on October 1, 1908. The most popular model (at least initially) was the five-passenger touring (top). It sold for $850. The Runabout (center) cost $25 less. Weight was 900 pounds for the chassis, 1200 for the touring. The cockpit (bottom) was simple. Ford said that "Complete control of the Ford car may be had without removing the hands from the steering wheel."

left toes knew the pressure and angle to hold it in Neutral while you released the hand brake-cum-clutch-neutralizer. The idea was to shove in the pedal to get to low speed as fast as possible, because a slow application wore out the bands. When you judged the speed sufficient for the load and grade you eased back into High, controlling the gas lever at the same time."

That may sound easy, but the complete shifting drill is extremely complicated for the newcomer, who usually forgets that Lizzie isn't just another car and will invariably push the right pedal to accelerate and the left to declutch—with predictable results. As John Keats once wrote, it usually took at least a year of practicing before the novice Model T driver "could get into High without bounding down the road looking like a frog with St. Vitus' dance and sounding like a canning factory with something wrong with it."

Braking was an equally interesting exercise that novices invariably attempted even though a T is...well, so unbreakable (pun intended). If it does hit something, chances are it'll just bounce off. You'd think you'd stomp on the "B" pedal to stop—except that this rarely does more than slow the pace a little. The column-mounted handbrake/declutch lever is usually needed, and it doesn't hurt to jab the "R" pedal on occasion.

The seating position in any Tin Lizzie is towering. You actually look *down* on the hood from a perch level with the roofs of most cars built after 1955 or so. Roadholding, given the rudimentary suspension, is surprisingly good, though no Model T is really fast enough to tax it—only 40-45 mph tops. That's just as well, because who'd want to corner quickly in a car some 6½ feet tall?

Journalist-historian Mike Lamm, who drove a T in 1977 for *Special-Interest Autos*, felt that Lizzie's horsepower must have been underrated "because acceleration feels a lot stronger than any 20 bhp could make it. The car *does* move out, and it holds 40-45 beautifully—a speed that feels plenty fast for the T's braking and handling capabilities." Steering, at four turns lock-to-lock for the tight 28-foot turning circle, is acceptable even today. Said Lamm, "The front tires can be flapped from side to side with no problem." The only steering reduction was by a planetary gearset under the wheel. A bolt-on lever at the lower end of the steering shaft pushed or pulled a rod working the tie rods between the spindle arms.

Hills presented a special challenge. The typical T-driver approached one either flat out (with a running start) or—for steeper grades—in Reverse. There were two reasons for that. Reverse was geared higher than Low (4:1 versus 3:1), and the gravity-feed gas tank was higher than the carburetor, so unless the tank was full the car would stall going forward up a grade of more than one-in-five. And

there was a reason for *that*. The gravity/splash lube system wasn't fully effective at such angles. Ford had positioned the gas tank to eliminate the chance of oil starvation on steep grades!

Writer Stern records that the first production Lizzie was completed on September 24, though a few "pilot cars" were built earlier. George Brown, another of Henry's assistants, recalled that business: "After they got the Model T through the experimental stage they started building [it] at Piquette. I remember when they built the first one, which was practically a handmade car.... I guess it was Frank Kulick who took it out on the road and tested it.... In those years... you'd take it out on the rough roads and give it the works, and then they'd tear it down. They'd go over it and check over the wearing parts and the engine and tear it right down to pieces. In the early stages there were a lot of changes made.

"Anyhow, they got the car going. After they got the first one built, they started easy and got the number-2 built. [Then] they started placing orders for their stock. It was a slow proposition.... I remember Mr. Ford used to get out there and say, 'I wonder if we'll get up to number-10.'" Henry liked to joke.

He was also excited about the finished product. According to Kimes, when the first pilot Model T came down from the third floor at Piquette, "Henry's enthusiasm almost overwhelmed him—and everybody else. Perhaps too excited to drive the car himself, he asked associate George Holley to take him downtown. The pair coursed the streets of Detroit; Henry, drinking in the sweetness of revenge, made sure that the trek took him past the offices of [former partner]

Ford described the Model T as "Serviceable and of very pleasing appearance from every view point." And for its time, it was, although it looked so tall and narrow that one would expect it to tip over quite easily. Visibility out of the closed top (bottom) was marginal at best.

Alexander Malcomson. Returning home, he gave everyone within striking distance 'a kick in the pants' or a 'punch in the shoulders.' 'Well,' he said, 'I guess we've got started.'"

Yet despite its historic importance today, the Model T was just another new car in 1908, one that seemed likely to evolve into a Model U within a few years. Not that Ford didn't expect it to sell well. In a September 5 letter the company told its dealers that each of them would initially get only one demonstration car because demand was likely to outstrip production capacity.

Ten days later, on Tuesday the 15th, 13 branch managers from the U.S. and Canada plus two from Europe toured the Piquette Avenue plant as well as the new Ford factory going up in Highland Park, soon to be the world's biggest auto plant. On Wednesday they got their first look at the Model T in demonstration runs and registered their approval. Thursday began with a luncheon at the Detroit Yacht Club, followed by an outing on the Dodge brothers' steam yacht *Hornet*. That evening, at a banquet at the Detroit Country Club, Ford told its branch officials that 25,000 Ts would be built in the coming year, an unprecedented schedule for a new model. A good thing, that, as the managers were demanding at least 15,000.

When the first production T came off the line a week or so later, Henry Ford jumped in and took it on a hunting trip to northern Wisconsin. Jimmy Smith and Bert Scott went along to do the driving. Stern notes that after some battery trouble "they reached Chicago, 345 miles away, in 16½ hours, making an average speed of almost 21 mph. At Chicago, the local branch manager borrowed the car [to show] to a few selected people who had been told about it. The hunting party then went...to Milwaukee, where they saw the 24-hour automobile race being held there. Afterward they drove to northern Wisconsin, stopping in Iron Mountain [Michigan] on the way.... Henry Ford stayed on [there] while Scott and Smith drove the car back to Detroit. They had to go through a brush fire and nearly got burned up.... Otherwise the return trip was uneventful. They arrived in Detroit on October 2, where the mud-stained car was photographed."

On October 15, The *Ford Times*, the company's new monthly publication inaugurated in April to provide employee information and promote auto travel, detailed the trip. The first production Lizzie, it said, "behaved admirably, requiring not even a single adjustment in the entire 10 days. A punctured tire sums up the difficulties encountered.... The roads going were six inches deep in dust—returning after the rains the roads were wet and muddy, and the car when it arrived in Detroit looked as if it had been taking a mud bath."

By that point, the whole country

knew about the T, thanks to a pre-launch publicity campaign that was perhaps the most ambitious ever mounted by an American manufacturer. News releases, photographs, and sketches were sent to the press on an unprecedented scale, and the response proved commensurate with the effort. *Horseless Age* and *Motor Age* each published eight photos or diagrams of the car, along with highly complimentary stories. *Motor World* ran four large pictures and called the T "a credit to the genius of Henry Ford." A record amount of literature went to dealers, who sent back a torrent of orders by mail, telegraph, telephone, and personal visits.

Initially, Model T bodies came in several colors, but with black fenders. Early 1909 touring cars were usually red, but later in the year most were green. Note the complementary pin striping. Windshields and tops for open cars were at first optional at extra cost, but were later made standard. The Model T rode on 30×3-inch front tires, 30×3½ at the rear.

Ads soon appeared in trade journals, prompting a flow of urgent orders from general dealers.

But the topper was an ad in the October 3 edition of the *Saturday Evening Post.* Said *Ford Times*: "If we were flattered by the reception the trade tendered the T, and surely no announcement ever received so glorious an acknowledgement...much more were we elated by the response from the consumer. The ad appeared on Friday; Saturday's mail brought nearly 1,000 inquiries. Monday's response swamped our mail clerks and by Tuesday night the office was well nigh inundated. There isn't a state in the Union that has not registered its approval of the Model T and the Ford Policy." Branches and local agencies also beat the drums as never before, buying unusually large amounts of newspaper space to trumpet the new Ford.

Once loosed, the cascade of orders continued unabated. By winter, demand was running so far ahead of supply that the company said Ts would be shipped

only to those dealers who had sold off all their old models on hand, "rationing" unheard of in the auto business. By May 1, 1909, production was lagging badly enough that the company stopped taking orders for nine weeks and, according to Kimes, scaled back 1909 calendar year production to 18,257 units.

The final figure ended up 17,771, a startling 74 percent increase over the 10,202 units in transition 1908 (including K, N, R, and S models). But the rest of the industry spurted, too, from 63,500 to 123,900, so Ford's share hardly changed at all, remaining at a little over 8 percent.

It wouldn't stay there for long, though, for Model T sales would literally skyrocket over the next decade, in some years jumping more than a 100 percent from the year before. America's involvement in World War I broke the upward spiral from 1917 to 1919, but then came the T's heyday: six years in which annual domestic sales topped the one-million mark and one with more than two million.

The Model T had caused a sensation in 1908, and the clamor didn't die down in 1909. Additional body styles were added early in the year, the most expensive of which was the $1000 Town Car.

Also as previously noted, several changes were made after the first 2500 units. The most significant was the famous three-pedal transmission control to replace the original two-pedal/two-lever setup in which the wheel-brake and reverse bands were hand-operated from "mule ears" on the steering column. Ford evidently thought so much of the three-pedal arrangement that it issued a $15 conversion kit for early Ts. As a result, only one "two-lever" model was known to exist by 1955, according to author Philip Van Doren Stern, though several others turned up later.

Other early, "second thoughts" alterations included the aforementioned switch from water-pump to thermosyphon cooling, deletion of the "wings" flanking the embossed Ford radiator script (though this persisted on some cars built as late as 1910), steel instead of linoleum-covered wood runningboards, and 14- instead of 13-inch steering wheels. After this, changes in the T would be fairly rare and thus quite newsworthy.

Lizzie made her formal U.S. debut on the last day of 1908 at New York's Grand Central Palace, but she'd already had her coming out in Europe. A batch of eight Ts built in October was shipped off for the November Olympia (London) and Paris motor shows. *Automobile Quarterly*'s Beverly Rae Kimes observed that "press reaction in both cities was restrained," *The Autocar*, for example, merely citing Ford together with Cadillac as "two notable exponents of the small car." Still, 253 British showgoers placed orders for a Model T.

Ford was already doing business in both England and the Continent. Though non-American operations are beyond the scope of this book, a brief word on them is appropriate here because this was the period when Ford began to be a truly international company. Financial manager James Couzens got the ball rolling when he journeyed to London in August 1908 to set up a factory sales branch to take over for the successors to the Central Motor Car Company of London, the firm's British agent up to that point. To head it, Couzens named one of Central's managers, 31-year-old Percival Lee .Dewhurst Perry, later Lord Perry of Stock

Harvard. Couzens chose well. Perry would head Ford's British branch for the rest of his life save 1919-28, and would direct Ford plants all over Europe from 1931 through 1948. He was every bit as important as the loveable Lizzie in Ford's rapid overseas expansion.

The T's sturdy dependability and urging from thousands of dealers and enthusiasts induced Henry Ford to approve an official factory entry for a New York-to-Seattle race in the spring of 1909. Mining magnate Robert Guggenheim, who had arranged the cross-country run to promote the Alaska-Yukon-Pacific Exposition, imposed rigid requirements. Competitors had to check in at 30 points; could obtain new parts only in Chicago and Cheyenne, Wyoming; and were forbidden to travel on railroad tracks. Of the 14 vehicles entered, only five—two Model Ts, an Acme, a Shawmut, and an Italia—responded to the starting gun. The Fords reached St. Louis some two hours ahead of the nearest rival, and remained together until reaching Idaho. Then Ford No. 1, with Frank Kulick and advertising manager H. B. Harper aboard, forged ahead with a nine-hour lead. But they got lost twice because of misdirections and fell a day and a half behind. Ford No. 2 was piloted by Jimmy Smith and Bert Scott, who had driven Henry on his Wisconsin hunting trip the previous fall. They headed straight for Seattle, arriving at the exposition amid the cheers of some 200,000 people after 22 days and 55 minutes. The Shawmut arrived 17 hours later, followed several hours after that by Ford No. 1. The Acme reached Seattle a week later; the Italia had been withdrawn at Cheyenne.

This race was widely reported, and Ford lost little time in capitalizing on the high public interest in it. A booklet written by Harper, called *The Story of the Race*, was distributed to dealers by the tens of thousands. A large-scale newspaper and magazine advertising cam-

paign shouted the news, and flailed the many rival manufacturers who'd shied from entering. High stamina and low price were naturally the main talking points. One ad proclaimed the Model T "the one reliable car that does not require a $10,000 income to buy, a $5000 bank account to run and a college course in engineering to keep in order." Soon afterwards, the winning Ford was displayed at hundreds of dealerships on a 6000-mile swing from Seattle to Los Angeles and back to New York, where it arrived just in time to be exhibited at the Hudson-Fulton celebration.

But the boom of Ford's victory drums was soon muffled. Five months after the fact, the judges discovered that Smith and Scott had violated the rules by swapping engines in Ford No. 2 en route, and awarded first prize to the Shawmut. But Ford lost only a moral victory; the propaganda hay had been reaped long before.

A historical footnote: Fifty years later, in 1959, Ford reenacted this race for publicity purposes. A 1909 Ford stopped in 85 cities along the original route and was seen by tens of thousands of people. William Clay Ford, the youngest grandson of Henry Ford and a company vice-president, greeted the car and escorting vehicles at the future site of the 1962 Seattle World's Fair. According to the company's northeast regional office, which had major responsibility for it, the promotion was "the most important and successful program carried out by this office in recent years." Interest-

Durability, an important selling point in 1909, likely prompted Henry Ford to okay the official entry of a Model T in a New York to Seattle race run that spring. Two Fords competed. The one driven by Jimmy Smith and Bert Scott finished first. The one piloted by Frank Kulick, seated at the wheel (below), and H.B. Harper, came in third. The winning Ford was later disqualified. The 1909 Model T touring car (right) listed at $850.

The four-passenger Model T Tourabout, sometimes also called the Tourster, was introduced in mid-model year 1909 and lasted for only about one year. It was easily identified by the lack of rear doors, which were included on the five-passenger touring model. The Tourabout listed at $950, and the windshield, top, lights, and horn were standard. This model never achieved great popularity, at least in part because it didn't have the rear doors. Speaking of doors, only the coupe body style had front doors.

ingly, none of Ford's press releases, nor a film of the expedition released in 1962, mentioned that the "winning" Model T had been disqualified.

Henry's son Edsel had developed an interest in that other new field of the early 1900s, aviation, and it was in 1909 that Ford Motor Company first leaped into the skies with an airplane of its own. Alan Nevins briefly recounted this small initial venture in *Ford: The Times, The Man, The Company:* "The fuselage was of wood and metal tubing, the wings of spruce covered with silk and linen. A tricycle landing gear was constructed, with two turnable wheels in front. The wings had no ailerons [flaps] and were warped to effect turns.

"The plane, finished in about a year, was tested on the Ford farm in Dear-

born, where a plank runway was laid out on a gentle slope. The plane rose about four feet from the earth, but was too heavy for its motor. After being lightened, it would hop at times to a height of six feet, then drop.

"During the tests the crankshaft broke and the plane was blown into a tree, with mild injuries to Van Auken, who was piloting it. [Henry] Ford then ordered the trials discontinued, thus waving aside any opportunity to become a pioneer."

As with Kulick's motor-racing accident two years earlier, Henry was perhaps scared by the dangers of flying, preferring to leave that to his friends, the Wright brothers. Not until 1925 would Henry have another go with aircraft, and then only at his son's urging.

1 9 1 0

Lizzie was mechanically unchanged for 1910 except for some tinkering with the rear axle, but prices went up on a rearranged model group. The landaulet and Tourster/Tourabout were dropped, the Town Car went up $200 to $1200, and the touring car and three-passenger Runabout/roadster were hiked $100 as Ford standardized the previously optional windshield, headlamps, and top. A new offering was the racy Torpedo roadster with a more rakishly angled windshield that suggested speed (matched by a longer steering column), and the Torpedo was relatively fast, at least a bit quicker than other production Ts.

There were also two new utility offerings. The Commercial Roadster was essentially the normal Runabout with a "mother-in-law" seat that could be removed to create a flat platform for carrying cargo—a sort of embryonic pickup truck. It sold for $650 but came with absolutely no frills. Ford also began offering a $700 chassis for mounting of commercial delivery bodies built by outside firms.

Ford's calendar-year output saw another jump this year, to 32,053 units, a gain of almost 50 percent. Market share settled in at 17.8 percent, as total industry volume climbed by 57,100 units to 181,000.

Throughout its life, the Model T was known almost as much for its factory as its qualities as a car, and the factory was the mammoth Highland Park plant, which came on stream on January 1. Located in Highland Park, Michigan, then a community of 4120 surrounded by the city of Detroit, it was designed by Detroiter Albert Kahn, at the time America's greatest industrial architect. Size was what made it noteworthy: the world's largest auto factory and Michigan's largest building under one roof. But Highland Park was also the most aesthetically pleasing factory of its day in architecture, cleanliness, and arrangement. Measuring 865 feet long by 75 feet wide, the four-story building had more than 50,000 square feet of glass, which led some to call it the "Crystal Palace."

Ford publicists spared no effort in touting Highland Park as "the wonder of the automobile world," calling it the "largest single manufacturing institution in the world," and stating that it maintained the "largest machine shop in the world." A photograph showing some 12,000 of the 16,000 employees in front of the factory ran in many newspapers, accompanied by word that the picture was "the largest specially posed photo

ever taken and [is] far and away the most expensive, considering the employees' time and loss of production."

As time went on, the plant's size (the entire complex including a foundry covered 60 acres by 1913) evoked less interest than its production feats. To the Boston News Bureau, Ford's 1912 output (more than 78,000 units) was "remarkable," and the 1913 tally (over 168,000) was "simply phenomenal." Realizing that size alone could not account for such prodigious numbers, executives of other car

Early Model T Fords used a lot of wood, which can be seen on this 1910 model (top) in the cowl area and on the artillery wheels. When down, the top on the touring car was a rather clumsy affair (above), sticking out way behind the body of the car as it did. Note the flat-topped front and rear fenders. Nearly 17,000 touring cars were produced from October 1909 to September 1910 (including Tourabouts), making this easily the most popular body style that year.

companies hastened to Highland Park to see the techniques that made it all possible. They were generous in their praise. Karl Neumaier, general manager of Germany's famed Benz Company, told the press: "The Ford plant is the most remarkable in the world; it is the very best in equipment and method." Louis Renault, head of the French automobile firm bearing his name, declared the facility to be "the best organized in the country" and that he was "very much impressed by the ingenuity displayed in the manufacturing of cars."

The advent of mass production, begun with the Model T, is generally regarded as the greatest achievement of Henry Ford and his company. It certainly received a tremendous amount of public notice beginning in 1914. For much of the world, Henry Ford became a symbol of both the process and its rewards, a Messiah to those impressed by size, vast quantities of goods, and the high standard of living mass production made possible. But he was equally a devil to those who deplored the "triumph" of machine over man, those who found no worth in huge industrial operations and uniform products. Yet even many of these detractors drove Model Ts.

Engineering societies, business organizations, and dealer groups began visiting Highland Park as early as 1910 to see the "magic methods" they had read or heard about. Two years later, *Ford Times* reported that "the reception business is being systematized and soon will able to handle four or five crowds a day." A 24- to 30-man guide corps was organized once a concerted effort was made to encourage plant visits. It was evidently successful, as the *Christian Science Monitor* reported that "the competent corps of guides" had escorted "thousands of persons" through the plant in 1912. By early spring of 1914, an average of 150 guests were touring the factory each day.

By that time, the company had organized its Motion Picture Department,

As might be expected, the 1910 Model T was basically a carryover. It did receive some mechanical tweaks, however, among them an improved rear axle, which can be seen above. Also visible is the arced rear spring, which was of course mounted transversely. The heavy use of brass can be seen on these cars. Like the other Model T models, the touring car rode a wheelbase of 100 inches and had a 56-inch tread front and rear, with a 60-inch spread being optional until 1916. Overall length measured a modest 134½ inches. The 1910 touring car listed at $950.

which featured the factory and visiting celebrities in a nationally distributed newsreel believed to be the first ever made in an industrial plant. It was exclusive grist for what was called the "Ford Animated Weekly."

After the announcement of the five-dollar-a-day wage in early 1914, Highland Park became "a national landmark and a new Niagara Falls," a major Midwest tourist attraction, a must-see stop for every visitor to Detroit. President William Howard Taft thought the place "wonderful, wonderful," and Roger W. Babson, president of the Babson Statistical Organization, said his visit was like a pilgrimage to a shrine. That view was evidently shared by William Bausch, head of Bausch & Lomb, who, with 19 business friends, traveled 320 miles just to see the factory. Approximately 100,000 people visited during 1915, and the figure more than doubled in two years.

It was in the summer of 1910 that Ford resumed full-scale racing following its return to competition in 1909. Dealers were delighted; within a few months, many reported that racing had greatly stimulated sales. Frank Kulick was again a consistent winner, *Motor Age* magazine again ranking him as one of America's top drivers in 1910-11. Two other pilots

helped the Ford cause. R.P. Rice, manager of the Seattle branch, dominated Northwest tracks and held the Seattle-to-Portland road race record from 1910 to 1912. E. Roger Sterns, a Los Angeles dealer, was California's top driver in 1910, ousting Barney Oldfield (who had also resumed racing) and other leading professionals that year.

The Model T was handicapped in racing by its low price and good power-to-weight ratio. To compete against heavier, higher-powered cars whose defeat would count for something, the 950-pound Ford was required in certain meets to carry several hundred pounds of dead weight and cost hundreds of dollars more. On principle, Henry Ford refused to change his car just to satisfy classification requirements, for he regarded the T's lightness and low cost as its chief attributes.

But in one contest open to it, the little 20-horsepower stock chassis proved a match for the heaviest, most powerful vehicles in the land. Ford soon boasted that Kulick, "The Pride of the Company,"

could defeat anyone. When rain postponed an exhibition race between Kulick and Barney Oldfield, who'd have driven a specially built, 200-horsepower Benz, *Ford Times* was keenly disappointed: "Such is fate, and the honors that would have come to Ford were postponed for another meeting."

Following Ford's return to racing in 1909, the Model T notched many victories. Here, a 1910 model on the Munsey Tour (above). A new body style for 1910 was the sleek-looking—for a Model T—Torpedo Runabout (below). It sported a lower seating position, a longer hood, and a rear deck-mounted gas tank, rather than under the driver's seat as on other models. It cost $725.

1 9 1 1

During 1911 the Model T literally became a "Tin Lizzie," thanks to the arrival of sheet-steel bodywork for the best-seller touring car. Up to now, T-bodies had been made entirely of wood, though aluminum had been used for some parts. Only the touring car bodies in 1911 got the new metal panels over wood framing, but other styles would soon follow.

Many of those panels came from Briggs Manufacturing Company, which began supplying them along with stampings and trim under contract to Ford in 1910. Briggs later became Ford's principal body supplier in a relationship that would also involve styling (through 1939) and replacement parts (as late as 1950).

All 1911 models received new metal runningboards stamped with "Ford" script, as well as steering wheels enlarged an inch to a 15-inch diameter, presumably for better leverage and less steering effort. There were also several minor mechanical changes, and Ford began offering the Delivery Car with factory bodywork as well as a bare chassis for the same $700.

But the big news was a substantial price cut on passenger models, beginning what would become a long downward spiral toward the $500-so-anyone-can-buy-it figure that still loomed large in Henry's thinking. The touring went from $950 to $780 with full equipment, the Runabout and Torpedo Roadster (still with identical bodywork save doors on the latter) from $900 to just $680. Even the Town Car, the most expensive offering, tumbled from $1200 to $960 (though it still came with three oil lamps, a toolkit, and tubular horn). On open models you could save an additional $80 by forgoing windshield, top, headlights, and horn, which put the Runabout and roadster at a sensationally low $590.

Helped by the usual advertising support, these price reductions had a predictable effect on sales, which more than doubled the 1910 tally. Calendar-year output set a third consecutive record, climbing to 69,762 units. Ford's industry share almost doubled, too, reaching 35 percent of the 199,319 American cars built this year.

Not included in the counts were the first Fords built overseas, for 1911 saw 15,000 Model Ts completed at the firm's new British plant, erected the previous year at Trafford Park near Manchester in the country's industrial Midlands. Though initially an assembly operation using imported components in the form of "knock-down" kits, Trafford Park quickly moved to build most of the car itself, and what we now call "local content" soon approached 100 percent. As time went on, the Model T would prove as much a "world car" in point of origin as well as performance.

Branch assembly, as Beverly Rae Kimes observes, was Henry's answer to "the wasteful inefficiency in freighting fully-assembled cars in quantity to distances several thousands miles from Detroit," which naturally made sense for the vast United States as well. "By the summer of 1909," Kimes says, "the company had decided to establish branch assembly plants to which as many as seven knocked-down Ts could be shipped in a single ordinary [railroad] box car (alleviating the expense of special freight cars) and duly put together for distribution to dealers in the outlying region."

Ford's first such plant opened in April this year at Kansas City, an industry first that would soon be copied by rivals chasing Henry's price cuts. Ford would later build additional plants in other areas of the country. Overseeing all branch manufacturing operations was one William S. Knudsen, whose services Henry secured early this year with the purchase of the Keim Mills of Buffalo, New York. Knudsen would cause a lot of grief for Ford in the Twenties as general manager of the Chevrolet Division of General Motors. In 1911, however, GM was but three years old, Louis Chevrolet was still building his first car, and Knudsen was an able manager who would contribute much to Ford's prodigious production growth.

Through 1914, Ford made a curious and vain effort to paint its indomitable little rattletrap as something of a prestige item. Press releases told of English aristocrats who owned Fords, and stories appeared around the country under headlines such as "Swells Own Fords." *Ford Times* breathlessly reported that two Russian grand dukes and 19 princes owned Model Ts and that President Wilson had bought one for use at his summer home. Company publicists arranged for show business luminaries like Eddie Foy, Billie Burke, and Henrietta Crossman to be photographed in Tin Lizzies as testimonials. Similarly, dealers were asked to furnish pictures of well-known customers and their cars against backgrounds of "fine-looking residences."

But of course, this campaign was doomed. Henry was clearly not selling an automobile for the elite. As he himself had stated early in his career, "I will build a motor car for the great multitude, constructed of the best materials, by the best men to be hired, after the simplest designs that modern engineering can devise [and thus] so low in price that no man making a good salary will be unable to own one and enjoy with his family the blessing of hours of pleasure in God's great open spaces."

Latterday historians have pointed out that in making the motor car universal, Henry helped destroy the very "great open spaces" he treasured. But given the spirit of the times and the embryonic auto market, he could not have conceived a more intelligent marketing approach nor a more appealing message for consumers. The utilitarian Model T embodied his vision, and farmers and families were already discovering all kinds

Although Henry Ford had never liked the big luxury-oriented Model K of the 1906-1908 era, the Model T lineup included a luxury model of its own, the six-passenger Town Car. It had listed at $1200, but this year the price was knocked down to a more reasonable $960. Only 315 were built.

of uses for it quite apart from its role as a car. Then, too, the T's very inexpensiveness—not to mention becoming even cheaper as time went on—subverted the company's efforts to sell it on the basis of sensible snob appeal.

If not a prestige item, the Model T was a hillclimber *par excellence*. Certainly on a pound-for-pound basis there is considerable evidence to support the *Ford Times'* contention that it was "the greatest hill climber ever built." With no rivals in the low-price class, the T carried off honors time and time again against the most expensive and powerful automobiles.

During what we might call the hill-climbing era of the automobile's early years, virtually every navigable summit in the country was scaled, some with monotonous frequency. A victory in one of the more important events definitely boosted a make's fame and standing. Ford consequently focused on the "name" contests, particularly the one in Algonquin, Illinois, where it scored notable victories from 1910 to 1912. Meantime, dealers and owners carried the Ford banner in numerous minor climbs.

Some dealers were so eager to demonstrate the T's capabilities this way that they advertised for competition. Consider this typical notice posted by a Columbia, South Carolina, agent: "CHALLENGE—Regardless of price, and including Steamers, July 5, '09, The Ford Model T cleaned up every automobile sold in Columbia in a Hill Climb. If you want to make a little more sport for Labor Day, the Ford is ready."

The 1911 Model T touring car (above and left) listed at $780. It received a new body this year, as construction changed from all-wood to sheetmetal over wood framing. All 1911 models also adopted new metal running boards stamped with the "Ford" script, and a larger 15-inch steering wheel gave drivers better leverage in parking. Opposite, bottom: Licensed in New York, this 1911 coupe looks ready to go (left); this dusty driver is shown competing in the 1911 Glidden Tour (right).

Between contests, many dealers drove their Fords up and down a variety of near-perpendicular surfaces. A Model T climbed Ben Nevis, Britain's highest mountain, in 1911, generating widespread publicity in both Great Britain and the U.S. In Nashville, before thousands of spectators, the local Ford dealer drove a car up the 88 steps of the Tennessee capitol building. The Duluth agent covered a $100 bet by persuading a T up three flights of courthouse steps, and a Los Angeles dealer used dynamite to blast his way in and out of the Grand Canyon.

Ford never worked up quite the same enthusiasm for long-distance reliability demonstrations, likely regarding them as too tame. As *Ford Times* complained, "Endurance runs are that only in name; in actuality they are joyrides that accomplish nothing except a holiday for the contestants and advertising orders for the newspapers." The monthly also grumbled that many entrants who finished with perfect scores had cheated, and suggested that each car should carry "a moving picture machine and a talking machine to see what the driver and observer are up to."

Despite this, the company, some of its branches, and many of its dealers participated in hundreds of contests during 1907-12. Fords were frequent winners in their class and occasionally showed well in the sweepstakes competition of important tours. For example, a Model T finished second in the 1910 Munsey Tour, and a three-car team ran fourth

ahead of Cadillac, Marathon, and Flanders in the 1911 running of the prestigious Glidden Tour (first staged in 1905). Perhaps the T's greatest triumph came in Russia, where it was the only one of 45 European and two American entries to earn a perfect score in a 1954-mile test conducted by the Imperial War Department. Czar Nicholas II personally inspected the winning T and recommended that Fords be purchased for the Russian army.

Regardless of the factory's disdain, Ford dealers often staged special endurance tests to show how their cars could withstand the roughest treatment. A Rochester, New York dealer sponsored January tours over hundreds of miles of snow-covered roads. Others loaded Model Ts with a dozen or so passengers for parades down Main Street. This sort of stunt reached its climax in 1911 when a Flivver was driven around Payne, Ohio, carrying 34 boys weighing a combined 3492 pounds.

A Wichita dealer started a minor craze by introducing "auto polo," played with two Model T chassis as field cars and two touring cars as goaltenders. "Endurance runs, speed races, hill climbs and other contests are mere parlor games in comparison," the enthusiastic agent assured the company. The Wichita team staged exhibitions all over the country, concluding with a match in Madison Square Garden.

Meanwhile, Ford and its ace driver/road tester Frank Kulick bowed out of track racing at the Michigan State Fair in

September 1911. In an exhibition single-miler, Kulick defeated some of the sport's biggest names and broke the track record. Immediately afterward, a delighted Henry Ford pressed a $1000 bill into Kulick's hand.

Though this would be his last appearance on a race track, Kulick drove twice more before retiring. In January 1912 he took a second "999" racer over the measured mile in 33.4 seconds on the ice of Lake St. Clair, the fastest anyone had run on ice since Henry's feat of 1904. Come summer that same year, he made "the automobile world stand aghast" by winning the celebrated Algonquin Hill Climb in record-breaking time. His performance so embarrassed big-car manufacturers that they threatened to boycott the 1913 event unless Kulick and his machine were barred—a threat averted when the driver and Ford Motor Company announced they were finished with competition.

Ford kept that promise, though not forever. Still, it would be a long time before the firm backed another racing entry—not until 1935, in fact. With few exceptions, Ford dealers also abandoned the sport in those years. In their stead, private owners and auto accessory firms continued campaigning hundreds of Ts that came to dominate the country's small-town dirt tracks—especially the so-called Fronty-Fords equipped with the powerful Frontenac cylinder head.

In addition, three Frontys qualified for the 1923 running of America's premier auto race, the Memorial Day Indianapolis 500. To the delight of guest official Henry Ford and the surprise of racing fans everywhere, all three finished. The fastest Fronty averaged 82.58 mph to place fifth, an exceptional showing for an inexpensive modified stock car. The machine-gun blast of the backfire through the open exhaust of these racing Fords was heard less after the Model A was announced in 1927, but Ts would continue to compete on dirt tracks until well into the Thirties.

Hillclimbs and reliability runs went into a slow decline in 1910-13, then rapidly fell off as cars became powerful enough to whisk up most any hill and durable enough to manage long distances. Economy runs survived much longer, but they were never as popular as other forms of early automotive competition and Ford entered only a handful. Winning performances were based on a fuel-to-weight ratio that the company deemed unfair to its light, economical Lizzie. Its suggestion that weight should not be a factor elicited no response among economy-run sponsors.

Ford's early and successful participation in track racing, hillclimbs, and more practical forms of competition convinced many motorists that the Model T was spirited, dependable, and economical to operate. It did much to ensure the Tin Lizzie's sales leadership in 1911.

New for this year's Model T was availability of what we'd now call an option: separate front doors for the ubiquitous touring, in which form it was called the "Fore-Door." But the name was quite misleading because the left front "door" was just a solid panel painted to look like it opened. The car actually had only three working doors: one in front, on the right, and the usual two at the rear. However, both the dummy and genuine front doors could be removed if desired to create the familiar "open-front"-style touring. "Fore" doors were also applied to the Town Car as standard equipment, only both of these opened (and were also removable).

Elsewhere, styling changes apparently intended to reduce the number of unique parts among the various body styles made the Torpedo Roadster higher, tubbier, and more like other Ts. Its dashing raked windshield was gone, replaced by the flat, folding affair used on the runabout. Buyers evidently didn't approve, for the model would not return in 1913.

Despite its "changeless" reputation, the Model T actually received quite a few minor interim modifications in its early years. Typical of Ford, these were not made according to any schedule, nor heavily advertised. This year saw a raft of changes effective with April production. "Early" (pre-April) 1912s were identical to their 1911 counterparts except for a one-piece dashboard (previously two-piece) and "Ford" radiator script that was embossed in the metal rather than being a separate nameplate affixed to it. "Late" 1912 changes included the aforementioned "fore" doors and Torpedo Roadster restyling, plus smooth-sided open bodies with seat bases no longer extending beyond the body sills. At the same time, Ford reverted to its pre-1911 practice of selling open models with windshield, top, and horn, and including these items in the advertised prices.

Henry Ford was now fully convinced that price reductions were by far the most important factor in Model T merchandising. He often said he gained 1000 new customers each time he trimmed a dollar from his prices, and justified the practice by relating these cuts to rising sales.

Henry was the boss, so prices came down again in 1912, this time by $80 on all models save the Town Car, reduced $60, and the Delivery Car (a.k.a. "Delivery Wagon"), which remained at $700. Thus, the touring car (with or without

"fore" doors) listed at $690 while the Runabout, Torpedo, and Commercial Runabout were tagged at $590.

The boss was proved right by yet another volume increase in this, the final year before the advent of the mass-production assembly line. For the calendar year, Highland Park cranked out 78,440 units, 8678 more than in 1911, a 12.4 percent hike. Corresponding industry production, however, jumped by more than a third to 356,000, so Ford's piece of the pie shriveled to just 22 percent, versus 35 percent a year earlier. The assembly line would soon put Ford back on top in both volume and production share. Meantime, despite prodigious efforts, the company was still hard-pressed to meet demand. Ford's price cuts were generously reported. Wire services, which rarely carried automotive news, flashed stories highly favorable to Ford following the reductions this year and next. *Harper's Weekly*, weighing the contribution of these to the T's success, opined that Henry "has thought out the best advertisement, and made the deepest, most sensational appeal to human nature he could have made."

Besides prices, Model T advertising from 1912 to 1916 emphasized the company's "winged pyramid" trademark. This was described by advertising manager Glen Buck as "a happy combination of two of the oldest Egyptian symbols: the pyramid symbolizing strength and stability, the scarab wings symbolizing lightness and grace." The pyramid

literally permeated the Ford organization for several years. "Here is the new sun of the Ford advertising system," Buck rhapsodized in one of many articles extolling the logo. "It shall be the 'blazing flag' around which the Ford forces shall rally."

The company certainly did its best to make sure the pyramid was seen. More than half the space in some Ford ads was devoted to it. Dealers were ordered to paint it on their sales windows and strongly urged to use it on their letterhead stationery. All Model T number plates bore the logo after October 1912. Within a year, the pyramid was "widely established all over the world," according to one latterday expert, and was of "enormous value" to the company. It was used consistently until late 1916, when for some reason the firm's Operating Committee questioned whether it should be continued. The matter was naturally referred to Henry himself. According to secretary Ernest G. Liebold, the boss abolished the symbol after being told that "scarab is another name for dung beetle."

It may surprise younger readers to learn that the Model T was the only car built before World War II to be subjected to market research. Ford first surveyed public opinion in early 1912, when 1000 owners (a one-percent sample) were asked, "Just what reason or reasons were foremost in your choice of a Ford car?" Twelve respondents indicated low price as their primary motivation, 39 pointed

to a "sound ignition system," 108 referred to low maintenance cost, and 842 reported that they had purchased on recommendation of other owners. The same question was asked in another poll, but the results have been lost.

The company soon abandoned this pioneer work, ironic in view of what happened in the Fifties with development of the Edsel. If Henry didn't actually say "The public can have any color it wants so long as it's black," that statement surely expressed his attitude toward customer opinion in years when the Model T dominated the market. Henry would be compelled to answer growing buyer demand for more colorful and stylish cars in the mid-Twenties, but the firm wouldn't formally resume public opinion research until the late Forties.

Opposite page: The 1912 Model T touring saw the price cut by $80 to $690. It was now available with front doors, though the left one was a fake. This page: Take a 1912 Torpedo Runabout (top), remove the windshield and the panel between the running boards and body, and paint it bright yellow. What do you have then? Speedster! Henry Ford (above left) took time to pose at the wheel of a 1912 "Fore-Door" touring. The Torpedo Runabouts (above) are shown plain and fancy.

1913

The 1913 Model Ts would be the last available in a choice of colors until 1926, when Ford would finally offer an alternative to black. Changes this year were few. The old "open-front" tourer was dropped, leaving the "fore-door" style with its non-working left front "door," plus a newly fixed rear tonneau that made this a true four/five-passenger body. Henry had decided an opening left door was unnecessary because the outboard handbrake hindered access on that side. However, Canadian tourings built through 1925 had two working front doors. The reason was that although most Canadian models were also left-hand drive, some had to be equipped with right-hand drive for certain provinces as well as export to various British Commonwealth markets. As noted, the Torpedo Runabout was also dropped this year, while the Runabout was given a tapered "turtleback" rear end that looked quite smart.

Common to all models was a change from a metal to a wooden ignition box on the cowl and a switch from brass to painted steel for windshield frames, steering wheel spoke assemblies, and all exterior lights excepting their bezels. It was all for the sake of keeping price down, of course, as was this year's switch from leather to leatherette on interior door panels.

Though not "factory," a good many Model T chassis were now being fitted with custom "Closed-Cab Pickup" bodywork, high-built wooden affairs that had no doors despite the name. In modified form, this utility style would eventually find its way into the Ford catalog.

Prices continued tumbling per Henry's desire that the Model T be within the financial grasp of more and more buyers. Price-leader for this year's line was the Runabout at $525, down $65 from the year before. The touring was newly listed at $600. The Town Car, now sporting a slim fixed window on either side of the front compartment, started at $850, then dropped during the year to $740. It also had somewhat smoother body lines.

As if to celebrate Henry's 50th birthday in late July, the Highland Plant began experimental operation of the world's first mass-production automobile assembly in April. For industrial history it was an event of tremendous significance. It would not only make Henry Ford the "father" of the automobile industry as we know it today, but would also change the face and pace of the nation. The Model T was the first car built by the

Although protection from the elements was somewhat lacking, the 1913 Ford Speedster (above) cut a dashing figure with its bright colors and wire wheels with large tires. A winter shipment of 1913 Model Ts to a New York dealer (below) paused long enough to have this picture snapped. Some people would call the 1913 Model T Runabout (far right, top) a "jaunty jalopy," and at $525 a bargain to boot. Production came to 33,129 units. The 1913 Town Car (far right, bottom) was st most expensive in the line, listing for $800, a drop of $100, but even at that price only 1415 buyers chose to drive one ho

thousands, not one at a time, on a moving assembly line with sequentially placed work stations. It was thus also one of the earliest cars to employ the principle of interchangeable parts successfully pioneered by Cadillac's Henry Leland. These factors and its simple design enabled the Model T to be sold at very low prices well within the reach of vast numbers of Americans who had never been able to afford a car. And that, of course, is the reason automobiles became universal.

Small-scale assembly methods and standardized parts had been in use well before this, both at Ford and elsewhere. The idea of a moving production line was probably conceived by Ransom Eli Olds, whose cars were once the country's top sellers. But it was Henry Ford who perfected the idea.

Toward the end of their lives, the Ford Models N and S had been built by means of a "sequential floor plan," by which machines and manpower were strategically located to "add" to each car as it proceeded on its orderly way through the Piquette Avenue factory. As author Beverly Hae Kimes noted, "A hundred cars a day could be easily built that way. But Henry Ford was thinking bigger. What was needed to build thousands was *movement*, continuous and carefully timed movement throughout the

production procedure. . . . It was not until the move to the newer and larger Highland Park plant . . . that the idea could be given full attention and the awkward beginnings made." Henry later attributed the idea to foreman William C. Klann, who was inspired by "the overhead trolley that the Chicago meatpackers used in dressing beef."

Accounts vary as to how Ford's assembly line evolved, but it seems that parts were merely pushed around at first. "It wasn't a conveyor-type thing at all," Klann recalled for Philip Van Doren Stern. "They had the stock in piles all along [the way]." Ultimately, the notion was expanded to having not just parts but sub-assemblies and then partly completed cars move slowly past workers on belt- or chain-driven conveyors, each worker performing a specific task over and over again.

This process was refined through several stages. By October 13, Ford had managed to cut chassis assembly time in half—from 12.5 to less than 6 manhours. Within two months it was down to an unheard-of 1 hour, 34 minutes.

The result was staggering. From 78,440 cars in calendar 1912, Ford output zoomed to 168,220 in 1913, then shot past the half-million mark just three years later. Through mass production, Ford factories would spew forth more

than 16 million Model Ts through 1927, a single-model record that would stand until the 1960s, when it was surpassed by another "universal car," the Volkswagen Beetle. Speaking of universal, U.S. Model T assembly from knockdown kits was begun this year at a new facility in Bordeaux, France, the start of the French Ford subsidiary that would last into the early Fifties.

In 1913-14, some people thought that inexpensive "cyclecars," small, lightweight two-passenger runabouts that were sort of a cross between car and motorcycle, might make a dent in Model T sales. Deciding to nip this budding trend, Henry had his shop build a small Model T, neat and streamlined, the construction of which greatly interested son Edsel. When it was finished, Henry told him, "Now you take it down and park it in front of the Pontchartrain Hotel." Edsel obeyed. A curious throng gathered, saw the Ford name on the radiator, and naturally concluded that Henry was about to bring out a cyclecar—which ended the threat.

As in other years, Model T promotion in 1913 was closely tied to current events. For example, when trouble with Mexico was anticipated this year, company publicists said that American battleships should carry Model Ts so Marines could "charge on Mexico City from

Vera Cruz in record time." The idea was hailed in metropolitan papers all over the country. Actually, Model Ts did figure in a 1917 Mexican border skirmish, which inspired a juvenile novel, *Charge of the Model Ts*. At one point, the board of directors told one of its members to arrange for a Ford to be the first car to pass through the new Panama Canal. The mission must have been unsuccessful, though, for the company never published an account of any such milestone.

The Model T has been the subject of more slang names than any other car in history. Of course, it's still best known even today as the "Tin Lizzie" and "flivver," though the origins of both those handles are unknown. Historian Beverly Rae Kimes once noted that "Lizzie perhaps arose from 'lizard,' the Model T

sharing the attributes of the hardy, fast little reptile, or perhaps from the frequent appearance of the name for one's favorite horse or aunt; flivver might have been derived from a 'for a liver' joke about the T."

But over the years, the Model T has been known by at least 48 other informal monikers, each briefly popular, most quite literal. Here's a rundown of the nicknames: T-bone, Detroit Disaster, Michigan Mistake, Flapper Flivver, Chicken Coup, Bone Crusher, Bouncing Betty, Cattle Hack, Fresh Air Taxi, Galloping Snail, Prince of Snails, Gref Zep's Uncle, Henry's first go-car, Lazy Lulu, Leaping Lena, My Lizzie of the Valley, Navigatin' Nancy, Noah's Ark, Old Faithful, Passion Pot, Puddle Jumper, Road Louse Exterminator, Rough Rider,

The Model T touring car was the most popular 1913 offering: 126,715 built. It listed for $600. Design changes meant that sheetmetal now encircled the entire passenger compartment from the top of the cowl to the rear. This model had three doors: two on the right side, as one might expect, but only a back door on the left.

Satan's Nightmare, Silly Symphony, Spirits of Bumps, Spirit of Detroit, Spirit of Jolts, Spirit of St. Vitus, Madame Elizabeth, Henrietta Elizabeth Van Flivver, Henry VIII (capacity four gals), Gilda Gray—shimmy expert, September Morn, Toonerville Trolley, A-Cute Digestion, Little Asphalt Annie, Little Bo-Creep, Rolls Rough, Tacks Collector, United Parts of America, Baby Lincoln, Lincoln's Baby, Lincoln's Relation, and the Missing Link in Lincoln.

1914

For this and the next 11 years, the Model T would be sold in only one color: black. The reason was the particular kind of black Henry Ford favored: a new kind of enamel that dried more quickly than other paints and thus helped speed up production. Thus, fashion notwithstanding, it was "any color, so long as it's black," though buyers still had the option of natural-tone or blue-painted wood wheels.

The 1914s would also be the last Ts to carry the acetylene headlamps, cherry-wood dashboard, and straight-top rear fenders of the 1908-09 original. A minor appearance change brought rounded bottom door corners, which enabled Lizzie to shed a bit of her "antique" look.

Ford again lowered prices in its relentless pursuit of affordability. The cuts weren't quite as large as those of past years in raw dollars—$60 for most models—but as all Fords were now sold with windshield, top, horn, and so forth, the effective reductions were as much, if not greater. The Runabout remained the price-leader, and was down to $440; the touring came in $110 upstream. The Town Car now sold for $690, $260 less than what a touring had cost only a few years before. A new body style arriving very late in the year was the $700 "Coupelet," what we'd now call a convertible coupe. Very few were built this year and demand would never be high, so it would last only into 1917.

But 1914 was another smashing year all the same. Ford's calendar-year production set yet another record at 308,162 units, about 100,000 more than all other automakers combined and some three-fifths of this year's 548,139-unit industry total.

Henry Ford and James Couzens were becoming fabulously rich as they gave the public ever-cheaper Model Ts. As they continued paying their executives higher and higher salaries and bonuses, they began to ask themselves, "What of our workers?" Their answer came this year in the celebrated "five-dollar workday," announced on January 5 and effective from January 12. Besides this unprecedented doubling of Ford's basic wage—which had been $2.34—the workday itself was reduced from 10 to eight hours. A third shift was added at Highland Park to make up the difference in production time.

Coming as it did in the midst of a mild worldwide depression, this announcement was instant page-one news across the world. Forty years after the fact, the London *Economist* termed it "the

Although the 1914 Model T touring car didn't look much different, the doors were now inset into the side panels, a practice that would be continued for more than a decade. This was the year that you could have your Model T in any color—as long as it was black, another practice that would last for over a decade. Buyers snapped up 165,832 touring cars for 1914, an increase of almost 40,000 units.

most dramatic event in the history of wages." The distinguished French intellectual, Father R.L. Bruckberger, went further in 1959: "I consider that what Henry Ford accomplished in 1914 contributed far more to the emancipation of workers than the October Revolution of 1917 [in Russia]....He took the worker out of the class of the 'wage-earning proletariat' to which Ricardo and Marx had relegated him...and made every worker a potential customer." Curiously, Ford and Couzens, who regarded the five-dollar day as the "greatest revolution in the matter of rewards for...workers ever known," were fully aware that it would be of great advertising value, yet they vastly underestimated its strong, immediate worldwide impact. It was easily the biggest news story ever to come out of Detroit. The statement was issued at mid-morning that January day. By noon, cables and telegrams from wire services and newspapers were pouring in from all over the globe. By the following morning, every daily paper in the country and thousands more abroad had carried the news. Over seven days the New York City press alone devoted 52 columns to the profit-sharing plan and to Ford, most of it being front-page space.

Many papers hailed the five-dollar day as an economic second coming. The Cleveland *Plain Dealer* editorialized that it "shot like a blinding rocket through the dark clouds of the present industrial depression." The New York *Sun* described it as a "bolt out of the blue sky flashing its way across the continent and far beyond." The New York *Herald* called it "an epoch in the world's industrial history." Some papers were so impressed that they made a special point of plugging the Model T. The East Boston *Free Press* suggested that, "When you see [Ford's] modest little car running by, take your hat off." The Cleveland *News* ran a large photo of a Model T touring car beneath the headline "The Car Humanitarian Henry Ford's Making."

With this "ocean of publicity," Henry Ford was the world's best-known industrialist by mid-1914. One newspaper went so far as to predict that he would become "one of the best-known men that America has ever produced" and that his name would be "famous until the sun takes its first chill." Henry enjoyed headlines, but none more than these. He'd already developed a strong appetite for publicity that would help him sell Model Ts and, later, Model As and V-8s.

Of course there was much more to the five-dollar day than just charity on Henry's part. The big Highland Park moving assembly line was now producing in high gear, so Ford could easily afford the pay raise because the man hours required to produce a Model T had been cut from more than 12 to about 1.5. And it should be noted that turnover at the new plant was tremendous. According to

Keith Sward in *The Legend of Henry Ford*, it had reached 380 percent by December 1913, which meant that Ford had to hire 963 men to keep 100. In fact, when Ford Motor Company decided to give employees with at least three years seniority a Christmas bonus that year, only 640 out of some 15,000 qualified. Clearly, Ford could save a lot of money in hiring and training with a more stable labor force, and Henry did comment later that the five dollar day was "one of the finest cost-cutting moves we ever made."

Little noticed in the excitement surrounding the news of the five-dollar day was the fact that the base wage actually remained at $2.34. The other $2.66 was labeled profit sharing, to be spent or saved in a way that would be "of permanent benefit" to the employee and his family. Home ownership, for example, was strongly encouraged. And to be sure that the workers used the profit sharing money properly, Ford formed a "Sociological Department," whose inspectors visited workers' homes. Not only did the inspectors check on matters such as health, hobbies, religion, citizenship, savings, and life insurance, they also assisted the workers and their families in bettering themselves. One example might be advice on how to improve the family diet. And since more than two-thirds of Ford's employees were foreign born, Ford in 1914 made English-lan-

guage classes mandatory for those who needed them. The lessons took place after work, and if an employee didn't attend, he lost his profit sharing money.

In 1914, the Tin Lizzie figured in one of the most striking sales promotions in the annals of American business. It was Ford's announcement of July 3 promising to rebate $40-$60 in cash to each Model T buyer if company sales exceeded 300,000 units over the following 12 months. Coupled with this was the aforementioned across-the-board price cut and a pledge not to cut prices again until August 1, 1915.

Unfortunately for Ford, its rebate announcement came at one of the worst times imaginable: the start of World War I. Metropolitan newspapers, particularly on the eastern seaboard, buried the story to make room on front pages for news about the outbreak of hostilities in Serbia and the German Kaiser's ultimatum to Russia. *The New York Times*, in an editorial titled "Well Devised But Ill Timed," apologized for putting the refund story on page five, conceding that it deserved as much prominence as the widely heralded five-dollar day.

They may have pushed it aside, but virtually every newspaper in the land ran the Ford rebate story somewhere. The smaller dailies and country weeklies gave it comparatively greater exposure—and rave notices. Such responses were pre-

Ford listed the weight of the 1914 Model T touring as 1200 pounds, and the bare chassis at 960 pounds. With its skimpy body, which added little weight, the Speedster was the "hot rod" Ford. Note the round "monacle" windshield. It didn't stop much wind, but it sure looked good!

cisely what sales manager Norval Hawkins had had in mind when he proposed the idea to Henry. In many communities during the rebate period, the best Ford salesmen were those who had bought Model Ts after August 1914.

As promised, the company released its sales results on August 1, 1915. For the 12 months, it said, the total was exactly 308,213 vehicles. The per capita rebate was accordingly set at $40, about nine percent of the average Model T's purchase price, and "profit-sharing" checks totaling nearly $15.5 million were duly mailed to most every American hamlet, town, and city over the next few months. Many newspapers, acknowledging the refund "a game in which Ford had everything to win and nothing to lose"—except money, of course—congratulated the firm on its "sales-promotion genius" and its customers on their good fortune in climbing aboard the "rebate wagon." Those checks, later called "the most virile crop of goodwill seeds ever planted," naturally made hundreds of thousands of friends for the Model T,

Henry Ford, and Ford Motor Company.

It was just as well, because Ford had lost a few friends as an unanticipated consequence of the five-dollar day, which may have been another reason for Hawkins proposing the rebate. On January 6, the day after the new wage was announced, some 10,000 men, many of them unemployed, showed up at the Highland Park gates seeking the 4000-5000 jobs that would be created by the new third shift. A tense atmosphere became even more so when company officials hesitated to address the crowd. When they did, they turned them all away, and rather brusquely, too. The incident naturally made news, and the reports tended to dim the magnanimous luster of the previous day's announcement. Of course, the Ford wage was a powerful attraction for any worker. The economy in general and the farm sector in particular were showing signs of distress. Wall Street was being wracked by periodic tremors. On February 1, 1912, the Dow Jones Industrial Average had dropped 6.91 points to 88.52, which amounted to a 7.24-percent loss in its total value, the 11th largest on record. This year, on July 30, the industrials dropped 6.9 percent in value, the 15th largest percentage loss on record, skidding 5.3 points to 71.42. Then, a "Big One." On December 12, the DJIA plunged 17.42 points to 54 even, a 24.4-percent loss that has yet to be exceeded. Clearly all was not well with the economy. The incident at Highland Park was merely a hint of much greater troubles to come, though they'd take a long time to surface.

On the eve of World War I the Model T was selling at a quarter-million units per year and enjoyed a worldwide renown like no other car. As the Indianapolis *Star* put it, "While the Constitution may follow the flag, or the flag the Constitution, all depending on the viewpoint with reference to the foreign policy of the United States, the Ford Motor Company has beaten out both the flag and the Constitution in carrying civilization into the wild places of the world."

A few examples serve to back that statement. Twenty Model Ts were used in construction of the Amur River Railroad in Siberia. Thirty Indian princes rode in Model Ts, interspersed with elephants, camels and horses, at the Delhi coronation of King George V. A Model T was delivered to the Tasha Lama of Urga after a 700-mile trip across the Gobi Desert. A T won the Johannesburg-Bereeniging race in South Africa. French troops used Ts in pursuit of brigands in Morocco.

By mid-1914, more than 550,000 Model Ts were on roads the world over, traveling 10-million miles daily. And there would soon be more, thanks in part to the establishment this year of a branch in Argentina under Ellis Hampton, who would soon set up dealer groups in

The 1914 Model T Runabout (top) sold for an even $500, and 35,017 buyers were impressed enough to claim one as their own. This model sported a handsome "turtle deck" at the rear. The touring car (above) outsold the Runabout by a ratio of almost five to one despite its $50-higher price tag.

Brazil, Chile, Venezuela, and Uruguay. "A car that is seen as often as the Ford must be right," declared *Ford Times* predictably, "or its very presence would kill it."

Lizzie's prodigious numbers were, in fact, an advertising asset. Every car bore the name "Ford" in bold script on the radiator, and the Model T's distinctive design was recognizable a half-mile away. In a day when every automobile purchase and virtually all out-of-town trips were reported in the "personals" section of small-town newspapers, Fords were naturally mentioned thousands of times, certainly more than most other cars. A few samples: "W.H. Judd is now riding around in a new Ford car, which he recently purchased. These [sic] are a very

neat little car...." "Our genial and efficient mail carrier now delivers the mail on his route in a stylish and comfortable runabout of the Ford make whenever the conditions of the roads will permit." "R.E. Rice is sporting a fine Ford runabout which he purchased from Agent Fred Scott of Coalton." "Mr. and Mrs. John Inglebrecht and children, of near Jefferson City, drove over to Eldon Saturday in their Ford to visit Mr. and Mrs. R.J. Rush."

Sometimes, though, this publicity backfired. The Elgin (Illinois) *Courier* reported that the "funeral of William Kiel, who was killed last Friday from being tipped in the Ford automobile, which he and Joy Seyle were driving, was held Sunday."

The Model T inspired more than 60 melodic tributes, with "The Little Ford Rambled Right Along," written this year, perhaps the most popular. Many titles

Ford wasn't building station wagons yet, but outside body firms were happy to create special body styles for the Model T, such as this 1914 Depot Hack. Other than being quite airy, it flaunted a handsome woody look that's still appealing today. Ford's calendar year output for 1914 set a new record: over 308,000 units.

attempted to capitalize on contemporary Model T jokes, of which there was no shortage. Typical were "I Didn't Raise My Ford to Be a Jitney," "It's a Rambling Flivver," and "Let's Take a Ride on the Jitney Bus." Others had a more romantic flavor. "The Packard and the Ford" suggested that Mr. Packard and Miss Flivver marry and give birth to a Buick, while "The Scandal of Little Lizzie Ford" depicted a demure T garaged with a rakish sports car. "On the Old Back Seat of the Henry Ford" promised that the moon would smile on couples spooning in flivvers.

Henry's humble creation was also the subject of a serious musical composition called "Flivver Ten Million," which "created a furore" when performed by the Boston Symphony Orchestra and attracted a record crowd at New York City's College Stadium when played by the New York Philharmonic. Written by T.S. Converse, a professor of music at Harvard, the 14-minute "joyous epic" described the assembling of the 10-millionth Model T—announced by a motor horn, full blast—and followed its wandering across the country. After a "necking party" and joyride (interrupted by a collision), "Phoenix Americanus," said the program notes, "righted and shaken, proceeds on his way with redoubled energy, typical of the indomitable spirit of America." At first, Boston Symphony conductor Serge Koussevitsky protested some of the score's honks, rattles, squeaks, and crashes, but Converse insisted they were essential. The composer was vindicated by favorable reviews in the Boston *Transcript* and *The New York Times*.

The last Model T songs were suggested by the car's demise in 1927. Typical of these ditties was "Henry's Made a Lady Out of Lizzie," which alluded to the new Model A, of course, and the wistfully titled "Poor Lizzie, What'll Become of You Now?"

1 9 1 5

Two new body types appeared in this year's Model T stable. One was the previously mentioned "Coupelet," a two-seat convertible replacing the fixed-roof coupe. Though introduced in late 1914, it didn't become widely available until this year. The other newcomer was the "Center Door" sedan, a high, upright closed model with full-length bodywork, three windows per side, and a door positioned slightly behind the center point of the wheelbase on each side.

All 1915 Ts exchanged old-fashioned bulb horns and acetylene gas headlamps for a hand-operated Klaxon horn and brass electric headlamps powered by the magneto. The former straight-topped rear fenders were newly curved, though front fenders remained as before and, without exception, were lipped. Hood louvers and an unbraced windshield appeared for the first time, and steel re-placed cherrywood for dashboards. Wire wheels, which had been coming into vogue as an "aftermarket" accessory for several years, were newly available from the factory. Less noticeable alterations included slightly reduced engine compression, ribbed-surface floor pedals (no longer lettered), larger coils, round lenses for cowl lamps (still oil-fueled) and taillamps, and a new differential housing.

Prices continued to fall. The touring, still far and away the line's best-seller, dropped to $440, the Runabout to a sensationally low $390. A $740 price tag made the new Center Door sedan this year's costliest Lizzie. The Coupelet listed for $590. The Town Car was still around, now at $640. Subtle changes over the years had made it frumpy-looking, and by 1915 its sales were mostly to taxi operators rather than private buyers.

Ford passed a production milestone in 1915 by building more than a half-million cars for the calendar year. The precise number, 501,462, was no less than two-thirds of this year's total industry volume, which reached 895,930.

There was another production milestone this year: the one-millionth Ford, completed in September. To the company's chagrin, the event went unnoticed. It was really Ford's own fault, and a bit surprising given Henry's sense of history. But as *Ford Times* explained: "With twenty-five assembly plants...and with a big factory in Detroit assembling so many Ford cars a day, we passed the million mark without knowing it."

Nevertheless, Ford managed some publicity from the event, however belated. Henry himself presented the milestone car to one of his favorite dealers, Stanley Roberts of Toledo, who had requested it. Roberts in turn displayed and raced the car at numerous northwestern Ohio county fairs. It was later wrecked with his brother at the wheel, and then apparently disappeared. A 1983 search, including old-timer's recollections, con-

Ford's 1915 Model T lineup included an interesting closed model, a two-door sedan—often referred to as the "Center Door" sedan (below, left and right). Its doors were located just behind the center point of the wheelbase. It cost $975, but late in the year the price fell to $740. The $440 Runabout (bottom left) ended the year at $390. The Town Car (bottom right), meanwhile, went from $690 to $640.

The Coupelet bowed late in the 1914 model year, so only a few were built. It was basically what might be called a convertible coupe nowadays, offering top-down fun or snug top-up protection against the elements. This 1915 model listed at $750, but that was reduced to $590 later in the year. Less than 2500 were built for 1915.

ducted in cooperation with the Toledo *Blade*, turned up nothing.

Another highlight of Model T promotion this year was a striking demonstration of auto production at San Francisco's Panama-Pacific Exposition, where 18 to 25 cars were built each day on a model assembly line running on a three-hour "shift." Easily the fair's most popular industrial attraction, the Ford exhibit garnered nationwide notice and huge crowds. It also earned a special gold medal for its contribution to the Exposition's success.

You didn't have to be a Ford worker to make money putting Model Ts together. In *All My Best Friends*, comedian George Burns, recalling the "freak" acts of vaudeville—"one-of-a-kind, step-right-up-and-buy-your-ticket type of acts"—notes that "Even the sophisticated Palace Theatre [in New York] once booked 'The Twelve Speed Maniacs,' a team of a dozen men who would assemble an entire Ford Model T in exactly two minutes. Their big finale was driving it offstage." But they had nothing on the 15,000 workers at Highland Park, who'd been turning out Lizzies at the rate of one every 30 seconds since June 1914.

Still believing strongly in the potential for mechanized farming, Henry put together at least 12 experimental tractors this year. Like his first "Auto Plow," these were built largely around car parts—from the Model T, of course—but

period photographs show the emergence of a basic design not unlike that of farm tractors we know today. After tests at Henry's Dearborn farm, the prototypes were publicly demonstrated at the Michigan State Fairgrounds in the fall. In October came word that Ford had purchased a site in Dearborn for construction of a tractor factory to be operated by a new subsidiary company.

Even more significant for Ford Motor Company's future was its July acquisition of 1000 acres on the banks of the Rouge River near Henry's birthplace of Springwells Township, southwest of Detroit. On it would soon rise a new factory that would eclipse Highland Park as the world's largest manufacturing complex. Because it was effectively a port, the Rouge location furthered Henry's goal of making Ford a self-sufficient company controlling all materials and means needed to manufacture and distribute its products.

This fiercely independent bent stemmed from Henry's rural upbringing as well as a basic unwillingness to trust others with even the tiniest part of his fate. He was also a pacifist at heart and thus deplored the war raging in Europe. War, he believed, was immoral not least because it enabled a few to profit from the deaths of many.

Such was the thinking that led to the abortive "Peace Ship" mission that Henry sponsored in late 1915. During the fall he'd learned that 20,000 soldiers had died fighting in Europe on one particular day, yet he realized that this carnage made absolutely no difference to the course of the war. Deciding that he *could* make a difference, Henry pledged to spend up to half his entire fortune to end the hostilities as soon as possible.

If his aim was noble, his method was naive. Believing mere persuasion would suffice, he formed a delegation of peace-minded politicians, business leaders, and other notables, put them aboard the ocean liner *Oscar II*, and set sail with them from New York on December 5. But arguments broke out en route about both mission and method, and by the time the ship reached Europe the delegates were in total disarray, thus ending the effort before it began. Initially, this failure left Henry with only heartfelt personal regrets and a little public embarrassment. "I wanted to see peace," he said. "I at least tried to bring it about. Most men did not even try." Some newspapers thought he shouldn't have tried at all. Said the Boston *Traveler*: "It is not Mr. Ford's purpose to make peace. He will assemble it."

But the Peace Ship would have two more damaging consequences. The first was the prompt resignation of financial manager James Couzens, who strongly disagreed with his boss' views. The second was what would turn out to be a protracted and mean-spirited libel action brought by Henry in 1916 against the Chicago *Tribune*, which had branded him an anarchist for sponsoring the mission. When the suit was finally heard in 1919, Henry's testimony created the unfortunate impression that he was ignorant if not illiterate. (It was here that he huffed those now-famous words, "history is bunk.") Ford won the verdict, but lost in the courtroom of public opinion. As Beverly Kimes wrote, it was a "sorry affair" that "would have been better forgotten."

Henry Ford reportedly said that the Coupelet, here a 1915 model (top), was the most practical two-passenger model the company had ever built. As before, the touring car (center) was the most popular 1915 offering. At $490, it was a good buy, and nearly a quarter million were built for the model run. Ford owners often altered their cars, witness this "hack" (bottom).

1 9 1 6

Lizzie was about to see big changes, but most wouldn't be made until September of this year (see *1917*). The initial 1916 models were thus the last Model Ts with dinky brass radiators— the "brassies" so beloved by today's T-enthusiasts—of which only 800 were made. Likewise would the familiar brass headlamps and horn be phased out for pressed-steel equivalents—painted black, of course. The small boxlike hood would persist but was fashioned of steel instead of aluminum. The transmission cover also switched from aluminum, becoming a cast-iron piece, while the speedometer was no longer listed as standard equipment in still another bit of cost-cutting.

No new body styles appeared this year, but all models were now delivered with 56-inch-wide track dimensions. Previously, cars sold in the South could be ordered with a 60-inch tread to match the width of road ruts common in that part of the country.

If Lizzie's looks seemed nearly constant, so did Henry's practice of cutting prices nearly every year. August brought yet another round of reductions. This time, the touring was lowered by $80 to $360, the Runabout dropped to an unbelievable $345, the Center Door sedan eased by $100 to $640, and the Coupelet was trimmed to $505.

Another Ford constant, fast-rising production, also continued, hitting a new calendar-year high of 734,811 units— more than the entire U.S. industry had built just two years earlier. Of course, it helped that Ford had by now established no fewer than 28 branch assembly plants throughout the country. But industry volume almost doubled in 1916, breaking the one-million barrier to reach 1,525,578. As a result, Ford's market share dropped 14 points to "only" 48 percent.

Elsewhere, Model T assembly began in Buenos Aires this year (at a former cigarette factory, which must have pleased Henry), and Percy Perry formed Automobiles Ford as the firm's new French subsidiary, expanding on the branch operation in Bordeaux. The Henry Ford Trade School opened in Detroit on October 25, about a year after the new Henry Ford Hospital received its first patients. Over the next 36 years, the School would train hundreds of managers, engineers, and assembly-line workers, most of whom stayed with Ford Motor Company. On November 1, just six days shy of his 23rd birthday, Henry's son Edsel married Eleanor Lowthian Clay.

The very next day, November 2, brothers John and Horace Dodge, who'd started building their own cars in 1914 but remained Ford suppliers and major shareholders, sued the company for $25 million. At issue was Henry's right to stop paying special dividends, as he'd just announced. He preferred to take such funds—and some of the $58 million in profits that had accumulated—and plow them back into the company. Beverly Rae Kimes reported that Henry "had some rather tart things to say about stockholders being non-producers receiving unearned dividends from profits which belonged rightly to the workers and their work."

The Dodge suit, which sought "reasonable dividends," took three years to settle. Kimes notes that Henry berated the brothers "for the absurdity of challenging a policy that had escalated their $10,000 worth of stock into $50 million. In the end, the courts declared the Dodges were entitled to their dividends—a landmark decision, by the way—which a miffed Henry had to promptly pay."

Despite embarrassments like this and the Peace Ship, Henry Ford was a national figure of enormous achievement and wide popularity. It was thus only natural that he would be targeted occasionally as a prospective political material. That's just what happened at this year's Republican National Convention, where Ford's name showed up on the first ballot for presidential nominations. His supporters were obviously in the minority, though, as nothing more came of this "draft Ford" movement.

The period between 1914 and 1920 was the heyday of the "Ford joke," similar to the Jeep and Volkswagen Beetle jokes of a later era. In these half-dozen years Ford jokes were as much a part of everyday conversation as the news, politics, the weather, sports, shop talk, and office gossip, and were as likely to be heard over tea at a church social as over beer at the corner saloon. They were as universal and numerous as America's time-honored yockers about mothers-in-law, Pat and Mike, and the farmer's daughter. To vaudeville monologists they were the staff of life, to toastmasters a rock of refuge for sure-fire introductions and after-dinner speeches. Salesmen opened solicitations with them, clergymen punctuated sermons with them, physicians carried them as part of their pharmacopeia of cheer.

Not surprisingly, Ford jokes were the subject of scores of books, some of which sold by the tens of thousands. Most were cheap paperbacks hawked for five, 10, or 15 cents apiece, but some featured contributions by the nation's leading humorists and cartoonists, including Ring Lardner, Irvin S. Cobb, Bud Fisher, Chic Jackson, and H.T. Webster.

While its exact origins are unknown, the Ford joke was a logical evolution of the automotive humor that became a stock-in trade of vaudeville performers after about 1902. Essex, Saxon, and even the high-priced Pierce were among the first targets. One gag that always brought a laugh at Franklin's expense was this description of a buck-toothed girl: "She wouldn't be so bad-looking, but she's got Franklin teeth. They're air cooled."

Another view, shared by advertising manager Charles A. Brownell, was that competitors started Ford jokes in the Model T's early days. "It's not a car," rival salesmen allegedly told potential buyers. "It's just a Ford." (Volkswagen used nearly the same words in its late-Eighties U.S. advertising.) Some of Ford's own 1907 advertising supports this opinion. "The Ford 4-cylinder ($600) runabout owes half its unparalleled popularity to the misrepresentation of jealous rivals," read one ad. Another asked, "Had you ever noticed that it is a weakness inherent in disciples to disparage their leader? Some makers affect to discount the achievements of FORD."

Indeed, vanadium steel was criticized by many rival automakers, who predicted Ford's "flimsy contraption" would quickly fall apart—until the alloy was adopted for armor plating on American warships. There was also what some termed an organized "mud-slinging propaganda campaign." Observed the Ft. Atkinson (Wisconsin) *Union*: "The best wits were hired to write the material, and many were the editors who were caught by it. It came in a blank envelope, apparently from nowhere, and usually had concealed somewhere a thrust at the 'Tin Lizzie,' coupled with a cute story."

Self-conscious Ford owners were undoubtedly one source of the quips and gibes. By joking about their car's small size, low price, and so on, they "could laugh off any joshing the owner of a bigger and higher-priced car might be disposed to give him."

The Model T's very cheapness and versatility must have spawned many jokes. Almost everyone knew that more than half the pieces in a Ford engine sold for a dime or less. News stories frequently told of a stationary Model T powering motors that ran everything from newspaper presses to water pumps.

The T's toughness was also widely discussed. One Texan was said to have abandoned his car to escape Mexican bandits, who hacked and burned it into a wreck that the owner later retrieved and drove away. One Ford, although buried six years in the muck of a California river bed, still had gas in its tank and ran "as good as new" once starting wires were installed. Another true story concerned the Ford whose engine had been removed to pump water and whose body was drawn by a burro. The moral, as the press was quick to point out: "You may dissect a Ford, but you cannot kill it."

Such tales led the public to feel that a

Model T could do almost anything—hence the countless jokes that bordered on the ridiculous but still seemed to have a trace of plausibility. No doubt many of those who invented or repeated them fully shared the opinion expressed by crusader Ida Tarbell in 1915: "I have never in all the world . . . seen so much to cause me to laugh and weep, to wonder and rejoice, as I have at the Ford."

Many accessory manufacturers generated additional jokes by their advertising. While Ford's own ads proclaimed the Model T to be as flawless as any car ever made (Henry sure thought so), gadget and parts makers spent huge sums convincing the public that their wares made the car a much better performer, easier-riding, or more economical. After reading that their cars drove like trucks, Ford owners were promised that a certain kind of shock absorber would make them ride like Pullmans. Buying a $2.50 crankcase support was alleged to save $20, for otherwise the crankcase would surely break and entail a $22.50 repair bill. Starting difficulty was emphasized in ads suggesting that old-fashioned blowtorches be replaced by special firetraps for the intake manifold. Then there were all the "anti-rattler" devices for silencing every one of the T's many potential rattles—though no mention that these could also work loose and add to the clatter. Surely no consumer product has had its shortcomings, both real and imagined, more thoroughly exposed than the Model T.

That this should add fuel to the Ford joke craze is hardly surprising. Consider the farmer who had no use for a speedometer in his Model T because "when I go 5 miles an hour . . . the fenders rattle; when I go 15 miles an hour my false teeth drop out; and when I go 25 miles an hour the transmission drops off."

Ford jokes followed several patterns. Perhaps the most numerous were those concerning the Model T's diminutive size. Postmen were reportedly upset about a rumor that Ts would be shipped by mail. A garbage collector bemoaned how tricky it was to sort out dead cats, broken bottles, and Fords. A patron who asked for Model T tires at a large department store complained of being directed to the "Rubber Band Department."

Lizzie's "loose-jointed" qualities inspired much "shake and rattle" humor. Henry Ford was reputedly a better evangelist than Billy Sunday because he'd shaken hell out of more people than Sunday ever saw. Asked if his car always made a racket, a T-owner innocently replied, "Oh, no. Only when it's running."

The belief that Fords were made entirely of tin prompted "Tin Lizzie" jokes. Question: "What time is it when one Ford follows another?" Answer: "Tin after tin." It was said that Ford was going to build cars without doors—but would supply can openers. A man hitched his cocker spaniel to a balky flivver and was

arrested for tying a tin can to a dog. A farmer, knowing that Ford needed lots of tin, shipped a battered tin roof to the company; he then got a letter saying, "While your car was an exceptionally bad wreck, we shall be able to complete repairs and return it by the first of the week."

Another theme involved the T's inferior social standing, and these jokes went something like the following. Question: "Why is a Ford like a bathtub?" Answer: "Because you hate to be seen in one." A Ford reportedly ran over a chicken, which then got up and said "cheap, cheap, cheap." Henry Ford once refused $1.50 for repairing a farmer's car, saying he had all the money he needed. "You're a liar," the farmer shot back. "If you had plenty of money, you'd take some of it and buy yourself an automobile!"

Offsetting the ridicule were jokes testifying to the T's sturdy dependability. A man told friends he wanted to be buried with his Ford because it had always gotten him out of every hole he'd ever been in. Owners of Cadillacs, Pierces, and Packards were said to carry Fords in their trunks—to pull the big cars when they bogged down. A Ford was like a motion to adjourn—always in order. And did you hear about the Model T that left the plant without an engine? It ran for a month—on its reputation.

Ford's mass-production techniques, five-dollar workday, $40 rebate, and other innovations inspired jokes complimenting the company. For example, Ford had to use asbestos crates to avoid fire risks when shipping Model Ts because they came off the line so fast that their metal was smoking. Two flies could "manufacture" 48,876,552,154 new flies in six months, but they didn't have anything on two Ford factories. A Ford assembly-line worker reportedly dropped his wrench and 20 Model Ts whizzed

For 1916, Ford's fast-rising production would reach dizzying heights: 734,811 cars for the calendar year. The Coupelet, however, didn't share in the bounty— only 3532 were built from August 1915 through July 1916. It would thus be dropped during the 1917 model year.

past before he could pick it up. Did you know that Fords were going to be painted yellow and sold in grocery stores? That way they could be hung like bananas and sold in bunches.

Most Ford owners enjoyed the jokes, and were among the more inveterate spinners of them. Even if some of the humor rubbed them the wrong way, they could, as one of the joke books pointed out, "always pat their pocketbook, let in the clutch and ride serenely on their way, proud of their possession and confident of their good judgment."

But there were those who never quite got used to the incessant teasing. One long-suffering Englishman, in a widely reprinted 1920 letter to a British motoring publication, voiced the anguish that this minority had suffered over the years: "In our opinion it is quite time that we Fordists should strongly protest against the jokes and insults which have been hurled at us. For years we have been the stock joke of the vermillion-proboscis-tinted 'comedian'; sneered at by the nut whose sole ambition in life soared to the height of his socks matching his coachwork, and the glossiness of his hair equaling a seal emerging from the water; held in contempt by the chauffeur of a big 'six,' doubtless because a Ford has passed him on the hill; treated with brusqueness by many a garage man—such has been the experience of most of us.

"I took delivery of my earliest Ford ten years ago, and at the first garage at which I stopped I was strongly advised to

At its new low price of $440, sales of the 1916 Model T touring car skyrocketed to over 360,000 units (built from August 1915 through July 1916). By 1916, the T had been stripped of virtually all brass trim, making Lizzie look more somber all in black. Minor changes saw the aluminum hood and transmission cover switch to steel and cast-iron.

have fitted a tray under the chassis. Innocently I asked the reason. 'So that it will pick up the nuts,' came the reply. I have lost count of the number of times people have told me that they would not be found dead in a Ford.

"But what angers me most is when we are classed as a God-forsaken, poverty-stricken lot. 'He has to put up with a Ford because he cannot spring enough to buy a car.' That is what I frequently hear. Could anything be more insulting? Could anything be more remote from the truth?

"Many a Fordist could buy up a majority of the revilers; many a Fordist is their intellectual superior; many a Fordist possesses more gentleness and character. Therefore, should these lines reach the eye of a Ford scoffer, I will tell him plainly that he is a snob. And a snob of the worst order."

Advertising types were constantly asked whether Ford jokes helped or hindered their sales. Until the early 1920s, most agreed that "every knock was a boost," that the ubiquitous one-liners only made the Model T that much more

popular. When a New York banker was asked in 1927 to put a value on Ford company stock as of 1913, he testified that the jokes were "an important asset" and that any manufacturer with a sense of humor would have welcomed them. Newspaper editorials echoed that view.

So did Henry Ford, who delighted in the jokes and, according to his advertising manager, told more of them than anyone else. (His personal favorite was the one about the man who asked to be buried with his T.) Some publications, knowing Henry had a fresh one for every reporter, even credited him with concocting the best jokes during his leisure moments. Toastmasters invariably bantered about the Model T at banquets Ford attended, and no one enjoyed the witticisms more than Henry himself. He did not, as rumor often had it, subsidize any of the joke books, though he often made a considerable show of buying them. "The jokes about my car sure help to popularize it," he once remarked. "I hope they never end."

But all things end, even bad jokes. By the early 1920s, with Chevrolet, Dodge, Essex, and Willys all moving up rapidly in sales, the Model T was an anachronism and the jokes about it began to boomerang too often to be a plus. They just weren't funny anymore. Owners began realizing that the critics were dead earnest, and fewer of them could laugh off the barbs. The nationwide Keith-

Albee vaudeville organization, perhaps the country's leading arbiter of street-corner humor, even banned Ford jokes from its stages.

Advertising experts also sensed the shift in public mood and suggested that Ford ought "to give the T prestige... to take the joke out of the car." A number of company executives, including Edsel Ford, agreed. Thus, after a lapse of several years, the company resumed advertising the Model T on a broad scale in 1923, aggressively promoting its car as "a quality product" with "a high social standing."

But for all practical purposes, the Ford joke died with the Model T. Its successor, the Model A, arrived in December 1927 and was too highly regarded to be funny. "With her," observed the New York *Sun*, "he who goes to josh remains to praise."

Still, Ford jokes lingered on for many years afterward. There were even a few new ones. In 1953, for example, the owner of a 1909 Model T was fined for speeding. His widely reported courtroom comment was in the best Tin Lizzie tradition: "It was only hitting on three. If it had been hitting on all four, I doubt you would have caught me."

But perhaps the most durable Ford joke is the one that neatly sums up the entire phenomenon. Question: "Heard the last Ford story?" Answer: "I hope so."

1917

Even without America's belated entry into World War I on April 6 of this year, 1917 would have been an unusually busy year for Ford Motor Company. Besides a facelifted Model T, the firm offered its first true truck and the first of its now-famous Fordson farm tractors. And lest we forget, an event of major significance for the firm's distant future occurred on September 4, when Edsel's wife Eleanor Clay Ford gave Henry his first grandson, Henry Ford II.

This year's Model T, first seen in September 1916, was a striking departure from previous flivvers—so much so that the New York *World* felt compelled to state above a photo of the car that "Yes, it's a Ford." It almost seemed like an all-new Lizzie, comelier and sturdier, and it generated considerable excitement. A crowd in Chicago stampeded through a showroom window just to get a better look at it.

Early Model Ts with their squarish hoods and brass radiator caps were as much a part of everyday Americana as baseburner stoves and kerosene lamps—and looked just as old-fashioned by now. But the more stylish '17s scarcely need blush in the company of other cars. "This comparatively tremendous advance in styling," as historian Leslie R. Henry would later write, "served to set the pattern for most of the succeeding decade."

Announcing an almost streamlined hood was a larger radiator suitably recast to match and more pleasing in shape. A separate shell of painted pressed steel made it stronger than the old one-piece radiator, simplified repair, and enhanced cooling capacity. It was also set higher to blend with the newly rounded hood, which in turn swept back more gracefully to a shapelier cowl. Curved, crowned fenders were, shall we say, the crowning touch. The last brass trim was banished, replaced by black enamel except on radiator cap and hub centers, which were adorned with shining nickel plate.

Ford may have been late in following rival makes to the "painted look," but the changes were worthwhile, giving the T a more modern, integrated appearance. They also hurt business for those companies that had been selling crowned fenders, vee'd radiators, and other embellishments to style-conscious T owners. ("More Class for Your Ford," one promised. "Makes It look like a $1000 Car.") But dealers were delighted as the trade-in value of older Ts declined significantly.

Prices, for once, did *not* decline, but they didn't go up except on the Center

There was big news regarding the Model T for 1917, that being new—and definitely more modern—styling. Highlights included a larger radiator and a newly rounded hood that swept back more gracefully into a shapelier cowl. The 1917 Runabout (below) saw production increase to 107,240 units. Henry Ford (above) is seen in what appears to be a rather pensive mood.

Door sedan, which rose a mere $5. Completing this styling evolution was the return of a fully enclosed coupe model, a smart-looker tagged at $550.

Yet despite all this, Ford suffered its first drop in calendar-year production, output falling more than 112,000 units to 622,351. War jitters may have kept some buyers away, but the industry as whole didn't suffer at all, with volume rising by better than 200,000 units to 1,745,792, which diminished Dearborn's market share to about 36 percent.

Unlike Ford's previous commercial vehicles, this year's new truck, sometimes called the Model TT, diverged quite a bit more from the passenger car on which it was based. And the differences were significant: a wheelbase extended no less than 24 inches to 124 overall, a suitably longer and stronger frame, a stiffer rear suspension with reinforced wheels, and solid rubber tires (to handle heavy payloads) and, as already used on some commercial T-conversions, a sturdier worm-drive rear axle. Only the most rudimentary of cabs was provided, as private converters were still offering a variety of special-purpose commercial T-bodies, but the TT did share the new passenger-car front end. More complete, integrated factory bodies would soon evolve. Early TT production figures are hard to come by, but it is known that Ford delivered some 39,000 cars, trucks, and ambulances to the U.S. military and the other Allies during World War I.

Ford also delivered some 7000 tractors during the war, this being the new Fordson model that bowed on October 8 of this year when the first one rolled out of the new Dearborn tractor plant. The name Fordson stemmed from the subsidiary Henry had formed to build the new workhorse: Henry Ford and Son, incorporated on July 27.

The Fordson set the pattern for tractor design over the ensuing 60 years

Henry Ford's concern for the American farmer undoubtedly motivated him to develop the Fordson tractor. It was a trend-setter whose powertrain effectively doubled as a chassis. Riding a 63-inch wheelbase it was powered by a 247-cid, 20-bhp four. Henry is in the center of the photo.

in that its powertrain effectively doubled as the chassis. The driver sat above the transmission's tail end, well back of the engine and just forward of a rear axle linking wheels that were about one-third larger than those in front. Wheelbase was just 63 inches, overall height 55 inches, width 62 inches, and length 102 inches. Turn diameter was a trim 21 feet. Power was supplied by a purpose-built L-head four that was larger than the Model T's, displacing 247 cubic inches on 4 × 5-inch bore-and-stroke dimensions. Designed to run on kerosene, it delivered 20 horsepower at 1000 rpm.

Only 254 Fordsons would be built in 1917, and they didn't stay in America. Germany's submarine warfare had put England on the brink of starvation, so a concerned Henry earmarked initial production for export sale to alleviate the plight. To ensure ample, steady supplies for the UK, he also decided to set up a tractor plant in Ireland's County Cork, the Ford family's ancestral homeland, under a new Henry Ford & Son, Limited affiliate company, but the war ended before the plant became operational.

Ford Motor Company halted paid Model T advertising early this year, and did not buy a line of space (tractors and Lincoln cars excepted) until 1923. This reflected the policy established in 1910 where advertising expenditures (or lack thereof) were prorated according to the number of orders in hand. Ad manager Charles A. Brownell notified branch managers in February: "Today, we have instructed our advertising agency to wire immediate discontinuance of all Ford advertising. This is done because we are now from 40,000 to 50,000 cars behind orders, and it is simply a waste to continue advertising when production is behind." Similar messages went out the following May and November. Almost all national magazines were dropped from the schedule after 1914, and motoring magazines were omitted beginning in 1916. That year, the company spent only $6000 on paid advertising, virtually all of it for tiny newspaper ads. Car companies often rise and fall on their advertising today, and many did in the Teens as well. But the Ford policy reflected Henry's belief that most paid advertising was simply unnecessary. While conceding that it was "absolutely essential to introduce good, useful things," he felt it "an economic waste" for products already on the market. "If you really have a good thing," he often pointed out, "it will advertise itself."

Henry also liked to say that "our best advertising is free advertising" and that he would rather have a news story on the front page than pay for space elsewhere. Ad executives were at a loss to refute him on that. As *Printer's Ink* lamented in 1926, the auto magnate had for years found it "a simple matter to break into the front pages of newspapers almost at will." But though it could hardly be objec-

tive on the subject, the magazine also thought that such publicity was largely worthless, for it "does not tell the full story of the Ford car to buyers" or "firmly fix it in the consciousness of the buying public." Others, however, were convinced that the Model T profited from Henry's activities. Indeed, the firm owed much of its considerable success to the Ford name being so much in the news.

Of course, the reason the company could afford to do without ads in these years was continuing strong demand for the Model T. The flivver market had most always been a seller's market, and wartime production cutbacks contributed to the shortage well into 1920. Demand fell off alarmingly during a short but severe recession in the winter of 1920-21, but bounced back so vigorously in the spring of 1921 that the company had to strain for two years to meet it. This situation embarrassed advertising types, "some of whom," said *Printer's Ink*, "would have felt inclined to chip in if Ford had passed the hat, just to get away from the task of trying to answer reactionaries who pointed to Ford's nonadvertising success."

But the fact was that although Ford Motor Company itself did not advertise, its dealers did. Indeed, the irascible Henry, despite his statement about "economic waste," actually required dealers to run ads as a condition in their contracts. For many years dealers handled their own advertising. Then, in late 1916 at the company's suggestion, outlets in larger cities began "clubbing together," taking full-page ads (listing all their names) in metropolitan dailies and dividing the cost according to each dealer's sales.

A number of agents balked at mandatory local advertising, claiming Ford was using them "to pay its bills." Others, because they thought the investment sensible as well as necessary, went along without complaint. From 1917 to 1923, Ford dealers bought space at an annual rate of $3 million, a figure that in the company's view ranked Ford among the nation's largest advertisers. Strictly speaking, the firm spent only a few thousand dollars a year on materials for those dealers who would use them.

Headquarters wasn't ordinarily concerned with a dealer's choice of media or copy appeals, but did insist that its trademark signature, the famous Ford script, in use continuously from 1903, appear in all local ads. It also strongly reprimanded dealers who resorted to unfair practices. Referring to an ad that showed a broken-down competitive car over the caption, "Sell it and buy a Ford," Brownell angrily told branch managers, "This is an unwholesome type of advertising which has long since been taboo, and we certainly feel that Ford dealers have enough good things to say about our cars without knocking the other fellow." We could use more of that kind of honesty today.

1 9 1 8

After the sensational 1917 restyle, Ford saw no reason to change the Model T this year. Ditto the new Model TT truck. Offerings did change, however. The slow-selling Town Car was phased out despite its relative popularity as a taxi, though private operators would continue converting Fords for the purpose. The Coupelet was also dropped as buyers began showing a marked preference for fully closed body styles. Government-ordered civilian production cutbacks and the start of Ford's wartime production on May 7th reduced the firm's calendar-year output by nearly a third, down 200,000 cars to some 436,000. Total industry volume dropped nearly 50 percent to 943,436, which increased Ford's market share to some 46 percent.

In addition, tractor volume jumped way up this year as 34,167 Fordsons were completed. With the immediate need for tractors in Britain largely satisfied, Henry had applied to the U.S. Agriculture Department for a farm-equipment manufacturing license. It was approved in late June.

Ford's contributions to the war effort included making the famous Liberty aircraft engine as well as howitzer guns, gas masks, field helmets, caissons, and mobile kitchens along with Model T ambulances and TT trucks. It also built the "flivver tank," a small, lightweight armored vehicle based on the Model T, and the Eagle submarine chaser (the first of which was launched on July 11) for the U.S. Navy. The latter was built on the world's first boat assembly line, set up at the new River Rouge site. Reflecting his patriotism, Henry Ford leased his new Detroit hospital to the government at only $1 a year for the duration, but this magnanimous gesture was rendered somewhat token when the war ended with the signing of the Armistice on November 11.

Little Lizzie Ford came marching home as something of a war hero, a number of battlefield dispatches citing Model

The Model T cruised into 1918 little changed, hardly surprising in light of the changes for 1917. The two-passenger coupe (top) listed at $505, the same as in 1917, but production jumped from a little over 7000 units the year before to almost 15,000, this in spite of lower overall production brought on by World War I. It was a sign that more and more people wanted closed cars. Also seen here are a 1918 Ford Police Wagon (center) and a Model TT truck (bottom).

Ts for "gallantry in action." Ten machine gun-laden Lizzies were used to drive Germans from an entrenched position on the Marne, and the sturdy little car was the only vehicle that could get through to wounded men during the first days of fighting in the Argonne Forest. "Without a doubt the best car for the advance (ambulance) work is the Ford car," ran a 1918 medical report published more than 60 years later in *Antique Automobile* magazine. "It is small, light, easy to run, easy to maintain, simply constructed, economical in the consumption of gas, does not take much road space, and can be handled by one man when necessary.... I am firmly convinced that the Ford ambulance...can operate in any place where troops go.... In no case have I known where a Ford was blocked for more than a few minutes. On account of this fact, should the car accidentally run into a hole, it may be literally lifted out." So much for Lizzie's reputation as a frail, temperamental creature.

In Africa, the T saved a detachment of British soldiers from starvation by providing motive power for flatboats. General Edmund Allenby attributed the success of the Palestine campaign to "Egyptian laborers, camels, and Ford cars." According to newscaster Lowell

Thomas, then lecturing on the Middle Eastern campaign, Allenby rode in a Rolls-Royce, but always had a Ford on hand as a kind of insurance.

"Hunka Tin," a wartime-inspired takeoff on Rudyard Kipling's "Gunga Din," brought down vaudeville houses after its publication in the *American Field Service Bulletin* and was used in Ford dealers' advertising all over the country. Termed by *Printer's Ink* as the most effective product advertising to emerge from the war, the poem concluded with a rattling stanza fully worthy of its subject:

> Yes, Tin, Tin, Tin,
> You exasperating puzzle,
>   Hunka Tin,
> I've abused you and I've flayed
>   you,
> But, by Henry Ford who made
>   you,
> You are better than a Packard,
>   Hunka Tin.

Henry was nothing if not iconoclastic. He may have hated war, but once it was thrust upon him he didn't hesitate to throw the full weight of his company behind America's military effort. A political cartoon appearing this year with the title "The Fighting Pacifist" depicted Ford, sleeves dutifully rolled up, hurling from

Although there was a war raging in Europe and the U.S. government had ordered cutbacks in auto production, that didn't stop Ford dealers from participating in auto shows. In this case, White Bros. Inc. had set up a display at a 1918 show, although it's not clear where this particular event took place. Behind the Model T coupe in the foreground is the display area for the Mitchell, a make that would expire in 1923.

Detroit all manner of vehicles, vessels, and ammunition across the Atlantic to batter the German Kaiser, who was saying, "And he makes Americans out of foreigners yet."

But it was this very single-mindedness that prevented Henry from the political career that his position and accomplishments might have otherwise given him. Thus, when President Woodrow Wilson persuaded him to run for a vacant Michigan Senate seat this year, Ford said that while he would mount a campaign, he wouldn't spend a single cent on it. Evidently, he thought no more of touting himself than he did advertising the Model T. His intransigence cost him the primary, though not by much—a mere 2200 votes. One can only wonder how history might have been changed had he spent a little on campaigning and gone on to serve in Washington.

Though little changed in appearance, the 1919 Model T finally followed the rest of the industry by offering an electric self-starter and demountable rims as new optional equipment. Initially available on closed models only, they were linewide extras by June. (The Model TT truck wouldn't get the starter until 1922.) The starting system was what we'd now term conventional, comprising a battery and generator, plus a combined ignition/light switch on the dash and an electric taillamp to replace the previous oil-burning item. Actual ignition, however, was still accomplished via the familiar four coils, commutator, and flywheel-mounted magneto.

Hand-cranking had always been especially troublesome on the Model T. As old-time auto writer Murray Fahnestock related in 1924: "Mr. Smith... climbs in by the right-hand door (for there is no left-hand door by the front seat), sets the spark and throttle levers in a position like that of the hands of a clock at ten minutes to three. Then... he gets out to crank. Seizing the crank in his right hand (carefully, for a friend of his once broke his arm cranking), he slips his left forefinger through a loop of wire that controls the choke. He pulls at the loop of wire, he revolves the crank mightily, and as the engine at last roars, he leaps to the trembling running board, leans in, and moves the spark and throttle to twenty-five minutes of two. Perhaps he reaches the throttle before the engine falters into silence, but if it is a cold morning perhaps he does not. In that case, back to the crank again and the loop of wire." For the simple T, the "self-starter," as pioneer Cadillac called it, was a comparatively great advance.

Ford also advanced on the production front, turning out a record number of truck chassis at both its U.S. and Canadian plants (including the 100,000th one-tonner) and almost doubling calendar-year car output to 820,455 units. The industry as a whole began a modest recovery from war-depressed 1918 by building 1,651,625 passenger cars. But that 57 percent gain was more than offset by Ford's increase, so the Dearborn automaker ended the year three points higher in market share at 49 percent. Completion of the three-millionth Model T this year only highlighted Ford's continuing dominance. Fordson tractor production also reached a new high in 1919, helped by the April 4 start-up of the new Irish plant in County Cork.

Significant non-product events this year included the birth of Edsel and Elea-

The Model T became a far more civilized car for 1919 with the adoption of an electric starter (along with battery and generator) as standard equipment for closed cars, and optional on open models late in the model year. Also new were demountable rims for easier tire changing. The coupe (top) now cost $750 because of the new standard equipment. This Model T roadster pickup (above), and others, worked as service vehicles at Ford factories.

nor Ford's second son, Benson, on July 20, and the March 15 resignation of engineer C. Harold Wills, who left Ford with $1.6 million in back pay to start an automaking venture of his own that would result in the short-lived Wills Sainte Claire. On January 1, Ford raised its workers' wage to an unprecedented six dollars a day—significant, if not nearly as newsworthy as the five-dollar day had been back in 1914. June saw the formation of a new Danish subsidiary near Copenhagen per recommendation of assembly operations boss William S. Knudsen, himself a Dane. From just 14 cars per day in October 1919, this plant would be producing 140 units daily by the summer of 1924. This

prompted construction of a so-called "miniature Rouge" factory in the South Port area that came on stream in November 1924.

Speaking of the Rouge, 1919 saw Ford's future riverside factory colossus begin taking shape in earnest. The deep-water port facilities set up there as part of wartime Eagle boat construction were enlarged to accommodate Great Lakes freighters that would eventually deliver huge quantities of iron ore, lumber, coal, and limestone to feed Ford's automaking machine. Also this year, the boat plant was retooled to make car bodies, several coke ovens were completed, and work was begun on a huge powerhouse and several blast furnaces. Meantime, Ford

signed its first contract, for car bodies, with the Edward G. Budd Manufacturing Company, which would soon to become one of its largest suppliers.

But by far the biggest Ford event of 1919 was the complete reorganization that left the company entirely in the hands of the Ford family. It was signalled by Henry's talk this year of building another car, the first and only time he would mention this possibility during the Model T's long career. His real aim was to outflank fellow stockholders as a prelude to buying them out.

Henry loathed stockholders, equating them with drones and parasites, people who "gave nothing but money to an enterprise." The wily tycoon decided that it was past time to rid himself of them for good. The surprise first step in his master plan came on December 30, 1918, when he submitted his resignation as company president effective the very next day. His stated reason was "to devote my time to building up other organizations with which I am connected," though he didn't name them. But he tellingly retained his seat on the board and got his son Edsel elected president.

Soon afterwards, while vacationing in California, Ford told a reporter that he intended to build a new and better car

that would undercut the Model T—now selling at an average $466—by $100-$200. What's more, it would be built and marketed by a concern other than Ford Motor Company. His "old" firm? "Why, I don't know exactly what will become of that," he said vaguely. The story was page-one news across the country. A bit later, Ford allowed that this "new car is well advanced, for I have been working on it while resting in California." Speculation mounted as to what he had in mind. One wire service reported that Harvey Firestone would be a partner in the rumored $200 million venture. *Printer's Ink* speculated the new car would be called "Flivv Junior," while the Washington *Herald* was sure that the name would be "Flivverette."

Within two weeks, Henry's loose comments had started to panic many Ford dealers, forcing Edsel to send them a soothing letter. "A new car may be manufactured," he wrote, "but . . . [it] could not possibly be designed, tested out, manufactured and marketed in quantities under two or three years' time." He admonished dealers to get busy selling Model Ts and stop worrying about this possible competitor.

Company shareholders were equally worried, concerned that Henry would

The 1919 Ford Model T Center Door sedan (both pages) listed at $875, some $230 more than in 1918. It also weighed 1875 pounds, up 160. Both were the result of the new additional standard equipment. The extra heft also meant that the 20-bhp inline four (right) had to work harder for a living. To accommodate the electric starter for 1919, the T got a new engine block, flywheel, transmission cover, and other related components.

actually make good his threat, thereby depressing the value of their stock. They were thus softened up for the calls from financial agents acting secretly on Henry's behalf. The buyout was completed by July. It cost Ford $105 million, $60 million of which was borrowed, though he knew the price was reasonable. When emissaries told him that they had completed their stock-buying mission, Henry reportedly "danced a jig all around the room." Of course, he immediately abandoned plans for his Model T rival—assuming he ever had any. Thus ended a brilliant maneuver that would be the most adroit "acting" performance of his entire career.

But coming up with the money wouldn't be nearly so easy. Curtailed civilian production during World War I led Henry to count on unprecedented demand and high prosperity for his firm in

from $525 to $975. Averaging $148, the reductions were, in percentage terms, the largest in industry history.

Once more, a Ford announcement was front-page news. Not untypically, the Sidney (Delaware) *Record*'s three-deck headline read, "Henry Fires a Bomb," "Just like Him," "The Ford is The Thing and Everybody Can Afford to Buy a Ford." Several papers suggested that the industrialist be made "general manager" of the nation, since he seemed to be the only one with the courage and ability to give the public relief from inflation.

The rest of the industry was incensed. Representatives from several firms including General Motors, Dodge, Maxwell-Chalmers, Hupp, Hudson, Essex, and Paige met in Detroit and solemnly announced that prices should not be lowered, because buyers would then expect further reductions and all buying would cease. Such statements only made Henry's halo glow all the brighter. Though reluctant, a number of rivals led by Franklin, Studebaker, and Willys-Overland found it expedient to follow Ford's lead. By October 9, 1920, some 23 automakers had lowered prices, 28 had not.

For a time it appeared that Ford's pricing strategy might succeed, as more than 100,000 Model Ts were sold that October. But November sales were off approximately 10 percent, and the December total sank to less than 50 percent of the November figure. During the first 24 days of December, Ford produced 78,000 Model Ts—some 35,000 more than dealers could sell. The firm duly closed its plants "for inventory," promising to reopen January 5, 1921, but the hiatus actually extended to February 1. Meanwhile, rumors that Ford was in financial straits spread throughout the country. Many were genuinely alarmed at the automaker's plight, and Model T owners "rallied like bees" to a suggestion by the chief of the Columbus, Ohio, Western Union bureau that each lend $100 to Henry to tide him over.

Ford declined all such offers, recalled workers, and in February 1921 assembled 35,000 Model Ts from parts on hand. These cars, along with 30,000 unconsigned vehicles produced in late 1920, were immediately shipped to dealers. As was then industry practice, dealers had to pay for the cars upon arrival or forfeit their franchises. In most instances they went to their bankers, got the money they needed, and watched demand gradually use up the excess supply. Instead of borrowing money himself, Henry had effectively forced dealers to borrow for him.

Fortunately for all concerned, the recession proved short-lived, and Model Ts were being built and sold at a record-breaking rate by the spring and summer of 1921. Henry had outwitted Wall Street, finagled his way out of trouble, and risen to new heights as a folk hero.

the postwar era. The Ford company, which had sold from one-third to one-half of America's cars up to the end of the war, built a record-breaking 750,000 units for model year 1919—fully 40 percent of the national total. But then came a sudden economic slump in mid-1920 and auto sales, including Ford's, began falling. Now it was Henry who was concerned. By April 1921 he needed $25 million to pay off his 1919 loan; he also owed $18-$30 million in taxes, and was determined to pay $7 million in employee bonuses in January 1921. Yet in the summer of 1920, he had just $20 million in cash to meet all his obligations.

To maintain production and income, Henry decided to fall back on a familiar ploy: reduce prices so drastically as to shake up the industry and startle the nation. Over the objections of key executives, he instituted price cuts on September 21, 1920, ranging from $105 to $180 on his five models, which had been priced

1 9 2 0

everal minor changes took Lady Lizzie into what would soon become known as the Roaring '20s. Steering wheels switched from wooden to composition and grew from 15 to 16 inches in diameter, while oval-section gas tanks replaced the former cylindrical units and square-end springs appeared. The one-ton TT truck was again essentially unchanged.

Ford calendar-year car production changed for the worse, however, falling by some 50 percent to 419,517 units even though the industry as a whole tacked on a quarter-million cars to finish at just over 1.9 million. As a result, Ford's market share also dropped by half, skidding to just 22 percent. Truck sales remained strong, however. Ditto demand for the Fordson tractor, production of which was shifted during 1920-21 from the original Brady Street plant in Dearborn to the new River Rouge complex, whose main blast furnace was finally completed on May 17.

Continuing Ford's rapid international expansion, assembly operations chief Bill Knudsen formed a Spanish subsidiary this year with leased factory space at the southern port of Cadiz. Within two years this plant was making a satisfactory profit on annual volume of 10,000 cars and 500 tractors.

Nineteen-twenty also saw the advent of the Ford Educational Library of Films as a successor to the firm's Animated Weekly newsreels and the Educational Weekly series of historic and instructional films. Over 50 of the longer and more ambitious Library productions would be completed through 1925, when the series was discontinued due to mounting expense.

There was never a question about the value of promotional films, and Ford continued to crank them out for its dealers, who would use them to good effect throughout the Twenties. One sales representative reported that in Pound, Wisconsin, a village of 400, more than 2000 people flocked in from the surrounding area to see such movies at the Ford dealership every Wednesday night. The Bridgeboro, New Jersey, dealer showed the movies in a nearby grove to an eager audience of 1800-2000 farmers every week. Many branches and dealers even kept specially equipped Model Ts on the road, complete with projectionists. Said the Silbee, Texas, Ford dealer: "We've given more than 40 shows with an average of 200 to 250 [people] on hand, and are creating goodwill by the bushel." But then, these were the first motion pictures many people had ever seen, a number of dealers reported. Besides dealer showrooms, they were sometimes shown in prospective buyers' homes and, in many small towns, on the side of a billboard or building. Of course, these were all silent movies. "Talkies" were still a few years away.

Henry Ford did far more than run the "Model T Company" in the Twenties. Indeed, he would develop America's first vertically integrated, highly diversified industrial empire, in line with his desire that Ford Motor Company be a totally self-sufficient enterprise. The firm ultimately mined coal, iron ore, and lead; owned timber lands, sawmills, dry kilns, a wood distillation plant, a rubber plantation, and a series of "village industries"; operated a railroad, blast furnaces, coke ovens, foundries, steel mills, and lake and ocean fleets; produced glass, artificial leather, textiles, gauges, paper, and cement; built airplanes; farmed 10,000 acres; and made Lincolns in addition to Model Ts, trucks, and Fordson tractors. Ford also prospected for oil, bought dolomite lands with the production of magnesium in mind, took steps to produce abrasives, bought acreage in the Florida Everglades with the intention of planting rubber trees, and experimented with generating power by burning coal at the mine and making charcoal iron. These activities received wide attention in the Twenties and contributed to the popular belief that Henry Ford had a daring and highly original mind, virtually unique technical skills, and a ceaseless devotion to mankind.

The Model T chugged into 1920 with only minor changes. Among them was an oval gas tank (rather than round), which allowed for a lower seat. Also new was a composition (rather than wood) steering wheel that now measured 16 inches in diameter (up one inch). The price of the two-passenger coupe (top) came down $25, to $850, but production was way up over 1919: from 11,528 units to 60,215 in the August 1919 to July 1920 period. The Runabout (bottom), seen here with a rather serious-looking couple aboard, listed at $650 with starter and demountable rims, but on March 3, 1920, the price was slashed by $100. Nearly 100,000 were built for the model year. Where optional, the starter sold for $75 dollars, demountable rims for $25.

Except for bodies with slightly lower profiles, the Model T didn't change for 1921. Its production figures, however, did, and definitely for the better, which must have been a relief to Ford accountants. In fact, calendar-year output set a new record by more than doubling to 903,814. The key factors were a modest upturn in the general economy during the third and fourth quarters as well as the price cuts Henry ordered this year in part to finance his stock buyout of 1919. As total industry volume declined by well over 400,000 units to 1,468,067, Ford's market share swelled some three-fold to a commanding 61.5 percent.

It was just as well, because the company lost ground in shifting tractor production to the new Rouge complex, a process that took fully six months, and by buying the Detroit, Toledo & Ironton Railroad (DT&I) on March 4 for $5 million. But both setbacks were only temporary. The much larger Rouge facilities boosted potential tractor volume to a quarter-million units annually, while a raft of capital improvements soon made the DT&I a money-maker.

Yet amongst these gains, one 1921 loss could not be made up and would eventually come to haunt Ford in the not-too-distant future. This was the December departure of William S. "Big Bill" Knudsen following a series of policy disputes with Henry. Knudsen was well known as the architect of the rapid expansion in Ford's assembly operations both at home and abroad, and his talents had not gone unnoticed at General Motors, now under the stewardship of the equally canny Alfred P. Sloan. After being wooed, Knudsen joined GM's struggling Chevrolet Division and vowed to get even with Henry by making Chevy sales at least equal, if not superior, to Ford's. It was a promise he'd keep within a mere six years.

Nineteen twenty-one was the year that saw the emergence of "Ford Days" in hundreds of small communities throughout the country. Town merchants, at the instigation of the local Ford dealer, would set aside a day and invite every Model T owner or driver in the surrounding area to come in. Businesses offered special bargains, and a carnival atmosphere prevailed as Main Street was taken over for parades, band concerts, vaudeville performances, dancing, queen crownings, and Model T and athletic contests. Prizes were awarded to contest winners and owners of the cars carrying the biggest load of produce, the most children, the five prettiest girls, and so

on. Model Ts turned out by the thousands for Ford Days and virtually took over some towns, inasmuch as drivers of other cars were usually fined if their vehicles appeared on the streets. Ford Days continued until 1931, and Model Ts continued to make up a large proportion of the participants even after production ceased.

This year also saw the continuation of an unofficial consumer boycott against the Model T, the first ever waged against a car. It came in response to a notorious, 91-week anti-Semitic campaign launched in 1920 by Henry Ford's weekly magazine, the *Dearborn Independent*. Ford whose anti-Semitism stemmed more from ignorance than deep-seated bigotry or malice, believed that Jews wanted to gain control of the nation's finances, commerce, and politics at the expense of Christians, and thought he was performing a great service in exposing it. Jews thought otherwise, of course.

Although no Jewish groups declared a formal boycott of the Model T, many firms and individuals stopped buying Fords nonetheless. So did some other companies doing business with Jewish concerns and dependent on their goodwill. Jews in Hartford, Connecticut, staging a 400-car parade in honor of Dr. Chaim Weizman and Albert Einstein, ordered "Positively no Ford machines in line."

Ford's branch mangers and dealers, particularly in cities with large Jewish populations, complained bitterly about the sales resistance and economic pressure resulting from the *Independent*'s campaign. The manager of the second-ranking dealership in the New York branch

Ford saw production more than double to a bit over 900,000 for 1921, pushing market share to a commanding 61.5 percent. A good part of the reason for that was Henry's stimulation of the marketplace with newly instituted price cuts. For example, the Center Door sedan (above) sold for $795 after September 22, 1920, a drop of $180.

went so far as to suggest that everyone would be happier if Ford put the money spent on anti-Semitic articles into making better cars. Some dealers were threatened with eviction by Jewish landlords, but got little sympathy from Ford's personal secretary. Replying to a Minnesota dealer who urged the articles to be stopped, he suggested that dealers should own their own buildings so as not to be vulnerable to such pressure. Ford himself was similarly unmoved. His stock answer: "If they want our product, they'll buy it."

It's difficult to determine the number of Model T sales lost to this situation. Though sales had dropped sharply during the last half of 1920, the main reason may have been a general economic decline that affected the entire industry. Sales then reached new highs as the economy trended upwards in 1921-23. Unquestionably some Jews condemned Ford's actions but still bought his products. As Will Rogers pointed out, the boycott "may not be a complete success yet—but it will be as soon as someone learns how to make a cheaper car." While the Model T was definitely a better buy than any competitor at this point, it wouldn't be in the mid-Twenties and Henry would learn he could no longer be complacent when he launched a second anti-Semitic campaign.

As impulsively as he had begun it, Ford ordered the *Independent* articles discontinued in January 1922. The reasons are not altogether clear. One possibility is that his New York manager finally convinced him of the difficulty of selling Model Ts in areas with large Jewish populations. Another is that Ford was swayed by William Fox, president of Fox Film Corporation, who threatened to show choice footage of Model T accidents in his newsreels if Ford persisted in attacking the character of Jewish film executives and their motion pictures. In any event, Henry called off the campaign, though he retracted nothing. Indeed, he later boasted that the articles had opened the minds of Americans to possible evils.

In 1924, the *Independent* launched its second series of anti-Semitic articles under the general title "Jewish exploitation of Farmer Organizations." Henry thought that a Jewish group was trying to obtain control of American wheat farming. One of those attacked, Aaron Sapiro, a prominent Chicago attorney, filed a million-dollar defamation of character suit against him—but not the *Independent*. Ford settled out of court in July 1927, and published both a personal apology to Sapiro and a formal retraction of

all past attacks on Jewish people. His motives for issuing the apology were complex. An important factor undoubtedly was the critical changeover from Model T to Model A production at a time when much of the sales force was complaining that Jewish hostility was hurting business.

Many Jews resumed buying Ford products after this, only to be alienated again in 1938 when Ford, on his 75th birthday, accepted the Grand Cross of the Supreme Order of the German Eagle, the highest honor Hitler's Third Reich could bestow on a foreigner. An accompanying citation observed that the medal was given to recognize Ford as a pioneer of motorcars for the masses. But his acceptance of the award, plus other anti-Semitic and pro-Nazi accusations against him, led to an active and effective boycott of Ford products in the years leading up to World War II by Jews and other Americans unsympathetic to his views.

The resulting sales slump was particularly acute in the company's Eastern sales region, which had the country's largest Jewish population. As region manager W.K. Edmunds wrote in 1944: "Mr. Edsel Ford understood this situation thoroughly, and just prior to the time we discontinued making automo-

As ever, Model Ts—like the attractive Depot Hack—were available in 1921 with bodies built by outside suppliers. A bare chassis was available for $360 that year, and lowered to $345 before the year was out. A heavier duty chassis listed at $455, later $440.

biles, he had allotted us a special fund [some $50,000] to be used for sales promotion and advertising in this area to improve our sales and counteract the existent antagonism." A company investigation also revealed that in Hollywood "Jewish interests...agreed to ban all Ford units from their studio lots and forbade employees and stars to buy Ford products." The report added: "A few stars are in a position to disregard the order, but many sales are being lost."

To this day, many older Jews and their descendants have not forgiven Henry Ford, refusing to buy Ford products and critical of those who do. Since the late Forties, however, almost all Jews have been gratified by the friendliness of the Ford family and company toward the Jewish community. "The new generation of Fords," declared an influential Jewish editor in 1970, "looks back at the era of their grandfather with a sense of deep regret, rejecting whatever smacked of prejudice and anti-Semitism."

1922

The trusty T was again largely the same this year, but the Center Door Sedan with its distinctive oval rear window was dropped. The door's position had made for awkward entry/exit, and the car was considered top-heavy, slow, and expensive. Closed models received mechanical window latches to replace the previously used cloth retaining straps, the Runabout's removable rear deck was slightly enlarged, and the T's wooden frame was now covered in steel for greater durability. The only change for this year's one-ton TT truck was availability of the passenger cars' optional battery-based electrical system with self-starter.

With the Twenties now starting to roar, Ford calendar-year car production reached unprecedented levels—the first of five straight years which saw production of over a million units each year. This year's total of 1,173,745 was not only a full 77 percent better than the 1921 tally but represented close to 52 percent of the 2,274,185 units built by the industry as a whole. Truck volume remained strong, as did demand for the Fordson tractor. The latter, now priced at $395, saw 66,752 copies for the calendar year; another 2233 were built in Ireland, after which production there was terminated. In all, some 200,000 Fordsons had been built since 1917.

It's interesting to note that some eight percent of U.S.-built Ford cars were being exported by this time and that Ford's European operations together accounted for more than half the firm's foreign sales. The Model T was now the second best-selling car in Australia, and Ford would remain number-two in that market into the 1980s, at which point it would take over first place. Furthering Ford's fortunes overseas were two new assembly plants built this year, at Antwerp in Belgium and Trieste in Italy.

The T scored its most highly publicized hillclimb victory in this year's fourth annual world's championship contest held on Pikes Peak near Colorado Springs, Colorado. The win had rags-to-riches overtones worthy of the T. The winner was a 21-year-old small-town Nebraskan, Noel E. Bullock, who had driven up the mountain only once before the race. The car itself, named "Old Liz," was unpainted and hoodless, and had been "home brewed" by the youth in a blacksmith's shop in 1918. Though berated publicly by several competitors as a "tin can" and a "cross between a kiddie-car and a pushmobile," it bested the elite of road racing and many of America's premium-priced makes. Bullock planned to race up Pikes Peak again in 1923 but was blacklisted nine days before the event for participating in a non-sanctioned dirt-track race in South Dakota. No other Model T ever won on the mountain.

The "Lizzie Label" craze—painting humorous comments on flivvers—reached its peak during the early- and mid-Twenties. It was particularly popular around land-grant colleges, where small-town smart alecks and country clowns had an abundance of dilapidated Model Ts as "canvases." While the exact origin of Lizzie Labels is obscure, they were likely popularized by *Judge*, a widely quoted satirical weekly that gave this peculiar folk art the dignity of humorous literature by paying five dollars each for the best of them.

Like Ford jokes, Lizzie Labels had certain discernible patterns. Many were borrowed quotations, such as "Abandon home, all ye who enter in" and "I do not choose to run." Others were more contemporary, such as "Barnum was right" and "Our booz'em friend." Another group parodied advertising slogans and the titles of songs, plays, and movies. Some were in the form of notices, like "Quiet please, violent ward" (on hood) or "Night calls by appointment only." There were also plenty of good old-fashioned wisecracks: "Follow us, farmer, for haywire"; "You may pass me, big boy, but I'm paid for"; "Heck of the Resperus." Sex was perhaps the most prevalent theme: "Girls, watch your step-ins" and "For fastidious flappers" are examples.

Meanwhile, Edsel Ford was fascinated by aviation, yet his father mostly thought flying was dangerous. Nevertheless, Henry bought a stake this year in the Stout Metal Airplane Company, which he would buy outright in 1925, paying each of the co-owners twice their original investments. Among other things, this purchase resulted in the construction of a Ford airport in Dearborn, complete with lodgings for weary travelers—the historic Dearborn Inn, which still hosts many visitors to nearby Greenfield Village and the surrounding area. Years later, one historian observed that to many, Ford's investment in the Stout Company "meant aviation had come of age."

But Ford made an even more significant acquisition when it bought Lincoln Motor Company on February 4 this year, thus gaining another car to supplement the Model T for the first time, albeit one with much smaller volume. Lincoln had been organized in 1917 by Cadillac founder Henry M. Leland and his son Wilfred to produce Liberty aircraft engines for the war effort. The firm then turned to automobiles, but its Model L didn't reach the market until September 1920, when auto sales were shrinking from prewar levels. And though this car was mechanically one of the soundest made in America, it lacked style. Add lofty prices in the $5000-$6000 range and it's easy to see why Lincoln was handicapped from the outset. Sales totaled only 752 units in 1920, and the firm proved unprofitable during 1921. By November of that year the firm was in receivership and offered for sale at a court-ordered price of $8 million.

Price cuts were the order of the day at Ford in the early Twenties. Consider the five-passenger touring: $440 on September 22, 1920; $415 as of June 7, 1921; $355 on September 2, 1921; $348 as of January 16, 1922; and $298 as of October 17, 1922. The final price was upped to $393 with starter and demountable wheels—still a bargain. This '22 touring sports a shiny front end.

Into the breech stepped Henry Ford, who could well afford that price. On the surface it seemed an unlikely move: the father of the Tin Lizzie selling a car that cost 10-15 times as much—but it was, in fact, entirely in character. Ever the canny businessman, Henry was no doubt intrigued by the prospect of being able to compete at opposite ends of the market, and he took advantage of Lincoln's plight by buying the firm at the receiver's sale in February. "We have built more cars than anyone else," he told the press in announcing his purchase. "Now we are going to build a better car than anyone else."

It would take a man with Ford's determination to get hold of Lincoln anyway. The company was heavily in debt; the state of Delaware, where it had been incorporated, tried to block the sale; and the U.S. government had a bill for $4.5 million in back taxes (later revised to $500,000). But Ford persisted, with strong urging from son Edsel. The Lelands didn't. Though under the impression they would continue to run the plant, they resigned within six months of the Ford takeover. The proximity of such strong figures as Henry Leland and Henry Ford just couldn't last.

One reason was the Lelands' fear that Ford would lower their high standards, though that would prove groundless. Lincoln's mechanical excellence would be maintained, while its styling would be considerably improved under the aegis of Edsel Ford, who promptly began enlisting the services of Le Baron, Willoughby, Dietrich, and Locke to supplement the coachbuilt bodies already available from the houses of Brunn and Judkins.

The Ford buyout and Lincoln's meager resources precluded many changes in the 1922 Model L though Ford did manage to raise production. Of the 5767 completed for the calendar/model year, 5512 were Ford-built, a fact proclaimed on radiator badges for a time. After the Lelands departed, Ford engineers tackled overheating tendencies by giving the L-head V-8 a cooler-running cylinder head. They also phased in a timing chain and sprocket and switched from cast-iron to aluminum cylinders.

In typical Ford fashion, Lincoln's 1922 prices were cut in a search for sales. Standard-body models, styled by Brunn, began with a basic seven-seat touring car that was newly listed at $3800; other styles ranged to $4900. Custom bodies proliferated, with Judkins and Brunn still fielding a variety of sedans, berlines, limousines, and coupes newly repositioned to $4600-$7200. Most of this year's Lincolns employed the longer, 136-inch-wheelbase chassis. The 130-inch platform was in its last season, offered only with a choice of six Lincoln-built open and closed bodies.

To no one's surprise, Ford immediately began a publicity and advertising campaign to promote Lincoln as a car of the highest quality. Exhibits at auto shows and in hotel lobbys, frequently called the Lincoln Salon Petite, strove to create an aura of snob appeal. "Guests," many of whom were sent engraved invitations, were greeted by "doormen and other attendants appropriately uniformed and carefully schooled in the proprieties." They were then escorted to the display, "a picture of exquisite appointments, floral decorations, and perfumed fountains, further enhanced through ar-

tistic lighting effects." "Charmingly costumed" pages and tuxedo-clad salesmen, each wearing a white carnation, were on hand to serve, while liveried drivers waited outside to demonstrate the "chauffeur-driven equipage."

Ford spent more than $400,000 on Lincoln advertising in 1923-24. Much of it went to 10 "class" magazines such as *Vogue, Vanity Fair, Town & Country, Spur,* and *Motor Life.* Aside from print advertising, Lincoln's leading sales-promotion medium was a monthly magazine simply called *The Lincoln.* Introduced in December 1922, it was designed to appeal to "people of taste and culture," with little of the "hard-sell" copy that had become common in *Ford Times.* The periodical was sent to Lincoln owners and prospective buyers as well as to "many of the finest clubs" in the country. Circulation stood at 70,000 by 1924.

Lincoln was not an outstanding sales success in its early years as a Ford Motor Company product, an average of some 7000 cars being retailed each year through 1930. Packard and Cadillac, competing at the same price level, outsold Lincoln more than three to one, while Pierce-Arrow marketed almost as many units despite considerably higher prices.

This page: Henry Ford loved the great out-of-doors, and often went on camping trips. He is seen here (far left) with his famous friend Thomas Edison (next to Henry). The large touring car in the background is no Model T—perhaps it's a Lincoln, as Ford bought that firm after it went into receivership in late 1921. Opposite page: Model Ts served in all kinds of roles, this '22 as a "Fire Chief Runabout." The "B" on the hood is the current owner's last initial.

1 9 2 3

This year brought the first major appearance alterations to the Model T in nearly five years. Most obvious were higher radiators and bodies set lower on their chassis. Two new closed styles appeared: two- and four-door sedans. The latter, tagged at $725, was predictably marketed as the "Fordor," a play on the name Ford. The former, wearing a $595 price tag, was called "Tudor" for consistency, though the spelling had nothing to do with England.

Both new sedans and the familiar coupe (now $530) featured a larger, rectangular rear window, thus considerably improving visibility astern, while rotary window regulators, cowl ventilator, and square fuel tanks were adopted across the board. Save the Fordor's rear portals, doors on closed models were newly hinged from the A-pillars instead of "suicide" style from the B-posts—a surprisingly modern feature. Open cars had new tops that could be erected or folded by one person, and their windshields were set at a more jaunty angle, with the upper section pivoted at the top of the frame. The coupe's rear compartment was now integral with the rest of the body. The runabout ($365) retained the detachable rear "turtleback" section that allowed easy conversion to "pickup delivery."

Dearborn's calendar-year car production set another record this year—a smashing 1,817,891 units, still about half the industry total (up to 3,624,717 cars)—but the Model T was looking decidedly old-fashioned and looking more so all the time. This partly explains why Ford resumed Model T advertising. During the previous six years the company had bought no ad space at all, leaving individual dealers to carry the ball. But this left much to be desired in that sales pitches were neither uniform nor consistently seen in all parts of the country. As a result, Edsel Ford announced the reestablishment of an advertising department in August following a conference with branch managers.

Ford was one of the nation's biggest ad buyers in the mid-Twenties, spending nearly $15 million between September 1923 and October 1926. About eight percent of the total budget was scheduled for women's and "prestige" magazines, as the advertising staff sought to imbue the Tin Lizzie with "an atmosphere of 'Pride of Ownership'...of class and quality." As with prewar attempts to establish the Model T as a prestige item, this aspect of the campaign met with little success. In fact, a Ford now likely

Ford gave a slight nod to modernizing the Model T by giving the '23 a higher radiator and hood and lowering the body slightly on the chassis. The touring (top) listed at $298, or $393 with starter and demountable rims. Buyers chose the latter by a margin of nearly six to one. With side curtains, the touring (bottom) not only looked terrible, but visibility was lousy. Two new body styles debuted for 1923, the "Fordor" sedan (center) and the "Tudor," both with conventionally placed doors (unlike the Center Door sedan).

evoked less "pride of ownership" among women and prestige-conscious men than any car on the market.

Henry Ford's basic dislike of advertising again surfaced in June 1926, when he told his dealers to fend for themselves once more. From then until the Model A's introduction in late 1927, the company bought virtually no advertising space. Dealers in many metropolitan areas again banded together, retained advertising agencies, and resumed campaigns on a local basis.

There were no changes of consequence in Ford's commercial vehicles this year, but more of them were built. Truck production totaled 193,234 in the U.S. and another 31,874 in Canada. On top of this came nearly 102,000 Fordsons, a new single-season high for the tractor.

Elsewhere in 1923, the company began construction on its first true engineering center, a faint sign that perhaps it was time to think about replacing the Model T. Located in Dearborn about a mile from the Ford family's Fair Lane estate, it would be the birthplace for many future Ford vehicles. This year also saw the hiring of one Dale Roeder, a young engineer who would be a key figure in designing many of Ford's commercial vehicles in the Thirties and Forties.

Ford built a total of about 929,000 touring cars for 1923. While that figure included foreign production, it's still an impressive number for a single body style (top). The Town Car (above left) continued as Ford's "prestige" offering, but takers were few. Truck sales were healthy, however, with over a quarter of a million built for 1923, among them this platform stake model (above). Prices started at $380 for the chassis, while a cab could be had for only $65. The Model T by now was beginning to look decidedly old fashioned, so Ford resumed advertising in 1923.

1 9 2 4

Lizzie turned "Sweet Sixteen" this year, and Ford celebrated with two production milestones. The first came on June 15 with completion of the 10-millionth Model T. Soon after leaving the Highland Park line it led parades through towns and cities along the Lincoln Highway (New York to San Francisco) and along Route 66 (Chicago to Los Angeles). Several million people saw the car, which was "greeted" by governors and mayors at each stop along both routes. A documentary film of the tour titled "Fording the Lincoln Highway" was widely exhibited in the mid-Twenties.

Next came the 11-millionth Ford, which was presented to the Prince of Wales during his visit to Highland Park in October. The Prince also spent some time at Fair Lane, the Ford family estate in Dearborn. A photo taken there of the Prince with Henry and Edsel would serve as the model for a life-size statue of the automaker that would be installed in front of Dearborn's Henry Ford Centennial Library in 1974. Said sculptor Marshall Frederick: "This pose, the thoughtful look, represents him in the best way. I like to see him thinking."

There was one physical change in the evergreen T for 1924: a shallow "apron" below the radiator (also fitted to some very late 1923 models) that helped tidy-up appearance. Passenger-car production for the calendar year eased by about 68,000 units to 1,749,827, but industrywide volume dropped by some 400,000, so Ford was still way out in front with about 50 percent of the market.

Nevertheless, Henry had sharpened his pencil for another round of price reductions, and the figures were truly astonishing: an unheard-of $265 for the Runabout and a mere $295 for the touring, both all-time lows. The Tudor and Fordor sedans went down to $590 and $685, respectively, while the coupe was reduced a fiver to $525. Despite the bargain-basement rates, Ford made an average of $50 per car and netted a $100 million total profit for 1923-24.

But the competition was preparing to put an end to the T's incredible market domination. General Motors, reorganized after the 1920 recession by Pierre duPont and Alfred Sloan, was readying a Chevrolet only slightly more costly than the Ford, yet far more modern and better looking. It would take some time to halt the Model T juggernaut, but it's interesting to note that 1923 would be the peak year for Ford sales. From here on, the trend would be inexorably downward.

Slightly fewer truck chassis rolled out this year—172,221 U.S. units—but this was tempered by the arrival of Ford's first factory truck bodywork. Announced in October 1923 but not widely available until January 1924, this was an all-steel "express" type with a new-design cab ahead of an open pickup-type box. Panels were initially supplied for dealer assembly and installation from Ford's own Highland Park plant, the

This page: Even if the Model T was growing old, the 1924 Speedster still looked speedy—even with the top up. Opposite page, left column: The Model T chassis (top) was both tough and versatile. Adapted for truck applications, it wore an endless variety of specialized bodies, several of which are seen here. A Model TT screenside delivery (second from top) featured roll-down side curtains and short running boards. The delivery van bodies of the Century Floral Shop and Pioneer Tea Company trucks (third and fourth from top) seem quite similar at first glance, but a closer look reveals a great number of differences. Ford's 1924 advertising (right side) often pitched the virtues of owning a Ford at women.

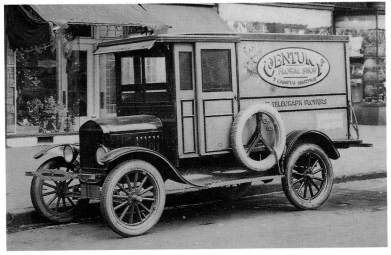

The Model T coupe for 1925 (above) was a "five-window" model that found wide acceptance in the marketplace. Listing at $525 that year, it weighed 1760 pounds and, of course, came with the electric starter and demountable rims as standard. Helped by the attractive pricing, production rose to a total of 327,584 coupes for the calendar year. Edsel Ford during these days spent a great deal of time trying to improve Lincoln styling and generally upgrading the marque. He is shown here (left) with wife Eleanor. Needless to say, the car behind them is a Lincoln.

Budd Company of Philadelphia, and Simplex Manufacturing Company of Kansas City. Beginning in 1925, Ford would deliver the entire body mounted on the chassis.

The express came in three basic forms: the no-frills open model, priced at $490 f.o.b Detroit; a "curtained" version with a full-length aft-cab roof atop four vertical supports; and the same with fixed side screens. The latter two were tagged at $520 apiece. A buyer could also get both screens and curtains for an additional $25. Regardless of configuration, cab design was unmistakable with its slightly raked, divided windshield and distinctive "half-moon" or C-shaped window openings.

In our cynical day and age, it's worth noting that Ford decided to offer its own truck bodies reluctantly, fearing that this might cost a lot of goodwill among the many independent firms who'd long built bodies for the TT chassis. But the market seemed big enough for all, and a wide variety of special truck bodies continued streaming forth from all manner of concerns, everything from light-duty panel deliveries to stake bodies, dumpers, tank trucks, even fire engines.

The main manufacturing event of 1924 was the launching of what has been called the "Ford Navy": a company-owned fleet of large freighters ferrying coal, iron ore, and limestone from various Great Lakes ports to the new River Rouge plant via the Detroit and Rouge Rivers. This "navy's" two initial flagships, the *Henry Ford II* and the *Benson Ford*, were completed early in the year, and joined several older vessels already in service. Typical of Ford Motor Company, which never did anything on a small scale in these years, the two new ships were the largest diesel-powered Great Lakes vessels of their day.

1925

For only the second time in its long life, Lizzie was treated this year to a major facelift—at least by Ford standards. Included were larger fenders and a newly optional nickel-plated radiator shell. Balloon tires, size 4.40 × 21, arrived as a new accessory at $25 apiece and made the Model T look almost modern. They also improved handling and ride due to their greater width (4.4 inches versus 3/3.5 inches) and lower inflation pressure (32 versus 80 pounds per square inch). Other new factory extras included a slower steering gear that was included with the new tires, and a hand-operated windshield wiper.

Some of the reduced prices instituted in late 1924 were trimmed a little further still. The Fordor remained the most expensive model in the line, but was now $20 cheaper at $660. Next came the Tudor, $10 lighter at $580, followed by the coupe, reduced another five-spot to $520. The open runabout and touring remained at $260 and $290, respectively.

Selective sliding-gear transmissions, usually with three speeds forward, were coming into more general use by now. Ford dealers, finding the Model T's planetary unit an increasingly tough sell, clamored for a change. So did many urban owners. But Ford clung to the old gearbox like a kid with a well-used toy. In fact, he seemed to have something of a prejudice against sliding-gear transmissions. Consider that back in 1910 a Ford test driver had crashed into a telephone pole with a vehicle equipped with such a gearbox, which was suspected of being partly to blame for the mishap. "Mr. Ford was tickled to death," recalled an associate. "He was glad it was smashed up, and he never had anything to do with [sliding-gear transmissions] until we came to the Model A."

Though the Model T still hardly seemed to be in sales trouble, calendar-year production declined again in 1925, this time to 1,643,295 units, about 110,000 fewer than in 1924. As the industry as whole built about that many more cars—some 3.74 million in all—Ford's market share slipped to just 44 percent, a loss of six percentage points. Nevertheless, the year saw a noteworthy production achievement when a record 9109 Model Ts were built in a single day.

Extra commercial-vehicle output made up for some of the passenger-car decline. In fact, domestic calendar-year truck volume set another record at 268,411 units.

To the basic cab-less TT chassis, now reduced $5 to $365, could be added a new "Closed Cab" with roll-down plate-glass door windows. It cost $20 more than the $65 "Open Cab" introduced the previous year. Either was suitable for mounting the many special-purpose bodies still available from outside firms as well as Ford's own express bodies, which garnered 28,266 calendar year orders. Also new was a factory-supplied eight-foot platform-bed model available with or without removable stake sides, the latter configuration measuring five feet wide and 26 inches high inside.

Perhaps more significant was the April 15 introduction of Ford's first light-duty American pickup. Predictably, this was the familiar Model T runabout carrying an accessory cargo box instead of the usual "turtleback," only here the box was fixed and not removable. It wasn't vast, measuring just 56 inches

The Model TT trucks remained popular, and just as adaptable. Heavy tires were often used at the rear (top left) and crude-looking cabs were hardly uncommon. Ford began offering its own truck bodywork for 1924 on a pickup-type express body (bottom left). Initially dealers finished the assembly work. Ford continued to spend part of its advertising dollars on women—a June 1925 ad in The Ladies' Home Journal tempted them to "revel in June air."

June, 1925 — The Ladies' HOME JOURNAL

Get all the Joy out of June

Every woman who loves Nature—and what woman does not!—should enjoy all the "rare days" of this perfect month in the open air.

With a Ford car at her disposal she can revel in June air and scene to her heart's content. Distance is covered and her time and strength conserved.

For not only is a Ford car pre-eminently dependable and easy for any woman to handle, but its economy prevents all worry as to expense—either of original cost or upkeep.

FORD MOTOR COMPANY, DETROIT, MICHIGAN

| Runabout . $260 | Coupe . . $520 | Fordor . . $660 |
| Touring . $290 | Tudor . . $580 | All Prices F. O. B. Detroit |

On Open Cars Starter and Demountable Rims are $85 Extra
Full-size Balloon Tires Optional—Closed Cars $25; Open Cars $45

Ford
THE UNIVERSAL CAR

MAKE SAFETY YOUR RESPONSIBILITY

For the second time in its long history, Lizzie was treated to a major facelift. Noticeable were larger fenders and, on some cars, a newly optional nickel-plated radiator shell. New also were balloon tires, offered for $25 extra, as well as a factory-installed, hand operated windshield wiper. The coupe (top) sold for $520, the Fordor sedan (above) for $660. Prices for other models in the 1925 lineup were: five-passenger touring, $290; two-passenger Runabout, an incredibly low $260; two-door sedan, $580; and the pickup, $281.

long by 41 inches wide by 13 inches deep, but utility combined with Model T ruggedness for a low $281 attracted a healthy 33,795 calendar year sales, beginning a winning truck tradition that continues at Ford to this day. Interestingly, you could still get the passenger-model Runabout with the optional "Pickup" body, which now cost $25 complete with adjustable tailgate and a pair of stake pockets on each of the longitudinal box rails.

This was a busy year for Ford in other ways. The firm opened a new Mexican assembly operation that ended the need for exports to that country from Los Angeles and Houston. Ford also began selling cars in Japan, opening a plant in Yokohama. Meanwhile, Ford Canada moved squarely into the Southern

Pacific market by establishing Ford Motor Company of Australia Pty. Ltd. Based in Geelong near Melbourne, this subsidiary also comprised new assembly plants at Brisbane, Adelaide, Freemantle, and at Granville near Sydney.

Back in the U.S., Ford opened new car plants at Louisville, Kentucky, and St. Paul, Minnesota; dedicated its new Engineering Laboratory (in January); and added several ocean-going vessels to its Great Lakes freighter fleet. On May 21, the River Rouge factory turned out the half-millionth Fordson tractor, one of 104,168 domestic units built this year, still the all-time record for that vehicle. And on March 14, the Ford family welcomed Edsel Ford's third son, William Clay.

This was also the year that Ford's recently acquired Stout Metal Airplane Division introduced its Trimotor airplane, soon to become famous as the "Tin Goose" owing to its mostly metal construction. A high-wing design, it mounted a single engine in the nose and one underwing engine fairly far forward on each side of the fuselage. The initial version, officially designated 3-AT and developed from Stout's single-engine 2-AT, had a traditional open cockpit. After the first few examples, however, this was changed to the more familiar—and practical—closed-cockpit configuration for the production model 4-AT-A, which offered seating for up to eight passengers and a crew of two or three. Its three engines were all Wright J4 "Whirlwind" units producing 200 horsepower each.

First flown on June 11 of this year and certified by the new Civilian Aviation Administration 15 days later, the Trimotor was publicly unveiled July 30 to mark Henry Ford's 63rd birthday. Like the Model T it seemed to evoke, the Trimotor was quite rugged. Many would remain in service long after Ford stopped building them.

In 1929, however, when Ford completed no fewer than 89 units, the Trimotor became the mainstay of Transcontinental Air Transport, the forerunner of today's Trans World Airlines, which that year began offering the nation's first regular cross-country air travel package. These coast-to-coast jaunts weren't exactly easy. Reliable instrument navigation devices were still some years away, so passengers could only fly by day; at night they had to travel by train. But the service was soon streamlined to a two-day flight with one overnight stop in Kansas City.

Ford gave up designing and building its own aircraft in 1938, but not before playing an important pioneer role in making air travel safer and more affordable for the general public. Henry may have mistrusted airplanes, but if people had to fly, he'd at least make sure they could do so without worry. Today, air travelers the world over owe him a debt of thanks.

1 9 2 6

Slumping sales prompted Ford to spruce up the aging Tin Lizzie even more this year. Closed versions, and later open models as well, were newly available in a choice of colors for the first time in over a decade, though this reflected not just marketing considerations but the advent of new colored lacquer paints that dried fast enough to match the Highland Park line rate. You could still get basic black, of course, and you got it on the fenders even with one of the new colors, which were applied only to body, cowl, and hood.

The bodies themselves again sat slightly lower on their chassis (this time by 1.5 inches, thanks to revised springs with raised spindles). Running boards were widened a bit, fuel tanks were relocated to the cowl area except on Fordor sedans, and a larger 11 × 1.5-inch parking brake was adopted along with an engine-mounted coil box and vaporizing intake manifold. Head/taillights were more stylishly mounted on the fenders instead of the frame, and the nickel-plated radiator shell became standard on closed models (it remained optional for the touring and Runabout). Wire wheels were an accessory that complemented the balloon tires introduced for 1925.

Inside, steering-wheel diameter was enlarged once more, to 17 inches, and there were new rectangular brake and clutch pedals. Finally, the touring at last received an opening left front door; no more sliding in from the passenger's side or hopping over the driver's-side gunwale.

If not exactly abundant, the new hues were poetically named: Gun Metal Blue, Highland Green, Phoenix Brown, Fawn Gray. So finished, the faithful Tin Lizzie reminded one of a prim but made-up spinster out on a fling.

But this and other recent alterations made no difference: the Model T was on its last legs. As we've seen, Ford accounted for more than half the cars and trucks sold in the United States during 1921-25. Its best sales year before 1955 was 1923, when it sold more than two million vehicles. But the T had been an anachronism long before, and buyers had begun defecting to other makes by 1924.

The trend continued this year as Ford's calendar year car output fell nearly 17 percent to 1,368,383 units. Though total industry volume gained only about 50,000 units, Ford's percentage share slipped to 36 percent, down eight points from 1925.

Low price and a reputation for utility and sturdiness had served the Model T well in an era of poor roads and equally unsophisticated yet higher-priced rivals. But these selling points began to pale once hard-surface highways and mechanically sound cars became more commonplace in the mid-Twenties. Furthermore, although Ford had cut prices $100 since 1922, Chevrolet had slashed prices $140, Overland $300, Maxwell $490, and Dodge $890.

Most important of all, public tastes were changing. Rising affluence and new values made many car buyers—especially women, who'd come to have more influence in car sales—increasingly style-conscious and interested in more comfort and convenience. Many men insisted on the latest mechanical innovations as well as speed and power. The Model T had little style, while convenience features and mechanical refinements cost extra, if they could be had at all.

Sensing the shift in attitudes, a number of manufacturers instituted extensive consumer research programs. General Motors surveyed hundreds of thousands of motorists to find out what they liked and didn't like, then skillfully designed and effectively promoted its new models accordingly. Noting Ford's lack of activity in this area, one magazine found it "difficult to imagine Henry Ford asking one motorist for advice, let alone taking it." Ford, perhaps the only automaker to conduct formal market studies before World War I and once so attuned to the public's needs, stubbornly ignored the winds of change.

But even Henry couldn't ignore the sales figures, and they told a disturbing tale. From 1924 to 1925, Ford dropped from 1,870,000 to 1,675,000 units while Chevrolet advanced from 280,000 to 470,000. In response, Henry cut prices twice in 1926. He also made the electric starter, battery, and demountable balloon tires standard for open models effective June 19. But the trump failed for the first time in Model T history and deliveries ran almost 400,000 units behind the 1925 total. Meanwhile, Chevrolet gained an additional 260,000 customers.

By early summer, it was clear to most everyone in the Ford organization—except Henry and a few other

Although the Model T was decidedly more modern looking in 1926 than it had been earlier in the decade, by now Ford was selling it largely on price. An ad catering to women (left) pictured the Runabout and prominently displayed its $290 base price, as well as giving a pitch for accessories to dress it up. The 1926 touring (below) listed at $310, and is shown here with the optional bumpers and wire wheels, the latter available in January 1926.

Ford promoted the 1926 Model T as "Meeting every modern need of transportation." Modern was a term Dearborn was using more, in part because the T was freshened up for 1926 with a lowered chassis, plus new fenders, running boards, hood, and bodies (except for the Fordor). The Fordor (above) looked a bit brighter with the now standard shiny radiator shell, and besides black it could be had in Fawn Gray, Highland Green, and Royal Maroon. The Runabout (opposite page) could be had in black, Gun Metal Blue, or Phoenix Brown.

executives also wearing blinders—that the Model T was faltering. Despite an improved market, sales in the April-June period were 154,000 units below the comparable 1925 total, a fact not lost on the press. Noting Chevrolet's 33-percent increase and its plan to expand production capacity to a million units annually by 1927, many observed that the Model T's market dominance was being seriously threatened for the first time.

Speculation began immediately as to how Henry would turn things around. First reports were that he would replace the four-cylinder T with a six-cylinder car. When he denied this, it was next rumored that he'd bring out a "Sheik Car" (*a la* Rudolph Valentino) to satisfy women's demands for more style. Again Ford said no, remarking that he'd already given the Model T colors and a nickel-plated hood. Said a New York dealer: "Yes, you can paint up a barn, but it will still be a barn and not a parlor."

More rumors popped up for the rest of the year and into 1927. Ford would replace the T's planetary transmission with a selective-gear unit; he would add a fourth speed; he would adopt a new carburetor capable of 30 mpg; he would produce an eight-cylinder model priced under $1000; he would enter the medium-price field with a car named Edison; he would build a "Superflivver," a two-cylinder car with as much power as a four. Ford was invariably asked to comment on these and other rumors and, just as invariably, he denied them all. The Model T, he said, would endure.

Aging design also hampered the T-based trucks in 1926, production falling 30 percent to 186,062 units. Even the Fordson tractor wasn't immune, output sliding to 88,101 units. The truck line saw no major changes until mid-June, when standard equipment was expanded to include balloon tires and demountable rims—but not the electric starting system, which remained a $50 option.

Despite production setbacks at home, Ford continued its overseas expansion in 1926, beginning Model T assembly at new plants in Bombay, India, and Singapore, Malaysia. Meantime, the French subsidiary under manager Maurice Dollfus moved from Bordeaux to a larger new facility outside Paris.

This year also saw the start of German Ford production in rented warehouse space at Berlin-Plotzensee near Cologne. In 1929, Ford would gain approval to build a full-scale manufacturing plant in Cologne, helped by tax incentives and low-cost real estate deals engineered by mayor Konrad Adenauer, who would become chancellor of postwar West Germany. Henry Ford laid the cornerstone for the new factory in October 1930. Initially, Cologne built the U.S. Model A, then turned to somewhat smaller cars better suited to European conditions though still based heavily on American Ford designs.

After nearly two history-filled decades, the Model T reached the end of its long road in 1927. Despite all the cosmetic freshening of the previous 10 years, the last Lizzie to roll out the door really wasn't all that different from the first ones built in late 1908. That was one of her problems, of course, the thing that ultimately did her in, but it's also one of the many reasons why we remember the Model T with such affection more than 60 years later. Cars built during this final year were equipped with the previously optional wire wheels as standard, replacing the old wood-spoke "artillery" types, and maroon and green were added to the color chart.

It was in mid-February of this year that Henry Ford admitted for the first

By 1927, the Ford Model T was in its swan song year. About the only changes were the standardization of wire wheels and the addition of two new colors. The touring car (above) was priced at $380 that final year. Notably, the 15-millionth Model T rolled off the Highland Park assembly line on May 26, 1927. The '27 Model TT truck chassis listed at $325 and $375—this one (below) having been equipped for fire fighting duty.

time that he needed a new car. While acknowledging that he'd already given some thought to its design, he refused to name an introduction date, claiming that "a statement at this time on the matter... might do serious injury to my competitors."

A fresh crop of rumors sprang up at once. By early spring it was generally assumed that the new Ford would be faster and have a sliding-gear transmission. It would also appear soon, some said as early as late June, but Henry still said nothing. Competitors complained that his silence caused a mild sales slowdown as prospects postponed buying until they saw what Ford had in mind. "The result is getting on everyone's nerves," said an Ohio newspaper, "as Ford himself probably realizes." Henry soon gave in. On the evening of May 25, 1927, Ford Motor Company confirmed that it would indeed build a new car.

As if to punctuate the announcement, the 15-millionth Model T rolled off the Highland Park assembly line the following afternoon, May 26. The milestone was marked in an appropriately

simple manner. There were no bands, no bunting, no speeches. With Edsel at the wheel and his father beside him, the car led a motorcade of company officials and 15 reporters and photographers to the firm's Engineering Laboratory. On the plaza in front of the building, under gray skies, were Ford's earliest automobiles and the first Model T. After Henry drove the older cars around the plaza for the benefit of motion picture cameras, the ceremony was over.

Most newspapers and magazines commented on the Model T's demise and what its successor would be like. There were, as the Louisville *Times* predicted, "acres of humorous writing devoted... to 'hunky Elizabeth, chunky Elizabeth, spunky Elizabeth Ford.'" Said the Baltimore *Sun*: "Since the Model T makes as much noise as any 10 other cars and the new Ford cannot possibly be noisier than the old, life will be pleasanter, we will all live longer."

Nevertheless, most of the press regarded the T's passing as a momentous event and treated it with a certain solemn sentimentality. To the New York *Herald-Tribune* it was "The End of an Epoch." The Dayton *News* said a "world institution" was being "Retired with Honors." The Roanoke (Virginia) *News* spoke for many: "It will be long before America loses its affectionate, if somewhat apologetic, remembrance of the car that first put us on wheels. We probably wouldn't admit it to anyone, but deep in our hearts we love every rattle in its body."

Of course, many were reluctant to see Lizzie go. Hearst newspaper executive Arthur Brisbane, on adding a new Ford sedan and truck to the several he already owned, wired Henry that he should keep one plant running indefinitely to make half a million Model Ts a year—he thought they could easily be sold at higher prices by mail order. A Ford dealer in Newark, "believing in the great merit of the Model T and the continued demand for same," sought to arrange for its manufacture and/or assembly in New Jersey. Newark citizens, he assured the company, would willingly finance the scheme.

The May 25 announcement prompted many owners to begin taking better care of their flivvers, eager to prolong their lives. One elderly lady of means in Montclair, New Jersey, purchased and stored away seven new ones so that she needn't be without a T for the rest of her life. A man in Toledo bought six, and only wore out the last of them in 1967.

Time would only increase affection and respect for what was once called "the first log cabin of the motor age." Archibald Henderson, writing in 1930, was typical in declaring the Model T's impact "greater by far than that of the telegraph, the telephone, rural free delivery, the phonograph, the radio, or electric light and power." E.B. White and Richard

Lee Strout in their classic 1936 epitaph "Farewell, My Lovely" called the T "hard-working, commonplace, heroic... the miracle God had wrought. And it was patently the sort of thing that could only happen once." To Philip Van Doren Stern, writing in 1955, the Model T "was, as no car before or since has been, truly the people's car... part of the fabric of American life, celebrated in song and legend and folklore." In 1959, *Fortune* magazine reported that 100 of the world's leading designers, architects, and design teachers had ranked the T as the 82nd "best designed mass-produced product of modern times"—higher than all other Ford cars except the 1940 Lincoln Continental, voted sixth, and the 1955 Thunderbird, rated 41st. In 1974, the T was named "the world's greatest motorcar" by the readers of *Motor Trend*.

That the T helped to change America's psychology, manners, and mores as well as the national economy is beyond question. No other single device did more to induce people of a provincial mind to begin thinking in regional and national terms. None did more to knit together different parts of the county, state, and ultimately, the nation.

Ford produced 15,007,033 Model Ts in the United States through May 31, 1927, the figure and date most often cited for total output and the end of production, though another 477,748 were assembled during the summer of 1927. Ford of Canada had built 747,259, Ford of England an estimated 250,000.

Automotive historians and journalists once believed that the T's production mark would stand unchallenged. "No other model was ever produced in such numbers," asserted Allan Nevins and Frank Ernest Hill in their authoritative 1957 book *Ford: Expansion and Challenge 1915-1933*, "and it is safe to say that on this score alone its record will never be matched." But Germany's Volkswagen, amid much fanfare, produced its 15,007,034th Type 1 Beetle on February 17, 1972, then smashed the T's world-wide production record the following year. For decades, the Lizzie shared honors as the longest-lived car with the Rolls-Royce Silver Ghost (1907-27). In the Sixties and Seventies, however, several European models including the Beetle, the French Citroen 2CV, and Italy's Fiat 1100 would exceed the T's production life.

No matter. There had never been anything quite like the Model T before, and there'd be nothing like it again. If people chose to remember its undoubted personality, filtering out the bad to dwell on the good... well, it was only human nature. And maybe that's what separates the T from most every other car ever built, for in some ways it was as human as legend and flivver jokes said it was.

Its storied durability would certainly prove out. As of March 1927, exactly 11,325,521 Ts were still registered in the United States. Despite its cheapness, the T lasted longer on average than other

The Runabout was the least expensive model in the 1927 Model T lineup, just $360. This one is fitted with bumpers, which cost an extra $15, but not the nickel-plated radiator shell. Options were relatively inexpensive: rearview mirror, $.75; top boot, $4.00; dashboard lamp, $.60; brake light and switch, $2.50; windshield wiper, $.50 if manual, $2.00 when vacuum operated; shock absorbers, $9.00.

cars (eight years vs. 6.3) because of its low-cost replacement parts, ease of repair, and Ford's vast dealer network.

Naturally, the number of Ts in daily use declined rapidly with the end of production, but some 5.4 million still plied the nation's highways as late as 1931, an estimated 600,000-800,000 a decade later. In 1948, when R.L. Polk and Company made the last actual count, 73,111 Model T cars and trucks were still registered. Of course, many additional Ts were unlicensed by then, stored in garages and farm buildings. Others could be found rusting where they'd stopped running years before. In 1953, Ford estimated the number of surviving flivvers at 100,000. Eighteen years later, historian Leslie R. Henry, taking into account large-scale T restoration, put the total at 300,000. As Henry observed, "If an antique buff finds a 'T' frame with a serial number on it, he's got enough to start building a car."

Many of the Lizzie's 4830 parts and some accessories are still readily available from old-car parts houses, some new old stock (NOS), others newly made reproductions from companies cashing in on the steady demand. The Sears-Roebuck catalog, which once devoted more space to T parts and gadgets than women's clothing, listed engine gaskets as late as 1975, though perhaps more for sentimental than business reasons. Today, every restored or restorable Model T sells for many times its original

purchase price; even "basket cases" cost more than they did new.

Two international organizations serve Model T owners: the Model T Ford Club International, founded in 1952 and thus one of the oldest old-car enthusiast groups, and the Model T Ford Club of America, established in 1966. The former, headquartered in Chicago, has 53 chapters whose members own more than 10,000 Ts. The latter has 66 chapters and 6000 members, many of whom also own more than one Lizzie. Both organizations publish bimonthly magazines that keep alive flivver knowledge and lore. Virtually every old-car museum in the land has at least one Model T on view. The Henry Ford Museum displays one of the first examples, the 15-millionth T, and several historically significant flivvers. Various individuals also have impressive T collections.

To this day, the Model T continues to generate considerable attention. Since 1948 it has been given full chapters in at least 15 books and has been the subject of six fiction and seven nonfiction works, not to mention a few movies and dozens of reprint owner and service manuals, parts catalogs, and sales brochures. Lizzie was a focal point of Ford Motor Company's 50th anniversary celebration in 1953. She was heavily publicized again in 1958, the 50th anniversary of her introduction; in 1963, when Ford marked the centennial of its founder's birth; and during the company's 75th anniversary in 1978.

Ford and other companies still invoke the Model T on occasion to make advertising points. In announcing its new Pinto subcompact for 1971, Ford ads signed by chairman Henry Ford II declared it "the new Model T. The first Model T stood for sensible, simple motoring; it was lively and easy to handle

and fun to drive... [T]his new [model] stands for the same things." It would even be available in "Model T Black." The campaign's early TV commercials showed a Model T being overtaken on the road by its Model A successor, then a Pinto. Rival automakers like VW and a few non-automotive companies have also looked to the T, invariably complimenting it and, in effect, saying "me too." A modern example: "What do the Apple personal computer and the Model T have in common? Ease of operation and affordability."

Over the years, "Model T" has become a way of saying "old fashioned." The instances are too numerous to list. It also comes up when durable, inexpensive, or widely accepted products are discussed. Douglas Aircraft's DC-3 and Ford's own Trimotor airplanes have been referred to as "the Model T of aircraft," and Eastman Kodak once described its product as "the Model T of cameradom."

The term has also long been associated with simplicity, success, even quality. For example, a 1979 United Press International story said that the cooling plant for the Three Mile Island nuclear reactor "will use the same natural circulation process Henry Ford used to cool the Model T engine." The Detroit *Free Press* reported at about the same time that the owner of a local shirt-printing company aspired to be "the Henry Ford of T-shirts" and was well on his way "to becoming Mr. Model T." An ad for a Japanese typewriter boasted a machine "jam-packed with quality like the Model T Ford and just as simple to repair." Such is the impact that has made the Tin Lizzie part of America's thinking and vocabulary.

Nowadays, it's positively stylish to own a Model T, especially one of the early "brassies." Many old-car buffs would have no other antique. Perhaps more than any other object from our past, the T still occupies a special place in American hearts. Many seniors had their first "automobiling" experience driving or riding in a flivver. Today, the sight of one bobbing along warms them like a ray of sunshine. Most smile; some may even yell, "Get a horse!" If the car is parked, they may reminisce with the owner about the "good old days" and perhaps recall a Ford joke or two. If asked to take a spin, they'll immediately climb in. If asked to drive, many accept, eager to prove they still remember how to manipulate the T's pedals and levers. Some younger people are similarly moved.

In the end, the Model T simply outlived its usefulness. But it hasn't been outlived by time. In its way, it has become almost immortal, as much a part of the country's heritage as the Fourth of July, a mixture of folk legend and nostalgic affection tinged with bittersweet humor. Few cars, let alone one so humble, can claim as much.

1928

As the curtain fell on America's most successful wheeled invention, the whole world wondered what "old Henry Ford" was going to do for an encore. Nearing 64, yet trim and youthful from a well-disciplined daily routine, he was still in the prime of an extraordinary life. His handsome 34-year-old son Edsel was showing promise of following in his father's footsteps. The company had nearly $250 million cash on hand, and total assets of the far-flung Ford empire stood at just under a billion dollars.

But the ingenious Model T, the very foundation of this fantastic success, had run its course. As 1927 opened and his company's sales continued sinking, it was all too clear that Henry Ford would have to work another miracle to bring forth a replacement with similar potential.

The "wizard of motors" had already been burning the midnight oil even as news of the Model T's demise swept the nation. Though he still steadfastly refused the notion that his beloved Lizzie was really finished, Henry was determined to come up with something just as revolutionary to succeed it.

For several years he'd been tinkering with different engines that might power such a car. By far the most radical was the L-head "X-8," built in 1926. As the name implied, it had four cylinders facing up, as in a V-type configuration, and four facing down where an oil pan would ordinarily be. Other unusual features included two roller main bearings, combined starter/generator, and a supercharger run off the flywheel. To Henry it seemed a logical successor to the T's legendary four-cylinder engine. He also saw the X-8 as a chance to one-up competitors instead of merely bringing out another inline four or six. Unfortunately, extensive engineering and testing showed the X-8 far too complex for mass production, too heavy, and too prone to lower sparkplug fouling by dust and mud. By the end of 1926, his hopes dashed that it could ever be made practical, Henry reluctantly halted development work.

A year later, pondering the Model T's imminent demise, Ford and a handful of his most trusted aides began a top-secret rush to develop a replacement car along more conventional lines. Edsel being much closer to both dealers and the sales department, presented the case to his father. What Ford urgently needed was a car that would appeal to the same customers that the Lizzie had in her salad days, yet could beat the best current competitors—namely Chevrolet, Hudson's Essex, and Willys-Overland's Whippet. It would have to be faster, smoother, more durable, not at all quirky, and must possess features buyers were demanding.

One thing was sure: Henry's cherished planetary transmission would have to go—an orthodox select-shift unit was long overdue. Urban owners in particular wanted one, and dealers had long complained of sales lost to the T's difficult, pedal-operated gearbox. Buyers were choosier than ever, roads were getting better, and there were more women drivers. Customers were now simply not inclined to lay out cash for a car that required a pedal held down hard just to select low gear or Reverse. Though Henry staunchly defended his patented planetary gearbox and other Model T features, he understood the language of sales. After great deliberation, he finally gave the order to design a car entirely new from stem to stern, fender to fender.

Meantime, Henry faced the challenge of closing his many plants and scrapping the well-oiled Model T production lines to retool, which meant losing incredible sums of money. The grade-school-educated motor king had a well-known disdain for formally trained engineers, preferring his own seat-of-the-pants approach. This plus the Model T's relative lack of change over a long 19-year production run had left him remarkably shy of engineering and styling talent to handle the tremendous amount of work the transition would involve. What he *did* have was a disciplined manufacturing operation led by one of the toughest, smartest men in the business.

As production chief, Charles E. Sorensen had long been top man at Ford Motor Company—apart from Henry and Edsel, of course. Starting in 1905 as a pattern maker, the tall Dane had always been a good idea-spinner, and after gaining a role in management became one of the key figures in developing the moving assembly line. A stern taskmaster with dynamo energy, he'd been a mainspring of Ford's amazing worldwide expansion, creating new manufacturing and assembly techniques, building new plants at home and abroad, and carrying out Henry's orders with rapid-fire precision.

Sorensen and another top production expert, Peter E. Martin, were part of the inner circle from the very beginning of the secret new-car project. By the time the basic concept had pretty well crystallized, three other engineers had joined up, selected quietly from the various experiments that were always in progress around Dearborn. In charge of overall design was Eugene Farkas, head of the stillborn X-8 project and the longtime Ford engineer who'd had a major role in developing the Fordson tractor. Assisting him would be Frank Johnson, chief engineer at the Lincoln plant, and Lawrence Sheldrick, a young engineer who had caught Henry's eye on another assignment.

Henry himself was basically a chassis man by inclination. Intensely practical, he'd always cared far more about how a car ran than how it looked. His son Edsel, by contrast, was more concerned with appearance—he had a natural eye for it—as well as comfort and features. With fast-rising Chevrolet as an example, Edsel also knew the marketing wisdom of updating models each year, something his father had stubbornly resisted with the flivver.

Partly because he was impressed with the job his son was doing with Lincoln, but mainly because he was occupied with chassis ideas, the elder Ford gave his son responsibility for the new car's body design. Assisting him would be Joe Galamb, the highly respected engineer who for all intents and purposes constituted Ford's entire "styling department" at the time. The amiable, Hungarian-born veteran had laid out the first Model T and, when he wasn't called on to make an occasional change on it, had been in charge of experimental engineering.

Edsel was widely known as a gentleman with class, and he and Galamb hit it off immediately. Young Ford would outline what he had in mind. Galamb would interpret it in sketches and clay models that the pair would then discuss in great detail. From the start they favored a sort of scaled-down Lincoln, with the same finely sculptured lines, rounded corners, just the right amount of nickel trim, nicely turned door handles, and a comfortable, well-appointed interior. "He [was quite critical] of the interior and the instrument work," Galamb later recalled. "When we made the first body sample, Edsel was very particular about the trimming and the material. He knew what he wanted and insisted that we get it." Maybe so, but nothing was approved at Ford Motor Company without Henry's critical—and often creative—contribution.

An example of the cut-and-try engineering that characterized all of Henry Ford's cars was the decision involving the height of the first prototype Model A bodies. Veteran production man W.C. Klann was also in on the project by that point: "The sample bodies were being built at the Highland Park plant," he recalled in a 1956 interview. "I built six bodies there.... They were always under lock and key. We would bring the panels down [to Engineering] and assemble them and get the height of our seat cushions. Well, Henry Ford wanted to fit himself and Mr. Sorensen; Edsel Ford wanted to fit Mr. Martin and himself." Klann related how the elder Ford insisted that he should be able to get in and out without knocking his hat off. The shorter Edsel supported Galamb's first drawings that called for a lower profile. Henry had the last word, of course, so Klann

The revolutionary Model A Ford was far more complicated than the old Model T. For example, it had nearly 2000 more parts (about 6800), so it's hardly surprising that it cost more. The 1928 standard coupe (top) sold for $550, exactly the same as the Tudor sedan (bottom). The Model A closed-cab pickup listed at $445, but a chassis model was available for specialized bodies, as on this Wisconsin Telephone Company truck (center).

made up a prototype 1½ inches taller. "When Henry Ford saw it," Klann remembered, "[he said] it looked like an old hayrack. He said, 'Scrap that. It looks terrible.' So it remained the same as before."

Initial styling efforts revolved around the mainstay coupe and Tudor sedan. The work had progressed far enough by March 1927 that a contract for a special set of body stampings was quietly given to the Murray Corporation of America. It was also Henry's nature to leak a clue now and then, and secrets are hard to keep in Detroit. In any event, it was the first tangible evidence that the Fords were working on a new car. The press soon speculated that besides refined body lines, the new mystery Ford would be introduced with a select-shift transmission and modern distributor ignition.

On May 26, Henry once more sparked instant national excitement by casually announcing that he'd been planning all along the shutdown of the entire Ford system to retool for a brand-new car. "We began work on this model several years ago," he told the press with some truth. "In fact, the idea of a car to succeed the Model T has been in my mind much longer than that. But the sale of the Model T continued at such a pace that there never seemed to be an opportunity to get the new car started."

The changeover would have enormous impact on a national economy in which Ford had owned nearly half the new-car market. Thousands of workers at 36 assembly plans across the country were immediately laid off, the Model T accessory industry went into a tailspin, many suppliers and parts houses went broke, and only the strongest Ford dealers managed to survive. Meantime, thousands of buyers decided to wait for the "new Lizzie," so dealers could do little more than wring their hands in frustration as the old T's gathered dust in their showrooms. Some of the more optimistic dealers put up big, colorful posters: "We are taking orders for the new car...speed, pick-up, flexibility, beauty, comfort, stamina—coming soon!" But as summer wore into autumn, then into winter, the new Ford was nowhere in sight.

In Dearborn, Henry and his team were working night and day toward a tough, spirited, smartly fashioned automobile that the average man could still afford. In design it was so new that it had already been christened "Model A," echoing the first production Ford of 1903—in effect, signalling a new beginning for Ford Motor Company.

Engineer Harold Hicks, who was transferred from airplane work to help on the new car's engine and chassis, was awed by Henry's driving ambition and the way he could still coax the best from his staff. As an engineer, he was even more impressed with Ford's uncanny ability to shortcut extensive development time by being a bear for simplicity:

"I remember that they had too many bolts holding the carburetor together. Henry Ford said to me, 'Cut those bolts down!' I had the Zenith company get out a design in which two bolts held the carburetor together. I felt quite proud that they had reduced it from about 14 little screws down to two bolts. I showed him the design. With his characteristic trait he said, 'Two is too many! Make it just one bolt!' So the carburetor came out with just a simple bolt down through it."

Henry often made up for his technical and educational shortcomings by overwhelming a problem with men and machines. Theodore Gehle recalls how this even rubbed off on Henry's chief lieutenant. Gehle worked in Ford's Pressed Steel Department as the first Model A bodies painfully took shape in mid-1927: "Mr. Sorensen said, 'Now you go down...and you just live there until you get the first bodies out. When you see daylight for the first bodies, why, you just let me know'.... The quarter panel was what was holding up the bodies most, and fenders were second."

As one of the company's experienced production experts, Gehle worked virtually around the clock trying to straighten out the kinks. At last he reported to Sorensen that while he wasn't having much luck, he did have an idea: "I suggest you [order] Pressed Steel to run off 100 sets of stampings, the best they can make. Some of these are going to be horrible. Then [order] the Body Plant to build 100 bodies with these sets of stampings. They will probably have to be scrapped, but it will give them knowledge. By relaying information back and forth [between departments] maybe out of the next 100 bodies you may get a good one." Gehle was amazed that the headstrong Sorensen went along with it: "These first 100 bodies were assembled and scrapped. On the next 100 bodies we saved about 10. From there we started Model A production, the bodies having been the bottleneck."

But there were other bottlenecks too, and they proved almost countless. By the end of May 1927, thousands of toolmakers, millwrights, and die and pattern makers had been hired or recalled to begin the massive overhaul that would have to be completed in record time, often without final plans and in many cases requiring duplicates for installation in the various assembly plants. In some departments, engineers and their assistants would work in relays, 24 hours a day, just correcting mistakes and designing or redesigning special tools.

What's more, the Highland Park plant, once described as "the most productive piece of ground on earth," had to be gutted to the walls because most manufacturing and all car assembly operations for that territory would be transferred to Ford's new showcase River Rouge complex. Giant machines weighing as much as 240 tons had to be completely redesigned or rebuilt. Thousands of smaller tools and precision instruments had to be manufactured.

Then, too, the Model A would comprise some 6800 different parts compared to fewer than 5000 on the Model T, so a multitude of supply sources had to be established. Engines, some body stampings, rear axles, and brakes were among parts to be made at the Rouge. Shock absorber parts would come from Buffalo; bumpers from Chicago; wood body parts from the Ford mills at Iron Mountain, Michigan; wood floorboards from a supplier in Vancouver, Washington; wheels from Ford facilities in Hamilton, Ohio, and Memphis; glass from Dearborn and New Jersey; radiators from Ford's big plant at Green Island, New York.

To supply the wide variety of new body types being drawn up by Edsel and Galamb, the company would contract with outside firms for most stampings and built-up bodies. Briggs Manufacturing Company, a longtime Ford supplier that also built custom coachwork for other automakers, was assigned to tool and produce bodies for the new Model A coupe. Major contracts were also signed with Murray and the Edward G. Budd Manufacturing Company. Briggs would come to specialize in pressings for sedan, coupe, Victoria, and panel delivery bodies, and would also furnish fully built

In 1928, Ford offered open cars in both the car and truck lines. The rakish Model A roadster pickup (above left) was the least expensive '28 Ford at $395. The phaeton, meanwhile, was the cheapest model in the car line, $460, and fairly popular, too—production during calendar 1928 reached 47,255 units.

and trimmed bodies for the later convertible cabriolet. Murray did much the same, plus assembly and finish on the wood-bodied station wagon that would arrive for 1929. Budd would become an invaluable source of special stampings and commercial bodies.

By late summer of 1927, the Fords were sufficiently satisfied with their progress that Edsel promised the press that the new car would be available within a few weeks. The Model A was an "accomplished fact," he said on August 10. Two months later, Edsel declared that production was but a few days away, and that dealers had taken deposits for 125,000 cars. "Tests already made show that it is faster, smoother, more rugged and more beautiful than we had hoped for in the early stages of designing," he declared. "Experiments have been made with a wide variety of color schemes and body designs, and all these have been decided upon."

As it turned out, reporters would wait a few more months for their first official peek, though they might have noticed that experimental cars, thinly disguised as Model Ts, had been on road trials out of the Ford Engineering Laboratory since early spring. By the end of October, as many as 150 such prototypes, all with hand-built chassis, had been driven at night around the firm's only test facility—the streets and countryside of Dearborn.

After nearly a year's effort and millions of dollars, the first Model A engine approved for full production was built at the Rouge late in the afternoon of Thursday, October 20. Its number was ceremoniously hand stamped into the block by Henry Ford as his son, Sorensen, Martin, and two longtime employees, August Degener and Charles Hartner, looked on. The next day, this engine was installed in a chassis rolling slowly down the pilot assembly line. At last, the tired auto magnate had his first real opportunity to stand back and assess his latest creation.

If the Model T chassis had been a paragon of simplicity, the Model A's was ideal. True, the flivver's familiar basic layout was retained. A single semi-elliptic transverse spring straddled the front and rear axles, buggy-style; the "wishbone" radius rod, acting as a front-end stabilizer, was plain to see; and the overall spindly appearance seemed almost the same at first glance. But every suspension piece, from the spring perches and 21-inch welded steel-spoke wheels to the feather-light frame and forged axles, had been completely and ingeniously redesigned for extra strength and nimbleness. And for the first time, a Ford had shock absorbers, double-acting Houdaille hydraulic units, and rod-operated four-wheel brakes, with 11×1.5-inch internal-expanding drums for safer, smoother going. Balloon tires (4.50×21) were carried over as standard equipment, but base prices now included front and rear bumpers.

Though still an L-head engine with aluminum pistons and three-bearing crankshaft, the A's cast-iron four-cylinder was also totally new. On 4.22:1 compression it produced a rated 40 brake horsepower at 2000 rpm and 128 pounds/feet peak torque at only 1000 rpm. Bore and stroke measurements of $3\frac{7}{8}$ by $4\frac{1}{4}$ inches gave total displacement of 200.5 cubic inches. That's right, it was no larger than the Model T unit, but it was obviously twice as powerful and, not so obviously, lighter. And sure enough, it bolted not to a heavy, complex planetary transmission but to a modern, three-speed gearshift unit with H-pattern floor lever. From there, drive passed to a multiple-disc dry clutch, though this gave way to a single-disc unit during the model year. Torque-tube final drive was also carried over, albeit with stronger, entirely new components. Out back was a three-quarter floating live axle with roller bearings and spiralbevel gears.

As predicted, engineers adopted a modern, less costly battery and ignition system that did away with a lot of engine compartment clutter. In place of the old time-honored magneto with its four vibrator coils and maze of wires running from dash to sparkplugs were just two wires: the high-tension lead from the coil to the distributor, and the low-tension lead to the ignition switch. A specially designed distributor sat atop the cylinder head and was gear-driven by a vertical shaft off the center of the camshaft, whose tail end drove the oil pump. The molded plastic cap with its pair of winged extensions gave the Model A distributor a character all its own. The wings encased the plug leads, connected via simple brass straps secured with round finger nuts.

Assisting the smartly styled fin-and-tube radiator for cooling was a centrifugal water pump and two-blade fan, driven off the front crankshaft pulley by a V-belt that also drove the "powerhouse" generator on the engine's left side. And, to please the stylists, the respected engine crank handle that had always dangled below Ford radiators was now removable.

As he watched that Tudor sedan body being tried on the first model chassis, Henry Ford may have felt special pride in his ingenious fuel system. Though the 1926-27 Model T had used something similar, this would prove to be one of the Model A's most controversial features (insurance companies blindly labelled it explosion-prone). The gas tank, still a 10-gallon affair, was simply part of the cowl, forming the roll over the front body from below the windshield to the hood beltline, and was filled via a knurled screw-cap on top. Fuel fed by gravity to the Zenith double-venturi carburetor, flowing first through a handy in-line sediment bulb. The cowl was designed so that on the engine side it formed the firewall and mount for the hood and, on the interior side, held the instrument panel.

Less than a week after the first Model A was completed, production began inching upwards as assembly problems were doggedly solved. By November 1, 1927, the daily rate was up to about 20 units. Two days later, selected reporters and Ford dealers were at last invited to have their first formal look. Describing early Model A assembly line action, veteran auto journalist Fay Leone Faurote would later write: "I stood and watched the men for a time. The job is new to them and they 'make haste slowly.' There are stops for fittings. Stops for minor parts and minor adjustments. In fact, the assembly line is just now crawling. But with each new machine a slightly faster pace is evidenced."

Arthur Hatch, Ford's Chicago branch manager in 1927, reminisced in his retirement years about some of the trials and tribulations in beginning Model A production at his plant: "Finally we got a car assembled and I took it out for a spin. I actually blocked the whole city of Chicago with the crowds that developed to see Henry Ford's 'well-kept secret'.... We got into production and the next morning my wife calls me at my office. 'I've stalled!' she said. 'The car won't run! I've frozen my feet and hands trying to get it started!' She no more than hung up than I began to get calls from Ford dealers all over Chicago. They were complaining that the new cars wouldn't run. So I went out in the plant and the superintendent said, 'There must be something wrong with the engineering.... The cars are being put together right.' I called the Ford operator in Detroit and said, 'Get me Sorensen!' Sorensen came on and I said, 'I've just blown the whistle.

Shut the whole plant down. My wife is stuck in the park. I've got 300 calls this morning that people are stuck all over town!' Sorensen said, 'Don't leave the office! You stay right there! I'll fly six of our people over there that were supposed to have designed this automobile. Are you sure you're right?' I said, 'I'm dead sure!'"

In Dearborn, Henry himself took one of the newly assembled cars home for lunch with wife Clara. When he got back in, it wouldn't start. The same thing happened to Sorensen. "Mr. Ford sent out an order at once to stop production," Hatch recalled. "It didn't take them long to find the problem. It was in the regulator which controlled the cutout between the battery and the engine so it [the battery] wouldn't overcharge. He had all the assembly plants ship the faulty regulators—they cost about $4.50 each—back to Detroit, where he made his engineers pile them up in a big heap. I went down there and he had them piled up higher than the roof of the engineering laboratory. He'd lead you out and say, 'Look at those things. Look at all the dummies I've got around here!'"

Though production problems continued, Henry wouldn't sell the Model A until it was right. At the end of November 1927, Edsel cautioned the press that it was "doubtful that the new Ford would be available to purchasers before the first of the year." He also projected that it would be months before the factories could turn out Model As on "anything like a peak production schedule," noting that the company had only shipped about 500 cars up to that time. Asked who was getting them, Edsel let it slip that none were being sold but were, at that very moment, speeding to different parts of the country for the forthcoming announcement shows.

The stage was set. On the morning of Thursday, December 1, 1927, readers of 2000 daily newspapers across the nation found a full-page advertisement that read in part: "We believe the new Ford car is as great an improvement in motor car building as the Model T was in 1908." So wrote Henry Ford in a $2 million ad blitz that hit the day before his long-awaited Model A went on sale. "In appearance, in performance, in comfort, in safety, in all that goes to make a good car, it will bear out everything I have said here...."

News spread like wildfire that the car would be shown in major cities on Friday, December 2, and hundreds of thousands lined up for a look. In New York City, a crowd began gathering outside Ford's big Broadway showroom at 3 a.m. By midday it had grown so large that the manager had to move his display to Madison Square Garden. Observed the New York *World*: "Excitement could hardly have been greater had Pah-wah, the sacred white elephant of Burma, elected to sit for seven days on the flagpole of the Woolworth Building."

It was easily the greatest new-model introduction ever, an event that rivalled Lindbergh's historic transatlantic flight as the top news story of the year, if not the decade. In the U.S. alone an estimated 10 million flocked to see the Model A in the 36 hours after its unveiling. Some 100,000 descended on Detroit showrooms the first day, mounted police had to be called out to control the throngs in Cleveland, and an overeager mob in Kansas City nearly burst the walls of Convention Hall.

Merrell "Mo" Jordan, later a successful California dealer, was an Illinois teenager when the Model A debuted: "You couldn't get near the car on introduction day. My dad owned the Ford agency, but that didn't help me. I remember the long lines of people waiting to take a ride. We had a special route laid out that ended by crossing a plowed field. That first car would do 50 in second, and I swear to this day that it was a faster model than the later ones." As a wide-eyed youngster, Jordan knew everything that went on at his dad's dealership—or thought he did. Seeing those early Model A demonstrators being taken into the shop and worked on all night, he probably thought that they were doctored to go faster. More likely the mechanics were just trying to keep them running.

Still, the Model A was surprisingly quick: 5-25 mph in a little more than eight seconds and up to 65 mph tops (against the T's 43 mph). Much of that acceleration, which compared favorably with that of even the best sixes and eights, could be attributed to modifications worked out by Harold Hicks. The A was so quick that on the day after its public debut, the state of Massachusetts declared that in the interest of safety it would "require all Model T drivers accustomed to the planetary transmission to take a test before they can operate the new models."

The Model A was not a sensational looker by standards of the day, but it did have plenty of charm. From the shape and contour of its nickel radiator shell and sweeping hoodline to the body details and the way the large, fully crowned fenders hugged the wire wheels, the family resemblance with Edsel's elegant Lincolns was unmistakable. By borrowing some of the big car's finesse, adopting a 3.5-inch longer wheelbase (103.5 inches) and incorporating a higher beltline that reduced window height, the designers fashioned a car much lower and prettier than the tall, boxy Model T.

The A bowed with a choice of five body styles: Tudor and Fordor sedans, coupe, roadster, and four-door phaeton (replacing the old touring car). Trim and equipment variations made for 10 models in all. There were four coupes: a $525 business model with rubberized roof cover and integral trunk; a Special version with leather top and back, also $525; a Standard business coupe with

fabric top and steel back, priced at $550; and a rumble-seat Sport Coupe wearing a canvas top with non-functioning landau irons, also $550. Roadsters numbered two: a Standard business model with trunk, and the rumble-seat Sport Roadster, both priced at $480. The Tudor sedan listed at $550; the Fordor cost $35 more. All closed models wore smart cadet-type sun visors and rounded roof corners, and all bodies were nicely enhanced by pinstriping and ample reveals for delineating contrast paint (fenders were still finished in black regardless of body color). Naturally, Edsel's artistic eye was behind the four initial color selections: Niagara Blue, Arabian Sand, Dawn Gray, and Gunmetal Blue.

Inside was an instrument panel that nicely married form with function. Shaped roughly like a diamond and finished in satin-nickel, the main cluster mounted to the back of the cowl/fuel tank and contained a direct-acting float-operated fuel gauge. An 80-mph speedometer was set off at the bottom of a vertical oval, with the ignition switch at the left, an ammeter to the right, and an instrument lamp in the center. As on the Model T, spark and throttle levers lived on the steering column, but their quadrants were gone. A floor accelerator pedal supplemented the customary hand throttle. Nearby on the panel's lower right was a combination fuel regulator/choke rod extending directly from the carburetor. Surrounding the horn button at the lock nut of the hard-rubber steering wheel was the headlight switch, a multi-position lever. Several grades of fine cloth upholstery were used in the various closed models; door panels, pleated door pockets, and side walls were trimmed in the same material. Open cars

came with imitation leather trim. Roadster and phaeton doors opened via internal levers, as there were no outside handles at first. Windows in all models that had them were crank-operated.

All this in a Tudor sedan that cost less than a comparable Chevrolet, which listed at $585, and just $15 more than a Whippet, was the attraction that had all those folks standing in line. A bonus was an impressive list of standard equipment that now included the aforementioned bumpers and speedometer, electric tail/stoplight, motorized windshield wiper, Spartan horn, and one-piece swing-up ventilating windshield.

Also standard in the Model A was safety glass all around, an industry first. This came about because of an auto accident during Model A shakedown testing, the severity of which hospitalized the driver and resulted in a long convalescence period. The incident convinced Henry that all of his cars should be equipped with this all-important safety feature.

It's an auto seller's dream when customers literally break down the doors, but Henry had laid down the law dictating that none of the early Model A demonstrators would be sold. As Ford worked to increase production through December, dealers were only allowed to take deposits on future deliveries. In the meantime, they fended off every kind of offer for the one or two "bolt-down" cars in their showrooms. It seemed that everyone from house painters to poli-

The most popular Model A body style in 1928 was the Tudor sedan. It saw production of 208,562 units during the calendar year, way ahead of the runner-up Fordor sedan, of which 82,349 were built. The wheelbase was 103.5 inches, up 3.5 over the T.

ticians wanted to be the first to have a Model A, but couldn't for love or money.

The record is a bit hazy, but the first Model A owner was probably Thomas Alva Edison. The famous inventor was invited to drive the first car off the Kearney, New Jersey line on December 19, and it was immediately turned over to him as a gift from longtime friend Henry Ford. James Couzens, one of Ford Motor Company's founders and by now a senator from Michigan, got the first car delivered in Washington D.C. It bore serial number 35, the same as his original 1908 Model T, and was another gift from Henry.

But the person officially publicized as Model A "Purchaser Number One" was swashbuckling movie idol Douglas Fairbanks, who bought a sport coupe as a Christmas present for his equally famous wife, actress Mary Pickford. As arranged by Edsel, this car was delivered on December 26 from a Beverly Hills dealer where it had been a demonstrator. "America's Sweetheart" thanked Edsel by sending him a photograph of her posing with the car. She signed it "Mary Pick-a-Ford."

When it was all over, Henry concluded he'd spent $100 million on bringing out the Model A. But while dealers had taken orders for 727,000 of them by the beginning of 1928, deliveries still

amounted to only a trickle, and it would be another full month before dealers would have even one of each body style for display. "We probably gave back half our deposits eventually," recalled long-time dealer John Eagal. "People would wait five, six, or seven months and then buy something else. In fact, delivery took so long that we never did locate some of the buyers to give back their money!"

One of the main production hang-ups was controversy over the new single-system rod-operated brakes. Motor vehicle departments in several states objected to the design, in which both the service and emergency brakes worked off the same pressure. The first cars had the emergency brake lever to the left of the driver, but the ruckus over the safety issue got so loud that Henry ordered a redesign. By the end of January 1928, some plants had started building cars with the lever mounted ahead of the gearshift and independent of the service brakes. By mid-year all Model A cars and Model AA trucks would have this modification.

As time dragged on, a confident Henry Ford urged his dealers to be patient. "The new car is coming along fine," he told them in a mid-February letter. "You can't get a great plant overhauled and converted from one type product to another in a day. It is easy to design a car.

It is a tremendous task to get into shape to produce it right in every detail and great quantity."

Slowly, week by week, Model As finally began appearing on American roads. It was soon quite fashionable to be seen in one. New York Governor Franklin D. Roosevelt bought a roadster to use at his Hyde Park estate. Actress Delores Del Rio gadded about Hollywood in a chic sport coupe. Humorist Will Rogers and movie moguls Cecil B. DeMille and Louis B. Mayer bought Tudors to run around in. Billie Dove, Wallace Beery, Lon Chaney, and Lillian Gish were other film celebrities who joined the Model A craze.

More than was ever true of the Tin Lizzie, the Model A offered not only more features, colors, and accessories, but more body styles. The Fordor sedan was in full production by May 1928, and nearly every month for the balance of the calendar year saw additional variations, culminating with the December 13 introduction of the elegant Town Car. Another of Edsel's creations, it featured a separate chauffeur's compartment, luxurious interior, and more formal styling, just the thing for well-heeled customers who wanted to ride around in style without flaunting their wealth. Budding actress Joan Crawford preferred a Lincoln away from the studio, but bought one of the spiffy

Town Cars just to be one up on all the other Model A owners in Tinseltown.

With its overwhelmingly enthusiastic reception, the Model A marked Ford Motor Company's 25th birthday in a grand way. It also marked major changes for the truck line. Designated (not surprisingly) Model AA, the new fleet was still largely car-based, if somewhat less so than in the TT days.

There were now two distinct groups of trucks: the light-duty "70-Series" models with bodywork derived from that of the passenger cars, and the "80-Series" heavier-duty models built on a stronger version of the car chassis with an extended 131.5-inch wheelbase and nominal 1½-ton payload capacity. Besides more massive construction, the latter featured a heftier front spring; dual 13- or 16-leaf cantilever rear springs, mounted longitudinally; larger 14-inch-diameter rear brakes; and special 20-inch spoke wheels carrying high-pressure truck tires. There was also a stronger driveline with two-piece propshaft, larger radius rods, and a larger worm-gear final drive. Exclusive to the 80-Series chassis was a new option called "Dual-High," basically a two-speed planetary gearset bolted behind the normal three-speed gearbox to give six speeds forward and two reverse.

Light-duty models began with open-

and closed-cab pickups combining front-end sheetmetal from the new Model A cars (save black-enamel instead of chrome headlight shells) with carryover Model TT cargo boxes. Respective prices were $395 (later $455) and $445. A smart newcomer was a Budd-built panel delivery with twin folding seats and twin center-opening rear doors. Its cargo bay was 57 inches long by 50 inches wide by 46.5 inches high.

Factory bodies proliferated greatly for the 80-series chassis. These ranged from the do-all closed-cab flatbed (a 97.5 × 68-inch platform) to stake-side, panel delivery (introduced in August 1928 at $850), and Ford's first bus body. Of course, independent builders rushed to supply specific "vocational" types for both new chassis, so the customer's choice was wider than ever. The bare 80-Series chassis was introduced at $460 but went to $540 in the spring of 1928. It came without a cab or seats, but you did get the passenger-car cowl, instrument panel, and front end, plus abbreviated running boards.

The long changeover and halting production startup make Model A and AA production figures a little hazy. However, for calendar 1928 it appears that Ford built some 110,000 trucks of all kinds in the U.S. (plus another 26,000 or so in Canada) and a little more than

Almost as popular as the 1928 Model A Fordor sedan was the roadster. It came in two guises: standard two-seater business roadster or two/four-passenger rumble-seat roadster (above). Both cost $480. The one seen here has the rumble seat, as did 30,129 others out of the total 81,937 roadsters built in calendar 1928. Note the step plates on the bumper and rear fender of the car pictured—climbing into the rumble seat was clearly for the young and agile. This car sports a number of extra cost items: exterior trunk, stone guard over the radiator, and spare tire cover.

633,500 passenger cars. Comparing the last with the industry's substantially higher car output of over 3.8 million units (versus just under 3 million in 1927), Ford's market share ended up much lower than the previous year, being just 16 percent. For all the excitement surrounding the Model A and AA, the days of Dearborn's overwhelming market dominance were over.

So were its days in the tractor business—increased competition, a shrinking market, and the need for extra car capacity led Ford to abandon U.S. tractor production in February 1928 after just 8001 calendar-year assemblies and nearly 740,000 American-made units in all. However, the workhorse Fordsons would continue to be built in Ireland where the need for them was comparatively greater and labor costs lower.

1929

All Ford assembly plants were again running full steam as 1929 opened, but they were still behind the steam-rolling demand for the Model A. A thousand boxcars a day moved in and out of both the Highland Park and Rouge facilities to supply the mammoth assembly system as production soared beyond 100,000 units a month. In January alone Ford built 159,786 units worldwide, a pace that would make this its biggest production year before 1949. Even rail shipments proved too slow at the height of the Model A buying binge this spring, so Ford sent one of its freighters, the *Lake Benbow*, on an emergency rush with parts for its San Francisco plant. Loaded at Chester, Pennsylvania, it sailed via the Panama Canal.

The 1929 models debuted with little fanfare, probably because they weren't outwardly much different from the '28s. Even the factory failed to clearly distin-

guish between them, persisting with its traditional Model T policy of making running improvements as needed. What parts and sheetmetal had been modified the previous year were designed to fit the new models, so it was very common to see late-1928 cars with 1929-model parts and early '29s with leftover 1928 items. The most noticeable difference was the belated arrival of external door handles for open models, both trucks and passenger cars, though there were many other subtle changes. One sure way to tell them apart was the '29s' sportier trim and colors.

January brought two additions: the convertible cabriolet, introduced at the New York Auto Show on the 16th, and the Delivery Car, an addition to the 70-Series Model AA commercial line, announced on the 24th. The latter was basically the Tudor sedan with blanked-out rear side windows, a swing-out rear door, left sidemount spare and no back seat. Initially sold only on a special-order basis at $595, it offered a useful cargo hold measuring 35 inches long by 42 inches wide by 43 inches high. More glamorous by far was the new $640 cabriolet, Ford's first true convertible since the old Model T Coupelet. When buttoned up it looked much like the rumble-

seat sport coupe, though its landau top irons were functional, of course.

Two more body choices arrived on April 25: the Town Sedan and America's first assembly-line station wagon, both four-door models supplied by Murray and priced at $695. The former featured a small side window aft of each rear door instead of closed roof quarters as on the ordinary Fordor sedan, plus a rear center armrest, standard cowl lights, and even a curtain for the back window. The wagon, though technically part of the truck line (where it was designated Model 150A), came with passenger-car appointments and seating for eight within a body constructed of hard maple with birch panelling. Ford's own Iron Mountain, Michigan, mills provided the raw tree wood and also built the body's sub-assemblies for

This page: Some samples of the 1929 Model A Ford lineup and their prices: standard phaeton (below left), $460; rumble-seat roadster (below right), $450; standard business coupe (bottom left), $525; and the station wagon (bottom right), $695. Opposite page: An interesting 1929 Model A offering was the Briggs-built Fordor "leatherback" sedan (top), which utilized leather or leatherette on the back and top. Also new for 1929 was the $670 convertible cabriolet (bottom), Ford's first true ragtop since the Model T Coupelet.

shipment to Murray. The Model A wagon wasn't a big seller at first, but in later years its "first-of-the-breed" status would allow Ford to proclaim itself with some justification as "America's wagonmaster."

Station wagon aside, the commercial line was unchanged for most of 1929, though February brought a switch from welded-spoke to "six-hole" steel disc wheels as standard equipment for the 80-Series 1½-ton chassis. More substantial improvements occurred beginning with October production: The "Dual-High" transmission option was dropped, a four-speed gearbox replaced the previous three-speeder, the worm-drive rear axle gave way to a tougher bevel-gear design, front suspension components were strengthened, front-brake diameter was enlarged to 14 inches, and wheels changed to positive-offset "five-hole" rims.

Nineteen twenty-nine looked like a prosperous year for Ford and the nation as a whole. Symbolizing the Model A's soaring popularity and Ford's return to full operation was the completion of the one-millionth Model A on February 4. It was quickly followed by the 2-millionth (a new cabriolet) on July 24, a milestone achieved less than 18 months after the first Model A was built. Recovering smartly from 1928, Ford's calendar-year car production and market share both doubled, to just over 1.5 million units and

32 percent of the 4.59-million-unit industry total.

Henry also turned a handsome profit by selling his DT&I railroad to a subsidiary of the Pennsylvania Railroad on July 1 for $36 million, fully $31 million more than he'd paid back in 1920. On October 21, the new Henry Ford Museum was dedicated as part of the automaker's new Greenfield Village historical complex in Dearborn, the celebration marking the 50th anniversary of Edison's invention of the incandescent light.

Exactly one week later, Wall Street, as one newspaper put it, laid an egg. On October 28-29 and November 6, the Dow Jones Industrial Average suffered its third, fourth, and fifth largest percentage losses in history, losing 94.5 points to create financial earthquakes all over the globe.

Though Ford sales would naturally

suffer, Henry saw a positive side to the ensuing economic chaos. He believed that falling wages and building-material costs created a good opportunity to expand operations and lower car prices, while, at the same time, providing new construction jobs thereby helping to ease the general slump. As a result, new Ford assembly plants would open in 1930 at Long Beach and Richmond, California (the latter ultimately replacing the San Francisco point); Seattle, Washington; Buffalo, New York; and Edgewater, New Jersey. Henry responded more immediately by upping his workers' daily wage to $6 and reducing Model A prices $5-$35, both on December 1. But generous though these moves were, the economic situation was too vast and worsening too quickly for the efforts of any one person to have much effect, not even altruistic multimillionaires like Henry Ford.

Opposite page: Unlike the 1929 Model A Sport Coupe, with its canvas roof and fake landau bars, the regular coupe was a five-window model (top). It provided better over-the-shoulder visibility. The Tudor sedan (bottom), now $525, was again the best seller—output soared to 523,922 units for the calendar year. This page: At 2525 pounds, the Town Car (above) outweighed the wagon by 25, and cost $1400, $775 more than the Fordor. Other '29s included the closed-cab pickup at $445 (bottom left) and the $695 Murray-bodied Town Sedan (below).

1 9 3 0

Arriving the first week of January, this year's Model A attracted almost as much buyer attention as the debut 1928 edition, though the crowd was quieter and smaller, estimated at just over nine million. Rumors of major changes had been flying for some time, and Ford watchers weren't disappointed.

They began with a higher, smoother hood-to-body line that gave a more pleasing appearance via elimination of the prominent cowl stanchion (first seen on the 1929 cabriolet). Smaller 19-inch-diameter wheels and larger tires gave a more up-to-date stance. Also new was Ford's first use of stainless-steel brightwork, encompassing radiator shell, a new cowl finish strip and headlamp, cowl lamp, and taillamp buckets and the doors. Rounding out the style updates were more generous fender shapes and roomier interiors. Colors and trim selections were again upgraded per established policy. The result of all this was breathlessly advertised as "The New Beauty of the New Ford."

Model choices expanded by two. Arriving very late in the year was a new close-coupled closed two-door called the Victoria, with a slightly lower roofline than the basic Tudor sedan and snappy canvas-covered top and back. The other newcomer was a smart DeLuxe-trim two-door version of the Standard four-door phaeton equipped with left side-mount spare, trunk rack, and genuine leather upholstery as standard. It sold for $625 versus the price-leading Standard phaeton at $440. Other prices were roughly the same as in 1929, ranging from $490 for the popular Tudor to $645 for the convertible cabriolet.

The Model A's reputation for taking hard knocks had become almost legendary by now—like the tales told about the banged-up 1930 roadster that faithfully carried champion rodeo rider Alice Sisty from show to show. Before awestruck crowds, it served as a barrier over which she jumped a matched pair of horses in the daring "Auto Roman Standing Jump." The Model A was also becoming popular with the budding "hot rod" set on the dry lakes of California, where names like Riley, Winfield, and Cragar were pioneering some great new speed equipment, thus setting the stage for the next generation of backyard mechanics and weekend racers.

More testimony to the Model A's fortitude came in February from an almost humorous accident near Spokane, Washington. Two city officials were hurrying across frozen Fernan Lake in a

This page: The bargain of the restyled 1930 Model A Ford lineup was the roadster (top), which sold for $435 in standard trim, or $495 as a DeLuxe. This one is well optioned with a radiator stone guard, rear-mounted trunk, and the "Quail" hood ornament. Of the 122,703 roadsters built during the model year, only about 12,000 were the DeLuxe. The $490 Tudor (above) was again the most popular body style, with 425,124 rolling off the various Ford assembly lines. Opposite page: Curiously, the five-window coupe (top) cost the same as the Tudor, or $50 more as a DeLuxe. It was popular, too, notching up production of 262,341 units. The Model A's trusty inline four (bottom left) displaced 200.5 cubic inches and developed 40 bhp, twice as much as the Model T. The instrument panel (bottom right) featured a "Cyclops-eye" speedometer.

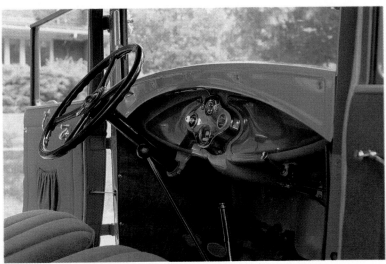

1929 coupe (to greet Army aviators, who had just landed after completing a sub-Arctic test flight) when they suddenly hit a layer of thin ice. The passengers managed to bail out in time, but the poor Ford sank quickly to the bottom. Twelve days later, the ice had hardened enough that a crew could bring a tow truck to the spot, where a square was cut through the 14-inch-thick floe. The coupe was located with a grappling hook and hauled to the surface. After water was drained from body, crankcase, and fuel tank, it was towed to the Ford garage in nearby Coeur d'Alene, Idaho, and given fresh oil, gasoline, and a new battery. The only mechanical work deemed necessary was cleaning spark plugs, fuel bowl, and distributor. The Model A dutifully fired up and was driven back to Spokane, a little soggy but good for many more miles.

Despite the economic downturn, this was another banner year for Ford. Though volume for the calendar 12 months was down some 450,000 cars to 1,155,162, the industry lost even more, plunging some 50 percent (versus Ford's 23 percent) to just over 2.78 million. As a result, the make's market share rose nine points to 41 percent. For the model year, Ford finished comfortably ahead of surging challenger Chevrolet with 1,140,710 cars versus some 641,000.

But even Ford wasn't immune to the growing economic blight, and in late summer some serious holes began show-

This page: This 1930 Model A roadster (top) has the DeLuxe features of cowl lights and twin taillights. Note also the trunk rack. The convertible (bottom), which cost about $200 more than the roadster, had roll-up windows. Note the sturdy A-pillars. Opposite page: The '30 Ford pickup (top) cost $435; 86,383 were built. It's believed that this '30 Phaeton (center) had its bodywork done by LeBaron. Optional vent wings adorn this '30 coupe (bottom).

ing up in the once-predictable sales patterns. On August 16 it was announced that strong demand had prompted the Chicago plant to step up production by 5000 cars per month. Four days later, though, assembly was drastically cut back at Louisville, Kentucky, because sales in that region were off 33 percent. It was an early symptom of the faltering economy and a contracting car market.

There were other problems, too. The main one was the competition, especially Chevrolet, which had not been idle during the Model A boom. Chevy engineers had been hard at work in 1928 on a new six-cylinder engine, and it arrived that Christmas in an attractive line of cars priced only $100 above comparable Fords. The 1929 Chevys were just right for a market that wanted something a little different, backed by a strong advertising campaign intended to win four-cylinder (mainly Ford) buyers over to the "smoother smoothness of the six-cylinder car." Sales of America's second most popular make rocketed to over a million units in just eight months, and Chevy continued whittling away at Ford's lead in 1930.

The Model AA truck line had shown signs of sales distress before Ford's cars, and this plus the need to use up surplus 1929 front-end components explains why the 1930 models, including the Model A station wagon, didn't appear until June 9. The only change on the interim "1929½" offerings involved a new option for the 80-Series 1½-ton chassis: dual rear wheels with balloon tires.

With the changeover to the "true" 1930 trucks came most of the front-end styling enhancements applied to this year's Ford passenger cars, plus a wider array of factory bodies, a redesigned closed cab, and a third chassis choice. The last was a 157-inch-wheelbase job answering demand for a Ford chassis that would accommodate 11- to 12-foot-long bodies without add-on frame extensions. Like its 131-inch companion, this "AA-157" was rated at 1½ tons and available with factory platform, stake, and express bodies, the last returning for the first time since 1924. A handsome new panel van offered as an "AA-131" model was quite distinct from its smaller, car-based sister. Ford also offered its first factory dumper bodies in versions for both the long chassis, albeit with many supplier-sourced components.

Elsewhere, the Delivery Car was no longer a stripped Tudor sedan but a roomier Budd-bodied workhorse, still on the basic Model A chassis but with its own higher roof, side panels, and rear end. This year's station wagon was much like the debut 1929 edition apart from the new front-end styling, but its wood bodywork was now built by Briggs and the Baker-Raulang company as well as Murray. As before, hood, cowl, and windshield frame were finished in golden Manila Brown to complement the natural-tone tree wood used behind.

Contemplated but never offered for 1930 was a separate Ford "Commercial Car" line comprising taxi, delivery car, panel delivery, Town Car Delivery, pickup, and service/tow truck on a special 118-inch wheelbase. The swanky Town Car Delivery, a novel idea that would be offered in volume for 1931, made it as far as three 1930 prototypes, all with Briggs bodywork on the standard 103.5-inch Model A car chassis. Featured were the expected blank side panels as well as an open front "chauffeur's" compartment and little "carriage lamps" high up on the B-pillars. If nothing else, these experiments showed Ford's determination to remain number-one in truck sales by giving customers the widest possible range of choices.

1 9 3 1

Arriving amidst widening economic gloom and increased competition was a 1931 Model A sporting several appearance updates: redesigned radiator shell with painted indentation, restyled instrument panel, and one-piece running board splash aprons. Typical of Ford model changeovers, any old parts that fit the new cars were used until stock was exhausted, so it wasn't unusual for early '31s to have, say, the old two-piece splash aprons. Bowing in March was a more distinctive Town Sedan with a racy and noticeably different slant windshield of the sort first seen on the 1930 rounded-back Victoria. It was accomplished by trimming back the front roof header a bit and bringing the windshield base slightly forward.

Arriving in June was a new open model, the Convertible Sedan, a sporty, five-passenger all-season two-door. It, too, wore the slant windshield, but stood apart from the convertible cabriolet by having fixed side window frames that left the full door and rear-quarter glass available for fending off the elements even with the canvas top lowered. Its roof folded away neatly over the body, behind the back seat, and could be covered by a tailored boot.

Offered only in DeLuxe trim with genuine leather upholstery in a fancy dark tan, the Convertible Sedan was tagged at $640, versus $595 for the cabriolet and $475 for the curtained DeLuxe roadster. As before, the latter two were available with a choice of trunk or rumble seat at no difference in price. The same applied to the fixed-roof Sport Coupe, still a cabriolet look-alike listing at $500 this year, and the $525 DeLuxe

coupe, still a "five-window" design with rear quarter panes. Rounding out this year's DeLuxe offerings were the $580 two-door phaeton, blind-quarter Fordor and "six-window" Town Sedans at $630 for either, and the popular Tudor sedan at $490. The more formal-looking Victoria listed at $580, either with or without an all-canvas top. Standard-trim models comprised four-door phaeton ($435), "three-window" coupe (with trunk only, $490), Fordor (with "six-light" roof, $590), and the price-leader no-frills roadster ($430).

Expansion hardly seemed prudent in 1931, yet that's just what Ford did with its truck line this year. There were no cosmetic or mechanical changes of note, but factory body types proliferated greatly to encompass everything from pickups to paddy wagons, funeral cars to school buses. This was a welcome turn of events for body suppliers Briggs, Budd, and Murray, whose business with Ford and other makes was tailing off with the rapid decline in the passenger-car market. Only trouble was, demand for most of the new Ford trucks wasn't high enough to make up the sales difference. The much-broader line was certainly an expensive proposition in the withering truck market of 1931, and Ford would trim offerings substantially for 1932.

Notable among the commercial newcomers was a production Town Car Delivery with special wood-framed aluminum bodywork behind the doors, plus B-pillar carriage lamps and a right sidemount spare with chrome-ringed metal cover. With birch veneer paneling lining the cargo compartment, it measured 45 × 45 × 42 inches. A snap-on canvas cover was provided for weather protection of the open driver's compartment. However what's really significant here is the price—at $1150 f.o.b. Detroit, the Town Car Delivery was Ford's first production vehicle to break the $1000 barrier. Perhaps not surprisingly, only 196 were called for as "hard times" continued getting harder.

Yet, sales were helped by a roomier new cargo box for the popular Model AA pickup. Supplied by Briggs, it boasted 22.2 cubic feet of load space versus the previous unit's 16.8. Ford also revived the canopy top as a pickup option and built a limited run of DeLuxe AA pickups (initially for General Electric) with integrated box/cab structure, a portent of

Opposite page: The '31 Ford pickup (bottom) found nearly 100,000 customers. It shared its 103.5-inch wheelbase and 40-bhp four with the cars. The heavy-duty AA trucks (top) used the same engine. This page: The '31 pickup (top) had a payload of 750 pounds. The DeLuxe Town Sedan (center) cost $630; the standard Fordor, which didn't have cowl lamps, listed at $590. A new '31 model was the convertible sedan (bottom), aptly named as it embraced features of both. Its easy-to-use top rode on tracks above the windows. At $640, it was the priciest '31; only 5072 were built.

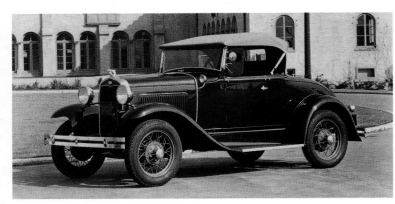

the later "car/pickup" idea. The foundation for these and other light-duty Ford trucks was the basic Model A Commercial Chassis, priced at $340 this year. As before, it was available with either open or closed cab, with the latter continuing to outdistance the former in buyer preference.

There was also a novel new station wagon spinoff for 1931, the Natural Wood Panel Delivery. Built by Baker-Raulang and priced at $615, it substituted solid wood panels for curtained windows and had two doors instead of four. Typical of the low demand for many of Ford's special-bodied commercials in this period, only about 900 of these would be built from December 1930 through March 1932.

The promotional highlight of 1931 was the nationwide tour of the 20-millionth Ford, a Town Sedan that rolled out the Rouge door on April 14. After an official send-off from Henry and Edsel Ford, it went to New York where Governor Franklin Roosevelt's wife, Eleanor, took it for a short spin. Then, accompanied by a flock of other new Fords, it headed west for whirlwind publicity stops at hundreds of welcoming dealers. Along the way, it paid a visit to "Andy Gump" comic strip creator Sidney Smith, received the checkered flag at the Indianapolis Motor Speedway, was inducted into the Sioux tribe, and became the first private car to descend to the bottom of Hoover Dam. It also passed through various state capitals, picking up specially minted "20,000,000" license plates and gubernatorial signatures in its logbook. Among other notables signing in were World War I hero Sergeant Alvin C. York, explorer Admiral Richard E. Byrd,

and husband-and-wife film stars Douglas Fairbanks and Mary Pickford. Fairbanks also drove the car in Los Angeles' 150th anniversary parade. On its return to Dearborn, the milestone Model A went on display in Henry Ford's new museum and was honored as the most widely traveled and photographed car in America.

But no amount of publicity could prop up Ford production, which ended the calendar year at just a third of the 1.5 million units built in 1929—a bit under 542,000 in all. At about 1,973,000 units, the industry as a whole was down again, but not as much as Ford, whose percentage share shriveled to a bit over 27 percent. Worse for Ford, Chevrolet won the model-year production contest, building about 4000 more 1931 models (619,500 against 614,500).

Such was the background for rumors that began abounding in the trade that Henry was working on a new car to replace the faltering Model A as a counter to Chevrolet's six. Some said it would be a small V-8 model named "Edison" in honor of his longtime friend.

Meantime, Henry had decided that something had to be done in the face of falling Ford sales. Accordingly, on July 29, the day before his 68th birthday, he laid off 75,000 workers and closed 25 of his 36 U.S. assembly plants until the economy showed some kind of improvement. But the economy did anything but improve. On September 24, the stock market suffered yet another setback as the Dow Jones Industrials lost 8.20 points—a bit more than seven percent of their total value (and still the 13th largest loss on record)—to close at a dismal 107.79. Henry responded again by quiet-

ly cutting his workers' wages, reverting to a $6 day in October. Employees doubtless grumbled, but at least they were still employed, something fewer and fewer people could say as the Depression set in.

But the wily auto baron already had something new up his sleeve, for he certainly realized by now that it was all over for four-cylinder cars. Consider that when the Model A was introduced in December 1927, there were still about a half-dozen fours on the market, the most prominent being Dodge, Chrysler, Willys, Durant, and Chevrolet. Willys would continue with a four and barely survive the Depression; Durant wouldn't. Meanwhile, the fours from Chevy, Dodge, and Chrysler were old designs nearing the end of their careers, and all three would be replaced by sixes for 1929. Other than Ford, only Plymouth—which debuted in July 1928, about a half-year after the Model A—would successfully rely on four-cylinder power into the Thirties, in this case through 1932.

Fortunately, Ford was well along by 1931 with what would prove to be his last personal product triumph. As a result, the last Model A rolled off the Rouge assembly line with relatively little notice on November 1, thus clearing the way for America's first low-priced V-8.

Despite the tightening grip of the Depression, Henry at least had the pleasure of driving the 20-millionth Ford, a '31 Town Sedan (top right), off the Rouge assembly line. The car then went on tour throughout the U.S., after which it went on display in the Henry Ford Museum. Other models for '31: the handsome $580 Victoria (top left), of which 36,830 were built, and the ubiquitous roadster (bottom row). The DeLuxe model seen here sold for $475; 56,702 were produced.

1 9 3 2

In the summer of 1930, on returning from a trip to Germany, Henry Ford sent a trio of his most gifted experimental engineers to a small rustic building deep within his Greenfield Village showplace in Dearborn. He housed them in his replica of Thomas Edison's Fort Myers, Florida laboratory, authentic right down to the old steam engine of the type the prolific inventor had used.

One of the three, 28-year-old Emil Zoerlein, had been in on a number of Ford's pet projects. "There are two more fellows working back there," Henry told him. "What you work on and what you see back there I want you to keep to yourself and not say a word to anybody about it. We are designing a V-8 engine. What do you know about electricity?"

"I think I know quite a lot about it," Zoerlein replied.

"Then," said Ford, "I'd like to have you work on the ignition system for this engine—the generator and starter and so forth. You work along with those two boys back there."

V-8s were nothing new in 1930. The French Antoinette had such an engine way back in 1900, and Rolls-Royce had one running in 1905. But just as he'd tinkered with the X-8 for the Model T's successor, and a bit later with an inline five, Henry Ford again wanted something truly revolutionary to replace the Model A. The most radical aspect of this new project would be coming up with what the experts said couldn't be done: a *low-cost* V-8 car. Henry had already decided in late 1929, when he gave the first order for the development of a V-8, that it *could* be done.

Zoerlein found colleagues Carl Schultz and Ray Laird already at the drawing board, pondering rough sketches they'd made of Henry's suggested ideas for a small V-8 that could—in theory—be mass-produced. "Schultz had already made a layout...showing a box [distributor] in front with about the same position and shape as we finally developed," Zoerlein recalled in a 1972 interview. "I worked with him to get the basic configuration first of all. We designed a distributor with two pairs of breaking points and a four-lobe cam for an eight-cylinder engine....It was the same principle as the Model K Lincoln...except for a new housing."

Looking to Lincoln was understandable, given Ford's growing experience with the large, Leland-designed V-8. But using a smaller version of that engine was scotched by high manufacturing costs. As a low-price car built in huge vol-

ume, the Ford had of necessity used a simple four-cylinder engine that could be cast and machined in one piece. One reason the big Lincoln sold for 10 times as much was the labor-intensive production methods dictated by its complicated V-8, which had a 60-degree block and 180-degree crankshaft. That block, magnificent though it might have been, had to be cast and machined in pieces and the whole engine carefully bench-assembled.

Initially, Ford told no one what he was up to, not Charles Sorensen, his closest aide, nor even son Edsel. Instead, he casually directed his three engineers for nearly a year. While Zoerlein experimented with the new engine's electrical system, Schultz and Laird wrestled with the real puzzle: designing a complex V-8 block that could be cast in one piece.

Making life difficult for engineers was one of Henry's more peculiar habits, but it seemed from his belief that over-

The big Ford news for '32 was, of course, Henry's new low-cost flathead V-8. Not to be overlooked either was the new, more streamlined styling. Although a four-cylinder Model B was still available, the '32s seen here are Model 18 V-8s, as noted by the V-8 emblems on the headlight bar and hubcaps. The DeLuxe rumble-seat roadster (top) cost an even $500, the Sports Coupe (with the fake landau bars) went for $535 (center), and the cabriolet (bottom) sold for $610—remarkable value for the get-up-and-go of a V-8.

coming obstacles often prompted new discoveries. This explains why his V-8 was devised under relatively primitive conditions when his fully equipped Engineering Laboratory sat just a few hundred yards away. Eventually, the team was allowed to recruit Herman Reinhold, head of the pattern shop, with whose help they secretly built molds and then cast the first experimental block at the Rouge foundry. The result was deemed satisfactory, and by early 1931 it was machined and fitted for running at the Greenfield Village workshop.

"We didn't have any instruments in our Fort Myers lab whatsoever," Zoerlein recalled. "We didn't even have an electric motor.... I asked Mr. Ford if we could set one up. At that time we only had direct current, which was supplied by a generator driven by a steam engine at one end of the shop. The steam engine also drove an overhead line shaft [that] provided power via belts to the various shop tools. Mr. Ford said he didn't want any electrical motors in this building even if direct current was available. He didn't give me any reason for that, and I didn't ask for it."

Because of the antiquated equipment they had to work with, the team faced another problem: how to test their engine. Henry wouldn't allow any bolts or nails in the planking of his cherished Edison building, so the trio devised a wooden test stand. They braced it on the floor by running wood beams to the ceiling in such a way that it was forced to stay in position without nailing directly into either surface.

Finally, the moment of truth. "We put a pulley on the back end of the engine and ran it up to the steam-powered transmission shaft to get it started by belt drive," Zoerlein remembered. "We were so busy getting [things] set up that it wasn't until the last moment ... that we noticed that we lacked a carburetor. We sent one of the engineers running and he came back with one that we stuck on.... The engine started and the whole building shook. As it ran, it would drive the line shaft and the steam engine, to give it load, until the belt slipped off. We were very happy, because before starting the thing, we didn't know whether it would run forwards or backwards!"

While that experimental V-8 ran not only backwards at times but very roughly, Henry was sufficiently satisfied to have Edsel and production bosses Sorensen and Peter Martin out for a look in June 1931. Also invited was Lawrence Sheldrick, who'd exhibited such talent in the Model A's development that he now headed the Ford Engineering Department.

Edsel was quickly convinced of the new engine's potential, but the others flatly declared that a 90-degree block with right-angle crank throws simply could not be cast in one piece at mass-production speeds—and that attempting to do so was a good way to go broke. Henry listened impatiently to their arguments, then groused: "Anything that can be drawn up can be cast!" With that, he ordered them to get the V-8 into production.

By early August, Henry was personally working full bore on the project, just as he had to perfect the Model T and Model A. On through the fall, more people were brought to the task of engineering, casting, and testing the blocks. For every success there were a hundred failures, from core shifts to pinholes. But Ford was sure he was on the right track—so sure, in fact, that in the first week of November he halted Model A production to allow his plants to prepare

for its V-8-powered replacement.

Thus began a $300-million race to solve the casting problems so the new car could be introduced without undue delay. As one industry veteran said much later: "It was an awful gamble. There isn't a man in the business today who would—let alone *could*—make that bet."

"We were scared because of the rush," one foundry worker said later. "I worked night and day. We even forgot to go home, right through Christmas season. One day . . . we had exactly 100-percent scrap. Everything was wrong. Not one engine came out right. Just think of this: there were 54 separate cores in that mold—54 sand cores that had to stay put exactly right for the valve sections and cylinders and everything in that engine block."

As the Rouge shops raced to ready the new V-8, Edsel and Joe Galamb teamed again to style a full line of open and closed bodies for the chassis it would power. Once more they took their cue from the imposing Lincolns that so embodied Edsel's artistic taste. Their objective was a smaller-scale adaptation incorporating the same sculptured lines and fine detailing. Body design was coordinated with a new chassis being developed under Henry's close supervision by engineers Eugene Farkas and Emery Nador. Also heavily involved were body suppliers Briggs, Murray, and Budd, who fine-tuned the approved stampings in anticipation of fat production contracts.

Farkas contributed the major chassis innovation, his design proving both novel and functional. It originated in an idea first sketched by Galamb, whereby the side rails functioned like traditional running board splash aprons. Farkas cleverly developed this so that the production rails were stamped out extra deep and with a long contour on their outer faces. With the body installed, they would provide a natural enamel finish between the underbody and running boards. The methodical Hungarian also had the task of designing a conventional fuel tank, which would be relocated from above the driver's knees, as in the Model A, to the rear. Ford gas tanks had been up

front since 1926, a feature that had drawn much criticism due to largely unproved allegations that the cowl mounting constituted a fire hazard. As with the frame, Farkas and Galamb designed the tank so that it neatly formed the enameled sheetmetal to finish out the lower rear body.

But while all this was going on, Ford's great plants again lay mostly idle. Their only serious activity by the end of 1931 was making replacement parts and assembling Model AA commercial vehicles, which continued to find a ready market. As this near sequel to the events of mid-1927 unfolded, the entire Ford organization edged closer to the brink of financial disaster. Its cash flow had all but dried up, its trained labor force had been largely laid off, and already hard-pressed dealers were either struggling to stay alive selling parts and used cars—or going broke. Compounding the losses from having no cars to sell was the new model's enormous tooling expense. "The cost was incredible," recalled one V-8 production man. "If it wasn't for Henry Ford's great personal wealth, the company could have gone broke in casting that engine."

Quickly grasping the gravity of the situation, Charlie Sorensen set aside his reservations about the V-8's casting complexities, rolled up his sleeves and pitched in. Armed with his knowledge of pattern making (as noted, his first job at Ford 27 years earlier), he barked orders, made changes, and drove his employees relentlessly. The last stubborn problems were soon resolved, largely through his personal initiative, for which he soon became known far and wide as "Cast Iron Charlie."

Confident that he could now actually mass-produce and sell his low-price V-8 car, Henry began promoting it after months of rumor and speculation. As he told the press on February 11: "I have just got back my old determination to get the price of an automobile down to the mark where the public can buy it." Besides introducing the new V-8 line within weeks, he said his company would also offer a four-cylinder version to satisfy

those who had written in urging that a "Four" be continued. What he *didn't* say was that it was also a hedge against the V-8's failing.

Full details came together on March 9, 1932, when the first V-8 model authorized for production was driven off the assembly line. Within three weeks, every Ford dealer had at least one car for display. Finally, on March 31, the wizard of Dearborn unveiled his latest mechanical marvel.

Despite growing unemployment, some 5.5 million Americans turned out to see the long-awaited Ford V-8. It was a subdued crowd, but one nevertheless enchanted with the idea that they could now buy a Ford with twice the usual number of cylinders. From a distance, the '32 didn't seem all that different from the Model A, but closer inspection revealed it to be all-new from radiator cap to taillight. Edsel and all who'd helped him could rightfully feel proud, for this was far and away the best-looking Ford yet—an opinion soon confirmed by the nation's youth, who would covet the '32 "Deuce" for hot rodding above all other cars.

No wonder. Here was the first Ford that could boast both performance and beauty. As an impressed newsman wrote after the San Francisco preview: "In the new Ford car the eye is caught by the bright beauty of the rustless-steel headlamps, and travels along the bead on the side of the hood toward the rear of the car [that gives] the impression of an arrow in flight. The bodies are fresh and modern, from the gracefully rounded V-type radiator to the rear bumper. The convex lamps, full-crowned fenders and long, low running boards harmonize

Opposite page: More '32 Ford V-8s: $600 Victoria (top), $645 DeLuxe Fordor sedan (second from top), $575 DeLuxe three-window coupe (third from top), and $650 convertible sedan (bottom). The last saw only 1142 built. This page: In 1932, Fords went to town for the first time without exposed radiators— they were now covered by a stylish vertical-bar grille. The cabriolet (left) had fixed A-pillars, as compared to the roadster's fold-down windshield (right).

with the balance of the design." A wheelbase extended 2.5 inches to 106 inches enhanced not only external appearance but internal room.

And for a Ford, the new V-8's interior was almost as revolutionary as its exterior. While the light switch remained at the horn button, as on the Model A, the key and ignition switch were sensibly combined in a single anti-theft unit at the steering column bracket. With the ignition toggle "Off" and the key removed, the steering gear locked the front wheels for parking. It was a wonderful idea (still in use today), though it took getting used to. The uninitiated were forever removing the key before stopping, thus running into all sorts of locked-up trouble—sometimes literally. Instruments, including an 80-mph speedometer, were grouped in a handsome, engine-turned oval housing trimmed with a stainless bead strip and mounted in a mahogany-color panel. Sun visors were arranged to swing out of the way, while the usual top-hinged windshield now opened on a pair of adjustable arms. Following now-customary Ford practice, fine wool, mohair, and leather upholstery were offered. Also per tradition, fenders on all models were dipped in black enamel, while bodies came in a fair choice of colors with contrasting reveals and pinstriping.

Models numbered no fewer than 14, arrayed in Standard and DeLuxe series at prices from $460 to $650. Base-trim offerings comprised the expected Tudor and Fordor sedans, three-window coupe with trunk, roadster, and four-door phaeton. To these the DeLuxe series added the Victoria coupe, convertible sedan (still with fixed side-window frames), convertible cabriolet, and sport coupe (again with dummy landau top irons).

Under the hood sat the ingenious flathead V-8, sized at 221 cubic inches on bore and stroke dimensions of 3.06 × 3.75 inches. Because its twin four-cylinder banks were cast integrally with the crankcase and flywheel housing to permit a short crankshaft, this more powerful 65-horsepower engine took up about the same space as the old four had in the Model A. Up front was a single belt, adjusted by turning a nut (1932 only) on the generator post mount, driving a pair of water pumps and a combination generator/fan off the crank pulley. The aluminum intake manifold was topped by a Detroit Lubricator carburetor, and a fuel pump that worked by means of a pushrod operating off the camshaft. Engine pans were initially cast aluminum, later stamped steel.

This compact powerplant was mounted on rubber in a double-drop frame of all-new design. Suspension was by Ford's familiar twin transverse leaf springs, but the rear one was now behind the differential, which helped lower frame height by nearly two inches from the Model A. That and the smaller 18-inch-diameter

wire wheels gave the V-8 chassis better handling, the cars a smarter road-hugging appearance. The front axle was "stabilized" via a radius-rod wishbone, a Ford feature since the Model T. Rods and levers operated four-wheel mechanical brakes. Shock absorbers were by Houdaille. At the rear, the gas tank neatly formed the underbody finish; above was the spare tire mount, which also served as a frame member. The transmission was again a three-speed unit but with synchronized second and high.

Catering to "four-banger" believers was an updated version of the Model A engine, now rated at 50 bhp, and there were sound business reasons for continuing on with the four-pot. One was the persistent—and the unpublicized—problem of casting perfect V-8 blocks. Another was the high number of buyers who needed a lot of convincing that an eight could be as cheap to run as a four. Of course, the four-cylinder cars were assembled on the same line as the V-8s, since they shared bodies and basic running gear. Their only noticeable difference was lack of V-8 emblems on headlamp bar and hubcaps, the latter bearing "Ford" script instead. For parts identification purposes, the 1932 V-8s were designated Model 18 and the fours Model B, but the latter somehow prevailed for the entire line, and the first V-8s are still often erroneously termed Model Bs.

Production snags prevented V-8s from being fitted to all but a relative few 1932 Ford commercial vehicles, but there was still plenty new in this year's revised Model BB line. Front-end sheetmetal again followed new passenger Ford styling, and both the 131½- and 157-inch chassis were redesigned, acquiring heftier, seven-inch-deep frame members and 50-inch-long parallel semi-elliptic rear springs (replacing cantilevered elliptics). Fuel tanks were enlarged from 11 to 17 gallons and repositioned beneath the seat, again allegedly for greater safety. Some, but not all, bodies were restyled, both factory and proprietary, but there were now far fewer choices than in 1931. Among the casualties were the Deluxe Delivery and the fancy Town Delivery.

Meanwhile, the basic Delivery Car reverted to its original form as a stripped Tudor sedan *sans* rear side windows. Though priced at a reasonable $520, it garnered but 401 model-year orders. The station wagon returned in both passenger and windowless commercial ver-

sions, but the former, tagged at $600, saw only 1400 copies. The open cab pickup, now in its waning days, saw a production run of only 593 units. The popular closed cab pickup, priced at $435, remained the truck line's volume leader, and gained extra hauling volume via a longer 69.1-inch cargo bed.

For all this, Ford truck sales kept on falling, skidding to their lowest point since the historic TT-to-AA changeover of 1927. Here, too, fast-rising Chevrolet was closing the gap, and in just one year, Ford would relinquish its truck sales leadership to the GM brand in 1933.

The passenger-car picture was no brighter. Nicely tooled and beautiful though it was, Ford's fast new V-8 proved terribly tough to sell. Aside from arriving near the very depths of the Depression, when consumer dollars were scarce and competition from other makes doubly fierce, it had an unproven engine about which buyers were either wary, uninformed, or both. Typical of the reactions were "Twice the cylinders take twice the gas!" and "Cylinders layin' on a slant like that will wear out on the down side!" Rural folk were among the most skeptical, brushing off the V-8 as a passing fad that could never replace their trusty four.

Some doubters weren't far off the mark. Within days of taking to America's roads, Ford's V-8 began earning a reputation as an oil guzzler. Then it was discovered that oil in the pan would surge away from the crankshaft bearings in hard turns, causing engine seizure. Worse yet, pinholes were found in many of the early blocks, prompting a widespread dealer recall for engine replacements. Laurence Sheldrick, Ford engineering head, had to admit that "The V-8 development was very hurried, and the public was the testing crew." This would, of course, hurt V-8 sales as the public learned about the V-8's teething problems.

All this naturally worried Henry Ford, so while his engineers hurried to correct problems, he directed his outlying branches to begin sponsoring reliability events in an effort to counter the mounting adverse publicity. The most widely reported was staged this summer in California's Mojave Desert, where veteran racer Eddie Pullen, driving a stock V-8 Victoria over a 32-mile course, logged 33,301 miles in 33 days without engine failure—and averaged 20 miles per gallon.

"After the first run of orders, we had some very difficult selling of the V-8," recalled long-time Stockton, California, Ford dealer John Eagal. "With the excessive oil consumption on the early deliveries, it was a hard thing to explain to customers . . . and hurt the V-8 cars more than anything else. It was during this period also that Ford lost the [sales] lead to Chevrolet. With the engineering problems, production lagged behind. . . . The dealers couldn't get cars and the salesmen became discouraged. Chevrolet simply out-produced Ford."

And so it was. Though both makes were well down for the model year, Chevy cranked out 313,404 of its stylish six-cylinder cars, compared to Ford's 210,824 cars. It should be remembered, however, that the late production start-up gave Ford what really amounted to a seven- or eight-month model year. For the calendar year, Ford's 1932 passenger-car volume sank to just over 287,000 units (of which about 90,000 were fours), the lowest since 1914.

Thus, what should have been a great new-car launch ended up a mediocre one. Even lending a fleet of V-8s as official cars for the Indianapolis 500 failed to generate much response (Edsel Ford drove a Lincoln as the Pace Car). With sales sluggish and dealers going broke in droves as business conditions worsened, word finally came down from Dearborn to get V-8s into the public's hands—fast.

To accomplish that, dealers began staging "Ford Open Air Salons" this summer, carnival-style shows that attempted to spark buyer interest via demonstration rides, movies about Ford assembly, lectures on the V-8's finer points, and similar activities. As an example, the Marysville, California, event was held at a lighted peewee golf course so customers could come in after work. Besides a selection of new models to try, the local dealer brought in Eddie Pullen's Victoria, fresh from its Mojave run. This year's Michigan State Fair was chosen as the site for the company's own exhibit. Alongside a modest cluster of tents shading a display of new cars and trucks was a graded and fenced half-mile oval track where visitors could sample the "smooth" V-8. By fair's end, some 63,000 visitors had taken test rides.

But the nation's economy was still plummeting, and no amount of stimulation seemed to reverse the industrywide sales slump. Toward the end of the year, the V-8 regained some of its lost momentum and was outselling its four-cylinder linemates by nearly nine to one, and outselling Chevrolet as well. Nevertheless, most of the firm's assembly plants were down to a four-day week by the first of August, operating at just a fraction of total capacity. As if to punctuate this gloomy situation, the Dow Jones Industrials recorded their 12th largest percentage drop in history on October 5, losing 7.15 percent of their value by sinking 5.09 points to close at just 66.07.

More somber news arrived in a terse statement from Ford Motor Company on November 7: "As the situation has stood, we have been operating plants two or three days a week, getting out from 50 to 100 cars a day at each plant. This is neither good from a manufacturing point of view, nor does it provide workers with a liveable wage. We are, therefore, for the time being, concentrating our production at points where shipping factors are more advantageous."

In other words, Ford was gearing down. Over the next two months it closed all but six of the 30 plants that had been operating that summer. With a turnaround nowhere in sight, Henry faced the first of what would become a series of yearly challenges to stimulate the market.

Though its effect on sales is unknown, Ford had another kind of bad publicity to contend with in 1932. It came on March 7 when some 3000-5000 unemployed workers staged a "hunger march" to dramatize the impact of Ford's layoffs, believing the huge firm was obligated to provide jobs, medical care, and emergency relief. The apparent trigger for the protest was Henry's statement of 1931 that "the average man won't really work unless he is caught and cannot get out of it"—hardly a tactful thing to say when you're closing factories and putting people out of work.

The marchers were unarmed, but firemen had been called and were ready to douse them with water as they gathered at the Rouge plant's Gate 3. Then, somehow, it all turned ugly. Demonstrators began throwing rocks and pieces of coal. Dearborn police and Ford guards shot back with tear gas, then guns. When it was all over, four demonstrators lay dead and another 50 to 60 persons were wounded. Among the injured was one Harry Bennett, the strong-armed former prizefighter Henry Ford had hired to head his so-called "Service Department" company security squad. Five days later, some 60,000 persons sang for the victims in a funeral procession through downtown Detroit. By one account, their voices "vibrated throughout the city."

And while some of the marchers hemorrhaged blood, Ford Motor Company hemorrhaged red ink, which would be used to record a loss of nearly $75 million for the year. There were few winners in 1932.

Opposite page: Ford offered two V-8 phaetons for 1932, the $495 standard, and the $545 DeLuxe. The car seen here (left) is the latter by virtue of the cowl lights and pin stripes. So is the rumble-seat roadster (right). The open cars didn't fare well saleswise in 1932: only 2705 phaetons, standard and DeLuxe, and 8996 total roadsters, in both trim levels and with or without the rumble seat. This page: Henry Ford's new 221-cid V-8 was a technological marvel because of its one-piece block, which made it cheap to manufacture.

1 9 3 3

For Henry Ford, changing models every year was "the curse of the industry." In the summer of 1932, he was barely beyond the ordeal of his multi-million-dollar V-8 launch when he had to start revamping the design for 1933. Badgered by bad news from all sides and falling further behind Chevrolet in the sales race, he apparently realized at last that if he couldn't sell his V-8s on performance alone, he'd have to try a combination of speed and sporty good looks.

Ever the motor and chassis man, Henry worked on improving the V-8's running gear while his quietly artistic son Edsel and stylists Joe Galamb and Eugene T. Gregorie rushed to create a new look. This time, though, they'd get valuable assistance from body suppliers Briggs, Murray, and Budd, all of whom were accomplished enough by now to provide clients like Ford with ideas and mockups expressing the latest, most fashionable styling.

Actually, however, Gregorie must be given most of the credit for styling the 1933 Ford, which Ford dubbed Model 40. The basic design came from the British Ford Model Y, a 90-inch-wheelbase family car designed to compete with the little Austin Seven and small Morris. Gregorie had done the body design for the Model Y and, according to Paul R. Woudenberg in *Ford in the Thirties*, it "was, in simplest terms, a streamlined [1932] Model 18.... The importance of Gregorie's work on Model Y cannot be underestimated, for it was no one less than Edsel Ford who, upon seeing the prototype Model Y, gave immediate orders for Gregorie to proceed with the development of the design for the 1933 full-size Ford.... In any event, the basic layout of the Y—especially the restyled Y which appeared in summer of 1932—was expanded by Gregorie into the 40. In recent years, upon first seeing the Y and its successors, Americans automatically presumed that it was a shrinking of the contemporary big American Ford models. At the beginning, at least, the precise opposite was true, and the British Ford led the way for American styling."

Though cars were becoming more streamlined on the drawing boards, the technology did not exist to produce them in mass quantities. Thus, the design Edsel approved for 1933 wasn't the teardrop shape it might have been. But it *was* more graceful, with the sort of racy, low-slung lines characteristic of the early- and mid-Thirties, the remarkable era that produced some of America's all-time classic automobiles.

Thanks to a strike at Briggs, plus the problems associated with getting out a second new design in less than a year, Ford's 1933 Model 40 line didn't bow publicly until February 9, two to three months behind the rest of the industry. But it was beautifully executed, as one journalist summarized: "With much roomier bodies, [this year's Ford V-8 has an] entirely new and decidedly attractive appearance.... Its beauty is enhanced by the rakish angle of the radiator grille which coincides with those of the wind-shield, hood, and door lines. Fenders are of modern design, with wide skirts, and their construction eliminates the need for the old splash aprons below the radiator and above the running boards. Wire-spoke wheels have been reduced to 17-inch in [diameter], and [full-width] bumpers front and rear are styled with a painted horizontal stripe and a slight dip in the center." Not mentioned here was Ford's new 112-inch wheelbase. Not only was it the longest in Ford's history, but for the first time it was longer than what

Chevrolet or Plymouth had to offer (by two and four inches, respectively). Also not mentioned was the fact that all doors on all body styles, save the rear doors on the phaeton, were now rear-hinged to open from the front—"suicide doors," as they would come to be called.

With most of its engine block problems ironed out by now, the V-8 was treated to several changes that boosted horsepower by 10 up to 75. Improvements included aluminum cylinder heads, higher compression (boosted from 5.5 to 6.3:1), and improved cooling and ignition. More surprising was a stiffer new X-type frame, still with transverse springing. Aided by axles stabilized with radius rods, it afforded great flexibility over rough roads and an exceptionally soft ride. And for better off-the-line performance, a 4.44:1 rear axle ratio was added as an option to the standard 4.11:1 gearing.

In answer to lingering doubts about the V-8's gas mileage, Ford undertook a number of economy runs in 1933. Driv-

Like it or not, competition forced to Ford to adopt the annual model change in the early Thirties. Thus, the 1933 Ford had an all-new look. The four was still available, but seldom ordered. The V-8, now Model 40, gained 10 horsepower, to 75. Opposite page: As in previous years, the Tudor was the best seller in the line—output rose to 426,389 units. The DeLuxe (top and center) listed at $550, and sported cowl lamps and dual horns. The $500 standard, such as the one on the economy run (bottom), did without them. This page: Other 1933 Fords: the $640 station wagon (top left), $610 DeLuxe Fordor (top right), and the $510 DeLuxe roadster.

ing cars under tough and varied conditions, from the floor of the Mojave Desert to the top of the Catskill Mountains, Ford V-8s averaged from 18.3 to 22.5 miles per gallon. These "real world" results were intended to convince potential buyers that they could do as well in normal, everyday driving.

Buyers who weren't impressed could still opt for less costly four-cylinder versions of all body styles. Commonly referred to as the "Model C," these were officially designated Model 46 and cost about $50 less than their V-8 counterparts. As in 1932, they were easily distinguished by their lack of V-8 emblems on hubcaps and grille. Across-the-line prices ranged from $425 for the Standard-trim four-cylinder roadster to $610 for the V-8 DeLuxe Fordor sedan, with most models selling for around $500-$550. The wood-body wagon, still technically part of the truck line, now listed at $640.

BB continued to denote Ford's 1½-ton truck chassis in 1933. The V-8 was now genuinely available throughout the line, and both it and the four-cylinder engine shared the mechanical improvements accorded the passenger-car versions. The commercials also received the new car styling ahead of the firewall. Special-purpose body choices were again reduced, reflecting the need to cut costs in the face of a shrinking truck market. Otherwise, both offerings and prices were much as before.

Though Ford's 1933 passenger cars were brilliant, they never achieved the success they deserved, thanks to their late introduction and lack of any real price advantage or publicity buildup. Together with Ford's long-standing policy that prohibited his dealers—now 9000 strong—from using high-pressure sales tactics like most rivals, these factors enabled high-rolling Chevy to lead the low-price field by another commanding margin—and for Plymouth to strengthen its hold on third place. Though Ford's calendar-year car output ended some 48,000 units ahead of 1932, output for the 12 months of 334,969 units was still way behind Chevy's model year production of just over 486,000. Plymouth, meanwhile, had surged to just under 300,000 units for the model year on the strength of its new styling and L-head six.

The Model 40s took to the road amidst signs that the V-8 was catching on at last, especially among the nation's leadfoots. Dirt-track and speedboat racers were among the first to discover that with only a few simple modifications a Ford V-8 could outperform most everything else its size and weight. In fact, its success on amateur and professional racing circuits from the Detroit River to Pikes Peak would set off a flathead speed craze that continues to this day.

Stock-car drivers, in particular, had found that by stripping the running boards, fenders, and top from a regular V-8 roadster and making a few chassis adjustments they could beat just about anything on the dirt tracks. At the 1933 running of the nationally famous Elgin (Illinois) Road Race in August, stunned onlookers watched as seven stripped Fords took the first seven places against a highly touted pack of Chevrolets, Plymouths, and Dodges. The winner, in a '33 roadster, was 1932 Indy 500 champion Fred Frame, who led the field over the tricky 8.5-mile course for 203 miles at an average of 88.22 mph.

This victory proved a tremendous tonic for Ford sales. Two months later, Henry invited his suppliers to Detroit for a special Exposition of Progress where Frame's car was the featured attraction. Encouraged by this happier turn of events, he began stepping up advertising and promotion while directing Model 40 refinements for the coming year. Equally happy for Ford was the formal opening June 12 of his Greenfield Village historical park, a tribute to an America that Henry, perhaps more than any other single individual, had changed forever.

On the political front, the Germans received a new Chancellor, Adolph Hitler, on January 30, 1933. Americans, meanwhile, had already voted their hopes for economic recovery by electing a new president. Soon after his inauguration on March 4, Franklin Delano Roosevelt unveiled a sweeping series of measures aimed at quieting public concern and giving the country a "New Deal." Among the first of what would create a potful of new "alphabet soup" agencies was the National Industrial Recovery Act, passed by Congress on June 16, Ford Motor Company's 30th anniversary. Included in its provisions was a requirement that participating businesses allow workers to unionize, something the paternalistic Henry stubbornly opposed as unnecessary and, in his case, unwanted. He naturally opposed the NRA. The agency's "Blue Eagle" compliance symbol, he said in July, was really a "Roosevelt Buzzard."

Wall Street seemed unimpressed as well. Perhaps reflecting investor skepticism that even a new President couldn't pull the country up by its bootstraps, the Dow Jones average, having crept up a bit from its rock-bottom level of October 1932, lost nearly eight percent of its total value on July 21 this year, still the ninth largest loss on record.

Henry must have thought he could do what Roosevelt couldn't, for on August 10 he opened the new Manufacturers National Bank in Detroit. His evident reason was that people would need to have more confidence in their now-shaky financial institutions before they'd start buying cars again, or anything else for that matter. Of course, that was precisely the President's logic—hence his declared "bank holiday" early in the year—but Henry was surely loathe to admit that he'd follow Roosevelt's path. Now 70 years old, America's premier motor magnate was making a sharp turn toward political and fiscal conservatism, and his increasing crustiness would impede Ford Motor Company's own recovery as the Thirties wore slowly on.

With V-8 power, it's hardly surprising that Fords went racing, even though not under official Ford sanction. Still, the V-8s, running with stripped bodies, were quite successful. This photo is believed to have been snapped at the famed Elgin, Illinois, race track.

1 9 3 4

On December 6, 1933, one day after the end of Prohibition, Henry and Edsel hosted reporters at the most publicized event of its type since the onset of the Depression: a Dearborn preview of the nicely updated 1934 Fords, Series 40A. Held a month earlier than other automakers' press shows, it was praised as much for the cars as for being the first time Henry served tobacco and alcohol at a company function. And as the beer and cigarettes were passed around, the motor scribes seemed enthusiastic indeed.

This event was also notable in that it marked the first time that Ford had made a normal December new model introduction since 1929. The late 1932 and '33 introductions, in particular, had hurt sales, and Ford was apparently determined to resume a more timely model introduction schedule.

The reviews that soon followed the preview were flattering. Said *Automotive Industries*: "Changes in the appearance of the attractive car include new hood, radiator and grille lines, a new instrument panel, and luxurious new upholstery treatment. The curve in the grille has been eliminated, and there is a new ornament surrounding the radiator cap. Hubcaps and the spare tire-lock cover are also new, as is the V-8 insignia on the grille. The fashionable bodies have the new 'clear vision' ventilating system similar to that in the new Lincoln cars." The last referred to a redesigned window-winding mechanism that first moved the

The Ford line received a mild facelift for 1934, the most obvious changes being a revised grille with a thicker surround and a new hood. Inside, one sat on richer upholstery while facing a new instrument panel. A popular option this year was the graceful greyhound hood ornament. The DeLuxe five-window rumble-seat coupe (top), which cost $570 and weighed 2450 pounds, found 26,879 buyers. Meanwhile, the DeLuxe three-window coupe (center), which sold for the same price, garnered almost the same number of orders: 26,348. The DeLuxe roadster (bottom left) listed at $525. Ford often emphasized the economy of the V-8 in its advertising (bottom right).

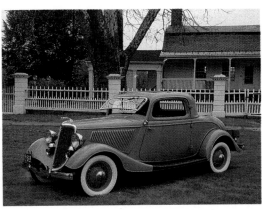

front door glass slightly rearwards to a "vent" position before lowering it vertically. A response to GM's "No-Draft" ventilation system, it required a design change to the door window frame; the '34 closed bodies therefore differed slightly from those of the previous year. Other little noticed changes were the straightening of the hood side vents, shallower headlight shells, and two (rather than one) latches on each side of the hood. DeLuxe models received three (rather than two) body pin stripes this year, plus dual taillights, cowl lights, and handsome twin exterior horns.

The most obvious interior change was the deletion of the engine-turned instrument panel insert in favor of a plain painted dash of similar layout. New accessories for 1933 had included either a glove compartment-type or ashtray-mounted radio, dual wipers, and heater. To these were now added a beautifully cast radiator cap in the image of a running greyhound, much like Lincoln's mascot. And for the first time in Ford history, body-color fenders were standard, though black fenders were still available at no charge. The paint this year was enamel, replacing lacquer, which had required buffing and hand polishing.

On the mechanical side, the V-8's Detroit Lubricator carburetor was replaced by a better-engineered Stromberg dual-downdraft unit on a new double-deck, two-runner intake manifold. It not only boosted horsepower to 85, a gain of 10 bhp, but made for a smoother-running V-8. So did a new fully counterbalanced cast-alloy steel crankshaft, an industry first. Other engine changes com-

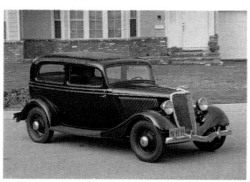

prised a new water pump, water-line thermostat, open-skirt pistons, and minor fit and wear improvements to existing hardware. Chassis alterations ran to a revised steering ratio, springs, and shock absorbers, plus the availability of a new "economy" 3.54:1 rear axle ratio for gas-conscious buyers.

But one item was missing from the '34 Fords: a four-cylinder engine. With growing public acceptance and the worst of its reliability problems long since solved, the versatile 221-cubic-inch flathead V-8 was now Ford's mainstay en-

gine—and would be through 1942—though not its *sole* powerplant.

With all the good press and the company's renewed interest in promotion, sales began taking off once people had a chance to drive the '34s. And drive them they did, to the first 10 places in the Gilmore Cup Race on February 24. No wonder the V-8's earliest champions were police officials who used their explosive speed to chase crooks—and the crooks who stole new Fords to outrun them. Infamous bank robber Clyde Barrow was one unabashed admirer who took time

from his criminal pursuits to praise V-8 virtues by writing to a surprised Henry Ford. Postmarked Tulsa, Oklahoma, and dated April 10, 1934, his letter read:

Dear Sir:

While I still have got breath in my lungs I will tell you what a dandy car you make. I have drove [sic] Fords exclusively when I could get away with one. For sustained speed and freedom from trouble the Ford has got ever [sic] other car skinned, and even if my business hasn't [sic] been strictly legal it don't hurt enything [sic] to tell you what a fine car you got in the Ford V-8.

Yours truly,
Clyde Champion Barrow

As fate would have it, Clyde and his wife Bonnie would meet their maker in a 1934 Ford sedan, gunned down in a sheriff's ambush.

May 26 saw the opening of Ford's exhibit at the Century of Progress exposition in Chicago. The firm's most ambitious undertaking of this kind, it sprawled over an 11-acre landscaped site fronting Lake Michigan and was dominated by a magnificent gear-shaped building, the Rotunda. Along the lake shore ran a .4-mile "Roads of the World" where visitors could ride over short reproduction stretches of historic thoroughfares from around the globe. The Rotunda and an adjoining industrial wing housed a dazzling display of Ford's latest automaking technology, plus supplier exhibits, live demonstrations of parts manufacturing, and displays of antique models as well as the newest Ford cars and trucks. As a centerpiece, three fully equipped V-8 Victorias were hung as on a chandelier from one 17-inch-diameter wheel, thus demonstrating the strength of its welded steel spokes.

It was Ford's greatest show ever, and few would forget the sights and sounds, the free souvenirs, and the beauty of the cars. The 1934 models seemed to have just the right blend of ingredients, something that would assure their place in the hearts of car fans everywhere as among the classiest Fords of all time.

With Franklin Roosevelt now firmly in charge at the White House, it began to seem as if "happy days" really might be here again—or if not, at least just around the corner. After hitting rock bottom in 1932-33, most automakers began to see a slight recovery this year. Ford was no exception despite eliminating its cheap four-bangers and posting slightly higher prices on V-8 models. Chevrolet and Plymouth had posted larger increases, however, which left Ford with about a $60 price advantage over the competition. Calendar-year car output jumped fully two-thirds, from about 335,000 units to nearly 564,000. Ford also won

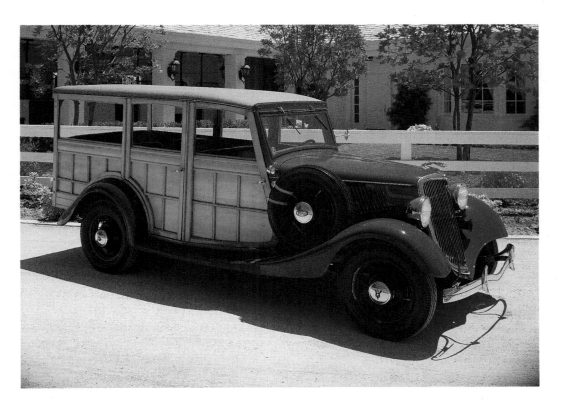

Opposite page: More '34 Fords: two trucks, the $470 pickup and a fire truck (top row); $520 standard Tudor (middle row); $615 DeLuxe Fordor (bottom). The closed-cab pickup was so dominant by 1934 that only 347 open-cabs were built. The Tudor sedan continued to dominate the popularity chart as 246,566 were built for the model year, 124,870 of them standards. That compared to 124,662 Fordors, of which 102,268 were DeLuxes. This page: The $660 station wagon was still very much a specialty model—only 2905 were built.

the model year production race with Chevrolet, besting its archrival by about 12,000 cars. Topping off Ford's recovery was production of its one-millionth V-8 car in June, barely 18 months after the first, a remarkable achievement all things considered.

Even more heartening, perhaps, was the happy circumstance that Ford moved back into the black in 1934, showing a profit of $3.8 million. Author Paul R. Woudenberg noted that "It was about time—losses from 1931 to 1933 had totaled $120,000,000—a figure which would have demolished all but a handful of American companies. The way Mr. Ford's mind worked, it was only a bookkeeping problem." The rosier financial situation also allowed Ford to restore the $5 day at his factories. Wages had plummeted during the Depression, of course, but this raise was probably intended as much to calm labor unrest as it was to improve workers' living standards.

Ford didn't fare as well in truck sales this year. The firm completed just under 192,000 U.S. units (plus another 12,300 in Canada), but was nipped by Chevy and pressed hard from below by Dodge and International-Harvester, all of which had newer models. Dearborn's offerings were again updated along passenger-car lines. Four-cylinder power was phased out during the year, and body choices were further thinned as Ford continued to focus more on the really popular types.

For the first time, however, the commercial line began diverging from

Ford cars mechanically. A new full-floating truck-type rear axle was adopted for the senior 131- and 157-inch chassis. There was also a separate truck V-8 with new low-compression heavy-duty cylinder heads that not only improved low-speed lugging power but permitted using gasolines with a wider range of octane ratings, both important considerations for commercial operators. The old-fashioned open cab was in its final year, attracting but 347 orders. Pointing the way to the future was a new Closed Cab Front End, the basic BB chassis supplied with cowl, windshield, and front sheetmetal for ready mounting of special-purpose "vocational" bodies or, for use as a semi-trailer tractor, a simple two-passenger cab.

As before, the everyday pickup was Ford's best individual seller. At $470, it was one of the firm's cheapest products this year, and all the '34s gained appeal by having the more reliable V-8 as standard equipment, the four-pot engine having been dropped for the little hauler.

The Tudor-based Sedan Delivery also shared the 112-inch passenger-car chassis, but its U.S. production ended at 9021 units, of which just 281 had the old four-cylinder engine. The woody wagon benefited from the same longer wheelbase in that it could now carry nine passengers, one more than before. But sales amounted to only 2905, all but 83 V-8-equipped. Such rarity combined with pleasing period design explains why Ford "commercial cars" of this era have long been sought-after collector's items.

1 9 3 5

A dwindling number of automakers fought for a dwindling number of sales in the mid-Thirties, so cars had to be updated each year if a company hoped to survive what had become the fiercest competition ever. Ford was no exception, and had little choice in any case. As General Motors had proven—mainly at Dearborn's expense—the annual model change was an essential sales tool, one long since widely accepted in the industry. Ford had inaugurated a two-year design cycle in 1933 that would be maintained for the rest of this decade. Accordingly, its 1935 offerings received a heavily revised chassis and fresh styling—enough to justify a new Model 48 series designation.

"Greater Beauty, Greater Comfort, and Greater Safety" was the theme. Styling was more rounded, with longer and wider bodies, narrow radiator, more steeply raked windshield, higher-crowned and more deeply skirted fenders, and smaller, 16-inch-diameter wheels. Inside was a handsomely restyled dashboard. All models reverted to front-hinged doors, a definite safety plus, though back portals on four-door styles remained the "suicide" type.

A significant body change not strictly related to styling was the arrival of built-in trunks for Tudor and Fordor sedans. The '34 Victoria had been a step in this direction, though its integral trunk didn't have much space and was extremely awkward to reach because its bottom-hinged lid didn't tilt open very far. This year's new "bustle" trunk was more useful (if less pretty). Even better, it added a mere $20 to the cost of the regular fastback sedans. The "trunkback" style, as it was first called, would prove enormously popular, not just at Ford but throughout the industry.

The 1935s would mark the end of several longstanding Ford features: standard wire-spoke wheels, external horns, and outside radiator cap. The parking lamps, now housed within the headlights were one of the items moved inside. And there was a first in 1935 as Ford began manufacturing its own sub-assemblies for station wagon bodies. Previously, the Mingel Company of Kentucky had supplied the wood panelling, with Briggs or Murray in Detroit handling assembly. Hereafter, wagon panels would be fabricated in a plant at Iron Mountain in Michigan's Upper Peninsula, an ideal location because Ford owned nearby hardwood forest acreage that minimized transportation costs. Final assembly took place at the company's own branch assembly plants.

Ford's 1935 model choices were broadly the same as before, but there was a smart newcomer in a reborn convertible sedan, the year's most expensive offering at $750. Unlike its Model A predecessor, it had four doors instead of two, removable rather than fixed centerposts, and no permanent side window frames. Still around were the glamorous DeLuxe phaeton at $580, the rumble-seat convertible cabriolet at $625, and the youthful DeLuxe roadster at $550. Interestingly, both the cheapest and the priciest DeLuxe models were soft tops. Prices across the entire line now ranged from $495 for the Standard two-seat five-window coupe to $670 for the DeLuxe woody wagon.

In all, the '35 was a sleeker and more

Ford trotted out all-new styling for 1935. Two of the most interesting models were the $580 DeLuxe phaeton, which required side curtains in bad weather, and the new $750 convertible sedan, which had wind-up windows. Output was 6073 and 4234, respectively.

obviously streamlined Ford, although George H. Dammann in the *Illustrated History of Ford* described it as looking "heavier, plumper, and more solid." But to the ultimate benefit of Dearborn sales, it wasn't nearly so radical as the Chrysler/ DeSoto Airflow, launched the previous year and destined to remain a marketing disaster.

However, Ford did follow the Airflow in one key respect by putting rear as well as front passengers firmly within the wheelbase to deliver a smoother overall ride on the same 112-inch span. Advertised as "Center-Poise Ride," it was achieved by the same means Chrysler had used—namely, shoving the engine/transmission assembly forward, in Ford's case a full 8.5 inches, thus necessitating the restyled bodyshells.

Naturally, it also changed front/rear weight distribution, which prompted a heftier frame that utilized more box sections and heavier bracing. The chassis also boasted a beefier rear axle, better "self-centering" mechanical brakes, nicer steering via a new transversely mounted linkage, and slightly wider front and rear track dimensions.

Springing, however, was still handled by single semi-elliptic leafs mounted transversely at each end, an archaic arrangement that would persist at Dear-

born for the next 13 years. But in spite of Henry Ford's insistence on "buggy springs," engineer Laurence Sheldrick was able to move the front spring forward of the front axle, much as the rear spring of the '32 Ford had been shoved back, resulting in a "springbase" of 123.1 inches, more than 11 inches longer than the wheelbase. That, and the 7.5-inch-wider front spring and softer spring rates front and rear made the Ford competitive ride-wise. Paul R. Woudenberg commented in *Ford in the Thirties* that "The new car was very much softer on the road, and Mr. Ford's transverse springs once again seemed to have caught up with the new IFS [Independent Front Suspension] technology. This technology, especially in the Chevrolet, was faulty in the beginning and the Dubonnet suspensions were not indestructible, lacking the support and geometry of the wishbone system."

The use of mechanical brakes was another area in which Ford was behind the times, but old Henry refused to believe that *any* of his ideas were outdated. The new self-centering brake shoes were coupled with floating wedges, and while the brake contact area remained at 186 square inches, the cooling ribs were increased 40 percent to improve efficiency. Woudenberg noted that "The brakes were good, but two problems were steadily reducing effectiveness. The first was weight....by 1935 sedan weight had increased from 2512 [pounds in 1932] to 2849 pounds. The second problem was speed. The new Model 48 was the fastest Ford yet, and the brakes were likely to have more work to do, especially since highway conditions were improving steadily allowing higher speeds.... For one more year, Ford could offer mechanical brakes without undue competitive problems because the GM hydraulic changeover in their various makes was not complete." Chevy converted to hydraulics in 1936; Plymouth had had them all along, since 1928.

Mechanically, Ford's 221-cubic-inch flathead V-8 remained at its nominal 85 bhp, as it would through 1940, but featured a reprofiled camshaft, improved crankcase ventilation, a new cast alloy crankshaft, and copper-lead bearings. Rounding out drivetrain modifications were a new "easy-action" centrifugal clutch, revised gearlever and propshaft, and roller-pinion gear bearings.

According to Woudenberg, this year's styling was largely the work of Phil Wright at bodymaker Briggs Manufacturing Company. "There were two styling sections at [Briggs]," he commented, "one headed by John Tjaarda being charged with experimental car-design exercises, while the [second] group did speculative designs for Briggs' regular customers, notably Ford and Plymouth. Phil Wright reportedly did the renderings for the 1935 Ford at his home, then showed them to his boss, Ralph

Roberts, who in turn showed them to Ford management including Edsel Ford. Ford officials were so pleased that the order went out to go right to a full-scale mockup of wood, rather than through the customary 1/24th clay scale models. Famed stylist Bob Koto, a compatriot of Wright...was later assigned to facelift the '35s into the following year's 1936 Model 68."

All this talk of styling may seem strange for the company that once built the seemingly changeless Model T. But, as noted, style—high style, done with taste—had become a key sales factor in the Depression market. More importantly, Edsel Ford wanted it, perhaps because design was one of the few areas where he wasn't much interfered with by his father. Further proof of that, as well as the growing importance of styling to Ford's fortunes, came this year when Edsel asked Eugene T. "Bob" Gregorie, a young draftsman he'd hired back in 1932, to head up Dearborn's first, formal in-house design group. Initially comprising only three or four, it would grow to a staff of 20 by 1938 as Ford followed the lead of Harley Earl's pioneering Art & Colour Section at General Motors (founded in the late Twenties).

Woudenberg observed that by the end of the 1935 selling season, "Ford had decisively regained industry leadership in sales with 826,519 [units] compared to Chevrolet's 656,698 and Plymouth's 382,925." Calendar-year production figures are a bit different but tell the same story. Having surrendered sales supremacy to Chevrolet in the harried transition to the V-8, Ford was back on top for '35:

	Ford	Chevrolet	Plymouth
1932	287,285	306,716	121,468
1933	334,969	481,134	255,564
1934	563,921	620,726	351,113
1935	942,439	793,437	442,281

While good styling surely played a part in this winning performance, so did Ford's redesigned chassis. The result for all passengers was what Ford termed the "Front Seat Ride," plus extra legroom. Further enhancing comfort, back seats were widened by 1.5 inches, the fronts by 4 to 5.5 inches depending on model.

The new chassis not only made the '35 Fords smoother-riding but nicer to drive. Drivers could appreciate the greatly reduced effort of the newly revised clutch, and V-8 performance was as impressive as ever, particularly for the price. Said Britain's *Autocar*: "Anyone who has not had previous experience [with this type car would] be astounded by the ease of the running at 40 to 50 mph...and by the way in which the speedometer literally shoots across the dial."

Still, braking remained a weak point. Despite claims of offering "The Safety of Steel from Pedal to Wheel," Ford's mechanical binders just couldn't be as effective as Plymouth's hydraulics. And although they were probably no worse than Chevy's mechanical setup, they still tended to groan, shudder, and pull to one side. As for ride quality, Ford's solid front axle just couldn't cope with road conditions as well as rivals' independent front suspensions, improvements notwithstanding. Obviously, these deficits hardly hurt sales. But as Josiah Work commented in the December 1989 issue of *Special Interest Autos*, the '35 Ford sold "not because but in spite of its outmoded suspension and brakes. Its appeal [came from] performance (meaning speed), looks and price—probably in that order."

The '35 Fords were introduced at the prestigious New York Auto Show in late December 1934. It had been 25 years since Ford had exhibited at that annual affair, and the company went all out to garner attention. Besides a bevy of sparkling cars, it had special "motion" exhibits on all three levels of the hall. Drawing throngs of admirers, they included a motorized "exploded" V-8 engine and chassis, and an engine assembly race against the clock by two workers from the big Rouge plant.

Ford also starred at Indianapolis this year, one of the sporty new convertible sedans acting as Pace Car for the annual 500-mile racing classic. But the big event was the California-Pacific International Exposition in San Diego, where the company put on a huge show in a specially erected building.

Other corporate highlights included production of the two-millionth Ford V-8 engine (fittingly on June 16, the firm's 33rd anniversary), the opening of Ford's first test track (a 2.5-mile concrete road near the Dearborn engineering lab), the formation of a soybean plastics plant at the Rouge (reflecting Henry's longtime interest in finding new applications for

farm products, which in this case would help make soybeans America's number-two cash crop), and relocation of the firm's 1933-34 World's Fair Rotunda building from Chicago to Dearborn, where it would remain part of Ford's corporate landscape until destroyed by fire in 1962. Equally significant for Henry, the Supreme Court declared the National Industrial Recovery Act unconstitutional, thus eliminating a source of pressure to allow his workers to unionize. History does not record whether the motor mogul danced another jig, but the news undoubtedly made him happy.

With a commercial fleet that again benefitted from most of the changes applied to its passenger cars, Ford reclaimed industry leadership in truck sales for 1935, ousting Chevrolet for the first time in three years and increasing its lead over Dodge. The line divided into the half-ton Model 50 station wagon, delivery car, sedan delivery, and pickup, plus the 1½-ton Model 51 pickup, panels, platforms, and driveaway chassis, the last available with the same basic array of factory bodies. Missing from the catalog were the two long-wheelbase panel trucks as well as four-cylinder power and the outmoded open cab.

The changed series designations reflected the newly revised chassis and front-end styling as well as more modern-looking cabs and aft bodywork. Steel was used more extensively on Model 51s, the workhorse pickup now featuring all-steel construction for the first time (no more wooden cargo-box sub-floor). With drivetrains repositioned forward, all models retained the same-length cargo floors despite reduced front overhangs that trimmed overall exterior length by several inches.

As for specific offerings, this year's 112-inch-wheelbase "driveaway" chassis without cab listed at $360, the 131-inch version for $500. The pickup, now with more integrated styling, sold for $480; a similarly revised panel delivery cost

One 1935 Ford ad (above) pointed out that, according to a national fleet owner, the V-8 was 12- and 31-percent cheaper to run than the Model A and T. The DeLuxe five-window coupe (below) listed at $585 with rumble seat. The V-8 was still rated at 85 bhp.

$565. On both, another $15 bought DeLuxe equipment that included full interior trim, twin horns, silver-finish grille, and chrome rearview mirror and single windshield wiper (vacuum-operated like the passenger cars' two). Tagged at $585, the sedan delivery could be equipped with bumpers and spare tire for $28, front passenger seat for $10, and a new roll-down window for its side-hinged rear cargo door at $2.

As ever, outside suppliers turned out numerous purpose-built vocational bodies for both the 131- and 157-inch Ford chassis, including buses, dumpers, tankers, service/wrecker trucks, and stakesides. Many of these were equipped with dual rear wheels, a factory option since the early Thirties.

1 9 3 6

Continuing its two-year design cycle, Ford issued a modestly facelifted 1936 lineup in mid-October 1935. Detailed to enhance the V-8 engine's growing reputation for performance, the new Model 68s sported a number of minor styling changes that, taken together, imparted a smart, graceful new look. This was accomplished via new fenders, hood, and grille. Since contemporary industry design trends dictated hiding some previously exposed components, horns were now concealed behind little round "catwalk" grilles in the front fender aprons. The hood grew longer and more pointed, the grille more prominently vee'd to match, giving the car a less stubby look from the side view. To most eyes, the styling changes were a definite improvement, and to this day the '36 is a favorite among Ford fans and collectors.

A major development involved the wheels, which were changed from Ford's patented welded wire-spoke units to modern drop-center steel rims with larger hubcaps. The new wheels, now five pounds lighter, reduced unsprung weight by 20 pounds, which had the same effect in improving ride quality as if the body had been made 200 pounds heavier. They also helped give the '36 Ford a more substantial look.

Ford's 1936 lineup consisted of 21 models, and was the first to list two distinct series. This was accomplished by making the cars with the optional DeLuxe-trim package a separate model group. The base models were still prosaically called Standard. As had been the case since the first Model A, the main differences on the DeLuxe were fancier cabin appointments and extra exterior chrome.

This year's Standards comprised five-window coupes with trunk or rumble seat, four-door woody wagon, and Tudor and Fordor sedans in fastback and trunkback form. Prices ranged from $510 for the trunked coupe to $670 for the wagon. The DeLuxe group included all but the last, plus a brace of three-window coupes and no fewer than four different open styles, with prices starting at $560. Arriving in March was a new five-passenger DeLuxe Convertible Club Cabriolet, with a longer top to cover its back seat. The regular two-place DeLuxe cabriolet and roadster were still around for those who preferred rumble seats ($25 extra), though fewer people did by this time. Prices were $675, $625, and $560, respectively. Topping the line at $780 was a new Convertible Touring Sedan with trunk. Models with the integral trunk were referred to as Touring Sedans and cost $25 extra. The trunk was a popular option despite the high, awkward decklid, and its growing presence throughout the industry prompted cancellation of the stylish but less practical Victoria.

Though not earthshaking, this year's engineering alterations were important in the neck-and-neck sales battle with Chevrolet, where every little talking point counted. Among them were an extra 3.5 inches of rear elbow room, created by recessing the interior side trim, and new pivoting rear quarter windows for Fordors. Steering effort was reduced by 13 percent for 1936 via a 17:1 steering ratio and a longer spindle arm, but this meant more turns of the wheel lock-to-lock. To alleviate the overheating problems that still dogged the V-8, radiator cooling area was increased a bit and cooling system capacity returned to 22 quarts. Other refinements included helical-cut gears for low and reverse (actually begun in mid-1935) and shorter shift throws because of a higher shifter tower.

As usual, most of the mechanical and style changes accorded Ford passenger cars were found in this year's truck line, but there were no significant differences otherwise. Showing the continuing close relationship, half-ton commercials now rode the exact same chassis as passenger models, so they, too, were now Model 68s. Light-duty Model 51 offerings were retagged Model 67. These and the "non-car" Model 68s looked just like their 1935 counterparts save exterior details changed mainly for the sake of identification. Prices stayed about the same, as did factory-built body choices.

The pace of razzle-dazzle promotion quickened as Ford put on big shows this year at the Texas Centennial in Dallas, at the Atlantic City Boardwalk, and at the Great Lakes Exposition in Cleveland.

The '36 Ford DeLuxe Tudor trunkback sedan (above) sold for $590; the skirts were aftermarket items. The cabriolet (bottom left) cost $625. Brewster, a New York coachbuilder, built specially bodied Fords.

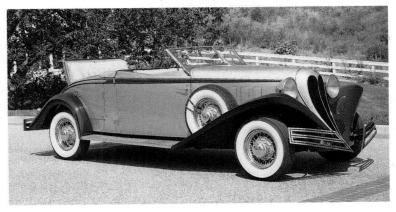

Those attending saw parades in which a float bearing a new roadster proclaimed Ford's ride to be like a "Car in the Clouds." Another crowd-pleaser was the "Human Ford," a '36 roadster that appeared on stage to answer audience questions in a "mystical" voice (no doubt supplied by a local ventriloquist).

Ford logged two production milestones in close succession during 1935-36. Its two-millionth V-8 car had rolled off the line in June 1935. Less than 12 months later, in May of this year, the three-millionth was built. The V-8, it appeared, was here to stay.

Though the country was now only inching its way out of the Depression—and slowly at that—Ford was rolling right along, surely a tribute to the inherent "rightness" of its 1936 model cars. In fact, Ford again bested Chevy in model-year production, building some 820,000 cars against 548,000 for its GM rival. Chevy, however, won the calendar-year race with 975,000 units to Ford's still substantial total of some 764,000. Ford also bowed to Chevy in truck sales, mainly because its rival offered new-design cabs as well as hydraulic brakes and full-floating rear axles on some models.

Significant for future gift-giving was the establishment this year of the Ford Foundation by Edsel Ford and wife Eleanor. Partly a response to the Depression, it had the avowed purpose of disbursing some of the Ford family's considerable largesse to provide "a chance for people to help themselves." Its actual intent, however, seemed far different. For one thing, its first grant went to one of Papa Henry's favorite causes: The Edison Institute, the umbrella organization for both the Henry Ford Museum and Greenfield Village (which Henry had built with some $10.4 million of his own money). For another, 95 percent of Ford Motor Company stock was immediately transferred to the new Foundation, which made the tax-exempt entity controlled entirely by the Ford family look like nothing more than a tax dodge. This resulted in the creation of two classes of stock: non-voting "A" shares for the Foundation, and voting "B" stock, all in Ford family hands.

By the Fifties, however, the Ford Foundation would become one of the nation's largest and most influential philanthropic organizations, supporting all manner of scientific and artistic endeavors at the urging of Henry Ford II. It was HF II who would also overturn tradition by again making Ford a publicly held company, with shares openly traded on the stock market beginning in early 1956.

Nineteen thirty-six also saw the opening of Ford's Rotunda, newly relocated in Dearborn, as a visitor center. This year's biggest corporate development, however, was the Lincoln-Zephyr, the car that would save Ford's premium make from death by the Depression. Technically and historically, the Zephyr

For 1936, Ford built about 7500 sedan deliverys (top). They were basically the Tudor sedan with a longer roof, blanked out rear side windows, and a rear door. Rarer still, was the convertible sedan—only 5601 were built. It listed at $760, or $780 with trunk. More popular was the $570 DeLuxe three-window coupe, which listed at $595 with rumble seat. A total of 21,446 were built, including the standard models.

is a significant product, so a brief review is appropriate before we leave this year.

Introduced in November 1935, the Zephyr was Lincoln's reply to the Packard One Twenty and Cadillac's LaSalle, a medium-priced "junior edition" created to sell in high volume and thus keep its maker afloat until the luxury market recovered from "hard times." As the One Twenty did for Packard, the Zephyr boosted Lincoln's annual production from a few thousand units to tens of thousands, something the impressive but expensive V-12 K-Series could never hope to do.

The Zephyr's basic concept originated with the radical Sterkenberg, a largish sedan penned in 1933 by Dutch-born designer John Tjaarda (pronounced CHAR-dah) of Briggs Manufacturing Company. It major innovations were a teardrop-shape body built in unit with a sophisticated chassis featuring all-independent suspension and a rear-mounted engine. W.O. Briggs, one of the first industrialists to take Tjaarda's advanced ideas seriously, suggested he show his sketches and a scale model to Edsel Ford with the hope of winning a substantial

new production contract for Briggs. "Lincoln business had practically come to a standstill," Tjaarda wrote later. "Relations between Briggs and [Ford production chief] Charlie Sorensen were strained because Sorensen felt that Briggs paid more attention to their Chrysler business.... As far as Briggs was concerned, something had to be done, [so they] hired me away from GM [to work on] Ford in particular." It was soon after that Tjaarda met with Edsel.

Intrigued by the Sterkenberg, Ford's president instructed the engineer to devise a prototype with volume production in mind. Working in complete secrecy from both Ford and Briggs executives, Tjaarda came up with a full-size, Sterkenberg-based wood mockup on a 125-inch wheelbase. Shown the following year at Chicago's Century of Progress Exposition, it sported a louvered fastback roof with a small dorsal fin, weighed about 2500 pounds, and carried a Ford V-8 in its tail. Top speed was estimated at 110 mph—unheard of for an 85-bhp car at the time.

Ford itself then built a running, front-engine prototype in 1934. Tjaarda recalled that at least two more were built, though some sources say one was rear-engined. Regardless, public response was overwhelmingly favorable, which was enough for Edsel. However, only 50 percent of those who saw it expressed any interest in a rear engine, which was enough for Henry. And typically, the old man insisted on making it simpler and more conventional still, so the Zephyr emerged not only with the familiar front-engine/rear-drive format but with Ford's traditional transverse leaf springs and solid axles at each end, plus a three-speed manual transmission (instead of the automatic Tjaarda had envisioned)—and, worse yet, mechanical brakes.

Tjaarda's original snub-nose styling implied the compact Ford V-8, but Edsel wanted something more. The existing Lincoln V-12 was too large, so he decreed a new engine for reasons of "prestige" and superior smoothness. His father didn't object but, ever the frugal tycoon, dictated using as many V-8 components as possible. The job was assigned to veteran engineer Frank Johnson, but the resulting powerplant wasn't that great. An L-head unit with four main bearings, it employed the expected monobloc casting with an exhaust core between the cylinders—more a "12-cylinder V-8" than a purpose-designed twelve. Displacement was 267.3 cubic inches on bore and stroke of 2.75 × 3.75 inches. Rated horsepower was 110 at 3900 rpm, a rather high power peak for the day, but the torque curve was quite flat, with at least 180 pounds/feet on tap from 400 to 3500 rpm, which made for fine top-gear flexibility.

Though similar to the Sterkenbergs from the cowl back, the Zephyr was more attractive, thanks to a longer,

handsome new prow front grafted on by Ford designer Eugene T. "Bob" Gregorie, mainly to make room for the longer engine. Briggs built the unit body/chassis while Ford handled final assembly, adding drivetrain, front sheetmetal, upholstery, trim, and paint. Edsel told Tjaarda that Briggs might as well have done it all, since the Zephyr assembly line was only 40 feet long!

Tjaarda had mostly guessed at stress factors, crucial with unit construction, so the Zephyr was the first car subjected to aircraft-type stress analysis. It proved rock solid. Tjaarda later declared it "the strongest [yet] lightest car of its size ever built." Weighing about 3300 pounds at the curb, the Zephyr was 940 pounds lighter than a Chrysler/DeSoto Airflow, yet could sustain nearly twice the impact loads of conventional body-on-frame cars. It also proved aerodynamically efficient, though evidently not shaped with the aid of a wind tunnel like the Airflow. Again, Tjaarda had guessed right.

Arriving as a two- and four-door sedan, the Zephyr offered typical Lincoln quality in a roomy, smooth-riding, and more manageable package with up-to-the-minute style and down-to-earth prices ($1275/$1320). For a Lincoln, it sold like hotcakes, accounting for better than 80 percent of the make's total 1936 volume and lifting Lincoln from 22nd to 18th place on the industry production list, the first time Lincoln had ever cracked the top 20. The Zephyr was also the fastest Lincoln yet. Despite a mediocre power-to-weight ratio and a short 4.33:1 final drive, it could do up to 90 mph and 0-50 mph in 10.8 seconds while averaging 16-18 miles per gallon.

By providing timely sales salvation, and as the future sire of the grand and elegant 1940 Continental, the Zephyr makes 1936 a watershed year in Lincoln history. With its new Depression-fighter, Ford's finest proved that it not only deserved to survive, but could still pioneer, much as it had in the Leland days.

When convertible sedan production began for the '36 model year, it was built as a flatback. However, buyers were by now demanding luggage space, and many wanted the spare tire out of sight, so at mid-year the convertible sedan became a trunkback (top left). This one is painted in Light Fast Maroon. The Fordor sedan (top right) was Ford's second most popular 1936 body style. Buyers could choose from four models: standard and DeLuxe, with or without trunk. The DeLuxe trunkback sedan, seen here in Gray Vineyard Green, sold for $650, $25 more than the flatback. Unfortunately, the liftover height was very high, and the rear-mounted spare tire made loading and unloading very cumbersome. Compared to the standard, the '36 DeLuxe panel (below) featured twin chrome horns, aluminum-finish grille, body-color wheels, and more body insulation.

1 9 3 7

Clean, fresh styling and several new features made this a vintage Ford year. Billed by company publicists as the most stunning Ford yet, the '37 marked the start of another two-year design cycle—and a big departure from past design practice.

The '37 was more evidence of Ford's new interest in streamlining, pioneered with the '36 Lincoln-Zephyr. Almond-shaped headlamps were firmly integrated in the "catwalk" areas flanking the grille, which was prominently vee'd, stretched, and sloped back. The hood was pointed to match, and a new two-piece vee'd windshield echoed the entire ensemble. Slim louvers aping the grille's fine horizontal bars adorned the sides of the hood, which was now hinged at the rear to open "alligator" fashion, as on the Zephyr. Fenders and rear ends were more curvaceous, and adding to that were newly available rear fender skirts. Hot rodders then, as now, loved them.

It added up to one of the decade's handsomest cars. Even President Roosevelt bought a '37 convertible sedan for use at his Warm Springs, Georgia, retreat. In a year of questionable styling for the industry as a whole, Ford was a standout—proof that streamlining didn't have to mean ugly. It might have been even lovelier had Henry Ford not personally ordered a four-inch reduction in overall length from the original prototype, most of it ahead of the cowl. The trunkless "flatback" sedans probably suffered most from the resulting stubby look. Paul R. Woudenberg noted in *Ford in the Thirties* that "Bob Gregorie is generally credited with the 1937 Ford design, but he later denied it, perhaps due to the unfortunately small following that the '37s have among Ford buffs."

Still, styling was one of Ford's few strong points by this time. Old Henry, the rural inventor who'd brought the automobile to the masses in his prime, was now a hardened man in his mid-70s. Though famed as an industrialist of stupendous achievement and beneficence, he was equally a mean and curmudgeonly capitalist who once declared that the Depression might be "good for the country," particularly if it taught people to be more frugal and industrious. Though son Edsel had been president since 1919, Henry still ruled Ford Motor Company with an iron hand, stifling new product developments with his stagnant attitudes and fighting Edsel's ideas most every step of the way.

Henry was also still adamant about refusing to let his workers unionize, and his right-hand man, Harry Bennett, em-

ployed a sort of private army to ensure they never would. By one estimate, Bennett by now commanded 800 full-time "troops" and had 8000-9000 regular employees as part-time "spies." Yet the vast majority of Ford workers had ample reason to seek shelter beneath the United Auto Workers banner. With sales difficult in the depressed market, production boss Charlie Sorensen was pushing workers harder than ever, speeding up assembly lines to a physically punishing pace when needed and forcing some workers to do more than one job at a time.

This worsening labor-management situation came to a head on May 26, 1937 with the infamous "Battle of the Overpass." Four UAW organizers, including Richard T. Frankenstein and Walter Reuther, set out to distribute union handbills on an elevated pedestrian walk near Gate 4 of the Rouge factory. Reporters and photographers were on hand to cover what was supposed to be a peaceful, routine bit of recruiting. Then, seemingly out of nowhere, Bennett's "Service Department" thugs rushed in and administered a bloody beating to Reuther and Frankenstein, seemingly oblivious to the fact that their actions were being recorded. The incident was naturally page-one news across the country, and it only further tarnished Henry's waning public image. Equally damaging was the subsequent hearing by the National Labor Re-

lations Board that found the company guilty of criminal charges brought by the UAW. Henry appealed the Board's decision all the way to the Supreme Court, but the verdict handed down in February 1941 went against him.

On a happier note, the 25-millionth Ford came off the line on January 18, 1937, and the company observed a quarter-century of truck production on July 27 by announcing that Rouge facilities would be expanded for that purpose. Happy days, however, were not quite back again, as the stock market reminded everyone on October 18. Almost eight years to the day after the Great Crash, the Dow Jones average "celebrated" by losing 7¾ percent of its total value, the 10th largest loss in history, as it fell 10.57 points to close at 125.74.

But optimism was hardy in those days, and Ford's 1937 new-model introduction proved it by being one of the splashiest ever seen. On the morning of November 6, 1936, some 7000 Ford dealers from all over the country piled into the Detroit Coliseum. The mood was one of excitement and anticipation—at long last, the nation's economic gloom seemed to be lifting, at least a little. After the auditorium darkened, a slim shaft of light picked out a large V-8 emblem at the center of an elevated stage, where golden-haired "elves" then unwound themselves up from the floor, one at a time, and

Sporting a new swept back grille and rounder, fuller fenders with the headlights faired in, the '37 Ford began a new two-year styling cycle. The five-window two-passenger standard coupe, which weighed in at 2275 pounds, was priced at $529. Note the painted windshield surrounds and the single windshield wiper.

began tossing various car parts into a big cauldron. Steam rose as engine components, wheels, radiators, and other bits and pieces were thrown into the brew. Then, in a fantasy of light and color, the fumes cleared, the elves vanished, and a new 1937 club coupe drove up a ramp, traversed the stage, and then rolled down onto the main floor. It was a new way to introduce cars, one that would be widely imitated as the industry became increasingly enamored of such razzmatazz. Certainly those dealers must have come away feeling that 1937 was going to be a banner year.

And in most respects it was. For the first time, closed body styles lacked the traditional fabric roof insert as Ford followed GM's 1936 move to all-steel construction (which GM called the "Turret Top"). Also new was a smaller, 136-cubic-inch version of the flathead V-8 (bore and stroke: 2.60 × 3.20 inches) rated at 60 bhp. Originally conceived for Britain and France, where it had powered locally built Fords for more than a year, it was prompted by European tax laws based not on vehicle size but engine displacement (in Britain, on bore). But here, this "V-8/60," as it was called, was marketed as an economy option, available only on Standard models as an appeal to buyers seeking a full-size car. William Cowling, Ford's sales manager, boasted that the new V-8 would deliver speeds of over 70 miles per hour with super economy, but in reality it was underpowered. And with a final drive ratio of 4.44:1, engine revs were too high at highway speeds, thus compromising longevity. This engine was in fact a "revver," but this characteristic alone made it ill-suited for American-style driving where low-end torque for acceleration and minimal gear-shifting were strong selling points. As it turned out, the little V-8 failed to garner many sales despite lowering list prices by $10 to $57. Ford would wisely give up on it in the U.S. after 1940, although it would continue to be used in Europe for many years.

In stark contrast to the anemic V-8/60, the bigger V-8 powered Ford to a win in the European Monte Carlo Rally in 1937, a feat that Ford would repeat again in 1938.

This year's other mechanical changes were more successful. The larger 85-bhp V-8 offered improved cooling via a larger, relocated water pump. Insert bearings were enlarged, pistons changed from aluminum to cast steel, cylinder heads from aluminum to cast iron. Carried over as running changes from 1936 were a heavier crankshaft with replaceable main bearings and a more restrictive "economy" carburetor that took five horses from the oft-quoted 90-bhp figure, hence the "V-8/85" moniker. Ford still clung to self-energizing mechanical brakes, but their old rod actuating system was ditched for a modern cable linkage within a protective conduit. Finally, the steering ratio was again lowered (raised

The '37 Ford pickup (top) changed from a vertical-bar to a horizontal-bar grille, traded the one-piece windshield for a two-piece unit, and got a four-inch-longer cargo box. The DeLuxe '37 Fords could be told by the bright trim: windshield surround, grille bars, and on the running boards. The Tudor (center), $674 and $699, saw output hit 107,373 units, the new five-passenger $719 Club Coupe (above) reached 16,992.

numerically) to reduce effort at the wheel, though it made for an unseemly number of turns lock-to-lock, making slow-speed maneuvers easier but quick cornering more difficult.

Counting V-8/60 versions, the '37 Ford line numbered 26 separate offerings in three series: V-8/60 Model 74 and V-8/85 Model 74 Standard and 78 DeLuxe. Body styles with clumsy side curtains continued to suffer dwindling sales throughout the industry as the decade wore on, so this would be the last year for the true Ford roadster, which had been effectively supplanted by the more popular convertible cabriolet with roll-up glass. The DeLuxe phaeton was still listed (at $750), but would last only through 1938. New to the catalog, and also quite popular, was the aforementioned club coupe, a four-passenger five-window DeLuxe style priced at $720. Its roof length was halfway between that of the conventional Tudor sedan and the normal coupe, which acquired rear quarter glass to become a five-window style, too. Still limited to Standard trim, the woody wagon again came with roll-down front door windows and side curtains in lieu of rear door and quarter glass. However, all-glass windows were available for only $20 more, $775 total. Repeating at the top of the line was the glamorous DeLuxe convertible sedan at $860.

In all, the more modern '37s lived up to customer expectations—aside from persistent comments that they would have been safer with hydraulic brakes,

like those on most competitors. The sales race saw Ford beaten by Chevrolet by a mere 2000 cars. However, Ford trucks sold better, which put Dearborn ahead in combined production. Ford also led in model-year car output, besting its GM foe by some 125,000 units (942,000 to 815,000). Alas, Ford wouldn't do as well for the next dozen years.

The new economy V-8/60 also appeared in this year's commercial line, available in the Sedan Delivery (but not the station wagon) for just $10 less than the V-8/85. It was also offered for all 131-inch-wheelbase trucks save dump-body models. Returning from Model T times was a pickup box as a new utility option for the Standard coupe. Prompted partly by the success of Chevrolet's 1936 "Coupe Pickup," this simply slid into the normal cargo hold once the trunklid was removed. The Sedan Delivery naturally received the new prow-front passenger-car styling. All half-ton and 1½-ton trucks also presented a fresh face via a slim new barrel-type grille, lower headlamps, two-piece windshield, and revised ornamentation. Cab and body styling was otherwise unchanged, but instrument panels were modified to include a new pushbutton starter, an electric fuel gauge became standard, and the previous in-cab fuel filler moved to a safer and more convenient outside location. Batteries were newly mounted underhood.

Enhancing the appeal of Ford's popular pickup were a redesigned box with a four-inch longer floor (73 inches in all)

Ford touted its brakes at 1937 auto shows (top left): "... all steel from pedal to wheel." The '37 Sedan Delivery (top right) started at $585 and came with either the new 60-bhp V-8 or the 85-bhp unit. Both used a two-barrel carb. Fords were popular with police departments throughout the nation (bottom left). The woody wagon (bottom right) listed at $775.

and full-width rod-actuated tailgate latch (replacing a crude three-strap arrangement). In V-8/60 form the pickup listed at $470, the Sedan Delivery at $585. The basic 131-inch driveaway chassis for vocational use sold for $505. As before, buyers could order a package of "Deluxe" cab features, which this year included driver's reading lamp, dual wipers, and twin sun visors. A sliding rear cab window remained optional for the appropriate models.

Ford's main commercial-vehicle news for 1937 was the belated arrival of the Transit Bus, which had been under development for several years. This rode a unique 141-inch-wheelbase chassis with V-8/85 power and "forward control," the driver sitting above and well ahead of the front axle. The predictably plain, boxy body, built under contract by the Union City Body Company of Union City, Indiana, could seat up to 25 people, who entered via double doors on the right. The Transit was initially quite popular. Ford delivered 500 to the City of Detroit in late 1936 and early 1937. Many other municipal orders soon followed.

1 9 3 8

Ford tried a new marketing ploy for 1938: different styling for Standard and DeLuxe cars. The former, now labelled Model 82A with V-8/60 power and 81A with the V-8/85, were essentially warmed-over versions of the '37 Model 78 DeLuxe, though the grille's upper horizontal bars were now swept back almost to the cowl, thus eliminating the separate hood louvers. The 1938 DeLuxe, the 81A, retained separate vents but got a longer hood that curved down into a heart-shaped grille that was now rounded at its upper corners, plus fuller, more rounded front fenders and flush almond-shaped taillights.

If not exactly ugly, the '38 Fords were arguably less attractive than the striking '37s, a not unexpected result when styling is changed for the mere sake of change. "The 1938 Ford deserved a better reception than it received in that gloomy recession year," commented Paul R. Woudenberg in *Ford in the Thirties*. "It was a more handsome car than its predecessors and should have sold well against the unchanged Chevrolet and Plymouth . . . [but it] has always lived in the shadow of its successors, for though it had the outward appearance of the new, underneath it was still the old."

A search for broader market coverage prompted the appearance distinctions between the DeLuxe and Standard models because demand for cheaper, more austere standard cars remained sizeable as the Depression dragged on. The price differential between a Standard Fordor with the 85-bhp V-8 and the DeLuxe Fordor came to $60, an 8.5-percent difference. In tough economic times, that price spread made a difference. Ford would persist with this DeLuxe/Standard dichotomy through 1940.

The instrument panel for 1938 continued with two large round gauges in front of the driver, one for the speedometer, the other for fuel level, oil pressure, etc. New however, were recessed knobs (a safety feature ahead of its time) and a specific spot for the radio speaker in the center of the dash. When specified, the clock was mounted on the glovebox door on the right-hand side of the panel. Fords still came with a crank-out windshield, and would through 1939, although Chevy had already dropped this feature.

Engineering alterations were almost nonexistent for a substantially shuffled model line. Standard offerings were pared to just a five-window coupe and a pair of sedans. These were duplicated in the DeLuxe series, which added phaeton, convertible sedan, and convertible club

coupe, plus a fixed-roof club coupe and, for the first time, the station wagon, newly and officially transferred from the commercial fleet.

At $825, the wagon now came with all-round glass windows as standard, although it could still be ordered without the window glass. Very few left the factory that way, however. The woody also received a revised bodyshell with a new

Although the '38 Ford used '37 bodies, it was heavily restyled at the front end. The DeLuxe models sported a more sloping hood and a new grille. It cost $770 to drive home a DeLuxe Fordor (top), and 92,020 customers did just that. The convertible sedan (center) was a bit pricier at $900 and far rarer: only 2743 built. The Standard models received a modest rehash of the '37 front end. At $595, the coupe (bottom) was the year's price leader; output came to 90,347 units.

117

steel floorpan and, in another first for a Ford, lockable doors, window, and tailgate. Also new for the wagon was an inside spare tire, replacing the traditional outside mount. Non-wagon '38s came with a built-in trunk; the old "flatback" sedans and rumble-seat roadster were dropped due to poor sales. Fender skirts were continued as an option, and they suited the open cars particularly well, especially the romantic phaeton, now in its final year.

Ford's relative lack of newness for '38 suggested that something was going on in Dearborn—besides old Henry's usual railing against progress, that is. And indeed there was; the firm was busy preparing not only an all-new '39 Ford but a separate new "companion" make. In a way, then, this year's styling split was a preparatory move designed to provide an orderly price progression between the Ford line and the forthcoming Mercury. As we know now, the latter would emerge as a slightly larger and more powerful version of the '39 Ford, intended to give Dearborn a more direct medium-price competitor against Pontiac and Oldsmobile from General Motors, and Dodge and DeSoto from Chrysler Corporation.

A sharp, unexpected recession blunted the pace of the nation's economic recovery in 1938. Though car sales slipped industry-wide, Ford model-year volume plunged even further to just about half its '37 level, some 410,000 units in all. Chevrolet also sank, but not as much, finishing some 55,000 cars ahead. This result largely reflected the fact that Ford was still way behind the times in several areas, its old-fashioned transverse-spring suspension and mechanical brakes being the most glaring anachronisms. But the old man was still in charge and, ignoring all advice from Edsel on down, he refused to follow what he considered to be engineering "fads." Though most everyone *but* Henry could see it, his intransigence had already set the company on a long, steady decline that wouldn't be reversed until it was almost too late.

If change was lacking in Ford's 1938 cars, the truck line more than made up for it, being not only completely redesigned (save the car-based sedan delivery) but broader than at any time since the onset of the Depression. Cab and panel-delivery styling was smoother and more modern, dominated by a large oval "barrel-nosed" grille sporting horizontal bars, flanked by headlamps more firmly nestled in the adjacent "catwalks." The hood was suitably reshaped and newly hinged at the rear, "alligator" style, a truck industry first. Fenders were also revised. Accessory rear fender skirts appeared, too, a new option for the handsomely restyled panel delivery. And for the first time since 1931, there was a completely reengineered pickup body.

And there was more. Following an

The '38 Ford trucks were noted for their "barrel-nose" front end styling. Listing at $685, the panel delivery came with the 60-bhp V-8 standard. In that guise it weighed 2985 pounds, but heft increased to 3012 pounds with the 85-bhp V-8. Output was a modest 6447 units for that recession-plagued year.

SAE recommendation that frame widths and cab-to-front-axle (CA) dimensions be standardized, Ford spread all its truck chassis rails to 34 inches and upped wheelbase on the 131-inch 1½-ton chassis to 134 inches, giving a five-foot CA. The long 157-inch platform was retained, as its CA was already "even" at near seven feet.

But the big news was a much-needed "in-betweener," a line of one-ton models called, appropriately, One-Tonner. The first such Ford offerings with this payload rating since the Model TT, they comprised pickup, panel delivery, platform, and cab/chassis models, all with a four-foot CA from a new 122-inch wheelbase. The latter was 10 inches longer than that of half-ton models but 14 inches shorter than that of the new 134-inch 1½-tonners, which were now termed "Regulars."

One-Tonner bodies were essentially upsized versions of their half-ton counterparts. The pickup, however, featured a longer, 96-inch cargo box and sturdier overall construction, plus standard side stake pockets and a hardwood load floor with metal skid strips. Pricewise, One-Tonners ran $120 to $165 above comparable half-tonners: $730 versus $590 for the basic V-8/85 pickup, $850 versus $685 for the like-engined panel delivery. As before, the small V-8/60 was available throughout most of the commercial line, but it only saved buyers about $10 on lighter-duty models in exchange for much poorer low-speed lugging power compared with the V-8/85. And that wasn't all, as James K. Wagner pointed out in *Ford Trucks Since 1905*: "The outstanding success of the '60' in the market place during 1937 was of no benefit [in 1938] since this inadequate powerplant made more enemies for the company than friends."

Ford broadened its truck line even further for 1938 by trotting out its first factory-built cab-over-engine (COE) models in the spring of 1938. Initial offerings divided between two wheelbases: 134 inches, a modified Regular chassis, and a compact new 101-inch span that gave a highly maneuverable five-foot cab-to-axle dimension. Though derived from the conventional "engine-front" design, the COE cab was seven inches wider and 7.6 inches higher, the latter to ensure adequate engine clearance. Engine access was via a tall lift-up nose hatch carrying a gaping oval grille, again with horizontal bars. Headlights perched in pods atop the front fenders.

Despite all these new choices, Ford truck production suffered mightily in 1938, falling to its lowest point since 1934. The recession was partly to blame, but so was growing buyer resistance to Henry's dogged persistence with mechanical brakes, though that would change soon enough.

Meanwhile, America paused on Saturday, July 30, 1938 to honor the world's most influential motor man. Henry turned 75 that day, and luminaries from around the world came to Dearborn to pay homage. This grand and happy celebration would be one of the last in Henry's life. Adolf Hitler was on the march in Germany, and despite the sincere efforts of British Prime Minister Neville Chamberlain, there would soon be no more "peace in our time."

1 9 3 9

Overshadowed by the October 1938 introduction of the new medium-price Mercury were several significant developments for the '39 Ford. Aside from pretty new lines for the Series 91A DeLuxe, the big attraction—really major news, coming from Ford—was hydraulic brakes. Old Henry had finally given in—three years after Chevrolet and 11 years after Plymouth. But though the new Lockheed system answered one long-standing criticism, the antiquated chassis was again basically untouched.

Ford's work on hydraulic brakes had begun in 1938 at Henry's direct order. But the aging motor magnate suffered a stroke soon afterwards, and would be less and less involved in running his company and developing its products. Still, he continued to have the last word on important matters—just as he continued to rely less on son Edsel and more on Harry Bennett for advice.

Nevertheless, Mercury was mainly Edsel's idea, and he named it as well. Though new from the ground up, the Mercury was really a "super deluxe" Ford with scaled-up price, proportions, and power. At 116 inches, its wheelbase measured four inches longer than Ford's, although the stretch was ahead of the cowl. Still, the Mercury boasted a nicer ride, and since the steering wheel and front seat were moved forward a bit, the Mercury gave the impression of having more interior room as well. It should be noted that some Mercury developments spilled over to this year's Fords, especially the DeLuxe. For example, Mercury's bored-out flathead V-8 had larger-diameter bearings, heavier rods and crankshaft, and other strengthened internals, most

of which were adopted for the Ford unit. There was also an obvious styling kinship between the first Mercury and the '39 Ford DeLuxe, especially at the front. Both wore low vee'd grilles, the former with horizontal bars, the latter with vertical ones. Headlamps on both cars were completely absorbed into the front fenders and retained the almond shape of previous years (circular sealed-beam units were on the way). At the same time hoods were deeper and bereft of side louvers.

This year's Ford Standard, more tactfully advertised now as simply the "Ford V-8," was another mild rehash of the previous year's DeLuxe, with busier grille and hood detailing in contemporary fashion and smaller hood louvers. Model 92A denoted V-8/60 offerings, a coupe and two sedans as in 1938. The step-up

Series 91A V-8/85 line began with this trio as well as a reinstated base-trim wagon. The DeLuxe range contracted as the phaeton, club coupe, and convertible club coupe all disappeared. The lovely convertible sedan was in its final season and no longer alone at the top of the line—the DeLuxe wagon carried an identical $920 price. Curiously, the four-door convertible would resurface for 1940—

For 1939, Ford switched to a vertical-bar grille and saw the headlights moved further apart. The DeLuxe convertible coupe (above), which weighed 2840 pounds, retailed for $788 and found 10,422 buyers. The woody wagon (below) was the year's second most expensive model: $916. And at 3095 pounds, it was the heaviest. Wagons weren't nearly as popular in 1938 as they would be after World War II, thus only 6155 were built.

and for that year only—as a Mercury.

New brakes aside, Ford cars saw few engineering changes. The V-8/85 retained its customary power rating despite the stronger internals and a new Ford-built dual-downdraft carburetor, though some tests suggested it was slightly more potent than before. Torque, however, was up to a peak of 155 lbs/ft. Shift lever throws were a bit shorter this year due to a higher shift tower, and DeLuxe models got a new, lower radiator with cooling area increased to 384 square inches, although coolant capacity remained at 22 quarts.

In what was expected to be a better sales year than it was, Ford sold over 481,000 cars, trailing the heavily redesigned Chevrolet by nearly 100,000 units. Worse yet, third-place Plymouth was closer than ever on the strength of its smart new '39 styling. There was also strong new competition in Studebaker's fleet, low-priced six-cylinder Champion, designed by Raymond Loewy. Ford was doing well enough, perhaps, but so were most rivals.

Which only made Mercury's sales assistance all the more timely. The new make was certainly overdue. Conceived to fill the yawning price gap that had long separated Ford and Lincoln, it also reflected a certain Ford yearning to be a multi-make manufacturer like General Motors and Chrysler. Early ads declared Mercury "the car that dares to ask 'Why?'", implying a clean-slate approach. But as historian Beverly Rae Kimes later wrote: "Another question [was] why Ford Motor Company hadn't introduced [it] sooner. The answer to that one undoubtedly was that it had taken that long for Edsel to convince his father to build it."

Old Henry certainly wasn't chasing innovation as he had so successfully in the past. But his son was. Edsel knew that Ford needed a medium-price product for loyal customers looking to move up—an alternative to the popular Pontiac and Dodge. Mercury was thus adroitly priced just below the Oldsmobile Eight and the DeSoto. While it wouldn't approach Pontiac/Dodge/Olds volume in the Forties, it usually matched or exceeded DeSoto's, averaging about 80,000 units a year, easily above the breakeven point. More important, this was mainly "plus business" at a time when Ford as a whole was faltering. Before Mercury, most buyers moving up were lost to GM and Chrysler.

Mercury bowed as a single series comprising a Fordor-like Town Sedan and three two-door body styles: sedan, convertible, and a slim-pillar "coupe-sedan." Prices ran around $1000, curb weights around 3000 pounds. As mentioned, power came from a larger, stronger version of the Ford flathead, with a wider 3.19-inch bore (on the same 3.75-inch stroke), yielding 239 cubic inches and 95 horsepower, specifications that would run unchanged through 1948. Stylist Bob Gregorie used the longer wheelbase to

make Mercury look more balanced and "important" than Ford—more like this year's Lincoln-Zephyr, which embodied this same, basic new corporate look. Interior appearance also aped Ford's, including a dashboard with an arced strip-type speedometer.

With its favorable power-to-weight ratio, Mercury soon became known as something of a hot rod, befitting not only its name (after the winged messenger god of Greek mythology) but the concept Edsel had thought right for it. Early Mercs were quicker than comparable V-8 Fords in stock, well-tuned form. Even the debut '39s were capable of close to 100 mph, yet were remarkably frugal. Ads claimed close to 20 mpg, though not for leadfoots, of course.

This year's Ford trucks also received the new hydraulic brakes and stood to be a lot more saleable for it. But they didn't prove as popular as Chevy's, which beat Ford in calendar-year production by a substantial 40,000 units. The real problem was that Ford's commercial line had nothing really new for 1939 except the more effective brakes, which were old news everywhere else.

Still, there were two more fairly important developments. One was yet another new gap-filler series. Awkwardly

named "Three-Quarter-Tonner," it offered the same model choices as the One-Tonner, with which it shared wheelbase and cab/chassis design. The newcomers' only distinctions were use of smaller passenger-car brakes, wheels, and tires plus different rear-axle ratios and, of course, somewhat lower prices. The year's only other truck news was availability of the new Mercury V-8 as an extra-cost option for the "Regular" 1½-ton conventionals and COEs, as well as the Transit bus, all of which needed it. The stronger engine was also available to special order on lighter-duty trucks and Ford police cars.

Public interest in Ford Motor Company was heightened throughout 1939 by the firm's exhibit at the futuristic New York World's Fair, which opened this year. As at Chicago, Dallas, and San Diego, the Ford story was showcased in a special building. This time, however, there was something quite extraordinary: the "Road of Tomorrow," an elevated highway completely encircling the structure, where visitors could take all of Ford's newest for a spin. Meantime, Dearborn logged two more production milestones: the 27-millionth Ford vehicle, completed at Richmond, California on February 15, and the six-millionth Ford V-8 engine, built on May 1.

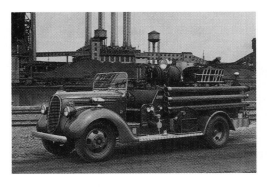 

The decade then coming to a close had been exceedingly difficult for the entire nation and no less so for Ford, its technical advances with the Model A, flathead V-8, and the Lincoln-Zephyr offset by Henry's growing eccentricity and the loss of low-price sales supremacy to Chevrolet. Yet, after years of hasty, often confused new-model programs, Ford seemed to be sorting out its various problems while looking forward to the real prosperity that was presumably just around the corner.

But the year movie buffs remember for *The Wizard of Oz* and *Gone with the Wind* also brought the outbreak of a new war in Europe as Adolf Hitler's armies invaded Poland in September. Canada declared war on Germany almost immediately, and Ford's Canadian plants swiftly turned from civilian to military production, initially building a small field truck with a high degree of parts interchangeability.

Personally, Henry Ford was furious at the brazen and brutal *Blitzkrieg*—enough to forget his well-known pacifism. "They don't dare have a war," he fumed, "and they know it." With that kind of reaction, the question as the Forties opened seemed not so much *if* America would get involved, but *when*.

Rumble seats were nearly extinct in Detroit by 1939, but Ford still had one on the DeLuxe convertible coupe (top row). The convertible sedan was a disappearing breed by 1939, but Ford continued to list one. A DeLuxe model (second row, right), it cost $920, a price tag high enough to help limit production to just 3561 units. Ford's heavy-duty trucks were pressed into service for many varying purposes (third row), such as fire fighting—the unit shown working at Ford's River Rouge plant—and hauling soft drinks for the bottling industry. At $702, the '39 DeLuxe five-window two-passenger coupe (bottom) enjoyed a production run of 37,326 units. It came with the 221-cid 85-horsepower V-8 standard. Although this example sports whitewall tires, not too many cars in 1939 rolled out of the factory so equipped.

1 9 4 0

The 1940 Ford DeLuxe is still fondly remembered, mainly due to its looks, because it certainly wasn't remembered for the few engineering improvements of which there were few. Workmanship, never a Ford selling point, *was* improved, perhaps because the company was now producing all its own car bodies, owing to labor problems at suppliers. Still, Ford trailed somewhat in fit and finish. But, oh, that styling!

And it *was* good—so good that these Fords remain today as some of the most desired cars ever built. Executed by Bob Gregorie with guidance, as always, from Edsel Ford, the DeLuxe was dominated by a crisply pointed hood meeting a handsome, chrome-plated vee'd grille of delicate horizontal bars, flanked by painted sub grilles. Headlamps—circular sealed-beam units for the first time—nestled in neat chrome nacelles that followed fender curvature. The fenders themselves were artfully shaped to complement the body contours, and the rear units could be skirted for an even more streamlined look. Distinctive chevron taillamps adorned the "beetle back" rear end. Completing the package were standard pivoting front ventpanes, a second response to GM's "No-Draft" ventilation and a boon to interior comfort on hot days. This deft facelift of 1939 styling worked amazingly well. Even the cheap Standards looked new and far less frumpy, distinguished by body-color headlamp housings (with the new "safety" lights) and a '39 DeLuxe-type vertical-bar grille with a simple chrome cap on the prow.

This would be the last year for Ford's old/new series split and the never-popular V-8/60. Unveiled in October 1939, the 1940 line continued with the price-leading, small-engine Standard series, designated O2A, and the V-8/85 series 01A comprising both Standard and DeLuxe models. The one remaining open body style was the rakish DeLuxe convertible coupe, priced at a reasonable $850. The demise of the convertible sedan left the wood-body wagon as this year's costliest Ford—$950. Club coupes gave way to five-window business coupes with fold-up rear jump seats and a large trunk. Sometimes referred to as the "opera coupe," this body style came in three forms: "60" Standard, "85" Standard, and "85" DeLuxe, respectively tagged at $640, $680, and $742. The outwardly identical three-passenger version was still around in these guises, now at $619, $660, and $721. In future years these coupes would be popular hot rod material.

On the technical front, Ford switched from floor to column-mounted gearshift, as did Mercury. Of course, Chevy and Plymouth had already done so a year earlier. Also on hand was a new two-spoke steering wheel. V-8/85s acquired a front anti-roll bar to "stabilize" a longer front spring, while V-8/60s picked up the larger-engine models' nine-inch centrifugal clutch, crank-driven fan, lower and wider radiator, and two-brush generator with voltage regulator. In all, nothing major.

The same could not be said for this year's truck fleet, which was fully overhauled with a more modern suspension for all models and fresh cab styling for all but COEs. The revised chassis abandoned Ford's traditional, heavy torque-tube drive for the lighter, open "Hotchkiss" arrangement in which the rear springs control lateral and longitudinal axle movement caused by acceleration and braking torque. Accompanying this change, rear frame overhang was sliced 11.4 inches for most 1½-ton models.

Heavy-duty rigs adopted the twin-longitudinal-leaf front suspension previously used on some light-duty models, though this remained a non-independent setup with solid axle. An extra inch in wheelbase stretched the longest chassis to 158 inches in that dimension and ex-tended cab-to-axle distance to a full seven feet for both conventional and cabover models. Last but not least, vacuum-actuated power brakes arrived as an option for all commercials save the half-ton, 112-inch-wheelbase offerings.

Seeking greater variety in truck appearance, Ford redesigned all conventional cabs (including dashboards) and styled half-ton front sheetmetal to be virtually identical (though not wholly interchangeable) with that of its 1940 passenger cars. In a departure from past practice, the faithful sedan delivery shared its handsome grille with the new DeLuxe, while the pickup's face aped that of this year's Standard.

Larger conventionals also boasted new, though slightly different cabs, with roof, cowl, and A-pillars stamped as a single unit to incorporate a fixed windshield and cowl-mount wipers, a truck-industry first. Front fenders were unchanged, but a reshaped hood and a lower, wider new vertical-bar grille made for a completely fresh look—one of the sharpest Ford trucks ever. Again like Ford cars and most all other 1940 U.S. vehicles, sealed-beam headlamps were featured across the line.

More completely transformed still was Ford's Transit Bus, which switched from a front to rear-engine configuration on a longer 148.5-inch wheelbase. A three-speed transmission and 11-inch clutch took drive to the rear wheels from a 95-horsepower flathead V-8 through a right angle via a short, open propshaft—a fairly compact power package that made eminent sense in a bus. Union City again supplied the body, still practically square but more modern-looking, thanks to slimmer pillars and larger windows.

This revised Transit is significant not only as Ford's first rear-engine production vehicle but the first practical out-

Ford Motor Company celebrated 1940 by building its 28-millionth Ford, a DeLuxe Fordor sedan (left) that had been assembled at the company's Edgewater, New Jersey, plant on April 8, 1940. The DeLuxe convertible coupe sold for a very competitive $849. Note the handsome chevron-style taillights that were used in 1940.

come from a series of rear-engine experiments conducted by Henry Ford and selected engineers beginning in 1937. Interestingly, these were initially oriented to passenger cars, likely inspired by the work of contemporary Europeans including Dr. Ferdinand Porsche, who employed the rear-engine layout to create his latterday Model T, the *volkswagen*—the low priced "people's car" which was commissioned by Adolf Hitler.

On April 8, the 28-millionth Ford car, a DeLuxe Fordor, rolled out of the firm's Edgewater, New Jersey, plant, then toured the country, stopping in major cities and state capitals over the next few months to collect the obligatory special license plates and celebrity logbook autographs. Another production milestone came on June 4 with the completion of Ford's seven-millionth V-8 engine.

Ford's 1940 sales were encouraging. Model-year car production climbed to almost 542,000 units, about 10 percent up on 1939. But Plymouth and Chevrolet had been busy, both now featuring all-new roomier and more modern bodies. They were truly cars of the Forties, and both scored healthy sales gains. As ever, Ford's problem was that it wasn't as up to date as the opposition—its body, for ex-

The '40 Ford DeLuxe convertible coupe (below) has been highly prized by Ford enthusiasts for many years, due in large measure to its handsome styling. The ragtop was relatively popular when new—23,704 were built for the model run. Although the U.S. was inching toward war in 1940, Ford assembly lines were still running at a normal pace. Seen here (bottom left) is a trio of standard Tudor sedans nearing the end of the line. Magazine ads for 1940 (right) fell back on the line that had been used as far back as 1907: "Watch the FORDS go by!" Also highlighted was the 28-millionth Ford car, seen with other milestone models in the background. Model improvements were also hyped.

Watch the FORDS go by!

THE TWENTY-EIGHT MILLIONTH FORD CAR

22 Important Improvements in THE NEW FORD CARS for 1940

ample, dated back to 1938. The 1940 Ford was in reality a car of the Thirties.

Against this, Dearborn's commercial vehicle output reached its highest level since 1937 and Ford scored the industry's biggest percentage gain in truck sales. But the new war in Europe was beginning to affect U.S. industry in general, and all truckmakers enjoyed substantially increased sales. Thus Ford's performance, improved though it was, still wasn't enough to dislodge Chevrolet as America's number-one truck.

Despite White House assurances of strict American neutrality, the nation began gearing up for war in 1940, slowly but inexorably. Ford did its part, breaking ground in September for a new Rouge facility that would eventually turn out Pratt & Whitney 18-cylinder radial aero engines. In the meantime, Ford Canada cranked up military truck production, as

did the British subsidiary in Dagenham. By June, when France fell to the Nazis, Ford England was also producing Rolls-Royce Merlin aircraft engines in Manchester. Ford was not, however, realizing income for production in Denmark and the Benelux countries, which had been overrun as well, nor from its plant in Cologne, Germany, which Hitler had requisitioned for his deadly war machine.

On a happier note, the exquisitely styled, immensely romantic Lincoln Continental stood out as the glamour leader of this year's Dearborn show. As most enthusiasts know, it originated in 1939 as a Zephyr-based custom commissioned by Edsel Ford for his annual winter vacation in Palm Beach, Florida. Enamored of European design, Edsel had directed designer Bob Gregorie to create a car along "strictly Continental" lines (hence the name), complete with Euro-style outside

Ford claimed 22 "Important Improvements" for 1940. Among them were a new column-mounted "finger-tip gearshift" and sealed-beam headlamps, both embraced industry-wide. Also touted for closed models was "controlled ventilation," which consisted basically of hinged ventwings. The novelty was that the divider strip lowered with the larger window "out of line of vision." The priciest model of the year—and indeed most years—was the DeLuxe station wagon (above), which listed at $950. Not too many buyers in 1940 liked the high price so only 8730 were ordered. The $765 DeLuxe Tudor (opposite) proved to be the most popular model in the 1940 lineup: 171,368 were produced.

spare tire. Gregorie, who admired the smooth shapes favored by John Tjaarda and others, had already penned several Ford-based cars for Edsel, all with long curving fenders and tall peaked grilles. The Continental would be merely an extension of these themes.

First came a scale model based on '39 Zephyr convertible dimensions. Edsel liked everything about it except the sloped Zephyr tail, which looked awkward with an exposed, upright spare, so he had Gregorie raise the deck and square it up, resulting in a more finished appearance that looked "as if they planned it that way," as one Ford stylist later said. With this, Edsel told Gregorie to prepare the actual car. This began as a '39 Zephyr convertible with 12 extra inches spliced in ahead of the cowl and suitably altered front fenders. It looked "sectioned" in profile because it was. Four-inch horizontal strips were removed from each door and the doors welded together again, thus reducing their overall height. Other new body panels, like the deck, had to be hand-hammered over wooden forms by skilled metalworkers. Not widely known is the fact that two more Continental

prototypes were built for Edsel's eldest sons, Benson and Henry II, once 1940 Zephyr sheetmetal became available in mid-1939.

Completed by March 1939, wearing Eagle Gray paint and a gray leather interior, Edsel's latest custom duly went to Palm Beach, where it attracted scores of admirers. Ford's president returned with over 200 requests that amounted to orders. Too astute to let them go, he ordered a run of 500 cars to see what would happen.

Scarcely four months later, the "Lincoln Zephyr Continental" (though bearing only "Zephyr" script) went on sale following a massive effort by production and body engineers. Besides the rakish cabriolet at $2840, there was a $2783 club coupe version. (A four-door had been sketched in September 1939, but never made production.) At that, the Conti-

nental was quite affordable, unlike most exotic "traffic builders." And build traffic it did, despite model-year production of but 54 cabriolets and 350 coupes. These were all basically Zephyr conversions that required a tremendous amount of hand labor: cutting, welding, patching, refinishing, leading, and forming.

Destined to become a Classic (as defined by the Classic Car Club of America), the 1940 Continental (and the little-changed 1941 version) remains an elegant tribute to Edsel Ford, the quiet enthusiast, the pursuer of luxury, the great judge of excellence in both cars and people. It wasn't his only legacy, of course, but it would have been enough to assure his permanent place in the automotive hall of fame. It was certainly a brilliant follow-up to his successful '39 Mercury. Edsel, in fact, was now at the peak of his career. Sadly, it wouldn't last much longer.

1 9 4 1

Despite the worrisome war raging abroad, many Americans were happy at the end of 1940. The Roosevelt Administration's New Deal had put a good many workers back on the job—though war mobilization efforts since 1939 was doing as much, if not more—and the country was hopeful that it could stay clear of the European conflict while producing its way out of the Depression. Ford Motor Company body painters made good wages for the time: $1.10 an hour. Fender-stamping repair workers had it even better: about $1.15.

This cautiously optimistic climate formed the backdrop for the rollout of Ford's 1941 models at a big Dearborn press reception in September 1940. Henry Ford was 78 now, and this would be the last time he would preside at such an event. Reporters must have sensed this, for nearly 500 turned out to see and hear the elder statesman of the American auto industry. True to form, Henry had little to say. Instead, he escorted the party to a nearby site where his workers were erecting a huge new factory that would turn out fighter aircraft engines. Like many other companies, Ford was now involved in a growing number of defense projects as Washington geared up not to fight, but to supply European allies with war materiel.

The '41s were the biggest Fords yet: longer, lower, wider, flashier, and heavier. Wheelbase stretched two inches, bodysides ballooned outward, interior space increased, and a stouter frame lived underneath. Curb weights rose by an aver-

age of some 300 pounds over the lithe 1940 models. Styling was evolutionary, marked by a rather busy front end with a vertical center grille flanked by low-riding "scoop" grilles, all with vertical chrome bars. At the rear were vertically mounted rectangular taillights.

"Probably the most outstanding advancement in this year's car," said *Ford News*, "is improved riding, made possible by a number of factors including a wheelbase increased to 114 inches. That the 1941 Ford is a big car is indicated by the fact that the front seat in the Fordor Sedan is a full seven inches wider than in any previous Ford car. The front seat width is why so little running board shows outside. The unusually wide bodies, with doors that round out at the bottom to cover all but a narrow strip of the running boards, are trim and sleek. Headlamps are mounted far apart on the massive front fenders to increase nighttime

visibility, and the separate parking lamps are set high on the fenders."

Ford was right in step with its big new '41. Rivals Chevrolet and Plymouth had enlarged their cars substantially the previous year, a move that met with considerable buyer approval. If Dearborn had been behind the times, at least it was beginning to catch up. The '41's clean, ready-for-action look was quickly accepted as the latest in high-fashion motoring.

The big engineering news was Ford's first six-cylinder engine since its Model K

Henry Ford experimented extensively with industrial uses for soybeans in the '30s and early '40s. He's seen here (above) trying to bash in a "soybean" trunklid to demonstrate its strength. The '41 Ford boasted bigger, roomier bodies, as on the $818 Super DeLuxe Tudor (left). A 1941 ad (below) discussed how women influenced the design of automobiles.

This is not "A Man's World" by a long shot!

unit of 1906-08. An undersquare L-head design typical of Detroit in those days, it displaced 226 cubic inches (bore and stroke: 3.30 × 4.40 inches) and produced 90 bhp at 3300 rpm—5 cid and 5 bhp more than the familiar V-8/85. A viscous-type crankshaft vibration damper marked a first for Ford. Otherwise, the six was typical of Dearborn design with its cast-iron crankshaft, direct-drive front-mounted distributor, and a front main-bearing cap with integral oil pump.

The new six was prompted by initial reaction to the '39 Mercury from Ford dealers, many of whom felt that a Ford Six would have been a better seller than that puffed-up V-8 car. Besides, Chevy, Plymouth, and others had long been making sales hay with sixes. Edsel Ford, always respectful of his dealers and often sympathetic to what they said, promised them one posthaste. He even managed to get his father's approval for it in one of those strange turnabouts for which Henry was noted.

Effectively, this six was an alternative to the V-8/60 in a revised '41 line comprising Series 1GA Six and Series 11A V-8, each with the same body styles and trim levels. The former Standard coupe and Tudor/Fordor sedans were retitled Special. They were bare-bones models that came dressed only in Harbor Gray paint. Further, they had only a single taillight, windshield wiper, sun visor, and horn. The DeLuxe was now the mid-level trim offering, adding a business coupe and the woody wagon body styles. They came in a choice of colors, along with dual visors and horns, better trim, and a locking glovebox door. At the top was a new Super DeLuxe group, with all the DeLuxe styles plus convertible coupe and a new two-door six-passenger Sedan-Coupe. Standard equipment included more chrome (including the outer grilles and running board edges), trunk light, clock, wheel trims, and painted stripes. Mid-year changes added chrome strips to all four fenders and around all the windows.

With its more modern design and greater power, the new six must have been a slight embarrassment to Ford, and buyers were quick to notice that it actually cost $15 *less* than the V-8 model for model. Prices ranged from $684 for the basic six-cylinder Special coupe up to $1013 for the V-8 Super DeLuxe wagon. The latter marked the first time in a decade that a regular-line passenger Ford had broken the psychologically important thousand-dollar price barrier.

Ford made up for lost time in another way this year. It may have been late with hydraulic brakes, but it now had the industry's largest: 12 inches in diameter. Other engineering alterations began with wider front and rear transverse leaf springs that allowed softer spring rates and softer shocks for a more cushioned ride. The springs were also located further apart, providing a springbase of 125

The '41 Ford pickup (top) listed at $605, although customers could save $15 or $20 by buying a six or four. The Super DeLuxe Fordor (above) cost $859.

inches, which also helped smooth out the bumps. Improved body mountings, meanwhile, made that going quieter. Numerically higher gear ratios, borrowed from the previous V-8/60 transmission, were adopted for both six and V-8, mainly to make up for the expected performance losses from the new models' greater heft. The result was comparable low-end getaway at some expense in low-speed flexibility in second and third gears.

Paul R. Woudenberg, in *Ford in the Thirties* summed up the new '41 Ford by noting that "The end result was a car with a new solid feel, greater insulation from road noise, and the familiar Ford mechanical sounds hardly evident. It was a car much more like its principal competitors, but in the process it lost many of the characteristics of the Ford in the Thirties.... Plymouth and Chevrolet owners could now feel more at home in the Ford."

Having been substantially reworked for 1940, this year's Ford trucks were predictably little changed. There were minor chassis modifications for all but half-ton models, whose wheelbase remained at 112 inches. In fact, the sedan delivery, in an odd departure from usual practice, was a virtual carryover, sharing none of the bigger and brighter new 1941 passenger-car design. Cabovers received a mild front facelift and "V-8" logos disappeared from bodies and hubcaps across the line even though the proven V-8/85 remained the mainstay powerplant. The new six was also offered here, though it found relatively few takers.

Ford's oddest truck development for '41 was availability of a new economy engine to fill in for the now-discontinued V-8/60. This was a small inline four lifted directly from Ford's new-generation farm tractor that had arrived in 1939 to replace the old Fordson (production of which had resumed in the UK in the late Twenties,

with some being sold in the U.S.). Rude and humble though this sounds, the tractor mill made a certain amount of sense in a Ford truck. Mainly, it was cheap to build, being essentially half a Mercury V-8 with the same pistons, rods, valves, and cylinder dimensions. Displacement thus worked out to 119.7 cubic inches, good for 30 brake horsepower on lowly 6.0:1 compression.

Of course, that was quite a few horses down from the V-8's 85, which is why the four wasn't offered in anything heavier than One-Tonner models. Even so, it surely had to work harder than any V-8/60 even though it produced slightly more effective torque. Too little engine for too much vehicle pretty much negated any economy advantage and explains why the four saw far fewer truck installations than even the slow-selling V-8/60. The Model N would be boosted to 40 horsepower for 1942, and would then quietly disappear.

More intriguing—and predictive—was the so-called "plastic Ford" that surfaced on August 13 this year. A compact, 2300-pound fastback two-door with V-8/60 power and a 110-inch wheelbase, it was an outgrowth of Henry's investigations into industrial uses for soybeans and their by-products, begun back in 1932. Strictly speaking, soybeans had nothing to do with this experimental. Its windows were made of Plexiglas, while the body comprised 14 separate panels (of $3/16$-inch section) made of an embryonic phenol-formaldehyde cellulose plastic reinforced with straw, hemp, ramie, and pine. Henry himself had tested this material in decklids fitted to various of his recent personal cars. One famous company photo shows him bashing one with an ax to demonstrate the panel's toughness. What he envisioned was a total damage-proof car body, one that could, conceivably, bounce off of anything it hit with nary a dent—not to mention being impervious to rust. Again, Henry was thinking way ahead.

But though plastics were already being used by several automakers for small parts like steering wheels and interior knobs, the technology just didn't exist in the Forties for practical, low-cost mass production of all-plastic car bodies. Then, too, Ford's cellulose compound was too brittle to sustain shunts without damage, a trait that would also have complicated the attachment of metal parts like hinges and handles. And according to one writer, the stuff "smelled like a mortuary."

The big problem, though, was prohibitive material cost. One company estimate put the price of even a compact car body at a dollar a pound in plastic versus just eight cents a pound for conventional sheet steel. So though *The New York Times* rushed to declare (on August 24) that a plastic Ford with a probable $400 price was on the way for 1943, the prediction was wildly optimistic. "Plastic" cars

The Super DeLuxe convertible (top left) was easily the sportiest model in Ford's '41 lineup. It retailed for $946, and found 30,240 buyers. Although it had the same roofline as the three-passenger coupe, the Sedan Coupe (top right) got a rear seat and room for six—if they were very good friends. It came only as the $849 top-line Super DeLuxe; 10,796 were built. The 112-inch-wheelbase half-ton '41 pickup (above left) enjoyed a production run of 70,190 units. Compare its styling with the 112-inch one-ton express (above).

wouldn't appear until well after World War II, during which a sturdier, more practical material called fiberglass was perfected. Even then, fiberglass shells cost more to make than comparable steel bodies, which partly explains why the pioneering mid-Fifties Kaiser-Darrin and early Corvettes ended up as high-priced limited editions that were consequently tough to sell.

There was no shortage of sales in 1941, but Ford's competition remained formidable. In the auto arena, a heavily revamped Chevrolet—still regarded as one of the best Chevys ever—was particularly strong. Third-place Plymouth, fielding a restyled version of its new 1940 design, managed to pull within 100,000 units by some accounts, while Chevy out-

sold Ford by 10-7, far wider than usual. Overall model-year totals were about 692,000 for Ford, slightly over a million for Chevrolet, and some 546,000 for Plymouth. Ford managed to step up production for 1941, but Chevy was climbing even faster.

Ford also trailed Chevrolet in truck volume—again—building more vehicles than it had in 1940 but falling just short of its 1937 high. The gain was fueled mainly by growing military demand, but Ford was not alone as total U.S. truck output surpassed a million units for the first time ever.

To some extent, Ford's disappointing '41 results reflected the problems of the company itself. The empire was going to seed under the aging Henry, who had never allowed Edsel enough latitude or managerial control—despite the fact that Edsel had been the "President" of Ford Motor Company for more than two decades. The only difference now was that the decay was starting to show. Against a mostly new Chevy, even an all-new '41 Ford was no more than a runner-up.

Ford might have done better had it not been for a wildcat strike that began April 2 after a handful of workers were fired for unionizing activities in the

Rouge rolling mill. A United Auto Workers team managed an effective auto blockade at all five entrances to the huge complex, effectively shutting it down in an action affecting some 50,000 employees. Nine days later, Edsel pleaded with his father to permit union elections. Henry grudgingly agreed, and 97 percent of his workers voted to join the UAW.

But then, perhaps hoping to wear them all down, the stubborn old man stalled, refusing to sign the contract presented to him in June. Wife Clara finally threatened to walk out herself unless he changed his mind. Reluctantly, Henry did, saying, "Don't ever discredit the power of a woman." To his own credit, Henry's good nature seemed to return once this inevitable die was cast. On June 20 the UAW and Ford Motor Company signed the American auto industry's first closed-shop contract, the first of many pacts that often left Ford workers better off than any others in Detroit.

Labor difficulties didn't preclude another important Ford milestone. It came on April 29 with production of the 29-millionth Ford vehicle. It would, however, be the last such observance for several years. America was about to enter World War II.

1 9 4 2

Historially, Detroit cars received only a mild reworking for the second year of an all-new design, and for 1942 Ford was no exception. But this would hardly be the usual sort of model year for the American auto industry. Ford unveiled its '42s on September 12, 1941. Less than three months later, the nation was at war.

The fact that civilian production would shut down after December 7 was inevitable. Contrary to popular belief, not everyone in Detroit had planned on America's entry into the war—least of all Ford, which had geared up for a big 1942. But Henry Ford, ever the pacifist, had felt the winds of war blowing from Europe, and like so many others his company had been gradually turning to war work long before the Japanese bombed Pearl Harbor. After that, the nation's industrial machine shifted into high.

Underscoring America's sudden involvement in the war, Ford closed its Rotunda visitors' center in Dearborn on January 28, 1942. No sense having foreign spies and saboteurs sneaking around the grounds of a major military contractor.

It was on December 4, 1941, three days before the attack in Hawaii, that Ford and other automakers had been ordered to freeze all civilian projects and cut back on excessive use of brightwork. These restrictions became even more ominous with Washington's sudden declaration of war against the Axis powers on December 8, which implied the total mobilization of U.S. industry. The implication became fact on February 10, 1942, when the government halted civilian car production for the duration. Only 43,307 Fords had been built since January 1. With just 160,432 units for the model year, the '42s would be the rarest Fords since 1910.

Ford advertised the '42s as "America's Most Modern 6 ... America's Lowest-priced 8." They were definitely more important-looking Fords, marked by new fenders, hood, and grille that gave the front end a more cohesive look. Running boards were newly concealed beneath deeper lower-door sheetmetal. Per prevailing industry trends, the grille, again with fine vertical bars but surrounded by a heavy-looking frame, was lower and wider—close to full-width, in fact. Above it were rectangular parking lamps in what remained of the front fender "catwalks." The only vestige of the prominent '41 central grille was a chrome divider bar running down from the hood.

Fenders were now one-piece units, like the grille, and taillights changed from vertical rectangles to horizontal ovals. A revamped dash highlighted interior changes.

Though not readily apparent, the '42s rode an inch lower than the '41s thanks to a reduced-height frame with a new welded central X-member. Spring rates were softened in a continuing quest for competitive ride comfort, which prompted the addition of a front track bar to assist the existing stabilizer in roll control. Other detail chassis changes included a heavier steering column jacket and revised engine and exhaust-system mounts.

Model choices stayed the same except that the low-price Specials were now strictly Sixes. As before, DeLuxe and Super DeLuxe offerings could also be had with the V-8. Ford dealers must have tired of explaining why the six had more horsepower than the V-8, because the latter was now rated at the same 90 bhp even though it was virtually unchanged. Prices *were* changed—up about $100 across the board—making the $1080 Super DeLuxe convertible the first Ford other than wagons to sell for more than $1000 since the Model A Town Cars of 10 years earlier.

Per Washington decree, Dearborn's final '42s had many parts that were painted rather than chromed. Military applica-

The '42 Ford received new front fenders and a wider, lower single-unit grille. Taillights changed from vertical rectangles to horizontal ovals. The Super DeLuxe Sedan Coupe (above left) increased by $61 to $920 with the 90-bhp V-8. With the six, also 90 bhp, it cost $910. Output came to 13,543 before the war interfered. The $825 sedan delivery (left) received a longer rear roofline, allowing for a 92.5-cubic-foot cargo area. Access was through a rear door. Only 1316 were built. In a prophetic statement, a '42 Ford ad said "here is new style that will stay good for years."

tions had priority for supplies of chrome and other "strategic" metals and led to a growing number of spot shortages in the civilian sector. The resulting "blackout" '42s are thus the rarest of a rare breed, something true for all Detroit cars built in the final days of this abbreviated model year.

They'd have to last, too, for there would be no more new American cars for four very long years. Buyers may have sensed this—or read about a Japanese gent named Tojo. Whatever the reason, demand soared as buyers scrambled to get 'em while they could. A gradual government-ordered slowdown in passenger-car production beginning in late 1941 only heightened the showroom rush.

Lincoln got much of Ford Motor Company's product emphasis this year, with heavy facelifts and more horsepower for Zephyr, Custom, and Continental. Mercury was also heavily restyled for a more massive look, but not significantly changed otherwise. Still on its year-old 118-inch wheelbase, the Merc remained miles more impressive than a Ford, yet cost only a few dollars more. Dearborn once boasted that Mercury had "made 150,000 owners change cars." What it didn't like was that a lot of them had changed from Fords.

Despite mounting military work in 1940-41, Ford found time enough to make some fairly major changes for its 1942 commercial line. Most affected were the half-ton models, which now began moving away from their passenger-car sisters to become more like their heavy-duty truck brothers in styling and engineering. This mainly involved a heftier new chassis with four crossmembers and straight siderails. Wheelbase now measured 114 inches, same as on the passenger cars, but suspension was now like that of the larger Regulars since 1940. This meant a front I-beam on parallel longitudinal semi-elliptic leaf springs and a similar arrangement for the carryover ¾-floating rear axle, now with open Hotchkiss drive. A new flexible radiator mount and revised spring shackles were featured across the line, cabover models included.

Stylewise, the sedan delivery fell back into line with Ford's passenger cars. Conventional cabs gained a new look via a revised hood, vertical-stripe grille, and higher, squared-up fenders with flush headlamps. The pickup gained a slightly wider cargo box that increased both load-carrying ability and versatility.

Years of gradual, considered expansion had by now swelled Ford truck offerings to 126 separate body/chassis combinations. It was a strong, solid lineup: conventionals and cabovers spanning three engines (four, six, and V-8), four wheelbases, and half-ton, ¾-ton, one-ton, and 1½-ton payload ratings. As with passenger cars, however, everyone built far fewer trucks for 1942—at least for civilians—and Ford's were as rare as any.

The DeLuxe was Ford's mid-range offering for '42, noted by a badge on the vertical grille bar. Five body styles were offered, among them the $885 Fordor (top). Super DeLuxes were badged to the left of the grille; the wagon (center) sold for $1125. The newly styled half-ton pickup retailed for $675 with V-8.

It hardly needs saying that Ford Motor Company was vital to America's ultimate victory in World War II. Though it had ceased to be the nation's top-selling automaker in the Thirties, it remained a vast corporation with huge resources. Henry and Edsel Ford saw to it that those resources were quickly mobilized.

Dearborn's war record was as proud as any in American industry. Its huge new factory at Willow Run, southwest of Detroit, turned out the famous B-24 "Liberator" bomber by the score. Testifying to its efficiency, B-24 production reached 5000 by July 1944. Output hit its peak the following August 31: An incredible 432 of the planes were built that single day.

Ford also turned out the Army's new light utility car, the Jeep, designed by the failing American Bantam Car Company of Butler, Pennsylvania, which proved unable to cope with the tremendous demand. Willys-Overland also built them, of course, as it would after the war, when it successfully modified the design for the civilian market. Ford's Jeeps stood apart from both the Bantam- and Willys-built versions by virtue of their vertical-bar grilles, curved front fenders, and elliptic bodyside cutouts.

Also spewing forth from Dearborn was a dizzying array of vehicles ranging from amphibious and armored personnel carriers to light tanks and conventional and all-terrain trucks. With government approval, the firm also built a limited number of 1942-style cars, mainly base-trim Tudor and Fordor sedans. Most saw service as military staff cars, but some remained stateside for "essential" civilian purposes.

The war years witnessed a leadership crisis that would have a profound effect on the company, its operations, and products in the postwar period. It was precipitated by the untimely passing of Edsel Ford on May 26, 1943, at the age of only 50. Never a robust figure, he was claimed by a combination of undulant fever, ulcers, and stomach cancer—hastened, perhaps, by Henry's continued reliance on Harry Bennett, whose strong-arm tactics had not only produced labor unrest but dissention among top company executives. Though overshadowed to the end by his legendary father, Edsel had nevertheless emerged as his own man, an auto executive of rare taste and ability. In particular, he almost single-handedly established styling as a distinct and important function within the Ford organization. His absence would be keenly felt.

On June 1, just five days after Edsel's death, Henry Ford, about to turn 80, was reelected to another term as company president, a term he would not live to complete. His resumption of day-to-day control was not universally welcomed. As *Automotive News'* Richard Johnson recounted in late 1985, "There was lingering concern among certain members of the family and allies of Edsel Ford that Bennett's influence on Henry I could be the downfall of the company. Bennett, fearing the grandson's looming presence, sought to have Henry Ford's will rewritten to provide that the company be run by a board of trustees for 10 years after his death.

"Not only was the family worried about the company, so was the U.S. government, which had huge war contracts with the drifting, poorly managed auto manufacturer. There was even talk of nationalizing the company to protect the government's investment."

Accordingly, Navy secretary Frank Knox, with President Roosevelt's blessing, arranged an early discharge for ensign Henry Ford II, Edsel's eldest son, then only 26. The express understanding was that he would take over from his grandfather as soon as possible. But the old man wasn't about to turn over the reigns so quickly, not even to his own namesake. Thus, as Johnson records, "The young man moved into his father's office and was eventually titled 'vice-president,' although he did not have any specific assignment at first. The company continued under the iron hand of Bennett...."

All this only hastened a breakup of the company's top managerial staff. Trouble had been brewing as early as 1939, but it didn't come to a head until

Edsel Ford, ever in the shadow of his father, died on May 26, 1943, at the age of 50. He'll always be revered for his sensitivity to excellence in design.

several top designers walked out on September 13, 1943. Among them were engineer Lawrence Sheldrick and stylist Eugene T. "Bob" Gregorie. Their departure, as historians Allan Nevins and Frank Hill noted in *Ford: Decline and Rebirth*, were "body blows to the Ford Motor Company" that considerably weakened both areas.

"Cast Iron Charlie" Sorensen was another casualty. He'd become too ambitious. He'd wanted to be Ford president, and Henry wouldn't have it. Sorensen thus departed on March 3, 1944, quickly becoming president of a still-troubled Willys-Overland.

The way now seemed clear for Bennett, but he hadn't counted on the Ford family. Clara Ford seemed the only one willing to tell her husband he was wrong. He must now resign and let their grandson take command, she said. Henry, wrote Nevins and Hill, remained "peevishly reluctant."

Meantime, Henry II had thrown himself into learning the family business from the ground up. "There were plenty of surprises," notes Johnson. For example, the young man "was dumfounded to learn [that] the company's more than $680 million in cash holdings were in bank accounts which did not bear interest.... The company not only needed an injection of financial discipline, but the revival of production discipline at the Rouge complex. It was widely believed Ford Motor Company was buoyed only by its defense business and was on the verge of collapse from wayward management."

Deciding it was time to do something about that—and rid himself of Bennett—Henry II began working to put himself firmly in charge, strongly supported by his mother, Eleanor Clay, and grandmother Clara. Johnson notes that a key figure in this was John Bugas, "an ex-FBI man who had fallen out of favor with the man who had hired him, Harry Bennett.

"During dinner at the Detroit Club in early 1945, Henry II met with Bugas and Mead Bricker, head of production at Willow Run, to plot a strategy.... For starters, Bugas advised Henry II to get his grandfather to agree that no company official could be dismissed without the young man's consent. With that, he began dismantling Bennett's vast network of cronies and accomplices. The young vice-president took on a high profile and there was growing pressure on the old man from his wife and daughter-in-law...to make way for his grandson. The elder Ford resisted until Eleanor threatened to sell her one-third share of the company and bring down the empire. With that, the infirm, increasingly senile founder agreed to resign." On January 23, 1944, HF II was appointed executive vice-president, then a relatively token title that nevertheless marked him as old Henry's heir apparent.

Still, it wasn't until late 1945 that

Henry II actually took over. The transition of power began in August, when he was summoned by his grandfather to the family's Fair Lane estate. He knew what he was up against: "I told him I'd take [over as president] only if I had a completely free hand to make any changes I wanted to make. We argued about that, but he didn't withdraw his offer." Thus did Henry Ford at last submit his resignation as president on September 20. The Board of Directors accepted it on the 21st and named Henry II to succeed him. Bennett stormed out that same day with the window dressing of a one-month directorship.

The leadership crisis and the atmosphere of murky intrigue that pervaded Ford Motor Company in the mid-Forties only made it more difficult to plan for the return to civilian production—but not impossible. In fact, proposals for a wholly revamped 1943 corporate line were well along before Pearl Harbor. Despite the press of military work, not to mention uncertainty over the war's eventual outcome, designers still found time in this period to refine those ideas and develop new ones. Some would be seen in the all-new 1949 Lincoln and Mercury; others would appear in overseas products.

Gregorie recalled Ford's wartime design activities in a 1970 interview with Michael Lamm of *Special Interest Autos* magazine. Naturally, the outbreak of war abruptly ended advanced planning for 1943-45: "All at once, the whole company changed gears and got down to war work. . . . Yet in the backs of our minds we knew that after the war we were going to have to start building cars again. At the beginning, nobody knew whether the U.S. would win or not, but there seemed little point in planning on any assumption except that we would. So slowly, in between wartime assignments, this little skeleton group we held together would

go back to the sort of nebulous business of designing after-the-war cars.

"The Ford lines were the ones we worked on most, because they were past due for a change. [Lincoln, having been heavily facelifted for '42, would have seen only detail alterations.] Edsel Ford was very busy with war production matters in 1942, but did spend what time he could with us on future planning. This lasted until his illness and death in the spring of 1943. The elder Mr. Ford took virtually no interest in design or styling activities, leaving this phase of operations to Mr. Edsel Ford and myself. There were no committees, etc., as is the usual practice. Decisions were quick and simple, which possibly accounts for some of the cleaner, simpler, straightforward styling we were able to accomplish. Mr. Edsel Ford and I were usually pretty much in agreement.

"What was intended as the larger Ford became the first all-new postwar Mercury," Gregorie continued. "At the time, we considered this design for the Ford of that era. Then, an entirely new Ford was developed, with lighter construction, new suspension, etc., and this became the 1949 Ford.

"One idea we had back then, and it came to fruition in 1949, was to associate the Mercury more closely with the Lincoln via certain body interchanges, as well as tie them together in advertising, sales, etc. Before, the Merc was based on the Ford. We figured the Mercury might gain some prestige by becoming a baby Lincoln rather than a blown-up Ford. So, during the war, our Lincoln designs did have some importance toward that end. We laid down the basic lines for what would become the 1949 Mercury in a painting that [illustrator] Ross Cousins did in 1943 . . . showing a five-passenger coupe driving past the Rouge plant. We called it a Lincoln, but the profile is very much what the 1949 Mercury became.

Then too, all those early Lincoln clays show a lot more of what we had in mind for the Mercury, as well as the Lincoln Cosmopolitan.

"As for the Continental," Gregorie said, "we didn't know whether it would be continued after Mr. Edsel Ford's death in 1943. We made some renderings and full-size models of the Cosmo with a spare tire mounted on the trunk, but it was too ponderous and clumsy to project the true Continental image. I think the only reason Ford Motor Company kept the Continental after the war was because they already had the body tooling. If the 1946-48 Continental hadn't used 1942 tooling, it probably wouldn't have been built those years. With the strong demand for postwar cars, the Continental did sell, and it really carried Lincoln prestige into the postwar period and to later Continentals. After Mr. Edsel Ford's death, though, no one had the heart to come up with a completely new Continental design."

The upgraded Mercury to which Gregorie refers wasn't supposed to resemble the '49 Lincoln. Through early 1947, Ford planning envisioned no fewer than six distinct corporate platforms: a 100-inch-wheelbase compact to be built by a separate new division, a standard Ford on a 118-inch wheelbase (same as the 1941-48 Mercury), a two-tier Mercury lineup on wheelbases of 120 and 123 inches, a 125-inch Lincoln (perhaps continuing the Zephyr name), and a top-line Lincoln Cosmopolitan and Continental on a 128-inch chassis. The erstwhile Zephyr would have had the baby-Lincoln styling Gregorie mentioned, while the '49 Mercurys would have continued as more luxurious Fords.

Dearborn wasn't the only Big Three producer with designs on a compact. GM and Chrysler had similar projects underway, stemming, like Ford's, from earlier

Despite his pacifistic leanings, Henry Ford thrust the might of Ford Motor Company into the war effort in the Forties, just as he had done in World War I. Among many achievements was the erection of the huge Willow Run complex 30 miles west of Detroit, which built B-24 "Liberator" bombers (opposite) by the hundreds. Henry II, recalled from the Navy in 1943, is seen here with Henry I and a model of the River Rouge plant (above).

studies done in response to the Depression. All these early-to-mid-Forties efforts were based on fears that a recession, like the one that followed World War I, was inevitable, thus making cheaper, smaller cars a necessity once peace returned.

Ford's postwar compact originated in 1942 and owed little to the small, plastic-bodied experimental of 1941. First thoughts centered on a low-price four-cylinder car with the dimensions, power output, weight, and price of the prewar Willys-Overland. Later, some executives apparently wanted a size/price rival for Studebaker's Champion. Of course, the Champion had a six, and its dimensions had grown since Raymond Loewy's 1939 original. As it turned out, Studebaker fielded a warmed-over '42 Champion for 1946, then bowed dramatically styled all-new models for '47.

In the late spring of 1944 a group of

Dearborn executives led by sales manager John R. Davis and the aforementioned Mead Bricker came up with the idea of forming a separate team to prepare new postwar products. This became the Engineering Planning Committee, representing key departments ranging from manufacturing to market research. Hudson McCarroll took the lead in defining these products and their technical makeup. Among them was what he saw as a new kind of economy car designed to sell at two-thirds the price of the standard Ford.

To this end, the committee reviewed Ford's last small-car experiment. Known simply as project 92-A, it was completed in 1938 by a team under Eugene Farkas, who'd played a big part in designing the Model A and the 1932 Ford. This car was quite small, about 600 pounds lighter than the contemporary Ford, with a shorter wheelbase and a narrower track. Farkas proposed using the small V-8/60 rather than tooling up a new four or six. But in the end, 92-A was scrapped due to production costs that would have been too close to those of a standard Ford for the compact to have a significant price advantage and still be profitable. Now, in the mid-Forties, company planners realized that the cost/profit problem would be even more troublesome postwar.

Ford had produced a variety of purpose-designed smaller cars in Europe before the war, starting with the four-cylinder British Model Y/Junior of 1932, a Sheldrick design. But all were deemed too small for American buyers, and there was nothing technical that could be applied to a new U.S. compact. Clearly, a new small American Ford would have to be designed from scratch in Dearborn.

Frantic and furious work brought forth many ideas, some intelligent, others less so. For example, one proposal envisioned front-wheel drive and a four-cylinder engine installed transversely in front (ahead of the wheels), a layout that's since become nearly universal. The radiator was placed slightly higher than the engine and behind it, backed by a cowl structure carrying the fuel tank, as on the Model A. The result was a short hood and a low, flat floor for unusually generous interior space. Also considered was a conventional rear-drive chassis with a longitudinal inline five—the elder Henry's doing. Though not directly connected with product engineering by that point, the old man had maintained a private laboratory where he'd toyed with such unorthodox ideas since about 1936.

The experimental department soon hummed with new powerplants, air-cooled fours and sixes among them. Cast-aluminum blocks were tried for several water-cooled units, including the five-cylinder job, but were ruled out as too costly. A rear-engine layout wasn't even considered, perhaps because of Henry's objections to it on the original Zephyr prototype, and front drive was ultimately discarded because of its many unknowns, as well as its higher cost.

As time went on, the small V-8 was increasingly preferred, along with other basic elements of Farkas' 1938 proposal, and a new prototype incorporating these features was completed by mid-1944. In September, Henry II announced that Ford planned to introduce this smaller, lower-priced car for the postwar market.

By the time the Engineering Planning Committee ordered full-scale versions that winter, Gregorie had already been doing small-car sketches and clay models for about two years. A 98-inch wheelbase was selected, and a fastback two-door sedan was the first body style developed. What emerged was quite similar to the '42 Ford in overall proportions but was more modern in appearance, with slab sides and a lower, wider grille. A continuing flow of fresh market information led to several more prototypes that differed from each other in many ways. These were further modified, and a 100-inch wheelbase was tried. Although the five-cylinder engine was still in the running at that point, the V-8/60 was more or less assumed. By January 1945, a more precise package definition prompted planners to settle on the 100-inch platform. Within six months, the five-cylinder engine was scrapped and development proceeded around the V-8 alone. The frame would be a smaller version of the forthcoming '49 Ford/Mercury design, complete with its new coil-spring independent front suspension and parallel rear leaf springs, both firsts for a Dearborn car. Clyde R. Paton, one time chief engineer at Packard, was hired to direct the project through to the production-ready stage. Assembly was slated to begin within six months after the end of war in Europe. (V-E day turned out to be May 11, 1945.)

But Paton soon ran into the same snag that killed Farkas' project: cost. Hudson McCarroll, promoted to engineering director in 1945, didn't know what to do and ended up listening to everybody. Sales manager Davis said he already had buyers for every standard Ford. Why put a lot of money into a compact that the public might not accept? He saw no need for a smaller car, even as a loss leader, until 1948-49 at the earliest. In that event, Paton thought an updated design might be needed, preferably with unit construction. With all this, the 100-inch-wheelbase prototype was shelved.

Paton and company then went to work on two larger versions of what was now being called the "Light Car": a 106-inch-wheelbase Ford and a 112-inch Mercury. To handle development and production, Ford created a new Light Car Division on April 12, 1946. (At the same time, brief thought was given to buying the shattered remains of Hitler's Volkswagen factory at Wolfsburg in the southern part of the new state of West Germany, but the idea was dismissed as a waste of precious funds.) By this time, the program was seen as so important that no one questioned the need for a new corporate entity of this size.

Then a new problem appeared: material shortages. Steel, copper, lead, zinc, and other metals were proving hard to come by even before war's end, and Henry II knew it wasn't good business to add a whole new model line that would vie for scarce resources with cars that were already selling well. Although management didn't officially curtail the small-car program in 1946, the Product Committee told the Light Car Division to defer production plans. The result was the same: The Light Car was dead, even though the 106-inch-wheelbase design

was fully engineered—effectively a production prototype.

Enter Maurice Dollfus, president of Ford France, who'd argued that the Light Car should be built in Europe, if not the U.S. Now, he finally got his wish. The engineering department released all data and blueprints to him in June 1946, and the 106-inch prototype was reworked at the subsidiary's Poissy factory, near Paris, for production on metric tools, with specifications adjusted for locally produced components. Named Vedette, the car started coming off the lines in the fall of 1948, but proved a sales disappointment due to relatively high fuel consumption and stiff competition from class rivals.

There was a funny thing about all these wartime machinations, and Gregorie summed it up perfectly: "It never dawned on any of us that, right after the war, anything on wheels would sell, whether it was restyled or not. We just never sat down and thought about it enough to figure that out. So we went right ahead as though the first thing we'd have to do...was restyle the Ford and Mercury, not realizing until the last minute that a suitable facelift would do as well. In fact, we had until about 1948-49 before we'd have to come up with anything really different."

Gregorie was only half right. The immediate postwar years did witness an unprecedented seller's market reflecting the huge pent-up demand for new vehicles in the wake of a four-year production hiatus. And, like most everyone else except the independents, Ford got along just fine by reprising its '42 models through 1948.

By model year 1949, however, when the majors completed their postwar design overhaul, Dearborn was in serious financial trouble. Aside from long impeding technical progress, old Henry had left his company in financial chaos, reflecting his long-time distrust of accountants. Thus, his grandson inherited not only an aging product line but a company laden with debt, fiscally out of control, and lacking broad, strong leadership in several key areas. On top of all this, Chrysler Corporation had taken over as number-two in industry production behind General Motors.

As a result, 1949 would shape up as a do-or-die year for Dearborn. And strange as it may seem now, there were many at the time who didn't give Ford more than a 50/50 chance of making it.

Ford Motor Company was seemingly without leadership after Edsel Ford's death. Henry Ford (left) resumed the presidency of the company, but the government, concerned that the firm might not be able to honor its wartime contracts, sent Henry II (right) home. But it was Henry's wife Clara (center) that became the heroine of the situation when she threatened to leave her husband if he didn't turn over the reigns of the company to young Henry. Grudgingly, old Henry did.

1 9 4 6 - 1 9 4 8

With the war just about over, the government okayed the resumption of auto production in mid-1945. Quicker to start up than most, and like everyone else, Ford fielded warmed-over '42s. A horizontal-bar grille (with red stripes in the bars) and revised rear deck trim were new. Ford also got Mercury's 239.4-cid, 100-bhp V-8—thus wiping out Merc's performance advantage. The Super DeLuxe Coupe Sedan (top) sold for $1307. Topping the line was the woody Sportsman (center): $1982. As ever, Fords were popular with the police (bottom).

American industry had turned to military production with lightning speed in the early Forties. It returned to peacetime business just as quickly with V-J Day and the end of war in the Pacific theater on August 3, 1945—a bit before, actually, thanks to Washington.

The transition would be fraught with significance for Ford Motor Company. The war years had brought the untimely death of Edsel Ford, the loss of several brilliant designers who had gravitated to him, and the end of his father's reign. Now, under Edsel's son Henry II, the troubled company entered the postwar world with the formidable task of essentially starting over. The postwar years were critical in that they would either be a new beginning or a beginning of the end at Ford.

It follows then that when Harry Bennett, old Henry's mercenary lieutenant, stormed out of Dearborn in 1945 after failing in his bid to become company president, he angrily told young Henry, "You're taking over a billion-dollar organization here that you haven't contributed a thing to!" However, Henry was about to start contributing in a big way. Aided by a cadre of bright young managers and accountants, he began guiding Ford back to its late-prewar position as a near rival to the General Motors colossus. He'd been shocked by the state of the business now under his care. Aside from losses that reached $10 million a month by the first quarter of 1946, budgets and accounting procedures were either in total disarray or non-existent. One department reportedly calculated its accounts payable and receivable by measuring the height of the paperwork!

Ford's new president began looking for help. He found it in late 1945. It came in the person of Charles B. "Tex" Thornton, who cabled him after reading a *Life* magazine story about the troubled company that summer. Thornton offered his services and those of several talented officers as young as HF II himself—just 26 to 34 years old. All were about to be discharged from the Army Air Force's Office of Statistical Control. To Thornton's surprise, Ford hired them on the spot, thus bringing in the "Whiz Kids"—the brainy systems specialists who would help turn Ford's fortunes around—originally called the "Quiz Kids" when they arrived in Dearborn, owing to all the questions they asked.

Besides Thornton, the "kids" comprised Wilbur R. (Gene) Andreson, Charles E. Bosworth, J. "Ed" Lundy, George Moore, Robert S. McNamara, Arjay R.

Miller, Ben Davis Mills, Francis C. Reith, and James O. Wright. Both Miller and McNamara would later serve as Ford president, while Reith and Mills would respectively head up Mercury and Lincoln in the mid-Fifties. Wright would succeed McNamara as general manager of Ford Division in 1957.

But HF II wasn't finished recruiting. Evidently feeling that one way to compete more effectively with General Motors was to hire from its ranks, he enticed Ernest R. Breech to come over from Bendix, then a GM division, in July 1946. Breech would serve young Henry in the same way that Bennett had served old Henry—until he was suddenly fired in 1959. In the late Forties, though, Breech had no reason to leave Bendix other than his stated desire to make Ford "the leading automobile manufacturer in the United States." True to his word, he followed his new boss by throwing himself into learning every aspect of the company

and its deep-rooted problems.

By the following autumn, Breech and HF II had taken on a whole slew of GM designers, engineers, and managers. Among the more notable: engineers Harold T. Youngren (from Oldsmobile) and Earle S. MacPherson (inventor of the famous strut suspension); designers John Oswald, George Snyder (also from Olds), and Eugene Bordinat (previously executive stylist at Chevrolet); and Lewis D. Crusoe, GM's expert assistant treasurer.

With that, designer Bob Gregorie, who'd briefly returned to Dearborn as chief stylist, resigned a second time, mainly over the '49 Ford program (see *1949*). Replacing him was none other than Tom Hibbard, who brought impeccable credentials to the job. Hibbard had first joined Ford in 1941 after partnering with Ray Dietrich since 1920 in the famed LeBaron coachbuilding firm (purchased by Briggs, Ford's long-time body supplier, in 1927). Later he joined with Howard A.

"Dutch" Darrin in the Paris-based Hibbard & Darrin, another renowned builder of exotic custom bodies. After just two years, though, Hibbard would resign as Dearborn's chief stylist, replaced by George Snyder.

Most U.S. vehicle makers faced a dilemma toward the end of World War II: Should they return to civilian production with warmed-over prewar models or put the rush on new postwar designs? Studebaker, after a brief run of 1942 look-alikes for '46, did the latter; however, Ford and most everyone else did the former. Henry Ford II had no choice. Though financed to the tune of nearly $700 million, his company was heavily in debt and faced the massive cost of winding down its war machine. Above all, Ford needed to get back to civilian production as quickly as possible, and indeed Ford wasted no time in advertising that "There's a Ford in your future." Still, the path to postwar profitability was going to be long and tough.

Among the first product decisions made by the new man in charge were the Ford Sportsman and its uptown cousin, the Mercury Sportsman. HF II reasoned that if Ford's first postwar models couldn't be all-new, at least some of them could be strikingly different on the surface—enough to lure buyers into newly reopened showrooms filled with cars that were otherwise quite familiar. Paneling convertibles in maple or yellow birch with mahogany-veneer inserts looked a pretty good way to do that.

Gregorie had designed just such a convertible before he first departed Dearborn (see *1943-1945*), and HF II had liked it. Ford certainly didn't lack for wood. It owned a massive forest and timber processing plant up at Iron Mountain, Michigan, that had supplied raw materials for station wagon bodies since 1936. Because the panels would be grafted right onto existing convertible shells, a woody ragtop would be no more difficult to build than a woody wagon. Not that Sportsman panels were mere appliques. They were, in fact, structural body elements made from solid wood blocks, mitered and fitted with handcrafted precision,

and handsomely finished with several coats of varnish.

Wood is nature's product, not man's, so no two Sportsmans were exactly alike. The Fords used three different types of trim during their two-year production run. Enthusiast Dr. Thomas B. Garrett noted that "'Style A' had horizontal pieces running full length across the doors and quarters. In the 'B' and 'C' styles, the full-length members ran vertically from top to bottom. All 1946 Sportsmans used the 'A' panels, whereas '47s were divided between all three." (Ford lists only 28 Sportsmans sold for 1948, all reserialed '47s.)

There was just one problem: the production '46 rear fenders, which wrapped around enough to cut into the wooden trunklid. The solution was using '41 Ford sedan delivery fenders and taillights on both the Ford and Mercury versions. Otherwise, the Sportsmans were largely the same as their non-wood running mates. Like its conventional counterpart, the Ford Sportsman came only in Super DeLuxe trim with the L-head V-8, the latter in deference to its greater weight. Exclusive standard equipment included hydraulic window lifts and vanity mirrors on both sun visors.

"Outside and inside, there never was a car like this before!" Ford boasted, conveniently overlooking the new Chrysler Town & Country woody. "The new Sportsman's Convertible is really *two* cars in one! Ford designers have combined the paneled smartness of the station wagon and the touch-a-button convenience of the convertible!" Hollywood actress Ella Raines took delivery of the first Ford Sportsman on Christmas Day 1945, a scant three months after Henry II had assumed the presidency. Despite only incidental publicity, it was a fair success considering it cost $1982 in 1946, $700 more than a comparable Fordor sedan and $500 more than the regular all-steel ragtop. A total of 3487 were built for the three model years, along with 205 Mercury Sportsmans, offered only for '46.

Performance was not a Sportsman asset. The Ford version, for example, weighed about 100 pounds more than the steel-body convertible and 200 pounds more than an equivalent Fordor—so it moved well enough but wasn't sensationally quick. Typical figures for both

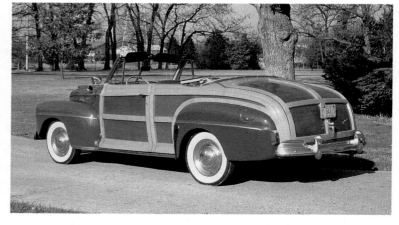

Sportsmans were about 85-mph maximum and a bit less than 20 seconds for the 0-60 mph dash. Both showed definite understeer, but handling was adequate considering the antediluvian front and rear transverse leaf springs. They even cope well with today's roads and traffic conditions, including freeways. Most examples are unusually solid for convertibles, testifying to their careful construction. Whether Ford or Mercury, the Sportsman is an entertaining piece—Dearborn's most notable production cars of the early postwar years.

Aside from simplified frontal styling that featured a bold horizontal-bar grille and revised decklid trim, the '46 Ford was essentially the '42 reborn. However, there were minor chassis changes that slightly improved both ride and braking, and V-8 performance was perceptibly better as the old 90-horsepower, 221-cubic-incher was replaced by the 100-bhp, 239-cid Mercury unit—much to the chagrin of Mercury's sales and "hot rod" persona. Even better, the V-8 featured useful revisions comprising a new pressurized cooling system, improved ignition, longer-life bearings made of silver alloy (developed for wartime airframes), and the return of aluminum pistons. Ford's 90-bhp six entered the postwar world unchanged. The prewar Special group of low-priced sixes was eliminated, leaving six- and eight-cylinder DeLuxe and Super DeLuxe series as before. Body styles comprised Tudor and Fordor sedans, coupe, wagon, and standard and Sportsman convertibles.

This basic package was little changed for the next two model years. Reshuffled nameplates, removal of the red stripes from the grille bars, and round parking lights mounted below the headlights were the main alterations for '47½. At the same time, an updated six gained 5 bhp thanks to higher 6.8:1 compression, modified combustion chambers, improved manifolding, vacuum spark advance (replacing centrifugal), and a new external-mount oil pump and conventional distributor driven by a common shaft. This was apparently enough to prompt Ford to advertise that "There's a finer Ford in your future." Pushed by postwar inflation, prices rose each year by an average $100.

While all this sounds boring, no styling or engineering changes were really needed for the booming postwar seller's market. From July 3, 1945, when it resumed civilian car production (with a Super DeLuxe Fordor) to the end of model year '46, Ford built just over 468,000 cars, almost 100,000 more than Chevrolet. One reason for that accomplishment was that General Motors was shut down for 113 days by a nationwide steel strike in 1946—such walkouts plagued all American industry in the early postwar years as workers sought to bring their wages in line with escalating postwar prices. Volume slipped to just under 430,000 units for 1947, then dropped below 236,000 for '48. The last wasn't a sign of trouble (though it could have been)—only an early end to 1948 model year production. Realizing the

need for a truly modern car, Ford had started work on an all-new design in early 1946. Set to debut for 1949, it would be a car of major importance to the still-struggling company.

With Breech and all those other ex-GM'ers on the scene, no one was surprised when Ford began reorganizing along GM lines. One of the most lasting results of this was the creation of Lincoln-Mercury Division on October 22, 1945. As an entity separate from Ford Division (formally established February 11, 1949) and the short-lived Light Car division, it had its own engineering, purchasing, production, and sales departments and dealer network.

This in turn prompted a new approach to product planning that would eventually see Mercury clones of certain hot-selling Fords, like the "glasstop" Sun Valley/Skyliner (1954), Comet/Falcon compacts (1960), the Cougar/Mustang "ponycars" (1967-73), and the Eighties Cougar/Thunderbird. To some extent, competition between Ford and Lincoln-Mercury was now inevitable, but it was good, healthy competition. It still is, so long as Dearborn doesn't fall into GM's recent habit of badge-engineering exact copies of most everything in the corporate stable. (The distinctions between today's Sable/Taurus and Mark VII/Cougar/Thunderbird suggest Ford recognizes the importance of avoiding that trap.)

Initially, divisionalization meant a closer design and engineering relationship between Mercury and Lincoln, albeit

Opposite page: Mercury had good luck with its six-passenger coupe (a close-coupled two-door sedan), which accounted for 30-percent of 1946 output. Ford also did well with that body style (top left), and even though it came only as a top-line Super DeLuxe, 70,826 '46s were built. The Super DeLuxe Sportsman (top right) didn't do as well, but it was a specialty model—only 1209 were produced. Ford gave its trucks all-new styling for 1948, although the only clue on the step-van (bottom left) was the grille, this one in chrome. San Diego police must have felt close to their captives in the '48 Coupe Sedan (bottom right). This page: Ford's '48 season was a short one because the 49's debuted early, but the $1972 wagon (above) still attracted 8912 customers. A modest restyling involving grille (no red stripes), parking lights, and rear deck trim took place in mid-1947 (below).

within well-defined price sectors, though the makes were still quite separate in '46. The job at hand was getting product out as fast as possible, and, like Ford, the quickest way to do that was to issue warmed-over versions of the '42s. That's just what they did, returning to civilian production the same day the new division was formed. L-M began formal operations on April 1, 1947 (a date no doubt chosen unintentionally), and its organizational structure and chain of command were in place by May.

With that, the formidable team assembled by Ernie Breech began determining Ford's future in earnest. With Crusoe handling Finance, Youngren heading up Engineering, and Al Browning in charge of Purchasing, Ford was probably in more competent hands than it had ever been before—as it had to be: They faced a titanic job. Their cars were obsolete, even next to the equally aged competition. The only way to regain market share—and build on it—was an entirely new corpo-

rate line.

At a Policy Committee meeting on August 23, 1947, Crusoe declared that the 118-inch-wheelbase Ford proposed during wartime should instead be the new postwar Mercury. The planned Merc, in turn, would become the next Lincoln, while the '49 Ford would be redesigned on its existing 114-inch wheelbase. As previously noted (see *1943-1945*) consolidation occurred at each end of the line, the "Light Car" compact being dropped for U.S. sales and the Continental slated to disappear after 1948. Breech concurred wholeheartedly, and that was the end of it.

If Ford, Mercury, and Lincoln were among the least changed of early postwar cars, the reason was Breech Discussing plans for '49, he told the Policy Committee: "I have a vision. We start from scratch. We spend no time or money phoneying up the old cars, because this organization will be judged by the market on the next *Ford* it produces, and it had better be a radically new one." According to Ford chroniclers Nevins and Hill, Breech claimed to have received divine guidance the night before, when, after praying, he was "told" to "Start afresh!" Of course, that's what they *had* to do—particularly in the case of the breadwinning Ford.

The factors that made new-design cars unnecessary in the early postwar years mostly applied to trucks as well, so Ford, like other makers, merely trotted out its '42 products at first. Once the tide of war began turning toward the Allies in 1944-45, and given a rapidly aging vehicle fleet at home, Washington began authorizing gradually increased non-military production. Accordingly, Dearborn was allowed to start turning out civilian trucks again on January 1, 1945, a full

seven months before building its first postwar cars, and somewhat in advance of other truck makers.

Though the improved 239 V-8 featured from the start, materials shortages and continuing military production made Ford's 1945 commercial line quite a bit leaner than its '42 fleet, limited to half-ton pickup, 1½-ton cab/chassis and stakes, and the 194-inch-wheelbase school bus chassis—42 offerings versus 126 prewar. However, improving sheet steel supplies after V-J Day allowed most missing models save ¾-tonners to return for '46, including a sedan delivery modestly restyled along passenger-car lines. In June of that year, 1½-ton conventionals and COEs with two-speed axle, oversize tires, and reinforced frames were up-

139

rated to two-ton status as "Ford officially recognized what most truckers had known for years," in the words of one writer. The '46s were also the first Ford trucks with advertised gross vehicle weight (GVW) ratings—i.e., the vehicle with its maximum permitted payload.

Changes were virtually nil for 1947, but historians took note on January 21 when the veteran Highland Park plant began building trucks for the first time in 20 years. The booming demand for cars had put a premium on space at the Rouge complex, hence the transfer of most truck output to the old facility.

Trucks had necessarily worked much harder than passenger cars on the wartime home front and thus needed replacing that much sooner once peace returned. This explains why America's first all-new postwar trucks arrived before most of the new-design cars, being introduced in late '47 or early '48 for the 1948 model year. Ford weighed in on January 16, 1948, with a handsomely updated line of new "Bonus Built" models offering more choices than ever—139 different variations.

Though not greatly changed behind the cowl, both conventional and over-engine cabs were easily identified by their new frontal styling. This involved broader, squared-up front fenders (with complementing rear fenders on pickup, express, and panel delivery), plus new door ventpanes and revived one-piece windshields. Both cabs presented the same basic face for the first time since 1941. And distinctive it was: a simple square, horizontal-bar grille centered within a heart-shaped opening, flanked by headlamps at the upper corners. Above were block letters spelling F-O-R-D; above that, on the hood, a divided oval suggested "nostrils." A long slot framed in chrome adorned each hoodside, with the left one concealing the hood release. Interior width swelled to 65 inches for roomier, more comfortable driving, aided by a redesigned dash and a new seat "suspen-

sion" made up of pads and rubber-mounted links.

Running gear and basic chassis specs weren't appreciably changed, though COE cabs sat slightly more rearward than before to give all models the same cab-to-axle dimension. Also, six-cylinder power was available in the tall ones for the first time. Advertised payloads were slightly higher across the line.

Model nomenclature was now completely different and much simplified. Half-tons were called F-1, while F-2 denoted a revived ¾-ton chassis, the first since '42. The F-3 was the previous one-tonner re-rated as a "heavy-duty ¾-ton." The true one-tonner, labelled F-4, was built on a "de-rated" version of the 134-inch-wheelbase 1½-ton chassis. F-5 was the "regular" 1½-tonner, F-6 the two-ton chassis. Wheelbases were 112 inches for F-1, 122 for F-2 and F-3, and 134/158 for F-4 through F-6. GVWs ranged from 5700 pounds for F-2s up to 16,000 on F-6s. Though F-5/F-6 were advertised as "Heavy-Duty" models, they were really mediums.

And that was because Ford now had burly new "Big Job" models, the F-7 and F-8—its first foray into the heavy-truck field. Essentially ground-up fresh, they carried the most powerful truck engine in Ford history: a rugged new "stroker" of an L-head V-8. Sized at 336.7 cubic inches (bore and stroke: 3.50 × 4.38 inches), it delivered 145 bhp at 3600 rpm and 255 pounds/feet peak torque at 1800 rpm on 6.4:1 compression—good for GVW ratings of up to near 40,000 pounds. (With slightly higher compression, this engine would also power the upcoming new '49 Lincolns.) Features included a forged crankshaft with three main bearings and viscous damper, hydraulic valve lifters, and a twin-venturi Holley carb with integral distributor-controlled speed governor. Other V-8 trucks carried the smaller 239 flathead, basically the revised passenger-car unit but here called "Rouge 239." The sturdy six was an alternative for the

F-1 through F-6 series. Cabovers were available only with V-8 as F-5s on up.

Matching their mightier missions in life, F-7/F-8 had the longest wheelbases—135, 159, and 195 inches—as well as the largest clutches, new five-speed transmissions, higher-rate springs on heavier axles, and the most powerful brakes. Appearance was basically the same as that of lesser models except that conventionals shared the 10-inch-greater overall cab width found on all COEs (82.3 vs. 73 inches). Speaking of COEs, this year's redesign prompted an incidental change affecting the semi-trailer tractor version (F-6 through F-9): a wheelbase stretched nine inches to 110.

Conspicuous by its absence from this extensive new lineup was the familiar sedan delivery, dropped after several years of declining sales (though Chevrolet's continued to sell well and would persist through the Fifties). Somewhat making up for it was a redesigned panel delivery, available only on the F-1 chassis. Though necessarily more "trucky" in appearance, it was longer, wider, and thus roomier, offering a full 160 cubic feet of cargo space. Also limited to the F-1 line was the popular pickup, whose familiar sidemount spare was relocated to beneath the floor of the same basic cargo box used since 1938. Rounding out F-1s were a trio of vocational-body platforms: Chassis with Cowl, Chassis with Windshield, and Chassis with Cab. These were also available in the F-2/F-3 series, which offered an eight-foot express pickup and 7½-foot platform and stake models.

Helped by its head start in 1945 and the prolonged steel strike the following year, Ford beat Chevrolet in 1946 model year truck output, then returned to its customary runner-up spot once GM got back to working full-time. Ford again finished second in the '48 race despite its broader, redesigned line, partly because Chevy (and sister division GMC) had gotten a six-month jump on Dearborn with

all-new trucks of their own. Still, Ford remained comfortably ahead of GMC as well as Dodge, Studebaker, and International.

Besides those already mentioned, corporate developments in this period reflected the generally expansionist mood of the time as well as Ford's struggle for recovery. In 1946, the firm broke ground for three new assembly plants (at Atlanta, St. Louis, and Metuchen, New Jersey). Despite losing $8.1 million that year, 1947 saw production of Ford's millionth postwar vehicle, its five-millionth truck, and ground-breaking ceremonies for a new Research and Engineering Center in Dearborn—and a $64.8-million profit. Expansion was also evident north of the border as Ford Canada added two car lines in 1946 aimed at broader, more appropriate market coverage. Lincoln-Mercury dealers received the Mercury 114, essentially a Ford in a Mercury suit, thus giving them a cheaper, higher-volume product. Ford dealers took on the Monarch, a Mercury in Ford dress, thus extending their range into the lower reaches of the medium-price class.

That same year, Ford Canada introduced a companion line of light-duty trucks under the Mercury label. Like equivalent Canadian Ford models, these carried only the smaller 221 V-8 (though with most of the recent improvements made to the U.S. 239), but had somewhat different, rather GM-like front ends. The Mercs became more like their U.S. cousins with the '48 redesign, differing mainly in trim and badges plus a slightly different model mix.

Yet, the most noteworthy event came to pass on April 7, 1947: America and much of the rest of the world paused to mourn the passing of Henry Ford at age 83. It was a time to reflect on his colorful life and historic achievements—a stupendous legacy by any standard (see sidebar). But it was more a time for looking ahead. Ford Motor Company could no longer trade on its past. The future was at hand and, with it, the fate of a once-mighty empire. For millions around the globe, the question now was whether a new young Henry could restore that empire to the greatness it had known at the peak of his grandfather's career. One way or another, the answer would be known soon enough. In model year 1949, Ford would either do or die.

Opposite page: By 1948, the price of the Super DeLuxe Sportsman (top) had escalated by $300 to $2282, an increase of 15 percent. That's hardly surprising, though, as inflation was high in early postwar years. While 1947 was the best year for the Sportsman, with 2250 produced, the short 1948 model year would see only 28 built. Henry Ford II (bottom) had his work cut out for him in reviving Ford Motor Company, but he looks totally in charge in this 1947 photo. This page: Henry Ford I died on April 7, 1947, and despite his frailties much of the world mourned his passing, remembering him for all that he had accomplished.

End of an Era:
The Passing of Henry Ford

The passing of Henry Ford in April 1947 closed a momentous era not only for the firm he had founded but the entire motor industry, which so many believed he alone had fathered. The bitterness and disappointments of his later years would not be forgotten, but they were overshadowed by towering achievements that are untarnished to this day. And to the end, he remained irascible, unpredictable, enigmatic—endlessly fascinating.

Ford was never easily characterized. Wrote Michael Lamm in the Ford 75th Anniversary Issue of *Automotive News* in 1978: "Almost anything anyone says about . . . Henry Ford contains a contradiction. Newton's third law of motion applies about equally to physics and to the elder Mr. Ford. It seems that every action . . . had an equal and opposite reaction. . . . [He] was an immensely complicated man, consistently inconsistent, and his personality changed not only from day to day but a good deal over the course of his long life. Men close to Ford could read his mood by the lines around his mouth and the color of his complexion. When his face looked gray and furrowed, people tended to stay out of his way.

"It's hard to believe that a man enlightened enough to revolutionize labor via the $5 Day of 1914, revolutionize industry through the moving assembly line, who believed in lowering profits, who tried to stop World War I with the Peace Ship of 1915, who supported Wilson and the League of Nations and paid all bills for the Neutral Conference on Continuous Mediation; who founded schools, a hospital, an orphanage, and a museum; who ultimately gave away at least a third of his life's net income—it's hard to believe that [this man] would later harass his workers with a private police force; resist the National Recovery Act; come to despise Roosevelt; admire the Nazi government and accept a citation from Hitler in 1938; lash out at Jews, banks, and Wall Street and fire most of his closest colleagues." Hard to believe maybe, but that was Henry Ford.

If ever a folk hero emerged from the ranks of motor moguls and other industrial tycoons, it was surely Henry Ford. Along with the Wright Brothers and his friends Thomas A. Edison and Harvey Firestone, he was an inspiration for millions: a symbol of the dreams, drive, and inventiveness that sparked America's unparalleled growth and prosperity in the first half of the 20th Century. After establishing Ford Motor Company purely on venture capital and an idea, he watched it blossom into a multimillion-dollar worldwide organization. He had taken just five years to produce a mechanical device that enabled a nation to conquer her vast size. No geographically large country had ever built a world-class economy before—for her's, America was in his debt. No less important were his manufacturing and product innovations, such as the simple, reliable Model T, and engineering benchmarks like the monobloc flathead V-8, which pioneered a whole new approach to affordable transportation.

For a man who once remarked "History as written is more or less bunk," Henry Ford certainly did more than enough to earn a permanent place in it.

1 9 4 9

Ford Motor Company was a bit late with its first all-postwar cars, largely owing to the massive corporate reorganization instigated by Henry II and Ernie Breech. But it had been an all-out effort once plans were finalized, and management hustled its new models to market as soon as it could. Thus, the all new Lincoln and Mercury went on sale in April 1948, Ford in June.

Yet because General Motors hadn't finished updating its fleet and Chrysler was still peddling prewar designs, Ford wasn't really that far behind. And in some cases it was ahead. The '49 Ford, for example, appeared several months before this year's Chevy, and the new Mercury was available before the competing Pontiac, Dodge, DeSoto, and Oldsmobile 76/88. Lincoln trailed Cadillac, whose all-new '48 styling helped tighten its iron grip on the luxury trade, but closed the production gap with a model year record: 73,507 units. That was fewer than 20,000 behind Caddy, though that was as close as Lincoln would get for a long time.

One cause for Cadillac's increasing lead was a United Auto Workers strike against Ford that occurred in May 1948, just when the firm needed maximum '49-model output. The union, complaining that management had again perpetrated a "speed-up" at both the Rouge and Lincoln plants, halted production for 24 days. Mercury, however, was unaffected and would enjoy another record year. In fact, Dearborn's middle make skyrocketed in model-year volume to 300,000 units, good for sixth place in industry standings, just behind Pontiac. For the calendar 12 months, Mercury managed 200,000-plus, but Lincoln only 33,000.

It's difficult to overstate the importance of this year's Ford. For one thing, it represented a historic design departure for Dearborn—the most dramatically different Ford since the Model A replaced the Tin Lizzie a generation before. Wrote veteran auto tester Floyd Clymer at the time: "It is no more like the prewar Ford than day [is like] night. It does not operate like any previous Ford car, and in its road-ability, ease of operation, and control, there is just no comparison between the new and old models." More importantly,

The all-new '49 Ford was a reflection of the all-new Ford Motor Company. The $1886 Custom convertible (top), the sportiest model in the line, attracted 51,133 customers. Thought was given to offering a '49 Sportsman (center and bottom right), but these plans were ultimately shelved. The most popular '49 model was the Custom Tudor (bottom left): 398,060 built.

the '49 was the car that literally saved Ford Motor Company. Had it not succeeded as it did, the firm might not have lived to see its 50th birthday.

The '49 Ford was the product of two key figures: design consultant George W. Walker and engineering vice-president Harold Youngren (as noted, a Breech recruit from Oldsmobile, where he'd worked on that division's brilliant new overhead-valve V-8, also introduced for '49). Although wheelbase stayed the same and engines were altered only in detail, the rest of the package was completely different from 1942-48: three inches lower, fractionally shorter and narrower, and much sleeker, thanks to new flush-fender styling. Shoving the engine forward a full five inches produced extra legroom despite the more compact dimensions. Youngren's staff also managed to increase seat width by half a foot, maintain headroom, and enlarge trunk space by 57 percent. Careful attention to detail kept curb weight below 3000 pounds, though the target was 2900. Still, only the convertible and woody wagon were slightly heavier than before. By contrast, no '48 Ford scaled less than 3000 pounds, and some were over 3500. The '49s were

thus a bit livelier despite their little-changed engines.

They were also different underneath in a way that would have upset old Henry. First, his beloved beam front axle and transverse-leaf-spring suspension, a feature of Ford cars since 1908, were finally discarded. Up front was a fully independent setup with coil springs and double wishbones (unequal-length A-arms). Out back, parallel, longitudinal leaf springs now supported the live rear axle. Both arrangements had long been used elsewhere. Final drive was now of the hypoid type instead of spiral-bevel, and the heavy old torque tube was replaced by open Hotchkiss drive (as on Ford trucks from the late Thirties).

The transmission was also completely reengineered, and the old two-speed rear axle gave way to a modern optional overdrive. Ford had planned to offer an optional automatic purchased from Studebaker, but South Bend refused. Developed with Borg-Warner, it appeared on the '50 Studebakers. Meanwhile, Dearborn was forced to develop its own automatic, which is why it didn't appear until 1951.

Brakes remained hydraulically actuated drums all-round, but had greater swept area to cope with the extra weight of the more forward engine mounting. Finally, the antiquated X-member chassis gave way to a lighter, more up-to-date ladder-type frame, except on the convertible, where X-bracing was retained for the greater structural rigidity demanded by that body style.

Though Ford engineering was still pretty agricultural in this period, Youngren did what he could to make the flathead V-8 more competitive. A major focus was the cooling system, a bugbear since 1932. Water was now pumped from the radiator straight to the back of the block without any baffle detours. This, plus a larger radiator, lowered running temperatures some 12 degrees but didn't completely eliminate the familiar hot spots, overheating, and vapor-lock problems. New valve guides helped cut oil consumption, another longstanding problem. Main bearings were changed from floating to the locked-in type, and manifold massaging, both intake and exhaust, improved breathing, and hence economy. Even so, peak horsepower remained at 100, though it occurred a bit lower in the rev range, 3600 rpm instead of 3800.

Ford debuted the '49 Fords at the Waldorf Astoria Hotel in New York City. A revolving turntable (top) highlighted four Custom models: station wagon, Tudor, convertible, and club coupe. A rotating display, meanwhile, showed off the new chassis, a good way to call attention to the independent front/ parallel leaf rear suspension and ladder frame. Onlookers (middle) showed great interest in the new Custom club coupe. A '49 Custom Fordor (bottom) was posed alongside a Model T to show far Ford had come since its early years.

It's a Dream Wagon...this '49 FORD
with its (heart) of steel and the new FORD "FEEL"!

Ford did a bit of an about-face with its 1949 station wagon. First of all, it was a two-door, a switch from the four-door models previously offered. Ford tried to make a virtue of this by saying that it had two "wide" doors rather than four "narrow" ones, "a blessing to parents of small children." Secondly, it was made of steel: "Yes, it's all steel—even under that gleaming molded plywood paneling."

Improved serviceability prompted several other changes. The old camshaft-driven "crab" distributor was remounted above the head on the right front cylinder bank to be shaft and gear driven. The oil pan was redesigned, as was the clutch. The latter allowed the transmission to be removed without dropping the engine as well. Of course, all this was merely patchwork stuff. What Ford *really* needed was a modern ohv engine, but it was still a few years off.

Because development time was so short, Henry Ford II told engineer Bill Burnett to forget last-minute efforts toward noise reduction and to concentrate instead on solving the steering and front-end geometry problems caused by the new engine location. But according to *Special Interest Autos* magazine, the engineers "kept right on improving the car after introduction, insulating it, changing the fan pitch, the camshaft, body mounts, and exhaust system for less noise." By the time the facelifted '50 debuted, they had made it a very quiet automobile.

The new Hotchkiss drive was a definite improvement, enhancing driveline smoothness and making for a less intrusive transmission hump with no sacrifice in ground clearance. Pushing the engine ahead allowed the rear seat to come forward off the axle for a more comfortable "Midship Ride," as Ford ad types termed it—and with far better springing. Again, however, these features were new only to Ford in 1949, and they weren't without problems. Consultant Walker usually gets credit for the styling and tended to claim it himself, one reason he was hired to head Ford corporate design in 1955. But it wasn't really his—and thereby hangs a tale.

Youngren's dimensional package for what was called project "X-2900" (after the target curb weight) was completed quite early, certainly no later than the winter of 1945-46. It was then turned over to two design groups: the in-house team under Bob Gregorie, and Walker's freelance crew that included Elwood Engel (destined to be chief of design at Chrysler in the Sixties) and "silent" Joe Oros (who'd figure heavily in the original '65 Mustang).

Walker ordered quarter-scale clays from both Engel and Oros as well as Richard Caleal, then in Walker's employ but recently associated with the Raymond Loewy consultant team at Studebaker. Caleal, whom friends called "the Persian rug salesman" because of the hard work he put into "selling" Walker on his designs, ran into trouble with the front and rear styling, so he sought the help of two pals from the Loewy staff, Bob Bourke and Holden "Bob" Koto. It was the latter who actually completed the model late one night on the kitchen table of the Caleal home in Mishawaka, Indiana—where it was reportedly cured in Mrs. Caleal's oven and created quite a stink. Professional ethics prevented this

Ford had completely redesigned its trucks for 1948 (as had Chevy, GMC, and Dodge), so the '49s were basically carryovers. Although stake models were available in a number of series, the F-5 (top) was a good bet for those needing a 1½-ton capacity. The F-3 parcel delivery chassis, with standard front end to the door opening, was new for '49. Most had a 104-inch wheelbase, a ¾-ton rating, and a GVW of 7800 pounds.

story from coming out for many years. Curiously, Koto never considered it one of his best designs.

But it carried the day on August 1, 1946, when four quarter-scale clays—three from the Walker team and one from Gregorie, all four-door sedans—were reviewed by Breech, HF II, John Bugas, Lew Crusoe, Mead Bricker, and J.R. Davis (recently put in charge of Ford's California plants). Without knowing which designer had done which model, they picked the Koto/Caleal proposal but ordered that elements of Gregorie's design be incorporated, notably the roof and door treatments. This wasn't enough for Gregorie, though, and in 1947 he resigned from Ford a second time, returning to his former career as a yacht designer.

Walker made two other changes to

the winning design. First, he turned its vertical taillights horizontally, then put them in accenting "pods," with a "character line" for each run forward along the fenders to add visual interest to the slab sides. With that, a full-size clay—a two-door sedan, painted yellow—was prepared for production engineering, which commenced September 1, 1946. As assembly began April 8, 1948, the '49 Ford had gone from drawing board to production in record time—only 19 months.

Studebaker influence was obvious in the new "bullet-nose" front, where a large central circle divided a full-width horizontal bar that seemed to "float" in the grille cavity. This was, as Bourke noted, "similar to the component on Studebaker front ends for 1950-51," but not nearly so sculptured and far more

Although Ford's V-8 (above) was basically the same for '49, it did receive an updating: new valve guides to cut oil consumption, locked-in type main bearings, massaging of the intake and exhaust systems for better breathing, and an improved cooling system to eliminate hot spots. The '49 F-1 eight-foot panel truck (bottom left) cost $1504 and boasted a cargo capacity of 160.3 cubic feet. Most of Ford's 1949 ads said "There's a NEW Ford in your future" (bottom right).

pleasing. Glass area was increased 12 percent to improve outward vision, helped further by slimmer roof pillars and much wider back windows. What we'd now call a "notchback" rear combined with a four-inch-lower roofline to make for a far more rakish Ford than the old fastbacks.

The interior was equally successful, especially the new "MagicAire" heating and "air conditioning" system that offered a choice of fresh and/or heated breezes. It was far superior to what most competitors had, and rendered the old-time cowl vent virtually superfluous. Controls were a bit clumsy, but the rest of the new "aircraft-inspired" dash was clean and functional, grouping gauges within a single backlit unit and offering handy chromed knobs for most other functions. Interior trim—broadcloth in most models—could be had in any color so long as it was medium gray.

Ford still had a soft spot for limited-edition specials, and gave brief thought to a new Sportsman. At least one '49 club coupe was mocked up as such, with identifying front fender script and a long woody-look "frame," possibly metal, running from just above the rocker panel to about mid-bodyside, split longitudinally by a thick chrome molding. It

also wore rear fender skirts and a low-hanging windshield visor. Unlike the 1946-48 Sportsman, side trim here was strictly decorative, a highlight really, and the inserts were painted body color. Though doubtless a prelude to the spiffy Crestliner that would appear for 1950, it would have made an interesting addition to the line.

What *was* offered for '49 were the usual sixes and V-8s in a two-tier, nine-model lineup. The base-trim series, officially nameless but sometimes called Standard, consisted of Tudor and Fordor sedans, long-deck coupe, and stripped business coupe. The upper-level Custom group deleted the last, but added a convertible and a new two-door wagon, replacing the previous four-door style. Prices were up across the board, ranging from $1333 for the business coupe to $2119 for the wagon. The latter, incidentally, was identical from the cowl back with a new Mercury counterpart, both with partial wood construction at the rear.

The '49 Ford was an expensive program for an automaker trying to recover from a lot of lean years: 10-million man hours and $72 million. It arrived well ahead of the model year because Ford literally couldn't afford to wait for the usual fall debut. But it did the job Dearborn needed it to do, and handsomely, too. Helped by the new Lincoln and Mercury, Ford recorded a gratifying $177 million profit for calendar 1949. Just as heartening, Ford bested Chevy in model year production by over 100,000 cars—nearly 1.12 million in all.

To give the '49 Ford the big sendoff it needed, Henry II staged an extravagant six-day press party at New York City's Waldorf Astoria Hotel beginning June 8, 1948, just 10 days before the public unveiling. An estimated 300 reporters attended, brought in by car or train at company expense along with almost every high-ranking Ford official. The resulting

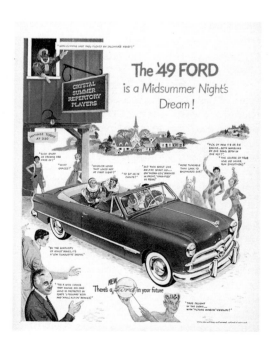

Like other manufacturers, Ford had by 1949 moved development of its new models from the streets to the laboratory. Here a '49 Ford is undergoing cold-weather tests to assure easy winter-time starting.

barrage of favorable publicity primed an already eager public, and an estimated 28.2 million visitors choked dealer showrooms in the first three days, more than 100,000 placing orders on the first day alone. For sheer impact, it was an introduction to rival the Model A rollout of 30 years before.

The '49 V-8, about as quick as its immediate predecessor, was no slouch, especially when compared to the six-cylinder Chevys and Plymouths. *Popular Science* reported 0-60 mph in 16 seconds. *Mechanix Illustrated*'s "Uncle" Tom McCahill needed 16.5 seconds with a straight-stick and stock 3.63:1 final drive, 15-15.5 seconds with overdrive and its shorter 4.10:1 rear axle. Ford's rival took 4-6 seconds longer to 60. Both magazines cited mediocre cornering as the '49 Ford's worst feature, but at least this new Ford didn't wander on straightaways anymore. Top speed came in at about 92 mph.

If there was a rush to claim credit for Ford's '49 styling, no one seemed willing to admit to engineering the new bodies, which made these Fords among the poorest built cars of their time and gave

many owners ample reason to trade for a 1950 Chevrolet. Doors didn't fit properly and often unlatched under body torque on rough roads. Hood hinges provided all the support of a sardine can and sometimes let the panels fly open, though they held somewhat better than the door latches. Decklid latches tended to pop, too, and dust and water leaks were common around trunk openings. Leaks also occurred around the windshield, and the foam seat cushioning was anything but durable, crumbling at about 30,000 miles. Trim and paint didn't measure up to Chevy and Plymouth. Lack of adequate body bracing was perhaps the worst deficit of all. Squeaks and rattles were numerous, and early shells tended to fall apart after three or four years, though later '49s were somewhat sturdier. Then, too, quality varied greatly between assembly plants, the best-built cars coming from Texas, the poorest from Chicago.

But many of these problems would be rectified; indeed, a number of corrective running changes were made during 1949 production per Ford tradition. The wonder is that bad word-of-mouth advertising didn't prevent Dearborn from climbing out of the red and into the black—but then, new styling was about all you needed for good sales in 1949 and most every American make did well that year.

Ford's "Bonus Built" trucks were

only a year old in 1949 and thus saw little change per industry custom. There were, however, more of them, as models expanded by 25 in the summer. Notable among the newcomers was a forward-control F-3 parcel van, a basic chassis/windshield "building block" with six-cylinder power on 104- and 122-inch wheelbases. There were also more choices in medium and heavy-duty wheelbases with the addition of a 176-inch F-5/F-6 platform and 147- and 178-inch chassis in the F-7/F-8 series. All this brought total variations to 164. Two-speed rear axles gave way to single-speed units on F-5s and F-8s, and other equipment, both standard and optional, was shuffled a bit across the line. For example, an optional new heavy-duty three-speed transmission arrived as an alternative to the familiar four-speed in the volume-leading F-1s, and wider factory-fitted tires were offered at extra cost on many models.

Unhappily for Ford, its truck output for 1949 hit a three-year low, in part because the supply/demand equation in the commercial market had changed to favor buyers again. The car market would be similarly affected by 1951. By that time, the vast reservoir of early postwar sales had run dry. From then on, Detroit competition would be increasingly market-driven, which among other things implied less room for wrong decisions and product mistakes. It was a lesson Ford would learn all too well all too soon.

1 9 5 0

Although the 1950 Fords looked much like the '49s, they were much improved in strength and quality. This year, Chevrolet debuted its Styleline DeLuxe Bel Air convertible hardtop, a model that appealed to 76,662 customers. Ford didn't have a hardtop, so it brought out the Crestliner (above), a Tudor sedan dressed up with a vinyl roof, striking two-tone paint, special wheel covers, fender skirts, and a fancy interior. At $1711, it found 17,601 takers. The more mundane Custom Fordor (below) cost $1558, and 247,181 were built.

The peace so hard won in World War II seemed increasingly fragile as the Forties waned. Almost as soon as hostilities ended, the dark veil of Communism—what Sir Winston Churchill ominously termed the "Iron Curtain"—descended on Eastern Europe, shutting off the light of personal liberty and free enterprise for millions. Then the Soviet Union blockaded West Berlin in 1948, testing whether Britain, France, and the United States were truly prepared to hold onto their portions of that newly divided city. The Allies were, launching an unprecedented round-the-clock airlift that eventually broke the Russians' resolve.

Now, in 1950, came a new test of wills between East and West. This time the setting was Korea, where Communists from the North attacked Nationalists in the South on June 25. President Harry S. Truman, determined to contain Communist expansion wherever it occurred, dispatched U.S. air and ground forces to support the new United Nations in what was termed a "police action." It wasn't exactly a world war, but it certainly wasn't peace, either.

Washington responded by stepping up military production and ordering cutbacks in the civilian sector, prompting many Americans to predict that the hardships of 1942-45 were about to return. They weren't, but the events of 1950 strongly suggested that a new austerity was at hand, and people stampeded to buy new cars, fearing that the auto production spigot might again be turned off at any time. The result was record passenger-car sales of more 6.33 million units during the calendar year, some 1.49 million above the record 1949 total and about 40 percent above the prewar high-water mark of more than 3.85 million, set in 1929.

Ford Division rode the crest of this

Among the body styles Ford offered in 1950, the Tudor (above) was easily the most popular: 275,360 DeLuxes ($1424) and 398,060 Customs ($1511). The '50 trucks, meanwhile, were now in the third year of their styling cycle, including of course this F-5.

wave as high as anyone in American industry, tacking on a little more than 100,000 cars to finish the model year at just over 1.2 million. The 1949 figures had been skewed, of course, because of the four-month longer model year. Archrival Chevy, with a normal 12-month model year both years, had an even better ride; it regained the number-one position by building close to half a million more cars than it had in '49, almost 1.5 million in all.

But Ford Motor Company could take comfort in its steadily improving market share. In 1950 it rose to 24 percent—the highest since the mid-Thirties—compared to a postwar low of about 18 percent just two years earlier. GM advanced too, so it's clear that most of Ford's gain came at the expense of Chrysler, which had been sliding since 1946—down from over 25 percent that year to 17.6 percent in 1950. Of course, it hardly hurt Ford

that Chrysler suffered a 99-day strike in 1950 or that Chrysler's first new postwar cars were boxier and less appealing than either Dearborn's or GM's.

Though advertised as "50 Ways New...50 Ways Finer," the 1950 Fords bore little outward change. A minor facelift supervised by Gilbert Spear brought lowered parking lamps in chrome housings that wrapped around the fenders, a classier hood ornament, and a simple crest to replace the block letters over the bullet grille. That medallion, which also rode the decklid, stemmed from some delving into 17th-Century Irish history and purportedly evolved from the Ford family's actual coat of arms. It soon replaced the famed blue oval in domestic Ford print ads and on dealer signage.

Model offerings were initially the same as before: DeLuxe (*nee* Standard) sedans and business coupe (but no club

coupe); Custom coupe, sedans, convertible, and semi-wood wagon. The wagon gained a lower-priced running mate late in the year called Country Squire, with a fold-up "stowaway" back seat instead of a fully removable one. Despite continuing inflation, prices stayed virtually the same across the line, starting again at $1333.

All models, with the exception of the V-8-powered ragtop, received the 95-bhp six as standard; the V-8 was optional across the board. Of interest to today's collectors was the first of the police packages called "Interceptor," a name that would also become familiar on some Ford engines into the Sixties. As one would expect, the new law enforcer was built around the more powerful, 110-horsepower Mercury V-8.

Ford's 1950 ad slogan was no exaggeration, for its cars *did* feature about 50 detail changes. Some were needed fixes

left undone from '49, hence another catch phrase: "The Ford in Your Future—With a Future Built In," which at least implied better quality. Other changes were cosmetic enhancements aimed at greater "showroom appeal" to counter the '49's poor quality image. The latter included more durable foam seats clothed in nicer fabrics ("a decorator's dream," Ford boasted), new pushbutton exterior door handles with rotary locks ("anchored at both ends" with "the grace of fine silverware"), a cover for the trunklid lock, and a gas filler concealed by a side-hinged flap. Less apparent—but more important—were newly strengthened bodies, hoods, trunklids, and doors that were also better sealed against dust and water. Other interior revisions included a newly designed emergency brake lever, larger defroster vents delivering greater air volume, a higher-capacity heater, extra

"Test drive' a '50 Ford" implored the ad (right), "You'll FEEL the difference!" And as far as good looks were concerned, Ford was quick to point out that "...again in 1950, New York's famed Fashion Academy has named [Ford] 'Fashion Car of the Year'!" Other talking points included the 35-percent easier-acting King Size Brakes and the solid comfort of the Mid Ship Ride. Riding a 114-inch wheelbase as all Fords had since 1941, the '50 Tudor (above) weighed in at 3015 pounds, compared to 3263 for the Custom convertible (top right), which had an X-braced frame to beef up the roofless body. Listing at a reasonable $1948, the ragtop was driven home by 50,299 happy buyers.

sound-deadening material, and wider sun visors.

Mechanical refinements under-scored' the comfort and convenience im-provements. The veteran 239 flathead V-8 was smoother and quieter—but no

more powerful—thanks to a new compo-sition timing gear, revised pistons to elim-inate cold-start "slap," and a new cam-shaft to reduce tappet noise. Intake valve stems got rubber O-ring seals to forestall oil leaks, and conrods acquired little squirt holes for better cylinder-wall lubri-cation. Some, but not all, of these modifi-cations also appeared on an otherwise un-changed Ford six. A three-blade fan replaced the four-blade unit on V-8s, and fan speed was lowered to 9/10ths of en-gine speed, thus reducing roar.

The '50 Ford also handled a bit better than the '49 thanks to some up-front pound-paring that yielded marginally better fore/aft weight balance, aided by the addition of a front torsion-bar stabi-lizer, transversely mounted between the lower A-arms. While overall weight was up slightly, fuel economy remained about the same. With the optional overdrive and its longer-legged rear axle, a '50 V-8 did 21 miles to the highway gallon and averaged 15.2 mpg overall in *Motor Trend*'s tests. Performance, likewise, was hardly affected.

The tremendous tooling costs of the all-new '49 design had precluded Ford from responding to that year's new pillar-less "hardtop convertibles" from GM. This rakish body style boasted the safety and security of a steel roof, and sported the open airiness of a convertible when the side windows were rolled down (due to the elimination of the B-pillars). Not only that, the new hardtops—as they would commonly be called—looked quite sleek, even with the windows up. This mid-year innovation had found imme-diate favor with buyers, who began snap-ping up Buick Rivieras, Cadillac Coupe de Villes, and Oldsmobile Holidays as quick-ly as dealers received them. More impor-tant for Ford was the fact that Chevy got a hardtop for 1950—the stylish Bel Air. Alas, even Ford's newly reinforced body was too willowy to go around without B-posts. A hardtop could have been derived from the convertible with its sturdier X-braced chassis, but Dearborn had more pressing priorities in its march to recov-

ery and hadn't slated a hardtop until the planned corporate redesign for 1952.

What to do in the meantime? Why not a spiffy Tudor sedan with the look, if not the function, of a true hardtop? George Walker's staff went to work, the result being the Crestliner, which bowed late in the 1950 campaign as an addition to the Custom series.

The Crestliner's colorful styling was influenced by the late Gordon M. Buehrig, famed designer of Classic-era Au-burns, Cords, and Duesenbergs. Buehrig, another recent recruit to the Dearborn design team, likened its two-tone paint treatment to the dashing "LeBaron sweep" of the custom-body period of the Thirties—a reference to the dashing el-liptical chrome moldings delineating the contrast color area. A matching vinyl roof covering emphasized the "convertible" intent, and standard rear fender skirts further set Crestliner apart from lesser Fords. Final touches included gold-ano-dized front-fender Crestliner script and a luxurious two-tone interior keyed to three exterior color combinations: Sportsman Green (chartreuse) body with

151

Quality suffered because the 1949 Ford, seen here in the body-drop assembly stage (right), had been rushed to production. By 1950, the situation had improved immensely. Most people in their '40s should remember the F-1 Ford Good Humor ice cream trucks (below).

black roof and color panel, maroon with black, and bronze with brown.

At $1711, the Crestliner was Ford's most expensive 1950 sedan, some $200 above the Custom Tudor, but it did include the V-8 as standard. Despite the price and the late introduction, this "factory custom" scored respectable sales of 17,601 units. Today, it's a highly prized collectible. Still, there was little joy in Dearborn because Chevy moved nearly 77,000 of its new 1950 Bel Airs.

Ford trucks also saw only detail changes this year. The all-new "Bonus Built" '48 line had marked a return to the firm's traditional policy of making running improvements without waiting for the next model year, and this practice continued for 1950.

Nevertheless, Ford's 239 truck V-8 now received most of the improvements of this year's passenger-car version, and maximum GVW ratings increased in some series. Model offerings rose to 175, helped by the arrival of a new-block six-cylinder option for the F-6 series. This was a modified edition of the existing 254-cubic-inch motorcoach unit, tuned here for 110 horsepower at 3400 rpm and 212 pounds/feet peak torque at a low 1200 rpm. Mated with a heavy-duty clutch and four-speed gearbox, this "Rouge 254" proved quite popular, accounting for no less than 50 percent of 1950 F-6 sales.

The year also brought two other truck developments of note. Arriving very late in the season was an F-5 parcel van. Available only on a "domestic special order" basis, it was much like its lighter-duty F-3 sister but used the heftier frame, springs, and front axle from the F-5 cabover, plus a larger driveshaft and a 10,800-pound-capacity rear axle. Ford also bailed out of the motorcoach—but not school bus—business in 1950, selling out to Marmon-Herrington after several years of declining sales.

War worries fueled truck sales as much as car demand in 1950, and Ford's calendar-year commercial output hit a 21-year high by reaching close to 346,000 units. But Chevrolet once again scored another production victory with combined car/truck volume that broke the all-time single-make record set by Ford back in 1923.

There was more profound sadness in Dearborn as Clara B. Ford, wife of the company founder, died on September 29 at age 83, the same as that of her late husband. Her passing came nine days after a happier occasion: an all-time daily Ford production record—a startling 9000 units. If Dearborn wasn't quite out of the financial woods—and it wasn't—the light of a clearing was not all that far ahead.

1 9 5 1

Just as it seemed that Ford Motor Company was on solid financial ground and moving ahead, the Korean War intensified and Washington ordered production cutbacks that immediately affected the firm's building program. For example, a proposed Lincoln-Mercury assembly plant in Wayne, Michigan, was turned over to Westinghouse for Navy jet-engine manufacture. On top of this came materials and market-share allocations that Ford felt were biased in favor of Chrysler and the independents, the former being awarded a 21.76-percent market share to Ford's 21.43. But as Ford vice-president Bill Gossett remarked: "If the controls were lifted, we would very quickly demonstrate who is entitled to the second place." He was right. Even in 1952, with controls still on and Chrysler overselling its quota, Dearborn would outproduce its rival, and Chrysler has not reclaimed second place to this day.

Still, the semi-war footing meant lower production for all Ford makes. It was probably just as well: the 1949 designs were in their final year at Ford, and the great seller's market was starting to wane.

The sales picture was predictably mixed. Ford closed its model-year gap with Chevy by about 73,000 cars, but both were down about 200,000 from their 1950 totals, Ford ending at just over a million units, Chevy at about 1.2 million, leaving GM's breadwinner in the number-one spot for the second year running.

But none of this dimmed the luster of a mildly facelifted Ford line now starring a true pillarless hardtop. Called Victoria, it was billed as being "Smart as a Convertible...Snug as a Sedan." It resided in the upper-level Custom series, boasting a plush, convertible-like interior; standard V-8; large three-piece rear window; and dashing appearance—the work of the late Gordon Buehrig. In a nation gone ga-ga for airy-feeling hardtops, the Victoria was a guaranteed hit despite a late debut (on January 28, 1951) and a $1925 price tag, just $24 below that of the

The '51 Ford was more heavily facelifted than the '50, the most obvious change being the twin-spinner grille. The Country Squire wagon now sported badges on the doors (it had received the name in 1950). Output of the woody increased by 6725 units to 29,017.

real convertible. In this first battle of the low-priced hardtops, Ford built 110,286 units to beat both Chevrolet's Bel Air and Plymouth's new Cranbrook Belvedere, which recorded output levels of 103,356 and about 30,000 units, respectively. Naturally, the Victoria's success made the Crestliner redundant, and the pseudo-

hardtop was dropped after a run of only 8703 cars.

A more substantial restyle than in 1950, again crafted under Gil Spear, gave all '51 Fords a new face, dominated by a thick horizontal grille bar with two smaller bullets at its outboard ends instead of one big central bullet. Headlights were now slightly recessed within new bezels, a winged hood ornament appeared, hubcaps were redone, and taillights were now twin-point affairs. Customs had side trim newly wrapped around at the rear, plus chrome accents on the bodyside "windsplits" leading rearward to the taillamps. Inside was a handsomely redesigned "Safety Glow" dash featuring a "Chanalited" gauge cluster and a new asymmetrical layout lacking the old-fash-

The '51 Country Squire wagon (above) retailed at $2029, making it the only model above $2000. New for '51 was Ford's real answer to Chevy's popular Bel Air convertible hardtop. Ford called its handsome $1925 pillarless coupe, which had been designed by the late Gordon Buehrig, the Victoria (opposite, bottom). Although it appeared a bit later then the other '51s, it was instantly popular—production came to 110,286 units, enough to nose out Chevy's Bel Air. Henry Ford II (standing) is seen here (top right) discussing business with brothers Benson and William Clay Ford.

ioned starter button—starting was now accomplished by a simple turn of the key. Fabrics and seat cushions were again improved for better durability and support, bolstered by non-sag springs providing "Automatic Posture Control." Alas, there

still wasn't much in the way of color selection, just the usual browns, grays, and greens.

As if to compensate, exterior designers conjured five new color schemes for the slow-selling Crestliner: Greenbrier metallic upper and black lower, Sportsman green and black, Hawaiian bronze metallic and brown, red and black, and all-black. Some people thought that the bodyside trim and color panel area had been made too elaborate, maybe even a bit garish.

The big mechanical news for '51 was the arrival of the three-speed Ford-O-Matic Drive, a new automatic transmission option to answer Chevy's two-speed Powerglide of 1950. Developed in cooperation with the Warner Gear Division of Borg-Warner, it listed at $159, about $70 more than the extra-cost overdrive. Ford-O-Matic combined a hydraulic torque converter with a planetary gearset, but only second and third gears were automatic; Low range had to be selected manually. In spite of that and a late arrival, Ford-O-Matic was a much-praised transmission, *Motor Trend* rating it the best automatic it had tested to that point

and much smoother than Powerglide. Another new '51 feature, though less highly touted, was "automatic ride control"—variable-rate rear springs teamed with "Viscous Control" hydraulic shocks front and rear.

Ford retained its classic, monobloc flathead V-8, still rated at 100 horsepower but boasting new valve rotators, chrome-flashed top piston rings, offset piston pins, revised camshaft, waterproof ignition system, and larger-capacity fuel pump. The 226-cid L-head six was standard on all but the Custom Victoria, Crestliner, and convertible, still ready to deliver 95 horses. It benefitted from a new torsional vibration damper, aluminum timing gear, level-mount intake manifold, and heavier main bearings. The new Victoria aside, model offerings stayed the same. The only two-door Custom wagon was now the Country Squire, its name newly displayed in bodyside script on the front doors. Prices again stayed mostly the same, too. The line-leading Deluxe business coupe was tagged at just $1324, the Fordor at $1465. Customs started at $1505 for the Tudor or club coupe and ran to $1925 for the

Opposite page: The Crestline (top), Ford's interim answer to Chevy's Bel Air hardtop, was continued into 1951. It featured revised bodyside chrome and two-toning. At $1595, it cost $330 less than the Victoria, but wasn't nearly as popular: only 8703 built. After 1951, it was gone. Ford output slipped about 200,000 units for '51, a down year for the industry, but over a million were shipped, among them these three Customs (bottom): convertible, Victoria, and Tudor. This page: All '51 Fords, including this Custom Fordor (top), were given a final inspection. For the first time since '48, Ford freshened up its light-duty trucks, most notably with a more aggressive-looking grille and a new cargo box with a "grain-tight" tailgate. The F-1 pickup, here a V-8 (right), was the most popular model: 117,414 produced.

new Victoria, $1949 for the convertible, and $2029 for the Squire.

Victoria was billed as the "Belle of the Boulevard...smart as a convertible... snug as a sedan"—which, of course, is why it sold so well. The brochure also pointed out that it was the only low-priced hardtop with a standard V-8, a not inconsiderable selling point at the time.

Motor Trend's testers gave good marks to a Custom Fordor with the new automatic, noting improved ride and handling and much better workmanship overall. The car wasn't faultless, though, and Ford-O-Matic's basic drawback spoke for itself: 0-60-mph runs took a lengthy 18.9

In addition to the revised grille, the '51 Fords sported a new hood ornament and slightly "Frenched" headlight bezels, restyled hubcaps, and chrome "jet pods" that merged into the freshened-up taillights. The '51 convertible, which listed at $1949, came with the V-8 as standard. Although output was down over 9000 units, it was still popular as 40,934 were built.

seconds in straight Drive, and a scarcely better 17.8 seconds shifting manually from Low. Still, this was good enough to outrun stick-shift Chevys and Plymouths, and significantly quicker than a Power-glide-equipped Chevrolet. The Ford's top speed was reported as 88.5 mph. Mileage? A so-so 18.4 mpg at a steady 60, 18.2 over-all. Still, *MT*'s Walt Woron was moved to write: "When it comes to controllability

on new cars, the Ford is hard to beat. On long, open stretches or over curving, climbing grades, the car is extremely easy to handle. Body sway is at a minimum. The only slight objection in this category would be the amount of wind noise (with windwings open) at about 60 mph."

Tom McCahill over at *Mechanix Illustrated* ran a '51 Crestliner in Dearborn and quickly seized on both the improved quality and more refined V-8. He also lamented the lack of punch with automatic, but pulled no punches when it came to one of the greatest weaknesses of the first postwar Fords: "I don't know of a car on the road that has less traction in mud, snow or ice. A one-legged kangaroo on a greased pole has more forward push than a current model Ford bogged down on ice

or snow. This is because they shoved the engine so far forward—to get 'Midship Ride' for your mother-in-law in the back seat—that a Singer's midget can almost lift the rear wheels off the ground." Maybe "Uncle" Tom should have driven with a hefty bag of salt in the trunk.

But even if they were never fully debugged, the 1949-51 Fords pulled Dearborn through its most dire financial crisis since the Model A changeover of 1927. Clean styling, exceptional smoothness, and competitive pricing were enough to move no fewer than 3,340,601 of these "recovery" models, thus assuring Ford's survival and laying the foundation for even greater success in the future—no mean feat when you think about it.

Ford also facelifted its "Bonus Built"

trucks for '51, an interim measure to tide the commercial line over to its next major redesign, scheduled for Golden Anniversary 1953. Both conventionals and COEs wore front fenders reshaped for a new grille comprising a larger, full-width cavity filled by a thick horizontal bar mounting outboard headlamps and a trio of large, bullet-head vertical dividers in between. Cabs were updated too, becoming "Five Star" jobs with 50-percent larger rear windows, standard dual wipers (a first for Ford trucks), and a revised dash with gauges grouped in twin circular dials. Optionally available was a new "Five Star Extra" deluxe features package, Ford's first since 1938. This bought many features which included: chrome moldings around the windows and grille; foam-filled seat with two-tone trim; interior door trim panels; sound-deadening on doors, floor, and rear cab wall; an acoustic headliner with 1.5-inch glasswool insulation; dual sun visors, armrests, and horns; plus a cigarette lighter, a door-activated dome courtesy light, and a glovebox lamp.

Truck versions of both the 226 six and 239 V-8 received the same basic improvements as their 1951 passenger-car equivalents—most notably, the new waterproof ignition system—but a new updraft carburetor brought the big six-cylinder Rouge 254 down to 106 bhp—a loss of four horses—and 210 pounds/feet torque. There was the usual shuffling of transmission gearing, axle ratios, and tire sizes across the line, and the heavy haulers now wore "Big Job" exterior badges. Additionally, the top-selling pickup reverted to a wooden floor for the slightly wider cargo box with a better-sealed "grain-tight" tailgate. F-1 through F-3 models acquired new bumpers, while brakes were revised on F-2/F-3s. All engines now featured "Power-Pilot Economy," a spark advance system with more closely tailored air/fuel ratios for extra economy.

Ford's new emphasis on truck comfort and convenience merely reflected changing buyer tastes in all segments of the market. An expanding highway system and the ever-increasing importance of trucks to the national economy meant that mediums and heavies were being operated over longer and longer distances, thus making long-haul comfort and easy operation necessities rather than luxuries. At the same time, the light-duty field was beginning to attract buyers who were trading in cars and thus demanded car-like style, appointments, and refinement. Ford wasn't alone in responding to this trend. Competitors, especially Chevy, were taking note, too. As total market demand would remain relatively stable over the next few years, the sales battles would increasingly hinge on which trucks were the most accommodating, not just the toughest or cheapest.

1 9 5 2

This year saw a resurgent Ford Motor Company carry out its second corporate restyle in only three years, and its second since the war. The timing was fortuitous, as it enabled Ford to one-up GM and Chrysler. Ford also one-upped most of the independents—Hudson, Kaiser, Studebaker, and Packard. There were two exceptions, however, as Nash traded in its "bathtub" styling for an all-new

Pinin Farina-based notchback design, and Willys reentered the automotive marketplace for the first time since 1942 with its compact Aero. Thus, most of Ford's competitors would still be pedalling first-generation postwar cars in '52, though Ernie Breech and Henry Ford II likely didn't know that when work commenced on the second-generation postwar models in 1949.

Ford's financial situation was still somewhat shaky then, and the ultimate success of its postwar "recovery" models had yet to be seen. The result was a cautious, economy-minded approach to product planning that relied on far more component-sharing than before. For example, new overhead-valve V-8s as well as a novel new ball-joint front suspension

system designed by Earle MacPherson were to have been featured across the entire '52 line. However, continuing plant expansion coupled with the outbreak of the Korean conflict and government-ordered production cutbacks postponed these developments for Ford and Mercury until 1954. Only Lincoln got them for '52.

Cost control explains the close styling similarities among all of Dearborn's 1952-54 cars, as opposed to the 1949-51 models that were derived from differing concepts: Bob Gregorie's wartime "bathtub" for Lincoln and Mercury versus the slab-sided Ford of Dick Caleal/George Walker. Key elements of the new "corporate" look were a basically boxy lower body with fenders about the same height

as hood and rear deck, rounded green-houses with large glass areas and one-piece windshields, and a center gas filler concealed behind a pull-down license-plate holder (termed "Center-Fill Fueling" by Ford Division ad writers). Ford and Mercury even shared bodyshells,

Ford stole the march on the competition with all-new styling and a number of engineering innovations for 1952. The Crestline Sunliner convertible (below, top right, and bottom right) was the glamour model of the lineup. It retailed for $2027, but output was down to 22,534 units, largely because of production cutbacks brought on by the Korean conflict. Right, second and third from top: The bottom-line Mainline Tudor was a bargain at $1485; the $1925 Crestline Victoria was a bit pricier. Production came to 79,931 and 77,320, respectively.

As was common in the '50s, owners often loved to doll-up their cars with extra chrome, in this case a '52 Sunliner (above). It flaunts rocker panel moldings, wheel trim rings, and a big V-8 emblem around the Ford crest on the decklid. Note the overdrive badge—OD was still quite popular on Fords in 1952. The '52 F-1 pickup (left), now $1425, was basically a carryover.

thus returning the latter to its original status as a "senior Ford," a major change from its 1949-51 stint as a "junior Lincoln." The usual extra wheelbase length was now entirely ahead of the firewall. The Ford was styled under Bob Maguire, whose design group included the late Gordon Buehrig and L. David Ash, as well as Joe Oros from George Walker's consultant group. Basic body structure and chassis design were also common to all three, good for production economics, however not for marque distinction and image, especially Lincoln's.

Hyped as the "Big '52," the new Ford reverted to the center-bullet grille theme of 1949-50, but with the solitary horizontal bar now slotted instead of solid. A pair

The '52 Ford ragtop, now called Sunliner, was part of the new upper-crust Crestline series (not to be confused the 1950-51 Crestliner). Weighing 3339 pounds, this one (above) sports the optional full-disc hubcaps new for '52. The 1952 wagons boasted all-steel construction and the availability of four-door models after a three-year hiatus. The 3617-pound, $2060 Country Sedan (right) was a V-8-only model.

of similar outboard "spinners" housed the parking lamps. Discreet bulges around the rear wheel openings helped relieve the slab sides; their thrust-forward leading edges were decorated on some models with moldings suggestive of air scoops, imparting a sense of motion. The rear deck, almost as squared-up as before, was flanked by small round taillights, a motif Ford would use for the next several years. The larger, curved one-piece windshield and larger wraparound rear windows provided "Full-Circle Visibility" and conferred an airy look, though they also accentuated height. The pillarless Victoria was especially attractive because the new styling had been created with hardtops in mind. All this moved Tom McCahill of *Mechanix Illustrated* to term the '52 "the best looking Ford ever built."

Nevertheless, the '52 Fords had something of a pseudo-GM look, perhaps because Dearborn styling was still very much under the thumb of Engineering at the time and the key engineers were now ex-GM'ers. Moreover, Earle MacPherson and Harold Youngren had set down some very specific dimensions. Admittedly, the '52 Fords appeared as engineers might design cars, high and boxy (also true of

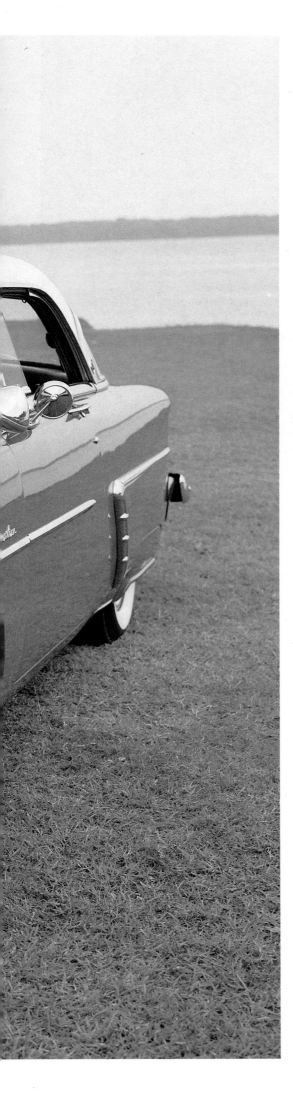

Mercury and Lincoln), however they were actually a bit wider and longer than the 1949-51s, and no higher. Wheelbase spanned 115 inches, an inch longer than before. Still, the '52 somehow managed to look smaller—not a plus given the bigger-is-better buyer mentality of the day. But at least it was clean, trim, and fresh at a time when Chevy and Plymouth were still pushing warmed-over '49s.

Inside, drivers operated new "Power-Pivot" brake and clutch pedals that were suspended instead of going through the floorboard, and consulted a pleasingly simple new GM-style dash dominated by a large cluster ahead of the wheel with white-on-black gauges. Ford called it the "Flight-Style" panel. Despite the changed external dimensions, passenger room was about the same as before, seating similarly upright.

Ford's '52 lineup comprised three series for the first time since 1942, and models increased by one, to 11, despite the departure of the slow-selling Custom Crestliner. Mainline replaced the former bottom-line Deluxe series, while the Custom group was retitled Customline. Tudor and Fordor sedans appeared in each, along with a $1389 price-leader Mainline business coupe and a more nicely appointed Customline club coupe. The three-tier series lineup would persist through 1956, then expand to four for 1957. Victoria hardtop, Sunliner convertible, and Country Squire wagon were put

Although the styling of the '52 was somewhat boxy and upright, it was also clean. The grille reverted to a single spinner, now flanked by slots in the grille bar. The parking lights looked like spinners too, so some people thought of the '52 as having a triple-spinner front end. New also: deeply Frenched headlights. The Crestline Victoria (left) was a popular choice in '52 as 77,320 were produced. This car sports spotlights, fender skirts, full-disc hubcaps, and a dealer- (or owner-)-installed strip of chrome atop the rear side sculpture. Apparently the blue Customline Tudor (above) passed inspection.

in a new top-shelf series called Crestline.

Though old-hat most everywhere else, all-steel station wagons were also new to Ford for '52, a bit surprising for the make that had pioneered wagons as far back as the late Twenties. The design, largely credited to Buehrig, came in three forms: a new two-door in the Mainline series called Ranch Wagon, a four-door six-passenger Country Sedan in the Customline group, and the aforementioned Squire. Though still an eight-seater, the last now boasted four instead of two doors and simulated instead of genuine tree wood on bodysides and tailgate— metal frames with decal inserts. At $2186, the Country Squire was the priciest '52 Ford. Regardless of style, Ford bodies were much sturdier for '52, prompting the "Coachcraft" sobriquet in advertising. Instrument panel and toeboard were welded to the cowl side panels

The Houston police ran at least one '52 "Radio Patrol" car in their fleet, a V-8 of course. Curiously, it was a mid-range Customline and a Tudor. Most police cars were Mainlines, which cost $85 less, and Fordors, often with a mesh screen between front and back seat.

for the first time, and the rear parcel shelf was newly tied to the C-pillars. Floorpans had several heavy-gauge channel sections welded on for extra support, then were welded to the sills and rear wheelhouses to further increase rigidity and seal against dust and moisture. Door openings, footwells, and upper pillar joints were all rounded for increased strength and better sealing. Primary bolts mating body and frame employed heavy use of rubber insulation to reduce noise and vibration. For the same reason, insulation was more generously used at key points throughout the structure.

Beneath the new bodies was an equally new chassis. Called the "K-bar" frame, it featured five crossmembers welded to box-section side rails and was claimed to be more rigid than the previous ladder chassis, a variation of which was continued for the Sunliner, Victoria, and wagons. At the rear were longer, stronger "Para-Flex" variable-rate multileaf springs and shocks remounted diagonally (like "sea-legs") to reduce side way in turns. Front shock valving took account of weight differences among the various models, with two sets of calibrations covering wagons and four for other models. Brake seals were redesigned for better protection against dust and water.

At the front were "Hydra-coil" springs that allegedly made for more precise handling and easier steering (up to 25 percent easier, according to Ford).

Altogether, this new chassis/suspension package provided what was described as "automatic ride control," aided by a lower center of gravity and tracks widened about two inches front and rear. Extra weight may have helped: up by about 100 pounds on the Victoria, for example, and 70 pounds on the convertible, reflecting the beefier bodies and chassis. About the only remaining criticism of Ford handling involved steering, which went from a slow 4.5 turns lock-to-lock to an even more tedious five, though this was somewhat offset by a new and stiffer steering linkage.

A totally different criticism of the '52s surfaced soon after buyers drove their shiny new Fords home: the very thin "Korean War chrome," particularly on the grille. After only a few polishings, it wore through, leaving the car looking old before its time. This, of course, was an industrywide problem that year.

Ford's big engine innovation for '52 was an all-new "Mileage Maker Six" derived from the new corporate ohv V-8. Standard for all Mainlines and Customlines save the Country Sedan, it was quite "square," with near-identical bore and stroke dimensions of 3.56 × 3.60 inches. Its crank was longer than the flathead V-8's, but stiffer. So was its block, due to an oil pan that dipped down 2¼ inches below the crankshaft centerline. This earned the nickname "I-Block," for the engine's appearance head-on. Despite modest 7:1

compression and only 215.3 cubic inches, horsepower totaled 101 at 3500 rpm—hot enough that the time-honored 239 V-8 had to be given a power boost to keep pace. The Ford Six now handily outperformed the "Blue Flame" Chevrolet, and with minor modifications could even give a Hudson Hornet fair competition.

As for the fabled flathead, newly dubbed the "Strato-Star" V-8, it was standard for all Crestlines and the Country Sedan, and basically the same as the '51 edition. However, compression boosted from 6.8 to 7.2:1, a reprofiled camshaft, and a new-type Holley carburetor combined to lift horsepower from 100 to 110 at 3300 rpm. Carried over from 1951 were such improvements as valve rotators, closer-fitting expansion-control aluminum alloy pistons, full-pressure lubrication, and automatic choke.

As before, both six and V-8 came with three-speed column-shift manual transmission and could be teamed with stick-overdrive for an additional $102 or three-speed self-shift Fordomatic. The last, despite a $170 surcharge, went into nearly one-third of '52 production. Convenience options included speed governor, turn indicators, windshield washers, engine compartment light, spring-wind or electric clock, five-tube DeLuxe or seven-tube Custom radios, wheel covers, rocker panel trim, and MagicAire heater. However, lights for glovebox, trunk, and Fordomatic selector were—ahem—glaring omissions.

Interestingly, road testers found little to choose between the new six and the old V-8 for performance or economy.

Output of the six-passenger four-door Country Sedan (top) was modest the first year, 11,927 units, but when the eight-passenger Country Squire and two-door Ranch Wagon were added in (5426 and 32,566 units), the 49,919 wagon total beat 1951 by 172 percent. Marmon-Herrington converted Ford F-1 panel trucks into the seven-passenger Ranger (center), which featured four-wheel drive, plus rear seats and side windows—much along the lines of the Chevy Carryall Suburban. The $1570 Customline Tudor (bottom) was the second-most-chosen '52 Ford. With 175,562 produced, it was nosed out by the like Fordor by 12,541 units.

its day, it remains an obscurity among collectible Fords.

For all its improvements, the '52 Ford was a sales disappointment, though this wasn't the car's fault. Further production cuts prompted by the continuing Korean conflict hampered all automakers in '52, and the new Ford got off to a late start, not being introduced until February 1 of that year, then phased out December 12 for the Golden Anniversary '53s. As a result, total production ended up at 671,733 units versus the previous year's 1,013,381. The only consolation was that Chevy dropped by about the same amount.

Ford's truck line received minor mechanical and styling changes this year (including the return of identifying block letters up front), but was mostly a rerun save two significant developments. One was the Courier, a revived sedan delivery based on the new two-door Mainline Ranch Wagon. Aside from the usual blank upper side panels, Courier differed from its wagon parent in retaining the traditional side-hinged rear door. Appointments were even more spartan than on Mainlines. For example, there was just one seat—for the driver, of course—and interior rear side panels were of utilitarian gray masonite as on the truck-based panel delivery. Still, the Courier was arguably Ford's best-looking sedan delivery since 1941. Available with six or V-8, and stick, overdrive, or Fordomatic, it proved quite popular.

Of greater significance was the arrival of three new overhead-valve truck engines: a replacement for the small six—the same "Mileage Maker" available in '52 passenger Fords—and two derivatives of the new Lincoln V-8, taking over from the old 337-cid L-head in the F-7/F-8 heavies. Marketed in truck form under the "Cargo King" label, the V-8s comprised a 317.5-cid F-8 unit (bore and stroke: 3.80 × 3.50 inches), basically the Lincoln engine with lower 7:1 compression giving 155 bhp (versus 7.5:1 and 160 bhp); and a smaller 3.56-inch-bore 279 for F-7s with 145 bhp (also on 7:1 compression). GVW ratings in both series were raised slightly from their L-head predecessors—up to 41,000 pounds on F-8s.

Both V-8s employed the same deeply skirted crankcase design as the Mileage Maker Six. Extended well below the crankshaft centerline, this gave extremely stiff crank support and a distinctive Y-shape in head-on view, prompting the generic nickname "Y-Block" for this car/truck engine family. Other Cargo King features included five crankshaft mains, hydraulic lifters, cast rocker arms, and Holley's new-design "Centri-Flo" two-barrel carburetor with concentric air cleaner.

Elsewhere, the Mileage Maker Six ousted the old L-head unit as base power in F-1 through F-5 conventionals and all parcel vans. The familiar 239 flathead V-8 remained optional for these models but

Motor Trend, in a blinding bit of deduction, declared the overhead-valve six to be Ford's engine of the future, mainly because the fabled flathead had reached its performance limit. And that was true insofar as the V-8's stock compression never went above 7.2:1. The six, by contrast, would reach 8.6:1 by decade's end. But Fifties Detroit was a V-8 world, and the six never gained widespread popularity, amounting to little more than 20 percent of Ford's total car sales through 1954. A much underestimated engine in

Ford rear styling for 1952 (top left) featured round taillights, which would be a Ford hallmark through the '50s, except for 1958. An all-new short-stroke overhead-valve six debuted for '52. It could pretty much keep up with the V-8. Many important decisions at Ford were made under the portraits of Edsel and Henry I (bottom left). The honchos at this 1952 meeting were (right to left): W.T. Gossett, L.D. Crusoe, D.S. Harder, Henry II, E.R. Breech, J.S. Bugas, Benson Ford, T.O. Yntema, and J.R. Davis.

was unchanged save a new trade name: "World Famous." The Rouge 254, now aptly named "Big Six," returned for all its previous applications save the F-6, where it was now the only engine available. Retuning gave it a bit better power and torque: 112 bhp and 217 lbs/ft.

For all this, Ford's share of U.S. truck sales sank to a postwar low in 1952. The main reason was the production curbs and materials shortages stemming from the Korean War, but stronger competition and a generally stagnant market were also factors.

Nevertheless, the years leading up to Ford Motor Company's Golden Anniversary were exuberant and prosperous ones. Busy, too. The firm broke ground for a new Kansas City assembly point in January 1951, and opened a new engine plant in Cleveland that September. On March 5 that same year, the company purchased Fair Lane, the Dearborn estate of its late founder. Then in April 1952, a companion Cleveland casting plant came on line, and on October 13 Lincoln-Mercury belatedly began production at

Wayne, Michigan.

Ford's early postwar difficulties may obscure the fact that the company was still a global giant of immense power and influence. The 39-millionth Ford car was built in 1952, and the company's total worldwide output for the calendar year was a record.

Still greater success was just ahead, but Henry Ford II had been thinking expansively even before his firm turned the profit corner with the '49 Ford. In fact, had it not been for Korea, Dearborn might have introduced an entirely new make for 1952.

In 1948, Henry had told his Executive Committee that Ford needed a new car line to bolster Mercury in the medium-price field, and ordered studies to investigate its feasibility. Research confirmed his hunch: Dearborn was indeed losing out to GM and Chrysler, each of which offered three medium-priced lines to Ford's one.

With that, the committee authorized work toward a new middle-market "E-car"—"Experimental"—in 1949, with in-

troduction slated for 1952. Little is known about this effort, but given Ford's finances of the time it likely would have produced just another variation of the evolving, cost-conscious '52 corporate platform, perhaps sized between the eventual 118-inch-wheelbase Mercury and the 123-inch Lincoln—say, a 120-inch chassis. The concept was no doubt either a "super Mercury" or a "junior Lincoln" a la the old Zephyr. In any case, there was little money to spare for launching an entirely new make. Then Korea intervened, bringing lucrative new military contracts and renewed curbs on civilian production. Add in all the new plant construction and preparations for the rest of the planned new '52 fleet, and it's easy to see why E-car got lost in the shuffle.

But not permanently. Though the E-car had no chance for 1952, studies resumed that year under the aegis of the Forward Product Planning Committee, which then threw the ball to Richard Krafve at Lincoln-Mercury Division. It was the genesis of the ill-fated Edsel, a story we'll pick up again later.

1 9 5 3

This was a historic year for Ford Motor Company, marking not only the firm's 50th Anniversary but the end of the fabled flathead V-8 (at least in the U.S.; it would continue in Canadian Fords for one year more). On top of that, Ford debuted its most totally changed truck line in two decades.

Since 50th Anniversaries don't happen every day, the relative lack of change in this year's Ford cars may come as something of a surprise. Still, there were plenty of useful updates.

Starting with the front suspension, new support plates and rubber compression bumpers gave the '53s almost twice as much total wheel travel as the '52s. The bumpers were small cone-shaped pucks, one each between the chassis and a lower A-arm. Again in the interest of ride comfort, the A-arms themselves were lengthened, rear leaf springs were made a bit softer, and shock absorbers were re-calibrated all-round. Alas, there was no change to the slow steering gear, but the linkage was again stiffened for more positive control.

Inside, the dash received detail alterations, while interior fabrics were made more durable and better-fitting than the '52 versions, which were pretty good already. There was a wider choice of both interior and exterior colors this year, plus thoughtful new touches like two-stage door stops, counterbalanced hood and trunklid, and a curved front seat track that slightly lifted the seat bottom as the seat was moved forward. Engines were unchanged save a higher-capacity cooling system for the six. June brought two welcome new options: "Master Guide" power steering ($125) and power brakes ($35).

Styling didn't change much, either, but it didn't need to. The grille exchanged its central spinner for a prominent bullet on a slimmer crossbar, and gained a lighter look via a thinner chrome "header" molding above. Parking lights changed from circular to rectangular and moved down and slightly inboard. The "jet-tube" taillights were modestly reworked to be visible from the sides. A horizontal strip of stainless steel adorned the rear fender bulges of Customlines and Crestlines, giving them an even closer resemblance to Lincoln, and the Victoria hardtop lost its twin rear window divider bars early in the model run. The trunk emblem/lock was also changed. The capper, however, was a special commemorative horn me-

The '53 Fords were changed only in detail: a new bullet-style grille, revamped taillights, and the addition of a horizontal chrome spear on the rear quarter panel of the Customlines and Crestlines. The two-door six-passenger Ranch Wagon (opposite page, top) was part of the Mainline series, so it didn't get nearly as much chrome trim. It retailed for $1917 and was easily the most popular choice among the three wagons: 66,976 produced for the model year. The Mainline Tudor sedan (right) listed at $1497; with 152,995 built, it was chosen twice as often as the Mainline Fordor. The most glamorous '53 Ford was the Crestline Sunliner (below), which cost $2043. It came with the V-8, but the Fordomatic automatic transmission, as noted on the decklid, added $184 to the price.

The $1941 Crestliner Victoria (above) cashed in on the booming demand for hardtops in 1953 with a production run of 128,302 units, a Ford record. The V-8 was standard, but many buyers added extras such as fender skirts, backup lights, and full-disc hubcaps.

Fifty Years Forward on the American Road

Beauty is only half the picture!

OF COURSE they're proud of the beauty of their car. We think you would be, too. But we wish we could give you the rest of the picture –take you over a Ford car, step-by-step, and point out some of its quality features.

First, we'd call your attention to a detail of body construction. We'd show you that there isn't a single exposed seam to catch and hold water. It costs more to build bodies this way but the weather stays out, the paint stays on and the beauty lasts.

Next we'd show you the way the doors fit, and we'd let you hear that good solid sound when they close. You'd see that each door is weather-stripped with a band of sealed foam rubber. Then we'd show you how easily the doors unlatch by just the pressure of your thumb on a button in the door handle. And, show you, too, how the Silent Doorman holds

the front doors open in your choice of two positions, two-thirds or full open.

Now we'd ask you to Test Drive it and let you feel some of the things about the Ford car that you can't see. First off you'll notice the "hushed" silence in which you travel and, then, the relaxed comfort you enjoy. (Ford engines, both V-8 and Six, are actually so quiet you can barely hear them as you drive along.) Ford bodies, too, are "quiet". . . floor, roof and body panels are "sound deadened." Even the body bolts are insulated. As to the comfort . . . well, you can see that the seats are sofa-wide. But

you can't see the heavy foam-rubber padding over non-sag springs underneath that fine upholstery. These quality "extras" are standard comforts in all models.

Another item we'd point out would be the paint. Did you know that it is baked-on enamel . . . baked on over a complete rustproofing treatment? That's why Fords keep their fresh, youthful look far longer.

Why don't you get the whole Ford quality picture firsthand? Your Ford Dealer will be proud to let you see, Value Check, and Test Drive the 1953 Ford.

Ford Worth more when you buy it
Worth more when you sell it

dallion in the steering wheel hub that read "50th Anniversary 1903 • 1953."

Dearborn may not have made a lot of changes for Golden Anniversary '53, but it built a lot more cars, especially Fords. With the government now easing Korea-prompted production curbs, Ford made the fateful decision to "blitz" its dealers in an all-out bid to challenge GM, shipping cars in record numbers seemingly without regard for orders. This, combined with increasing competition in the medium- and high-price segments, created a surfeit of Mercurys and Lincolns, though not for long. The public had liked all the new '52s, and it bought even more of the same in '53.

The "blitz," of course, was primarily intended to benefit Ford in its perennial sales battle with Chevrolet, and to some extent it worked. The division built nearly 1.25 million of its '53 cars, up nearly 50 percent from '52 and less than 100,000 behind Chevy. The effort peaked in 1954, when swamped dealers again advertised new Fords at less than cost.

"Dream cars" were popular with manufacturers in the Fifties, and Ford built its share. Henry Ford II (in the foreground) is seen here (right) in 1953 with brothers William Clay and Benson along with two futuristic cars, both of which were to have a strong influence on future Ford styling. The black car was known as the Continental "Nineteen fifty X"; the red one was called the XL-500.

Trouble was, the onslaught didn't at all damage Chevrolet, which simply cut prices in reply. It did, however, deal a mortal blow to Chrysler and the independents, which couldn't afford to discount nearly as much. Today, the Ford/GM price war is generally regarded as one of the key factors in the independents' postwar decline. In particular, it precipitated Packard's ultimately fatal acquisition of Studebaker and the Nash/Hudson merger that formed American Motors, both of which occurred in 1954. It also hastened the demise of Kaiser-Willys, which abandoned the U.S. market late that same year.

Simple though they were, Ford's '53 suspension revisions were heartily approved by motor-noters. Said *Speed Age*: "These changes have done wonders for cornering ability. Body pitch is reduced considerably, thereby keeping weight distributed more evenly over the wheels. After driving into a few turns at speeds that normally would be considered unsafe, and coming out with the feeling that

there was something to spare, one develops a healthy respect for a frame and suspension that makes this car safer for John Q. Public."

Motor Trend's praise was even more lavish: "Ford engineers have tackled the ride and handling characteristics with good results. To a large extent, in this car at least, they have proved that a good ride can be achieved in a lighter car. A heavier car is not necessarily [better riding]....In our test we gave this new 'miracle ride' a good workout: driving rutted, bumpy roads; taking dips at a fast clip; traveling winding mountain roads with numerous sharp curves. Our car took the rutted roads in stride and took all dips without bottoming and with minimum oscillation after rebound. In the mountains the

The Sunliner (left) weighed in at 3334 pounds, the heaviest non-wagon in the lineup. It found favor with 40,861 buyers in 1953. The woody-look Country Squire eight-passenger wagon (below) was both the heaviest and priciest '53 Ford: 3609 pounds and $2203. This one is equipped with extra-cost overdrive and has a badge to that effect on the tailgate. The Courier sedan delivery (bottom) was basically a Ranch Wagon with blanked-out rear side windows and a side-hinged rear door. It cost $1515 with the I-Block six—those fitted with the V-8 received a front fender badge.

steering was light and positive, and the car hugged the road well, with no tire squeal on the turns taken deliberately at above-average speed."

For its day, the '53 Ford was quite something for a low-priced car. The flathead V-8 was positively ancient in design terms, but it was never better than in this swansong year—almost totally silent beneath its fiberglass-insulated hood. Body insulation was so good, door and window fit so tight, that little noise of any kind could be heard at highway speeds. The smoothest Fordomatic to date shifted without hesitation and could hardly be felt. Foam seat cushioning was even thicker than in '52. And anything a '53 Ford V-8 lacked in performance or economy was more than offset by a ride so comfortable that the extra cost of a Mercury or Lincoln could be justified only by snob appeal. Buyers evidently agreed, even if they did need a little "force-feeding" from the factory.

Throughout all this, Dearborn indulged itself in a year-long birthday party. First came the "50th Anniversary Press Forum," a lavish to-do for members of the Fourth Estate on May 6-8 that included a preview of Ford's new styling center and scientific lab. The Ford Archives, opened in 1951 near Greenfield

Ford's truck line was all-new for 1953. The F-100 pickup (above) featured a set-back front axle, which resulted in a shorter 110-inch wheelbase. This one has the standard cab. The F-700 dump truck (left) has the DeLuxe cab, which among a number of comfort and trim features included the chrome teeth in the grille.

Village, was formally dedicated on May 7. Thirteen days later, newly elected President Dwight Eisenhower helped break ground for the company's new Research and Engineering Center, which would be completed in 1958. Rounding out the festivities, a specially trimmed '53 Sunliner driven by William Clay Ford, the youngest of old Henry's grandsons, paced the Indianapolis 500 on Memorial Day. A limited number of replicas was made available through dealers.

On June 14, Ford's 50th was observed coast-to-coast on Ed Sullivan's Sunday night TV show, then sponsored by Lincoln-Mercury. On June 16, the official anniversary date, the company reopened its Rotunda visitors center for the first time since January 1942, but not before dressing it to resemble a giant birth-

day cake. The following day, Ford hosted dinners for dealers all across the country. On June 22, the company announced plans for a new world headquarters building—the soon-to-be-famous "Glass House" in Dearborn. September 9 brought another production milestone as a new 1954 Mercury Monterey convertible became Ford Motor Company's 40-millionth vehicle.

It was a grand time. Dearborn had not only made it to 50 but had made one of the most dramatic comebacks in American business history. In six short years, Ford had decisively reclaimed the number-two position in industry production from a faltering Chrysler Corporation, and Henry Ford II had become a respected

industry leader, not least for his astute choice in managers, engineers, and designers, all of whom were hard at work laying ambitious plans for the future. An unexpected cause for celebration came when an overdrive-equipped Ford Six won the '53 Mobilgas Economy Run Sweepstakes with 27.03 miles per gallon overall and 56.7 ton mpg, driver Les Viland repeating his 1952 victory (in a Mercury V-8). Ford Sixes would continue to do well in the annual economy contests through decade's end.

Ford also commissioned a book to mark its Golden Anniversary. Many thousands of copies were sent out all over the country along with a cover letter from Henry Ford dated April 6, 1953.

The F-100 pickup (top) started at $1330, but this one got the extra-cost DeLuxe cab. It also had the six-cylinder engine, which can be told by the three-pointed star in the center of the grille. Note the new-for-'53 Ford truck crest on the hood. Moving up the line was the "Big Job" F-700 (above left), this one probably best described as a cab-forward rather than a cab-over. The '53 truck cab (above), this one a standard, was new and nicely designed, but it was relatively stark compared to car interiors.

"About a year ago," it said in part, "we asked the former managing editor of *Life* magazine to come in and put the book together for us. He and his staff, composed of some of the best photographers, writers and artists in the country, produced

The '53 Victoria (above and top left) and Sunliner (left) were easily outsold by the mainstay Tudor and Fordor sedans, but an industry-wide trend found buyers more and more style and luxury conscious. This trend would continue throughout the Fifties, and some makes would soon be selling more hardtops than sedans. The dashboard for '53 was basically a carryover, but it did receive added trim around the knobs flanking the half-moon speedometer. The gauges rode a semicircle above that. Ford steering wheels for '53 got a special commemorative horn medallion in the steering wheel hub that read: "50th Anniversary 1903 ● 1953."

the story and pictures you will find in 'Ford at Fifty'. When they finished the job, we felt it was not only a fine portrait of our company, but of a segment of American life as well." Published by Simon and Schuster, this book is coveted by collectors.

And so are the cars. Not only was the '53 nicely styled, but it was well built. It was the last of the flathead V-8s and the very pinnacle of its development. That the '53 was also an anniversary model and the Indy Pace Car only adds to its luster. Collectors are especially partial to the Sunliner convertibles and the Victoria hardtops.

The big innovation for this year's fully redesigned "Economy Truck" line involved new "Driverized" cabs with set-back front axles and wider track dimensions. The results were shorter wheelbases and increased front overhangs that conferred greater stability and easier maneuvering. Powertrains were little changed from '52, but all manual transmissions acquired synchromesh gears for the first time, and direct-drive and over-drive five-speed boxes were available in more models. Ford also shared in a truck industry first (with GMC) by offering au-

Ford's F-750 truck chassis was well suited to fire-fighting duties (left). Ford was hardly bashful in calling its 1953 lineup "Merely Terrific!" and "The New Standard of the American Road" (below). Talking points included the styling (a longer, lower, wider look), resale value ("better than any other car on the American Road"), the "famous" V-8 engine, Fordomatic Drive, "Wonder Ride" comfort—in all, 41 "Worth More" features. Who could resist? Ford even advertised "Great TV! Ford Theatre, NBC-TV, Thursday evenings."

The New Standard of the American Road

Merely Terrific!

And it hangs onto its value better than any other car on the American Road

"TERRIFIC" is the word for the '53 Ford.

A glance will tell you it's *your* dream car—come *true!* For this new Ford with its longer, lower, wider look is undoubtedly the style-setter of the '53 season. Here's beauty that's terrific... merely *terrific!*

When you take off for the open spaces you'll thrill to the wonderful "Go" of Ford's famous V-8 engine. And with Fordomatic Drive the shifting is done for you . . . and a sight better than you can do it by hand.

On highways or byways you'll find "top level" comfort with Ford's new *Wonder Ride* . . . a ride so harmonized that

you enjoy new freedom from jolt, pitch and roll—new smoothness and stability on straightaway or turn.

See this Ford and Value Check the 41 "Worth More" features. Test Drive it. Then you'll see why Ford is worth more when you buy it . . . worth more when you sell it. You'll agree it's the New Standard of the American Road.

Fordomatic Drive, white sidewall tires, optional at extra cost. Equipment, accessories and trim subject to change without notice.

See it...Value Check it...Test Drive it

'53 FORD

Great TV! Ford Theatre, NBC-TV, Thursday evenings.

---

tomatic transmission as a first-time option. Two important chassis changes shared by all models were adoption of parallel, rather than spread, frame rails and a switch in fuel-tank mounting from cab to chassis.

Model nomenclature was completely revised. Conventionals were now F-Series models, parcel vans became P-Series units, and new "cab-forward" models, replacing the former cab-over offerings, formed the C-Series. B-Series denoted the school-bus chassis. Suffix numbers signified payloads. Among conventionals, the previous F-1 became the new half-ton F-100, while the F-2 and F-3 were combined into a new ¾-ton series tagged F-250. F-350 was the former one-ton F-4, albeit with a wider choice of body types and lower maximum GVW ratings. From there, offerings progressed to the 1½-ton F-500, replacing the old F-5; two-ton F-600, taking over from the F-6; the F-700, the newly named "Big-Six" F-7; and the F-750/F-800 heavies, the V-8 versions of same. There was also a new "super truck," the F-900, the first Ford with a GVW above 26,000 pounds (the actual rating was 27,000 lbs.). The new front-end configuration boosted GVW ratings on several series, including the basic half-tonners, which now came in at 4800 pounds.

Dimensionally, the set-back front axles chopped four inches from the wheelbases of F-100 through F-600 models, three inches on F-700/800/900. F-100s thus rode a 108-inch span; F-250s, 118 inches; and F-350s, 130 inches. Conventional heavies came on wheelbases of 132, 156, 175, and 192 inches. These trimmer chassis in concert with revised steering geometry made for generally tighter turning circles, appreciated by operators who had to cope with increasing urban congestion.

This year's van series started with P-350s on unchanged wheelbases of 104 and 122 inches, and ended at P-500/P-600 versions on a 130-inch span. The new "cab-forwards" were limited to the 500 and 600 series.

Notwithstanding their "Economy" title, the '53s were the most civilized trucks in Ford history. The "Driverized" cab, designed with the aid of plastic scale models, featured a taller greenhouse, a slightly curved windshield of 55 percent greater area, and a rear window expanded to a full four-feet wide. Ahead was a squared-up hood/fender ensemble domi-

nated by a double-bar grille with outboard headlamps in a large inverted-U cavity. The bars joined at the center in a small "V" that presented an upside-down tri-star on six-cylinder versions (shades of Mercedes-Benz!) or a V-8 emblem on those models. Above was a modified version of Ford's new "keystone" passenger-car crest, with a lightning bolt below old Henry's famous signature instead of "family" heraldry. Name script also disappeared from pickup tailgates, replaced by big block letters.

So much for the conventionals. As for the new cab-forwards, they looked just like the tall conventionals they were, marked by a stubby, boxy hood with a functional air slot above the grille opening. Strictly speaking, the P-Series vans were now the only true forward-control models. Appearance wasn't vastly different from before save the new split-theme grille.

Vans excepted, Ford trucks now bore functional louvers in the right side of the cowl for feeding air to a newly optional "MagicAire" heater. Among new standard cab appointments were a wider seat with non-sag springs, "armrest height" windows, new-design dash, and safer rotary door latches.

With restrictions on civilian use of chrome finally being eased, Ford's '53 trucks could be a lot brighter than the

1951-52s. This involved ordering a Deluxe features option, basically the former "Five Star Extra" package but more easily identified by the sparkling little vertical "teeth" it added between the grille bars, three per side. In all, Ford's '53 truck line was quite impressive—and rather numerous too, now 194 models strong. The one offering that wasn't substantially changed was the new-for-'52 Courier sedan delivery, which returned with most of this year's passenger-car modifications.

Probably partly because it was Ford's Golden Anniversary year, Ford was selected to pace the 1953 Indianapolis 500 race on Memorial Day, May 30. William Clay Ford did the driving honors. Ford ran off a number of replicas to highlight the event. The Sunliner shown here wears rear fender skirts and has a "Coronado" dummy continental kit on the decklid. Both were popular Ford accessories in the Fifties. Two other options that would become nearly universal on Fords were added in mid-model year: "Master Guide" power steering and power brakes. They listed at $125 and $35, respectively.

1954

If 1953 had been a historic year for Ford, 1954 brought a milestone of another sort. After 22 years, Dearborn finally bid farewell to its fabled flathead V-8—beloved progenitor of low-priced performance, the engine of choice among hot rodders everywhere. This change (which also affected Mercury) made Ford the world's first automaker to offer a choice of ohv six *and* ohv V-8 engines. At the same time, Ford and Mercury became America's first popular-priced cars with ball-joint front suspension, a smaller version of the excellent new-for-'52 Lincoln setup.

Chief engineer Earle S. MacPherson did not actually invent that new suspension. A few European makes had used ball joints before, and Thompson Products had experimented with them in America as early as 1946. But it was Ford and MacPherson that made Thompson's system practical. The result proved so successful on the "Mexican Road Race" Lincolns of 1952-54 that it soon became the standard of the industry. Since the '52 Ford chassis had been designed to accommodate ball joints, few changes were required for its 1954 installation; among them was a half-inch gain in wheelbase.

Ed Sullivan probably did more than anyone to promote the virtues of "ball-joint" suspension, but what MacPherson actually did was to use rotating sockets instead of conventional kingpins and bushings. This eliminated 12 of 16 grease fittings. The ball-joint system also did away with a lot of unsprung weight, as "buff" magazines were quick to notice. Said *Motor Trend*: "It doesn't heel excessively on sharp, high-speed turns, and it doesn't feel like you're guiding a couple of sponges around a turn." The editors were so impressed that they declared Ford the most roadable car of 1954. In *MT*'s view, compact size and less weight made it an even better handler than the race-winning Lincolns.

The new Ford/Mercury V-8s were the last of four overhead-valve engines from the project initiated in early 1948 under Harold Youngren. The idea was to develop a common block that could serve as the basis for a new Ford six and a large Lincoln V-8, both of which arrived as planned for '52, as well as a smaller V-8 for Ford/Mercury, which for a variety of reasons had to be delayed until 1954. The program was completed with remarkable speed. Test engines were on the dynamometer by late '48, and final specifications were approved by mid-1950. Ultimately, some 400 prototypes were run the equivalent of nearly a million miles in the laboratory and on the road.

The smaller V-8s may have been late, but they were worth the wait. Though both were about the same size as their flathead predecessors—239.4 cubic inches for the Ford unit, 256 cid for Mercury's—they were much more efficient, had lots of room to grow (the flathead had reached its size limit), and boasted five-main-bearing crankshafts for greater reliability and smoothness. Both were modern short-stroke designs like their Lincoln and Ford truck relatives, and featured the same deep crankcase that gave them a distinctive Y-shape in head-on view, hence the nickname "Y-Block." Hanging the oil pan rail well below the crankshaft centerline added block strength and reduced chances of oil loss between the block and pan.

Y-Block engineering was principally the work of Victor G. Raviolo, who'd later become Dearborn's corporate chief engineer. In determining cylinder spacing, he'd aimed for a displacement range of 230 to 320 cubic inches. As it turned out, that wouldn't be enough to keep pace with the burgeoning "horsepower race," so a larger engine family was created for 1958.

Ford's Y-Block arrived with a bore and stroke of 3.50 × 3.10 inches, good for 130 horsepower with standard two-barrel Holley carb and 7.2:1 compression. This proved short of expectations, so an increase to 254 cid was ordered for 1955. When it was learned that Chevy would have a new 265 that year, Ford bored and

Ford introduced a novel new model for 1954, the "bubbletop" Crestline Skyliner (Mercury got a version it called the Sun Valley). It was basically the regular Victoria hardtop with a Plexiglas insert over the front seat. Tinted green to keep the interior at least reasonably cool, it also had a shade so that the sun could be kept out if desired. Priced at $2164, it cost exactly the same as the Sunliner ragtop. Hampered at least in part by the high price, only 13,344 were called for during the model year.

stroked to 3.62 × 3.30 inches for 272 cid and a more impressive 162/182 horsepower. There was also a 292 rendition for the '55 Mercury and Ford's new Thunderbird, with bore stretched to 3.75 inches. (The '54 Mercury engine, which used the Ford V-8's stroke but the 3.62-inch bore of the I-Block six, delivered 161 bhp with standard four-barrel carburetor and 7.5:1 compression, up 25 percent from the old flathead.)

Despite its ultimate size limitations, Ford engineers were quite proud of the Y-Block. It exhibited no valve bounce below 5500 rpm, while hard tappets, fully pressure-lubricated rocker arms, umbrella-type valve guides, and dampening coils on valve-spring ends contributed to quiet running and low oil consumption. Crankshafts were durable "semi-steel" affairs

derived from Ford's cast-crank technology. Following Ricardo principles, combustion chambers were kidney-shaped, with the larger ends away from the spark plugs. Combustion thus began there, progressing to the smaller areas where the mixture was cooled by head/piston contact. It was quite a contrast to the symmetrical combustion chambers of Chrysler's hemi-head V-8s.

With all the hubbub surrounding the V-8, one might expect the six to be carried over greatly unchanged, but that was not the case for '54. In fact, it was now standard for all models, including Crestlines and wagons. A bore job took it to 215 cid, and this along with compression hiked to 7.2:1 raised horsepower by 14 to 115—five horses more than the '53 V-8.

The new overhead-valve V-8 was

optional across the board at about $80. As before, both engine choices were offered with stick-shift, optional stick-overdrive, or Fordomatic. A little-known fact is that the 256 Mercury unit was also optional for the '54 Ford, intended primarily for police cars.

Ford styling changes were minor in this third year of the basic '52 design, mainly because management had decreed an extensive reskin for '55. Customlines and Crestlines now wore a near full-length stainless molding midway on the flanks, and the grille reverted to the three-spinner '52 theme, albeit with a toothy horizontal bar. Parking lights returned to small, circular housings outboard.

The biggest design change occurred inside, where a clean new instrument

Despite the Skyliner's debut, the '54 Sunliner convertible continued to sell well. Although output dipped some 4176 units to 36,685, it was clear that Ford's new fun-in-the-sun Skyliner wasn't stealing much from the Sunliner. Apparently those who really wanted the sun's rays preferred them unfiltered.

panel recessed most controls within a strip of tooled aluminum. The speedometer was a now an "Astra-dial," a dome-like affair with a green translucent plastic window on top. The idea was to illuminate the numerals from behind day or night, an early form of indirect lighting. Warning lamps replaced the usual oil and amp gauges and were much criticized at the time, though most other makes were also going in for "idiot lights." Last but not least, power windows and seats were added to the options list.

A further reflection of Dearborn's expansive new mood was the addition of three models to the '54 lineup: a two-door Ranch Wagon in the Customline series; a luxuriously appointed Crestline four-door sedan, a forerunner of the mid-Sixties LTD; and the unique Skyliner Victoria, a hardtop with a see-through roof—a novelty heretofore seen only on show cars.

Designers had been thinking about "bubbletops" since the late Thirties, when technical advances in the infant plastics industry began yielding stronger materials that could be used structurally, not just decoratively. The first such appli-

cation was executed by John Tjaarda for Briggs, a one-piece plastic top for a '39 Plymouth convertible sedan. By the end of World War II, the public had been titillated with promises of radical see-through cars from a number of companies, but nobody ever built any for sale—until Ford, that is.

The likely impetus for the Skyliner, and a Mercury companion called Sun Valley, was the late Gordon M. Buehrig, who'd come to Dearborn in 1949 to design the Crestliner and '51 Victoria. As noted, he also helped develop the all-steel '52 Ford/Mercury wagons, and would later handle body engineering for the beautiful Continental Mark II. Buehrig had previously worked at Studebaker with Raymond Loewy, a leading proponent of the see-through top, then became a freelance designer and created the still-born TASCO car, which had hinged roof sections of transparent plastic (basically the "T-Top"), an idea he patented. Buehrig was later moved to take issue with General Motors when it showed something similar on an experimental Corvette. "But I settled," he said. "They were too big to sue."

A more direct forecast was the fiberglass-bodied XL-500 show car of 1953, with a clear plastic top and pillars raked forward to form a "basket handle" roof band. The idea would resurface two years later on the experimental Mystere, where the up-and-over pillars served as the only structural roof members.

Ford's production bubbletops were

considerably less radical, of course—just the ordinary pillarless coupe with a Plexiglas insert over the front-seat area, tinted deep green to ward off heat and glare. The Skyliner listed at $2164 with standard six, $109 more than the normal Crestline Victoria. Mercury's $2582 Sun Valley cost $130 more than the equivalent Monterey hardtop. Aside from the plastic half-roof and minor identifying trim, both were virtually identical with their steel-roof counterparts.

Ford described the Skyliner in rather flowery prose, claiming for it "a freshness of view, a new gaiety and glamor, vast new areas of visibility, a whole new concept of light and luxury.... You're comfortably 'out of doors' all year long...with that wonderful feeling of being fashionably first." This happy puffery wasn't entirely accurate. The green tinting made for a kind of bilious, slightly weird interior ambience. Quipped *Motor Trend*'s Walt Woron: "It may cause many a young lady to check her makeup. She might as well switch to green lipstick."

A more serious problem was perspiring passengers. Though desert tests showed that the steel-roof hardtops were only about five degrees cooler inside, bubbletoppers undoubtedly *felt* much warmer on sunny days than that difference implied. And Ford didn't yet offer air conditioning. However, buyers did get an interior sunshade that snapped onto the headliner around the transparent section's perimeter, but it provided only partial relief.

Interesting though they were, the Skyliner and Sun Valley were predictably poor sellers. The former saw only 13,344 copies this year, the latter a mere 9761. By contrast, Ford moved nearly 100,000 Crestline sedans and over 95,000 conventional Victorias for '54. While excessive interior glare and heat buildup made many buyers think twice, price was surely a consideration, too. At $2164, the Skyliner cost exactly the same as the droptop Sunliner, yet looked little different from the more practical standard Victoria. Mercury gave up on the idea after 1955, while Ford would persist with decreasing success through '56. At least Dearborn was trying to give the public something it couldn't get anywhere else.

No '54 Ford was a true high performance model, but "Uncle" Tom McCahill reported that the new ohv V-8 brought 0-60-mph runs down to about 15 seconds with automatic, a healthy four seconds faster than a like-equipped '53 flathead. Manual transmission would shave off another second or so. Top speed was 92-94 mph, about the same as 1952-53.

It bears mentioning that Chevrolet and Plymouth would trail Ford by a full year in offering modern high-compression V-8s. As all the "Low-Priced Three" were basic design carryovers for '54, the new ohv unit was undoubtedly a factor in putting Ford on top in the industry production totals: a rousing 1,165,942 cars for the model year. The margin over Chevy was slim to be sure—22,381 units—but it was an important moral vic-

tory and an indication of just how far Ford Motor Company had come in a very short time. Of course, it didn't hurt that 1954 was another year of forced "blitz" production.

But Ford would have no need for such tactics after 1954. Nineteen fifty-five would prove a banner sales year for most automakers, and Ford shared the wealth by issuing even brighter and brawnier cars based on the winning 1952-54 design. Things wouldn't always

Despite the glamour of the hardtops and convertibles, Ford's best seller for '54 was the Customline Tudor sedan (above), which 293,375 customers ordered. Listing at $1744 with the 115-bhp I-Block six, it was good value for money and a reasonable compromise between the stark Mainlines and the fancy Crestlines. The last received a couple of embellishments to mark its top-line status in the Ford hierarchy, as on the Sunliner (below): Crestline badges on the rear-quarter body sculptures and three little hashmarks behind the stone shields ahead of the rear wheels.

Although the new two-seater Thunderbird would bow as a 1955 model, Henry Ford is seen here (top) previewing the new car in 1954. It would soon be capturing the imagination of millions of Americans, even though most wouldn't have the opportunity to own one. The price leader of the 1954 Ford line was the Mainline Tudor, available as either a business coupe or a sedan. The former sold for a low $1548, but found only 10,665 takers. The back seat in the sedan bumped the price to $1651, but it was far more popular: 123,329 were built.

go Dearborn's way in the years immediately following its Golden Anniversary. But by bolstering the success of the first postwar Fords, the 1952-54 models ensured that the firm would be able to weather most anything that came along. Henry Ford II and friends had every reason to be proud—and relieved.

Indeed, there seemed only one problem left to solve: grabbing a bigger share of the fast-growing medium-price market. Lincoln-Mercury chief Benson Ford asked, "From the viewpoint of the total Ford Motor Company, what should Ford owners graduate to? The next logical step would be a Mercury." The question was, was that enough? Increasingly, the answer seemed to be no.

Authors Nevins and Hill, in their seminal company history, state that Benson "had inherited a difficult situation. He had to sell in the medium-priced and high-priced field two models that had never become outright successes, although the Mercury had shown high promise. Benson was assisted by Stanley Ostrander, but [L-M] Division lacked an official who could push a point of policy against [executives] like J.R. Davis,

Since Ford Motor Company was headquartered in Dearborn, it's hardly surprising that the fire department depended on Fords. The ambulance was a specially equipped '52 Courier. In the mid-Fifties, the Ford F-750 chassis served as a very popular basis for fire-fighting equipment, but other series were also used for these specialized applications.

[Ernest] Breech, or Henry II. Nevertheless, the Lincoln-Mercury Division held possibilities through the improvement of existing models or the creation of a new one.... Other possibilities lay in the Lincoln Continental...." Dearborn was now on the brink of its fateful decision to form a multi-division structure in an effort to overtake General Motors.

It's not easy to buy the Nevin/Hills thesis that Mercury hadn't been an outright success to this point—unless they meant that it had yet to outsell, say, Buick. Since the war, Mercury had often exceeded 300,000 cars a year and ran sixth in the industry, remarkable given its prewar performance. The '54 line did well in a lackluster year for the industry as a whole, and a larger, more impressive Merc was on the way for '55.

But Dearborn managers seemed to want a new make no matter how well Mercury was doing. It was a matter of corporate pride. Thus, in the summer of '54, the "E-car" project, which had been pottering along since being resumed in 1952, was put on the proverbial front burner. While styling work began in earnest under Roy Brown, the Forward Product Planning Committee heaved yet another pile of research—a six-volume report—in management's direction. It all but mandated a companion for Mercury with a distinct, well-defined image and, perhaps, a slightly higher price. Robert S.

McNamara, then assistant general manager at Ford Division, asked a sensible question of the Executive Committee: "What is the new car intended to offer the car-buying public?" History shows that the ultimate answer wasn't fully considered.

Meantime, on October 16, William Clay Ford announced that a new Continental was in the works, not a revival of his father's original but a modern car of like character. Just six days later, Ford unveiled its reply to Chevrolet's sporting two-seat Corvette of 1953-54, the glamorous Thunderbird (see *1955*). Virtually unnoticed was the growing number of U.S. buyers turning to import cars. Granted, they numbered only 44,000 in 1954, but their ranks were swelling rapidly. It's thus a bit curious that Ford all but abandoned its French subsidiary this year, turning most of its interest over to a new organization with the acronym SIMCA, which would later become Chrysler-France. Still, the operation had been in trouble for several years—much like the French troops trying to bail out of the civil war going on in an obscure country called Vietnam.

Dearborn's truck designers took a well-deserved rest for '54. Not that many changes were called for: The new "Economy" line was doing splendidly. Chevrolet was still far and away the sales leader by dint of its greater manufacturing capacity, but Ford gained the most sales of any truckmaker in '54, ending the year with just over 29 percent of the market. Even better, the F-800 was the top seller in the 19,501-26,000 GVW class.

But there were some changes anyway. Prime among them was the arrival of two more ohv V-8s: beefed-up "Power King" versions of the new Ford 239 and Mercury 256 passenger-car units, thus

giving Ford trucks an all-ohv engine lineup for the first time. Replacing the old flathead V-8 as an option for F-100 through F-500 models, the 239 produced the same power and torque as its equally new automotive sibling but employed a heavy-duty air cleaner, a different oil pan, and special engine mounts. The 256 took over for the old Big Six in all its previous applications (F-700 on up), but was detuned from its Mercury spec, lower compression and Holley Centri-Flo carb resulting in 138 bhp and 226 lbs/ft torque. The Lincoln-based Cargo King 317 V-8 returned as standard power for F-800/900, while the ohv six got all the passenger version's improvements and a new name: "Cost Clipper."

Elsewhere, Master Guide power steering was newly optional for heavies, while F- and C-Series models sported a new grille comprising a massive slotted, convex horizontal bar atop two vertical struts. Ford reached further into the heavy-truck field with new T-Series tandem- or dual-axle models, 10-wheeler conventionals on the 700/800/900 chassis, identified by wider front fenders and appropriate hoodside nameplates. At the other end of the line, the smart Courier sedan delivery shared most of the changes with this year's Ford car, including the new ball-joint front suspension.

The brawnier, all-ohv engine lineup proved timely. After years of being America's only V-8 truck, Ford now faced head-on competition from Dodge, and Studebaker and Chevy/GMC would join the fray by early 1955. Worse, GM would introduce completely new "Task Force" models at mid-1955, while Ford hadn't scheduled its next truck redesign until 1957. Was Dearborn out of step? Not really, but overtaking Chevy was going to take some time.

1 9 5 5

Ford dealers got their first companion model this year, the sleek, two-passenger Thunderbird: a "personal" car with sports-car overtones. The standard line was hardly ignored, though, as it was restyled stem to stern and packed more power than any previous Ford.

The perennial Ford/Chevy battle was especially fierce in what proved to be Detroit's best year ever: 7.17 million total car sales. Ford again claimed second spot on the chart but enjoyed an impressive model-year volume of over 1.4 million units. Robert S. McNamara, one of the "Whiz Kids," was elevated to division general manager early in the year, and his influence would be felt well into the next decade. Two other key appointments occurred as Ernest Breech became board chairman on January 25 and George Walker was named Ford Motor Com-

pany's first vice-president of styling in May.

Other 1955 corporate highlights included production of the 20-millionth Ford V-8 engine, on June 24, and a one-day production record of 10,877 vehicles, set November 9. At year's end, Ford U.S. had completed a record 2,614,559 vehicles for the 12 months, and its work force numbered 181,616. Hourly employees earned average wages of $106.88 over a 44.2-hour week.

Wall Street lifted a collective eyebrow on December 21 as Ford announced its first public stock sale in over 30 years: 10.2 million shares of common stock held by the Ford Foundation. With approval from the Securities and Exchange Commission, the issue went on the block January 17, 1956. Ford thus became a public company for the first time

since 1919, when old Henry's "acting job" had put it exclusively in Ford family hands.

Significant for the future of car design, Ford awarded a $200,000 grant on September 2 to Cornell Medical College for research into ways of preventing and/ or minimizing auto-crash injuries. The following week, the firm hosted traffic specialists from around the country at a two-day National Safety Forum and Crash Demonstration, during which it publicly proclaimed its commitment to safer cars and reducing the nation's growing highway carnage.

Dearborn's steadily improving fortunes since 1949 had been accompanied by management's growing desire to take on General Motors product-for-product. For example, Jaguar, MG, and other sports cars had begun selling consistently

Ford's Mystere dream car (right) made the rounds of the 1955 auto shows, although it had actually been ready somewhat before that—Ford hadn't wanted to tip off the competition to its styling ideas. Many Mystere features found their way to production models, examples being the '56 Ford's parking lights, 1955-57 two-toning, and the '57's canted fins. The '55 Thunderbird (below) is an early prototype.

in the late Forties, though not in large numbers. Several American producers decided that home-grown models would do much better, owing to customer loyalties and the easier parts and service availability domestic makes enjoyed. Thus arrived the 1951-54 Nash-Healey and '54 Kaiser-Darrin, neither of which sold more than a handful. Neither did Chevrolet's new Corvette—at first. But *as a* Chevy, it represented a challenge that Ford couldn't ignore, hence the Thunderbird. Its impetus came from two directions. Ford Division styling director Franklin Q. Hershey, assisted by young William P. Boyer, had been rendering sports cars since 1950, hoping to interest management in a production model. Nothing much happened until division chief Lew Crusoe went to the '51 Paris Auto Show with George Walker, then an

outside consultant. Crusoe yearned for a Ford reply to the sporty two-seaters he saw there: the Spanish Pegaso, a revived Bugatti, the Jaguar XK-120, and GM's LeSabre show car. Turning to Walker, he reportedly asked, "Why don't we have something like that?" "Oh, but we *do*," replied Walker, who then grabbed a phone to tell his troops back home to get a sports car going. Ideas soon sprang from the drawing boards of both Walker's and Hershey's staffs, but there wasn't much urgency until the Corvette's 1953 debut, underlining Henry Ford II's determination to match GM in every market sector.

Designed largely by Boyer under Hershey's direction, the Thunderbird moved rapidly through the usual stages of renderings, clay models, and pre-production prototypes, during which its basic lines were gradually refined.

Among discarded notions were canted fins and taillights; a wide, eggcrate grille and high-set bumper; numerous scoops and scallops; and a bolt-on hardtop patterned on the roofline of the locked-up Continental Mark II. Scrubbed at the very last minute was a sweepspear side molding similar—but not identical—to that on the new '55 Ford Fairlane (though it did appear in two early ads). The result

The '55 Thunderbird was an instant hit, but Ford never called it a sports car. Rather, it was marketed as a "personal" car, and—unlike Chevy's Corvette— came with all the power amenities plus roll-up side windows, rather than drafty side curtains. The Bird rode a 102-inch wheelbase, 13.5 inches less than the big Fords, and its design was deliberately related to the looks of the '55 Ford in the hope that some T-Bird magic would rub off on the workaday models.

Designer William P. Boyer did a drawing (top left) of a "Ford Sports Car Equipped with 'Competition Windscreens'" in June of 1953. It looked remarkably like the production T-Bird. Styling similarities up front between the Bird and the regular Fords were similar headlamp bezels and mesh grilles (left), though the T-Bird's was lower and narrower. From the back (above), taillights and backup lights were shared, and the shape of the upper rear fenders was almost the same. The removable hardtop came standard.

was a timeless look that could hardly be improved upon. Production began September 9, 1954.

The Thunderbird met with generally favorable reviews. About the only things it shared with Corvette were four wheels and two seats. A touring *boulevardier* rather than purist sports car, it shunned snap-in side curtains for more convenient roll-up windows, fiberglass bodywork for traditional steel, and a six-cylinder engine for a potent V-8—this year's new 292-cubic-inch Mercury engine offering 193 horsepower with manual shift or 198 bhp with self-shift Fordomatic. With its good looks and ample zip, the T-Bird sold a respectable 16,155 units for the model year. More important in Ford's eyes, it soundly trounced Corvette, which sold a mere 674 copies this year.

But as a two-seater, the Thunderbird would never sell in sufficient volume to satisfy company accountants—or Bob McNamara. It would thus be transformed into the totally different four-seat "Squarebird" for 1958. According to Boyer and others, the Squarebird was underway even as the first two-seaters were being sold. Though the early Birds easily outsold the Corvette, the four-seaters did far better—enough to make money, which was what McNamara cared about. As most everyone knows, the changeover made the two-seaters "instant classics" that remain highly prized—and highly expensive—collector's items.

Having delivered the T-Bird, Crusoe moved over from Ford Division to become executive vice-president of the Car

and Truck Group, responsible for assembly and distribution of all Ford products. Here he picked up the services of Francis C. "Jack" Reith, fresh from the late Ford France, who set to work on new-model planning. One of Reith's first actions was to greatly enlarge the developing '57 Mercury (soon nicknamed "Reith's Merc" within certain corporate circles). This was in line with a new overall product strategy predicated on rapid growth. Reith told the board of directors that population and per-capita income were soaring, which implied an expanding car market. To capture a larger share of it, Ford

needed a broader range. "Too large a percentage of our business [is] in one car and one price bracket," he said. He wanted the evolving "E-car," initiated in 1954, to be slotted in *below* Mercury, not above, with a wheelbase of 118-120 inches, versus the 122 of his '57 Mercury. There should, however, be some overlap for the sake of dealers.

Reith's basic plan, which was accepted, contemplated not two corporate bodyshells but four: low-line Ford; E-car/Ford Fairlane; standard Mercury and maybe a higher-priced E-car; Lincoln and a new "super Mercury" (the last would materialize as the 1958 Park Lane). Ford would thus compete as usual against Chevrolet and Plymouth; the basic E-car against Dodge and Pontiac; the standard Mercury and higher-priced E-car against Olds, Buick, and DeSoto; the "super Mercury" against Chrysler and the Buick Roadmaster; Lincoln against Cadillac. Wrote Ford company chroniclers Nevins and Hill: "The plan seemed so convincing that no one was prepared to offer what might appear petty objections."

Accordingly, Lincoln-Mercury was

split in two in mid-April 1955. Ben Mills took over Lincoln, while Mercury was put under F.C. Reith. (You couldn't say he didn't have the courage of his convictions.) The E-car was handed over to Dick Krafve at the new Special Products Division where a talented team of stylists and engineers had been working on a reborn Continental since 1952 as "Special Product Operations." That program, with most of its staff, was now transferred to a new Continental Division. Overseeing all was newly named group director Benson Ford.

It was a grand plan typical of those sky's-the-limit days, though it was destined to be derailed by a boom market gone bust. But it does explain the '55 Ford: a continuation of the successful 1952-54 design intended to tide the division over until the "big" '57s. Though still overshadowed by a brilliant new Chevrolet, the '55 Ford was a fine package and a solid hit, lifting the division to unprecedented model-year car production of over 1.4 million units—less than Chevy's total but impressive all the same.

This high success was built on higher

performance and a facelift so extensive that the '55 Fords seemed all-new. The latter is properly credited to veteran designer Hershey, who with Bob Maguire, Damon Woods, John Najjar, and L. David Ash conjured up a complete reskin characterized by a rakish new look of motion. Like Dick Teague with his '55 Packard, Hershey managed the obligatory wraparound windshield by cutting dogleg A-pillars into the 1952-54 shell. Hooded headlamps, also *de rigueur*, rode above a smart new full-width concave grille. Artful "speedlines" provided interest around the wheel openings. Rear fenders hinted at fins in another concession to contemporary Detroit fashion.

Though still on the 115.5-inch wheelbase adopted for 1954, the '55 Fords were, again in the spirit of the times, slightly longer, lower, and wider than their immediate predecessors. Models now divided into four series, up from three. The low-end Mainline and mid-range Customline returned with two- and four-door sedans (plus a Mainline business sedan), but club coupes, a Ford mainstay since 1937, were dropped after

For 1955, the Fairlane took over for the Crestline as the top-of-the-line series. Six models were offered, ranging in price from $1914 to $2272. The Victoria hardtop (top) started at $2095, and output increased to 113,372 for the model run. The Sunliner (center and bottom), which came in at $2224, attracted 49,966 sun worshippers. In the 1952-54 era, the mid-range Customlines had been Ford's best sellers, but that changed in 1955 as Fairlane buyers snapped up 626,250 cars, 154,328 more than drove home in Customlines.

three years of declining sales.

Wagons more than made up the difference, increasing from three to six and put in their own separate series for the first time. This encompassed a pair of two-door Ranch Wagons, base and Custom, and a trio of four-doors: plain-sided Country Sedans with seating for six or eight, and an eight-passenger Country Squire with the now-customary woody-look trim. Chassis specs duplicated those of non-wagons save stiffer springs and shocks.

Replacing Crestline at the top of the heap was the new Fairlane series, named after the Ford family's Dearborn estate (but shortened into one word). It was identified by bold "swash" moldings that curved down from above the headlamps to a saucy dip at the A-pillars, then ran straight back at mid-body. The area thus defined—hood, rear deck, and upper bodysides—was painted to match or contrast with the roof when optional two-toning was ordered (only the roof was a different color on other models).

Fairlane offerings comprised two-door Club Sedan, four-door Town Sedan, Sunliner convertible, Victoria hardtop coupe, and the new hardtop-based Crown Victoria, available in steel- and plexi-top form (the latter taking over from the Crestline Skyliner). The Crown Vic sported a distinctive "basket handle" roof treatment inspired by Ash's work on the X-100 and Mystere show cars. Its wide, raked-forward chrome band wrapped up and over where the B-pillars would normally be located. Though it looked like a rollbar, it was merely applied trim, so it was not structural. And it didn't move with the windows to create the open expanse of a hardtop. Engineer Harold Youngren thought body flex sufficient to warrant specifying the stiffer X-braced convertible frame—which made for an unusually tight, solid-feeling car.

Like the '54 Skyliner, the bubbletop Crown Vic had a ¼-inch-thick Plexiglas half-roof (forward of the band). Compared to the normal Victoria—which was basically the upright Tudor sedan *sans* B-posts—both Crowns achieved a sleeker look via a flatter roof panel; longer, more rakishly sloped B- and C-pillars, and less rear-window curvature. Despite this, they actually offered slightly more rear headroom.

As the star of the new top-shelf series, the Crown Vic was well-equipped and typically two-toned. But the plexi-roof version, like the Skyliner before it, garnered far fewer orders than the steel-topper—1999 against 33,165—and for the same reason: formidable heat buildup despite heavily tinted glass. (A snap-in sunshade was still provided to ward off sunstroke.) Both versions would return for '56, but only 603 bubbletops and 9209 steel-roof models would be called for. The Crown Vic was thus abandoned as a bad bet, though Ford briefly considered retaining it for the all-new '57 line.

Of course, such gimmickry was typical of the age and Ford, in particular, had an unusual fondness for unusual roof treatments. Also typical, but necessary, was a wide array of solid colors and two-tone schemes. Ford had more of both for '55, and many of the more striking combinations were carried inside on Sunliners and Victorias, including Crowns. Among the most arresting were black and pink, pink and white, black and yellow, and white with aqua.

While inside the '55, buyers were sure to notice the most unusual Ford instrument panel yet. Another bit of period kitsch, it sported three large chrome-edged circles low in the center containing (left to right) heater controls, radio, and clock—all extra-cost items. The driver faced another "Astra-Dial" speedometer, a semicircular affair in a dash-top pod with a little window in its upper surface "for daylight illumination." First used for '54, it was now flatter and slightly lower to eliminate stray windshield reflections. Optional factory-installed air conditioning arrived at mid-year, but it was expensive at $435 and only 22,575 cars were so equipped.

Ford had stolen a lead on Chevy and Plymouth with its smooth, efficient new overhead-valve Y-Block V-8. The '55 "Trigger-Torque" version was slated to go to 254 cid but ended up a 272 as Ford increased both bore and stroke (from 3.50 × 3.10 to 3.62 × 3.30 inches) to counter Chevy's new 265 engine. Horsepower rose to 162 with Holley two-barrel carburetor and 7.6:1 compression, up 32 from '54. A newly optional "Power Pack" with four-barrel carb and dual exhausts lifted that to 182 bhp. At the other end of the spectrum, the rugged "Mileage Maker" six now delivered 120 horses, up five, thanks to higher 7.5:1 compression.

There were two other V-8 options. One was the bigger-bore 292 T-Bird/ Mercury unit, with the same 8.5:1 squeeze, four-barrel carb, and 198 bhp. This was part of a special-order package for Fairlanes and wagons that also included Fordomatic. (Only the T-Bird offered this engine with manual transmission.) Late in the year, a special 205-bhp "Interceptor" 292, ostensibly for police use, appeared on the list, an outgrowth of the factory's efforts in NASCAR stock-car racing. Here Ford was attempting not only to match its archrival in the horsepower race, but to prevent defection by speed merchants and hot rodders who quickly acclaimed the Chevy V-8 for its freer, higher-revving valvetrain and superior hop-up potential.

Automatic buyers—and their ranks were swelling like a tidal wave—applauded a new kickdown feature for this

The least expensive '55 Fairlane was the Club Sedan (top left), a $1914 offering that attracted 173,311 customers. Like all Fords that year, it came with the I-Block six, now at 120 horsepower, as standard. Most Fairlanes were optioned with the 272 Y-Block V-8, however, which cranked out 162 bhp, or 182 with a four-barrel carburetor. New to the model lineup was the Crown Victoria, available only in the Fairlane series. It wore a shiny tiara that went over the roof from door handle to door handle and came with or without the bubbletop Plexiglas roof insert. Priced at $2202 plain and $2272 with insert, the two models saw output of 33,165 and 1999 units, respectively. Apparently the public wasn't ready for bubbletops.

Station wagons were placed into their own separate series for 1955. At $2392, the eight-passenger Country Squire (top left) continued as the most expensive Ford offering (except Thunderbird); 19,011 were built. The Country Sedan (top right) could be had with either two or three rows of seats. Priced at $2156 and $2287, 106,284 found homes. The Fairlane Club Sedan (above left) weighed 3155 pounds, while the $1801 Customline two-door (above right) was 16 pounds lighter. With 236,575 built, the latter outpaced the Fairlane by 63,264 units. Note the I-Block six badge on the front fender and the small hubcaps.

year's Fordomatic. Combined with the added horsepower, it shaved up to three seconds off 0-60-mph trips. Flooring the throttle provided an automatic downchange into Low (manually selected on earlier Fordomatics, which started in Second). Said the brochure: "For a real 'speed-trigger' start, just press the accelerator to the toeboard and you'll flash away in low gear." Standard transmission for all models remained the usual three-speed column-shift manual, with overdrive optional as always.

Axle ratios were now touted as "Torque-Tailored"—matched to body style, engine, and transmission for "brilliant response at all driving speeds." Other mechanical alterations ran to Champion's new 18-mm gasket-less spark plugs (for improved driveability), larger-diameter "Magic-Action" drum brakes (up from 10 to 11 inches), harder

brake linings claimed to last 40-50 percent longer, and standard tubeless tires (6.70 × 15s). Last but not least, Ford's new-for-'54 ball-joint front suspension was given a slight rearward tilt to absorb road shocks from the front as well as vertically, a tweak advertised as "Angle-Poised" geometry.

Ford handling was better than ever in '55, as the chassis was now less prone to rear-end breakaway despite the more powerful engines. Acceleration was livelier, of course: the typical 272 with Fordomatic could scale 0-60 mph in just under 14 seconds and reach a shade over 100 mph. The steering, however, still needed work, as it was a little stiff for parking and too slow at 4.75 turns lock-to-lock.

Nineteen fifty-five marked the biggest expansion in Ford manufacturing operations since the Twenties, a reflection of the firm's strong comeback since 1949—and its high-flying plans for 1957-58. A new factory in Mahwah, New Jersey, took over for the old Edgewater point; northern California lost the old Richmond facility (seen in the 1988 film Tucker: A Man and His Dream) but gained a replacement in San Jose; and a new Louisville, Kentucky, plant was added. They were timely additions. With almost-all-new cars and the record-busting '55 market, Ford model-year car output was now the highest since 1923. Though it still trailed Chevrolet by a substantial 253,000

units overall, Ford was now America's undisputed wagonmaster, outpacing Chevy's volume by some 49,000 units.

Alas, the price of rapid expansion seemed to be a noticeable decline in workmanship. A Popular Mechanics survey found that while buyers liked Ford styling and performance, the '55s were riddled with squeaks and rattles. Some owners complained of ill-fitting doors that wouldn't close without slamming. Others endured water leaks, especially around the dogleg A-pillars and their new vertical ventwings, and many disliked the small, inefficient wipers that left a big blind spot smack in the middle of the windshield.

Poor fuel economy was another gripe: not much better than 10 mpg for the Fordomatic 272 in city traffic. Even the "Mileage Maker Six," named for its class win in the Mobilgas Economy Run two years earlier, lost a few mpg's. But Ford was likely as unconcerned about this as any Detroit producer, what with gas at two bits a gallon and buyers clamoring for horsepower. Overall, Ford fared extremely well in 1955. Though not appreciated as much as this year's new Chevy, the Fords have become worthy collector cars in their own right. The fast-looking Fairlanes, especially, have a lot going for them, and their values will surely climb higher as the years pass.

The same can be said for Ford's 1953-56 truck generation, the pickups having

become hot items among a growing number of commercial vehicle aficionados. Unlike passenger Fords, this year's "Economy" line saw only modest refinements: slightly higher GVW ratings on some models, minor engine mods, a revised group of deluxe features now marketed as the "Custom Cab," and a return to the '53 twin-bar grille style, albeit with a vee'd dip in the upper bar cradling either a V-8 emblem or, on sixes, a four-pointed star. The Cost Clipper Six was improved along Mileage Maker lines, though different carburetion left it with two fewer horses than the passenger-car six. The big Cargo King V-8s—still at 279 and 317 cid—returned with stronger valvetrains, pistons, timing chains, and exhaust-valve seat inserts, plus improved cooling,

though none of this changed outputs. Higher 7.5:1 compression and the new Champion plugs lifted the small 239 Power King V-8 to 132 horses. It ran cooler, too, thanks to a new high-capacity water pump.

Ford's most changed commercial this year was, of course, the Courier, which took on all the features of the basic '55 two-door Ranch Wagon, though it still had a one-piece swing-out rear door instead of a tailgate and metal panels instead of rear side windows. The I-6 continued as standard power, while the newly enlarged 272 V-8 replaced the 239 Y-Block as the step-up option. Appointments were a touch more lavish now, with seat, headliner, doors, and cargo-bay walls all covered in copper-tone vinyl.

Fords were always popular as police cars, and quite a few were also placed into taxi fleets (top). Some of these cabs have heavy-duty bumper guards and lack the original grille and parking lights. All '55 Fords, including the Sunliner (above left) rode a 115.5-inch wheelbase. Ford trucks received only a modest update for 1955, most noticeable in the mildly restyled grille. The F-100 pickup (above) listed at $1460, and was the truck line's best seller; 124,842 were built for the model run. Curb weight was 3080 pounds.

Despite a mostly holdover lineup, Ford grabbed no less than 30 percent of the 1955 truck market—a postwar high for the make. Ford also recorded a new "personal best" in one-year truck output, topping its previous record of 1929 by some 20,000 units.

This was a very busy year for Ford Motor Company. The firm opened its first desert proving ground, at Kingman, Arizona, on February 29, and Ford stock returned as a regular listing on the New York and other exchanges starting March 7. On March 27, Ford issued its first public annual report, hailing its "decade of growth" since 1946 and reporting record profits of $437 million for fiscal '55, as well as record sales and production. May 24 witnessed the first stockholders' meeting since the company's return to the public sector. Henry Ford II also decided to bring his firm into the Automobile Manufacturers Association, where he was promptly elected president.

Travelers and truckers alike had reason to cheer in 1956 when the federal-aid Highway Act was signed on June 29. It authorized the building of a 42,000-mile interstate highway system that was to be 90-percent government funded via the tax-supported Highway Trust Fund. Eventually, these roads would dramatically cut travel times in all parts of the nation.

On the product front, Dearborn's biggest event of 1956 was unquestionably the return of the fabled Continental. The new Mark II model was the first product effort for young William Clay Ford, then 26, but he was helped by an all-star team: engineer Harley F. Copp and designers Gordon Buehrig and John Reinhart.

The Mark II originated in 1952 via a committee called Special Product Operations (SPO), set up by Ernie Breech. An initial design was ready by December of that year, a long-hood/short-deck coupe inspired by Edsel Ford's 1940 original. Bill's brother, Henry II, took one look and said "I wouldn't give a dime for that." SPO went back to work. Four months later, management reviewed no fewer than 15 proposals. The unanimous winner was a Buehrig/Reinhart design combining the imposing front end of one SPO model with the molded-in spare tire deck outline of another. Copp devised a new 126-inch-wheelbase chassis dipped low between the wheels to provide chair-height seating within an overall height of only 56 inches. This "cow-belly" design left no room for exhausts, so he routed them through the frame rails. Locomotive and aircraft influence figured in the ultra-clean dash design. Lincoln's newly enlarged 368-cubic-inch V-8 was specified, but Continental engines would be specially pulled from the assembly line, then individually balanced and tested. Completing the driveline were Lincoln's

three-speed Multi-Drive automatic transmission and a 3.07:1 rear axle ratio.

With its elegant, "modern formal" styling marked by the trademark trunk treatment and a wide-quarter roofline, the reborn Continental was one of the handsomest cars ever. One designer termed it "a revival of the Duesenberg concept," which wasn't far from the truth. For mid-Fifties Detroit, it was unbelievable. But so was the price, a breathtaking $10,000. The Mark II thus sold sparingly. Only 1325 of the '56s would be called for, followed by another 444 of the little-changed '57s, after which Dearborn took another, more "cost effective" course.

Departing from usual practice, *Motor Trend* magazine bestowed its Car of the Year Award on Ford Motor Company's entire '56 line, honored "for progress in automotive safety and for focusing industry attention on the safety factor itself." Given the then-burgeoning horsepower race, Dearborn's decision to try making sales hay with "Lifeguard Design" might seem curious, but it really wasn't, for performance hadn't been forgotten at all.

After the major styling changes of 1955 and the debut of the Thunderbird, Ford gave both the regular models and the Thunderbird a modest facelift for 1956. This page: For the Bird the most notable alteration was kicking the spare tire out of the trunk onto the rear bumper (above). This increased trunk space, the major complaint regarding the '55s. The second most obvious change was the optional "porthole" windows in the hardtop (top). Opposite page: Sharp eyes would also note the vent flaps in the front fenders (to improve cockpit cooling) and the exhausts rerouted to the corners of the rear bumper (top). Base price was $3151. Posing together, the '56 Crown Victoria and T-Bird show off the "Ford family" styling themes.

In fact, higher compression lifted power ratings for all '56 Fords. A jump from 7.5 to 8:1 added another 17 horsepower to the Mileage Maker Six for a total of 137. The two-barrel 272 V-8 was also squeezed another half-point, gaining 11 horses for 173 in all. The Power Pack option was scratched, but the four-barrel 292 with dual exhausts was now readily available in all Fairlanes and wagons. Output here rose but fractionally to 200 bhp with manual transmission, 202 bhp with Fordomatic. Topping the chart was

Although Henry Ford I sold cars on utility and price, Henry II knew that even low-priced cars in the Fifties had to have glamour. The '56 Fords did, particularly the Fairlane Sunliner and Crown Victoria. The ragtop (left) listed at $2359, and even though it was a down year for the industry, production jumped 8000 units to 58,147. However, the $2337 Crown Victoria (above) skidded 24,000 units to a mere 9209. As the flagships of the Fairlane fleet, these cars were almost always two-toned and often heavily optioned, making them highly desirable to latterday Ford collectors.

a hot new Y-Block enlargement, the 312-cubic-inch "Thunderbird Special" (bore and stroke: 3.80 × 3.44 inches), offering 215 bhp in two-barrel form or 225 bhp with four-barrel, the latter restricted to automatic. It promised high excitement in a light Tudor sedan, since any engine was newly available in any model—and with manual shift. A twin-four-barrel 312 with 245 bhp was added at midyear as a Thunderbird option. The standard Fords weren't mentioned, but a few may have been built with it.

Otherwise, the '56 mechanical package was much like '55's. The electric system switched from six to 12 volts per industry trend, differentials were slightly modified, and all engines received increased valve lift and minor changes to carburetors and distributors in the interest of improved fuel economy.

Styling wasn't overlooked either. A cautious but pleasing update of the '55 exchanged the fine-mesh grille and its flanking "spinner" parking lamps for a wide-grate insert and large oval lights. Bodyside moldings and headlamp brows became more massive, and the round taillamps, a Ford fixture since '52, were enlarged and given bright trim rings. Roof crowns were flattened ¾-inch, and conventional hard-tops adopted the Crown Victoria's longer, more graceful rear greenhouse slope.

Though the plexi-roof Crown Vic de-parted shortly after the start of '56 pro-duction, three new offerings upped the net model count by two. Following GM's lead at mid-1955 (with Buick and Olds), Ford added a Victoria Fordor hardtop sedan to the Fairlane line, and threw in a two-door Customline Victoria for good measure. Joining the wagon train was the Parklane, a Ranch Wagon with Fairlane side trim and interior appointments, a half-hearted reply to Chevy's pretty but slow-selling '55 Bel Air Nomad. No mat-ter, the Parklane outsold the '56 Nomad 15,186 to 7886.

Common to all '56 Fords was a re-worked dash with a hooded instrument cluster presenting a conventional round speedometer and flanking pairs of small-er stacked circles housing gauges and warning lights. Control knobs protruded less than before, and the dash top was de-signed to facilitate installation of an op-tional vinyl-covered foam pad, one of Ford's new "Lifeguard Design" safety features.

The result of work with safety ex-perts at Cornell and other universities as well as the U.S. Air Force, Lifeguard De-sign aimed at reducing or preventing in-juries in a collision with certain standard or optional features that enhanced what we now term "passive safety." Specifical-ly, Ford standardized a deep-dish steering wheel that give way under impact rather than impaling the driver on the column; a positive lock to keep the front seat from sliding forward under sudden deceler-ation; and stronger "anti-burst" door latches. An extra-cost package combined

The '56 Crown Victoria's distinguishing feature was still the basket-handle chrome band that rose over the roof (below). Fender skirts were a popular option. The regular Victoria (above) retailed for $2194 and was far more popular with 177,735 built, but it too flaunted plenty of chrome (and stainless steel) trim.

the aforementioned dash padding with padded sun visors, a shatter-resistant plastic-back rearview mirror, and air-plane-type lap seat belts anchored firmly to a reinforced floor plate.

Ever the sober, practically minded executive, Ford Division chief Robert S. McNamara believed safety would help sell his '56 cars. But though the public ini-tially took to Lifeguard Design in a mod-est way, the rush to install seatbelts over-taxed Ford's supplier, so only 20 percent of the '56s got them. It may have been just as well, as Ford's own research showed that fewer than 20 percent of those who ordered seatbelts bothered to wear them. Ford would continue its strong safety pitch for another few years, but many dealers said performance was more important.

So was competitive pricing, with price tags this year ranging from $1748

for the stark Mainline business coupe to $2533 for the Country Squire. Though up $100-$200 from 1955, Ford prices had been remarkably stable since 1952.

Competitive pricing was also an im-portant point with a rising young Ford salesman in Pennsylvania named Lido Anthony Iacocca. Seeing that McNamara's safety campaign was doing nothing to turn on his mostly blue-collar prospects, Iacocca came up with a more compelling campaign of his own: "A 56 for 56"—meaning a '56 Ford for $56 a month. Helped by a Philadelphia ad agen-cy, Iacocca and company visited super-market parking lots, leaving little bags of potato chips on the windshields of late-model cars. Each bag bore this message: "The chips are down. Wujatake [so many dollars] for your car? We're selling '56 Fords for $56 a month." As silly as this sounds, Fords soon began selling in the

Philadelphia area like...well, potato chips. McNamara took note and, minus the baggies, applied the idea nationwide. He later said it helped sell an additional 72,000 cars.

Depending on engine and who did the testing, a '56 Ford could be a bit faster than a '55: 0-60-mph acceleration was down to around 12 seconds with 292 and Fordomatic. Mileage, on the other hand, was slightly better on average. Otherwise, there was little difference from behind the wheel—except for workmanship, which if anything was even worse. Rattles and squeaks, wind and water leaks were again in evidence, plus some new complaints: hoods and front fenders that shook at speed, orange-peel paint, inferior upholstery. It was all too bad, because the '56 Ford was quite pleasing mechanically. Though no Detroit make in these years could claim truly excellent workmanship—certainly not by today's standards—Chevy had an edge in this department over both Plymouth and Ford, particularly by 1957.

The most marked difference in this year's Thunderbird was a "continental" exterior-mount spare tire, a last-minute change likely made more to increase trunk space than to enhance styling, though it came off well visually. So did the now-famous porthole windows, a new option for the accessory hardtop. Though they didn't relate to anything else on the car, they improved over-the-shoulder vision, which may explain why buyers preferred them four-to-one over the blind-quarter hardtop. Finally, front fenders now sported flip-open ventilators, answering complaints of excessive engine heat in the '55 cockpit. The 292 V-8 returned with 202 bhp as standard with manual transmission, while the new 312 engine offered 215 bhp with optional stick-overdrive, 225 bhp with Fordomatic and, as noted, 245 bhp with the midyear twin four-barrel option.

Road tester Karl Ludvigsen judged the '56 T-Bird better balanced than the '55, mainly because slinging the spare out back resulted in a better front/rear weight distribution. Even so, the early Birds were not really sporting handlers. The quick steering and fairly stiff rear springs from '55 were respectively slowed and softened for '56 because most buyers wanted them that way. Thus, the '56 (and '57) plowed a bit more through corners, and steering response was rather vague, though not completely robbed of feel by excessive power assist. The all-drum brakes were adequate for normal driving if not track work. Still, the two-seaters seem entirely up to date today, giving away little in comfort or driving pleasure to cars several decades younger.

Despite their expected disadvantages as competition cars, early T-Birds not only raced but fared surprisingly well. In fact, they were far more capable than many appreciated. At the 1955 Daytona Beach Speed Weeks, for example, a car

Following trend-setter General Motors, Ford added a four-door hardtop (top) to the Fairlane line for '56. With 32,111 built, this $2249 Victoria was modestly popular. Another new model was the $1985 Customline Victoria (center), an answer to Chevy's mid-line Two-Ten Sport Coupe. Like the Chevy, it was overshadowed by the top-line hardtop; 33,130 were built. The $2533 Country Squire (bottom) saw output increase to 23,221 units.

sponsored by Tom McCahill of *Mechanix Illustrated* magazine and driven by Joe Furguson swept all honors among American production sports cars, averaging 124.633 mph on a two-way run to best every Porsche and Austin-Healey and all but one Jaguar XK-120M. For 1956, Ford hired ex-racing driver Pete DePaolo to prepare a flock of Birds for Daytona. Chuck Daigh's carefully set-up '56 won the production-class standing mile at 88.779 mph, very nearly beating a modified-class Corvette driven by Zora Arkus-Duntov to 89.735 mph. But the Birds weren't entered in the long-distance race, a Chrysler 300 won the Grand

National stock-car event, and the T-Bird wasn't competitive in road racing because of its soft suspension and indifferent brakes. The regular Ford was competitive, however, as it walked away with the Manufacturer's Trophy at the Pure Oil Performance Trials at Daytona Beach, Florida, in February.

In the all-important sales race, Ford pulled a lot closer to Chevrolet. Despite the industry's general sales retreat this year, the division ended the model year at bit over 1.4 million cars (including Thunderbirds), only some 42,700 units behind its banner '55 total. Chevrolet finished with 1.56 million, a decline of some 137,500 despite selling a record 3467 Corvettes. Thunderbird eased to 15,631 units, perhaps reflecting slightly higher prices (up to $3151 basic from an initial $2944). Now all that remained was to pull ahead of Chevy and stay there. Ford wouldn't do that, but it would outsell its rival in '57.

Wrapped windshields were all the rage on mid-Fifties Detroit cars, and if cars could have them, why not trucks? Chevy had answered yes with its new-generation 1955 "Task Force" fleet. Now Ford got into the act by notching in dog-leg A-posts to accommodate curved front glass on all truck cabs save P-Series vans. You could also get wraparound *rear* glass, though few buyers opted for this extra, mostly F-100/250 customers. Following its new custom of annual grille changes for trucks, Ford combined elements of the '54 and '55 designs to create a different yet still familiar look. With the Custom Cab option the face was chromed, the first bright face available on a Ford truck since 1938.

Yet another expansion of the engine chart lifted model offerings to 289, a new Ford record. At the bottom was a revised I-Block six, renamed "Cost Cutter" but again modified along Mileage Maker lines. Tuning and carburetion differences rendered it slightly less powerful than the passenger-car engine, with horsepower coming in at 133, torque at 202 pounds/feet. Replacing the base 239 V-8 in all 100-500 F/B/C-Series applications was a truck version of the passenger-car 272, producing 167 bhp with two-barrel carb and 7.8:1 compression. An upgraded edition with 158 bhp took over for the Power King 256 in F-600/700s, and optional four-barrel carb delivered 168 bhp. The F-750's old 279 was bored and stroked to 302 cid (3.62 × 3.66 inches) and treated to a number of internal upgrades including higher 7.5:1 compression. The result was 175 bhp and a healthy 279 lbs/ft peak torque. Powering "Big Job" 800s and 900s as well as a new tandem-axle T-750 line was a "Torque King" 332, essentially a bored-out 302 offering 190 bhp or, in "Special" tune, 200 bhp. At midyear these figures rose to 200 and 212, respectively, as Ford responded to interim heavy-truck power hikes by Chevrolet.

With all these "power plays," Ford's

The '56 Ford pickup sported the trendy wraparound windshield so popular on cars, plus another grille revision. Prices for the 6½-foot-box F-100 (top) started at $1577, but the example pictured has the optional V-8 (emblem on the grille), Custom Cab (emblem under the side window), wraparound rear window, and side-mounted spare. A new station wagon model was the $2428 Parklane (above and opposite, bottom), a response to Chevy's stylish Nomad. Some thought it a half-hearted answer because it was based on the two-door Ranch Wagon, but the Parklane was dressed in Fairlane trim inside and out and made for an attractive package for anyone seeking a luxury wagon. Buyers agreed, choosing it over the Nomad two-to-one: 15,186 versus 7886. Can you spot at least seven chrome options on this '56 Crown Vic (opposite, top)?

GVW ratings were slightly higher for '56, so transmission choices and axle ratios were adjusted to suit. The one other development of note concerned first-time availability of tubeless tires for models rated over a half-ton. The Courier sedan delivery again kept styling and engineering pace with this year's passenger cars, including the new Lifeguard equipment.

Considering the tough new competition and Chevy's continuing lead in manufacturing capacity, Ford's commercial line enjoyed another fine sales year. Though production for the calendar year was down substantially to just over 297,000 units, 1956 model-year volume was much higher, mainly due to an extra-long 15-month run beginning in September 1955. Many truck-watchers took this to mean that something new was in the works, and they were right on the money. In both cars and trucks, Ford Division was about to make its most sweeping overhaul in a generation.

1 9 5 7

Many enthusiasts still regard 1957 as the vintage Detroit year of that decade. Ford Division certainly contributed its share of the harvest: a line of totally restyled trucks and standard cars, a handsome facelift for the last of the two-seat Thunderbirds, and V-8s ranging from a mild 190-horsepower "272" to a supercharged 300-bhp 312. In short, Ford not only covered the market, but overwhelmed it.

Which was precisely the plan. If Dearborn couldn't beat front-running GM at its own game, then it would change the game. Of course, a massive product overhaul coming only two years after the major revisions of 1955 would be unheard of today—and prohibitively expensive. But most anything was possible in that extravagant era, and Ford's huge '57 investment paid off. The automotive sales race with Chevrolet, which fielded only a heavily facelifted line, was hard-fought as always. Some figures showed Ford ahead in calendar-year output for the first time since 1935, but the final tabulation had Chevy the winner by a scant 130 units. However, Ford scored a substantial victory in model-year production: better than 170,000 units. Its grand total of 1.67 million cars was a post-Model T high, and would not be bettered until well into the Sixties.

A big factor in Ford's '57 popularity was its powerplant lineup, one of the industry's broadest. At the bottom was the 223-cubic-inch ohv six, now rated at 144 horsepower; it was the base engine for most passenger models. V-8 offerings began with the 190-bhp 272, followed by a 212-bhp 292, standard for the Thunderbird. Then came a raft of 312s, commencing with a four-barrel 245-bhp version and extending through twin-four-barrel 270- and 285-bhp units. At the top were two supercharged 312s, rated at 300 and 340 bhp on 8.5:1 compression. While the latter's production is doubtful, the former appeared in a few Thunderbirds.

Standard Fords gained all-new bodyshells atop a Continental-style cow-belly chassis spanning two different wheelbases, and model offerings were rearranged into five separate series. On the shorter, 116-inch platform were the bottom-end Custom and flashier Custom 300 Tudor and Fordor sedans (replacing Mainline and Customline, respectively), plus two-door base and Del Rio Ranch Wagons, a brace of four-door Country Sedans, and the woody-look Country Squire. Also included was the Ranchero, the first car-pickup from a domestic maker since World War II. Based on the Ranch Wagon, it was prompted by the growing postwar demand for plusher, more car-like commercial vehicles.

The longer 118-inch wheelbase was reserved for two Fairlane series: a four-model standard line of two- and four-door hardtops and sedans, and the new Fairlane 500 with these styles plus the Sunliner convertible and the first (and last) retractable hardtop in American production, the unique new Skyliner. Ford's '57 styling originated in the Mystere show car, a space-age dreamboat typical of the age, created by Bill Boyer of the Advanced Styling Studio in the summer of 1954 expressly for the January 1955 Detroit Auto Show. Though it definitely influenced the '57 rear-quarter treatment and the new Fairlane 500's "swash" (bodyside) molding, the Mystere was a little *too* accurate a forecast, so it was withdrawn from the Detroit show "in order not to tip [our] hand," as Boyer recalled. "I don't believe it was shown until '56 or '57, then [only] as an idea car preceeding the '57 Ford."

Boyer also notes that the Mystere was developed at about the time that '57 development work began in earnest for both the Thunderbird and standard Ford, though it wasn't until 1955 that management decided to divide the passenger models between two different wheelbases. The original package thus became the Custom/Custom 300; the Fairlane/Fairlane 500 was a simple "stretch job."

The '57 Ford bore the imprints of several designers, so none of them can take exclusive credit for it. Boyer, for instance, was heavily involved throughout the program, yet Frank Hershey did much of the early drawing board work, assisted by Damon Woods. Later, Bob McGuire took overall charge, with L. David Ash, Chuck Mashigan, and A.J. Middlestead chipping in. Of course, de-

The two-seater Thunderbird sported its most extensive—and final—facelift for '57. It looked familiar from the sides (bottom left), apart from the canted fins, but a new grille and bumper (below) and squarer deck, larger taillights, and a new bumper (bottom right) could be seen front and rear. Inside resided a hooded instrument cluster (above left). Most of the styling changes were echoed in the big Fords. Supercharging came to the T-Bird in 1957 via a unit that spun out 300 horsepower (above).

sign vice president George Walker had the last word—aside from company president Henry Ford II.

Despite all the "chefs," Ford's '57 styling was settled on quite quickly and was particularly clean for the period: full-width rectangular grille, squarish front fenders brought down about even with a wider and flatter hood, and modest "blade" tailfins atop large, round taillamps. Rooflines proved troublesome. A number of proposals were drawn up ranging from delightful to dreadful. The one selected was crisp, graceful, and altogether right. Windshields wrapped more via pulled-back A-posts, and a switch from 15- to 14-inch wheels and tires, in line with an industry trend, contributed to a three-inch reduction in overall height. Overall length and width were noticeably increased, approaching Mercury dimensions of only a few years earlier. The instrument panel was all-new,

too, but still pleasingly simple. A curved ribbon speedometer flanked by fuel and temperature gauges sat beneath a deep visor just ahead of a slightly smaller deep-dish steering wheel placed a bit lower than before. The ignition switch was still to the left, per recent Ford practice. Climate controls, radio, and clock (the latter two remained accessories) were located in the top center of the panel. Interiors were naturally color-keyed to exteriors, vinyl and vinyl/fabric trims depending on model.

Ford's ball-joint front suspension was simplifed and refined for '57, with 33 percent fewer parts and newly swept back lower A-arms for a smoother softer ride. Rear geometry was also revised via two-inch-longer leaf springs pinned inboard of the frame rails for the first time. Extending from a new, tapered driveshaft was a reworked hypoid axle set further back to reduce rear-end acceleration

squat. This together with the new drop-floor chassis brought a small improvement in back-seat room.

It had been 25 years since Ford's first V-8, but '57 engine changes were comparatively minor, geared to improve both performance and economy. All V-8s received high compression, larger intake valves and manifolds, redesigned camshafts with higher lift, and distributors with combined centrifugal/vacuum timing advance (replacing full-vacuum mechanisms). Reduced hood height dictated new low-profile carburetors across the board, with simplified throttle linkages and more efficient design. As before, any Ford engine could be teamed with column-shift three-speed manual transmission, optional stick-overdrive or self-shift Fordomatic.

Reviving the '54 "bubbletop" name, the new Skyliner was Ford's most interesting '57 by far. Billed as the "World's only hide-away hardtop," it was introduced slightly behind the rest of the line. It didn't look that different from the Sunliner in top-down form, but its rear fenders were three inches longer and somewhat higher, resulting in an ungainly "bustle" look. Ford, on the other hand, claimed that "This additional length is evident in the longer, low-line silhouette of the rear deck area—a smooth expanse of metal that comes right up to the rear seat!" Still, the Skyliner was the ultimate expression of Fifties gadgetry, and Ford advertising played on it by asking a legitimate question: "How can it be a 'hardtop convertible' if the top doesn't go down?"

The concept had been broached by stylist Gilbert Spear, whose designs convinced William Clay Ford, then head of Special Projects Division, to earmark $2.2 million for development as part of the Continental Mark II project. When it was realized that development costs would never be recovered with a low-volume product, the idea was turned over to Ford Division in 1955, though only after another $18 million was set aside for testing. As the all-new '57 line was less than two years away by then, a crash program was undertaken to get the retrac out in time.

Much of the work involved the rear structure so as to make room for the roof (shorter and squarer than that of standard hardtops but still plenty big) and its hardware. The decklid was hinged in the

Ford debuted for 1957 boasting four series and two wheelbases. The top-of-the-line group was now called Fairlane 500 and rode a 118-inch span, up 2.5 from 1956. Weight was also up, by about 200 pounds. Least expensive among the half-dozen Fairlane 500s was the two-door Club Sedan (top), which featured much thinner pillars than normally seen on a sedan. Selling at $2281, it found favor with 93,756 buyers. Although it came standard with the 144-bhp six, most were ordered with the 190-245-horsepower 272, 292, and 312 V-8s. This car, however, runs a 312 with the extremely rare (especially on the big Fords) supercharger.

only possible way, at the back. A space-saving 10-inch-long flap was created at the front of the top; it folded under as the top slid back. The convertible chassis was modified with closer-set siderails to leave room for the top's control linkage. Remarkably, little rear leg space was lost. The gas tank took up valuable real estate under the trunk floor, so it moved aft of the back seat (an "accidental" safety benefit for rear-end collisions); the spare took its place. To compensate for the extra weight, the 272 V-8 option was made standard.

The Skyliner's "nervous system" comprised 600 feet of wiring and no fewer than 10 power relays, eight circuit breakers, 10 limit switches, three drive motors, and a safety interlock that prevented anything from happening with-

out the transmission in Neutral. It was complicated, but more reliable than generally believed. Here's how it worked: Pressing a steering-column switch with the ignition on (and, preferably, with the engine running to minimize battery drain) activated two (1957-58) or three (1959) switches to start the deck motor, which lifted the long lid via twin shafts at each edge. The fully locked-open deck then tripped the switch for another motor (behind the rear seat) that raised the package shelf to deck level. This started another motor that unlocked the top, after which two more motors (one on the '59) raised the roof and sent it back into the open trunk cavity. A separate servo folded the hinged flap as the roof eased its way down. A dashboard warning light glowed throughout, then extinguished

on completion of the sequence which could be reversed at any time. In case of failure, the point at which the sequence stopped told you where the trouble was. A hand-cranked emergency override was provided so you wouldn't have to drive with the top at half-mast.

Arriving at $2942, $437 upstream of the Sunliner, the Skyliner sold respect-

Ford was quite innovative with new body styles during the Fifties, but one of its "better ideas" was really a throwback to the Thirties, the car-pickup. Still, Ford was the first to offer one postwar: the Ranchero. Based on the 116-inch-wheelbase two-door Ranch Wagon, with rear roof and side windows removed, it came in standard or Custom trim. The '57 Custom (below) listed at $2149, and 15,277 were built (plus 6428 standards). This one has the "Style-Tone" paint job.

The '57 Fairlane 500 boasted all-new styling featuring a wide horizontal grille, heavily hooded semi-"frog-eye" headlights, stand-up hood ornament, and modified "Fairlane sweep" side trim with a gold anodized insert for the first two-thirds of its length. Among the more enticing Fairlane 500 offerings was the Sunliner convertible (above), a 3526-pound beauty that listed at $2505, or $3500 with typical options. The most sensational '57 Fairlane 500, however, was the Skyliner (below).

ably well for a specialty item based mainly on novelty value: 20,766 units for the model year. That nearly equaled this year's record two-seat Thunderbird volume and was more than twice the number of Corvette sales in 1960.

In the end, the Skyliner was doomed by inconvenience and high cost. Its near 20-percent price premium over the Sunliner, which had the same open-air appeal, grew each year. Worse, there was only 6.5 cubic feet of luggage space with the top down, and it could be accessed only by reaching over the rear fenders. Ford side-stepped the issue by saying that with the top down "there's plenty of room for week-end luggage," and with it up there was a "vast cavern" big enough to handle a cross-country trip. But the most telling factor was division chief Bob McNamara, who deplored "gimmick engineering" and steadily turned Ford toward no-nonsense products as the Sixties approached. The Skyliner—"the miracle car of this generation"—would thus be ditched after 1959 and 48,394 units in all.

The '57 Fords garnered mostly glowing reviews. *Motor Trend*, for example, timed a stickshift Fairlane sedan with the 245-bhp Thunderbird Special V-8 at 9.5 seconds 0-60 mph, two seconds quicker than its previous Fordomatic tester—"real rapid time in anyone's book." Roadability stood to be better, and *MT*'s editors judged it so. They started "on exceptionally rough roads and noticed a definite improvement in spring and shock action over '56." Smooth roads revealed "a minimum of nose dip when braking. The brakes seemed smooth and positive. Vio-

lent cornering brought out the advantages of a low center of gravity. The new Ford really sticks. Body lean is modest, and with the built-in oversteer, you get a feeling of confidence in the car's ability to do your bidding." *MT* later reported 11.1 seconds 0-60 for a like-powered Fairlane 500 four-door with Fordomatic, but was critical of quality.

Speaking of workmanship, 1957 marked the first use of "sculptured" body panels on a Ford—sheetmetal with sharper than ever edges, creases, and curves. But stamping processes were far from perfected at the time, so the panel rejection rate was very high. The "split-level" wagon roof with its notched, transverse character line proved especially tricky. Not until 1959-60 would Detroit learn to make such stampings reliably.

Rumors of a new, larger Thunderbird started circulating in '57. Some suspected that the two-seater was dead, while others hoped it would continue as a companion to the "family" Bird. The former proved correct, and Ford gave some consideration to the latter. In any case, the last of the "little Birds" was arguably the best. A serious facelift brought a bold bumper/grille (proposed by Bill Boyer for 1955 but deemed too radical and costly then), plus modest blade fins *a la* standard Ford flanking a longer rear deck. "We extended the trunk largely to get rid of the spare tire," Boyer remembered, so the '57 ended up four inches shorter than the '56. (An optional exterior spare was still listed, but found few takers.) Inside were a handsomely redesigned dash with telescoping steering column (revived from '55) and modified door panels repeating the T-Bird logo.

Though the '57 was the most "styled" two-seat Bird, designers resisted attempts to gook it up with extra chrome, two-tone paint, and creased sheetmetal. They deserve a lot of credit, because the result was good and still looks good today. Production ran longer than usual due to 1958-model delays, so the '57 was the most numerous of the two-seat generation at 21,380 units.

T-Bird mechanical changes included

a larger fuel tank (20 versus 17 gallons) and a new rear axle with straddle-mounted pinion gear. The strong frame and coil-spring front suspension were retained, but engineer Bill Burnett reverted to five-leaf rear springs (as on the '55, versus the '56's six-leaf) and wheel/tire diameter shrank from 15 to 14 inches. Considered but rejected were Edsel-style pushbutton automatic transmission controls in the steering wheel hub. Transmission choices stayed the same, but engine options expanded to include the aforementioned supercharged mills.

The Paxton-McCulloch blower was supplied at the behest of driver Pete DePaolo, who'd learned that Chevy might have a blower on its '57 Corvette. A $500 option, this centrifugal unit delivered up to six psi of compressed air to a sealed carburetor, and it did wonders for performance. While the 245-bhp setup would see 115 mph tops and turn 0-60 mph in 10 seconds, the blown Bird was good for 125 mph and well under seven seconds (closer to six by some accounts). Just 208 were built, plus another 1500 with the twin-four-barrel 270- and 285-bhp engines.

Ford wasn't doing this for fun. It was doing it for Daytona, and 15 of the 300-bhp Birds were run off to qualify as "stock" in time for the February 1957 Speed Weeks. Chuck Daigh recorded 93.312 mph in the standing mile, and a

private entry ran the flying mile at 146.282 mph one-way, 138.775 mph both ways. Four months later, the Automobile Manufacturers Association decided to deemphasize competition and the T-Bird's racing career was nipped in the bud, though it ultimately wouldn't matter. The lush personal Ford was about to become a full-bore luxury liner, albeit of sensible proportions, so a racing image would be even more peripheral to sales than before.

Fully modern styling, revived cab-over models, and a smaller group of more potent engines made Ford an even healthier competitor in the increasingly hard-fought truck wars. Conventionals adopted a squared-up, slab-sided look, with full-width flat hoods, blunt front ends, and simple slotted-bar grilles. Though pickups returned with a choice of 6½- and 8-foot cargo boxes as before, there were now two kinds: narrow sepa-

At $2942, the Skyliner retractable hardtop (above left) was easily the most expensive '57 Ford—and the most fascinating. Its all-steel top—with the help of 600 feet of wiring, 10 power relays, eight circuit breakers, 10 limit switches, three drive motors, and a safety interlock—hid completely in the trunk, or rose automatically as needed. Ford output jumped 225,000 units for '57, so a lot of haulers were needed to deliver them (above right). The $2157 Custom 300 four-door (below) attracted 194,877 orders.

Ford's base '57 series was the Custom, replacing the '56 Mainline. It rode a 116-inch chassis and included three models: a seldom-ordered $1879 business sedan (6888 built), four-door sedan (68,924), and a two-door sedan (top). The last, priced at $1991, found 116,963 buyers. Even this base series wore bodyside chrome, a practice begun in mid-1956 with the Mainline. The Fairlane 500 two-door sedan (center) shows how much more glitter the top-line series got. Entering its second year was the Victoria hardtop sedan, offered as a Fairlane or a Fairlane 500. The latter (bottom), priced at $2404, saw 68,550 built.

rate-fender Flaresides and wider new flush-fender Stylesides, the latter a no-cost option that mimicked Chevy's premium-priced, limited-production Cameo Carrier. The Styleside's smooth rear quarters were also highlighted on a restyled F-100 Panel Delivery that boasted a larger cargo bay and a "split-level" roof treatment *a la* this year's Ford station wagons. Windshields were more radically wrapped and larger, as were the flat and optional wrapped rear windows on conventionals.

As noted, the handsome Ranchero, a revival of the prewar "coupe-pickup" idea, joined the Courier as a new derivative of the two-door wagon. Buyers could choose from base and Custom models trimmed much like the standard and Del Rio Ranch Wagons, respectively. Both had the more potent, 144-bhp "Mileage Maker" six as standard. The 190-bhp 272-cid V-8 was optional for the base Ranchero, while Customs could also be ordered with the 212-bhp 292. As in passenger Fords, all engines could be teamed with one of three transmissions. Many other options were shared as well: power steering and brakes, electric seat and windows, whitewall tires, full wheel covers, left-hand outside rearview mirror, and for Customs, two-tone paint. No-cost features included a full-width, three-passenger bench seat and tough double-wall box construction. Customs came with extra exterior brightwork and a chrome steering-wheel horn ring.

With its car-like civility and prices starting at a low $1920, the Ranchero was a tempting alternative to an F-Series pickup for those who wanted a car but needed a truck. Once again, Ford was trying to give buyers something unique—"niche marketing" in today's parlance—and it worked: The Ranchero was more than a fair success with debut model-year sales of 21,705. That was about 1000 more than the gimmicky Skyliner generated—not bad for a much simpler concept. This good idea (Chevy was moved to copy it for 1959) would remain a fixture of the Ford truck line for the next 22 years.

The new C-Series cabover would prove even more enduring: Still in production into the early Nineties with no end in sight. Unlike the discontinued "cab-forwards," this new design was a true COE, positioning the engine almost directly above the front axleline and the driver well ahead of it. The glassy, almost cubical cab looked nothing like Ford's redesigned conventionals save a slight family resemblance in the grille. More striking still, the entire cab was hinged at the front to tilt forward for drivetrain access—not an industry first but a definite innovation for a mass-market maker like Ford, and destined to be widely copied. In fact, a few other companies would actually borrow the C-Series cab *in toto* and put it on their own chassis, paying Ford a royalty for the privilege.

Ford's truck chassis weren't substantially changed for '57 aside from the usual component upgrades, GVW adjustments, and appropriate tailoring of springs, brakes, steering, and axles. F-100/250/350 continued on a 108-inch wheelbase, with 118-inch span reserved for the cab/chassis and certain platforms and stakes. Mediums and heavies again comprised F500/600/750/800/900 conventionals on wheelbases of 130, 142, 154, 172, and 192 inches, plus T-Series tandem-axle models on the same platforms and equivalent C-Series tilt-cabs (including a 99-inch-wheelbase tractor with dual rear tires). One change occurred in the P-Series van line: the addition of a P-400 version on a special 137-inch wheelbase.

Engines weren't appreciably changed either, but there were fewer choices in the interest of production simplicity and reduced unit costs. The Cost Cutter Six remained standard power for F-100/250/350 but was up to 139 bhp via tighter compression and higher-lift cam as on the passenger-car Mileage Maker. Similar revisions were made to the step-up light-duty option, the 272 V-8, now at 171 bhp. An upgraded 181-bhp version was newly offered on "dualie" F-350s and as standard for all 500-700 mediums regardless of bodywork. The big 302 and 332 "Cargo King" V-8s continued in the "Big Job" 750/800/900 heavies.

All this enabled Ford to capture its biggest slice of the American truck pie in more than two decades—fully 31.3 percent of the total '57 market. With interim updates, this year's basic new conventional-cab styling would prove good enough to last all the way through 1979, by which time Dearborn would be firmly ensconced as America's truck sales leader. For the immediate future, though, Ford would still be chasing Chevy and its substantially higher production capacity.

Still, Ford racked up three more production milestones in 1957: the three-millionth Mercury (built June 4), the 2.5-millionth Ford tractor (on April 18, the 40th anniversary of the original Fordson), and the 25-millionth Ford V-8 engine, completed on December 15. The last came from the new Lima, Ohio, engine facility that had opened the previous May. Other corporate events of note this year included the appointment of young Bill Ford as vice-president for product planning and styling (on February 27); Robert S. McNamara's promotion to group vice-president of Ford Car and Truck Divisions (May 23); the opening of a new Michigan proving ground at Romeo, north of Detroit (also May 23); the donation of 50 acres of Ford land for a new Dearborn civic center (on January 9); and a gift of 75 acres of the Ford family's Fair Lane property to Henry Ford Community College (on June 6).

But most everyone in Dearborn was focused on the scheduled September 4 introduction of the long-awaited E-car, by now publicly known as the Edsel. The

Station wagons continued to be listed as a separate series for 1957, all on the shorter 116-inch chassis. A total of five models was still listed, even though the Parklane was gone, the slack taken up by the new Del Rio, basically a Ranch Wagon with fancier Custom 300/Country Sedan trim. At $2301, the two-door Ranch Wagon (top) remained the price leader, attracting 60,486 buyers. The volume leader was the four-door Country Sedan (center). The $2451 six-seater and the $2556 nine-seater (up from eight in '56) together garnered 186,889 sales. Output of the $2684 top-drawer Country Squire (bottom) came to 27,690.

Although this scene (above) may conjure up visions of scraping ice off the car in the middle of a Chicago winter, this '57 Country Sedan is actually undergoing tests in Ford's cold room—a good place to test components for severe weather driving. A new truck design for 1957 was the C-Series Tilt Cab (right). Available in many guises, it is seen here as a Big Job C-900 rated at 30,000 pounds GVW and 60,000 pounds GCW. Talking points included a double-channel frame, 9000-pound front axle, and a heavy-duty 332 V-8.

first consumer-oriented "teaser" ads for Ford's new middle-leaguer appeared in July, though speculative news stories had been running for well over a year. With anticipation mounting and the days counting down, Ford capped the publicity buildup with an elaborate Dearborn press preview on August 27-28, attracting some 300 newspaper and magazine writers. Unusual for such events in those days, the journalists were invited to drive home in an Edsel, and 65 accepted the offer. Unfortunately, several suffered breakdowns *en route*, a tellingly accurate omen of what was to come.

1 9 5 8

Divisionalization and Jack Reith's master plan reached fruition in 1958—and ran headlong into America's worst economic slowdown since World War II. A sharp recession beginning in 1957 put a big damper on everyone's sales, but Ford Motor Company was hit particularly hard. No wonder. Aside from Mercury and the standard Ford, everything in the corporate fleet was new. And the fleet was larger now with the advent of Edsel, the long-rumored "E-car." The one bright spot in Dearborn's dismal '58 picture was the new four-seat Thunderbird, the only car line besides American Motors' Rambler to score higher sales than it had in '57.

Contrary to popular belief, the Edsel wasn't a complete disaster. Its initial model-year output of 63,110 was respectable for a new make, and better than this year's totals for several established brands, including DeSoto, Studebaker—and Lincoln. But as most everyone knows, the seemingly boundless medium-price market of 1955 had evaporated by now. As one writer aptly put it, Edsel's "aim was right, but the target moved." The reason, of course, was that the recession suddenly altered buyers' perceived needs. Volkswagen and Rambler cashed in, the latter doubling its volume, mostly at the expense of the mid-priced stalwarts that had carried Detroit for years.

Then there was the name, little recognized by '58 and none too nice to hear. Edsel's ad agency had originally suggested 6000 possibilities, four of which generated good vibes in consumer testing—and were kept as series names. But they didn't satisfy, so more were solicited. Division chief Dick Krafve even hired poetess Marianne Moore, who came up with stunners like Mongoose Civique and Utopian Turtletop. Rejecting all, board chairman Ernie Breech casually said, "Let's call it the Edsel." When told that the company president didn't want the car named for his father, Breech replied, "I'll take care of Henry." He did.

Then too, despite 18 different models, two V-8s, and 100 color/trim combinations, the Edsel was not the advanced car many expected. It was really just a '58 Ford (Ranger/Pacer/wagons) or Mercury (Corsair/Citation) with a few interesting gimmicks, such as a drum speedometer and optional tachometer or compass. More to the point, it featured very controversial styling, especially its vertical "horse collar" grille. Senior models encroached into Mercury's price territory, which turned off some buyers, and quality nits were more plentiful than usual.

Some of these mistakes were corrected for '59, but by then it was already too late.

Ford Division gave its passenger cars a heavy facelift this year, declared that there was "Nothing newer in the world," and watched total sales volume drop to 987,485 units. Some blamed this on the styling, which wasn't particularly memorable. Quad headlamps, then an industry fad, and a big-mouth bumper/grille provided a visual link with the new Thunderbird. Additional flash came from wilder side trim and two-toning, nine longitudinal roof grooves (to strengthen the weak '57 panels), and a blunted tail with four oval lamps and a large, elliptical trunklid scallop. Model offerings were bolstered by a new four-door Ranch Wagon, and prices jumped by $50 to $220. The fascinating Skyliner "retrac" still topped the bunch, now at $3163 basic, $513 more than the soft-top Sunliner and a whopping $728 above the fixed-roof Fairlane 500 Club Victoria. Only 14,713 were built, some 6000 fewer than in '57.

Clumsy though it looked, the '58 was a much better Ford mechanically than the '57. Ride was softened via minor changes in shock calibrations, the front upper control arms, and rear spring rates. Ford's manual steering felt like power steering except when parking, yet turns lock-to-lock remained a tedious 4.5. The only difference was a 35-percent quicker ratio with power assist. Elsewhere, the 223 six got one extra horsepower; the 292 became the base V-8, albeit with seven fewer horses (205 in all); and the 272 and 312 V-8s were unceremoniously dumped.

But that was because Ford now offered its first "big-block" V-8s, a pair of "FE-Series" units sharing a gaping 4.00-inch bore. With a stroke of 3.30 inches, the smaller 332-cubic-inch unit was good for 240 bhp with two-barrel carb and single exhaust, or 265 with a four-barrel and dual pipes. A 3.50-inch stroke produced a 352, a high-compression (10.2:1) powerhouse cranking out 300 bhp at 4600 rpm with four-barrel carb and dual exhausts. So equipped, a '58 Ford could scoot from 0

Although many enthusiasts lamented the passing of the two-passenger 1955-57 Thunderbird, Ford president Robert McNamara didn't. He had taken a cold, hard look at the two-seater and realized that the market simply wasn't big enough for it to turn much of a profit—if any. He thus decreed that the next T-Bird would be a four-passenger car, and so it would be. And he was right as 37,892 '58 Birds left the assembly line (in a short model year at that), a bit more than the combined output of the 1956-57 models.

As before, the '58 Thunderbird shared some styling themes with the regular Fords: grille (top), fins (center), and quad taillights (bottom). The new "Squarebird," as it came to be called later, gained 700-800 pounds in heft, rode an 11-inch longer wheelbase, and cost $500 more for the convertible (about $250 additional for the hardtop). And, of course, the emphasis had changed completely from a sporty "personal" car to a "personal-luxury" cruiser. The new formula, which the T-Bird essentially pioneered, would be widely imitated in the Sixties.

to 60 mph in 9.5 seconds with either stickshift or this year's silky new Cruise-O-Matic self-shifter. But though respectably quick for the day, it wasn't any better than a 312/manual '57. Nor could it match this year's full-size Chevy with its new 348 engine that had 20 fewer horses.

The FE-Series (also offered as an Edsel 361 and Mercury 383) was devised principally by Robert Stevenson, named chief engineer at Ford Engine & Foundry in '57. Derived from the Y-Block, this new family incorporated all the lessons learned from previous Y-Blocks. Bore centers were chosen for a maximum displacement of 425 cubes, an arbitrary figure so far above foreseeable needs that long production seemed assured (as it turned out, into the early Seventies for the 390 version). The main improvements were bigger valves, intake ports, and main bearings, the last prompting a low-cost, precision-cast crankshaft. Combustion chambers were fully machined and located in the head (instead of the block), while overheating and valve warpage were minimized by having no two exhaust valves adjacent. Heads were smaller but intake manifolds larger than

usual, which allowed manifold passages of about equal length for more even fuel distribution. A bonus was added engine rigidity and elimination of separate tappet chamber covers. Serviceability was improved via relocated spark plugs and oil filter, and new-design valve rotators promised better lubrication and longer life.

There's still much confusion about the 332/352, the 390, and Lincoln 430 engines of this period. The 390, to be launched in 1961, was a high-performance mill that looked much like the 352, using the same heads and cam. However, it required entirely different head castings for its stronger bottom end and larger oil passages. The 430 wasn't related at all, though Stevenson designed it at about the same time as the FE-Series. Its pushrods poked up through tubes in the intake manifolds instead of the heads, and its combustion chambers were completely within the bores.

Ford's other big mechanical news for '58 was Cruise-O-Matic, a new three-speed, torque-converter "slushbox" based on Fordomatic. Initially an option only for Fairlanes and wagons, it offered "dual-range" drive like GM's early Hydra-Matic, with first-gear starts in position D1 and second-gear takeoffs in D2, plus a hill-holder that obviated the need for applying the brakes to keep from rolling backwards when stopped on an incline. In addition, Ford claimed that it gave up to 15 percent better fuel economy. Like the FE-Series V-8s, it would be around a long time.

The same cannot be said for the "Ford Aire" suspension. Another new option for Fairlanes and wagons, it com-

As expected, the '58 Ranchero received most of the styling changes seen on the passenger cars, the main exception being that the car-pickup kept the round '57 taillights. The deluxe Custom 300 (top) listed at $2236. Total Ranchero output slipped to 9950 units in recession-plagued 1958. Among the 116-inch-wheelbase "junior" Fords, the Custom 300 continued as the deluxe series. The $2210 two-door (center) trailed the four-door in popularity, but it notched up 160,360 sales nonetheless. Far less called for was the $2115 two-door business sedan (bottom); only about 3000 were built.

The Skyliner's top was a marvel to behold as it went through its various sequences to lift the decklid, raise the top, flip the front section of the roof, and lock everything securely in place. As a safety measure, the top could be operated only with the transmission selector in Neutral, and the sequence could be stopped and reversed at any point. Though complicated, the system was surprisingly reliable.

prised a 300-psi compressor and an air storage tank placed close together at the right front of the engine bay, plus a rubberized air "spring" or dome at each corner and three leveling valves (one for each front dome, one near the right rear dome covering the back). Front geometry differed little from that of the conventional coil-spring setup, but trailing arms appeared in back to provide the axle location of the normal semi-elliptic leaf springs. This set Ford Aire apart from GM's various air-ride systems that re-

quired more fully reworked geometry.

Alas, Ford Aire worked no better than others of this faddish ilk. Opening the door triggered solenoids (linked to the courtesy-lamp switches) that started air pumping to each dome as needed for proper ride height with a given load and weight distribution. Once underway, the leveling valves adjusted pressure within the domes to compensate for road surface and braking. That, at least, was the theory. In practice, Ford Aire proved so troublesome that only 100 or so '58s were so equipped. The main problems were leaky airbags and water condensing or sometimes freezing in the lines. No air-sprung T-Birds, Lincolns, or Mercurys were ever built, though systems were planned (the '58 Thunderbird's rear end was designed for a bolt-on installation) and Mercury advertised one. By 1960, only Cadillac and Rambler still offered air-ride options, though not much beyond that. Ford

wouldn't try one again until 1984.

In retrospect, T-Bird's change from two-seater to four-seater seems perfect in view of its surprising success in this difficult sales year—up over 50 percent from '57 and nearly 100 percent better than first-year '55. The '58 also pioneered the personal-luxury concept that would be widely imitated during the Sixties. But when the decision was made back in 1955, few knew for sure whether a four-seat Bird would "play in Peoria."

Product planner Thomas Case had recommended retaining a two-seater "to add some spiff to the ['58] program. It was not set up to be a profit program per se, although it turned out to be...." But McNamara wanted the T-Bird to pay its own way, and Case got a "chewing out" when McNamara heard he was angling to keep the two-seater. "It's dead," he told Case. "I don't want anybody to do any more about it." Yet without McNamara,

the Thunderbird might have died altogether at that point. Recalled stylist Bill Boyer: "He thought it was a good concept; he went in and fought for it [with the board of directors] and won." Of course, part of his pitch was that a four-seat Thunderbird would make *real* money, which it did.

Styling work began during 1955. Boyer stretched the proposed wheelbase from 108 to 113 inches, and development focused strictly on a low-slung hardtop coupe. A "formal" wide-quarter roofline was adopted to keep decklid height down for the ultra-low stance the sales department wanted. Setting off the blocky lower body—hence the "Squarebird" nickname later given this design generation—were a gaping mesh-filled bumper/grille, quad headlamps nestled under "gullwing" hoods, prominent side sculpturing, and a broad deck terminating in two wide rectangles, each holding a pair of large circular taillamps. Surprisingly, a convertible wasn't approved until May 1957 and didn't get to dealers until June 1958.

Ford's fascination with gimmicky roof features led to brief consideration of one for the four-seat T-Bird. A Skyliner-type retractable was most favored, but stowing the top and its associated linkages and wiring was even more of a problem in a car with a much smaller trunk. However, engineers managed to work up a "clamshell" top that broke in the middle as it folded down and over itself. Boyer recalls that this worked quite well, but it was doomed for all the reasons that led division chief McNamara to shelve the Skyliner after 1959, though its legacy can be seen in the rear-hinged decklid on the production soft-top convertible.

The Squarebird's extreme lowness suggested a trio of more practical ideas intended to facilitate entry/exit. One was a T-top with twin take-out panels over the front seats. Designer Gordon Buehrig had tried this very thing on the stillborn TASCO sports car project shortly before joining Ford in 1950, and Chevy would adopt it for the "shark-generation" 1968 Corvette. An early-1957 suggestion that the T-roof hardtop be Thunderbird's *only* '58 body style was rejected due to high tooling costs, so stylists proposed replacing the panels with flexible sections that retracted into the "T" like a rolltop desk. That one didn't even get off the drawing board. Next came small "flippers," which were abandoned almost as quickly. In the end, the most practical idea was the chosen: a sliding steel sunroof. Offered as a 1960 option, it didn't sell well and lasted only a year, but it marked a first in postwar U.S. production and T-tops would ultimately have their day, in the sun.

The new Bird's main innovation was unit construction, used by European producers since the Twenties and by Ford itself for the original 1936 Lincoln-Zephyr. Also known as *monocoque* construction and inspired by aircraft practice, it did away with a separate frame and resulted in a tighter, lighter platform. As unit construction was also ordained for this year's Lincoln and Continental Mark III—the largest such cars in history—Ford erected a new factory at Wixom, Michigan (opened April 15, 1957) to build all three. It made sense. Though these were low-volume luxury models, they generated enough combined volume to keep the one plant busy. This also made unit construction economically feasible, since the low individual unit volumes would have made separate frames far costlier than for a mass-market car like the standard Ford.

Despite the '58 T-Bird's fairly revolutionary nature, Ford allotted only $5 million for styling and body/chassis/engine engineering and $45 million for tooling. To economize on research and develop-

For 1958, the Skyliner had the dubious distinction of being the only Ford (aside from the T-Bird) of having a list price above $3000. And at $3163, it cost $221 more than the '57. The high price and weak economy combined kept output down to 14,713 units. Weighing 4069 pounds, the Skyliner was the heaviest '58, including T-Bird, so it got the 292 V-8 as standard.

ment, body engineering was farmed out to the Budd Company, the convertible to Wettlaufer Engineering. The ragtop arrived with a manually operated rear-hinged decklid that completely concealed the stowed top, which moved on a complex linkage similar to the Skyliner's. The system was made fully automatic (via a single dashboard pushbutton) late in the '59 model run.

Overall engineering was rapid-fire and often clever. Body engineer Bob Hennessy recalled that when the planned overall width was discovered to be insufficient for rear-wheel movement, "we were about two-thirds into engineering with die models. [So] we literally split the drawing down the centerline [and] spread it apart." The interior package envisioned a car considerably lower than the standard Ford, but it turned out to be surprisingly roomy. However, as Hennessy notes, "with a five-inch ground-to-floor-pan height, 2½ to three inches for a seat track and electric seat motor, plus four inches of actual seat height, the driver's fanny was only 12 inches off the ground. This left us with a high tunnel on the inside and, of course, the main integral frame sill section above the floor on the outside.... The front seats were literally in a deep well." Boyer took advantage of all this by creating the first tunnel control console. It's been *de rigueur* for personal-luxury cars ever since.

The '58 Thunderbird proved an instant hit, so much so that Ford had to put Wixom on heavy overtime to keep up

Opposite page: Some thought that Ford's expensive '58 facelift had been a step backward design-wise. Others approved of the kinship up front with the T-Bird and liked the quad headlights and taillights. The Fairlane 500 sported new side trim with a larger anodized insert. The $2435 Victoria suffered mightily this year, skidding over 100,000 units to 80,439. This page: The $2428 four-door was the most popular '58 Fairlane 500 (right): 105,698 built. Wearing Custom series side trim, the Ranch Wagon was the bargain among Ford wagons. It started at a modest $2397, and 34,578 practical buyers took one home.

with demand. "We were making money so fast we didn't know what to do with it," said engineer John Hollowell. "It came . . . to somewhere around $1000 per car." Hardtop production totaled close to 36,000 for the model year; late introduction held the ragtop to just 2134 units. What Ford really had here was a latterday Continental offering the same sporty elegance for less than half the price of a Mark II ($3631 for the hardtop, $3929 for the convertible). No wonder it did so well. *Motor Trend* agreed, naming the T-Bird its 1958 "Car of the Year" for "a new packaging concept that combines safety with performance and comfort with compactness." Even so, Ford Division finished the model year some 160,000 cars on the low side of Chevrolet, which fielded an all-new, one-year-only design that cost almost as much to bring out as the Edsel.

Showroom smash though it was, the '58 Bird was less successful on the road. *Motor Trend*, testing the fifth hand-built pilot-assembly car, reported an unimpressive 13.5 seconds 0-60 mph and a quarter-mile time of 16.8 seconds. Braking wasn't so hot either. Engineers had wanted better binders, but had to settle for little more lining area than on the much lighter little Birds. *MT* bemoaned the loss of the '57's tachometer and telescoping steering column and found visibility so-so. Ride, however, was judged good, and rear-seat access surprisingly easy, thanks to the industry's longest doors and front seatbacks that folded "far enough to squash a walnut," as Tom McCahill from *Mechanix Illustrated* put it.

McCahill was fond of the two-seat T-Birds, regarding them as sports cars. For him, the four-seater was a "sedan" having "ride and stability through corners and over dipped roads [of] typical family-car style, with not even a remote hint of 'sports car feel.'" And with tongue firmly in cheek he noted that a '58 had run at Daytona at "a surprising 107 mph, just 20 mph slower than my 1955 Bird." On the other hand, he reported a 0-60 time of 9.9 seconds. "In top-tuned condition . . . this car will break 110 mph, which today is typical of American family sedan performance. It is not the sharpest sedan ever written up [in *Mechanix Illustrated*] but, by the same token, not the slowest either."

Dearborn's two other newcomers, the Continental Mark III and a completely redesigned Lincoln, were also born in

the heated atmosphere of 1955, and, like Edsel, suffered in the cold of the withering '58 market. The Mark was now just a top-line Lincoln, with minor styling differences on the same enormous new unitized structure (wheelbase: 131 inches). Models expanded to four, and prices were dropped to the $6000 level in a search for sales. Sales they found, but some came at Lincoln's expense. That plus Edsel's poor showing put an end to Ford's multi-divisional dream. Thus, in January 1958, Continental Division was merged with Mercury, Edsel, and Lincoln to form the M-E-L Division. That would last only through Edsel's demise in November 1959, after which Lincoln-Mercury would be reinstated.

Ford sounded a more optimistic note in January '58 by trotting out its biggest, brawniest trucks ever. Labeled "Super Duty," they comprised F-Series conventionals, C-Series cabovers, and T-Series tandems on new 950, 1000, and 1100 chassis. Maximum GVW ratings were 36,000 pounds for the one-axle Fs and Cs, 51,000 pounds for tandems. Moving these new heavyweights was a trio of new oversquare Y-Block V-8s: a 401 (bore × stroke: 4.12 × 3.75 inches) with 226 bhp for 950s, a 477 (same stroke, 4.50-inch bore) delivering 260 bhp in the 1000s, and a 534-cid monster (4.50 × 4.20) pumping out 277 bhp in the 1100s. Respective torque outputs were both impressive and prodigious: 350, 430, and 490 lbs/ft—just what was needed in a big rig—all peaking between 1800 and 2300 rpm—just where

a trucker wanted them. Chassis specs weren't vastly different from lesser Ford heavies, just beefier. Air brakes were standard on some models, and there was a wide variety of purpose-built axles and transmissions. Arriving late in the season was a tandem-axle tilt-cab Super Duty, the CT-1100.

Elsewhere in the '58 truck line were revised powerplants for medium and "light-heavy" models, which now included an 850, essentially the 800 with the Super-Duty 401 engine. The 292 V-8 replaced the 272 in all its applications, packing 186 horses and 269 lbs/ft torque, while the 302 and 332 got slightly more power and torque. The 118-inch-wheelbase F-100 platform became more widely available, and all F-Series models acquired quad headlamps and checked grilles. Ranchero and Courier changes followed '58 passenger-car practice. The familiar I-6 remained standard for both, but the base V-8 was the revived 292, again with 205 bhp, while the new 300-bhp 352 became the top power option.

Americans bought import cars in record numbers this year: 372,000 in all. Many of these were Volkswagen Beetles and Renault Dauphines, but a few were Fords—mostly British-built Anglia and Consul models. Dearborn had been selling "captive imports" in the U.S. since 1948, mainly through Ford franchises, though it also signed some non-company dealers to handle them. Sales were always modest through the late Fifties due to lack of customers in those bigger-is-

Ah, the call of the wild! Barbeques and camping had become popular Fifties pursuits, and the '58 Country Sedan wagon (above) was there to help. Priced at $2557 and $2664 (six- and nine-passenger), 89,474 took to the road, many to idylic spots such as this. Ford one-upped Chevrolet in the truck field in '58. Chevy had debuted the flush-sided (no rear fenders) '55 Cameo Carrier, an expensive specialty model that sold poorly. Ford brought the smoother styling to the masses with the $1913 Styleside F-100 pickup (right).

better days, as well as only token promotion and spotty parts and service support. Then, too, domestic dealers used to making handsome returns on their "real" cars didn't like the narrow profit margins of small "furriners" selling in the $1500-$2000 range. So what if the nameplate read "Ford?" Real Americans bought American cars.

Looking back, it's too bad that Ford—and GM, too—didn't push harder with "captives" in these years. Not that the cars were at all spectacular. Ford's mainstay, the 100E-series Anglia, introduced in 1954, was a boxy little sedan or wagon of conventional design with an 87-inch wheelbase and a modest 37-bhp inline four. Then again, the VW Beetle was an even more humble affair whose main virtue was better-than-average workmanship. But given the aforementioned attitudes, not to mention a "not-invented-here" xenophobia that's still common among U.S. auto executives, captives would always be treated with an indifference that defied description—here one day, gone the next, back again just as soon as the sales department decided they needed another price-leading small car.

All the more curious, then, that April 2, 1958 saw the first German Ford sales through U.S. Mercury-Edsel-Lincoln dealers—the very American-looking 1.7-liter Taunus 17M with jazzy Z-shaped side moldings (like the '56 Mercury) and

available two-toning. It's unclear whether this was a response to GM's new emphasis on German Opels and British Vauxhalls or simply a sop to MEL dealers desperately seeking sales in a difficult market, but the effort was as half-hearted and peripheral as any such program. And when demand for domestic cars picked up in 1959-60, the captives were shunted aside in showrooms like the poor relations most dealers thought they were.

Captives would be more visible beginning in the mid-Sixties, but neither Ford nor GM would ever score really high sales with European imports, the exceptions being Ford's success in the Seventies with its Capri sports coupe and Fiesta minicar.

A more important forecast of the future arrived in July 1958 as Congress enacted its first piece of legislation affecting the auto industry. This was the Automobile Information Disclosure Act mandating the now-familiar "Monroney sticker"

price label, named after Oklahoma Democratic Senator A.S. "Mike" Monroney, the bill's chief sponsor. Effective with model year 1959, the Act required all manufacturers selling cars and station wagons in the U.S., including importers, to affix stickers listing the suggested retail prices for the base version of a given model and any options fitted, plus additional charges like freight. Trucks were initially exempt, but would be included later. The act also specified $1000 fines for each instance of non-compliance or "false endorsement." Removing or altering the label also carried a $1000 fine plus a one-year jail sentence.

This was a highly beneficial act from the standpoint of consumer protection—the goal being to eliminate "bait-and-switch" and other reprehensible sales tactics. But it also opened the door for much greater federal involvement in the way cars are designed and sold in America. As the coming years would show, it was a not altogether happy precedent.

1 9 5 9

After the doldrums of 1958, this year almost seemed a relief to Ford Division—but not Edsel, Mercury, Lincoln, or Continental, the only makes in the entire U.S. industry to produce fewer '59s than '58s. Mercury slipped to slightly under 150,000 units. And Edsel, of course, was destined for oblivion. In fact, production ceased in November after production of just 3008 Ford-clone 1960 models.

Import cars, meanwhile, scored 615,000 U.S. calendar-year sales—a new high—and American Motors' Rambler and Studebaker's new-for-'59 Lark compact garnered over 480,000 orders. Ford had seen the trend and was working on a compact of its own for 1960, but so were GM and Chrysler, thus setting the stage for a new Big Three battle royal.

Buyers had a clear styling choice among their low-priced standards this year: a radical new "bat-fin" Chevrolet, Virgil Exner's heavily facelifted "shark-fin" Plymouth, or a conservative,

With the '58 recession easing, 1959 promised to be a better year for the industry, including Ford. The Skyliner retractable (top), however, was in its last year, and while the price crept up to $3346, sales fell to 12,915. New for '59 was the top-line Galaxie series, posed here (center) to demonstrate that its roofline was clearly Thunderbird-inspired. Ford Motor Company offerings for 1959 (bottom) consisted of (top row) Edsel, Continental Mark IV (and companion Lincoln), and Mercury. Below them are the Thunderbird and a Ford Fairlane 500 hardtop. Robert McNamara, in the center, seems pleased with the new lineup.

squared-up Ford. Though Chevy emerged the victor in model-year production, by slightly less than 12,000 units (1,462,140 versus 1,450,953), it's clear the public preferred Ford, which outsold its perennial rival for the calendar year by about the same margin.

Much-changed 1957-58 inner bodies and new outer panels produced what Ford Division immodestly advertised as "The World's Most Beautifully Proportioned Cars." The claim was debatable to be sure, but Ford could point to winning the Gold Medal for exceptional styling from the Comite Francais de l'Elegance at this year's Brussels World's Fair. And its new look was considered handsome at the time, though so orthodox next to the new Chevy that one could easily conclude the two longtime rivals were aiming at different buyers—which might just have been the case, come to think of it.

Aside from extra trunk space, it's hard to say what the stylists had in mind for this year's standard Ford. "Silent" Joe Oros, chief project designer, never explained, and the free-thinking Alex Tremulis, who was there at the time, once condemned it as a worse mistake than the '58. Predictably, perhaps, company styling boss George Walker declared the '59 the best-looking Ford ever done under his direction.

Regardless, they must have been striving for a closer kinship with Mercury, and not only in appearance but size. All models now rode the 118-inch wheelbase, which swelled overall length by five inches on wagons and close to six on lowline sedans. Width was up fractionally, as were curb weights, while trunk volume ballooned by 11 cubic feet. Curving front glass upward as well as to the sides increased windshield area by 29 percent. Backlights were also higher and more noticeably wrapped.

Facial freshening involved quad headlamps with T-Bird-style "gullwing" hoods above a shallow full-width grille containing four rows of star-like ornaments. The front bumper was now separate but still massive, wrapping around to bullet-shaped outriggers housing turn signal/parking lamps. These were echoed in a cylindrical upper rear fender form extended from about mid-body. Ford continued to resist finny excess, though, settling for chrome-lined ridges atop the tubes, which terminated in backup lamps. Finishing the rear was a heavily sculpted "Flying V" center panel decorated by a full-width chrome molding on Fairlane 500s, a stubby gold-tone chevron on Fairlanes, and a large Ford crest on the rest. Taillamps became round again, nestled in huge "jello-mold" reflectors (for some reason advertised as "Iris eyes") that made for mile-away brightness. Inside were the usual reshuffled colors and trims, plus a restyled dash with the same basic layout as before and a large, square instrument cluster. It all looked nice, but the white-on-silver gauge markings were hard to read.

Initially, Ford fielded a leaner lineup. The Custom series was dropped and Custom 300 became the base group, offering the same three sedans. Fairlane lost both its hardtops. Then, previewing a shakeup in the 1960 line, T-Bird-type wide-quarter roofs were grafted onto the four closed Fairlane 500 styles at midyear to create a new top-shelf series called Galaxie, "A bright new personality in cars ... with Thunderbird elegance—family-size!" It absorbed the Sunliner and Skyliner via changed rear fender script. (Curiously, though, all Galaxies wore Fairlane 500 rear-deck identification.) The retrac, now on its last legs, saw production of but 12,915 units.

Like most of Detroit this year, Ford reacted to the '58 recession and buyers' new-found economy-consciousness by lowering compression ratios a bit so all engines could run on regular gas. The Mileage Maker Six returned at 145 bhp, but detuning dropped the 292 to 200 bhp, the four-barrel 332 was scratched, and the two-barrel version fell to 225 bhp. The 352 still ran 9.6:1 compression, so its 300 horses probably weren't too happy on low-calorie feed.

Supporting Ford's bulkier, heavier bodies was a heavier and stronger new frame with siderails bowed out to near track width for extra passenger room. There were a number of suspension tweaks, including a link-type front stabilizer bar and variable-rate rear leaf springs, nearly all directed at a softer ride. The result was excessive body roll in sharp corners that brought howls of protest from both the tires and the motoring press.

Ford listed two convertibles from 1957-59, but since the Skyliner (right) would be gone after '59, Ford would offer only one convertible for 1960-61. For 1959, the Sunliner (below) met with a warm reception, as output jumped by 10,000 units to 45,868, this despite a $200 price hike to $2839. The turquoise and white color combination seen on these cars was quite popular that year. The '59 Fords were noted for their squared-up, conservative styling, quite a far cry from the "batwing" Chevy and the high-finned Plymouth.

Cruise-O-Matic was slightly modified, too, but Fordomatic was completely reworked, becoming a two-speed transmission that was simpler (105 fewer parts), lighter (thanks to a new aluminum case), and cheaper than the previous

The '59 Skyliner retractable hardtop could be told from other Fords (as could the '57 and '58) by the changes made at the rear end to accommodate the disappearing top. Mainly, length was increased about three inches, the decklid altered so that it could be rear-hinged, and the rear panel was unique. From the doors forward, all parts were strictly '59 Ford. The side trim on the '59 Fairlane 500 and Galaxie was more akin to the '57 Ford than to the '58.

three-speeder. Answering Chevy's "Positraction" limited-slip differential was Ford's "Equa-Lock" axle, a new factory option priced at just $38.60.

Dearborn also took its first steps toward extended service intervals and reduced maintenance costs, an area where it would continue to lead in the Sixties. This involved standard aluminized mufflers said to last twice as long as previous types, full-flow oil filters that lengthened oil-change intervals from 1000 to 4000 miles, and "Diamond Lustre" enamel paint that wasn't supposed to need waxing.

Not surprisingly, the detuned '59s couldn't match 1957-58 performance,

though testers appreciated their greater economy. Most motor-noters also approved the "hatbox" styling, but complained that the high-rise windshield made wind buffeting a problem even with the windows closed. Happily, the '59s showed much tighter assembly and construction than the 1957-58s, and *Motor Trend* now rated Ford above Chevy or Plymouth in this department. "The outstanding feature . . . is the solid feel of the body," *MT* reported. "Doors close like bank vaults and give the feeling of extreme rigidity and safety."

Greater thrift, better build, and more acceptable styling helped Ford to very good sales in line with the industry's general '59 recovery. Adding Thunderbird style to the standard cars was clearly right on the money. Despite an abbreviated selling season, the four closed Galaxies garnered over 405,000 orders—better than 27 percent of the division's total model-year car production. Ford would again resort to this profitable ploy in the early Sixties.

Thunderbird, billed as "The car *everyone* would love to own!" in 1959, was refined with minor trim changes, a new engine option, and a redesigned rear suspension. The last was dictated by the many problems and consequent fast phaseout of "Ford Aire" suspension. The '58 had been designed to accommodate it via complex coil-spring/trailing-arm rear geometry. The '59 reverted to conventional rear leaf springs. Minor mechanical mods included a new auxiliary coolant

tank and radiator fan and a repositioned windshield washer system. The new engine was Lincoln's big-block 350-bhp, 430-cid V-8, largest member of the "MEL" family introduced the previous year. The 300-bhp 352 remained standard.

External revisions comprised thin-bar grille insert and taillight appliques (replacing the '58's honeycomb-pattern pieces), plus new front-fender ornaments, pointed chrome moldings on the lower-bodyside "bullets" (ousting the previous hash marks), relocated name script, revised wheel covers, and larger Bird emblems on hardtop C-pillars. White replaced black on instrument backgrounds, and the usual trim/color shifts were made. Prices rose by about $50, to $3695 and $3979 for the hardtop and convertible, respectively.

Of course, the successful "Square-bird" package didn't really need changing in its sophomore year—which is just as well, as there was little money available. As historian Richard M. Langworth records in *Personal Luxury: The Thunderbird Story*: "...The convertible tooling cost of $2.9 million...more than gobbled up the original $2 million tooling budget for late-1958-through-1960 changes. The revised tooling budget for *all* 1959-60 modifications was only $700,000. And you didn't buy much for that, even in the Fifties."

Though not intended as a performance machine, the Squarebird was decently fast. This year's base-engine 352

would scamper from 0 to 60 mph in 11 seconds, while the big 430 reduced that to about nine seconds—and hiked fuel consumption to about 12 miles per gallon. Though smaller and lower than most all contemporaries save Chevy's Corvette, it was no handler, with lots of plowing and body roll in corners. Braking and steering also left something to be desired. But the car itself was very desired, witness model-year production that moved up smartly to near 67,500 units—nearly double the '58 tally.

While competition exploits had never been a factor in T-Bird sales, the Squarebird carried Ford's colors in some NASCAR events in 1959, though for some reason it was considered a separate make, not a Ford. At the inaugural Daytona 500, run on the then-new International Speedway in late February, Johnny

Beauchamp's Bird was declared the winner in a three-way photo finish with Lee Petty's Oldsmobile and a Chevrolet. But the victory lasted just three days. After examining a photo of the finish, the judges decided that Petty should get the trophy. The follow-up Firecracker 250 on July 4 saw Fireball Roberts' Pontiac in Victory Lane, but six T-Birds were among the top nine finishers. By season's end, Squarebirds had racked up six NASCAR wins to Chevrolet's 14, Plymouth's nine,

Thunderbird flew into 1959 with the $3696 hardtop (below) and $3979 convertible (bottom). For their sophomore year, they received a minor facelift. Up front, the grille now sported horizontal bars, a theme that was carried to the back around the taillights. Along the sides, the five hashmarks on the door sculpture gave way to a fussy chrome projectile tip.

and eight for the standard Fords. Dearborn had better weapons for 1960 and beyond, but privately entered Squarebirds still managed an occasional first in minor, usually short-track races over the next few years.

This year brought the arrival of none other than James Nance, fresh from failure at Studebaker-Packard, to head up the newly formed Mercury-Edsel-Lincoln Division. Nance had had many good ideas in South Bend, but had tried to do too much too soon and without enough capital. In Dearborn he had plenty of capital but a negative mandate: consolidate, don't expand. "It was a difficult position," he said, "because we had to merge three formerly separate divisions into one, and inevitably that meant laying off a lot of people." No sooner had this been accomplished than Nance left to run a bank, saying, "One thing I learned from the auto industry: You can't do anything without money!"

Ford spent a fair amount of funds on its '59 truck fleet. Model choices expanded to 370 with the arrival of the firm's first factory-built four-wheel-drives, which effectively killed the well-known light-duty 4×4 Ford conversions offered by the Marmon-Herrington company for some 20 years. A response to Chevrolet's mid-1957 4WDs, the inaugural factory "four-by" Fords were limited to a 118-inch-wheelbase pickup and cab/chassis in the F-100 and F-250 series, but more would follow soon.

Elsewhere, F-100 through F-600 conventionals exchanged their checked grille for a four-bar horizontal affair of the same shape. Above was a reworked hood presenting a mesh-filled rectangular air intake bearing "Ford" in big block letters. F-750s on up used the same grille but had a smooth-faced "crowned" hood wearing a large "keystone" crest. Except for name script, the Courier now looked just like the two-door Ranch Wagon, adopting its full side windows and rear liftgate/tailgate for the first time. On hand as usual were most of the styling and mechanical changes featured

in equivalent passenger Fords, including "economy" V-8s and the longer 118-inch wheelbase. The Ranchero followed suit. It now came only in Custom form, albeit with higher-grade appointments from the Country Sedan wagon. Despite new competition from Chevy's copycat El Camino, Ranchero scored higher model-year sales, up from 9950 to 14,169. But even that was still way below the debut '57 total and would prompt a big change in Ford's "coupe-pickup" for 1960.

"Four-bys" aside, this year's "truck-trucks" saw no mechanical alterations of note, though the applications chart did. The passenger cars' new two-speed Ford-omatic was now the automatic option for F-100s, while a heavy-duty Cruise-O-Matic arrived at extra cost for F-250/350s. Special tractor packages designed to better meet the needs of semi-trailer oper-

ators became available for both conventionals and tilt-cabs on the 750-1100 chassis and for 850/950 tandem conventionals. Tilt-cab tandems expanded to include pairs of CT-850/950/1000 models, plus a single CT-850 chassis and a second CT-1100.

There were three highlights on the corporate front in 1959. The first came on April 29 with production of the 50-mil-

With the T-Bird in full production—and for the full model year—output took a healthy jump for 1959. The hardtop (opposite), which weighed 3813 pounds, enjoyed a model year run of 57,195 units—an increase of more than 20,000 units. The convertible (this page) saw a five-fold increase to 10,261. It boasted 3903 pounds of heft. The two ragtops below both sport a Continental rear tire kit. As in '58, the 300-bhp 352 V-8 was standard, the 350-bhp Lincoln 430 optional.

Stations wagons made an important contribution to Ford's success in 1959 as 269,338 units were built (55,000 ahead of Chevy). The Country Sedan (top) was still the favorite with 123,412 produced, three-quarters of them the $2745 six-passenger version. A deluxe camping kit (center) provided a pop-up tent atop the wagon, a sunshade to screen a compact stove/sink setup, and a detachable rowboat that flipped up to serve as a cover for the unit when traveling. The woody-look Country Squire (bottom) came only as a nine-passenger wagon; it listed at $2958 and 24,336 were built.

lionth Ford vehicle, a Galaxie. The second took up most of June: a reenactment of the famous New York-to-Seattle race of a half-century before, ostensibly won by a Model T. As noted (see *1909*), Ford neglected to mention that the original "winner" had later been disqualified in favor of another, since-deceased make, perhaps hoping no one would remember this 50 years later. But now as then, it was publicity that counted, and Ford did its best. Interestingly, the T used for the duplicate run had been specially hand-assembled from previously unused parts at the Mahwah, New Jersey, plant on October 23, 1958 to commemorate the 50th anniversary of the Lizzie's introduction. The factory-fresh 50-millionth Galaxie accompanied it along the original race route, with stops in 85 cities.

Also notable, if less historic, was the formation of Ford Motor Credit Company on August 24. This was patterned on General Motors Acceptance Corporation (GMAC)—no surprise, what with ex-GM'er Ernie Breech sitting as board chairman—and its purposes were roughly the same: namely, to finance new-car sales at company-owned dealerships and to represent Ford in the debt market. Old Henry would have been astonished.

1 9 6 0

The Edsel expired early this model year as production ceased on November 19, 1959. Ironically, some of its styling hallmarks would be seen on far more successful cars in the coming decade. For example, the vertical grille motif was used later by Pontiac, while the chiseled lower body of 1965-66 Chryslers owed much to the 1960 Ford/Edsel design, likely because Elwood Engel styled both. But the hard fact was that Dearborn had failed in its attempt to conquer fortress GM by expanding to five separate divisions.

According to John Brooks in *The Fate of the Edsel and Other Business Adventures*, Ford spent $350 million on the E-car, though $250 million is the sum traditionally bandied about. George Dammann, in *Fifty Years of Lincoln-Mercury*, says that the tooling bill alone came to $24,000 per car, but that multiplies to over $2.5 billion, which seems excessive.

If nothing else, the Edsel experiment taught Ford that not even number-two could compete with General Motors on the same broad, diverse scale. Ford took heed, and would never again stray from a two-division structure, thus avoiding the "corporate clone" sales hazard that would plague GM a quarter-century later. To have learned that lesson in 1960 was probably worth $350 million. And as Ne-

vins/Hill observed: "That the [firm] took the adventure in stride is proof of its sound financial condition." Even so, as Lee Iacocca would later record in his autobiography: "Looking around Dearborn for someone to admit responsibility for the Edsel project today is like old Diogenes with his lantern, searching for an honest man."

The Edsel offered another lesson to Ford and every other automaker, summed up nicely by Art Railton of *Popular Mechanics*: "Motivation research doesn't tell what's to come, only what has been." Yet the end brought a solid consolation, something long overlooked by most historians. Gearing up for Edsel had boosted Dearborn's total production capacity. Now, that extra volume was freed to benefit Ford's important new 1960

compact. A good thing, too, as the Falcon was a big hit right off the bat, helping to ease the embarrassment of the Edsel fiasco. Coming hard on the heels of the successful 1958-59 "Squarebird," the Falcon proved that Dearborn hadn't lost its marketing touch.

It was during the bottom of the 1957-58 recession that the Big Three were designing and readying their new compact cars for 1960. They were seen as a necessity in view of the exploding sales of small imports, plus the AMC Rambler and the '59 Studebaker Lark. Ford's offering, the Falcon, was easily the most conservative of the Big Three offerings, both in terms of styling and engineering. It was offered initially only as the $1912 two-door sedan (below) or the $1974 four-door sedan (bottom). Both of the cars shown are equipped with the $66 DeLuxe trim package.

The '60 Falcon wagons debuted later than the sedans, but since a two-door model was offered it was easy to come up with a Courier sedan delivery (above). Alas, it wasn't too popular; only 2374 were built in the short model year. The '60 T-Bird (below) received a new grille featuring one horizontal and three vertical bars with a finer eggcrate pattern behind.

Speaking of Mr. Iacocca, he took over as Ford Division general manager in 1960, one of three key executive shifts this year. The first was Ernie Breech's resignation on July 13, though it was really a firing by president Henry Ford II, who took over for Breech as board chairman. Robert S. McNamara was then named to succeed HF II as president on November 9. But McNamara wouldn't last long, resigning on December 12 to become defense secretary in the new Kennedy Administration. HF II filled in until April 1961, when he again vacated the chair for John Dykstra, who would serve only some 24 months.

Though his importance to Ford should not be overstated, Iacocca was a born car salesman with a keen sense of what turned on the public, and his contributions were undeniable. He would be the driving force behind the Mustang, Dearborn's biggest success of the Sixties, and spearheaded the memorable "Total Performance" campaign that injected ex-

citement into most every Dearborn car of this era. Such feats would propel him into the president's chair by 1970. But like Breech before him, Iacocca would be booted out (after eight years) by the temperamental "Henry the Deuce." As most everyone knows, Iacocca then rode off to save Chrysler Corporation, an accomplishment not his alone (he had a lot of help from many other expatriate Dearborners) but certainly equal, if not superior, to anything he did at Ford.

This year's new Ford compact was born in 1957 as the "XK Thunderbird," one of several small-car projects then in progress throughout the worldwide Ford organization. Another was the front-drive Cardinal, a stillborn 1962 U.S. project that was transplanted to resurface as Ford of Germany's 1963 Taunus 12M. Completed in a remarkably short 19 months, the Falcon arrived with Chevrolet's Corvair and Chrysler's Valiant as the Big Three's reply to the growing popularity of small imports like the Volkswagen Beetle in the economy-car craze spawned by the '58 recession.

The Falcon was deadly conventional next to Corvair: live-axle rear suspension and a front-mounted, water-cooled straight six versus all-independent suspension and an air-cooled flat-six at the back. About the only things they had in common were four wheels, drum brakes, and unit construction. But while Corvair's unusual specifications appealed

mainly to car buffs, Falcon's anvil simplicity proved far more saleable, and the little Ford promptly ran away with the compact market.

Riding a 109.5-inch wheelbase, Falcon bowed as a two-door and four-door sedan measuring 181.2 inches long, 70 inches wide and 54.5 inches high. Wagon versions arrived early in the calendar year and were a bit longer and heavier. (Base curb weights ranged from 2259 to 2575 pounds.) The Ranchero car/pickup was moved to this platform in a search for sales after somewhat disappointing results with the full-size 1957-59 original.

Unlike the Valiant, which featured European-style looks, Falcon styling was simple, almost severe: a large concave grille with single headlamps, attractive bodyside creases, rounded corners and fenders, and an unadorned rear with big round taillamps. Despite being 32.5 inches shorter overall than 1960 standard Fords, it was surprisingly roomy inside. Power came from a new 144-cubic-inch inline six with conventional pushrods and short-stroke cylinder dimensions (3.50 × 2.50 inches). Output was a respectable 90 bhp. Mated to it were standard three-speed manual or optional two-speed Fordomatic self-shift transmissions, both with column control. Interiors were plain (some said stark), but it was all part of the plan.

In a way, the Falcon was a latter-day Model A: simple, reliable, easy to buy, and

cheap to own. Reported fuel economy was upwards of 27 mpg, and prices ranged from just $1912 for the two-door sedan to $2287 for the four-door wagon. The Ranchero listed for a low $1875. There weren't many options available (though there would soon be), but that was part of the plan, too. And the plan worked beautifully. Corvair scored a quarter-million sales for the model year and the Valiant came in just under 200,000 units, neither of which was bad,

Thunderbird continued with only minor revisions to its bucket-seat-and-console interior for 1960 (above). The driver faced three round dials. New to the options list was a sliding metal sunroof (below), a first among postwar American cars. This $212 extra didn't prove too popular, however, as only 2536 T-Bird hardtops got one. Triple taillights replaced the dual units for 1960, and as in 1958-59 the grille pattern was used at the back as well. The chrome spears found on the door sculptures of the '59 were removed for '60 in favor of nine hashmarks on the rear fenders.

The big Fords were completely restyled for 1960, and it seemed almost as if they were chasing the radical "batwing" '59 Chevy (note the flat "fins"). Wheelbase stretched one inch to 119, length grew from 208 to 213.7 inches, and width swelled from 76.6 inches to 81.5. The result was a bigger car with no real gain in passenger room and a trunk with a narrow lid and an extremely shallow cargo compartment. The $2675 Galaxie Victoria hardtop sedan (all three photos) slipped by more than 8500 units to 39,215 for the model year. Ford dropped round taillights for '60, as it had done in '58, but would return to them the next year.

but Falcon saw nearly 436,000, which was stupendous.

The '60 Thunderbird, promoted as "The world's most wanted car," was left pretty much alone in this final year for the original four-seat design. New to the options list was a sliding metal sunroof, the first in postwar U.S. production, but at $212.40 it attracted only 2536 orders. Styling changes were confined to hash marks on the rear fenders, cleaner side trim, a large horizontal grille bar with three vertical dividers and square mesh behind, triple-taillight clusters, standard outside rearview mirror, polarized day/night inside mirror, revised interiors with built-in armrests, and new color combinations.

T-Bird prices rose this year, to $3755 for the basic hardtop and $4222 for the convertible. Nevertheless, popularity reached a new high with model-year production of nearly 91,000 units, a record that wouldn't be broken until 1964. Included were about 2500 special high-trim models with a gold-colored vinyl top. Most T-Birds again carried the standard 300-bhp 352 V-8; only about 3900 were equipped with the big-block Lincoln 430. Both units were unchanged.

Now that compacts were here, auto writers coined a new term for the largest U.S. cars like the Ford Galaxie: full-size. And this year's big Fords were even fuller, gaining a much longer, lower, and wider bodyshell. Wheelbase grew an inch, to 119 inches, where it would remain for the rest of the decade, but overall length was up 5.7 inches to 213.7 and width swelled by five inches to a massive 81.5 overall. Initially, the width actually made the car illegal in some states, though nobody seemed to notice. The new styling seemed a hastily contrived reply to the bat-wing '59 Chevrolet, but lead times made any similarity quite coincidental. Some experts persist in believ-

ing otherwise, though there is evidence to support their claims that Ford rushed out the new design a full year earlier than originally scheduled.

No matter. The Fords were prettier than the oddball Chevys. Headlamps moved down into a wide U-shaped grille fronting a much lower and broader hood. The old dogleg A-pillars gave way to straight posts and a taller windshield. Bodysides gained discreet contouring below a shallow, full-length beltline over-hang swept back into modest horizontal fins and a flat rear deck, which covered an extremely shallow trunk. Taillights this year were semi-circular. Altogether, Ford

was the arguably best-looking of this year's Big Three standards.

Big-Ford model choices didn't change much, but series names were reordered to read, from the bottom, Custom 300, Fairlane, Fairlane 500, and Galaxie. As before, offerings in the separate Station Wagon series paralleled these in trim and equipment. An attractive newcomer to the Galaxie line was an airy hardtop coupe called Starliner (reviving an old Studebaker name), with a gently curved roofline that almost qualified as a fast-back. There was more to this than just looks, for the sloped top was aerodynamically superior on NASCAR super-

One of the stars of the '60 full-size Ford lineup was the Starliner, "semi-fastback" hardtop that borrowed its name from a '53 Studebaker. More aerodynamic than the square-roofed Galaxie, it was also more effective on high-speed NASCAR race tracks. At $2610, its good looks attracted some 68,461 customers. The Starliner above sports accessory skirts and the then-popular half-moon headlight caps (or "visors").

tracks to other Galaxies' boxy, T-Bird-style roof. And indeed, winning races seemed the Starliner's main mission in life (at the risk of diluting Galaxie's distinct styling image). But with more than 68,000 sales, it proved to be one of the

more popular 1960 full-size Fords and is a favorite with collectors today. It wouldn't hang around long—only two years—but as one enthusiast observed, it was "the kind of car you never forget."

Engine choices still involved the familiar 292 and 352 V-8s. After a few dor-

The 1960 Galaxie Sunliner (top) continued its winning ways in 1960, with production down only slightly to 44,762 units for the year. Base list price was $2860, but that was with the standard 145-horsepower 223-cid six. Buyers ordering the 3791-pound ragtop, however, almost always opted for a V-8: the 185-bhp 292, 235-bhp 352, and 300-bhp 352. Among wagons, which were still listed as a separate series, only one two-door remained, the $2586 Ranch Wagon (center). This bare-bones model, awaiting shipment, has been scratched on the rear quarter panel. The Fairlane 500 series now encompassed only two sedans, and the $2388 Fairlane 500 Town Sedan (bottom) was by far the most popular big Ford with 153,234 units produced.

mant years following the AMA's 1957 "anti-racing" edict, the Big Three were beginning to resume their race-track skirmishing, and Ford's maximum 300 bhp just wasn't enough. Accordingly, the division released its first performance engine in three years. Dubbed "Interceptor 360," it was a tuned 352 initially restricted to three-speed manual transmission, and pumped out the advertised 360 bhp with single four-barrel carburetor and 10.6:1 compression. *Motor Life* magazine got hold of an Interceptor-equipped Starliner prototype in the summer of '59 and was startled to find that the 4141-pound car would do 0-60 mph in 7.1 seconds and an honest 150 mph. A "new bomb," said the editors. By contrast, *Motor Trend's* 300-bhp/automatic Starliner needed 11.7-seconds 0-60. Perhaps the best thing about the Interceptor was its price: just $150 extra. The "Total Performance" era was at hand.

In the meantime, Detroit's general recovery from dismal '58 continued apace as production returned to the record levels of 1955—even above that in some cases. Not that everyone fared well in 1960. DeSoto was looking decidedly terminal and Lincoln none too healthy. Chevrolet seemed to be the one big winner, posting 191,000 more cars for the model year to increase its lead over Ford Division, which ended up some 11,500 units short of its 1959 tally.

It was becoming easy to get lost in Ford's commercial line. This year's fleet comprised 488 different models, up by no fewer than 118 from 1959. The expansion came in two areas: the addition of stake and platform models to the year-old four-wheel-drive F-100/250 series, and a wider choice of engine, axle, spring, and tire options for heavies and extra-heavies. Among the latter were new "economy" versions of the big 401 and 477 V-8s. Other Super Duty powerplants returned with slight detuning in line with this year's advertising pitch, "Certified Economy, Certified Durability and Certified Reliability." Two heavy-duty tractors, the 132-inch-wheelbase F-1100 and 99-inch C-1100, disappeared, while other 1100s were now equipped for off-road use only (via 29,000-pound rear axles and a nominal GVW rating of 36,000 pounds).

A yearly facelift for light-duty conventionals was well-established by now, and this year's treatment was dominated by a full-width "dumbbell" half-way up the face. Headlamps were mounted outboard in square recesses that tapered inward toward the dumbbell's horizontal bar. Below that was wide eggcrate latticework flanked by rectangular turn signal/parking lamps. A narrow full-width slot separated grille from hood, with the latter exchanging its mesh air intake for two "letter slots" either side of a large Ford crest. All this wasn't exactly pretty, but at least it was different. F-600s on up retained their more attractive 1959 treatment.

Most '59 Ford trucks had fronted a horizontal-bar grille, but a rectangular unit of similar shape took over for 1960. The F-250 4×4 (above) boasted stronger standard springs: 1200 pounds front, 1950 pounds rear. Meanwhile, the F-600 (top) could be optioned to a 21,000-pound maximum, a response to the Chevy 60H.

Though still trailing Chevy by a substantial margin, Ford again racked up substantial domestic truck production in 1960, topping 330,000 units for the fourth straight year. The exact total of 337,468 failed to equal the firm's postwar peak of 1955 but beat its '57 and '59 tallies. Besides the new Falcon-based Ranchero and a Courier parallel to this year's redone Ranch Wagon, the '60s included the last of Ford's traditional panel delivery trucks, a mainstay of the line for more than 30 years. The demise of this body type was due not so much to falling demand, though sales had been tapering off, but rather a "better idea" being planned for 1961: the Econoline.

Ford was certainly no stranger to simple, rugged vehicles. This was, after all, the company the Model T had built. It was thus fitting that Ford not only participated in producing the legendary Jeep during World War II but designed its replacement, the first of which was delivered this year. This was the M-151 Military Utility Tactical Truck—"Mutt" for

short. Under development at Ford's Special Military Vehicle Operations department since 1951, the Mutt looked much like the wartime Willys/American Bantam model but had more modern specifications. Its chief advances were fully independent suspension, an overhead-valve four-cylinder engine delivering 71 bhp, and somewhat tidier dimensions that allowed Mutts to be dropped safely by air to wherever they were needed. Wheelbase was a dainty 85 inches, overall length 132 inches, width 62 inches, and weight a svelte 2140 pounds.

Mutts began coming out of Ford's Livonia, Michigan plant on September 1 this year. Thousands would ultimately be built, seeing action in Vietnam and other trouble spots through the early Eighties. Many are still in service but, like the Jeep, the Mutt wouldn't last forever. Today's go-anywhere field car is the "HMMWV," short for "High Mobility, Multipurpose Wheeled Vehicle," commonly referred to as the "Hummer." It's a worthy workhorse, but it's not as loveable as a Mutt.

1 9 6 1

Another busy product year saw Ford introduce a new third-generation Thunderbird; trimmer, restyled full-size cars; and a fully redesigned truck fleet starring new Econoline compacts and high-built H-Series semi-trailer tractors. The division offered more horsepower up and down the line, from a larger Falcon six to a brawny new 390 passenger-car V-8 to retuned Super Duty heavy-truck engines.

These and a raft of mechanical and cosmetic refinements helped Ford slip past Chevrolet in model-year car production by over 20,000 units, the grand total being 1,338,790 units (versus 1,318,014). However, both rivals were down from model year 1960, Ford by 100,580 units, Chevy by over 335,000. Dearborn's truck output remained at its previous level, but was now closer to Chevy's, which lost some 52,000 units.

The new passenger-car 390 V-8 was essentially an enlarged 352, created by stretching bore 0.05-inch (to 4.05 inches) and lengthening stroke 0.28-inch (to 3.78). Dubbed "Thunderbird Special," it produced the same 300 horsepower as the previous high-compression four-barrel 352, but packed more torque (427 lbs/ft versus 381, both peaking at a lazy 2800 rpm). In this form, the 390 was the standard—and only—powerplant for the new Thunderbird and the largest big-Ford option. All Ford V-8s now bore the Thunderbird name regardless of whether they were actually available in the T-Bird. This applied to the 352, still around as a regular-fuel 220-bhp option, and the 292, now rated at 175 bhp.

There were two other versions of the 390: a police-only 330-bhp Interceptor engine and a "Thunderbird 390 Super," conservatively rated at 375 bhp. At mid-year, the single four-barrel engine initially offered was supplemented by one with triple two-barrel carbs and higher compression, good for a mighty 401 bhp.

In *Fearsome Fords*, author Phil Hall notes that the 390s differed internally from the smaller FE-Series engines: stronger castings, thicker main-bearing webs, enlarged oil passages, and larger intake manifolds. However, they retained the cast-iron exhaust headers of the 352 Interceptor and its larger dual exhaust outlets. The 375-bhp unit could be ordered in any full-size '61 Ford save wagons and was strictly for performance—power steering, power brakes, and automatic weren't available.

All this put Ford now firmly in the big-brawn league with Pontiac's 389 V-8

and the new Chevy 409. It was also a prelude to an important announcement by Henry Ford II in January 1962. Ford's chairman, then president of the Automobile Manufacturers Association, denounced the group's 1957 "anti-racing" edict as a "so-called safety resolution" that Ford would no longer abide by. That sounded the gun: A new horsepower race was underway.

None of this mattered much to Thunderbird fanciers, who were busy drooling over this year's swoopier interpretation of the personal-luxury theme so successfully established by the 1958-60 design. "Unique in All the World," said the ads, and it was.

Thunderbird had been following a three-year design cycle, so a new '61 was no real surprise. Two clay mockups were in contention: one by longstanding Bird designer Bill Boyer, the other by Elwood Engel, both working under corporate styling vice-president George Walker. Engel's crisp, angular proposal was eliminated when Robert McNamara, then Ford Division general manager, decided it should be the basis for the new "compact" 1961 Lincoln Continental, so Boyer's work was again the starting point for a new-generation Thunderbird.

Boyer remembered his model as "very rocket-like in concept—very much aircraft-oriented, with big round 'flower-pot' taillights. It had what I called a 'fleet-submarine bow.' We wanted to keep the thing very youthful, and of course that meant aircraft and missile-like shapes—a model as aerodynamically aesthetic as possible. In contrast, Elwood's was a very formal job, [thus] perfectly suited to Lincoln." But they had much in common: "Both featured very highly integrated bumper/grille combinations," said Boyer. "There was much similarity in the windshield and side glass, a lot of interchangeability." Tapered cleanly in plain view, the new Bird bore only a suggestion of tailfins. The 1958-60 roofline was retained but became a bit more rounded. The front end was a bit chromey, and remained so through grille-insert changes for 1962-63.

Interior design proceeded under 40-year Ford veteran Art Querfeld: "I wanted to emphasize and delineate the positions of the driver and front seat passenger, [so] I conceived of two individual compartments separated by a prominent console [that] swept forward to the dash [and] curved left and right, meeting the doors and continuing around on the door panels." This was finished in brushed aluminum with horizontal lines. Stuart Fry of the packaging team created a unique "Swing-Away" steering wheel that could be moved laterally 10 inches to the right (with the transmission in Park) to assist entry/exit. Pop-up roof panels were considered once more, but were again rejected due to complexity and high cost.

Dimensionally, the third-generation Bird wasn't vastly altered from 1958-60.

The customary hardtop and convertible retained a 113-inch wheelbase and 52.5-inch overall height but were half an inch shorter and about an inch narrower. Body construction followed the "dual unitized" principle, with separate front and rear sections welded at the cowl. The cowl structure itself was shared with the new Continental, which held down tooling and production costs and afforded greater rigidity than in previous models.

Most of the new Bird's engineering work involved a completely redesigned chassis featuring "controlled wheel recession"—lots of rubber bushings to allow fore/aft as well as up/down movement. Although already familiar Mercedes-Benz practice, it was another T-Bird first in U.S. production. Front suspension employed coil springs located above the upper wishbones. The lower control arm was now a single bar instead of a wishbone, with a strut running from its outer end to a body-mounted bushing. At the

rear, forward spring mounts were also carried in rubber, with arms from the leaf shackles to each bushing permitting fore/aft movement. Stability was improved by widening track an inch in front and three inches in back. A quicker steering ratio reduced turns lock-to-lock to 3.5 and allowed use of a smallish, 16-inch-diameter wheel. The power-assisted, self-adjusting brakes had 14 percent more lining area than in 1960.

After trouncing the '60 Chevy Corvair and Plymouth Valiant by 186,000 and 241,000 units, respectively, Falcon sailed into '61 with a mild facelift highlighted by a more attractive convex grille. The four-door (right) sold for $1976, a $2 increase, but the DeLuxe trim package was up $12, to $78, but it now included chrome trim around the bodyside sculpturing. Four-door production settled in at 159,761 units. The '61 Thunderbird boasted all-new "projectile-look" styling penned by William P. Boyer. The $4639 ragtop (below) still maintained its clean "bootless" look.

The full-size '61 Fords boasted a heavy facelift that gave it a more squared-up look. The grille was new, a star-studded concave affair with one horizontal bar, while the round taillights and little canted fins were reminiscent of 1957-59 styling themes. The Galaxie Sunliner (above), down $11 to $2849, saw output hold steady at 44,614 units. The $2599 Galaxie Starliner (below), also down $11, returned for its second and final year—and watched production skid to 29,669.

This thoroughly overhauled chassis gave the '61 Thunderbird much better handling than its predecessor. It took high-speed turns with little body lean, plowing heavily only in tight corners. The quicker steering was more responsive, the enlarged brakes had better stopping power, and "controlled wheel recession" made for the smoothest T-Bird ride yet. It was certainly the most comfortable American car on a wheelbase under 115 inches—and the best-engineered Thunderbird to date. Ford sold 73,051 of them, of which 10,516 were convertibles.

A heavy facelift left this year's full-size Fords slightly lighter and shorter than the '60s. Changes included a simple concave grille with a "pin-dot" pattern bisected by a horizontal bar carrying quad headlights outboard, bodysides recontoured just below the belt, shorter rear decks (and a deeper trunk), and large circular taillamps topped by subtle blade fins. Model choices stayed basically the same: two- and four-door sedans in base Custom 300, step-up Fairlane, and even nicer Fairlane 500 trim, plus the top-of-

the-line Galaxie series with these plus a pair of Victoria hardtops (two and four doors), Starliner hardtop, and Sunliner convertible. As before, the parallel wagon series comprised two- and four-door Ranch Wagons, six- and nine-passenger Country Sedans, and a nine-seat Country Squire, the last now also available as a six-seater. All closed Galaxies save Starliner continued with squared-off wide-quarter rooflines *a la* Thunderbird, which buyers definitely preferred. Starliner declined to under 30,000 units for the model year and wouldn't return for '62; only the Galaxie two-door sedan was less popular among non-wagons.

Ford again emphasized reduced maintenance by extending big-car lubrication intervals to a full 30,000 miles this year, made possible by a special new molybdenum-disulfide lubricant for key points newly protected by polyurethane caps or liners. Normal grease fittings were eliminated, replaced by threaded plugs that could be removed if needed. Oil-change intervals lengthened again, this time to 6000 miles. Other mechanical changes comprised thinner main leaves for the semi-elliptic rear leaf springs, recalibrated shock absorbers, and standard self-adjusting brakes. Less welcome was a 50-percent reduction in steering effort with optional power assist, which was now definitely too flaccid.

Falcon entered its second year with the same models, a more elaborate new convex grille, and a bit more chrome. Responding to Chevrolet's sporty Corvair

Monza of mid-1960 was the "1961½" Falcon Futura, a more uptown version of the standard two-door boasting bucket seats separated by a mini-console, plusher carpeting, higher-grade vinyl trim, and special emblems. Floorshift manual transmission was optional. The Futura pointed the way to success in the compact class, notching close to 45,000 sales despite an abbreviated sales run. Newly available for all '61 Falcons was a stroked, 170-cid version of the pushrod six with 101 horsepower. It would linger through the early Seventies and be used in Falcon's spiritual successor, the Maverick.

It's appropriate to pause here for a brief look at the new '61 Lincoln Continental, which in this and subsequent versions would become world-famous as the official car of American Presidents from Kennedy to Carter. It certainly marked a renaissance for Ford's luxury make—the first Lincoln since the original Zephyr that was advanced enough to leave the rest of the industry gasping. And like the Zephyr, it rallied the marque after too many years of decline. Arriving as a four-door thin-pillar sedan and convertible, it garnered 25,164 sales, Lincoln's best model-year tally since 1957.

Indicative of its design excellence, the '61 Continental received the Industrial Designers Institute Bronze Award, one of the few cars so honored. The citation recognized seven Ford stylists: Gene Bordinat (who succeeded Walker as corporate design director on May 18, 1961), Don DeLaRossa, the aforementioned Elwood Engel, Gayle Halderman, John Najjar, and Bob Thomas. Though the car was evidently a committee project, this group was laden with talent and couldn't have worked better together.

The heart of the '61's crisp new shape was the cowl-forward structure that housed its mechanical heart—electrics, air conditioning, powerplant—and was inherently the most expensive to create. As mentioned, this was shared with the new Thunderbird, a handy way of halving development and tooling costs for two relatively low-volume cars. Component-sharing wasn't new, of course, but it was a radical step for cars so different in size and style, even to the number of doors. It limited the Lincoln's size in only one critical dimension, overall width at the A-pillars, but that only dovetailed with the goal of a relatively compact luxury car, a complete reversal of past Lincoln practice.

But making such a car appear substantial and stable required extremely close attention to detail. As John Najjar noted: "By creating the top edge of the body side and defining it with thick chrome trim, the appearance of stability and width was achieved. An additional benefit of this clearly defined longitudinal edge appeared from the driver's seat: The fenderline was visible from front to back. [The wide "shoulders" also helped make the greenhouse look "nestled," adding

The '61 Falcon rolled merrily into 1961 with output up almost 40,000 units to 474,241. Wagons alone climbed 45,728 units to 120,038—87,933 of them the four-door (top). Base price was $2270. The best seller among the big Fords was the $2592 Galaxie four-door sedan (above), which watched production spurt to 141,823 units.

further to the impression of stability.] By introducing curved side glass, we were able to achieve what was probably the greatest angle of tumblehome [inward curvature] on a car of this type."

The new convertible sedan, a style not seen in U.S. production since the 1951 Frazer, was adopted to one-up Cadillac with what was seen as a more saleable soft-top. No fewer than 11 mechanical and hydraulic relays were needed to open its rear-hinged deck, unlatch its top, and lower it into the trunk. But because the top did fold flush, the stylists were able to bring the flat rear deckline right up to the passenger compartment, much as Dutch Darrin had done with his memorable '51 Kaiser. The lack of B-pillars above the beltline prompted the use of throwback center-opening "suicide" rear doors hinged at the back.

Classy looks aside, the '61 Lincoln was renowned for its high-quality craftsmanship, largely promulgated by Harold C. MacDonald, chief engineer for the Car and Truck Group. Shunning rampant innovation, he concentrated on proven techniques: the most rigid unit body/chassis yet produced, the best sound insulation money could buy, extremely close machining tolerances, an unprecedented number of long-life components, sealed electrical system, extra rust and corrosion protection. These Lincolns also received the most thorough testing yet seen in Detroit. Each engine was run at 3500 rpm (equal to 98 mph) for three

hours, then torn down, analyzed, and reassembled. Every transmission was tested for 30 minutes before installation. Each finished car took a 12-mile road test, during which it had to pass 200 individual checks. Black light was used to visualize a fluorescent dye in lubricants to check for leaks. Backing it all up, Lincoln offered an unprecedented two-year/24,000-mile warranty.

Public response was immediate and satisfying. Though the new Continentals didn't appear until quite late, sales exceeded 25,000 units, putting Lincoln ahead of Chrysler's Imperial for keeps. Note that this was accomplished with just two models to Imperial's six. The sedan predictably accounted for the bulk of production; convertible output was just 2857 units. Against Cadillac, Lincoln had essentially one model to counter 12, hardly a toe-to-toe match, but the Continental was so good that it outsold all but one of the Caddys and stole at least 10,000 sales from the GM division.

Ford's truck line became even more bewildering for '61, now numbering 619 individual models, 131 more than the previous year. Most significant of the newcomers from the standpoints of sales volume and industry impact were the new Econoline compacts, a pickup, windowless panel van, and "windowed" passenger/delivery van built around Falcon chassis and mechanical components. Power was supplied by an 85-bhp version of the 144-cid Falcon six, placed between the

As always, the Country Squire (above) reigned at the top of the station wagon line. For '61, it came in six- and nine-passenger form, listing at $2943 and $3013, respectively. The former found 16,961 buyers, while the nine-seater enticed 14,657. The Ranchero (left) received the same updates as the '61 Falcon, and priced at a reasonable $1887 it attracted 20,937 customers, about the same as it had in 1960.

driver and front passenger in a new for-ward-control unitized structure. Wheel-base measured 90 inches, a full 19.5 inch-es shorter than Falcon's. Overall length was 168.4 inches, width some 75 inches overall, height about 79 inches. Base GVW rating was 3600 pounds, and a 4350-pound package was optionally available.

The Econoline was Ford's response to the Volkswagen Type 2 "Microbus" and pickup that had attracted sparse but steady sales among short-haul light-duty commercial users, especially in cities, as well as families seeking a roomier alter-native to the traditional station wagon. However, Ford made a key departure by retaining a conventional front-engine/rear-drive format instead of using the rear-engine/rear-drive layout of the German import—or Chevrolet's similar "Corvair 95" models that also bowed for '61. And the Econoline's engine was a simple, water-cooled six versus VW's air-cooled flat four and Corvair's complex, less reli-able air-cooled flat six. Chassis specs were equally conventional: an I-beam front axle on semi-elliptic leaf springs, live rear axle on same, recirculating-ball steering, and all-drum brakes.

Per VW (and Corvair 95) practice, the Econoline panel came with two front doors and a pair of center-opening right-side doors—all the better for curbside de-liveries and passenger loading. The side doors were optional for the window ver-sion, which was advertised as the "Sta-tion Bus." Another pair of doors provided rear access on both models. Maximum cargo space was a bit more than 204 cubic feet, impressive for the trim external size. The pickup featured an airy cab with the same large windshield as the vans, plus a flat rear window flanked by curved panes in the roof quarters. Behind, the cargo box was fully integrated with the body and measured 85 × 63 × 23 inches. The tailgate wasn't full-width, but opened much closer to the ground than on a con-ventional pickup. The spare was carried inside the box at the extreme right rear.

In all, the Econoline was a timely ad-dition to Ford's truck line—and a profit-able one. Helped by a large order from Bell Telephone, which thus helped to ad-vertise it among non-commercial pros-pects, the Econoline way outsold the VW Type 2. It also handily beat the Corvair 95, just as the Falcon had trounced the

passenger Corvair. Testifying to its suc-cess, the Econoline would be copied by both Dodge and Chevy/GMC within three years.

Ranchero's increased popularity as a Falcon-based compact prompted a similar downsizing of the full-size Courier. The result was the new Falcon Sedan Deliv-ery, also bearing painted metal where glass would be on the parent two-door wagon, but with the same drop-down tailgate and roll-down back window. Trim remained spartan—this was a com-mercial vehicle, after all—but a full-width front bench seat was included. Like their passenger cousins, both these Falcon "trucks" could be ordered with the new 170-cid six at extra cost.

Moving up the line, all models with quad headlights reverted to dual 7.5-inch-diameter units, and conventional cabs were treated to a front-end facelift. The latter involved a large, square "face" on heavies (750-1100), matching their taller build, surmounted by "Ford" in block let-ters and a slightly setback hood with four wide air slots in front. In addition, these models as well as the T-700 tandem ac-quired bolt-on (instead of integral) front fenders and grilles, plus substantially re-duced front overhang. Other conven-tionals used a shallow loop grille with a wide, narrow slot bearing a block-letter nameplate. Styleside pickups sported slightly longer and wider cargo boxes newly integrated with the cab for a smoother, more car-like appearance. Sep-arate running boards reduced step-up height on F-Series mediums (500-700), while wider, squared-up front fenders made them look a bit more like their heavy-duty brothers.

Engineering changes were diverse. Wheelbases grew two inches on most conventionals; the two F-100 chassis, for example, now spanned 114 and 122 inches. There was also a new 212-inch-long chassis in the F-700 and -750 Series; a 175-inch C-700 was another new offering. Modern high-strength/low-alloy (HSLA) steel was adopted for redesigned frames beneath some tandems and extra-heavy tractor models, and non-powered trailing or "pusher" third axles became available late in the model year on the F/T-950/1000 chassis. F/T-700s now came with a 302 V-8 as standard, while a "big six"—a beefy new enlargement of the I-Block 223 developing 152 bhp—returned to the line as a V-8 alternative in the C-550/600 cabovers and F-600. The five Super-Duty V-8s received minor adjustments that gave each a bit more power and torque, ranging from 206 bhp and 341 pounds/feet on the two-barrel 401 to 266 bhp and 481 lbs/ft on the burly four-barrel 534. Capping it all off, Ford extended basic Super Duty warranty coverage to 24 months/100,000 miles.

Last but not least was an entirely new group of high-built tilt-cab tractors, the H-Series. Designed for efficient operation and long-term durability on the nation's growing Interstate highway system, they were the first Ford trucks available with diesel power: whopping 672- and 743-cid Cummins V-8s. Ford's own gasoline engines were also available. Initial H-Series offerings included the 850, 950, and 1000 chassis, both single- and tandem-axle. A diesel-powered 850 tandem was thus termed an HDT-850. Factory wheelbases differed from those of the low-cab C-Series, comprising spans of 126, 134, 146, 158, and 176 inches.

Ford made a major business deal this year that would prove a major headache: the $28-million takeover of Electric Autolite, well-known maker of spark plugs and other automotive components. This may have reflected Ford's continuing desire to be more like General Motors, which had long owned both AC spark plugs and Delco Electric. Whatever the reason, the Justice Department evidently felt that automakers already had too many suppliers under their wings, for it filed suit against Ford, charging that the Autolite acquisition violated anti-trust laws. Ford's attorneys must have been perplexed. "Why," they must have asked, "pick on Ford for buying an electrical supplier when giant GM already owns two?" The answer, of course, was politics. Being much larger than Ford gave GM commensurately more clout in Washington. Then, too, GM was more experienced at dodging trust-busters, who were still trying to figure ways to cut the giant down to size.

In any case, the suit wouldn't reach

court until 1967, and Ford was ultimately ordered to divest itself of Autolite (in December 1970). But it wasn't all bad, because Ford was able to keep Autolite until the suit was settled, and it reaped handsome profits from its Autolite Division (formed as Motorcraft Division on April 18, 1961, renamed on August 14). In all, not a bad way to lose. Oddly enough, the government did not oppose Ford's acquisition of Philco Corporation on December 11 of this year. Perhaps it decided that one suit was enough.

Ford faced another big problem on October 3 when it was threatened with a companywide strike by the United Auto

Ford's '61 pickups were new from stem to stern: lower, wider, and with a larger non-wraparound windshield. The F-100 (top) Styleside retailed for $1981. Newest addition to the Ford truck line was the Falcon-based Econoline. Riding a 90-inch wheelbase, the van boasted a 204.4-cubic-foot cargo hold, 40 percent larger than the typical half-ton panel. The $1880 pickup version (above) had a 85.9-inch cargo box.

Workers union—the first such action in what had been a generally cordial 20-year partnership. This time, however, a solution was swift and final: a new three-year contract signed October 20.

1 9 6 2

Dearborn's stable became even more specialized this year with introduction of the intermediate Fairlane and the first of the big performance Fords, the Galaxie 500/XL. The year also brought an important new small-block V-8, a near-revival of the two-seat Thunderbird, and improved truck engines.

Chevrolet reclaimed the number-one spot in model-year car production, outpacing Ford by some 500,000 units, partly on the strength of its new conventional compact, the Chevy II. Still, Ford's total was better than 150,000 cars higher than its 1961 tally—nearly 1.5 million.

The smaller, all-new Fairlane accounted for a good chunk of Ford's 1962 volume—about 20 percent, in fact. A kind of grown-up compact sized between Falcon and the standard Fords, it measured

Ford had been merely keeping up with its Big Three competition when it introduced the '60 Falcon. But a big size and price gap between the new compact and the ever-larger full-size cars prompted Ford to be first to fill it. Enter the mid-size '62 Fairlane: 115.5-inch wheelbase and 197.6 inches overall—figures that could have prompted Ford to shout, "Suddenly, it's 1955!" Ford president Lee Iacocca (top) stands proudly beside the new car. The top-line Fairlane 500 four-door (center) sold for $2304, the base two-door (bottom) cost $2154.

six inches longer than Falcon in wheel-base (115.5 inches), 16.5 inches longer overall, and 500 pounds heavier. Even so, it employed the same sort of unit construction, conventional engineering, and conservative styling, even the Falcon's optional 170-cubic-inch six as standard power. Models were initially restricted to two- and four-door sedans in standard and ritzier 500 trim.

Coincidentally, Plymouth and Dodge fielded smaller 1962 full-size cars of similar dimensions. Whether because of their size or oddball styling, they didn't sell well, and Chrysler hurriedly revived the big Dodge at mid-season. Fairlane had no such difficulty, selling more than 297,000 units for the model year. Even better, most of this represented "plus business" that didn't come at the expense of other Fords. Some auto writers observed that this Fairlane marked the return of a size not seen in U.S. cars since 1955. Its success wasn't lost on GM, which would field '55-size cars of its own in just two years.

Fairlane was well along in 1960 when Ford product planners determined that it would need an engine larger than the Falcon six as an extra-cost option. Unfortu-

Despite the Falcon compacts and the new intermediate Fairlanes, the full-size cars remained Ford's best sellers for '62. The most popular single model was the Galaxie 500 four-door sedan (top). It weighed in at 3650 pounds, listed at $2667, and 174,195 buyers drove one home. The price leader among the big Fords was now the two-model Galaxie series; the two-door sedan (center) started out at $2453 and 54,930 were called for. Among hardtops, the $2674 Galaxie 500 Victoria (bottom) was the favorite, and demand was strong enough that 87,562 were produced.

For 1962, the Thunderbird lineup doubled to four models, two of them convertibles. The regular ragtop (top row), now tipping the scales at a hefty 4370 pounds, got a price increase of $149, to $4788, hardly small change in '62. But that seemed modest compared to the $5439 sticker on the Sports Roadster (bottom). This new model boasted a fiberglass tonneau cover with headrests above the bucket seats; they tapered back over—and covered—the rear seat, thus reviving the concept of a two-seat Bird. Skirts were omitted to highlight the sporty chrome wire wheels.

nately, none of the firm's existing power-plants would fit the new in-between package. The big 223-cid six was getting old, while the smallest FE-Series V-8, the 292, was too thirsty. Accordingly, engineering director Harold C. McDonald convinced management to authorize $250 million for developing a new "small-block" V-8 of 220-230 cubic inches. The project was handed over to a team under George F. Stirrat, who had worked his way through the ranks at the Engine & Foundry operation after joining Ford in 1949.

Stirrat's major objectives were a 20-inch maximum block width and an installed weight of 450 pounds. He went to new extremes for the compact block, selecting a 3.50-inch bore and a short 2.87-inch stroke, plus correspondingly short connecting rods and low-height pistons. The block extended only as far as the crankshaft centerline. This didn't leave enough crankcase room for full counter-weighting, so 30 percent of the engine's total unbalanced forces had to be handled by external masses. Bore-center spacing was 4.38 inches, which allowed considerable room for later enlargement beyond the initial 221 cid. On 8.5:1 compression,

the new engine delivered 145 horse-power at 4400 rpm.

The small-block's valvegear design was new to Ford but familiar Pontiac/Chevrolet practice. Rocker arms were mounted on ball-studs that eliminated the need for rocker shafts, while valves were conventionally sized relative to bore, with head diameters of 1.59 inches for the intakes and 1.39 inches for the exhausts. Timing was fairly conservative. The weight target was met with new high-precision thin-wall casting techniques developed by Harold C. Grant, a leader in nodular-iron castings and the shell-molding process using resin-filled cores. This dealt a knockout blow to the aluminum-block engines then built in America. Buick's 215-cid V-8 and American Motors' six were lighter but cost more to build, as did Chrysler's heavier 225-cid six. Ford's cast-iron small-block sent these and other rivals scurrying to the foundries to copy its construction.

A step down the ladder, the compact Falcon carried on with an "electric shaver" grille, Deluxe-trim editions of all body styles, and a new Squire wagon with the same sort of imitation-wood side paneling found on the big Country Squire. The Falcon name also appeared on a base and Deluxe-trim Club Wagon, the renamed passenger version of the forward-control Econoline Station Bus.

The big Fords, still on their 1960 platform, were again thoroughly—and handsomely—restyled. They gained a bulkier look via more rounded sheetmetal, which discarded the little fins of 1961. The line-up contracted to make room for the new Fairlane. Galaxie was now the base series, limited to two- and four-door sedans; a new Galaxie 500 line came in above with a

Although the '62 Ford still used the basic 1960 bodyshell, styling was again heavily revamped. The front end was the least changed, keeping the shape of the '61, but the new flat, and somewhat ornate, grille made it look different—and more elegant, some said. The rear end, however, looked all new as the little canted fins disappeared in favor of a straight-through fenderline. The big round taillights that had returned for 1961 were reworked somewhat and lowered to beneath bumper level. The "grille" between them emphasized the width of the car. The Galaxie 500/XL was a sporty new bucket-seat-with-floorshift rendition of the regular 500, available as a Victoria hardtop or Sunliner convertible. The latter, introduced at mid-year, found favor with 13,183 buyers.

full range of body styles. The latter emphasized luxury and comfort: "The ride is silent as a secret," cooed the brochure. The wagon lineup returned, of course, but minus the two-door Ranch Wagon. Engine availability was unchanged at the start of the model year: standard 223-cid six, now at 138 bhp; optional 170-bhp 292 V-8, 220-bhp 352, and 390s with 300, 340, and 375 bhp.

A marketing technique favored by new division chief Lee Iacocca was the "half" model year, special trim and/or mechanical options to give familiar models added zest for the spring selling season, traditionally the year's busiest. Iacocca

continued the practice this April with three "1962½" offerings marketed as "The Lively Ones" (partly via a tie-in with a TV show of that name). All were keyed to the growing buyer interest in bucket seats, console, floorshift, and other youthful features popularized by Chevy's Corvair Monza. The trio comprised a revised Falcon Futura two-door with squared-off T-Bird-type roof; a Fairlane 500 Sports Coupe, the pillared two-door with buckets and special trim; and the similarly outfitted Galaxie 500/XL Victoria hardtop coupe and Sunliner convertible with standard 292 V-8. Some thought the letters on the last stood for

"Experimental Limited," but they meant nothing more than "extra lively."

Accompanying the XL was Ford's largest V-8 yet: a 390 bored-out by 0.08-inch to 406 cubic inches. Optional only in the full-size line, it was offered as a 385-bhp "Thunderbird High-Performance" unit with single four-barrel carb, and as the "Thunderbird Super High-Performance" with three two-barrel carbs and a rated 405 bhp—nearly one bhp per cubic inch. The latter was clearly not for the faint-hearted and cost a sizable $380. Still, the 406 gave the big bucket-seat Fords the go-power to match their sporty pretensions. Contemporary road tests showed 0-60 mph acceleration times ranging from the mid-6s to a bit over seven seconds—fantastic for quiet, smooth-riding freeway flyers weighing nearly two tons.

The 406 Galaxie would have been a fine stock-car racer but, aside from heft, it had a problem. As writer Phil Hall explained: "When the Starliner was dropped, so were Ford's superspeedway chances. The squared-off sedan roof just didn't cut through the air as quickly as the sleek Starliners." Ford attempted to recoup with the Starlift, an accessory hardtop that turned the big convertible into something resembling the now-departed Starliner. Though ostensibly available to the public as well as race teams, few were actually built, and NASCAR (the National Association for Stock Car Auto Racing) banned it as "not production" after only

one race. Ford would improve full-size aerodynamics with racing in mind, but not for another year.

It should be noted that Ford's NASCAR rivals all mustered more cubic inches in '62, which was the name of the game. Chrysler had a 426 "wedge," Dodge/Plymouth a 413-cid version of same, Pontiac a potent 421, and Chevrolet its burly (and increasingly celebrated) 409. When the dust settled, Ford counted only six Grand National wins, its lowest total in NASCAR's senior circuit since first seriously entering the lists in 1955.

Of course, "Race on Sunday, Sell on Monday" had long been an article of faith among Detroit marketers, and a competition connection undoubtedly helped move a good many of Ford's new "Lively Ones." But sporty features were of equal if not greater importance to most buyers, and these Fords delivered. All offered higher-grade carpeting, color-keyed vinyl on front bucket seats and interior side panels, chrome-like accents of mylar plastic, Thunderbird-type center consoles with auxiliary storage, and availability of the aforementioned floorshift control for both manual and automatic transmissions. Closed models typically wore vinyl roof coverings, a new styling fad then sweeping Detroit. The big XLs even included a "bucket-styled" back seat, bright-metal pedal trim, and additional courtesy lights. Naturally, there was a price for all this sportiness, but it wasn't exorbitant. At $2273, the little Futura

cost only $202 more than the workaday Falcon Deluxe two-door. The Fairlane Sports Coupe listed at $2403, $161 above the plain two-door 500. Even the big XL hardtop was a good buy: $434 above its three-speed six-cylinder Galaxie 500 counterpart, but still reasonable at $3108 base.

And interestingly enough, it was the Galaxie that proved the most popular of the Lively Ones. Buyers snapped up 28,412 hardtops and 13,813 convertibles, a total of 42,225 units for the model year. By contrast, the Falcon Futura garnered only about 17,000 orders, the Fairlane Sports Coupe about 19,600. But the racing action would increasingly shift to mid-size cars, so the sales action would too by mid-decade, making the heyday of sporty full-sizers like the big XLs relatively brief.

A big reason for this change was drag racing, notably the stock categories in NHRA (National Hot Rod Association)

As introduced for '62, the sportiest Falcon was the two-door, bucket-seat sedan, Futura (above left). Then in 1962½, just in time for the spring selling season, Ford sprung "The Lively Ones": Galaxie 500/XL, Fairlane 500 Sports Coupe, and a revised Futura (top right). The last featured a Thunderbird-style roof (vinyl top optional), unique hubcaps with a red-white-blue color band, and other minor changes. With the Starliner gone, Ford needed a more aerodynamic roofline for racing, so it came up with the Starlift top (bottom), but few were built and NASCAR banned it.

With the demise of the two-door Ranch Wagon, the full-size Ford wagon lineup for 1962 consisted of five models, all with four doors. The woody-look Country Squire (top), with seating for six or nine, listed at $3018 and $3088, respectively, and saw output reach 16,114 and 15,666 units. The mid-range Country Sedan (above), with price stickers pegged at $2829 and $2933, was the volume leader: 47,635 and 16,562 units.

competition, where lightness was crucial. As there was nothing much to run in the early Sixties except full-size cars, Chevy, Pontiac, and other makes began offering fiberglass, aluminum, and Plexiglas body panels to lower weight and thus the elapsed times. These pieces were customarily sold through dealers, but it wasn't long before they were combined with the biggest engines in lightweight, factory-stock drag packages. Pontiac and Dodge/Plymouth were particularly active in this area, but Ford would join them in earnest in 1964.

Less awe-inspiring, perhaps, but more significant for the "real world" was the more potent small-block that arrived at mid-'62 as a Fairlane option. Dubbed "Challenger 260," it put out 164 bhp via a 0.30-inch bore increase and higher 8.7:1 compression. It only hinted at the little V-8's development potential, which would be realized soon enough.

The third-generation Thunderbird was little changed in its sophomore year, a different grille texture and minor trim shuffling being the only visible changes.

There were, however, two interesting developments. One was an optional "M-Series" 390 V-8 with triple two-barrel carbs, 10.5:1 compression, and 340 bhp. So equipped, the Bird needed just 8.5 seconds for the 0-60-mph dash and could top 125 mph. Equally exciting was the Sports Roadster, a spiritual successor to the two-seat T-Bird. Ever since the final '57 models, Ford had received a steady stream of inquiries from dealers and customers who, although happy with the four-seater, longed for a new "little Bird." Iacocca was sympathetic but knew a separate model would cost too much. Stylist Bud Kaufman provided the solution: a fiberglass tonneau (with faired-in front seat headrests) to cover the existing convertible's rear seat area. Through careful attention to detail, the tonneau didn't interfere with raising or lowering the top, and the front seats were still free to hinge forward so luggage could be stuffed in underneath. But the tonneau had one big drawback: It was too big to carry in the trunk, so you had to leave it at home if you wanted to travel four-up. This and a

tall price—about $5500—limited sales to just 1427 for the model year.

Still, the Sports Roadster was dramatic, set off by Kelsey-Hayes wire wheels and skirtless rear wheel openings. (The spinner hubs made the wires too bulky to fit under the normal T-Bird skirts, and they were too pretty to hide anyway.) Rarity makes this the most desirable Sixties T-Bird today. The rarest, of course, are those with the M-Series engine, a mere 320 of the '62s.

Thunderbird had a second new "package" model this year. Called Landau, it was a high-line hardtop with vinyl roof and dummy rear-quarter landau bars—a Bill Boyer flashback to the Classic era. Priced at $4398, only $77 more than the standard model, it accounted for about a fourth of '62 T-Bird hardtop volume.

Ford was also touting its "Twice-a-Year Maintenance" plan in 1962. Owners could now drive 6000 miles between routine service stops, allowing for a savings in both time and service expense.

Not unexpectedly, the truck line saw relatively little change following the major makeover of 1961, though it wasn't completely untouched, of course. The little Ranchero and Falcon Sedan Delivery took on the new appearance of their passenger-car cousins as well as many of their mechanical improvements. Among the latter were larger brake linings, more durable aluminized mufflers, and optional availability of a four-speed manual transmission with floorshift. Port-side cargo doors were a new option for the Econoline van, as was the 170-cid six for both it and the pickup.

Moving up the range, F-100 through F-600 conventionals were newly identified by a revised grille bearing a wide, stylized star between the headlamps and "Ford" lettering moved up to just under the four air slots. Cruise-O-Matic replaced Fordomatic as the F-100's automatic option. Costlier repairs had led to complaints about the integral cargo boxes on '61 Styleside pickups, so this was phased out during 1962 production in favor of conventional separate cab/box construction, on 4WDs at first, then 4×2s.

Customer feedback also prompted several alterations among medium- and heavy-duty engines, though displacements and basic specs stayed the same. The 292 V-8 was treated to a more durable forged crankshaft, the 302 and 332 units became a bit thriftier via reduced compression and a switch from four- to two-barrel carburetors, and hydraulic lifters replaced solid tappets on all Super-Duty powerplants. The F-750 changed from "junior 800" to "Super 700" by taking on the latter's front sheetmetal and two-inch shorter wheelbases, and there was the usual annual shifting of GVW ratings on some models, mostly upward. Aside from this and the above-mentioned engine changes, the low-profile C-Series and high-build H-Series tilt-cabs were

Among trucks, Ford's H-Series tractors were the long-distance haulers, here an HD-900 diesel (top left). The bumper-to-back-of-cab dimension was 82 inches. The T-Series tandems, here a 950 diesel (top right) were also often fitted with the 266-bhp, 534-cid V-8. It is seen here with the central radiator shutters closed. At the light-duty end of the line were the F-250 4×4 pickup (above left) and the Econoline people-mover, now officially designated the Ford Falcon DeLuxe Club Wagon (above). It listed at $2287.

basically holdovers, as were tandem-axle conventionals and COEs.

Ford had another fine truck year, adding close to 36,500 units to finish at just over 375,000. But Chevy remained America's number one truckmaker in 1962, producing nearly 54,300 more to finish near 397,000 units.

Dearborn helped make history on January 26 of this year. That was the day Mercury astronaut Colonel John Glenn became the first American in space, and Ford's Aeronutronics Division played a key role in monitoring his pioneering sub-orbital circuit of the globe. Ford had entered the burgeoning aerospace field rather early, in May 1956, when it purchased Aeronutronic Systems of Newport Beach, California, a small but growing specialist in military and aerospace electronics. Like so many other auto chiefs, Henry Ford II had recognized the value of taking his firm into non-automotive fields as a hedge against the cyclical ups-and-downs of the auto business and as a source of extra income. It was this rationale that had prompted the Philco and Electric Autolite buyouts of 1961.

Initially a subsidiary, Aeronutronics became a full-fledged Ford division in June 1959, about two months after being named prime contractor for the U.S. Army's new "Shillelagh" surface-to-surface missile. Given the increasing importance of high-tech electronics to the nation's arms and space programs, it was a foregone conclusion that Aeronutronics would have greater involvement in both. Underlying its success and expertise in those areas was the announcement on December 14, 1962, that the Ford unit had landed the contract to develop a new camera scanning system for future Mercury flights and the forthcoming two-man Gemini missions. Under the later name Ford Aerospace, Dearborn would remain a key military and aerospace contractor until early 1990. It then unexpectedly sold the division (then employing 20,000 people nationwide) so as to concentrate more on its "core business" in a vastly improved international climate.

Ford's core business was definitely on the upswing in 1962. The Edsel fiasco was a fast-fading memory, Dearborn's newest products were selling well—very well in Falcon's case—and management seemed clear about the right course to steer toward a future that was looking rosier than ever. Finances were solid, and announcement of a 2-for-1 split made the annual stockholders meeting on May 24 even happier than usual. Symbolizing Ford's continued strength and optimism was the return of its famed script-in-oval logo, featured on the right-side door stepplates of most of its 1962 cars and trucks.

And the year brought yet another production milestone: the 30-millionth Ford V-8 engine, completed on July 2. In fact, the only really bad news for Ford in 1962 was the fire that destroyed its historic Rotunda on November 9. Originally built for the Chicago Century of Progress exposition some 30 years before, it had greeted 13.2 million visitors since being reopened in Golden Anniversary year 1953. Losing it was a shame.

Even in bucket-seat Futura trim, the '62 Falcon had remained a cheap-to-buy, cheap-to-run six-cylinder compact. It would still be that for 1963, but those wanting a jazzier compact were pleased at the outset of the model year with the addition of a convertible. Then at mid-year, a snazzy semi-fastback hardtop joined the roster, and so did the 260 V-8 and the sportier Futura Sprint, offered as a ragtop or hardtop (above). The latter, stickered $2320, did 0-60 in 12 seconds. Output came to 10,479 units. Ford, testing the waters for a sporty car for the masses, developed the mid-engine, two-seat Mustang I (below) to gauge public opinion. They liked it, but the production car would be a far more conventional four-seater.

Ford Motor Company observed two milestone anniversaries this year: its 60th as a company, and the centennial of its founder's birth. Ford Division celebrated in a big way. Larger V-8s, new styling, and additional body styles were featured across the car line, with the more exciting developments reserved for "1963½" debuts, and the truck fleet was again greatly expanded with new short-chassis high conventionals and wider availability of diesel power. In the production race, Ford built over 1.5 million cars for the model year—its best total since 1957 and a new record—though it trailed Chevrolet by a significant 600,000 units. Truck output jumped by nearly 50,000 units to nudge 425,000, a new postwar high, but Chevy built some 86,000 additional units to maintain its customary lead, ending at just over 483,000.

Per now-standard Ford practice, the '63 car line bowed with the same drivetrains from the end of the preceding model year. However, improved filters first used in 1962 increased oil-change intervals to 6000 miles on all engines. The chassis-lube requirement was longer, too: 36,000 miles across the board. There was also a welcome new transmission: "America's first fully synchronized 3-speed manual," replacing the old standard

"crash" boxes on Falcons, Fairlanes, and base-model standards.

Facelifts occurred throughout the car line, but the surest way to spot any '63 Ford was by its amber front turn-signal lenses, a new federally mandated item. So, too, was positive crankcase ventilation (PCV) on cars, an embryonic pollution-control measure. Not coincidentally, the California legislature began laying the groundwork this year for America's first serious emissions-reducing devices, which would be required on all domestic

cars sold in the Golden State beginning with the 1966 model year (1968 for imports). It was a faint sign of much stronger measures to come.

This year's Falcon sedans adopted the squared-up roof from the mid-'62 Futura, and all models displayed slightly pointier front fenders and a more pleasing convex grille. Futura replaced the previous Deluxe as a separate series, with two- and four-door sedans and a pretty new convertible, all identified by spear-like side trim. Both the 144- and 170-

cubic-inch Falcon sixes adopted hydraulic lifters. Brakes received thicker linings and were now self-adjusting. Electric wipers were newly standard across the line. Although the Falcon was America's lowest-priced six-passenger sedan in 1963, prices were now close to where Ford's low-line standards had been only five years before. They ranged from $1985 for the base two-door to $2470 for the new Futura convertible.

Billed as the "Super Torque" Ford, this year's Galaxie was heavily reskinned to become fractionally longer and wider (by 0.6 and 0.8 inches, respectively). Still intact were the basic body structure and 119-inch-wheelbase perimeter chassis introduced back in 1960, but the suspension was modified to put "Thunderbird velvet in the '63 Ford's all-new ride." The coil-spring front end got more built-in "give" via new "Compliance Link" geometry

The '63 Falcon sedan delivery (top left) could brag about a seven-foot cargo bay and a low list price of $2111. Although the Sprint stole the spotlight, the regular $2470 Futura ragtop (center left) found 31,192 customers. Holding down the middle rung of the full-size Ford ladder was the Galaxie. The $2453 two-door (bottom) garnered 30,335 takers. The high-flying big Fords were the four Galaxie 500/XLs. The only four-door was the $3333 Town Victoria (top right): 12,596 built. Output of the $3268 "slantback" XL (center right) was 33,870.

that allowed the lower A-arms to pivot for better road-shock absorption. Also changed toward the same end were the forward mounts of the rear longitudinal multi-leaf springs. Curb weights were up slightly—by 75 pounds on two-door hardtops, for example. A revised engine chart deleted the Y-Block 292 as the base V-8 in favor of the Fairlane's 164-bhp Challenger 260. Initial options comprised a single 352 with 220 horses and two 390s and a pair of 406s with respective horsepower of 300/330 and 385/405.

Highlighting the latest big-Ford restyle were a handsome new concave grille, more prominent round taillamps, and, on Galaxie 500s, twin bodyside moldings. A square-roof hardtop sedan joined the bucket-seat XL sub-series, while a pair of cheap "300" sedans, not strictly Galaxies, slotted in below the base Galaxie sedans as the new price-leaders. The latter were aimed mainly at fleet buyers like police departments and taxi operators. Again, sticker prices weren't radically different, running from $2324 for the 300 Tudor to $3518 for the sporty XL ragtop.

Though just a year old, the popular Fairlane intermediate achieved a closer resemblance to the big Fords, gaining a similar concave grille and front bumper, plus minor tinware reshaping. Two new body styles premiered: a trio of four-door wagons—fancy Squire with imitation-wood paneling and plain-sided Ranch Wagons in base and Custom trim—and a 500 hardtop coupe available with or without front bucket seats. The pillared 500 Sports Coupe disappeared. Fairlane toed the price line, too, spanning a narrowish $2150-$2500 range.

Thunderbird, now in the last year of its third-generation "rocketship" design, was promoted as "Unmatched . . . unmistakable . . . unique in all the world." For 1963, it acquired flat-top wheel openings and modest horizontal front-fender creaselines running back to three sets of slanted hashmarks on the doors, plus restyled wheel covers and the usual color and trim shuffles. Prices did change here: up about $130 over '62. The base hardtop now cost $4445, the convertible $4912, the singular Sports Roadster a cool $5563. The lush Landau returned at a higher $4548, still with standard vinyl roof (now in a choice of four colors) and mock walnut on door panels, console, and steering wheel. Only 14,139 were built, including 2000 Limited Edition models priced $200 above the regular Landau. Introduced in January, the LE boasted white paint and matching leather interior, plus a Rose Beige vinyl top and knock-off-style wire wheel covers (not to be confused with the Sport Roadster's genuine wire wheels). In keeping with the more international image Ford began portraying this year, the Limited Edition bowed in Monaco. Grace Kelly was on hand, hence this model came to be called the "Princess Grace" T-Bird.

As noted, Ford saved its most exciting developments for mid-season. Starting with Falcon, a graceful semi-fastback two-door hardtop arrived in Futura and new Futura Sprint form, the latter also is-

This page: The two-door '63 Galaxie 500/XL Club Victoria (top left) utilized the Thunderbird-style squared-off roofline. At 3670 pounds, it weighed exactly as much as the slantback XL and cost the same, but even though it was around for the full model year, output came in a bit lower: 29,713 units. The 500/XL Sunliner, which topped the XL price ladder at $3518, attracted 18,551 orders. As in 1962, the Thunderbird was offered in four models. The convertible (center) was falling in favor, with only 5913 built for the model year, even though the $4912 price tag was only $24 higher. As always, the hardtop (bottom) was the favorite Bird, with 42,806 produced for '63, and the least expensive: $4445. Opposite page: The operation of the T-Bird's top, seen here on a Sports Roadster, had since 1959 been based on the technology (somewhat simplified) of the 1957-59 Ford retractable.

After a successful first year, Fairlane charged into 1963 with four new models, now nine, and two new body styles. One of the newcomers was the Fairlane 500 Sports Coupe (above), a true hardtop. It sold at $2504; 28,268 were built. The price-leader $2154 Fairlane two-door sedan (below) saw 28,984 produced.

sued as a convertible. Besides bucket seats, Sprints came with four-speed floorshift manual transmission, dash-mounted tachometer—and the dull 170-cid six. But they could be made into honest performance machines with the 164-horsepower Challenger 260 V-8, a first-time Falcon option.

Car Life magazine termed the V-8 Sprint "Le Petite Sport," noting that its power-to-weight ratio was only 21 lbs/bhp, versus 31.4 for six-cylinder models. The editors termed the 260 "a willing engine. If it seems unaware of the choking restrictions of its single two-barrel

carburetor, it is because of somewhat generous valve sizes and relatively clean intake and exhaust designs. Its ability to readily surpass the 5000-rpm redline would have one believe it is fitted with mechanical lifters, but, of course, it isn't. The engine is completely devoid of fussiness, and exhibits a surprising amount of torque from rather ridiculous rpm levels. [It's] much happier in Falcon surroundings than it ever seemed to be in the Fairlane...." As proof, *CL's* four-speed test car recorded 0-60 mph in 12 seconds, the quarter-mile in 18 seconds at 75 mph, and a top speed of 105 mph.

As agile as its name, the Sprint had all the makings of a potential rally winner. Ford knew it, and sent a trio of specially modified hardtops to contest this year's Monte Carlo Rally. Prepared by the Holman & Moody works of stock-car-racing fame, each landed with a tuned, 260-bhp 260, close-ratio four-speed gearbox, ab-

breviated Galaxie rear axle with 4.51:1 final drive, heavy-duty suspension, and big Bendix/Dunlop front-disc brakes. Signed up to drive were Bo Ljungfeldt/Gunnar Haggbom, Anne Hall/Margaret McKenzie, and Peter Jopp/Trant Jarman. The results were mixed. Veteran Erik Carlsson was the outright winner in his two-stroke Saab 96, and the Hall/McKenzie team didn't even finish. But for the first time in the Monte's 32 years, one car won all the special stages: the Ljungfeldt/Haggbom Sprint. Icing the cake, Jopp/Jarman won the big-engine class and finished 35th overall, eight spots ahead of their teammates.

Ford reaped a lot of "Total Performance" publicity from this and other Falcon successes in 1963. For example, a factory-sponsored production car won the manufacturer's trophy in this year's Shell 4000 Trans-Canada Rally, though a Chevy II was the overall winner.

Fairlane kept pace for excitement with a new small-block option of its own. A bore increase to 4.00 inches took the 260 to 289 cubic inches, good for 271 bhp with four-barrel carb and 11:1 compression. (A 195-bhp 289 replaced the 260 as the base Galaxie V-8 at mid-year.) It was just the thing for the new hardtop Sports Coupe, which was decked out with the expected center console and deluxe wheel covers with simulated knock-off spinners.

The first evidence of Ford's announced intention to get back in the NASCAR wars appeared for 1963½ in the form of a new "slantback" Galaxie 500 Sports Hardtop. Offered in standard and XL guise, it sat about an inch lower than its square-top counterpart thanks to

a shallower greenhouse with sloped C-pillars and a smallish backlight. If not as smooth as the old Starliner, it was a step in the right direction for stock-car racing, and Ford proved it by turning in one of its best NASCAR seasons to date. Commencing with Dan Gurney's win at the Riverside 500 in January, the big Fords were in the winner's circle at every 500-mile event and took 23 Grand Nationals in all. Just as important to Ford, the XL was a winner in the sales race, seeing 12,596 square-roof four-door hardtops, 29,713 two-doors, and 18,551 convertibles. Helped by prices identical to those of the box-topped coupes, the new slantbacks were the most popular of all: exactly 33,870 XLs, plus 100,500 Galaxie 500s.

Matching competitors' moves in the big-inch wars, Ford again bored its FE-Series block, this time by 0.10-inch, bringing the 406 up to 427 cid. Output with single four-barrel carb was 410 bhp, and a new twin four-barrel setup with an aluminum intake manifold pushed that up to 425, both on tight 11.6:1 compression. Price was discouraging—the 410 cost $405 additional—but a beefed-up chassis and suspension and bigger brakes and tires were included. A four-speed manual transmission, first offered as a late 1961 option, was a mandatory extra with either version.

Ford also cooked up a limited-production 427 for the dragstrip, with 12:1 compression and a nominal 425 bhp, the latter mainly to satisfy the rulebook. By now, lighter mid-size cars were starting to rule in quarter-mile competition, but Ford tried to keep its big cars competitive by offering an S/S kit for NHRA's Super/Stock class, with fiberglass body panels and other changes that lightened front ends by some 160 pounds. The factory also turned out a handful of S/S cars with stripped interiors. Still, the smaller Plymouths and Dodges were faster, and the typical XL rolled out the door with a 390 and automatic.

The same applied to the interesting Thunderbird Sports Roadster, which saw a mere 455 copies in this, its second and final year. Of those, only 37 were equipped with the high-output M-Series 390—a modern rarity indeed.

Actually, personal-luxury buyers as a whole were moving away from convertibles, and it's significant that Buick offered its new-for-'63 T-Bird fighter, the Riviera, only as a hardtop. Ford had built 10,516 of the '61 T-Bird ragtops, 7030 of the conventional '62s, and now just 5913 of the '63s. To some extent, this reflected increased buyer preference for air conditioning and the greater safety and practi-

Of the 343,887 Fairlanes built for 1963, 104,175 were the $2304 Fairlane 500 four-door sedan (above). The top-line 500s sported flashier side moldings, chromed door window frames, and upgraded interiors. The three station wagons were new, the $2781 Country Squire (below) being the priciest; only 7983 were built.

cality of closed bodies, but price was also a factor. Convertible Birds in this period cost some $500 more than hardtops, with most of the difference accounted for by the complex top-folding arrangement. Sales would bounce back a bit with the advent of 1964's fourth generation, only to decline over the next two years. With the fifth-generation design of 1967, the convertible Bird would be gone. It hasn't reappeared since, but there must be many Bird lovers who hope that Ford will yet revive it.

Total Performance of another sort was evident in this year's Ford truck line.

The three-quarter-ton F-250 pickup, a beefed-up F-100, was offered as a 4×2 or a 4×4. This 4×4 Styleside (top), of which 1835 were built, has the separate cargo box. Wearing a new grille for '63, the F-100 pickups could be ordered as a fendered Flareside or smooth-flanked Styleside with integral or separate cargo box. This $2019 F-100 (center) has the former. The '63 Ranchero (bottom) listed at $1898, but the DeLuxe Trim Package cost about $100 extra. Of the 18,533 units built, 6315 got the upper-level trim.

It was the broadest ever, with more than 1000 individual models. The big news was the N-Series, a group of short-hood, high-rise conventionals with a basic cab derived from the familiar F-Series design but set 16.5 inches further forward. Aimed at budget-minded operators seeking a lower-cost alternative to the H-Series high-tilt cabovers, the Ns comprised 500/600 medium-heavies on wheelbases of 121, 132, and 144 inches; 700/750 heavies on spans of 121, 163, 181, and (750 only) 212 inches; and extra-heavy 850/950/1000/1100s' on wheelbases of 134, 146, 158, 181, and 212 inches. Model choices were further multiplied by tandem-axle NT versions of the extra-heavy offerings and a plethora of gasoline and diesel powerplants throughout.

In fact, Ford went in for oil-burners in a big way this season, expanding choices from two to eight. Smallest of these was a new 220-cid inline four (bore and stroke: 3.94 × 4.52 inches), supplied by Ford of England as an option for upper-series parcel vans, which duly tacked a "0" onto their model designations to become the P-3500/4000/5000. One step up was a derivative six with 330 cid from the same cylinder dimensions, packing 112 bhp and 265 lbs/ft peak torque on 16:1 compression. Billed as the "city-size" diesel, it was a new choice for C- and N-Series mediums, which were called 5000/6000s when so equipped.

Next came six massive Cummins diesels, beginning with a V-6 200 that delivered that many horses and 452 lbs/ft torque from 588 cubic inches (5.50 × 4.125-inch bore and stroke) and 17:1 compression. A new alternative in lighter H-Series rigs, it also powered Ford's first compression-ignition conventionals: heavy-duty F-950/1000/1100-D single-axles and T-850/950-D tandems. Designations for other medium and heavy diesels also tacked on the suffix "D." The big 672- and 743-cid V-8 "smokers" were still around, and there was a third choice in the Cummins V-8 265, a 785-incher derived from the V-6 200 and also named for its horsepower but belting out 685 lbs/ft torque. One step below was a pair of straight sixes, the Cummins NH 220 and 250, both similar to the existing NH 180. The 250 was an 855-cid biggie (5.50 × 6.00-inch bore and stroke) that also churned out 685 lbs/ft, albeit on 14.9:1 compression. The NH 250 and V-8 265 were also available in the H-Series, but this year's high-tilt offerings shrank to four as Ford deep-sixed a quartet of less popular versions.

Elsewhere, both the 302 and 332 heavy-duty gas V-8s were again offered with four-barrel carbs, albeit as an option, and gasoline sixes ran slightly lower compression for a bit better mileage. GVW ratings were upped on some medium and heavy F-, C-, T-, and CT-Series models, and a one-ton "Heavy Duty" payload package arrived as a new Econoline option. The latter brought maximum

Styling of the '63 Econoline pickup (top left) was unchanged, but the interior was upgraded a bit and five-leaf rear springs were new. At $1890, it cost $8 less than a Ranchero. The $2069 Econoline van (top right) weighed 2568 pounds. For '63, 48,620 regular Econoline vans were built, plus 11,394 pickups. Two more '63 trucks: the medium-duty F-600, here with the 12-foot stake-bed chassis and Custom Cab (above), and the 158-inch-wheelbase HT-950-D tractor (above right), now available with an 855-cid Cummins diesel.

GVW to 4850 pounds via heavier front and rear axles and a reinforced under-body structure. Naturally, the 170-cid six was also included. Still in the light-duty vein, Econoline vans acquired deeper roof grooving for improved body rigidity, and all models benefitted from wider (5.5-inch) standard wheels and matching tires, faster steering, slightly reduced turn diameter, five-leaf rear springs, and foam-backed driver's seats. Chrome bumpers and narrow-band whitewall tires (now 7.00 × 14s) remained Econoline extras, as did a Custom Cab package comprising chrome hubcaps, interior coat hook, additional sound insulation and, on vans, cargo-area headliner. Though badged as a Falcon now, this year's Econoline Station Bus was enhanced by the addition of a re-tracting side step for easier cargo-bay access. There were also two new offshoots: the Window Van, with fixed instead of opening rear side glass, and the Display

Van, really the blank-side delivery model with rear glass on the starboard side only.

This year's compact Ranchero and Falcon Sedan Delivery saw no significant changes beyond those made to passenger Falcons, but it's interesting to note that the midyear 260 V-8 option was also listed for these commercials, though installations were probably not too numerous. Finally, light- and medium-duty F-Series conventionals got their annual grille change, this one a simplified flat-face affair bearing four horizontal bars split vertically into five segments. Head-lights remained at the extreme ends, just outboard of larger square parking lights.

Besides observing two major birthdays this year, Ford Motor Company installed a new president on May 1. He was Arjay Miller, one of the original "Whiz Kids," who replaced John Dykstra to become only the seventh president in the company's 60-year history. At the end of the month, on Memorial Day, British driver Jim Clark hustled one of Ford's new bantamweight, mid-engine V-8 Indy racers to a second-place finish at the annual 500-mile classic. It was an impressive feat that underscored Ford's aggressive new commitment to racing and the lessons to be learned from it, the latter presumably going to improve Dearborn's road cars.

Another sign of that commitment was the attempt Ford made this year to

buy Ferrari, the great Italian sports-car maker. The bid was doomed by founder Enzo Ferrari, who wouldn't hear of selling out, least of all to Americans. Not that he needed to. Though small, his firm was on pretty solid financial ground at the time. What attracted Ford, of course, was Ferrari's enormous competition experience and lengthening victory record in Formula 1 and long-distance GT events, areas where Ford wanted to compete on equal terms with the best in the world. As Ferrari's owner, Ford evidently thought it could slap blue ovals onto the appropriate hardware, take trophies won back to Dearborn, and reap the publicity and sales benefits. But Enzo wasn't about to share his glory with anyone, and his refusal to sell irked Henry Ford II. Ford's chairman promptly sought revenge by ordering an all-out assault on Ferrari, with victory in the prestigious 24 Hours of Le Mans road race the principal focus.

As a company, Ford had always been quite conscious of history and its place in it, old Henry notwithstanding. On November 18, the firm demonstrated this anew by donating its entire historical film collection to the National Archives in Washington. Just four days later, history reeled: President John F. Kennedy was dead, assassinated while riding through the streets of Dallas in his Lincoln Continental limousine. America would never be quite the same again.

1964

Dearborn's biggest success of the decade arrived this year with the Mustang ponycar. Reflecting another of Lee Iacocca's favorite marketing schemes, it was an early offering for model year 1965, and is thus covered in the next section.

But Ford Division had lots to show for '64 proper: a brand-new Thunderbird, thoroughly revamped big cars, and facelifted Falcons and Fairlanes. All this coupled with fairly stable prices to make for a very good year: production up by well over 60,000 units to a bit over 1,594,000. But Chevy did considerably better, topping the two-million mark for the third straight model year and up more than 160,000 over 1963. The gap with Ford was better than 700,000, but Mustang would close that up substantially for '65.

Though you wouldn't think it from looking at them, the full-size 1961-63 Fords used the same inner body and pe-

rimeter chassis introduced for 1960. Ford now reskinned this platform one last time, achieving a distinctive if rather busy look compared with earlier models. Highlights included a flat-faced horizontal-bar grille with three distinct vertical peaks, more rounded front sheetmetal, a longer rear deck, busier back panel, and heavily sculptured bodysides with long, convex front-fender "pontoons" running back to mid-body.

No major changes occurred in big-Ford drivetrain specs or availability. Model choices were also basically as before, but the previous Galaxie and 300 names were replaced at the bottom of the

line by Custom and Custom 500. Galaxie 500 and its XL subseries continued at the top. Interiors were still dominated by the basic '63 dash with its simple, square-hood instrument cluster, but new thin-shell bucket seats did a better job of holding XL occupants in place—which was welcome. According to *Mechanix Illustrated*'s veteran tester, Tom McCahill, this year's XL cornered "like a snake in a rat hole."

The big '64 Ford may not seem historically significant—just a five-year-old design set to be phased out—but it's perfect for collectors. Author Tim Howley declared in *Special Interest Autos* magazine

that it "stands quite alone as the ultimate Total Performance Ford." *Motor Trend* evidently agreed, for the magazine bestowed its "Car of the Year Award" on the entire '64 Ford line "for engineering advancement based on high-performance testing in open competition." The sportier full-sizers delivered on the implied promises of the division's "Total Performance" ad theme as much as any '64 Ford. Indeed, *MT* found this year's XL "a big solid, comfortable family car, yet still slanted toward the sporty set." Howley also noted that this year's "styling had been carefully dictated by the aerodynamics of racing. Even the body panels

were designed to be lighter than the '63s."

As before, there were three 500/XLs: convertible and two- and four-door hardtops, the latter now with the slantback roofline from 1963½. Production totaled 58,306 two-doors, 15,169 convertibles, and 14,661 four-doors. Thanks to a strong quality-control effort begun in 1961, XLs and other big Fords wore like iron. Observed Howley: "All too many of them were driven for 10 years or 200,000 miles, and they just don't show their age. Rare is the low-mileage '64 XL, as this was not the kind of car you bought to put away in your garage." Economy was hardly impressive, but performance defi-

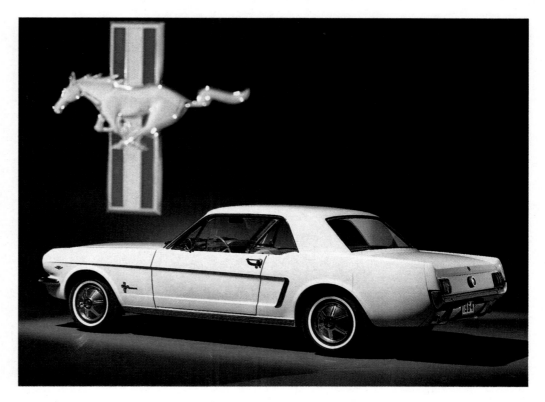

The Mustang made a splashy debut on April 17, 1964, but as far as Ford was concerned its new "ponycar," as it came to be called, was a '65. However, since there were subtle differences between the early Mustangs and the "proper" '65s, enthusiasts have for a long time referred to the those built before the fall of '64 as 1964½ models. The chief ingredients that went into the making of America's first ponycar were compact size, long-hood/short-deck proportions, sporty styling, bucket-seat interior, and an incredibly long list of options that allowed buyers to tailor their Mustang to anything from mild to hot or relatively conservative to overtly aggressive. Riding a 108-inch wheelbase, the Mustang carried a base price of $2368 with the standard six. The galloping pony, of course, symbolized the freedom of America's wide-open spaces.

For 1964, the junior-year Fairlane received a moderate freshening-up. Featured were a revised grille, new side trim that incorporated a fake air scoop, revised taillights and rear trim, plus rounded, finless rear fenders. That wasn't enough to stop output from tumbling to 277,586 units, although that was still respectable. The $2317 Fairlane 500 four-door (top and center) was still the best seller: 88,919 built. The $2612 Custom Ranch Wagon (bottom) found 24,962 customers. Both cars wear front fender V-8 badges.

nitely was. In a contemporary comparison test, a 390-equipped XL did 0-60 mph in 9.3 seconds, which was fair going, while a 427 clocked it in 7.4 seconds—remarkable for a two-ton luxury liner.

While the lighter and more competitive Fairlanes now carried Ford's drag-racing colors, the big cars continued doing well on NASCAR's senior-division Grand National stock-car circuit. Chrysler Corporation revived its fabled hemi-head V-8 for the '64 campaign, planning to beat back any Ford or GM threat. Ford cried foul—if the Hemi was legal, Ford ought to be allowed to run its new semi-experimental overhead-cam 427. Not quite, said NASCAR, but the production pushrod 427 could use a high-rise manifold and a higher rev limit, both of which Ford quickly attended to. The Hemis grabbed the limelight as Plymouths won the Daytona 500, the World 600 at Charlotte, and finished 1-2-3 at the Darlington 500. But when the smoke cleared, Ford had 30 NASCAR victories.

Dearborn's continuing assault on the Indy 500 was an equally glamorous sign of its commitment to performance "testing" in open competition. Alas, 1964 brought another near-miss at the Brickyard, this time with Roger Ward finishing second with a mid-V-8 Ford Indy racer. Were the traditional Offys impossible to unseat? Not at all, as Ford would prove the very next year.

Falcon entered its fifth year with new lower-body sheetmetal and an extra engine option, the 116-horsepower 200-cubic-inch "Special Six" introduced in mid-'63 as base Fairlane power (replacing the 170 there, though that six remained optional for '64 Falcons, which continued with a standard 144). Even pointier front fenders flanked a thrust-forward grille, bumpers were bulkier, bodysides took on prominent convex contouring and full-length character lines, and rear ends were squared up. The result was not altogether pretty; hardtops and convertibles probably looked best. The sporty Sprint hardtop saw more than 3000 additional copies this year, 13,830 in all, but the convertible dropped from 4602 to 4278 and would fall even further for '65. Too bad, because the Fairlane's light and lively 289 small-block was newly available at extra cost, making these the fastest Falcons ever.

No fewer than eight Falcon teams contested this year's Monte Carlo Rally, and the results were better than the car's debut outing the year before. New competition from Plymouth's V-8 Valiant prompted Ford to split its entries, half in the under-2500cc class, the remainder in the over-2500cc category. The latter ran tuned, 285-bhp 289 V-8s (two two-barrel carbs, 10:1 compression) and used more lightweight body components than the '63 factory cars, but the cars were otherwise similar. The Austin Mini-Cooper S of Paddy Hopkirk/Harry Liddon came home first, due partly to rules changes that favored small-displacement machines (less than 1.3 liters). But Bo Ljungfeldt was again fastest on all the timed stages (though he tied one with Hopkirk) and finished second overall and first in the upper division. Anne Hall capped the proceedings by taking the GT class. Rally rulemakers then banned the Sprints, but the point had been made: The Falcon was as much a "Total Performance" car as any Ford.

Fairlane was freshened up by being shorn of its tiny fins and adorned with oversize bull's-eye taillamps. Rear flanks picked up barrel-like sculptures terminating in chrome-capped, raked-forward dummy scoops; a large bulge appeared in the hood; and the grille insert was a bit more complicated. Model offerings stayed the same. Sales eased, but Ford's mid-size was still generating healthy sales volume of some 200,000 units a year.

To lead its quarter-mile assault against the mid-size Plymouths and Dodges, Ford trotted out the mid-year Thunderbolt, a factory drag car superficially resembling the workaday Fairlane two-door. According to Phil Hall in *Fearsome Fords*, some 54 were built by Dearborn Steel Tubing, then one of Ford's

The '64 Thunderbird boasted all-new styling, although there was a hint of the 1961-63 "projectile-look" up front. Gone, however, were the smooth sides, replaced by sharp sculpturing; new were the finless rear fenders and wide rectangular taillights. Of the three models, the favorite was the $4486 hardtop (below), of which 60,552 were produced. The $4953 convertible (top) enjoyed a rise in popularity as 9198 were called for. Although the Sports Roadster was gone, some '64s were fitted with its streamlined tonneau (right).

contractors for special projects like this. Thunderbolt's heart was a fortified "High Riser" version of the already potent 427, essentially the latest NASCAR engine, with stratospheric 12.7:1 compression, two four-barrel Holley carbs on an aluminum high-rise intake manifold, plus high-rise heads, machined combustion chambers, domed pistons, and high-lift cam. A modified Galaxie driveshaft mated to a Detroit "Locker" differential. Two transmissions were available: a very-heavy-duty four-speed with Hurst linkage or three-speed automatic.

The big-block V-8 was physically too large for the Fairlane engine compartment, so the stock front suspension and much of the 427 exhaust system had to be modified and/or custom-fabricated for the Thunderbolt. Weight was naturally removed wherever possible: fiberglass hood, front fenders, and doors; gutted interior; Plexiglas rear and side windows.

As Hall points out, the amazing thing about the Thunderbolt was that "you could order [it] through your dealer, race ready, for about $3900. Considering what you got, it was stealing." Of course, few knew about it except those who wanted to put Ford on the National Hot Rod Association throne. Their efforts were generally successful, though the automatic proved a handicap against the four-speed Mopars. Highlighting the

year was Butch Leal's Super/Stock class win at the Labor Day NHRA Nationals at Indianapolis Raceway Park. In what some said was the closest competition in memory, his Thunderbolt blasted through the quarter-mile traps in just 11.76 seconds at 122.78 mph. With this and other successes, Ford won the NHRA Manufacturer's Cup.

By contrast, this year's new fourth-generation Thunderbird made absolutely no gesture toward "Total Performance." The Sports Roadster was gone (though some dealers fitted a slightly restyled tonneau and wire wheels to 45-50 standard '64 convertibles). So was the M-Series engine. The plain 390 V-8 was again the only powerplant listed, with the same 300 bhp it had three years earlier. As before, it was teamed with only Cruise-O-Matic. Power steering and brakes were still standard, too, but power windows remained optional (with hand-cranked ventpanes).

Planning for the third-series four-seater evidently took note of the competitive challenge from Buick's Riviera, which Ford knew about before GM launched it for '63. Thus arrived completely new sheetmetal with busy bodyside sculpturing, a drop-center rear deck leading to wide rectangular taillights in a large twin-loop bumper, bulged hood, and a high, thrust-forward bumper/grille flanked by elliptical scallops housing the

The '64 Ford was now in the fifth—and final—year on the 1960 basic body and chassis. A major reskinning, however, largely disguised that fact. Up front, a full-width grille with three prominent vertical "vees" gave the car an aggressive stance, while new bodyside sculpturing, particularly a "bullet" flowing backward from the headlights, provided an illusion of length. Two series were offered, the low-buck Custom, with a more upmarket 500 subseries, plus the Galaxie 500, with the sportier XL subseries. The $3233 500/XL hardtop coupe was driven home by 58,306 customers.

headlamps. Wheelbase remained at 113 inches, and ride height stayed about the same despite a switch to low-profile 15-inch tires (replacing taller 14-inchers), the first such application on a non-compact.

Predictably, the '64 Bird put even more emphasis on luxury and refinement. For example, an automatic parking-brake release was now standard, as was backrest rake adjustment for the front-passenger seat, which along with the driver's chair adopted a "thin-shell" design (fiberglass frame with applied cushions) similar to that of this year's big XLs. The hardtop roofline retained its formal air but now incorporated "Silent-Flo," one of the first windows-up ventilation systems. Flicking a console-mounted lever activated a servo that opened a full-width vent beneath the backlight to pull

The '64 Ford four-door hardtop forsook its squared-off '63 roofline in favor of a semi-fastback look. Offered as a $2750 Galaxie 500 (right) or a sportier 500/XL at $3298, the plainer 500 won the sales derby by more than three to one: 49,242 units to 14,661. Note the lack of the medallion on the rear fenders. At $3495, the 500/XL Sunliner (bottom left) was the most expensive '64 big Ford, but it attracted 15,169 orders anyway. The optional 390 V-8 (bottom right), which was noted by front fender crossed-flag badges, came in 300 and 330 horsepower versions.

air through the car from the cowl into the low-pressure area behind.

Vying for attention with the new Bird's exterior was a jazzy cockpit dominated by a dash that looked like something out of "Buck Rogers." No serious driver liked the ornate speedometer with its red-banded drum pointer, or the chrome-trimmed minor gauges, or the plethora of highly styled buttons, knobs, and levers. But Ford would have the more straightforward Mustang for enthusiasts; Thunderbird buyers simply loved their cars. Despite strong rivalry from the elegantly muscular Riviera, the '64 broke the Thunderbird's 1960 sales record with 92,465 units, a mark that wouldn't be bettered until 1977. The '65 sold 74,972 copies; the '66 scored 69,176. No three-year generation did better until 1977-79.

Car Life said these Birds were "Begadgeted and bedazzling," which was a fair description, but there was more to them than that. The magazine thought its '65 Landau near-ideal for high-speed motoring: "So quiet and effortless was the running that the . . . speedometer too often crept well past the 80-mph mark. . . . This is precisely the type of service for which the Thunderbird was designed— covering vast distances between two points in the shortest legal time with the least extraneous intrusions upon the passenger's serenity." The magazine's test car ran 0-60 mph in 10.3 seconds, did 115 mph maximum, and returned 13-16 miles per gallon.

Road & Track, long a champion of sports cars and small imported sedans, was less sanguine than its then-sister publication, saying the '65 Thunderbird

had "more symbolism than stature. Only the blessedly ignorant view it as anything more than what it is: a luxury-class car for those who want to present a dashing sort of image, who worry about spreading girth and stiffening arteries, and who couldn't care less about taste." But it misrepresents *R&T* to quote out of context. "Even when viewed in that light," the editors continued, "the Thunderbird must be admired. It is extremely well done for its purpose. Its roofline, its bucket seats, and console have inspired dozens of lesser imitations which, by their very imitation, proved the Bird a better beast."

All '64 Fords were better in a more serious way: safety. Front-seat lap belts were standardized effective with January production, and rear belts were added to no-cost equipment the following month. The new Thunderbird encouraged you to buckle up via a standard dashboard warning light that glowered for a few seconds after starting up. Really concerned Bird buyers could plump for a "Safety-Convenience" package with four-way hazard flashers—blinking taillamps and parking lights, not mandatory then but a good idea for roadside emergencies—plus warning lights for inoperative flashers, door open, and low fuel. Another predictive feature lurked within the new Bird's

right front seat: an integrated headrest. Making up the top third of the backrest, it extended on two slim poles when the seatback was reclined. Though this aimed more at comfort than safety, one wonders whether it didn't inspire the more "anatomically correct" head restraints legislated for post-1967 cars.

Buyers applauded another round of reduced-maintenance measures for all '64 Fords, Dearborn continuing its recent efforts to make car ownership less expensive and bothersome. Chassis lubrication was now needed only once every three years or at 100,000-mile intervals, whichever applied, and front wheel bearings were good for 24,000-mile stints. The first fruits of advancing electronics technology showed up in a transistorized ignition system that was newly optional for some models. This was claimed to extend the life of spark plugs and points to 50,000 miles by shortening voltage-rise time and delivering higher plug voltage.

After the major changes for '63, Ford's truck team relaxed a little on this year's line. There were, however, significant substitutions on the engine chart. First, the old Y-Block gasoline V-8s gave way to fortified truck versions of the FE-Series passenger-car design labelled FT-Series. There were three sizes: 330, 361,

Opposite page: Falcon received a lower-body reskinning for '64, with bulkier lines and full-length bodyside sculpturing intended to make it look more "important." While not a big seller, the Futura Sprint returned for '64. The $2436 hardtop (top) and $2671 convertible (bottom) found 13,830 and 4278 customers. This page: In addition to the bucket seats and V-8, wire wheel covers were standard on the Sprint (top left). The base Falcon two-door (top right) cost $1996; 36,441 were built. Falcon won the GT class in the '64 Monte Carlo Rally (above). The $2047 Ranchero (above right) saw '64 output skid 50 percent to 9916 units.

and 391 cid. All ran 7.6:1 compression and two-barrel carbs except the 391, which had a single four-pot carb. Respective bhp numbers were 186, 203, and 235; torque ratings were 186, 330, and 372 pounds/ feet. The 330 was thus considered a me-dium-duty mill, the others heavy-duty. Also shared by all were high-durability internal features including forged-steel crankshaft, long-skirt pistons, stress-re-lieved heads with "Rotocoil" exhaust-valve rotators, pyramidal con-rod big ends, and stronger, twin-strand timing chains. Applications comprised the 600, 700, and 800 chassis among F- and T-Se-ries conventionals, high-tilt N-Series, low-cabover C- and CT-Series, and the B-Series school-bus platform. Incidentally, that 361 was basically the same engine originally developed for the Edsel—more proof that Ford's E-car experiment was far from a total loss.

Remaining engine changes involved more economical versions of the big Cummins diesels for heavy and super-

heavy models. The V6 200 thus gave way to a slightly less powerful V6E 195, the V8 265 was replaced by a V8E 235 (30 fewer horses), and the six-cylinder NHE 225 took over for the basically similar NH 250.

Other truck news concerned the usual GVW shuffles and the yearly cos-metic surgery for light- and medium-duty F-Series conventionals. The latter was more involved than usual. Besides a simple change of grille inserts—a more attractive affair comprising two rows of four rectangles—nearly all F-, T- and N-Series conventionals got inch-higher rooflines for increased headroom. Also not immediately apparent, Styleside pick-ups had redesigned frame-mounted cargo boxes (still fully independent from the cab) with vertical (instead of round) taillamps, sturdier double-wall construc-tion, and the industry's first one-handle tailgate latch. Rear wheel housings were flat-topped for greater utility, but interi-or box dimensions weren't vastly differ-ent (now 98.7 × 70.0 × 19.3 inches).

Additionally, long-wheelbase F-100 and 250 pickups rode a new 128-inch span (up six inches) selected to accommodate camper shells, then fast-rising in popu-larity. Also catering to the growing re-creational market, these same models could be ordered for the first time with the big 262 gas six, a good compromise between six-cylinder thrift and V-8 lug-ging power for the heavier loads of the typical camper-equipped pickup.

Comfort and convenience weren't overlooked. Factory air conditioning was

a new option for all light-duty models as well as sleeper-cab COEs, while F-100/ 250s received "deep-cushioned" seat-backs and 26 pounds of sound insulation. The Econoline's optional automatic transmission changed from two-speed Fordomatic to the new lightweight, aluminum-case C4 version of three-speed Cruise-O-Matic, a change that also affected certain Fairlanes and big-Ford passenger cars. Econolines were also nicer to live with, gaining color-keyed in-terior trim, cab headliners, locking glove-box, and spare tire. The basic Econoline van *sans* side windows and cargo doors was renamed Panel Van and marketed as a distinct model separate from the Win-dow/Display vans and the Falcon-badged Station Bus and Club Wagons.

The two Falcon-based commercials were naturally modified in step with this year's passenger compacts. Interestingly, the Ranchero gained no cargo space from the lengthier new rear-end sheetmetal, but the Falcon Sedan Delivery did, its floor length and maximum load volume going up slightly to 85.4 inches and 78 cubic feet, respectively (also true for Fal-con wagons, of course). Rated payload was now 690 pounds.

Ford just couldn't seem to beat Chevy in truck production no matter how hard it tried, and 1964 was no excep-tion. Though Dearborn built 33,855 more units for the model year—458,583 in all—GM's standard-bearer lengthened its lead by nearly 6800 units to 65,208. Ford would have its day, but not for an-other six years.

Detroit built some 10 million cars for model year 1965, its highest one-year total in a decade and its greatest single year ever. Dearborn accounted for over 2.5 million of them, but the ghost of F.C. Reith might have commented that Ford Division was still too dominant at close to 2.2 million. Mercury's production was only some 350,000, Lincoln's a mere 45,000.

If this lopsided situation led Dearborn planners to wonder over the wisdom of abandoning a five-division structure back in 1959, developments were about to confirm their decision. Harder times were at hand. A generation of young people would soon vanish from the market, their outlook altered by an unpopular war. And with them would vanish the "muscle cars" and the "ponycars" starting to make sales history. The government would begin demanding safety and emission equipment, contributing to inflation-fed price escalation. And a new threat of unprecedented proportions was already on the horizon: Japan, Inc.

Yet none of this loomed large in 1965. True, a Senate subcommittee chaired by Connecticut's Abraham Ribicoff began hearings into auto safety this year, prompted partly by continuing at-

tacks on the design of Chevy's rear-engine Corvair compact by one Ralph Nader, a zealous young lawyer who promoted himself as a "consumer advocate." But Nader hadn't quite finished writing *Unsafe at Any Speed* in 1965. Moreover, "The Great Society" was at hand under newly elected President Lyndon Baines Johnson, Toyota and Nissan were still unfamiliar foundlings as far as America was concerned, gas cost 30 cents a gallon, the Viet Nam conflict was still comfortably distant for much of the populace, and Watergate was just the name of a new hotel in Washington, D.C. And lest we forget, trucks sold in record numbers in 1965: over 1.5 million of them. More than a third were Fords. Unhappily for Dearborn, even more were Chevrolets.

Without question, 1965's most significant automotive story was the phenomenal success of Ford's Mustang, the

first of the new sporty compacts that were quickly dubbed "ponycars" in its honor (by *Car Life* magazine). Introduced at the New York World's Fair on April 17, 1964, it made more news than Barry Goldwater's sewing up the Republican Presidential nomination. America went wild over this affordable new personal car with lithe, long-hood/short-deck proportions. Ford had projected first-year sales of 100,000 units, but the model-year total (through August 1965) was an

One of the most popular convertibles ever built was the '65 Mustang. Although blessed with a long model year (which included the "1964½" model), output was a sensational 101,945 units. But at a very affordable $2614, perhaps that's not too surprising. The ragtop, which rode a 108-inch wheelbase like all Mustangs, weighed a reasonable 2789 pounds, and the 260 V-8 added only a modest $75 to the sticker price.

astounding 680,989. A legend had been born. And its base price was only $2368 f.o.b. Detroit.

The Mustang itself was born during 1961 in meetings of the Fairlane Group, an informal eight-man executive committee that met regularly at Dearborn's Fairlane Inn under the aegis of Ford Division chief Lee Iacocca. Their purpose was to explore a new youth-oriented car Iacocca wanted in order to capitalize on growing buyer interest in bucket-seat compacts with four-on-the-floor. Working under project code T-5, the group considered a revival of the 1955-57 Thunderbird (called "XT-Bird") as well as a production version of the experimental Mustang I, a light, open, mid-engine design of Triumph/MG dimensions with all-independent suspension and German Ford V-4 power. But both were rejected and for the same reason: only two seats. The team shrewdly realized that such a car would have limited sales appeal—none for young couples with children, or anybody else who occasionally needed a back seat. The decision was thus made to go with a so-called "median sports car," a four-seat proposal that established the new model's basic package. Now, all the stylists had to do was develop an appropriate look for it.

They produced scores of proposals beginning in late '61. The one that ultimately impressed Iacocca was a white-painted full-size clay model dubbed Cougar. It had been created by Joe Oros, Gale Halderman, and L. David Ash of the Ford Division studio, one of several teams competing in an intramural design contest Iacocca had set up. Cougar was a low, sleek hardtop with lines quite close to those of the eventual production car. Evolved from it for "testing the waters" purposes was a running prototype called Mustang II, with slightly exaggerated styling that hinted at the forthcoming production model without being too explicit. By the time it was first shown, at the United States Grand Prix in Watkins Glen in autumn 1963, the production model was largely locked up. All indications were that it would meet Iacocca's goals: 2500-pound curb weight, a base price of not more than a dollar a pound, and looks that said "young."

The Mustang was mainly a body engineering project, as Iacocca had directed that running gear and chassis components be off-the-shelf Falcon and Fairlane bits to hold down development costs, and thus retail price. At 181.6 inches overall, the Mustang was as long as a '64 Falcon, but its 108-inch wheelbase was 1.5 inches shorter. Hardtop coupe and convertible body styles were designed to accommodate the 170-cubic-inch Falcon six as standard and the efficient 260-cid Fairlane V-8 as an option. Additional no-cost features would include three-speed manual gearbox with floorshift, full wheel covers, padded dash, bucket seats, full carpeting, and color-coordinated interior.

A key part of the Mustang concept was a smorgasbord of low-cost options enabling each buyer to personalize the car to taste. On the menu were self-shift Cruise-O-Matic, four-speed manual, and three-speed-with-overdrive transmissions; three different V-8s; limited-slip differential; "Rally-Pac" gauges (tachometer and clock in a small pod atop the steering column); power and front-disc (late 1965) brakes; power steering; air conditioning (except with the Hi-Performance 271-bhp V-8); center console; deluxe steering wheel; vinyl roof covering; pushbutton radio; knock-off style wheel covers; 14-inch styled steel wheels; and whitewall tires. Then came the *packages*: Visibility Group (mirrors and windshield washers); Accent Group (striping and rocker moldings); Instrument Group (needle gauges and round speedometer); GT Group (disc brakes, driving lights, special trim); and a special handling package for V-8s. Air conditioning was the costliest individual extra at $283, but others were bargain-priced: $31 for the handling package, $58 for disc brakes, $180 for the Instrument Group and Rally-Pac.

The semi-fastback 2+2 (top row) wasn't available until the fall of 1964, but it proved immediately popular. In place of rear-quarter windows, it flaunted stylish side-louvered vents. Back seat room was skimpy, but that was made up for by a fold-down seatback that expanded luggage area. It cost only $35 less than the ragtop, but output nonetheless reached 77,079 units. As for the later '65s, the hardtop (bottom left) was available with the 289 V-8, as was the convertible (below). The wire wheel hubcaps cost $45.80 extra.

Engines determined any Mustang's personality, and offerings changed a bit during the long '65 model run. The smaller V-8 for the debut "1964½" cars was the 164-horsepower 260 small-block. Next came its bored-out 289 derivative (4.00 × 2.87), which had become standard on some mid-'64 full-size Fords and optional for other models save Falcon and T-Bird. This delivered 195 bhp with two-barrel carburetor, 210 with optional four-bar-

rel, or 271 bhp in "Hi-Performance" guise. After September 1964, the 260 was discontinued, a two-barrel 200-bhp 289 became the base V-8, and the four-barrel unit was boosted to 225 bhp. The four-barrel 289 cost $158 extra, the "Hi-Po" engine $276 when combined with the GT Group, $328 when it wasn't.

Developing 0.95 bhp per cubic inch and 312 lbs/ft peak torque at 3400 rpm, the 271 featured high-compression

Given all-new styling for '64, it's not surprising that the '65 Thunderbird didn't look terribly different. However, it could be detected via a new mesh grille with six vertical bars, vertical bars in the taillights, and simulated air vents in the front fenders. The 300-bhp 390 V-8 continued as the only available powerplant, and the 113.2-inch wheelbase remained the same. The Sports Roadster-style tonneau cover, though not often seen, was still available for those who wanted to individualize their T-Bird.

heads, high-lift cam, free-breathing intake manifold, free-flow exhaust, solid valve lifters, low-restriction air cleaner, and chrome-plated valve stems. Dealer parts counters offered even more go: $73 Cobra cam kit (306-degree-duration cam with 0.289-inch lift), $222 cylinder head kit (stock heads with extra-large intake and exhaust valves plus heavy-duty springs and retainers), $343 "engine performance kit" (matched pistons with the cam and head kits). A big-port aluminum manifold cost $120 with single four-barrel carb, $243 with dual four-barrels, and $210 with triple-twos. As a final touch, a dual-point centrifugal distributor was available for $50. Front disc brakes—one-piece Kelsey-Hayes cast-iron units with 9.5-inch-diameter rotors—arrived late in the '65 run at $58 and were worth every penny.

Mustang wasn't exotic, but it looked right. Its most criticized styling elements were the dummy "scoops" ahead of the rear wheel openings, and the shallow, high-set grille. Space utilization was poor for the wheelbase length, with only marginal rear seat room for adults. Some "buff books" also took issue with the driving position, the sloppy standard suspension, and the Falcon-like dash.

But properly optioned, the Mustang was a fiery quarter-horse. *Road & Track* magazine's 271-bhp car did 0-60 mph in 8.5 seconds, the standing quarter-mile in 15.6 seconds at 85 mph, and 120 mph

tops. Its optional handling package (larger front anti-roll bar, 5.90-15 Firestone Super Sports tires, quick-ratio steering) "eliminated the wallow we experienced with previous [plain] Mustangs [and tied] the car to the road much more firmly, so on a fast run the point of one's departure into the boondocks is delayed very considerably.... There is a certain harshness to the ride at low speeds over poor surfaces...a small price to pay for the great improvement in handling and roadholding." In all, said *R&T*, the Hi-Po 289 Mustang was "a big step in the right direction." Other publications agreed. *Motor Trend's* similarly equipped car did 0-60 mph in 7.6 seconds and ran a slightly faster quarter-mile. It was obvious that with the right equipment, a Mustang could be a most satisfying enthusiast's car.

Arriving in autumn 1964 for the start of the formal 1965 model year was a third Mustang body style, a semi-fastback coupe called "2+2." Priced about $200 above the hardtop and mere pocket change below the convertible, it had even less rear legroom but looked slick. Rear quarter windows were omitted for vents that functioned as air extractors for flow-through ventilation. The 2+2 sold over 77,000 for the model year against 102,000 convertibles and—the really stupendous figure—over half a million hardtops.

Arriving about a year behind the Mustang was an even stronger, limited-production offshoot: the memorable

Weighing in at a road-hugging 4588 pounds, the '65 Thunderbird convertible measured 205.4 inches overall, about five inches less than the Galaxie 500 ragtop that weighed 1200 pounds less. As in 1964, it stickered at a lofty $4953. Redesigned wheelcovers were observable, and closer inspection would reveal standard front disc brakes, sequential taillights, and reversible keys. In spite of a record sales year for the industry, output slipped 2352 units to 6846.

Shelby GT-350, a fastback heavily modified at Ford's behest by former race driver Carroll Shelby. One of the few truly dual-purpose American production cars, it was brilliant on the street, superb on the track. The impetus behind it was Ford's desire that Mustang have a solid performance image. And what better way to do that than by taking the Sports Car Club of America's B-Production championship away from Chevy's Corvette?

The GT-350 easily accomplished its mission as Jerry Titus won the B-Production national crown in 1965. Walt Hane won it again—with the same car—in 1966, and another GT-350 owned the class in 1967. The GT-350 was also successful in drag racing. It was, in a word, a thoroughbred. Today it stands as one of the most coveted Fords of all—surely one of the hairiest.

Shelby had been behind the equally memorable Cobra, the light and lovely British A.C. Ace roadster adapted for Ford small-block power (the 260 V-8 ini-

Topping the T-Bird Landau was the '65 Limited Edition Special Landau (above), resplendent in "Ember-Glo" metallic paint with matching wheel covers, parchment vinyl top, wood-look interior trim, and a plaque with the owner's name—all for less than $50 extra. Only 4500 were built. The ineptly reskinned Fairlane 500 Sports Coupe (below) cost $2538—15,141 were sold.

tially, later the 289). Introduced in 1962, it partly realized his dream of building the world's fastest production sports car (ultimately fulfilled in the brutal 427 models). Built in small numbers, the Cobra was never commercially important to Ford, but its numerous race wins had tremendous publicity value. Moreover, it established Shelby as a manufacturer. Indeed, he'd opened a small-scale assembly operation in Venice, California, by 1962. Thus, when Iacocca decided Mustang needed an extra dose of excitement, Shelby was an obvious choice.

His assignment was deceptively simple: make the Mustang a race car capable of winning the national B-Production crown. There were just two requirements. First, it had to be identifiable *as* a Mustang for Ford to realize any sales benefit (SCCA rules tended in this direction anyway). Second, it would have to see at least 100 copies annually to race as a "production" model. The latter prompted Shelby to devise two versions: a street machine, the GT-350S, and a ready-made racer called GT-350R. Both would be available through the network of Ford "performance" dealers Shelby had knit together to sell the Cobra.

Each GT-350 started out as a white fastback supplied from Ford's San Jose,

California, plant with the 271-bhp 289 and Borg-Warner T-10 four-speed transmission. Shelby added a High-Riser manifold, big four-barrel carb, hot cam, and free-flow exhaust headers to boost output to 306 bhp at 6000 rpm. A factory-installed Galaxie rear axle (replacing the stock Falcon unit) was located by trailing arms and brought 10 × 3-inch drum brakes that Shelby fitted with metallic linings. Koni shocks were used all around. The front suspension's forward mounts were relocated and the optional production disc brakes installed, along with quick-ratio steering box, a large anti-sway bar for extra roll stiffness, and a heavy steel-tube brace linking the tops of the front shock towers to eliminate body flex under high cornering loads. Shelby's own 15 × 6 cast-aluminum wheels were shod with Goodyear high-performance tires. The result of all this was near neutral handling instead of the

regular Mustang's strong understeer.

Outside, the standard Mustang's galloping pony was plucked from the grille, the stock steel hood replaced by a fiberglass replica with functional air intake, and the dummy bodyside scoops eliminated. Bright blue racing stripes appeared along the rocker panels, and a pair of much wider stripes rode over the hood, roof, and deck. Inside, the street Shelby was stock Mustang apart from three-inch-wide competition seatbelts, mahogany-rim steering wheel, full instrumentation, and no back seat (the last prompted by the way SCCA defined a production "sports car"). For those who occasionally needed to carry rear riders, a kit was available with a small bench seat that put the spare back in the trunk.

The full-race GT-350R was a more highly tuned S-model set up for the track. Its engine was the same except for special heads—basically the Cobra racing unit

rated at 340-460 bhp. To save weight, the transmission got an aluminum case and the interior was stripped except for a racing bucket seat, rollbar, safety harness, and necessary instruments. A heavy-duty suspension was used along with racing tires. Last but not least was a new fiberglass nose *sans* front bumper, leaving a rudimentary air dam with a large central slot that acted as an air intake for an oil cooler. Some R-models also had four-wheel disc brakes. Curb weight was only 2500 pounds, versus 2800 for the street machine.

The GT-350R was duly homologated for B-Production, which included small-block Corvettes, Sunbeam Tigers, Jaguar E-Types, and the occasional Ferrari or Aston Martin. Out of 562 completed as '65 models, no more than 30 were built to racing specifications. But since all the special parts were available over the counter (per Shelby philosophy), anyone could

turn the street car into the racer—as some did.

Announced at $4547, almost $2000 over the base V-8 Mustang 2+2 and $200 more than a Corvette coupe, the street GT-350 fell in the upper-middle range of the performance market, but came home first on the road. With 0-60 mph times averaging 6.5 seconds, a top speed of 130-135 mph, and race-car handling and braking, it drew rave reviews. Predictably, the first-year Shelby-Mustang would be the purest of the breed, and is thus the most highly prized today. Beginning with the '66s, it was progressively softened into a plusher, more stylized version of the production Mustang, something completely different from Shelby's original concept.

Mustang seemed born to race, and did even before it went on sale. In late winter of 1963-64, Ford prepped a team of rally Mustangs to take over for the newly banned Falcon Sprints, but their

Without the badges, few would have known the all-new '65 Fords, marked by their clean, angular styling. Overall sales spurted upward, but the $3233 500/XL hardtop (above) plummeted 52 percent to 28,141 units. Part of the reason was the plush new LTD, whose $3313 hardtop sedan (below) saw output of 68,038 units.

only major win came in the Tour de France, where Peter Proctor and Peter Harper finished one-two in class.

There was greater success on the dragstrips, where 2+2s stuffed full of big-block 427s racked up numerous wins in NHRA's A/FX class (Factory Experimental) and, less often, as "funny cars." The factory got into the act for the '65 season, fielding wild "altereds" with two-inch-shorter wheelbases. At the Pomona Winternationals in February, Bill Lawton's Mustang outlasted and outpaced a pack of Mercury Comets and Chrysler Mopars to win A/FX. Les Ritchey did the same at the Labor Day Nationals in Indianapolis, beating famed dragster Gas Rhonda.

Meantime, the big Fords were giving the division its best-ever year in NASCAR, winning 48 of the 55 scheduled Grand National events. A rules dispute prompted the factory Dodge and Plymouth teams to sit out most of the season, but these and other rivals were still represented by intermediates, which makes the big Ford's record all the more impressive. Veteran Ford pilot Fred Lorenzen won a rain-shortened Daytona 500 averaging 141.539 mph. Bobby Johns placed third, also in a Galaxie.

But the stockers bore little resemblance to this year's all-new showroom

As with the Galaxie 500/XL hardtop, the convertible watched production skid in a market where overall sales were booming. For the year, 500/XL ragtop demand diminished by 35 percent, slipping from 15,169 units to 9849. A $3 price increase to $3598 wasn't to blame—a shift in customer preference to luxury was.

their wagon siblings abandoned round taillights for large hexagonal lamps. There were few changes in the engine department, but a new 240-cid "Big Six" (bore and stroke: 4.00 × 3.18 inches) replaced the base 223-cid unit that had been around since 1952. No fewer than six V-8s were available, with horsepower ranging from 200 to 425 bhp, including two 427 big-block mills.

The posh LTD's debut forecast the future and hastened the demise of the overtly sporting XL, whose production declined to only 37,990 units after peaking at nearly 95,000 just two years before. By contrast, the LTD two- and four-door hardtops scored over 100,000 sales despite fairly hefty prices of $3233 and $3313, respectively. Though Ford's overall full-size sales were up for the third year running (to 978,519), buyer interest in bucket-seat biggies was obviously waning. From here on, the emphasis would increasingly be on luxury.

Nevertheless, this year's XL could be a formidable performer. For example, *Car Life* magazine's test 427 hardtop suffered a broken shock and other suspension problems, yet managed just 4.8 seconds 0-60 and an average 14.9 seconds at 97 mph for the standing quarter-mile—this with *no* special engine prep or trick tires. Top speed? A thrilling 136 mph. *Hot Rod* played with a similar mount, did a bit of tweaking, and rocketed through the quarter in 14.43 seconds at 108.04 mph. "The [427] Galaxie 500 XL is a reliable, fast car that will attract attention wherever those in the know hear that wicked idle," concluded *Hot Rod*. "At a going price of $4725 as equipped, it isn't cheap, but then quality and performance never are."

One step down was Fairlane, now in the last year of its original 1962 design. As Detroit so often does in such cases, the mid-size Ford got a bevy of alterations to keep customers interested. A lower-body reskin produced a more square-shouldered look, with some attempt at aping the new big-car appearance. Wheelbase grew half an inch (to 116) and there were minor increases to rear track, overall length, and width—and weight. The standard 200-cid six was reworked for this and all other applications with seven main bearings and gained four bhp for a new total of 120. Optional engines comprised three 289 V-8s, with the high-performance 271 still top dog. New to the list was a 225-bhp version with 10:1 compression and four-barrel carb. Base prices ranged from $2230 to $2648. But despite all the changes, Fairlane production dropped to a new low: 223,954 units.

Falcon retained its basic '64 styling and model choices. The Sprint convertible and hardtop remained the most interesting variants, but they weren't popular (Mustang saw to that) in what would be their final season. Respective production was only 2806 and a mere 300. However, they were still fine buys at $2337 and $2671. Falcon finally got the 289 V-8 (the

models, now billed as being "quieter than a Rolls-Royce." Pride of the line was the limousine-like Galaxie 500 LTD, two- and four-door hardtops with plush cloth-lined bench-seat interiors priced about $600 above their standard-trim counterparts. Though all big Fords acquired more square-cut body lines, the 500/XL hardtop coupe retained its semi-fastback roofline from 1963-64, and this undoubtedly contributed to Ford's supertrack victory streak.

Beneath its new styling and luxury demeanor, the full-size '65s were the most changed Fords since 1949. Author Phil Hall summarized their new engineering in *Fearsome Fords*: "The frame and concept were new. There were now coil springs front and back. The front units were redesigned for strength utilizing the experience from stock-car racing. Conventional coils were still between the upper and lower control arms. The design was so strong that it became the standard for NASCAR stock cars regardless of

make . . . right into the 1980s. . . . The rear coil springs were mounted just ahead of the rear axle with two control arms anchoring the axle and springs to the body. A third member was attached to the right-hand side of the differential. There was also a Panhard rod from the right side of the axle to the left frame member. . . . Frames contained torque boxes for added strength. In addition, bodies were strengthened similar to unitized bodies [and] the number of frame attachment points was reduced. . . . While this had little to do with performance, it did make for a quiet ride. . . ."

As in '64, this year's big-Ford line comprised low-line Custom and Custom 500 sedans, the full-range Galaxie 500 series (including the new LTDs), and parallel Station Wagon offerings. Styling was cleaner and more stately, announced by a horizontal-bar grille flanked by stacked quad headlamps. The fussy pontoon bodysides of 1964 gave way to more flowing sheetmetal, while non-Customs and

260 was dropped, as was the little 144-cid six), but it was just the easy-going 200-bhp version.

Thunderbird was only mildly face-lifted for this second year of the glittery fourth-generation design. A wide Bird emblem replaced block letters on the nose, chrome "C-spears" adorned the front fenders, and taillamps were chopped into thirds for sequential turn indicators, the segments lighting up in sequence from inboard to outboard to more graphically indicate changes in direction. More significant was standardization of front disc brakes, something this weighty personal car had long needed. Added in late March was a fourth model called the Limited Edition Special Landau. Technically a trim package, this featured "Ember-Glo" metallic paint and matching wheel covers, a vinyl top in parchment color, pseudo-wood interior trim, color-keyed carpeting and vinyl upholstery, and a console plaque bearing the owner's name. At just $50 above the regular Landau's $4589 sticker price, it saw only 4500 copies. Thunderbird model-year output slid by some 18,000 units to about 75,000.

Symbolizing "Total Performance" in a big way this year was Ford's spectacular showing at the Indianapolis 500. Dearborn's formal entry into Indy-car racing had hastened the swing to lighter new rear-engine machines, breaking the dominance of the traditional big and heavy Offenhausers. Still, success had been elusive in 1964 despite a more powerful new twincam version of Ford's 260 small-block, engineered, like the car itself, by Lotus in England under Colin Chapman. But there was no such problem in 1965. Ford entrusted its factory cars to the capable Leo Beebe, and Parnelli Jones proved their stamina in early rounds at Milwaukee and Trenton, New Jersey. Indy V-8s were also made available to other teams via Louis Meyer, a former Offy-car builder, so that on Memorial Day no fewer than 24 of the 68 contestants on the Indy starting line were "Powered by Ford." Jim Clark, the "Flying Scotsman," and Yankee veteran A.J. Foyt were the fastest qualifiers, and Clark simply ran away from the pack, averaging

150.686 mph to give Dearborn its first Indy 500 victory in a 1-2-3-4 Ford sweep.

Ford still longed for victory in the international Manufacturers Championship then dominated by Ferrari and Porsche. This involved long-distance contests for prototype sports cars staged on demanding road courses all over the world. Included on the schedule was the prestigious 24 Hours of Le Mans in France. After failing to "buy" its way into this elite game by acquiring Ferrari, Dearborn told its British subsidiary to develop a car that would beat anything the Italians or Germans could come up with.

The result was the GT40, a pretty and sleek mid-engine coupe built around Ford's Indy small-block and developed during 1963 under a new Advanced Vehicle Operations (AVO) department at Ford of England. The basic design came from Eric Broadley of the racing Lola concern, modified by Dearborn designer Roy Lunn (who also worked on the experimental Mustang I) and British engineer John Weyer. Packing 350 bhp, the first GT40 was completed on April 1, 1964, but aside from setting a new lap record at Le Mans, the car was singularly unsuccessful in its debut season.

The 1965 campaign went somewhat better. While AVO continued building GT40s in England, development was stepped up by involving Kar Kraft in Detroit and Shelby-American in California. A 289 with 390 bhp was installed, and Kar Kraft came up with a "Mark II" version for the big-engine prototype class carrying the 427 NASCAR engine tuned to 430 bhp. Ken Miles and Lloyd Ruby gave the GT40 its first victory, averaging 99.94 mph in a 2000-kilometer contest at the Daytona Speedway. Le Mans still proved elusive, however, for even though Ford set another lap record it had to watch all six of its entries—four GT40s and two Mark IIs—retire with gearbox failures. No matter. Much bigger things were just around the corner.

Ford's big truck news for 1965 was "Twin I-Beam" front suspension, a response to the recently introduced car-type independent front suspension on Chevy trucks. A highly touted Ford fea-

ture to this day and inspired by the French "Unic" design of prewar days, the Twin I-Beam system comprised a pair of pivoted, transversely mounted forged-steel drop axles that moved independently of each other on separate coil springs and radius arms. The idea was to combine the smoother ride of its independent front suspension with the ruggedness of solid axles, and it worked. Large front-fender nameplates heralded its initial use on two-wheel-drive F-100s and 250s, which rode inch-longer wheelbases as a result.

Other truck news involved a revised engine lineup and, at midseason, the first "SuperVans." The latter were windowless Econolines with 18 extra inches of rear sheetmetal grafted on to provide 23 percent more cargo volume. Underbody structure was stiffened to suit, and Ford threw in larger tires. There was also a Heavy-Duty version with still-wider rubber (7.00 versus 6.95 × 14), a front stabilizer bar, and higher-capacity rear axle and springs.

The 170 six was now standard power for Econoline and the little Falcon-based Ranchero pickup, albeit rerated to 105 bhp for truck applications thanks to higher 9.0:1 compression. The new passenger-car 240 Big Six arrived as the step-up Econoline option and as standard on F-100/250, replacing the old 223. There was also an even bigger 300-cid six as an option for F-, C-, and N-Series models through the medium-duty 600s, as well as for P-Series parcel vans. Ousting the six-cylinder 262, the 300 featured the same thinwall block construction and four-inch bore as the 240, as well as the same seven main bearings, stud-mounted rocker arms, and gear-driven camshaft. Its main differences were a 0.8-inch longer stroke (3.98 inches) and lower 8:1 compression, good for 150 horses and a substantial 234 pounds/feet peak torque. Also missing from the chart was the familiar 292 gas V-8 used in F-100-350s. In its place was a detuned version of the 1960-63 passenger-car 352, producing 208 bhp and 315 lbs/ft torque on 8.9:1 compression.

If competitors didn't rush to copy Twin I-Beam, they would be quick to imitate another '65 Ford innovation: the "Camper Special." An option package for F-100s, it recognized the growing number of owners who were converting pickups to live-in recreational vehicles via slide-in camper shells available from an increasing hoard of specialist suppliers. Included were heavy-duty radiator (to handle the camper unit's extra weight),

70-amp/hour battery, a large "Western" mirror on each door (for better vision astern), extended exhaust pipe, ammeter, oil pressure gauge, and appropriate front-fender badges. The package was tied to the 300 six or 352 V-8 with four-speed manual or self-shift Cruise-O-Matic—no problem, as most buyers ordered these anyway.

Up among the big rigs was a new 199-inch N600/750 chassis and several new "domestic special order" options: 99-inch C-8000 and 158-inch T-8000 highway tractors powered by a choice of three 464-cid Cummins diesels, and an extended four-door six-passenger "Crew Cab" for the F-250/350 chassis. At the other end of the line, the name "Ranger" was resurrected from Edsel days to denote a new bucket-seat interior option for F-Series Styleside pickups, while the Ranchero was now available with a two-tone "Futura Ornamentation Package"—'64 Falcon Futura-style side trim with a contrast-color insert keyed to the roof. Econolines gained slightly thicker bumpers, a less bus-like steering-column angle, and a lower, more comfortable driver's seat. This year's annual "facial" for lighter F-

Series models involved a grille with two rows of nine small boxes between the headlights, plus parking lamps moved above to flank "Ford" in block letters within a narrowed air slot.

Ford trucks had never been more popular than in 1965. Production rose a substantial 104,554 units to 563,137, a new record. But the total market was stronger than ever, too, and though Chevrolet turned out only a bit less than 96,000 more trucks than in '64, it had started from a higher level and thus maintained its lead over Ford with 619,690 units, though the margin was some 8500 units narrower.

A key executive promotion occurred on January 14, 1965, as Lee Iacocca moved up to vice-president of the Car and Truck Group, no doubt a reward for the phenomenal success of "his" Mustang. Donald N. Frey took over as head of Ford Division. Meanwhile, Ford's Philco subsidiary, which had been combined with the Aeronutronics unit in mid-1963, was pleased to note that it had largely designed and equipped NASA's new Houston Mission Control facility that opened in June.

More heavily publicized by far was the announcement that after 15 years, Ford's chairman would divorce his wife, the former Anne McDonnell, to marry a glamorous young Italian socialite, Maria Christina Vettore Austin. Tabloids had a field day with both the divorce and this year's wedding, painting HF II as the "bad boy" of American business. Whether one agreed with that depended on individual sensibilities, of course, but there was little doubt that Henry drew more attention to his personal life than most corporate bigwigs. In any case, he seemed to take all the furor in stride, though the same could probably not be said for his ex-wife or their three children, Charlotte, Anne, and Edsel II.

Falcon was at the end of its styling and bodyshell cycle in 1965. There would be no more hardtops or convertibles, so the '65s have some last-of-the-line collector interest, the Sprints in particular. But there were only 3106 built in total, as people looking for inexpensive, sporty Fords bought Mustangs. The $2226 Futura hardtop (top left) saw 25,754 units built; the ragtop (top right), just 6215. The convertible at the bottom has the 289 V-8.

1 9 6 6

F ord Division modestly touted 1966 as its "greatest year yet for Total Performance." Corporate advertising revived the famous blue signature oval while declaring that "Ford has a better idea." Both claims were not without merit, for Ford Division had a raft of new products this year: a totally redesigned Fairlane, an upgraded Falcon, a winsome Jeep-like sport/utility vehicle called Bronco, and a new W-Series line of high-built heavy trucks. The year also brought the largest extension of the venerable FE-Series V-8, still going strong after eight years.

The result was a very successful season—at least on the car side, with Ford retailing about 2.2 million to best Chevrolet by some 6000 units. Much of this reflected continuing strong demand for the Mustang, the mainstream big cars, and the new intermediates. Alas, truck volume declined by nearly 10,000 units while Chevy's advanced by some 2000.

Pontiac had created the "muscle car" back in 1964 with the GTO, basically that year's mid-size Tempest LeMans stuffed full of 389 V-8. It was an instant hit, so imitators were not long in coming. Oldsmobile, in fact, fielded its 400-cid 4-4-2, a

heated-up F-85 Cutlass, that same year, and Chevrolet dropped a 396 into its Chevelle during 1965 to produce the SS-396. But Ford had to sit on the sidelines because the original Fairlane hadn't been designed with sufficient underhood room for anything larger than a small-block. While that provided fine performance and made more sense from a weight/handling standpoint, the Fairlane was simply outclassed by GM's more muscular middleweights.

Introduced in August 1965, the Bronco 4×4 was Ford's reply to the Jeep CJ and International Scout. It was compact, riding a 92-inch wheelbase and measuring 152.1 inches overall. Power came from the Falcon 170-cid six, although the 289 V-8 was added late in the year. Three models were offered: Roadster, Sports Utility, and Wagon. The last (above) was the most expensive, $2625, and accounted for 12,756 units. The '66 Falcon was in reality a shortened version of the all-new Fairlane. The $2328 Futura Sports Coupe (below) accounted for 20,289 units of the 182,669 built.

Ford finally caught up with this year's new second-generation Fairlane. Though dimensionally similar to the 1962-65 models (save a ½-inch longer wheelbase), it could accommodate any big-block mill the engineers wanted to shove in. The new GT hardtop and convertible were the muscle models, packing a 335-bhp 390 with higher-lift cam, a larger four-pot Holley carb, and a lower-restriction air cleaner than the 315-bhp unit, next step down on the '66 chart. Standard gearbox was a three-speed manual, with overdrive optional, but most buyers chose either the floorshift

four-speed or new "Sport Shift" Cruise-O-Matic, the last denoted by special "GTA" badges on trunklid and front fenders. Sport Shift referred to a new-design range selector (with console mount) that permitted holding first or second gear to maximum rpm as with a manual.

By contrast, other Fairlanes seemed pretty tame. They ran with a modest 120-bhp 200-cid six, but could be upgraded with a 200-bhp 289 V-8, a 390 with 265 or 275 bhp depending on transmission, and the 315-bhp 390. GTs aside, model choices were comprised of the previous body styles in base and 500 trim plus a new 500

convertible. The last was also available along with a two-door hardtop as the 500/XL, with center console and all-vinyl front bucket seats as on the GT.

Fairlane's '66 styling was clean and contemporary, a complete break with the dowdy 1962-65 look. A new front-end appearance was achieved by stacking the quad headlamps either side of a wide, horizontal-bar grille, much the same as on the big '65 Ford. Fall-away front fenders swept back past a broad, flat hood to mildly kicked-up "Coke bottle" rear fenders that terminated in a shortish rear deck with neat vertical taillamps. Hard-

tops were graced by a nicely integrated semi-fastback roofline. Wagons picked up a 1965 big-car innovation: the dual-action tailgate with drop-down window. A clever hinge allowed opening the gate outward like a door or downward in the traditional way.

The hotter, smoother Fairlanes seemed to be the muscle-car warriors Ford needed, but competitors hadn't been idle. Pontiac, for example, offered up to 360 bhp in its '66 GTO, and Chrysler had a street version of its fabled 426-cid Hemi V-8—with 425 *very* strong horses—as the top power option for its mid-size Plym-

outh Belvedere/Dodge Coronet. Ford responded by running off about 70 Fairlane two-door sedans with the mighty 427, still rated at 410 bhp with single four-barrel carb or 425 bhp with twin quads. These cars, which also carried special fiberglass hoods with functional air scoop, were destined solely for dragstrip service. Interestingly, no GTs were built this way.

Despite lacking the ultimate power of its rivals, Fairlane scored near-sensational sales. Production totaled over 317,000 units, second only to the 1963 figure and an impressive 42 percent above lackluster '65. The GTs proved quite popular, outselling the tamer, less expensive XLs by some 8000 units, though the GT ragtop saw only 4327 copies.

Falcon was now more mid-size than compact, because planning had decreed that Mercury's counterpart Comet would share Fairlane tooling for '66. A wholly separate Ford compact would have been too costly, so this year's new second-generation Falcon was essentially a short-wheelbase Fairlane, nearly identical in structure from the cowl back but with different front and rear styling. One side effect was that sedans now weighed in about 150 pounds heavier, while wagons acquired an extra 400 pounds of heft. Alas, Falcon lost its hardtops and convertibles, the latter transferring to the mid-size line, but there was compensation in four-door and "club coupe" two-door sedans with sporty, Mustang-like long-hood/short-deck proportions, something missing in counterpart Fairlanes with their longer rear overhang.

Falcon and Fairlane wagons shared a 113-inch wheelbase, but Falcon sedans measured 110.9 inches between wheel centers, 1.4 inches longer than before but

5.1 inches shorter than non-wagon Fairlanes. The previous powertrain lineup returned without change. Sprints were history now, so the most interesting '66 Falcon was the Futura Sport Coupe, a pillared two-door with standard bucket seats. In all, Ford's latest compact—touted as "the best buy in compact history"—combined mid-size interior room and comfort with more manageable exterior size. But it wasn't that much cheaper than the Fairlane and was thus eclipsed by it in both marketing emphasis and sales, which amounted to just under 183,000 units.

The new Falcon/Fairlane relationship also affected this year's Ranchero, which followed Chevy's 1964 El Camino in being upgraded from compact to intermediate. Though Ford's car-pickup continued to share frontal styling with Falcon, it now rode a 113-inch chassis and borrowed rear-quarter panels and taillamps from the intermediate wagon as well as Fairlane wheel trims and 14-inch tires (versus 13-inchers on passenger Falcons). Despite its hybrid nature, this was the prettiest Ranchero yet, helped by a distinctive new rear window treatment with the glass slightly inset between short vertical pillar extensions flowing down into the top rails of the integral cargo box. And for the first time in several years there were two Ranchero models, base and Custom, the latter often equipped with bucket seats.

Ranchero engines were still the same as Falcon's: 200-cid six and 289 V-8s with two- or four-barrel carb. Each could be teamed with "three-on-the-tree" manual or self-shift Cruise-O-Matic, and V-8s could be ordered with four-on-the-floor. Base payload capacity was 850 pounds,

Given the Mustang's first year success, nobody expected it to change much for 1966, and it didn't, except for a "floating" Mustang emblem in the grille, altered fake side air scoops, and other minor details. The convertible seen here (left), which listed at $2653, has a number of extra cost options, styled steel wheels, trunk luggage rack, and the GT package among them. The $2607 2+2 fastback (above) also sports the GT package, as well as wire wheel hubcaps. Production of the two models came to 72,119 and 35,698, respectively, to which would have to be added the 499,751 hardtops that were turned out for '66.

Thunderbird flew into 1966 with a minor facelift (left), the major change being a reshaped checked grille with a wide-winged Bird emblem and taillamp lenses spread completely across the back. Mustang (above), meanwhile, held steady. The 200-bhp 289 V-8, as on this car, was the most popular engine choice.

but a 1250-pound option package was available for those who needed more. Overall, the '66 Ranchero was a unique and pleasing blend of sport coupe, pickup, and station wagon. And as events would prove, it would be unique in another way: a one-year-only model.

The Mustang was now in its sophomore year, and because change hardly seemed called for in light of its overwhelming first-year success, Ford noted simply that "we changed Mustang very carefully." The horizontal grille bar was ditched and thin bars replaced the previous honeycomb as a backdrop for the galloping-horse emblem. Windsplits decorated the simulated bodyside scoops (except on GT-equipped cars, where the scoops were eliminated), and fuel-filler cap and wheel covers were restyled. Inside, the standard Falconesque gauge cluster with strip speedometer gave way to the more comprehensive five-dial GT instrumentation. Engines were reduced to standard 200-cid six (the 170 was dropped) and 289 V-8s with 200, 225, and 271 bhp. The options list, with more than 70 choices, lengthened to include an eight-track stereo tape system and deluxe seatbelts with reminder light.

Mustang's model-year sales were

down because early introduction had made its '65 season longer than usual. But for comparable 12-month periods, the '66s actually sold better by some 50,000 units. One reason is that there was still no direct competition. Chevy was a year away from launching its Camaro, and sales of its Corvair were dwindling. Plymouth's hastily created Barracuda, which had appeared a couple of weeks before the Mustang, lagged way behind— just a fancy Valiant with a glassy fastback. Meantime, Ford happily counted the proceeds from 35,000 fastbacks, 70,000 convertibles, and nearly half a million hardtops. Testifying to this torrid sales pace, the one-millionth Mustang rolled off the line on March 2, 1966, less than two years after the ponycar's public debut.

Dealer and customer feedback prompted most changes to this year's Shelby GT-350. The most obvious ones were external: fixed Plexiglas rear side windows in place of the stock fastback's air-exhaust vents, functional side scoops for rear brake cooling in place of the windsplits, and the thin-bar production-'66 grille (still minus the galloping pony). Also, the 15-inch mag wheels (actually aluminum centers with steel rims) were replaced by 14-inch rims in no-charge choice of chrome styled steel or cast-aluminum alloy. Otherwise, there's no clear distinction between 1965 and early '66 GT-350 production. Shelby didn't always incorporate all changes with the start of a new model year anyway, preferring to use up parts on hand (shades of Model A days). Thus, the first 250 or so '66 models

After a successful four-year run, the Fairlane was completely redone for 1966. The sportiest—and most expensive—model was the 500/XL GT convertible (above), which listed at $3068, the only Fairlane to crack the $3000 barrier. And with only 4327 built, it was also the rarest. At a more modest $2378, the Fairlane 500 hardtop (below) was the favorite choice, as 75,947 people proudly drove one home.

were actually leftover '65s with the new cosmetics and the previous suspension, interior, and blue-on-white paint scheme.

Effective with the start of "actual" '66 production, colors were expanded to red, blue, green, and black, all with white stripes; the stock 2+2's optional fold-down rear seat became available; and batteries were left in their original under-hood location. The "true" '66s also used heavy-duty Ford-installed shock absorbers but retained the special Pitman and idler arms that gave the '65s such sharp steering. All '65s and early-'66s used rear traction bars that ran from inside the car to the top of the rear axle; late '66s used Traction Master underride bars. Early cars also had lowered front A-arms that altered steering geometry for improved cornering, but this was later discontinued as not cost-effective. Drivetrains remained the same, but the Detroit "Locker" rear end was made optional—as was automatic transmission.

If the '66 Shelby wasn't as loud or fierce as the '65, Carroll kept things interesting with a Paxton centrifugal supercharger as another new option. (A special GT-350 "S" was envisioned but never actually released.) Sold factory-installed at $670 or as a $430 kit, the blower was said to boost horsepower "up to 46 percent"—to beyond 400 bhp—which allegedly cut the 0-60-mph time to a mere five seconds. Few if any cars were so equipped, however.

Shelby planned increased '66 production so that every dealer who wanted cars could get them. He also sold the Hertz company on the idea of renting out a fleet of specially trimmed GT-350H models, most of which were finished in black with gold stripes. Hertz did so at major airports throughout 1966, but a good many returned from a weekend's use with definite signs of competition fatigue. Not surprisingly, Hertz found this program a mite unprofitable and soon bailed out.

Total '66 Shelby-Mustang production was 2380 units, including 936 Hertz cars and six specially built convertibles that Carroll gave to friends at the end of the model year. No R-model racers were constructed, though a few '65 leftovers were registered as '66s. Shelbys continued to race and win, though they were essentially the same cars that had run and won the year before.

Overshadowed by the GT-350's stunning early success in SCCA "club" racing was its performance in the Trans-American Sedan Championship. First run in 1966 as essentially an offshoot of SCCA's sedan-class events, the Trans-Am was intended as a series of "mini-enduros" ranging anywhere from 200 to 2400 miles and two to 24 hours, thus requiring pit stops for fuel and tires. As planned, it attracted Mustangs, Barracudas, Falcons, Dodge Darts, and a host of under-2.0-liter imports. By the end of its inaugural season, the Trans-Am had become one of the most popular series on the SCCA schedule, due partly to a good many factory entries. To make things more interesting, a manufacturer's trophy was awarded to the company whose cars won the most races. Driver egos took a back seat as each factory vied to establish or uphold its performance reputation.

Trans-Am rules were based on FIA Appendix J specifications for Series Production Cars (Group 1) or Touring Cars (Group 2). The senior class was limited to displacement between 2000 and 5000 cc (120-305 cid), a maximum wheelbase of 116 inches, and minimal mechanical modifications. Only four-seaters were allowed, so the GT-350, officially a two-seater, wasn't. Mustang hardtops did the honors instead.

The 1966 schedule had seven races, but the series was very close all season and the winner wasn't decided until the finale at Riverside, California. There, a huge blue Shelby-American van appeared with a Shelbyized Mustang hardtop for former GT-350 team driver Jerry Titus, editor of *Sports Car Graphic*. Titus qualified on the pole and won the race, thus giving Ford the manufacturer's trophy. But Shelby-American's 11th-hour appearance signaled a change in Ford's racing priorities, probably due to the realization that the 1967 GT-350 wouldn't be as competitive as the original R-model. From here on, the factory's Trans-Am effort would be carried out with Mustang hardtops.

Shelby-American extended race assistance to Mustang entrants early this season—logical, as the regular notchbacks and GT-350s shared virtually all mechanical components. But this support was soon withdrawn (probably because somebody felt that there wasn't enough product similarity), so Ford took up the slack with limited support of its own to outstanding non-Shelby teams. By season's end, Ford and Shelby-American were competing with each other.

For the full sized 1966 models, detail appearance changes were the order of the day. Featured were squared-up taillights, a grille and hood pushed forward some, bigger rear wheel arches, and a more sweeping roofline with a slightly concave backlight for two-door hardtops. The pride of the fleet was the new Galaxie 500 7-Litre, a bucket-seat convertible and hardtop coupe respectively base-priced at $3872 and $3621. The name reflected the metric displacement of their standard 428-cubic-inch V-8. This new engine was created by combining the 406's 4.13-inch bore with the 3.98-inch stroke from Mercury's 410 big-block. Swept volume actually worked out closer to 427 cubes, but Ford used "428" to avoid confusion with its high-performance big-block. Despite 10.5:1 compression, a big four-barrel carb, and hydraulic lifters, the 428 wasn't a muscle mill. Rather, it was a torquey, low-revving slogger designed for big cars growing ever heavier with the addition of more and more power accessories. Output was 345 bhp in standard tune, and a 360-bhp police version was theoretically available to civilians.

Despite its heft (over two tons at the curb), the 7-Litre was quite fast. *Car Life*'s automatic car ran 0-60 mph in a creditable 8.0 seconds. But though the 427 and

The Illustrated History of Ford *comments that "The Galaxie 500 LTD Limousine (top) was popular with governmental bodies that wanted to equip their fleet with a luxury prestige car, yet stay within taxpayer-set bounds." Far more common was the $3278 Galaxie 500 LTD four-door hardtop (above), a 3649-pound model that found favor with 69,400 buyers. This one has the 315-horsepower 390 V-8—the 289 was standard.*

four-speed were optional, the 7-Litre was really a luxury liner with just a hint of sport—much like the 500/XL in fact (even interiors were shared). Predictably, it found a limited audience, with only 8705 hardtops and a mere 2368 drop-tops built this model year.

The big 500/XL itself continued to decline, model-year sales falling off to 25,715 hardtops and 6360 convertibles, though that combined volume was triple what the 7-Litre generated. You only got a 200-bhp 289 as standard, but XLs cost less—$3231 for the hardtop, $3480 for the convertible—and you could get any optional V-8, including the brawniest big-blocks. But buyers seeking *real* performance were now looking to the mid-size muscle brigade, not heavy, big-inch standards. At least the 428 was successful. A popular option for other full-size Fords as well as the '66 Thunderbird, it would continue as such for several years. Other big-Ford powerteams remained as before. As a group, the big Fords did quite well for '66, with production topping the one-million mark for the first time in six years. As usual, the mid-line Galaxie 500 sedan and hardtop coupe were far and away the best sellers, but the posh LTDs were doing fine, too: 69,400 hardtop sedans

and 31,696 hardtop coupes.

A mild restyle and a couple of new options marked the last of the fourth-generation Thunderbirds. "... new ideas set the pace with boldness and brilliance," said the ad writers, referring probably to the reshaped checked grille with a wide-winged Bird emblem and taillamp lenses spread completely across the back, still with sequential turn signals. New to the lineup were the Town Hardtop and Town Landau, the latter with dummy S-curve landau bars on the rear roof quarters. Both differed from the normal hardtop in two ways: the first having C-pillars extended forward to the doors, thus eliminating the small, triangular rear quarter panes; and the second a standard warning-light console (optional on the base hardtop) above the windshield header. The new roof made for bulky-formal looks—even more so with accessory rear fender skirts—but proved popular with the style-conscious. Combined Town volume was well over 50,000 units; the plain hardtop tallied only a little over 13,000 sales.

The trusty 390 remained standard T-Bird power, now rated at 315 bhp; the 345-bhp 428 arrived at a modest $64.30 extra. Another new feature was a cruise-

Ford advertised in 1966 that there were "49 new ways to go Ford!" Among the full-size cars, 19 models were listed (including station wagons), and three of them were ragtops—the $2934 Galaxie 500 convertible, the $3480 500/XL (above), and the $3872 7-Litre (this one with a 345-bhp 428 V-8). The cheapest version saw output reach 27,454 units, while the more expensive variants managed only 6360 and 2368, respectively.

control system with buttons mounted in the steering-wheel spokes for convenience. Ford called it "Highway Pilot Control," later "Fingertip Speed Control." Leather upholstery with reclining front passenger seat came as a $147 extra, along with a combined AM radio/eight-track stereo tape player for $81.55.

Significantly, this would be the last year for the factory-built T-Bird convertible. Buyers in this market had long shown a preference for the greater comfort of closed models with air conditioning, reflected in '66 ragtop production of only 5049 units. Overall Thunderbird sales dipped to near 69,000 units, down some 5000 from 1965.

Ford trotted a second horse into its 1966 corral, a stablemate for the Mustang ponycar. But the new Bronco was a horse of a very different color: a light, compact multi-purpose vehicle with four-wheel drive, inspired by the long-running success of the civilian Jeep CJ and, more recently, the International Scout. The concept was simplicity itself: a spare, square-lined body (supplied by Budd) atop a welded box-section steel frame with a tidy 92-inch wheelbase. Overall length measured a trim 152.1 inches, while width was 68.6 inches, giving Bronco a somewhat wider stance, and thus greater

stability, than a Jeep CJ on and off the beaten path.

A notable chassis innovation was Bronco's "Monobeam" front suspension: a coil-sprung solid drive axle located by forged radius arms and a track bar. At the rear was another live axle on fixed-rate semi-elliptic leaf springs (changed to variable-rate at midyear). Drive was normally to the rear wheels, but a two-speed Dana Model 20 transfer case engaged all four wheels for maximum traction for bad weather or off-road driving after the front wheel hubs had been manually engaged. This was what we'd now call a "part-time" 4WD system, with choice of "high" and "low" ranges, the latter intended for severe low-speed conditions digging out of mud or maybe climbing trees. Brakes were drums all around and measured 11 × 2 inches in front and 10 × 2.5 inches out back. An optional 3300-pound towing package included 11 × 1.75-inch rear brakes from the F-100 pickup.

Bronco arrived in three body styles, though two were variations of the basic Jeep-type open model called the Roadster. This came with a rudimentary soft top, pickup-style drop-down tailgate, fold-flat windshield, and a simple front bench seat. There were no doors, but styled fiberglass inserts gave the square openings a more rakish look. The "Sports Utility" model came with functional doors as well as a squared-up half-length hardtop that transformed the Bronco into a mini-pickup. The Wagon featured a full-length top with fixed rear side windows and a separate opening rear liftgate. Prices were attractively low: $2355 for the Roadster, $2480 for the Sport Utility, and $2570 for the Wagon.

But that was just for starters, because Bronco options were plentiful. Initially, there was only one powertrain, the 170-cid six mated to a three-speed manual transmission, but the 200-bhp 289 V-8 became available from March 1966, and Cruise-O-Matic came along a bit later. Other extras included a two-person rear bench seat (easily removed for hauling chores), front bucket seats, radio, heater, and chrome plating for grille, bumpers, and wheel covers.

The Bronco earned high praise for its good performance and economy, high versatility, and nimble handling both on- and off-road. It didn't unseat the Jeep CJ as the four-wheeler's favorite, but it was a timely plus for Ford dealers. Just as important for corporate pride, it was another product with no counterpart at Chevy, which wouldn't get around to responding to this particular Ford for another three years.

Monobeam front suspension was also featured on this year's F-100 4WD pickup, which now came on the same two wheelbases as its two-wheel-drive counterpart and was newly available as a Styleside as well as separate-fender Flareside. The usual grille change for F-100s through 600s brought a two-tier insert between the headlamps bearing wide twin air slots above a slim eggcrate—which only made for a really fussy-looking front.

Ford's other major truck development this year was the W-Series, a new line of high-tilt cabovers replacing the H-Series. Single- and tandem-axle models were offered in no fewer than 1250 different variations, though all had diesel engines and resolutely box-like cabs made from simple steel sheet, matched by

a big flat windshield.

Changes elsewhere in the '66 truck fleet involved the usual chassis and drivetrain updates among mediums and heavies, plus full production-line availability of four-door Crew Cab pickups on the 147-inch-wheelbase F-250 and 152-inch F-350 chassis. Rooflines were raised on F-800/900/1000 and all T- and N-Series cabs for an additional 3.5 inches of headroom, and a new motorhome chassis derived from that of the P-Series parcel van became available to special order. Commercial Econoline vans were treated to standard seatbelts and windshield washers, and the line of car-like Falcon Club Wagons expanded with the addition of extended-length "SuperVan" derivatives.

Missing from the '66 lineup was the Falcon Sedan Delivery, a victim of lagging sales.

On the racing scene this year, Ford reveled in a second consecutive triumph at the Indy 500, thanks to driver Graham Hill and his Lola-Ford. Meantime, Dearborn's prospects for winning the Manufacturers Championship brightened considerably as the mid-engine GT40 notched victories at Daytona and Sebring in February. Continuing production in England meant that more GT40s were available to non-factory teams, and no fewer than 13 cars—eight big-block Mark IIs and five small-block machines—showed up for Le Mans in June. Shelby-American, Holman & Moody of stock-car

fame, and Alan Mann Racing of England were all on hand. Only three of the 13 Fords survived the 24 hours, all Mark IIs—but they were first at the finish, the lead car piloted by Bruce McLaren and Chris Amon.

It took time, but this was a fantastic feat for a relatively new car that may have been born in Britain but was rightly perceived as American. Ford had done precisely what it had set out to do: establish itself as a force to be reckoned with in the world's most brutal, most prestigious automotive competition. And if Ferrari's renown suffered by Ford's victory, so much the better. At least that's what Henry Ford II undoubtedly felt after being thwarted in his attempt to buy Ferrari a few years before. Actually, Ford took home two Manufacturer's trophies in 1966: one for the big-inch prototype class, with the Mark II, and the sports-car crown, won by the GT40.

Understandably, Dearborn was jubilant. So what if General Motors led in sales? Mighty GM hadn't won Le Mans. But Ford had—convincingly. And for many enthusiasts the world over, that made Ford the *real* number-one.

The full-size Ford station wagon lineup embraced five models for 1966, two of them the top-line woody-look Country Squire (above). With seating for six or nine, prices came in at $3182 and $3265. Production totaled 69,598 units, 60 percent of them being the nine-passenger unit. With the Ranch Wagon and the two Country Sedans added in, total big Ford wagon output came to to 195,153 units. Among the '66 pickups, the F-350 (left) was significant because of its nine-foot cargo box, which actually dated back to the 1957-60 era, and because 1966 would be its last year.

1 9 6 7

Enthusiasts tend to look wistfully at model year 1967—the last before the advent of federal regulations. Yet it was clear even at the time that Washington was bound to take a hand in the auto business. Air pollution was already a recognized health problem in places like smog-prone Los Angeles, the industrial Midwest, and the congested Northeast. And GM's palsied performance before Congressional safety investigators—and news of its secret investigation of consumer crusader Ralph Nader—convinced many people that automakers could not be trusted.

The Clean Air Act was already on the books in 1967, mandating reduced levels of harmful tailpipe emissions effective with 1968 models. On September 9, 1966, President Johnson signed the second part of the government's new 1-2 regulatory punch: the National Traffic and Motor Vehicle Safety Act. Among other things, this provided for Federal Motor Vehicle Safety Standards (FMVSS)—government-required devices aimed at increasing the chances of occupant survival in collisions.

From today's perspective, the first safety and emissions standards seem pretty simple and straightforward, but at the time they were quite controversial. Enthusiasts were dismayed by the prospect of losing performance to detuned engines and the extra weight of bigger bumpers and other safety equipment. But enthusiasts, vocal though they are, don't make up the majority of car buyers, and the fact was that the standards had wide popular support. In between these factions stood the automakers, some of whom declared that certain regulations would be impossible to meet, though they'd already voluntarily adopted several requirements such as seatbelts, dashboard padding, and splinter-proof laminated glass.

Only three things seemed clear: Regulation would almost certainly make cars more expensive, the regulations themselves would grow more specific and stringent, and Detroit could be counted on to fight Washington every step of the way. Yet for most automakers, the task for 1967 was simply to prepare for 1968. In some cases this meant replacing older designs that couldn't meet the new rules with fresh ones that would. Of course, some of the forthcoming standards were either known or virtually certain somewhat before 1967, and this partly accounts for the unusual number of new cars introduced that year. Among them were redesigned full-size models from GM and Chrysler, revamped intermediates from American Motors, and new-design Chrysler compacts.

Ford contributed to this busy picture with a totally new Thunderbird, plus Mustangs and big Fords restyled from the waist down. The new-for-'66 Falcon and Fairlane got only minor touch-ups, though the latter now offered its most powerful engines ever. Ford's truck line also saw a number of changes, including the first redesigned F-Series cabs in six years. Yet despite so many new offerings from all quarters, there was no great rush to buy. Quite the opposite, in fact. Compared with record 1965, the industry as a whole sold 1.2 million fewer cars, though truck sales held steady. In model-year car production, Ford Division finished at 1.7 million, down nearly half-a-million from 1966, itself a "pullback" year. The decline stemmed from reduced mid-size and big-car sales, as Mustang demand remained strong despite new Chevy and Plymouth competition, and the new T-Bird turned in a better sales performance than its 1966 predecessor. Chevrolet declined, too, but only by about 13,000 cars, and regained its usual spot as "USA-1." Ford fared somewhat better in trucks, producing 452,253 units. That was down about 11,500 compared to Chevy's loss of nearly 72,000, but Chevy's truck margin was still close to 97,500.

At least Ford could still find solace on the race track. A.J. Foyt was first in his Coyote-Ford at the Indy 500 in May, leading a 1-5 Ford-powered sweep to give Dearborn its third Brickyard victory in as many years. The following month, Foyt teamed with Dan Gurney under the Carroll Shelby banner to give Ford its second consecutive win at the 24 Hours of Le Mans, averaging 135 mph over 3251 miles. Their mount was the new Mark IV derivative of the interim GT40-based "J-Car." Packing a 500-horsepower 427 V-8, the Mark IV was easily identified by its larger and swoopier new body fabricated of aluminum honeycomb sections bonded and riveted together.

The Mark IV had won its first time out, at this season's Sebring 12-Hours. But Ford evidently felt that its point had been made, for it withdrew from Makes Championship competition after Le Mans '67. Dearborn wasn't finished with big-bore international racing, but on the GT circuit at least, its colors would henceforth be carried by private teams.

The posh, personal-luxury Thunderbird was a world removed from the all-conquering Mark II, but no less important to Ford because of an even more important race, the sales race. And it was the continuing quest for sales that had prompted discussion of a Thunderbird sedan beginning in the early Sixties. By mid-decade, however, Lee Iacocca and others at Ford Division realized that the Bird no longer need make even a token gesture toward sport, mainly because Mustang and the new Fairlanes would be catering to the younger, performance-oriented crowd.

Such was the rationale behind this year's new fifth-generation Thunderbird, perhaps the purest expression of the personal-luxury idea yet seen. The significance of the all-new '67 is that it firmly fixed the Bird's shape, size, and character for the next decade: larger, heavier, and plusher than any previous model. Replacing the convertible was "an historic first four-door," to quote Ford's ad writers, a Landau sedan built on a 117.2-inch wheelbase—nearly as long as the full-size Ford's. Base and Landau hardtop coupes,

with wide C-pillars and tiny quarter windows that slid back into them, returned on a 114.7-inch chassis, up 1.5 inches from the 1964-66 dimension. Powertrains stayed the same: standard 315-bhp 390 V-8 or optional 345-bhp 428. Both teamed only with Cruise-O-Matic, now with the manual-hold feature, renamed "SelectShift," as introduced on the '66 Fairlane.

Thunderbird returned to body-on-frame construction for the first time in 10 years, a move dictated by cost considerations. The '67 chassis comprised side rails joined front and rear by torque boxes. Rigidity lost through departure of unit construction was largely regained via stiffening ribs, sheetmetal crossmembers, and a full-length tunnel stamped into the floorpan. There were no fewer than 14 body mounts located all around the passenger compartment to reduce noise and vibration within.

According to a '67 Ford brochure, "When Thunderbird changes, the automobile world watches, for this will be the look of other cars tomorrow." And in appearance, the '67 Bird *was* quite fresh, though vestiges of the past could be seen in the rear-roof "sail" panels and at the rear. The drop-center decklid returned in muted form, and taillights still stretched all the way across the back, but rear fenders had fashionable hippy contours, bodysides were more massive, and hidden headlamps appeared for the first time in a large, "wide-oval" grille.

Long-time T-Bird stylist Bill Boyer recalled that the '67 design was actually the work of two separate studios: "It was a compromise in a way.... [L. David] Ash had at that time what I think was called the Corporate Projects Studio, which was

in competition with the Thunderbird Studio. [We] essentially did the roof, backlight, and rear half.... Dave was responsible for the front end. He had a design that he considered a giant Ferrari. Management liked [this] front end and our rear end with its hopped-up rear quarter. What we ended up with was an amalgamation, I would say just about down the middle."

A four-door T-Bird might seem like a contradiction in terms, and Boyer admits that it "just sort of happened.... We did a rendering in black cherry with a black vinyl roof, a four-door with center-opening doors and a sail on the rear door where it hinged to the body. Iacocca saw this and just about flipped. 'Let's get that four-door nailed down,' he said." And, of course, they did.

The '67 T-Bird sold well, mainly on the strength of its new looks and greater size. Interesting gimmicks also helped, like the new Tilt-Away steering wheel that moved out of the way laterally, like the 1961-66 Swing-Away wheel, but also tilted up to the right. The two-door Landau was the most popular offering, but the new sedan scored respectable sales of nearly 25,000 for the model year. But that would be the highest it would ever achieve, popularity falling with each passing year until the body style was dropped for the replacement sixth-generation design of 1972.

This year's full-size Fords, billed as the "Luxury leaders of the volume car field," got a heavy "mid-life" redo to carry their platform through two more years. While still massive, the new look was more flowing, with hopped-up rear fenderlines, elliptical wheel openings, and a two-element horizontal grille. Hardtop

coupe rooflines took on a faster slope. The LTD version had very wide C-pillars with vertical leading edges, while Galaxie 500 and XL hardtops had larger, triangular rear side windows and correspondingly slimmer pillars.

Powerteam availability for the 18-model big-Ford line was unchanged, but the 7-Litre hardtop and convertible were transmogrified into an XL option package. Priced at $515.86, it included the 428 V-8, uprated suspension, and power brakes with front discs. The 427 was still available, though on a more restricted basis, while the old 352 V-8 was honorably retired. New big-Ford features included Fingertip Speed Control, eight-track tape player, and SelectShift Cruise-O-Matic. The XL's standard engine remained the 200-bhp "Challenger" 289, but equipment now ran to "leather-smooth" all-vinyl trim, Thunderbird bucket seats, and "command" console with T-bar shift lever.

Big-Ford production declined 15 percent for the model year, and XL sales hit a new low: barely 23,300, including a paltry 5161 convertibles, just 2.7 percent of full-size volume. By contrast, the luxury LTD, now a separate series and bolstered by a new four-door sedan, scored over

This '67 Mustang (above) wears a GTA badge on its front fender, the "A" meaning that it has an automatic transmission. The base hardtop listed at $2461, but this well-equipped model sports about $1000 worth of options. The fifth-generation Thunderbird (right) not only boasted all-new styling, but a four-door sedan as well. Called Landau, it sold for $4825 and weighed in at a hefty 4348 pounds. The hardtop (there were no convertibles for '67) rode a 114.7-inch wheelbase, but for the four-door this was stretched to 117.2 inches.

For 1967 there were three Thunderbirds (top): hardtop, Landau hardtop, and Landau four-door sedan. The hardtop started at $4603, while the fancier Landau cost $101 more. The Falcon changed little for '67, hardly surprising since it was all-new for '66. It came in two series, base and Futura, and the sportiest model of the seven offered was the $2437 Futura Sports Coupe (above). It featured bucket seats.

110,000 sales. Once again, Ford's single most popular big car was the Galaxie 500 hardtop coupe: over 197,000 units.

The hot-selling Mustang finally got some ponycar competition for 1967. Chevrolet fielded its similar Camaro, and Pontiac debuted its Camaro-clone Firebird at mid-year. Plymouth's Barracuda, originally just a "glassback" version of the compact Valiant compact, received a handsome new look all its own, plus coupe and convertible body styles. Of course, Ford knew something of these plans, and had readied some new Mustang features for '67. Chief among them

was a bold engine option: the broad-shouldered four-barrel Thunderbird 390 packing 320 bhp. With the carryover 200-cid six and trio of 289 V-8s, available powertrains now numbered 13.

Though Mustang retained its 108-inch wheelbase, new lower-body sheetmetal imparted a beefier look. Overall length went up by two inches, width by 2.7 inches and—to make room for the 390—front track was widened 2.6 inches (which also improved handling response). The 2+2 became a true fastback, with an unbroken roofline instead of the previous semi-notch effect. Other changes included a concave tail panel and a few extra inches in the nose to match a more aggressive grille. And, oh yes: the single three-element taillamps were now split into three separate units. Engineers pitched in with new rubber bushings at suspension attachment points for reduced noise and vibration, and a general front suspension rework decreased understeer without the need for overly stiff

springing.

Mustang shed another vestige of its Falcon origins with a new "twin-cowl" dash dominated by a pair of large, circular dials ahead of the driver, surmounted by three smaller gauges. The optional tachometer eliminated the ammeter and oil pressure gauges in the starboard slot—a retrograde step. A new Competition Handling Package—stiff springs, thick front anti-sway bar, Koni shocks, limited-slip differential, quick steering, 15-inch wheels—was available with the GT Equipment Group but not commonly ordered, making it quite rare today. Still restricted to V-8s, the GT package comprised front foglamps, rocker stripes, dual exhausts, power brakes with front discs, and fat wide-oval tires. You could also get an Exterior Decor Group with thin bars on the back panel and turn-signal "repeater" lights in a special hood with dummy twin reversed scoops. And, as on the Fairlane, combining the GT group with automatic got you "GTA" badges on the lower front fenders. The T-Bird's Tilt-Away steering wheel was optional across the board. In fact, Mustang options now totaled "well over 100."

It was almost a foregone conclusion that Mustang sales would decline in the face of competition, and they did—by about 25 percent. The hardtop sustained most of the loss, but the convertible also suffered, trailing the fastback for the first time. Yet the model-year total of 474,121 units led the ponycar field by a wide margin. Interestingly, that was more than *double* the most optimistic estimates of Ford's marketing mavens for Mustang's *first* year.

Mustang's racy cousin, the GT-350, was altered along the same lines but, in typical Shelby fashion, Carroll went Ford one better with an even bigger big-block: a warmed-up 428 advertised at 355 bhp but closer to 400 by most estimates. As installed in the new GT-500, it boasted an aluminum intake manifold and a matched set of 600-cfm Holley four-barrel carbs. The GT-500 proved popular, outselling the smaller-engine GT-350 two to one. The latter still carried the Hi-Performance 289 with the usual Shelby tweaks save the steel-tube exhaust headers. Quoted power remained at 306 bhp, but it must have been less without the headers and straight-through muffler.

To keep weight down and appearance distinctive, Shelby stylists created a fiberglass front to complement the stock '67 Mustang's longer hood, and put two high-beam headlamps in the center of the grille. (Some cars had the latter moved outboard to comply with state motor-vehicle requirements for minimum headlamp distance.) Also added were a larger hood scoop, sculptured brake cooling scoops on the sides, and another set on the rear roof quarters for interior air extraction. The rear end received a spoiler and a bank of large taillights. In all, it was a busy but arresting package. Customer feedback and the '67's extra weight prompted power steering and brakes as new "mandatory options" (you paid extra for them but you couldn't get a car without them). There were also some special interior appointments not shared with the production Mustang: racing steering wheel, additional gauges, and a functional rollbar with inertia-reel shoulder harnesses.

Shelby-Mustang production forged ahead to 3225 units for the model year, much of it due to the new GT-500. The '67s saw little track action, though, and for a good reason. They were about equal parts luxury and performance, while the 1965-66 cars were more like thinly disguised race cars that could be used on the street.

But it should be noted that Mustang again captured the SCCA's Trans-Am championship. This sophomore season saw serious competition from Roger Penske's new Camaro team and Bud Moore's new Mercury Cougars, but Ford won the Manufacturer's crown as Jerry Titus scored four wins in Mustang notchbacks.

Only detail refinements attended this year's follow-up edition of the "Coke-bottle" mid-size Fairlane. There were the usual exterior trim shuffles involving badges and taillights, plus wider bodyside moldings and a reworked grille with a chrome horizontal divider bisected by three vertical bars. Engineering changes were minimal, but 390 V-8s were cut to a 270-bhp two-barrel unit and a 320-bhp four-barrel version. The 427 muscle motor was ostensibly available to give Ford an edge in advertised horsepower over the Pontiac GTO, Buick GS, Olds 4-4-2, and Chrysler's hemi-engine intermediates, but few were actually installed.

Ford ads pleaded with new car buyers in 1967 to "Join the Fairlaners...people who have more fun in the car that has more to offer." But the appeal fell on deaf ears as Fairlane sales skidded nearly 25 percent to 238,668 units, landing not far above the 1965 nadir. The 500/XL and GT convertibles were quite scarce: only 1943 and 2217, respectively. Their sister hardtops were more numerous, with respective totals of 14,871 and 18,670.

Falcon, faring even worse than Fairlane, saw output plummet 64.8 percent to 64,335 units—an all-time low. Perhaps that was due in part because Falcon also flew along with few changes. A new "cross-hair" grille bar marked the front, Futura back panels gained revised brushed-metal appliques, front fenders got twin speedline indents, and a four-barrel 225-bhp 289 V-8 joined the options list. As it turned out, that was hardly enough to convince buyers to "Go pert, peppy, and proud...in a Falcon."

The '67 Ranchero exchanged its Falcon instrument panel, front sheetmetal, and body trim for Fairlane components— no big deal, as the engineering similarity between the compact and mid-size pas-

senger cars made this transformation a simple bolt-on job. Its likely rationale was to make the Ranchero more identifiable as being derived from an intermediate car in the way that Chevrolet's contemporary El Camino was based on the midsize Chevelle. Model choices expanded from two to three: base, mid-line 500, and sporty XL, the last with the expected all-vinyl buckets-and-console interior, plus special exterior badges. In line with upcoming federal standards, Rancheros and all '67 Ford cars came with dual master brake cylinders and hydraulic lines (for "fail-safe" stopping should either circuit prove faulty), energy-absorbing steering-wheel hub (a big, ugly foam-filled cone bolted onto the existing dished wheels, a patchwork answer to an impact-protection rule), and four-way emergency flashers. Power brakes with front discs were a new Ranchero option.

Among the plethora of new vehicles tempting buyers in 1967 was a completely revamped line of Chevrolet light trucks with clean, smooth-lined styling. Ford's F-Series was overhauled, too, with new-

Ford simplified its '67 lineup of full-size cars by dropping the two 7-Litre models and by making the successful LTD a separate series (rather than a Galaxie 500 subseries). At $3493, the Galaxie 500/XL convertible (top) was the most expensive model offered, and with only 5161 built, the rarest of the big Fords that year. This one has the optional 345-bhp 428 V-8. The 500/XL hardtop (above) retailed at $3243 and enjoyed a production run of 18,174 units. The 200-bhp 289 V-8 and Cruise-O-Matic were standard equipment, as were bucket seats and console.

design cabs that unfortunately managed to look like a mere facelift of the old ones. But different they were. A shallower but wider windshield was one clue. Curved door glass was another. Up front rode broad-shouldered sheetmetal with the hood wrapped down at the sides and a deeper, simpler new horizontal-bar grille. Slim, tubular sheetmetal sculptures adorned front fenders and doors, and were carried all the way back on Styleside pickups. The medium/heavy cab (F-600 and up) was taller and had a commensurately deeper grille of identical design.

Drivers of any '67 F-Series were sure to notice the new cab's improved visibility, four more inches of shoulder room, and three-inch-wider seats, as well as new car-like conveniences including reversible keys (they worked either side up, a Ford innovation from 1965), keyless "slam" locking, higher-capacity cowl ventilation, and standard two-speed wipers.

Accompanying the new cabs was a raft of chassis updates. The main ones involved strengthened frames on two-wheel-drive F-100s and 250s; a new 131-inch wheelbase for 100/250 pickups, in-

cluding 4WDs, with the eight-foot cargo box (the old nine-footer was dropped); new F250/350 Crew Cab wheelbases of 149 and 164.5 inches; adoption of Twin I-Beam front suspension for F-350s; beefier spring and wheel/tire packages across the board; straight-through frame rails and wider front tracks on mediums; and auxiliary fuel tanks as a new option for light-duty pickups. Engine changes this year mainly involved the heavies: no more two-barrel 401 and 477 gas V-8s; a pair of larger diesels to replace the previous British Ford engines; a wider choice of proprie-

tary Detroit Diesels for F/T-8000 and new N/NT-8000 models. Also new to the heavy-duty line this year were a diesel-powered CT-8000 low-cabover tandem and a downrated gas-powered T-800 conventional tandem replacing the previous T-700/750.

Upgraded equipment and more model choices marked the sophomore edition of the little four-wheel-drive Bronco. The Sport Utility was renamed Pickup, and both it and the Wagon could now be ordered with "Sport" trim, which merely meant dual armrests and a chrome horn-

The '67 Fairlane was modestly restyled to look more like the big Fords. Thirteen models were listed, the most expensive being the $3064 GT convertible (left). Sharp eyes will note the "A" on the decklid badge, which means that this car is equipped with an automatic transmission. Not only were the GT ragtops rare—only 2117 were built—but this one boasts the rare 427-cubic-inch V-8 option (above), which developed a rousing 410 or 425 horsepower. The '67 Fairlane rode a 116-inch wheelbase.

ring inside and bright grille, bumpers, and window surround moldings outside. Lengthening Bronco's standard-equipment list were padded sun visors, backup lights, variable-speed wipers, and, at Washington's behest, dual-circuit self-adjusting brakes. Newly optional for all models was an 11.5-gallon auxiliary fuel tank with skid plate.

Ford was readying a new and bigger Econoline for 1968, so this year's final version of the original 1961 design saw few changes other than standardization of backup lights, two-speed wipers, and

occupant-friendly padded sun visors and armrests. The Econoline had garnered some 400,000 sales going into model year '67, and would add another 50,000 or so before bowing out.

Before leaving 1967, we should note the arrival of a second Ford ponycar, the new 111-inch-wheelbase Mercury Cougar. It's probably the most interesting Mercury of the Sixties, though it's been long overshadowed among collectors by the Mustang that spawned it. Of course, it was created to give Lincoln-Mercury Division a toehold in what seemed like, given the Mustang's huge success, an unlimited ponycar market.

Unlike Mustang, Cougar premiered only as a hardtop coupe, though with three different trim/equipment levels: standard, GT, and XR-7. At $2851, the base Cougar cost some $350 more than the equivalent Mustang but came with a 200-bhp 289 V-8 and such premium features as headlamps hidden within a distinctive "electric shaver" split grille, matching taillamps with sequential turn signals, vinyl bucket seats, sports steering wheel, deep-loop carpeting, and floorshift three-speed manual transmission (though most all Cougars were delivered with SelectShift Cruise-O-Matic). The $3175 GT added a 390 V-8, commensurate handling mods, wide-oval white-stripe tires, a serious-sounding low-restriction exhaust system, power front-disc brakes, and special

identification. Compared to Mustang, Cougar was 6.7 inches longer overall, a bit wider, and 200 pounds heavier, the last a partial consequence of its more generous equipment.

Perhaps the nicest Cougar was the pretty XR-7, a mid-year addition intended to lure a few people out of pricey imported sports cars. Crests on the C-pillars were the only exterior clue to this Cougar's special status, but the XR-7 cabin was decked out in contemporary Eurostyle, with leather-surfaced buckets and a woodgrained dash containing genuine needle gauges. Base price was only $3081, though the average XR-7 delivered for close to $3600. Even at that, this was a tempting price rival for open two-seaters like the Sunbeam Tiger and big Austin-Healey, and rather cheaper than a Corvette. It was a satisfying car, especially with the "Hi-Po" 225-bhp 289. That appeal was proven by XR-7 sales, which totaled close to 28,000 for the model year despite the late introduction. Cougar as a whole did about what management expected, selling upwards of 140,000 units, about 30 percent of Mustang volume.

Highlighting a busy corporate year were production of the 70-millionth U.S. Ford vehicle on May 3, and the belated retirement of Ernie Breech from the company's board of directors on April 21 (he'd been allowed to retain his seat even after Henry Ford II ousted him as board chair-

man back in 1960). This was also the year that Ford unveiled its first prototype electric car, saying that it expected such vehicles "to be commercially feasible within the next 10 years."

That prophesy would prove wildly optimistic, but there's evidence that Ford's interest in electrics reflected more serious concerns than simply presenting a good-citizen image. For example, 1967 saw Ford join with Mobil Oil in the Inter-Industry Emission Control Program, which aimed to find ways of reducing air pollution from refineries and factories. The program was later broadened by the participation of five more oil companies as well as automakers Toyota, Nissan, and Mitsubishi. Also this year, Ford was honored by no less than the National Wildlife Federation, receiving the organization's Distinguished Service to Conservation Award for efforts at reducing air and water pollution at U.S. Ford plants.

Cynics would no doubt say that however worthy, these efforts made good grist for the Ford PR mill and helped counter similar bleatings of environmental awareness emanating from GM and other companies. On the other hand, it could be argued that Ford was at least showing the same kind of social concern it had in the mid-Fifties with regard to auto safety. Back then, of course, there was no need to jump on that bandwagon because, as conventional wisdom said, "safety doesn't sell." But now, Washington was legislating not just safer cars but cleaner ones as well. The auto business hasn't been the same since.

Like its big brother Galaxie, the '67 Fairlane (top) sported vertically stacked headlamps. Vertical grille bars were new for 1967. The 500/XL (note the badge in the center of the grille) hardtop started at a modest $2724 and 14,871 copies were called for. The Fairlane Squire wagon (center) carried a base price of $2902, but only 8348 were ordered. The top-line Ranchero 500/XL (above) listed at $2768, which included bucket seats.

1 9 6 8

Dearborn still touted "better ideas" for 1968, but what Ford Motor Company actually offered this year was a lot of little good ideas and two big ones: revamped intermediates and a new Continental Mark. The government had a few ideas too, and they were quite visible. Like other automakers, Ford now had to provide certain "passive" safety devices like a shock-absorbing collapsible steering column, front and rear side marker lights, anti-glare interior trim, and non-protruding, tougher-to-open inside door handles. Other items would be required soon enough. Also, exhaust-emission standards now applied to all 50 states, not just California (where they'd been in force since 1966). Like everyone else, Ford was scrambling to find the best way(s) to meet those requirements.

Ford did well in what would be the American industry's best year yet. The division's model-year car volume rose by some 23,000 units to just over 1.75 million, this despite a lengthy strike in September-October 1967 that affected '68 production, and a considerable drop in Mustang demand. However, Ford still trailed league-leading Chevrolet by a

healthy margin, although helped a bit by Chevy's decline of some 60,000 cars.

Calling the winner in the '68 truck race is a bit trickier, because model- and calendar-year sales, production, and registration figures tend to be carelessly bandied about without labels. Ford itself claims 1968 was the year it regained sales supremacy over Chevrolet, but doesn't say whether this was for model or calendar year. One independent source states that Ford first beat Chevy in truck *sales* for *calendar* 1967, while another shows that Ford didn't *outproduce* Chevy until *model year* 1970. We'll go by the latter, as we believe model-year production is the most accurate reflection of how a manufacturer's products fare each year.

And on that basis, Ford still lagged in trucks for 1968. Though its total output rose a substantial 191,000 units to near 643,500, Chevy began at a higher level and produced sufficiently more units to end the model year at near 681,000. Ford, however, had closed the gap by over half, and the difference was now reduced to fewer than 38,000 units compared to 97,500 for 1967. And as implied above, Ford would continue closing in until it surpassed Chevy for 1970—at least in that particular statistic.

Car-wise, intermediates made news this year as each of the Big Three issued newly styled and/or engineered editions of these increasingly popular models. Ford was no exception. But just to make sure no one missed the fact that its midsizers *were* new, the division gave the

high-trim versions a new name: Torino, what Italians call their famous city of Turin. Described as "Ford's newest bright idea," Torino consisted of a six-model group: standard formal-roof hardtop coupe, four-door sedan, and Squire wagon, plus GT convertible, notchback hardtop coupe, and a new fastback hardtop. The Fairlane name returned on a lower-priced companion line with the same body styles in base and 500 trim. Chassis design and the 116-inch wheelbase (113 on wagons) carried over from 1966-67, but overall length grew by about four inches, width by half an inch, and average weight by some 120 pounds.

With dimensions and weight now approaching the full-size class, the new Fairlane/Torino was styled to bear a closer relationship with the big Fords. Rear fenderlines had the now-obligatory hopup, and bodysides were more radically tucked under, as on the Mustang. Front and rear ends were pleasingly simple. Quad headlamps reverted to side-by-side placement within a recessed grille cavity, and front fenders jutted slightly ahead to house combined parking/side marker lamps.

Ford revamped its intermediates for 1968 and renamed the top-of-the-line series Torino. Torino GTs came in three styles: hardtop, convertible, and a fastback hardtop (below). The last stickered at $2747, and with 74,135 built outdid the two other models by nearly three to one. Wheelbase measured 116 inches.

The new Fairlane/Torino fastback was a real head-turner, its roofline taken directly from the Mustang 2+2. But unlike previous sloped-roof intermediates, such as American Motors' Marlin, this one avoided looking fat and heavy via an upswept rear side windowline and a deep backlight. Reflecting the effectiveness of Ford's flow-through ventilation systems and the growing popularity of air conditioning, convertibles and all hardtop coupes lost their door ventwing windows. It made for a smoother profile—and a lot more wind buffeting when the window was open even a crack. Four-door sedans were similarly shorn of their fixed rear-door quarter panes.

If mid-size Ford dimensions were now closing in on the big-car line, so were prices. In fact, there was a surprising amount of overlap between Torino and that full-size mainstay, the Galaxie 500. The Fairlane group was quite distinct, coming in just above Falcon Futura at $2464 for the four-door sedan to $2880 for the Fairlane 500 wagon. But the cheapest Torino, the sedan, listed at $2688, the top-line GT ragtop at $3001. By contrast, Galaxies ranged from $2864 for the basic four-door to $3214 for the posh 500/XL convertible. Of course, intervening inflation means those dollar differences were more significant then than they are now, but it shows the direction the market was taking: "Smaller" no longer necessarily meant "cheaper."

Fairlane/Torino engines comprised the usual array, but there was a new number among V-8s: 302. This was simply the 289 with a longer 3.0-inch stroke. Rated at 210 horsepower and engineered with emissions standards in mind, it was standard for Torino GTs at the beginning of the year, then became a mid-year option when the two-barrel 289 took over. That engine lost five bhp to emissions tuning (down to 195), as did the optional two-pot 390 (now 265). The four-barrel 390 gained five ponies (for 335 total). Standard for non-GTs was the sturdy 200-cubic-inch six. It, too, fell victim to emissions controls, rerated to 115 bhp, five fewer than before.

Performance engines also changed during the year. At the start was one 427, a single four-barrel unit rated at 390 bhp via a milder cam profile and first-time use

of hydraulic lifters. But it was available only with automatic, not exactly what the drag set had in mind. Accordingly, it was phased out by spring in favor of the 428 Cobra Jet, a huskier version of the T-Bird/big-Ford engine. For drag racing and insurance purposes it was advertised at 335 bhp on 10.7:1 compression, but was undoubtedly much stronger.

After a lackluster '67 NASCAR season, Ford roared back, notching 20 wins—more than any other make and twice as many as it had seen in each of the previous two years. Ford pilot David Pearson won the driving crown. The new mid-size fastback was a big help, its superior aerodynamics having been conceived with an eye to long-haul superspeedway events. It was the same story in USAC, with A.J. Foyt's Fairlane on top, and Benny Parsons was king with his Torino in ARCA (Auto Racing Club of America). The only problem was that a rival, the new Mercury Cyclone fastback, was faster still in long-distance sprints because of its smoother front end, a fact Cale Yarborough and company rubbed in every chance they got.

But the sales race mattered more to Dearborn accountants, and in that contest the new Fairlane/Torino was a champ. Production climbed more than 50 percent over '67 to a record 372,000 units. Significantly, the most popular single model was the slick GT fastback at 74,135 units, and the Fairlane 500 version added more than 32,000 to that. Convertibles, on the other hand, were falling out of favor—only 5310 GTs and a mere 3761 Fairlane 500s were built.

Mustang, "the most exciting car on the American road" according to the ads, saw sales dip to 317,000 units, hardly great compared to earlier years. On

paper, the loss was difficult to explain. It was a generally good year for the industry as a whole and Ford in particular, and Mustang offered the widest selection of engines and convenience options in its brief history. The likely answer was continued competition, now rougher than ever. Besides GM and Chrysler, American Motors was a threat with its new Javelin and AMX. Also, Mustang prices were higher. The convertible now listed at $2814, for example, and a handful of options could quickly run that to over $4000, quite a sum at the time.

Familiarity may have been another factor, particularly since Mustang styling was little changed after 1967's major facelift. As before, the trademark simulated air scoops ahead of the rear wheels were integrated with the side sculpture via a creaseline running from the upper front fenders to behind and around the scoops, then down and forward into the lower part of the doors. GTs now accented this with optional "C-stripes" to impart a look of motion. All '68s carried a more deeply inset grille, the galloping horse still in a bright rectangle that was newly flush-mounted. Eliminating the horizontal grille bar allowed GT foglamps to "float" at the outboard ends of the big mouth cavity.

Otherwise, the Mustang GT package was essentially unchanged from '67. However, this year's edition included dual exhausts with chrome-plated "quad" outlets, a pop-open fuel-filler cap, heavy-duty suspension (high-rate springs plus heavy-duty shocks and front sway bar), F70-14 whitewall tires on six-inch rims, and styled steel wheels. Wide-oval tires were also available.

Mustang's initial '68 powertrains duplicated '67 offerings except that the four-speed was no longer available with the base 200-cid six. That engine and the optional two-barrel 289 were detuned per Fairlane/Torino, the four-barrel 390 similarly uprated by five horses. The latter, incidentally, was still available with heavy-duty three-speed. Also echoing the intermediates was the mid-year arrival of a two-barrel 220-bhp 302 to replace the high-winding 289. Here, too, it was a reasonable performance/economy compromise between the base six and the high-power V-8s—and just as reasonably priced at about $150 extra. Another mid-year announcement was Mustang's first optional six, a 250-cid derivative of the 240 Big Six offering 155 bhp for just $26.

Topping the chart was a new option to counter Chevy's growing escalation of the horsepower war, a four-barrel 427 big-block. Running on 10.9:1 compression, it packed the same 390-bhp wallop as in the mid-sizers (a conservative rating to appease nervous insurance companies) and was also restricted to Cruise-O-Matic. Still, with typical 0-60-mph times in the neighborhood of six seconds, the 427 made for the fastest showroom-stock Mustang yet. But the engine's heaviness tended to overwhelm the front suspension, and a formidable $755 surcharge precluded many sales. All big-block '68 Mustangs benefited from the addition of floating calipers to the power front-disc-brake option. They provided more stop-

ping force than the fixed-caliper '67 discs with the same pedal effort. The new design was also said to promote longer brake life and, with fewer parts, to be more reliable. Ford recognized the need for front discs in big-inch Mustangs by making them a mandatory option for all cars equipped with the 390 or 427.

As with Fairlane/Torino, the 427 was hastily retired from the Mustang program at mid-year in favor of the 335-bhp 428 Cobra Jet. A quarter-mile trip of 13.56 seconds at a trap speed of 106.64 mph caused *Hot Rod* magazine to sing its praises. Also announced was a fortified 302 with high-compression heads, larger valves, wilder cam timing, and a pair of four-barrel carbs. Humorously rated at a

240 bhp, it was clearly developed for Trans-Am racing, but Ford had trouble getting it into production after getting SCCA's okay, and few were actually made.

New to Mustang's lengthening options list was the Sports Trim Group, with woodgrain dash, two-tone hood paint (also available separately), Comfort-Weave vinyl seat inserts, and wheel-lip moldings on sixes, plus styled-steel wheels and larger tires with V-8. A spring/summer Sprint package offered GT C-stripes, pop-open gas cap, and full wheel covers; V-8 got styled wheels and wide-oval tires. Despite such go-go goodies, withering installation rates suggested buyers were shifting from pure sport to a

combination of sport and luxury. Other new extras included rear window defogger and Fingertip Speed Control.

Appearing this year only was a special limited-production Mustang, the California Special. Offered primarily in the Golden State and styled along Shelby-Mustang lines, it was basically the standard hardtop with a ducktail spoiler above wide Cougar-like taillight clusters, plus mid-bodyside tape stripes and a plain grille cavity with foglamps and no Mustang emblem.

The real Shelby-Mustangs got another facelift highlighted by a full-width hood scoop and hood louvers, larger grille cavity with square running lamps (not driving lights), and sequential rear turn signals, plus new convertible alternatives with built-in roll-over hoop. Luxury options like air conditioning, tilt steering wheel, tinted glass, and AM/FM stereo now outnumbered performance features.

With federal emissions limits in force, the GT-350 was switched to Ford's newly enlarged 302-cid small-block—and lost a lot of power, withering to a rated 250 bhp. The Paxton supercharger option returned from '66 to add about 100 horses, but again found few takers. The big-block Shelbys were still clearly preferred, outselling the GT-350s by two-to-one. The GT-500 initially retained its 428, re-rated to 360 bhp. A few, however, got ordinary 390 V-8s, reflecting a shortage of 428s due to an engine-plant strike. Buyers weren't told about the substitution because it was nearly impossible to spot. Mid-model year brought some redress in the GT-500KR—for "King of the Road." This had the new Cobra Jet engine, basically the 428 with big-port 427 heads, larger intake manifold and exhaust system, and an estimated 40 extra horses. Ford also tossed in wider rear brakes.

Shelby's 1968 volume, up for the fourth straight year, came to 4450 units. Convertibles were predictably much rarer than fastbacks: 404 GT-350s, 402 early GT-500s, and a mere 318 KRs. But 1968 would be the peak for Shelby GT production. The press mostly yawned at what was becoming a cushy cruiser, and Ford made no effort to race the '68s, or the '67s for that matter. Not that they'd have been competitive. They'd grown too big, too soft, too heavy—not at all the race-bred stormers their predecessors had been. And Ford only diluted their ap-

peal with Shelbyesque showroom Mustangs like the California Special.

A more important change for Shelby was the late-'67 production shift from Shelby's Los Angeles facility to Michigan, where stock Mustangs supplied from Ford's Metuchen, New Jersey plant were converted into Shelbys by the A.O. Smith Company under contract. From here on, Ford would handle all Shelby promotion, advertising, and model development.

The encore fifth-generation Thunderbird faced the world with a revised grille, minor trim shuffling, and a new engine. Sales dipped some 13,000 units to 64,931, the lowest since 1963. At the start of the season, the familiar 315-bhp 390 was standard. A new "Thunder Jet" 429 was the lone option, but only this larger V-8 was being fitted by the new year.

One of the "385-series" engines (so-called because of the first design's 3.85-inch stroke), the 429 was a cousin to Lincoln's big 460, also new this year. Both would soon spread to lesser Ford/Mercury models, including intermediates, because of their greater adaptability to emissions control. With bore and stroke of 4.36 × 3.59 inches, the 429 arrived with 360 horses, and would continue powering T-Birds well into the Seventies.

This year's full-size Fords were mechanically unchanged apart from emissions-tuned engines. They comprised the 240 Big Six, still at 150 bhp; the new 210-bhp 302 as base V-8; two- and four-barrel 390s, and the 428. The hoary 427, galloping more slowly now after the loss of 35 horses, was the top option only through December 1967.

Another round of lower-body surgery plus fresh nose and tail grafts yielded more massive-looking big Fords that still managed a flowing appearance. Hardtop coupes exchanged their previous semi-fastback rooflines for a more formal notchback design with slightly bulkier sail panels. An exception was the LTD version, where larger rear-quarter windows made C-pillars somewhat slimmer. New to the line were Galaxie 500 and 500/XL hardtop coupes with massive fastback superstructures *a la* Fairlane/Torino. LTD, XL, and the Country Squire wagon acquired headlamps hidden behind retracting lids, matched to a special cross-hatch grille.

Two equipment changes not only reflected the continuing decline of the big XLs, billed as the "top choice for active people," but actually seemed designed to hasten it. First, the standard powertrain was no longer a V-8 and automatic but the 240 six and three-speed manual. Few were ordered that way, of course, but it was a sign of the times. Then, from December 1967, the bucket seats and console that had been part of the big XLs since the first '62s were shifted from the no-charge to the extra-cost column. Though this lowered the price (the XL hardtop moved to just $104 above the equivalent Galaxie 500), it made for a

Mustang returned for 1968 with only a mild facelift that included an extra chrome surround inside the grille and altered simulated scoops ahead of the rear wheels. Base prices started at $2602 for the hardtop, although most were ordered with a V-8, power steering and brakes, and a host of other options that often upped the bottom line by $1000 or more. Output of the 2635-pound hardtop skidded an alarming 30 percent to 249,447 units as the ponycar craze was already beginning to wind down. The largest engine available early in the model year was a 390-bhp 427-cid V-8.

With Mustang sales sliding, Ford tried to add a little luster to its ponycar with the Mach 1 show car. Based on the 1967-68 Mustang bodyshell, it sported a lowered roof, rectangular headlights, big air scoops ahead of the rear wheels, racy-looking wheels, and a clean grille with a pony emblem. Note the streamlined mirrors and the flip-out "toll gate" side windows.

much less distinctive car.

At the same time, the 7-Litre package was replaced by a $205 GT Equipment Group tied to the 390 or 427 V-8s. This included heavy-duty suspension with front anti-roll bar and higher-rate springs, wide-oval tires, power brakes with front discs, the requisite emblems and rocker-panel stripes, mag-style wheel covers, low-restriction exhaust, and sprightlier 3.25:1 rear axle ratio. It all added up to the most overtly sporting big XL in years, nevertheless only a few were built.

Yet, demand for the big XLs shot up to its highest level since 1964: 56,114 units, a 140-percent gain. The convertible accounted for only 6066 orders, and total full-size Ford sales dropped fractionally.

Ford largely ignored the Falcon for 1968. The only cosmetic changes of note were a new twin-element mesh grille that would continue through the compact's demise in 1970 and square taillights replacing the round ones of 1967. As elsewhere at Ford, the 302 V-8 was an extra-cost alternative to the base 170 six and optional two-barrel 289, and the automatic transmission got SelectShift manual override. Buyers apparently agreed with the ads that touted the '68 Falcon as "The compact car for a big, fast country" because they snapped up over 130,000 samples, more than doubling 1967 sales.

The highlight of this year's truck fleet was...a 1969 model? That's right. The two-month strike that hit Ford in the fall of 1967 postponed the introduction of the new second-generation Econoline into the winter months. Lee Iacocca might have said this late arrival was a "1968½," but division marketers decided to go him one better by labeling it a '69, thus advancing that model year a full six

months. Not a bad sales tactic, really, and one that Ford would soon resort to again.

We'll talk about the new Econoline here because it was planned as a '68. It certainly gave dealers plenty to talk about, for this was a brawnier, more mature Econoline—and a mid-size truck rather than a compact. Better make that van, because the old pickup was no more, a victim of consistently sluggish sales.

The new Econoline's bigger size was dictated by a change in both body configuration and driveline layout, with the latter shaping the former. Where the first-series model had its engine almost directly over the front wheels and between the front seats, the new one moved the powerplant further forward and to the right. This, in turn, necessitated a stubby overhang ahead of the front wheels, complete with a shallow hood for access to the engine's front. Rear access still required stepping inside and unclipping a cover, though this was slimmer and closer to the firewall. Shoving the engine ahead opened up additional front-cab leg room and allowed for a less bus-like steering-wheel angle. It also meant that doorsills were behind the front wheels instead of ahead of them, which made for wider doors and easier entry/exit. A third benefit was that the extra up-front metal formed a kind of "safety zone" offering an extra margin of occupant protection in a frontal collision, something the previous forward-control design didn't.

With this basic change, Econoline wheelbases were stretched to 105.5 inches for standard-length models and to 123.5 inches for SuperVans, which now had fully integrated bodywork instead of the previous (and obvious) welded-on rear extension. Twin I-Beam suspension was installed up front, bringing a wider

track that enhanced stability. Rear leaf springs were lengthened to 52 inches to give passengers and cargo a smoother ride. Styling was simple and thus functional, with a plain horizontal-bar grille, a discreet full-length bodyside creaseline (for panel rigidity), curved windshield and door glass, and center-opening rear cargo doors.

Strong acceptance of the earlier SuperVan and Heavy-Duty Econolines prompted three available payload ratings for the new second generation. E-100 models had a maximum GVWR of 4500 pounds, E-200 denoted a 5400-pound capacity, and E-300s had a 7600-pound rating. There was only one basic body style, a box with two front doors and two center-opening right-side cargo doors. But plain and Custom trim was available, as were "windowed" Club Wagons—newly transferred from the Falcon line. The ritziest Club Wagons were badged Chateau and could be trimmed and equipped to rival a passenger car: air conditioning, stereo radio/tape player, tinted glass, full carpeting, middle and rear seats, and similar niceties were all listed. Standard engines were the 200-cid six for E-100/200 and the 240 for E-300 (optional on other models). The new small-block 302 V-8 was available across the board.

As expected, this year's Ranchero was restyled *a la* the new Fairlane/Torino,

adopting ventless side glass but retaining the basic 1966-67 cargo bed. It was a handsome package, especially the sporty GT, which was trimmed like equivalent Torinos—it replaced the '67 500/XL. Special badges, bodyside "C-stripes," and slotted wheels identified the GT visually, while optional 428 Cobra Jet power, complete with mean-looking hood scoop, made this one hauler that could really haul down the road. The base Ranchero and Ranchero 500, outfitted to match equivalent Fairlanes, continued to appeal to more cost-conscious buyers.

The rest of this year's truck line saw relatively little change. Light-duty F-Series models wore a simplified double-decker grille, with each deck holding eight floating bars arrayed in vertically stacked pairs. Some federal safety standards applied to trucks as well as cars, so all models sported electric front side-marker lights, rear-quarter reflectors, and more life-preserving interior features like soft control knobs, recessed door handles, and

anti-glare trim. Broncos even got "friendlier" bumpers: rounded at the ends instead of square. A swing-away spare tire carrier was a handy new option for the popular sport-utility.

Emissions standards prompted two new gasoline V-8s for light-duty trucks: a two-barrel 390, borrowed from the passenger-car line and tuned for 255 bhp, and a downrated version of the existing 361 called "360," taking over for the veteran 352. Front-disc brakes became optional for two-wheel-drive F-250/350s, integrated factory-installed air conditioning was a new extra-cost item for all F-Series through the 750 chassis, and F-100s adopted the F-250's "Flex-O-Matic" variable-rate rear springs as standard. Up among the heavies was a trio of new high-torque diesel V-8s developed for Ford by Caterpillar and designed for more economical urban running. Spanning 522, 573, and 636 cid and 150 to 225 horsepower, they were optional in 6000-8000 chassis in the F-, T-, and C-Series.

Mustang fastback sales took a beating in 1968 as production plummeted by 40 percent to 42,581 units. Base price came in at $2712, but this example (above) is optioned with the $147 GT equipment group. The California Special (bottom left) featured some Shelby Mustang styling touches. Meanwhile, the '68 convertible (bottom right) listed at $2814, but found only 25,376 takers, a drop of 43 percent from 1967.

Disputed sales and production figures notwithstanding, the truck market, especially the light-duty and recreational segments, were becoming as important as cars to the profit pictures of the Big Three companies. Ford recognized the trend this year by forming a special Motor Truck Operations section under future company chairman Philip Caldwell. One of its first programs was to set up a nationwide network of new Ford Truck Centers for sales and service of medium- and heavy-duty models exclusively. Some 43 of these would be in place by the end of 1969.

The '68 Thunderbird Landau sedan (top) listed at $4924 and demand remained relatively stable at 21,925 units, about one-third of total T-Bird output. The '68 Techna (above) was Ford Engineering's "experimental car of the future." It featured doors that opened straight out from the body for improved access, small power control panels in place of door handles, flush-mounted plastic bumpers, and high-level brake and turn signals located in the rear window.

Discretion being the better part of public image, Ford began easing away from "Total Performance" advertising in deference to the public's new safety consciousness. It was just as well, because Ford had a rather disappointing competition year on several fronts. For example,

an Offenhauser captured the Indy 500, thus ending Dearborn's four-year win streak, though Dan Gurney was runner-up in a rear-engine Eagle with stock-block Ford power. And there was another win at Le Mans, thanks to Belgian ace Jacky Ickx, who drove a GT40 prepped by the Gulf Oil-sponsored John Weyer team.

But there was frustration in Trans-Am competition. Group 2 rules had become difficult to manage, so SCCA now bent them a bit. Engines were still restricted to 5.0 liters (305 cid), but minimum vehicle weight was set at 2800 pounds and wheels up to eight inches wide were allowed. The schedule again included 13 events. Though Bud Moore's Cougar team was gone, Mustangs prepped by Shelby-American had to bat-

tle not only Roger Penske's Camaros but a pair of new factory-backed AMC Javelins. Jerry Titus, still the lead Shelby driver, finished first in the Daytona 24-hour opener. But Penske pilot Mark Donohue started to click with round two, winning that race and the next seven before Titus broke the string at Watkins Glen. By that time there was no catching Camaro, which eventually took the championship.

There was happier news on January 10 as Ford set a new one-day domestic production record: 14,333 units. Less than a month later, on February 6, Arjay Miller moved up from president to board vice-chairman.

But to fill Miller's post, Henry Ford II looked beyond Dearborn for the first time in a long time, and his choice was astonishing: none other than GM executive vice-president Semon E. "Bunkie" Knudsen. This was surely the most startling executive shift since Bunkie's father, William S. Knudsen, had left Ford for Chevrolet after an argument with Henry Ford I in the early Twenties. "Big Bill," of course, promptly built Chevrolet into a Ford-beater. Now his son, who had made Pontiac number-three before taking over as Chevrolet general manager in 1961, would try to make Ford more competitive with Chevy for the Seventies. Rumors of a drastic shakeup in Ford management began flying almost as soon as Bunkie arrived. Although some staff changes were made, he didn't instigate a wholesale cleanout, yet he had Ford looking a lot more competitive within a few months.

It was also in February 1968 that

Ford unveiled another timely experimental car: a high-mileage "clean air" prototype developed under the aegis of its Inter-Industry Emission Control (IIEC) venture with Mobil. Said to be the product of 11 years work and $32 million, it was reported to have tailpipe emissions "approaching" those being proposed for the early 1980s. But like everyone else in Detroit, Ford was only beginning down the long road to cleaner cars.

By any measure, 1968 was a vintage year for Lincoln-Mercury, both makes setting new production records. Dominating headlines was the return of the Continental Mark. Logically, it should have been called Mark VI, a designation that actually finished first in public-opinion surveys. But since it was seen as the direct successor to the Mark II, the embarrassing, overgrown Marks III/IV/V of 1958-60 were forgotten and the new model was tagged Mark III.

Officially part of the Lincoln line, this second Mark III is the Ford product most closely associated with Henry Ford II. Just as he'd rejected the first Mark II proposal ("I wouldn't give a dime for that"), the outspoken board chairman is said to have okayed the Mark III by saying, "I would like to drive that one home." But its basic concepts and premises are more correctly credited to Lee Iacocca, not yet company president but already playing an important role.

Like the Mark II, the '68 Mark III was the work of a stellar team, this time headed by L. David Ash, with Art Querfeld assisting and Ralph Peters the product planner. Also involved was Her-

mann C. Brunn, son of the late Hermann A. Brunn, the coachbuilder who produced most of Lincoln's prewar custom bodies. The project, started in September 1965, was entrusted to the Special Development Office at the Dearborn Design Center.

Iacocca insisted that, unlike the II, this new Mark must be a profit maker. The first production cars delivered for about $7000, about 30 percent below the Mark II's price. (Given the rate of inflation, the $10,000 Mark II would have been about $13,000 in 1968 dollars.) So this was very much a volume luxury car, as sales soon confirmed: 7770 for the abbreviated '68 model year, 23,088 for '69, and about 25,000 annually for 1970-71. (There's some confusion about model years. The Mark III was announced on April 5, 1968, ostensibly as a '69 model, but Ford records break out 7770 as '68s. This probably represents sales through the normal new-car introduction month of September.)

Though Iacocca likes to take credit for it, the Mark III's design theme was self-evident: a modern interpretation of the early, close-coupled Continental coupe, with similar long-hood/short-deck proportions, wide quarter roof, and some vestige of the trademark outside spare tire. By the time of the final clay model in October 1965, designers had settled on a squarish, "classic" grille flanked by panels hiding the headlamps, and clean, chiseled lines flowing back to a short deck on which the spare tire outline was even more pronounced than the Mark II's. The hood was the longest of

The '68 Ford F-100 Styleside pickup (top left) retailed at $2237, and some 285,015 were built for the model run. Because of a UAW strike, '67 Econolines were carried into early 1968, at which point the '69s were brought out. Seen here (top right) is the 12-passenger Chateau Club Wagon. Falcon entered 1968 with a seven-model roster. The priciest offering was the $2728 Futura wagon (above left), of which 10,761 were built. Further up the price scale was the $3206 LTD hardtop sedan (above); 61,755 were called for.

any American car. Parking lamps and taillights were neatly set into the fender edges. Wrapping it up was a choice of 26 colors, including four new "Moondust" metallics, and no fewer than 4752 trim combinations. Hermann Brunn contributed a five-pod dash with woodgrain accents and easy-to-reach controls, plus large, comfortable seats. The latter, he noted, "have wrinkles. We put them in deliberately because we think they denote comfort and luxury."

The Mark III rode a 117.2-inch wheelbase, about nine inches shorter than the Mark II's and the same as the four-door Thunderbird's. In fact, it was a T-Bird underneath, sharing basic structure and suspension. As it turned out, the Mark III wheelbase was close to that of Cadillac's new front-drive '67 Eldorado. Although the latter was more technically advanced, the Continental seemed to have more magic in its name. Despite Cadillac's big distribution/production advantages, the Mark III almost matched Eldo production in its four-year life span, and never trailed by more than 2000 a year.

1 9 6 9

Ads boasted that Ford was "The Going Thing" for 1969. There certainly was a lot going on at Ford Division: a new-generation Mustang, a larger small-block V-8, and larger, redesigned big cars. Also, some *very* hot intermediates arrived to carry Dearborn's performance colors on and off the track, while the Shelby-Mustang was about to depart. New engines were also featured in the truck line, where full availability of the new second-generation Econoline contributed to higher sales. Two major executive changes were in place by new-model announcement day: Bunkie Knudsen as company president, and John B. Naughton as the new general manager of Ford Division, replacing Matthew S. McLaughlin.

Production-wise, Ford's model year car total improved by about 75,000 units to a bit beyond 1.8 million (not counting 3150 Shelby Mustangs), the full-size line accounting for slightly more than a million. Chevrolet lost about 25,000 but still tallied a bit more than 2.1 million cars. Chevy also maintained its lead in trucks, but by the smallest margin in years, recording just about 26,000 more than Ford's 658,500.

Knudsen's arrival seemed to augur well for both Ford performance and performance Fords, the new president favoring lower, sleeker cars, with particular emphasis on fastbacks. In fact, he said that while "the long-hood/short-deck concept will continue ... there will be a trend

toward designing cars for specific segments of the market." While he denied Ford had any intention of building a sports car, he did hint that an experimental mid-engine car was being developed. (This turned out to be the Mach 2, a design exercise begun in 1966, making liberal use of Mustang components in a curvy two-seat coupe package.) He also assured the press that Ford's stock-car racing effort would continue.

The compact Falcon, which was advertised as offering "Big car benefits at a compact car price," celebrated its 10th birthday this year. It was virtually un-

changed, models stayed the same, and deleting the four-barrel 289 V-8 left the 220-horsepower 302 as the most powerful engine option. Production dropped to 95,015 units as buyers continued deserting compacts for slightly more expensive intermediates or smaller, lower-priced imports. But Ford had sensed the shift and was readying a new smaller compact. Falcon would hang on, unloved and unpromoted, through 1970, after which it would be unceremoniously dumped.

Few changes attended this year's Thunderbird, now in the third year of its styling cycle. Besides the usual grille, taillight, and trim shifts, the Landau hardtop lost its vestigial rear-quarter side windows, creating an all-time great blind spot. Meanwhile, minor chassis tuning gave two-doors flatter cornering and slightly lower ride height. The year's major new option was one that would soon spread through the U.S. industry: an electrically operated sunroof, harking back to the 1960 Bird. Bucket seats had moved to the options column for '68, and Landau sedan and hardtop buyers continued to show a marked preference for the now-standard front bench. Overall T-Bird production declined by about 15,700 units for the model year to slightly more than 49,000—the lowest since the abbreviated 1958 season. The picture wouldn't change much for the next few years.

Ford now filled a rather obvious displacement gap in its corporate engine lineup with a new 351-cubic-inch V-8, basically a 302 redesigned by Phillip A. Martel, who'd come to Ford from GM back in 1950 and who had also been responsible for the big 385-series engines of 1968. Directly descended from the original 1962 small-block, it used the 302's 4.00-inch bore and a half-inch-longer stroke (3.50 inches). Author Phil Hall observed in *Fearsome Fords* that actual displacement was 351.86 cid, but the company used "351" to avoid confusion with the earlier 352 Y-Block. The new engine was optional in 1969 intermediates, full-sizers, and ponycars—except the new Mustang Mach 1 (and Mercury's Cougar Eliminator), where it was standard.

It should be noted that the 351 being discussed here is the "Windsor" unit, not the more famous "Cleveland" engine. The former got its nickname from the Canadian plant that built it starting in the fall of 1968, a full year before Cleveland production began. While both had the same bore/stroke dimensions, the Windsor featured increased bulkhead strength, a deck height raised 1.27 inches, and a new crankshaft with larger main and crankpin journals. Its intake manifold

was of drop-center design, and its valvetrain included "positive-stop" rocker arm studs. As in the original Fairlane 221, 4.38-inch bore spacing was used for the Cleveland, which became the basis for nearly all of Dearborn's high-performance cars from 1970 through 1974. That relegated the Windsor to a secondary role, used mainly with low compression and two-barrel carburetion.

Ford spent some $100 million for tooling the Cleveland. Its block casting was unique, with an integral timing chain chamber and water crossover passage at the front, and deck height was exactly one inch higher than on the 302's block. Cylinder heads differed dramatically from the Windsor's, with valves canted 9.5 degrees from the cylinder axis for modified wedge-type combustion chambers. In addition, intake valves were tilted four degrees, 15 minutes forward and the exhausts backward for shorter port areas with more direct gas flow. The widest possible spacing was chosen for maximum valve size. Intakes had a 2.19-inch head diameter, while the forged-steel exhausts were 1.71 inches across their aluminized heads.

This year's big Fords were fresh from the tires up. Basic chassis and suspension changed only in detail, but wheelbase was stretched two inches, to 121 (where it would remain through 1978), the first such increase since 1960. Overall length went up from 213.3 inches to as much as 216.9 inches on some models, and there were fractional gains in track and overall width. And Ford wanted buyers to know the new models were big and plush, pointing out that they had a track as wide as a Cadillac, more headroom than an Imperial, more legroom than a Chrysler, and that the '69 was quieter than the '65 LTD that was, in turn, quieter than a Rolls-Royce.

The 21-model lineup again began with Custom and Custom 500 sedans and wagons, progressing through seven Galaxie 500s, two XLs, and the posh LTD sedan, hardtops, and Country Squire wagons.

Styling was a nice mixture of Lincoln-Mercury pretense and the svelte brawn of recent big Fords. Hoods were longer, rear decks shorter, bodysides more shapely. Headlamps were again concealed behind flip-up doors on LTDs, Country Squires, and XLs, which shared an imposing, full-width eggcrate grille with a protruding center. Lesser models wore a flatter, plainer face. The fastback hardtop coupe, again offered as a Galaxie 500 or XL, was renamed "SportsRoof"— as were all Ford fastbacks this year—and acquired tunnel-roof or "flying buttress"

The Fairlane/Torino lineup consisted of 14 models for 1969. At the top of the performance heap reigned the Cobra, a no-frills muscle machine answering Plymouth's popular '68 Road Runner. Cobra was offered as a $3164 formal notchback hardtop or as a $3189 SportsRoof fastback hardtop (left). Power came from a 335-horsepower 428-cubic-inch V-8, and along with that Ford threw in a four-speed manual transmission, heavy-duty suspension, six-inch-wide wheels, F70-14 wide-oval belted tires, plus a taxicab-plain interior. Options included automatic, Ram Air induction, tach, front disc brakes, and limited-slip differential.

styling, with a near-vertical backlight flanked by sloping outrigger sail panels. Inside was what Ford called the "Front Room," a cockpit-style dash curved in front of the driver and swept away to the right to give passengers, as the brochure boasted, "more room than Ford has ever offered before."

A redrawn big-Ford engine chart finally scratched the old 427 as the top option. In its place were two 385-series "Thunder Jet" 429s, one a two-barrel, 320-bhp version, the other a four-barrel, 360-bhp unit. Both ran 10.5:1 compression and required premium gas. The 150-bhp 240-cid "Big Six" was base power for all models except the LTD and Country Squire, which came with a 200-bhp 302. Also available were a two-barrel, 265-bhp 390 and—at mid-season—the new 351 Windsor in 250-bhp two-barrel form. A four-speed manual gearbox was still optional, but only with the four-barrel 429.

A new Mustang had been planned long before Knudsen set up in Dearborn. While he wouldn't have much influence on this or any other Ford product until the 1971 models, he was able to make a few last-minute changes for the '69 pony-car. He also lured stylist Larry Shinoda from his former employer to head Ford's Special Design Center. Working under GM design vice-president William L. Mitchell since the early Sixties, Shinoda had been involved with such stunning show cars as the 1960 Sting Ray racer,

Corvette Mako Shark, and Corvair Monza GT and Super Spyder. He favored wind-cheating shapes and eye-catching aerodynamic addenda: spoilers, front air dams, low-cut noses, voluptuous lines. These and other GM characteristics would show up on a variety of Dearborn cars.

The '69 Mustang was mostly finished when Shinoda arrived, with dimensions that marked a departure from the original sporty-compact concept. Though retaining a 108-inch wheelbase, it emerged four inches longer (most of it in front overhang), about a half-inch wider, and some 140 pounds heavier. Unit construction was retained for the all-new bodyshell, which continued successful appearance themes. Changes included a more prominent "mouth" grille with egg-crate insert that carried two extra headlamps at its outer ends in place of the optional (and mostly ineffective) foglamps of previous years. The old side sculpturing was erased, but rear fenders now bulged noticeably above the wheel arches. Taillights were still vertical clusters but no longer recessed in the back panel, which was less concave. The usual three body styles returned, and the newly named SportsRoof fastback acquired flip-out rear side windows. Driving range was increased by enlarging fuel tanks from 17 to 20 gallons.

Dimensional increases were also evident inside: 2.5 inches more front shoul-

The Talladega was named for the 2.66-mile Alabama speedway that opened in 1969, and the emphasis was on aerodynamics for high-speed track work. The key differences from the regular Fairlane/ Torino were up front: a six-inch longer nose, curved gently to meet a simple, flush-mounted grille (from the Cobra) above a sectioned Torino rear bumper. Some 754 Talladegas were built. Street models had the 428 Cobra Jet V-8.

der room and 1.5 inches more hiproom, thanks to thinner doors; a modified frame crossmember under the front seat added a significant 2.5 inches to rear legroom. Bubbly press releases claimed trunk capacity was larger by "13 to 29 percent," but it wasn't much of a gain because there hadn't been much to begin with. A Mustang trunk could still just manage a two-suiter and little else.

Mustang model permutations expanded by four. Two bowed at the beginning of the model year, the other two at mid-season. Priced about $230 over the standard hardtop was the Grandé, aimed at personal-luxury ponycars like Cougar and Pontiac's Firebird. Features ran to vinyl roof with identifying script, twin color-keyed door mirrors, wire wheel covers, two-tone paint stripes just under the beltline, and bright wheelwell, rocker-panel, and rear-deck moldings. Dash and door panels were decorated with imitation teakwood (a good copy of the real thing), and some 55 extra pounds of sound insulation were added.

More exciting was the new Mach 1 fastback. A $3139 intruder into Shelby territory, it wore non-functional rear-quarter air scoops, decklid spoiler, flat-black hood with NASCAR-style tie-downs, and a functional hood scoop. The last was nicknamed "Shaker" because it was attached to the engine air cleaner and stuck up through a hole in the hood where it vibrated madly, especially at high revs.

Mustang engine availability also expanded. The hardy 200 six was standard for all but Mach 1, while the 155-bhp 250 six cost $39 extra. V-8 offerings ranged from the 220-bhp 302 to the 335-bhp 428 Cobra Jet, available with or without Ram-Air induction. Mach 1 came with the new 351 in two-barrel, 250-bhp regular-fuel tune. This was available for other models, as was a high-compression four-barrel unit with 290 bhp. Rounding out engine options was a four-barrel 320-bhp 390 with 10.5:1 compression.

Naturally, the Cobra Jet was the choice for all-out performance. Developed by Ford's Light Vehicle Powertrain Department under Tom Feaheney, it was thoughtfully combined with a tuned suspension engineered by Matt Donner. Beginning with the heavy-duty '67 setup, he mounted one shock ahead of the rear axle line and the other behind it to reduce axle tramp in hard acceleration. Result: a street machine that handled like a Trans-Am racer. The big-engine Mustang still exhibited final oversteer, but it was more easily controlled with the throttle. "The first Cobra Jets we built were strictly for drag racing," Feaheney recalled. "Wheel hop was damped out by staggering the rear shocks. It was not a new idea, but it worked." As for straightline performance, a Cobra Jet Mach 1 would run the quarter-mile in about 13.5 seconds, making it one of the world's fastest production four-seaters.

Sixes also got a measure of attention with "center percussion" (forward located) engine mounts that greatly improved operating smoothness. Competition manager Jacque Passino was optimistic about the six-cylinder Mustang: "We've been putting [them out] kind of artificially since '64 to fill up production schedules when we couldn't get V-8s. I think there is a real market for an inexpensive hop-up kit for the 250-cubic-inch engine." But he was whistling in the wind. A kit never materialized, nor did a fuel-injected six he also predicted, though both probably should have.

Announced at mid-model year were two very exotic Mustang fastbacks: Boss 429 and Boss 302. The latter was created primarily to compete with the Camaro Z-28 in the Sports Car Club of America's Trans-American Sedan Championship racing series. Ford had even considered calling it Trans-Am, but Pontiac copped that handle for its hottest '69 Firebird. Ford had to build 1000 copies to qualify the Boss 302 as production, but ended up turning out 1934 of the '69s. Despite even

Although it still rode a 108-inch wheelbase, the '69 Mustang was bigger and heavier. Quad headlights, with two mounted in the grille, were new and there were more models to choose from, but sales continued to slide. The $2849 convertible, for example, saw output skid 42 percent to 14,746 units for the model year.

that limited number, the Boss brought people into Ford showrooms like the original Mustang had back in 1964. Knudsen knew what grabbed the public.

Shinoda's interest in "airflow management" was evident in the Boss 302's front and rear spoilers, effective at any speed over 40 mph. The four-inch deep front spoiler was angled forward to direct air around the car. The rear spoiler was an adjustable, inverted airfoil. Matte-black rear window slats *a la* Lamborghini Miura did nothing to enhance airflow but looked terrific. The aerodynamic aids resulted in a gain of perhaps 2.5 seconds per lap at Riverside Raceway in California with no increase in engine power.

Of course, there *was* an increase in power—a big one. The Boss 302's special high-output (HO) V-8 was said to produce 290 bhp at 4600 rpm, but estimates of actual output ranged as high as 400 bhp. It employed "Cleveland" heads with oversize 2.33-inch intake valves and 1.71-inch exhaust valves, which were inclined in the big ports to improve fuel flow. Other HO tweaks ran to an aluminum high-riser manifold, Holley four-barrel carburetor, dual-point ignition, solid lifters, four-bolt central main bearing caps, forged crankshaft, and special pistons. To help prolong engine life, Ford fitted an ignition cutout that interrupted current flow from the coil to the spark plugs between 5800 and 6000 rpm, thus preventing accidental over-revving.

Boss 302 hardware also included ultra-stiff springs, staggered shocks, a four-speed gearbox pulling a shortish 3.50:1 final drive (Detroit "Locker" dif-

ferentials were available with ratios of 3.50, 3.91 and 4.30:1), power brakes with 11.3-inch-diameter front discs and heavy-duty rear drums, and F60-15 Goodyear Polyglas tires. Traction-Lok limited-slip diff was optional, as were Autolite "inline" four-barrel carbs on a special "Cross Boss" manifold. Ford hadn't missed a trick. Even wheel wells were radiused to accept extra-wide racing rubber. On the street, the Boss was unmistakable, with matte black paint on hood and grille extensions, plus bold bodyside C-stripes with "Boss 302" lettering. It was the ultimate '69 Mustang.

Not counting the Boss 429, that is. This big-block brute was born of Ford's desire to qualify its new "semi-hemi" 429 V-8 for competition in NASCAR (National Association for Stock Car Automobile Racing). The rules said it had to be installed in 500 production cars, but didn't specify which models. So although the NASCAR racers were Torinos, Ford decided to side-step the rules by putting a street version of the new engine in the smaller Mustang. This *was* Knudsen's doing—Bunkie loved stock-car racing.

Besides semi-hemispherical combustion chambers—"crescent-shaped" in Ford parlance—the Boss 429 engine employed thinwall block construction, aluminum heads, beefed-up main bearings, and a cross-drilled steel-billeted crankshaft. There were actually two versions of this "820" engine: a hydraulic-lifter "S" unit fitted to the first 279 cars, and the later "T" edition, with different rods and pistons and either mechanical or hydraulic lifters. Both were nominally rated at

While 1969 was a down year for Mustang as a whole, fastback production more than tripled to 134,438 units, 60,046 of them going to the standard model, which started at $2635. A good many of them, of course, were upgraded with V-8s and bigger wheels and tires, and the rear-window slats were popular. Mustang continued with a triple-taillight theme, but the lights were redesigned for 1969.

360 bhp in street form or 375 bhp in race trim. But as with the HO 302, this was just to avoid raising the ire of insurance companies, which were then raising premiums for muscle cars of all kinds.

The semi-hemi was too large for even the '69 Mustang's bigger engine bay, so Ford farmed out Boss 429 assembly to Kar Kraft, the low-volume specialty constructor in Brighton, Michigan, that had become virtually a Ford subsidiary because of all its Dearborn business. There, a mini-assembly line was set up to shoehorn the engines into selected SportsRoof fastbacks, which required modifying front suspension and inner fender wells, adding diagonal braces twixt wheelhouses and firewall (to resist body twisting in hard acceleration), and moving the battery to the trunk (with the big-block installed, there was no room for it up front). For good measure, track was widened at each end (to 59.5 inches), and

wheel arches were flared to accommodate F60-15 tires on seven-inch-wide Magnum 500 wheels.

Other features unique to the Boss 429 included a big, functional hood scoop, specific front spoiler, and an engine oil cooler. Power steering and brakes were standard, as was a Traction-Lok limited-slip differential with 3.91 gearing, to help get all that torque to the pavement. A Detroit No-Spin axle was optional. Outside, the Boss 429 was far more subdued than either its small-block brother or the Mach 1: just discreet identification decals and a Boss 302-style rear wing.

For what amounted to a factory drag racer, the Boss 429 was surprisingly lush. Every one left Kar Kraft with the Decor Group that was optional on other Mustangs, along with high-back bucket seats, deluxe seatbelts, center console, and woodgrain dash trim. Ford also threw in the optional Visibility Group, comprising parking brake warning lamp, glovebox lock, and lights for luggage compartment, ashtray, and glovebox. However, automatic shift and air conditioning weren't available even as options.

At $4798, the Boss 429 was the costliest non-Shelby Mustang to date, which may explain why just 852 were called for. Only another 505 would be built to 1970 specs. A tamer 429 then became a regular

Mustang option, only to disappear after a single year.

Of course, neither Boss was intended to make money; these were, instead, specialty models that had to be built for homologation purposes. *Car Life* magazine tested both Bosses and found the little guy quicker to 60 mph—6.9 seconds versus 7.2. But the 302 lost in the quarter-mile at 14.85 seconds and 96.14 mph compared with 14.09 seconds and 102.85 mph for the 429. Top speed for both was shown as 118 mph. Obviously, the 429 was potent, but its chassis was simply overwhelmed in standing-start acceleration. It was fearsome as a starting point for those who wished to modify it for the strip, but on the street it was something of a disappointment. In fact, *Car Life* found it slower than the 428CJ Mach 1.

Not so the Boss 302, and it's interesting to note that the example tested by *Car Life* turned in the same quarter-mile time as the magazine's Camaro Z-28. *Car and Driver* pronounced the Boss 302 "the best handling Ford ever. . . . [It] may just be the new standard by which everything from Detroit must be judged. . . . It's what the Shelby GT-350s and 500s should have been but weren't." All of which made for something of a bargain, even at a not-inexpensive $3588.

Mustang's reach into the luxury and

performance ends of the ponycar field showed interesting results. Of 184,000 cars delivered in the first half of the model year, only about 15,000 were Grandés, but close to 46,000 were Mach 1s. On cue, division general manager John Naughton predicted "heavy emphasis on performance" for what he (or his press writers) saw as the "Sizzlin' Seventies."

Because Mustang changed this year, so did its Shelby GT cousins. Fastback and convertible returned in GT-350 and 500 form, differentiated from the weightier, lengthier, much busier new ponycar by a three-inch longer hood, reshaped front fenders, and a new nose with a big loop bumper/grille (all made of fiberglass to hold down weight), plus a clipped tail still bearing a lip spoiler and Cougar sequential turn signals. Scoops were everywhere—five NACA ducts on the hood alone—and wide reflective tape stripes ran midway along the flanks. Said *Car and Driver*'s Brock Yates: "I personally can't think of an automobile that makes a statement about performance . . . any better than [this Shelby]."

But brag is one thing, fact another. And the fact was that greater weight and stiffening emission controls rendered the '69s tamer than any previous Shelby. The GT-500 was no longer a "King of the

Road" but retained that '68 model's 428 Cobra Jet engine, still rated at a nominal 335 bhp, though actual output was down 25 horses by most estimates. The GT-350 adopted Ford's new 351 "Windsor" smallblock, with hydraulic-lifter cam, big fourbarrel carb, aluminum high-rise manifold, and low-restriction exhaust system. Advertised horsepower was unchanged from that of the previous 302—but then, this engine was standard in the new Mach 1 fastback, which cost much less than the Shelby.

And that was a problem. The Mach 1 was interference enough, let alone the Bosses 302 and 429. While the latter were no cheaper or more readily available than the Shelbys, they were "a curious duplication of effort," as Yates put it, and only dimmed what luster the Shelbys still had. Indeed, the '69 Shelbys were built at Ford's Southfield, Michigan, plant right alongside stock Mustangs. With design now being determined by production economics and marketing studies, proposed features that might have restored the Shelbys' distinction—things like fuel injection, moonroof, and reclining seats—didn't stand a chance. "The heritage of the [Shelby GT] is performance," Yates mused, "and it is difficult to understand why the Ford marketing experts failed to exploit its reputation."

A new Mustang model for 1969 was the $2866 Grandé, which was aimed at personal-luxury ponycars like the Cougar and Firebird. Features ran to vinyl roof with identifying script, twin color-keyed mirrors, wire wheel covers, beltline pinstriping, and bright wheelwell, rocker panel, and rear deck moldings. Dash and door panels were trimmed in imitation teak.

But fail they did, and Shelby production sank by fully 25 percent. As usual, fastbacks way outsold convertibles and the GT-500 maintained its lead over the GT-350. Model year production totaled just 3150 units, including a mere 194 GT-350 convertibles and 335 of the GT-500s. In Trans-Am racing in 1969, rules changed yet again for the 12-race '69 season, diverging even more from those for Group 2 sedans. As Mustang fastbacks were now legal, the new Boss 302 was the hot ticket, and Shelby's outfit prepared one apiece for Peter Revson and Horst Kwech. A second team fielded by Bud Moore had Parnelli Jones and George Follmer in the driver's seats. Massive factory engineering efforts produced semitube frame chassis (thinly disguised as roll cages), acid-dipped bodies, huge tires, flared fenders, spoilers, wings, and mindboggling horsepower.

The canted-valve HO engine made an impressive debut in the '69 curtain-

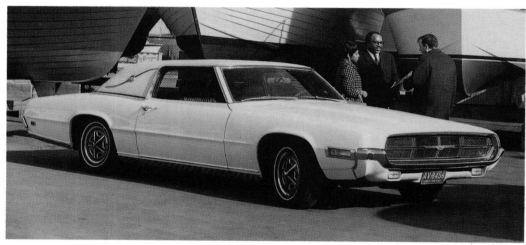

Thunderbird continued with a three-model lineup for '69. The hardtop listed at $4824, while the Landau sedan (top) was the priciest at $5043. Popularity of this model was beginning to decline, however, as output slipped to 15,695 units. Priced at $4964, the Landau coupe (center) was the year's best seller: 27,664 units. Among big Fords, the $2930 Galaxie 500 tunnel-roof hardtop (bottom) found 63,921 customers.

new 351 V-8, but there were two hot newcomers. One was the Cobra, a very different animal from Carroll Shelby's like-named sports car. This one was, as Ford put it, the "Newest, brightest, star-quality performer for folks who don't want anyone stepping on their tails." It was a no-frills muscle machine, and its mission was to step on the tail of Plymouth's popular Road Runner. Two models were offered: SportsRoof and formal notchback hardtops. Exact production isn't available (body designations were shared with corresponding Fairlane 500s), but likely most were fastbacks. Prices were attractive: $3164 for the notch, $3189 for the fastback. That money bought a 335-bhp 428, four-speed stick, competition suspension, six-inch-wide wheels, and F70-14 wide-oval belted tires—plus a taxicab-plain interior. The outside featured blacked-out grille and hood lock pins, and was devoid of doodads save small, cartoon snakes (decals on early cars, emblems on later ones) on the tail and front fenders. Options included a wide choice of axle ratios, Cruise-O-Matic, Ram-Air induction with broad hood scoop, bucket seats, console, tachometer, front disc brakes with power assist, and limited-slip differential.

Ford boasted that the "Cobra uncoils for action on command," and indeed it lived up to its name on the dragstrips, proving to be the fastest mid-size Ford ever. Typical quarter-mile time was 14.5 seconds, while the 0-60-mph run took a mere six seconds. Fuel economy was only eight mpg or so, but who cared when gas cost but 30 cents a gallon? The Cobra boosted Ford's performance image among the street-racing crowd. And most professional road testers agreed that of all the '69 supercars it was the tightest and quietest.

Ford would have its last big season for some time in NASCAR stock-car racing this year, thanks partly to the new limited-production Torino Talladega. Named for the 2.66-mile Alabama superspeedway that opened in '69, it featured body mods designed to solve the aerodynamic problems that had hampered the fastback Torino stockers in 1968. It was also Ford's weapon against the still-slippery Mercury Cyclones and Dodge's new winged warrior, the Charger Daytona. The key differences were at the front: a six-inch-longer nose curved gently to meet a simple, flush-mount grille (taken from the Cobra) above a sectioned Torino rear bumper. Developed with the aid of wind tunnel tests, these changes reduced air drag and made for higher speeds with no more horsepower.

Even so, Ford sought approval for its semi-hemi 429, but NASCAR disputed how "production" it was. As the rules didn't say that an engine had to be sold in the model being raced, Boss Mustang installations counted toward certifying the 429 Talladega. The rules also required a minimum of 500 cars, and Ford

raiser, where Jones was declared the winner after a post-race check of lap charts. Round two, at Lime Rock, Connecticut, went to Sam Posey in a Shelby-prepared Boss 302. But it would be the Shelby team's only victory this season.

That was enough for Carroll Shelby. The cars bearing his name were now being designed by committees instead of engineers, had become too soft and plush to be raced, and were being crowded out by Ford's own products. Accordingly, Shelby announced his retirement as race-

car developer and team manager on October 4. Soon afterwards, executive vice-president Lee Iacocca agreed to terminate the Shelby-Mustang program. Cars stranded in the pipeline—a little over 600—were given Boss 302 front spoilers, black-finish hoods, and 1970 serial numbers, thus ending one of the most remarkable chapters in high-performance history.

Ford's middleweight Fairlane/Torino returned for 1969 with only minor trim changes and optional availability of the

scrambled. While the 429 wasn't approved until late in the season, Ford built the requisite number of cars in time for the Daytona 500 in late February.

They proved formidable. After a 10-year association with Plymouth, driver Richard Petty was enticed to the Dearborn camp and won with the Talladega his first time out at the Riverside 500. Lee Roy Yarborough was victorious at Daytona despite being forced to run the old 427 wedge. David Pearson ended up with the NASCAR crown and Ford with 26 Grand National wins.

Altogether, 754 Talladegas were completed, including prototypes. The street models, built at Ford's Atlanta facility, had the 428 Cobra Jet and Cruise-O-Matic, power steering, power disc brakes, competition suspension, and F70-14 tires on six-inch-wide styled steel wheels. All had white bodies and flat-black hoods.

Elsewhere on the racing scene, Ford added four more laurels to its crown in '69. The first was collected in Victory Lane at Indianapolis. Mario Andretti averaged 156.876 mph in the Memorial Day 500 in a Hawk racer powered by a special Switzer-turbocharged 159-cid Ford V-8 that allegedly developed up to 675 bhp at 10,000 rpm. Andretti then went on in this machine to clinch the USAC Indy-car championship with a victory at Trenton, New Jersey.

Across the Atlantic, Jacky Ickx and the John Weyer team repeated their winning performance at Le Mans—with the same GT40 they'd used in '68. With that, Ford took home the International Makes Championship. Sadly, this was another performance story that would end in 1969, the GT40 having been rendered obsolete by a rules change limiting Group 6 prototypes to engines of no more than 3.0 liters (180 cid). But though effectively banished from the track, the GT40s, Mark IIs, and Mark IVs, as well as the special limited-edition roadgoing GT40 coupes called "Mark III," were destined to be highly prized collector cars. Today they can still be seen in the occasional vintage-car race looking as fresh and running as fast as they did when new—the epitome of "Total Performance" and glorious reminders of a unique period in Ford history.

Things were quiet on the truck front for '69. Only detail changes occurred among mediums and heavies, leaving most of the action in the light-duty end of the range. Starting with Ranchero, its base six switched from the 200-cid unit to the heftier 250, the 302 became the base V-8, and two- and four-barrel 351 V-8s arrived to supplement the continuing 390 and 428 options. Ranchero GTs exchanged their standard buckets for an ordinary bench seat, though the former were still available at extra cost. Naturally, all Rancheros wore the slightly busier grilles of this year's Fairlane/Torino, as well as their revised exterior and

Falcon fluttered into 1969 with the same seven-model lineup. The base station wagon (top) now cost $2660, a $43 hike, and 11,568 were built. The Futura Sports Coupe (center) listed at $2598, but output sunk to 5931. Although it rode a six-inch-shorter 113-inch wheelbase, the Torino Squire wagon (bottom) was styled along the same lines as the big Country Squire. But at $3107, it was $554 cheaper; 14,472 were built.

interior trim.

NVH—Noise, Vibration, and Harshness—was an increasingly common buzzword in Dearborn as engineers stepped up their efforts to eliminate these problems everywhere. Trucks were not exempt. The sturdy little Bronco was a case in point, becoming even sturdier this year via strengthened door frames, pillar junctions and hinges, plus a new fixed windshield instead of the previous fold-flat glass. Also for NVH reasons, the Roadster was cancelled (it hadn't sold that well anyway), Wagon and Pickup tops were no longer removable, and a previously optional steering damper—a shock absorber-like device in the steering linkage—became standard. Two-speed wipers were adopted late in the run as a no-cost extra, and the 302 V-8 was newly optional. Sport models now came with nicer interiors featuring aluminum door-panel appliques, parchment-color vinyl upholstery, and, with the accessory back bench seat, a rear vinyl floormat.

Turning to the more work-oriented

Full-size Fords wore two different grilles. The cheaper Customs, like the $2649 price-leader two-door sedan (top), had a simple horizontal-bar unit. The more expensive models, such as the $3661 Country Squire wagon (bottom) sported a far more ornate front end and also got hidden headlights. Output of this top-line wagon came to an impressive 129,235 units, while the base Custom found only 15,439 buyers.

light-duty trucks, E-100 Econolines were supplied with higher-rate front springs, and all-round heavy-duty springs as a new E-300 option. Indicative of where the van market was heading was a new mini-motorhome Econoline conversion, performed by an outside firm but marketed with Ford's full approval and sold by a good many Ford dealers.

The 302 was also the new base V-8 for F-Series pickups, where grilles took on horizontal bars by the simple expedient of removing the black vertical paint stripes that had formed the previous hashmarks. Power steering and the plush Ranger trim package were newly available on F-350s as well as 100/250s. This year's Ranger was identified outside by black-painted headlamp bezels and red-stripe center grille bar, inside by uprated vinyl trim and woodtone accents on dash and doors.

New for F-100/250 Stylesides were three "vocational" options: Heavy-Duty, Farm & Ranch, and Contractor's. The last featured full-length auxiliary storage bins atop the box siderails, plus heavy-duty springs, rear step bumper, dual "Western" door mirrors, and other on-the-job necessities. To this you could add an "Electric Power Pak," a self-contained 2500-watt underhood generator for running power tools at worksites without convenient electrical hookups. The Farm & Ranch package had most of the same chassis and cab features, but replaced the "contractor's boxes" with swing-up side boards for carrying tall or bulky loads like hay bales. The Camper Special package was still around for standard and Crew Cab F-100/250/350 Styleside 4×2s, but there was a new version: a 4×4 Crew Cab chassis with a 148.3-inch wheelbase.

Nineteen sixty-nine was the year that the new National Highway Traffic Safety Administration—NHTSA—first proposed "passive restraints" as mandatory automotive safety equipment. The idea was to keep occupants in place during a collision by means of a device or devices that would function without the car's occupants doing anything other than getting in the vehicle and closing the door. Significantly, the government didn't define "passive restraint"; any device would do so long as it proved effective. But increasingly the term came to be associated with the airbag, a collapsed cushion within the steering wheel or dashboard that inflated rapidly in response to crash forces.

NHTSA soon wrote passive restraints into law as FMVSS 208 and re-

quired them on all cars sold in the U.S. beginning with model year 1975. But as we know now, airbags would be delayed until the late '80s by squabbles over their complexity and hence likely reliability, as well as possible health hazards. (Ear damage from the explosive inflation of the bag and the unknown effects of the chemicals used for it were the chief worries.) In addition, automakers were irritated that NHTSA seemed closed to alternative restraint methods like passive seatbelts. Indeed, Standard 208 was long known as the "airbag standard." A compromise was eventually reached in this most controversial of Federal motor-vehicle standards, though even now the long-range benefits—and hazards—of 208 are only now being determined.

There were big doings at Ford's "Glass House" World Headquarters in 1969. An agreement with long-range consequences was reached this year with Toyo Kogyo of Japan, maker of Mazda cars and trucks, to act as Ford's Asian affiliate, which included supplying parts for certain Ford products outside North America. It seemed a modest relationship, but it would assume an importance that few Dearborners could have imagined in 1969. The year also brought word of a "rearrangement" at the Edison Institute, a $1.6-billion long-range development program that would largely refurbish both Greenfield Village and the Henry Ford Museum in time for Ford Motor Company's 75th anniversary bash in 1978.

But the big surprise was the bomb-

shell that exploded on September 11: a complete reorganization of the company's top-echelon management structure—including the abrupt dismissal of Bunkie Knudsen after less than two years as president. Chairman Henry Ford II told the press that "things just didn't work out," but would say no more. He said even less to Knudsen, showing him the door with a simple, "Bunkie, you'll be leaving."

Insiders surmised that like his father before him, Knudsen had caused his own demise by accumulating and wielding too much power. "Knudsen moved in and started doing things his way," wrote prominent Detroit analyst Robert W. Irvin. "Knudsen was almost running the company and [some said] he had alienated many other top executives. Others said Knudsen's departure was an indication of how the Fords don't like to share power." Tellingly, Irvin wrote those words in July 1978 as a comment on the firing of Lee A. Iacocca. Of course, one doubts that Iacocca liked sharing power any more than "Henry the Deuce," so it's logical to wonder whether he also didn't have something to do with Knudsen's firing.

In any case, HF II moved to soften the impact of this upheaval by announcing a presidential troika comprising R.L. Stevenson for International Automotive Operations, R.J. Hampson for Non-Automotive Operations, and Iacocca for North American Automotive Operations (NAAO). But that lasted only a year: Iacocca would become overall president in 1970.

1 9 7 0

Ford Division touched three very different bases this year, unveiling a replacement compact, heavily restyled intermediates, and new-design long- and short-cab heavy-duty conventional trucks. All these product initiatives, plus a prolonged strike against GM, put Ford on top in both car and truck production for the model year. On the car side, Ford went back above the two-million mark for the first time since 1966, building close to 2.1 million units to Chevrolet's 1.8 million-plus. Truck volume declined by some 18,000 units from 1969's level, landing at 640,647, but Chevy fell much further, losing better than 192,000 units to close at just over 492,500.

The new compact, called Maverick, bowed well ahead of the model year, on April 17, 1969. That date was chosen for luck: five years to the day after the launch of the phenomenally successful Mustang. Billed as "the first car of the '70s at 1960s prices," it was much the same package as the first Falcon, though slightly smaller. It featured resolutely ordinary engineering and a similar $1995 price tag (the original Falcon started at $1912), the only domestic Ford listing below $2000. Maverick also had a similar mission: to counter the small imports, sales of which had been creeping steadily upward since the mid-Sixties. Predictably, Maverick was pitched as a roomier, more powerful, more trouble-free import alternative. Its simplicity

Although the Big Three compacts of 1960-61 temporarily slowed import sales, by the end of the Sixties Detroit had largely abandoned the compact market and import sales were booming again. Enter Maverick, Ford's second attempt at an import fighter. Though bigger than a VW Beetle, it was indeed compact: 103-inch wheelbase, 2411-pound weight. The public responded by snapping up 578,914 units during the long model year.

certainly implied reliability, and indeed Ford advertised it as "Simply wonderful and wonderfully simple." The 103-inch-wheelbase chassis had a typical leaf-sprung live rear axle, twin-arm front suspension with coil springs, recirculating-ball steering, and all-drum brakes.

Under the hood it looked like 1961 all over again. The same 170-cubic-inch cast-iron six (rated at 105 bhp) that had been optional in that year's Falcon was the base engine; its 120-bhp, 200-cid enlargement cost a bit extra. A "three-on-the-tree" stick shift came standard, but most buyers opted instead for Cruise-O-Matic. Curb weight, in the vicinity of 2500 pounds, made Maverick quite a bit heavier than most rival foreigners, but lighter than other domestic compacts.

Arriving as a two-door fastback sedan, Maverick was contemporary in appearance, if a bit overdone. *Road & Track* magazine opined that "it looks like an American car. That isn't necessarily bad . . . and the overall impression is detracted from only by the tiny tires [6.00-13s], its fat-hipped look, and the rather unattractive grille. . . . The voguish blind-rear-quarter routine makes all three rear windows too small from both the visibility and styling standpoint." Trim and equipment were kept basic in the interest of low price. There were no instruments apart from speedometer and fuel gauge, for example, and a European-style under-dash shelf filled in for a proper glovebox. However, the plain bench seats were covered in a spunky tartan-plaid cloth, and armrests and full carpeting were standard. Interiors were color-keyed to five whimsically named exterior hues: Anti-Establish Mint, Hulla Blue, Original Cinnamon, Freudian Gilt, and Thanks Vermillion. It was all part of an attempt to make this an economical "fun" car for those on a budget—or those who didn't like imports.

And in that, Maverick succeeded admirably. Production for its extra-long 1970 model year totaled nearly 579,000 units, reflecting just how right it was for the market. Though it would be refined and modified as time went on, Maverick would continue to appeal principally to

mainstream buyers and, on that basis, must be considered one of Ford's more successful products of this decade.

Maverick's debut signaled the end of Falcon. The '69 models carried on into 1970 virtually unchanged, then disappeared after 15,700 had been built. Actually, the plan had been to drop Falcon once Maverick was introduced, but a brief sales upsurge in early '69 prompted Ford marketers to let the two compacts run side-by-side into model-year 1970. But Maverick's early high success showed there was no real need for that, so after a brief midyear return on stripped versions of the restyled 1970 Fairlane/Torino, the Falcon nameplate was honorably retired. (At least in the U.S.—it's still used by Ford Argentina for a descendant of the original 1960 American model, and by Ford Australia for very different, locally designed upscale intermediates.)

All-new styling "shaped by the wind" marked the 1970 mid-size Fords. Wheelbases grew an inch, to 114 on wagons and 117 inches on other body styles. Width ballooned by two inches, overall length by five. Interiors were redone, trim upgraded, windshield wipers concealed (beneath a rear hood extension), and comfort and convenience options were expanded. Basic engineering, however, was untouched. None of this was exactly earthshaking, but *Motor Trend* thought enough of the total package to name Torino its 1970 "Car of the Year."

The new look was certainly eye-catching: more sculptured and flowing than in 1968-69. Front fenders and hood were pointed, and knife-edge front fenderlines swept down to vanish in the doors. Bodysides took on a more rounded look, while the rear fenders "hopped up" a bit just ahead of the wheel openings. The rear flanks featured a nice blend of round and rectilinear.

Model-wise, a new top-shelf Torino Brougham series debuted, its mission being to move Ford's intermediates upmarket. Models consisted of a slope-roof hardtop coupe priced at $3006 and a $3078 notchback four-door hardtop. The previous base Fairlanes disappeared, leaving a Fairlane 500 trio (two-door hardtop,

four-door sedan and wagon) to anchor the bottom of the line at base prices around $2600.

As before, the hottest members of Ford's mid-size family were the Torino GT convertible and "SportsRoof" hardtop and the Cobra fastback. The last remained a budget muscle car, delivering a four-barrel 360-bhp 429 V-8 and appropriate chassis mods for just $3270 basic. The GT fastback listed at $3105, the ragtop at $3212, both with the 220-bhp 302 V-8. Power options ran through two- and four-barrel 351s, the Cobra's 360-bhp 429, and on to the 370-bhp Cobra Jet 429 with or without Ram-Air induction, the last also being available for Cobra. Highlighting Cobra appearance were standard

In hyping its 1970 models, Ford noted that the "Torino line serves as a plush way of transporting everything from people to saddles." The Brougham formal hardtop (bottom left), which was priced at $3006, included hidden headlamps, full wheel covers, luxury cloth and vinyl interior trim, and the two-barrel 302 V-8 as standard equipment. The vinyl roof was available in five colors. Output came to 16,911 units. The $3379 Squire station wagon (right), the priciest model in the Torino lineup, boasted 85.2 cubic feet of rear cargo space. Some 13,166 buyers apparently liked the woody look enough to drive one home. Catering to sun worshippers was the Torino GT convertible (below). With a base sticker price of $3212, it attracted only 3939 customers, making it the rarest '70 Torino. Note the styled steel wheels and the bodyside stripe.

NASCAR-style hood lock pins, black-finish hood and grille, and fat glass-belted tires. "Sports slats," backlight louvers *a la* Mustang Boss 302, were optional for both GT and Cobra hardtops. GTs wore hidden headlamps (as did Broughams and the Torino Squire wagon) and could be dressed up with reflective "laser" bodyside stripes, a center console, and spoked road wheels.

These mid-size Fords could be blistering street performers. A 300-bhp GT could touch 60 mph from rest in about eight seconds; the 370-bhp Cobra would do it in a mere six seconds. But the new styling proved less aerodynamic in superspeedway racing than that of the 1968-69 Torinos. The hardtop's concave backlight was said to be one of the problems. Ford had little choice but to run the older models in NASCAR this year, this time without the services of Richard Petty, who returned to the Chrysler camp. Ford took just six big-track events. On November 20, North American Automotive Operations announced that it would abandon the Grand National and most of its other racing programs, including the Trans-Am and international endurance contests.

For 1970, Mustang reverted to single headlights, and received recessed taillights and a minor shuffling of ornamentation. Powerteams stayed pretty much the same, too, although an optional Hurst shift linkage was now available. The most powerful engine offering was the 335-horsepower Cobra Jet 428, which is duly noted on the hood of this Mach 1 (left). This engine had a bore and stroke of 4.13 by 3.98 inches, a compression ratio of 10.6:1, and utilized a Holley four-barrel carburetor. It cost $376 extra with Ram-Air. With the standard 250-bhp two-barrel 351, the Mach 1 listed at $3271, and 40,970 buyers drove one home, down 43 percent from 1969. The Mustang hardtop coupe (below) started at $2721, and with 82,569 built, it was the best-selling model in the lineup.

The curvy new mid-size styling naturally graced this year's Rancheros, which expanded from three models to four with the addition of a fancy Squire version bearing the same pseudo-wood bodyside and tailgate appliques as the Torino Squire station wagon. Ford called it "The Ultimate in Personal Pickups," and it was pretty posh. The 155-bhp 250 six was now base power for all Rancheros. Options included most of the same small-block and big-block V-8s shown for Fairlane/Torino. Ranchero GTs came with "laser" stripes on tailgate as well as bodysides, but the buckets-and-console interior still cost extra. Vinyl roof coverings remained optional for all but base models.

Now touted as the "Number One" ponycar, Mustang faced more competition than ever in 1970. Dodge's beefy new Challenger and a completely redone Plymouth Barracuda companion appeared to do battle, followed at mid-season by a handsome second-generation Chevrolet Camaro and Pontiac Firebird. Despite an exciting lineup, Mustang model-year volume fell alarmingly to 190,727 units, down from nearly 300,000. Though this partly reflected the shrinking demand for ponycars in general, Mustang's design familiarity was probably also to blame.

Mustang's 1970 changes were predictably evolutionary. All seven models, including the pair of Bosses, continued with a tasteful facelift of the new 1969 styling, marked by a return to single headlamps plus minor ornamentation shuffling and taillamps recessed within a flat back panel. Powerteams stayed basically the same, and mechanical improvements were few. New appearance options for fastbacks included Boss-type backlight louvers, adjustable rear spoiler, and distinctive C-stripe tape treatment. An optional Hurst shift linkage was also new to Mustang.

With the advent of high-speed freeways and the growing popularity of air conditioning, it's perhaps not too surprising that convertibles sales were falling. That was also true of Mustang, as 1970 ragtop output sank to only 7673 units, off 48 percent from '69. Base price started at $3025; this car (top) has the 351 V-8. Ford dreamed up a little 1970 roadster called the Funabout (above)—perfect for the beach.

As before, the high-performance Mach 1 carried a standard 250-bhp two-barrel 351 and offered options up to the big 335-bhp Cobra Jet 428. The '70 got its own special grille with built-in driving lamps, plus a standard rear stabilizer bar. Mach 1s still came with the GT Equipment Group, but the package itself was eliminated as a separate option for other models, leaving enthusiastic drivers with only the Competition Suspension Package. This was now offered in two forms: one for four-barrel 351 and 428 V-8s with automatic; a second with staggered shocks for manual-shift 428s. New among option groups was the Drag Pack, available only with the 428 and comprising stronger con rods, heavy-duty oil cooler, and a modified rotating assembly. Detroit No-Spin differential was still on the order form with gearing as short as 4.30:1, so buyers who wanted to go like blazes in 1970 still could.

Further up the scale was the hot Boss 302, still a Trans-Am special built in very low volume: just 6319 for this model year. Sadly, withering ponycar demand and Ford's withdrawal from the Trans-Am series meant that the little Boss 302 wouldn't be back for 1971. Nor would the incredible Boss 429, of which only 505 were built to 1970 specs, all before the end of 1969. Again there were two engines: the 820T, essentially unchanged from late '69, and a new 820A with minor adjustments to its Thermactor emissions-control system, a sign of the times.

Mustang's luxury Grandé hardtop returned from 1969 with landau-style black or white vinyl roof, twin racing-type door mirrors, special identification, and bright wheel lip moldings. Like other Mustangs, it inherited the Mach 1's high-back front bucket seats, which added greatly to interior comfort. Of course, there were still "basic" Mustangs in 1970: hardtop, convertible, and SportsRoof fastback with standard 200 six or base

302 V-8. Prices hadn't climbed much since the early days. The six-cylinder hardtop listed at only a bit more than $2700, the V-8 convertible for as little as $3126. But ragtops were on the wane throughout the industry, and the number of open Mustangs built was only about 7700 this year. Continued buyer preference for air conditioning and closed bodies had conspired to reduce the popularity of soft tops, including Mustang's.

Thunderbird, promoted for 1970 as "The Thunderbird of Thunderbirds," got some radical sheetmetal surgery, though its basic 1967 body/chassis engineering remained substantially the same. New frontal styling reflected the influence of the now-departed Knudsen/Shinoda regime: an elongated hood terminating in a prominent vee'd snout. In the trade, this was often referred to as the "Bunky beak" or the "Knudsen nose." The effect was strikingly similar to the 1969 Pontiac Grand Prix—and must have confused some buyers. Headlamps were exposed for the first time since 1966 and separated from the wide thrust-forward grille. Hardtop coupes got slightly "faster" rooflines. Production ran marginally ahead of '69 levels, but the Landau sedan faded, production totaling just 8401 units, a little more than half its previous volume.

Ford had been heavily promoting the silence of the full size-models since 1965, and continued that theme for 1970 by beckoning buyers to "Take a quiet break." Continued also was the styling theme set down for 1969, although appearance was freshened via altered grille inserts and

new rear bumpers with integrated horizontal taillamps. LTDs, Squire wagon, and XLs sported a bulged hood and grille-center, the latter comprising small horizontal bars and flanked by eggcrate panels. Model choices swelled to 21 with the addition of a new Brougham LTD sedan and two- and four-door hardtops. Ready to bid farewell were the XL convertible and "tunnel-roof" fastback, which reverted to a standard V-8, the 250-bhp 351, in exchange for slightly higher prices: $3501 and $3293. Overall big-Ford sales were strong (though not as strong as Chevrolet's), with Galaxie 500s and non-Brougham LTDs again far and away the most popular. The LTD was now romping along at an annual rate of about 300,000. Of course, it had inspired competitors long before, notably Chevy's Caprice and the Plymouth Fury VIP. By contrast, the big XL was the last sporting full-sizer available anywhere. And with 1970 demand down to just 33,599 units, it's easy to see why Ford didn't persist with it after 1970.

Lincoln turned 50 this year but, curiously, the milestone was ignored—unless you count the introduction of a completely revamped big Continental. Mercury would soon have its own version of the Maverick, but L-M announced a more interesting new small car on April 17 this year. Borrowing Lincoln's old Capri name, it was a shapely, semi-fastback coupe on a 100.8-inch wheelbase that had been conceived by Ford of Europe as a Mustang for that burgeoning market. Ford had been peddling "captive imports"

in the U.S. with varying degrees of success since the late Forties, most recently the British-built Cortina that served as Capri's starting point. But where the Cortinas had been generally simple and dull, the Capri was Mustang-sporty yet decidedly European—and a lot more agile.

A sort of early, small-scale "world car," Capri was built in both Germany and England, where it was sold as a Ford with a wide array of engines and option "packs." What Americans got was a hybrid: a German-built car with the Cortina's 71-bhp 1.6-liter pushrod four. There were reasons for this. German workmanship was superior to Britain's, and the crossflow "Kent" engine was already emissions legal (Cortinas had been sold in the U.S. since 1964).

In initial U.S. form, the Capri was more penny pincher than hotshot, averaging an easy 25 mpg thanks largely to a svelte, 2100-pound curb weight. There was just one trim level, but it included

The '70 Thunderbird arrived with a beaky new front end. Reportedly it was Bunky Knudsen's idea, so the design came to be known as the "Knudsen nose" or "Bunky beak." The Landau sedan (top left), now $5182, saw output slip further to 8401 units. The $4961 hardtop (top right) fared even worse: 5116. Of the 50,364 '70 T-Birds built, 36,847 were the Landau coupe. All came with a 360-bhp 429 V-8. The mid-engine "Shelby Mk. V" (below) sports unusual gullwing doors over the rear compartment. Note the location of the spare tire. The badges on the sides and the plate at the rear read "Power by Ford."

The appearance of the 1970 full-size Fords was altered via grille inserts and new rear bumpers with integrated horizontal taillamps, and the lineup swelled with new top-of-the-line Broughams: sedan and two- and four-door hardtops. Making its last appearance was the sporty XL series, and so too did the tunnel-roof hardtop. The XL hardtop (top) sold for $3293 and attracted 27,251 orders. The LTD series sold far better, about 374,000 units total. Listing at $3579, the new Brougham hardtop sedan (above) weighed a road-hugging 4029 pounds. This one has the 429 V-8 to help move all that heft.

vinyl interior with front buckets, plus full carpeting, four-speed floorshift, and styled wheels with radial tires. This combination of sportiness, economy, and low price—just $2295 P.O.E.—proved immensely appealing, and L-M sold 156,000 Capris during the long introductory 1970 model year. Encouraged by this strong reception, L-M Division decided to order up bigger engines and more equipment from the European catalog, which would eventually encompass a peppier 2.0-liter four and, still later, 2.6- and 2.8-liter V-6s. In all, the Capri was a timely arrival, just the thing for a market seeking more rational substitutes for overblown ponycars and overpowered muscle machines. In fact, it

was probably ahead of the market, as events would soon prove.

Speaking of international happenings, 1970 was the year that brought the renowned Italian coachbuilders Ghia and Vignale into the Ford family. Both acquisitions were worked out through Automobili DeTomaso and its irrepressible proprietor, Alessandro DeTomaso. An expatriate Argentinean and former Maserati racing driver, DeTomaso had begun building cars under his own name in the early Sixties, the most recent being the mid-engine Mangusta sports car. Notably, it employed small-block Ford V-8 power and striking Ghia bodywork. Both Ghia and Vignale had fallen on hard

times, and DeTomaso wanted to snap them up as the centerpieces for a mini automotive conglomerate he hoped to create.

Ford, however, had designs on DeTomaso. Dearborn managers had been impressed with the Mangusta as a car of Ferrari caliber. There was even a suggestion that it be rebadged as a new Shelby Cobra. They certainly liked the idea of reliable, easy-to-service American mechanicals combined with exotic Italian styling. It looked like a great way to draw customers into Lincoln-Mercury showrooms. But the Mangusta ("mongoose" in Italian) had too many problems even for a "practical exotic," so Ford asked DeTomaso to come up with an improved version as a low-volume "image" car for L-M. DeTomaso complied, and the evolutionary Pantera came stateside for 1971.

To get the venture rolling, Ford helped DeTomaso buy Ghia and Vignale, then created DeTomaso, Inc. as a wholly owned Ford subsidiary to coordinate the activities of the three Italian firms, plus two others. But this combination would only last until 1974, when the Pantera's relative lack of success prompted a split. DeTomaso went his own way, eventually acquiring Maserati, and Vignale was closed, sad to say. Ghia, however, would survive as a European styling studio and prototype construction shop for both Ford Europe and Ford U.S., playing a part in developing such production cars as the 1974 Mustang II and 1979 Mustang. Ghia remains a vital source of design ideas and Ford concept cars to this day, though its name has been somewhat diluted since 1974 by careless sprinkling of Ghia badges on workaday Fords, mostly in Europe, but also in the U.S. for a time.

Ford's big truck news for 1970 was literally that: its first new long- and short-cab heavy conventionals since the early Sixties. They went by the name "Louisville Line" in honor of Ford's big new factory in that Kentucky city—the world's largest devoted exclusively to trucks, with 2.3-million square feet encompassing three parallel assembly lines. The model chart was just as big: some 650 different offerings arrayed among gas and diesel engines, single and tandem axles, and long and short cab/chassis configurations.

Specifically, the L-Line, as it came to be called, swept away all the old N-Series models as well as the F-based T-Series tandems on the 800-1000 chassis. Features included lighter yet stronger frames, wider axles of higher capacity, and more comfortable and spacious cabs. The last boasted a new integrated climate-control system, chair-height seating, and the latest in ergonomically designed instrument panels, which were hinged to facilitate service access. Cab styling was burly and square-rigged, marked by huge, hexagonal eggcrate grilles and windshields measuring a massive 1515 square inches. A bewildering array of powerteam combinations included Ford-built gas engines, Ford-Caterpillar diesel V-8s, and Cummins and Detroit diesels, and there were 6-, 10-, 13-, and even 16-speed transmissions for the first time in Ford history.

For all that, the basic Louisville lineup was somewhat simplified: L-Series single-axle conventionals, LT-Series conventional tandems, LN-Series short conventionals, LNT-Series short conventional tandems, and LTS-Series conventionals with setback front axles. Each was available as a gas-powered 900 model or diesel 9000. This nomenclature was also applied to the existing C/CT-Series low-tilt cabovers and W/WT-Series high-tilt COEs, production of which was transferred to the big new Kentucky plant. As a result, these models benefited from greater use of rust-resisting electroplated steel as adopted for the L-Line. N-Series Louisville "shorts" offered wheelbases of 138, 144, 150, 162, and 222 inches. The "longs" omitted the first two but were also available on spans of 174, 186, and 204 inches.

With all this, changes among Ford's light-duty models were relatively minor. Fiberglass-belted tires were more widely available, springs and payload ratings got the usual minor adjustments (mostly upward), two-tone paint and a ready-made "Electronics Service Interior Package" became optional for Econoline vans, and "Traction-Lok" limited-slip differential was added to the Bronco's option list. F-100/250/350 pickups received a split fine-checked grille and revised cab trim packages: Custom, the former base assortment; Sport Custom, a modestly upgraded version of the previous Custom; Ranger, slightly reduced in content; and new Ranger XLT, the previous Ranger package augmented by woodgrain tailgate panel, extra cab insulation and bright

Unlike the 1970 LTDs, the Galaxie 500 wore exposed headlights and had a flat (rather than peaked) grille. This is the four-door hardtop (top), which carried a base sticker price of $3096. Although only half as popular as the four-door sedan, output nonetheless came to 53,817 units. Ford tried to emphasize the roominess of the Galaxie 500's interior (above) by pushing the passenger's side of the dash forward. Note that the radio was mounted to the far left, where only the driver could operate it.

moldings, and plush cloth-and-vinyl upholstery.

Having enjoyed good success with it in 1969, Ford again offered a special Explorer package for F-100/250 Styleside pickups as part of a mid-season "White Sale" promotion. Besides the appropriate rear-fender nameplates, this year's Explorer came with full exterior chrome trim including wheel covers, rocker moldings and auxiliary box rails, plus a Shet-

land Plaid interior keyed to two exterior colors, "Grabber Blue" or "Explorer Green." It was sold in combination with both the Custom and Sport Custom cab and with reduced-price combinations of popular options like air conditioning, automatic transmission, and power steering and brakes. It was all part of the market's continuing move toward more car-like pickups, a trend that Ford would help keep accelerating in the years ahead.

1 9 7 1

A new minicar, restyled full-sizers, and the largest Mustang yet made 1971 a busy Ford year. In car sales the division was fresh from its best calendar 12 months since 1966, recording over 1.8 million registrations against 1.6 million for arch-rival Chevy. In 1971 model year car production, Ford fell short of its 1970 level by about 52,000 units, but its total volume of just over two million was still good enough to maintain an edge over Chevy, which was still recovering from its long 1970 strike, but up nearly 374,000 units to just over 1.83 million. Ford might have been struck too, but had quickly come to terms with the United Auto Workers, inking a new three-year pact on December 8, 1970, just two days before Lee Iacocca took over as company president.

That same month also brought significant revisions to the Clean Air Act that would have a profound effect on most all cars of the Seventies. These were the so-called "Muskie Amendments," named for Maine Senator (and erstwhile Vice-Presidential candidate) Edmund S. Muskie. As passed, these called for a 90-percent drop in both hydrocarbon (HC) and carbon-monoxide (CO) emissions for all cars effective with the 1975 model year, and an equal cut in oxides of nitrogen (NOx) from a proposed 1971 California standard, this to take effect nationwide for 1976. Detroit had balked at these stringent targets at a White House meeting in May 1969, contending they couldn't reach such levels until 1980 or '81.

In the end, the automakers got their way. After no little wrangling, the EPA agreed to less stringent "interim" levels in April 1973 that would hang on through the 1979 model year, after which the original 1975 standards would take hold. Even then, many 1975 and later cars had to adopt a new cleanup device, the catalytic converter, a sort of "afterburner" in the exhaust system that helped lower all three pollutants by using chemicals to foster more complete combustion and/or formation of less harmful substances (such as changing carbon monoxide to carbon dioxide).

But actually, the regulatory noose began tightening in 1971. First, fuel-vapor recovery systems, to prevent gasoline fumes from leaking into the air, became mandatory in all 50 states following a 1970 California regulation. More telling was General Motors' unilateral decision to lower compression on all its '71 car engines to permit operation on reduced-octane low-lead or no-lead gas that would

be needed to meet the anticipated 1975 standards. Ford, Chrysler, and American Motors would follow suit for '72. In a related move, all U.S. makers except Ford began publishing two sets of horsepower figures for '71: traditional SAE *gross* (dynamometer readings of engines without fan drive, exhaust system, or other ancillaries), and the more realistic new SAE *net* measure (with ancillaries installed as they would be in an actual car). Ford would grudgingly join in for '72.

The perennial Ford/Chevrolet sales fight was extended this year to the increasingly important subcompact arena. Ford's contender was the Pinto, a chunky fastback two-door sedan on a 94.2-inch wheelbase, Dearborn's smallest car yet. It arrived coincidentally with Chevy's Vega, a slightly larger small car on a 97-inch wheelbase with typically GM lines and a 2.3-liter (140-cubic-inch) overhead-cam four with unusual aluminum-silicon construction. Both had resulted from programs started in the mid-Sixties to develop direct domestic competitors for various small economy imports. Led by the quirky VW Beetle, import sales had climbed to 15 percent of the total U.S.

Ford's third import fighter, the '71 Pinto, was introduced on September 11, 1970. Described as "a frisky new little car [that] kicks up its heels" it came with a 75-bhp 1.6 liter four or an optional 100-bhp two-liter. The base two-door sedan (top) listed at $1919 and weighed 2115 pounds. The $2144 three-door Runabout (above) debuted at the Chicago Auto Show on February 20, 1971. The sedan had been criticized because of its small trunk and shallow decklid; the Runabout's hatch was far more accommodating.

market by 1970, too large a slice for Detroit to ignore. Pinto and Vega were intended to get some of it back.

Developed as project Phoenix, the Pinto stemmed from an earlier Ford program that envisioned a more radical mini. According to author Jan Norbye, this "G-car," as it was called, "had VW exterior dimensions and [would have been] powered by a transversely positioned inline four-cylinder water-cooled engine in the rear. The chassis configuration was [ultimately] discarded, but the G-car body was adopted for a new project . . . using a front engine and live rear axle." Phoenix envisioned use of certain components, mainly engines and transmissions, from

Ford's German and British subsidiaries in a package sized to compete head-on with the Beetle. Those ideas survived.

The result was a conventionally engineered Euro-American hybrid. Pinto's standard engine was the cast-iron 1.6-liter ohv four from the British Ford Cortina and L-M Division's newly imported Capri, rated at 75 horsepower. Optional (at $82 extra) was a 2.0-liter 100-bhp overhead-cam four from the German Ford Taunus (and newly available this year in U.S. Capris). Pinto's standard four-speed manual gearbox was imported, too. A three-speed automatic was optional.

Comparisons between Pinto and Vega were inevitable. *Road & Track* magazine said that while the Chevy is "by far the more interesting design . . . Pinto happens to be the more pleasant car to drive in everyday use—base model for base model—and carries a price tag some $172 less. To be sure, there is 'less car' in the Pinto; where the Vega has disc front brakes, it has drums; the Vega coil-and-link rear suspension, the Pinto simple leaf springs; it is somewhat less roomy, and in standard form it's not as quick as a stan-

dard Vega. But, thanks to a quieter and smoother engine, a superior gearbox, somewhat greater comfort for the driver and better finish throughout, it is subjectively the nicer car."

Even so, Pinto lagged behind Vega and many imports in several key areas. *R&T*'s initial 1.6-liter test car needed a leisurely 20 seconds in the 0-60 mph run, versus 16.5 seconds for the Chevy and a brisk 13 seconds for the lighter Datsun 510 from Japan. Also criticized were Pinto's sparse instrumentation, lack of back seat and trunk space, the long stopping distances and poor directional control of its all-drum brakes, and the tendency of the lightly loaded back end to hop around. And both the Pinto and Vega were handicapped because they did not offer a four-door sedan.

But it wasn't all bad. Said *R&T*: "Pinto is maneuverable and handles pretty well. Its rack-and-pinion steering . . . is not very quick . . . but it's a far cry from the wheel-twirling of the Maverick. Out on the road we found good cornering adhesion, at least in the dry (with the optional A78-13 tires on five-inch rims), and steering characteristics close to neutral. . . .

Lee Iacocca poses with a '71 Pinto, which is equipped with the optional vinyl roof. A Ford public relations handout noted that "With 'Pintopower' to spare, [the Pinto] excels at turnpike speeds and in tight passing situations. Small and light, Pinto gallops through the heaviest traffic and can wiggle into the tightest parking place." With a 94.2-inch wheelbase, the Pinto was nimble, but it was wider than most small cars. Also touted were Pinto's "styling and functionalism."

Mind you, it's no sports car, but for the economy-car class the handling can't be faulted." And economy was pretty good: 22 mpg in the *R&T* test versus 18.6 for the four-speed Vega, though both trailed the sprightlier, 25.3-mpg Datsun.

R&T later sampled a 2.0-liter with the $32 front-disc brake option and liked Pinto even more. The engine, they said, "makes it a proper car . . . smooth and quiet, much better than the Vega in these respects." And though 0-60-mph performance improved to a quite lively 11.4 seconds, there was no mileage penalty—the big-engine model actually proved 0.5-mpg thriftier than the 1600. As for braking, the car "stopped in less distance from

80 mph than the drum-brake Pinto did from 70!" Fade resistance was 50 percent better as well.

Over 350,000 buyers liked Pinto enough to drive one home this model year, which seemed to justify Ford's decision to stop selling imported Cortinas after 1970. This fine performance was achieved despite a recall to fix carburetors on early cars, prompted by a rash of reported underhood fires, and short supplies of the 1.6-liter engine, owing to a strike in Britain. Low price and a simple "owner-friendly" nature undoubtedly helped Pinto's fortunes. (The owner's manual showed how to perform an unusual number of routine maintenance chores, and Ford offered a special "key" that could be used as an emergency screwdriver and sparkplug gapper.) Also helping was the midyear arrival of an

identically styled "three-door sedan," a hatchback with standard cargo-area carpeting and fold-down back seat. Called Runabout, it answered one big Pinto failing: poor trunk space.

Pinto would have a long, 10-year production run during which it would re-

Mustang galloped into 1971 with all-new styling, increased size and heft, slightly more interior room, and a longer 109-inch wheelbase. Ford's ponycar was more "styled" than ever before, and although it maintained long-hood/short-deck proportions, one couldn't help but notice the sweeping, almost horizontal fastback roofline, full-width grille, and Kamm-style back panel inspired by the Shelby Mustangs. The Mach 1 (left) carried a base sticker of $3268, and for that one received the 302 V-8 this year. For only $93, however, a buyer could opt for the 351-4V V-8 (above). This was the "Cleveland" 351 with a bore and stroke of 4.00 by 3.50 inches, 10.7:1 compression, and Holley four-barrel carb. As with the exterior, the interior (top) was more highly styled than before. The tach and speedometer are the large gauges.

323

Mustang convertible sales had been declining ever since 101,945 ragtops had been built for the long '65 model year. And even in spite of new styling, 1971 wouldn't be any different as production slipped 1552 units—some 20 percent—to just 6121. The starting price this year was increased to $3227, up $202. Although the rear styling was new, Mustang clung to its now-traditional triple-taillight theme.

main a consistently good seller despite tightening emission controls, added weight from required safety equipment and, later, an unsafe fuel-tank design that drove Ford to court. Moreover, it would always outsell the Vega. Though Pinto wouldn't be enough to stem the import tide alone, it would serve Ford well through a difficult decade.

Ford's history-making ponycar was all-new for '71 and bigger than ever—as big as a Mustang would ever get. Its increased size stemmed from Ford's belief that sales would improve with more passenger room, presumably the reason that compacts were now generally outstripping ponycars. The familiar long-hood/short-deck proportions were retained on a one-inch-longer, 109-inch wheelbase, but the car was more "styled" than ever, aping Ford's Le Mans racers (and the tastes of the briefly employed Bunkie Knudsen and Larry Shinoda). Most noticeable were a sweeping, almost horizontal roofline on the fastbacks, plus a full-width grille and clipped, Kamm-style

back panel inspired by the now-departed Shelby-Mustangs. Closer inspection revealed a more acute windshield angle and newly hidden wipers. The advent of polyurethane bumper covers keyed to paint color made the front end even more interesting and better integrated. This was standard on Mach 1, along with a special twin-scoop hood (optional on other models) and a unique grille with a small running-horse emblem on honeycomb mesh, flanked by horizontal parking lamps styled to look like driving lights. On other models the rectangular opening was graced by the return of a chrome-framed horse and horizontal divider bar.

Mustang model choices stayed the same except for the new Boss 351. A substitute for the Boss 302/429, it carried a "Cleveland" 351 V-8 with four-barrel carb and 11:1 compression, good for 330 gross horsepower. It was more tractable than the old HO small-block and, since it wasn't as high-revving, more durable. Lesser models except Mach 1 started with the truck-based 250-cubic-inch six, this year rated at 145 horsepower (the old 200 just wasn't up to the '71's extra weight). Mach 1 was demoted to a 210-bhp 302 V-8 that remained the step-up option elsewhere (save the Boss 351, of course). Appealing to leadfoots were three other optional V-8s: a two-barrel 351 with 240 gross horses, a four-barrel version with 285, and the new four-barrel 429 Cobra

Jet, replacing the previous 428 big-blocks and rated at 370 bhp with or without Ram Air induction. There was also a Super Cobra Jet boasting 375 bhp. Though this made even the weightier '71 a real screamer, it garnered few orders.

Though ostensibly a performance machine as before, the Mach 1 could still be ordered with air conditioning ($407) and automatic transmission ($238), as well as a slew of convenience features more appropriate to a luxury car: power steering, tilt steering wheel, "sport deck" rear seat, AM/FM stereo, and intermittent wipers. Other extra-cost items included sports interior ($130), power front disc brakes ($70), center console ($60), and instrument group ($54).

In fact, liberal use of the options book could raise a Mach 1's $3268 base price to well over $5500. Standard equipment included integrated front spoiler, dual exhausts, and racing-style door mirrors. The 429CJ engine cost $436 extra, and made the Mach 1 undeniably quick. So equipped, it would do 0-60 mph in 6.5 seconds, 0-75 in about 9.0, and the quarter-mile in 14.5. With automatic and 3.25:1 final drive ratio, top speed was about 115 mph, fuel "economy" 10-11 mpg. "It is a decent mixture for those who want good performance and some comfort," wrote Chuck Koch in *Motor Trend* magazine, "but it still remains a little unwieldy for city traffic."

There was consolation in the Boss 351, however. Though it looked much like the Mach 1 save name decals, special mid-flank striping, and Boss-style front spoiler, it handled better on a standard "competition" suspension with uprated coil springs and hydraulic shocks up front, staggered rear shocks, and front and rear stabilizer bars. *MT*'s Koch also found it quicker than his 429 Mach 1, capable of 0-60 mph in 5.8 seconds and the quarter-mile in 13.8. However, a short 3.91:1 rear axle and a lack of overdrive gearing limited top speed to only about 100 mph.

With only 210 bhp, a 302 Mustang was no match for either the Boss or the Mach 1. Its typical figures were 10 seconds 0-60 mph, the quarter-mile in 17.5 seconds, and a top speed of only 86 mph (with 2.79:1 gearing and automatic). Yet this was hardly sluggish, and it returned

The '71 Mustang Mach 1 (top), which boasted bold bodyside striping, was bought by 36,499 sporting types. Thunderbird soared into 1971 with its beak still intact, but the grille itself was modified slightly. The hardtop (above) started at $5295 this year, but the $5438 Landau was twice as popular: 20,356 units versus 9146. The $5516 Landau four-door was down to 6553 units, and would be gone after 1971. An interesting new option was the Turnpike Convenience Group, which combined cruise control, reclining front seat backrest, and Michelin steel-belted radial tires. High-back front bench or bucket seats were available.

The Maverick two-door sedan waltzed into 1971 with two new stablemates, a four-door sedan (top) and the sporty Grabber (center). The former rode a wheelbase stretched 6.9 inches to 109.9, almost identical with the 1960 Falcon. Ford called it a "family-sized sedan" and crowed about the "substantially increased rear seat roominess." Priced at $2234, just $59 more than the base two-door, it attracted 73,208 orders. The Grabber listed at $2354, and for this the buyer received a two-door sedan decked out with a Charblack grille, twin nonfunctional air scoops on the hood, reflective tape stripes, racing mirrors, and a blackout treatment of the spoiler and rear end. Buyers snapped up 38,963 samples. The '71 LTD was treated to a mid-life restyle, which included a new grille. The hardtop sedan (bottom) listed at $3969.

decent gas mileage—up to 17 mpg. All things considered, the 302 was probably the year's best all-around Mustang power choice.

In retrospect, the '71 Mustang doesn't seem like a bad car, though it got a lot of bad press at the time. It was larger because buyers didn't like cars with cramped interiors. It was the thirstiest Mustang yet because, with gas still selling for only 30 cents a gallon, most buyers weren't too concerned about fuel economy. Yet despite its extra size and weight, the '71 actually rode and handled better than previous Mustangs. And with the competition suspension, understeer was reduced and roadholding improved. New variable-ratio power steering provided better road feel than previous fixed-ratio Mustang systems. And the low, flat-roof fastback was racy-looking and attractive in an era of uninspired styling.

But a good car doesn't necessarily mean good sales, as Ford Motor Company knew all too well. If Mustang wasn't losing customers to Camaro, Firebird, and Barracuda, it was definitely being outsold by the Maverick, Plymouth Valiant, Dodge Dart, and Chevrolet Nova. The ponycar market was fading fast, and greater size, copious options, and fresh looks just weren't enough. So despite its new design, Mustang again sagged in sales. Model-year production totaled less than 150,000. Hardtops dropped to 83,000, convertibles captured a bit more than 6000, and fastbacks held at about 60,000. Included in the last are an estimated 1800 copies of the Boss 351, which was dropped at mid-season—there was little need for it once Ford gave up racing. As one might guess, it's now the most collectible '71 Mustang.

The full-size Fords received a midlife restyle, introducing a basic look (ads called it "crisper") that would continue through 1978 on an unchanged, 121-inch wheelbase. A massive bumper/grille, again reflecting Knudsen's influence, featured deeply inset quad headlamps on each side of an eggcrate center section, and sharp horizontal creases appeared above slightly flat-topped wheel arches. Hardtop and sedan backlights were modestly curved; hardtop coupes had bulky sail panels terminating just behind the door glass, where tiny vertical panes filled the gap. A new instrument panel put controls in a large pod jutting out from the cowl. The sporty XL was history now, so Ford's lone full-size convertible moved to the LTD series and the 500 fastback was dropped. The engine chart remained the same apart from a new 400-cid V-8, basically the 351 with a larger, 4.00-inch bore. A relatively efficient engine with torque and emissions characteristics suitable for family-car applications, it would power a variety of Dearborn cars in the years ahead.

Broadening Maverick's appeal in the compact's sophomore year were a new four-door sedan and a sportier two-door.

The latter, modishly called Grabber, wore a jazzy two-tone hood with fake air scoops and partial matte-black finish, extra lamps in the grille, and no round center emblem, plus dual racing mirrors, reflective bodyside tape stripes, and flat hubcaps with wheel trim rings. Floorshift and high-back bucket seats were new options for Grabber and the base two-door. More practical folk were interested in the new sedan, built on a longer 109.9-inch wheelbase, making it about the same size as the Falcon had been. Both Maverick sixes, 170- and 200-cid, lost 5 bhp to emissions tuning, but the corporate 250 six with 145 bhp was newly optional, as was the 210-bhp 302 V-8. Other changes included larger 14-inch wheels and tires, extra-cost vinyl roof, and new colors.

After a decade, the Fairlane name was retired from Ford's U.S. roster as the mid-size Torino line was rearranged into base, mid-range 500, luxury Brougham, and sporty GT and Cobra models. The cars themselves weren't changed much apart from split grilles and minor trim twisting, but the Cobra lost a lot of its bite, downgraded now to a standard four-barrel 351 V-8 with 285 bhp. The 370-bhp 429 was still available, however.

The derivative Ranchero car-pickups saw as little change, but there was an interesting midyear edition for another of Ford's annual "White Sales." This was a specially priced mid-line Ranchero 500 decked out in one of eight select colors and supplied with black-finish hood and inner cargo box, black vinyl roof, dual body-color racing mirrors, broad bodyside tape stripes, F70-14 blackwall tires with raised white lettering, and Grabber-type flat hubcaps and wheel trim rings. All quite snazzy, and a money-saving alternative to a Ranchero GT.

Thunderbird also sailed along with few significant changes. Two-door rooflines reverted to the huge, blind C-pillars of 1966-69, and all models displayed more restrained, horizontal-bar fronts. Sales continued at their previous pace, but the four-door hit a new low of only about 6500 units. New to the options slate was a Turnpike Convenience Group combining cruise control, reclining front-seat backrest, and Michelin steel-belted radial tires. High-back front bench or bucket seats were also available.

Having just completed the tremendous job of launching the new Louisville Line, and its factory, Ford's truck department treated itself to a fairly quiet 1971. There were minor adjustments in availability of both Ford-built and proprietary (non-Ford) diesel engines among mediums and heavies, while the low-end 170- and 240-cid gasoline sixes were detuned to meet emissions levels *a la* the passenger-car versions. The F-500/600 platform-stakes were discontinued, but the lineup expanded beyond 1100 models with the addition of two F-600 cab/chassis and, for the construction trade, a new four-wheel-drive F-600. Crew Cabs were now

For the sophomore year of its styling cycle, the '71 Torino kept the same sheetmetal but received revised grille and trim. Or as Ford put it, "subtle styling refinements of the award-winning 1970 Torino design." The Torino Brougham continued as the luxury leader in the line, with the two-door hardtop (top and center) retailing at $3175. But it didn't sell well, so only 8593 were built for the model run. The Brougham hardtop sedan did even worse: only 4408 built. Buyers clearly preferred the less expensive base Torino and 500 models. Wagons sold reasonably well, but the top-line Torino Squire with its simulated wood and hidden-headlight grille was hampered by a $3560 price tag. As a result, only 15,805 were called for. It also weighed a hefty 3583 pounds, as much as a full-size Ford wagon dating back only a few years.

available on F-700/750 and diesel F-7000 form. A special-order Ford-built motor-home chassis announced in 1970 was re-designated the M-Series.

Among the volume models, Econo-lines and the lighter F-Series pickups sported new grilles: a broad dual-element eggcrate for the latter, a two-tier affair on the former. The F-Series' fancy Ranger XLT package got a few more interior touches not shared with the ordinary Ranger, and there were minor trim and equipment shuffles affecting the Custom and Sport Custom cabs. Econolines also received minor trim revisions inside along with standard molded foam front seats. Power steering was now standard on F-250/350s and a new option for Econolines. Light-duty Fs could be ordered with factory AM/FM radio for the first time. Missing from the extra-cost equip-ment roster were the special F-Series Contractors and Farm & Ranch packages.

Ford maintained its decisive truck sales lead in 1971, though it was even harder now to pin down exact totals. One reason was the growing number of recip-rocal shipments between Ford U.S. and Ford Canada. Back in 1965, Washington and Ottawa had signed a joint Automo-tive Trade Agreement that rendered the U.S.-Canadian border invisible with re-spect to vehicle tariffs. Thus, for the first time, U.S. plants could freely send vehicles to Canada, while Canadian operations were free to build and export U.S.-spec models. This, in turn, enabled car and truck producers to assign specific products to specific plants in either or both coun-tries depending on the demands of each market and even the quality levels achieved in the various plants—an enormous boost to manufacturing flexibility.

Dearborn was as quick to take ad-vantage of this as GM, Chrysler, or American Motors. Indeed, the tempo of cross-border back-and-forth had been stepping up since the Agreement was signed. But it also complicated the task of keeping tabs on production because ex-ports from either nation were counted as factory sales in the receiving country. So about the best we can say is that Ford's Ontario truck plant built at record levels in 1971 and that this surely played a part in keeping Ford first in trucks.

Ford's corporate birthday falls on June 16, but the company paused on June 4, 1971 to observe another milestone: 75 years since Henry Ford had built his em-bryonic Quadricycle. Here was a remind-er, should anyone in Dearborn have needed one, that the firm's own Diamond Anniversary was approaching—still more than six years distant, though not really *that* far off relative to Ford's long, rich history.

But events were about to make those coming six years seem a lot longer than usual, not just for Ford, but Detroit in general and the nation as whole. A radical change in the world economic order was at hand, and with that, America's place in it.

Ford F-100 pickup prices started at $2810 for a Styleside with a 6½-foot box. The eight-foot unit added $118 to the bottom line. The Ranger XLT (top) consisted of a Ranger package to which were added XLT trimmings. Together they made sure that the pickup had plenty of bright metal in and out, as well as fancier upholstery and other luxury touches. The Chateau was the top-line Club Wagon (center), a $3827 people-mover that was fitted with deluxe upholstery, full-length carpeting, and a good deal of bright trim. Some 5438 were produced for 1971. The '71 Ranchero started at $2851, but buyers could opt for AM/FM radio, "Laser" stripes on the $3273 GT model (bottom), or even a fire-breathing 429-cubic-inch V-8.

1 9 7 2

Another busy Dearborn year saw Ford Division present two completely new car lines for the second year in a row, plus a perky little compact pickup and worthwhile improvements to the Econoline and Bronco. Its Lincoln-Mercury Division had new products, too, including a successor to the Continental Mark III. Quipped *Motor Trend* magazine: "The Ford Motor Company executive who claimed 'the annual model change is dead' must be joking. Either that or he didn't get a good look at the company's plans. . . ."

Executives always look at year-end production totals, and they had reason to be pleased with 1972's results. Ford Division maintained a solid lead in truck deliveries for both the model and calendar years, and recorded substantially higher model-year car volume—up over 192,000

units to nearly 2.25 million. Lincoln and Mercury also enjoyed a production upsurge, both makes besting their previous model-year highs. Corporate net income set a record as well, making 1972 the most successful year in Dearborn history. The one sore spot was Chevrolet's return to number one in car production, outpacing Ford by almost 200,000 units for the model year.

Except for engines, this year's Ford Torino was all new from road to roof, switching from unit to body-on-frame construction for the first time. The idea

The full-size 1972 Ford lineup consisted of 19 models. Visual changes were minor, but one way to identify the '72s was by their simpler grilles and a new front bumper cross-piece, plus a higher rear bumper. The Galaxie 500, here a $3604 four-door hardtop (above and below), sported new rocker panel and wheel lip moldings. Output of this model was 28,939 units. The Galaxie 500 two-door hardtop was more popular, 80,855 units, but the four-door sedan outdid them both. A new option was an electric sliding sunroof and the 351 V-8 became the base engine as the "Big Six" and the 302 were scratched (except for fleet and taxi use).

was that the frame be fairly flexible, thus effectively becoming part of the suspension to isolate road shocks from the rigid body. Accompanying this change was a new four-link rear suspension with coil springs instead of the previous semi-elliptic leaf springs. Front-disc brakes with new single-piston calipers were now standard, and there was a new steering

The bigger and heavier '72 Torino boasted all-new styling. In fact, the wheelbase was stretched to 118 inches (except two-doors), just an inch shy of the big LTD's 1968 span. The $3094 Gran Torino Sport fastback (top left) featured a simulated hood scoop and two-tone argent grille. The notchback (below) cost $2878, but emphasized luxury. Respective outputs were 31,239 and 132,284 units. The $3486 Squire (top right), which found 35,595 buyers, boasted a three-way "Magic Doorgate" and semitransparent woody trim.

linkage, incorporated into the boost mechanism with power assist. Front suspension remained much as before: upper control arms, coil springs mounted on lower lateral arms.

Following GM's practice since 1968, Ford split its mid-size line along different wheelbases: 114 inches for two-door models, 118 for four-doors. Overall width grew by 2.5 and 4.6 inches, respectively. Front and rear track also increased, as did weight—by close to 300 pounds on average—thanks to the separate frame and added sound insulation. With all this, Torino was now about as large and weighty as a full-size late-Sixties Ford.

A slimmed-down model platoon counted just base Torinos and a new Gran Torino series, plus a pair of hardtop coupes called Gran Torino Sport. The Gran Torinos, essentially what the

Broughams had been, shared base-series body styles: notchback sedan, hardtop coupe, and five-door wagon. The two Sports—notchback and fastback SportsRoof hardtops—took over for the previous GTs and Torino Cobra. Convertibles were conspicuous by their absence. So were four-door hardtops, though Ford advertised four-door sedans as "pillared hardtops."

There was a reason for these omissions: an expected a new government "crush" standard for car roofs in rollover accidents that would effectively ban convertibles and maybe even pillarless closed models. Though this never materialized, Ford and other Detroit makers used the threat of it as an excuse to begin dropping convertibles, slow sellers anyway, while restoring B-pillars to hardtops and then crowing about their "improved safety."

Actually, there was another, more practical reason for getting rid of pillarless cars: B-posts made a more convenient outboard anchoring point for the new front-seat shoulder belts that were federally mandated this year.

But back to the Torinos, where prices were hardly affected despite more expansive dimensions and standard equipment. In fact, base stickers even went down $100 or so in some cases. As before, the base-series sedan was the price-leader, now at $2641. Topping the line, also as before, was the lush woody-look Torino Squire wagon, tagged at $3486.

Torino's '72 styling was dramatically different. Front fenders remained pointy, but wheel arches bulged, beltlines were hiked, rear fenderlines humped, and bodysides more heavily sculptured. All Gran models as well as the Squire carried a distinctive "mouth" grille nestled above a scooped-out bumper and flanked by quad headlamps; others carried a full-width face. Sports also donned a simulated hood scoop. Wagons continued with the two-way "Magic Doorgate" pioneered on big Fords way back in 1965. Special hinges allowed it to open laterally like a door or to swing down like a conventional tailgate.

Existing powerplants were detuned where necessary to run on regular gas, a sign of the times. Also emblematic of the age, Ford now fell in line with other U.S. producers (and SAE Standard J245) by quoting power and torque figures in more realistic SAE net terms instead of the old, optimistic gross measure. A 250-cid six and 302 V-8 were standard depending on model. Respective horsepower ratings were 113 and 130 bhp. Extra-cost V-8s comprised a brace of 351s (165-bhp two-barrel and 220-bhp four-barrel), a 400 borrowed from the big-car line (180 bhp), and one 429 (220 bhp). Most Torinos rolled out with SelectShift Cruise-O-Matic, but four-speed manual was available with the four-pot 351.

Other available options suggested that these new Torinos aimed far more at comfort and smooth-riding quiet than sporty performance. The one vestige of the "muscle" era was a $443 Rallye Equipment Group for Sports only. This gave full instrumentation, including tachometer, plus higher-rate springs and shocks, rear stabilizer bar, 14 × 6-inch wheels mounting G70 wide-oval tires, and manual transmission with Hurst linkage. The four-barrel 351 cost $127 extra. The 429 was $100 if ordered with the Rallye package. But brochures stressed the Torino's new kinship with the big LTD in matters of ride, luxury, and room, and this year's Sports would be the last "interesting" mid-size Fords of this decade.

Nevertheless, Ford seemed right on the money with these tarted-up Torinos, for they accounted for almost 27 percent of the division's model-year car volume. At 60,794 units, the Sport fastback was the line's third most popular offering,

after the Gran sedan and hardtop. Part of this initial success may have come at the expense of the big Ford, which sagged by about 100,000 units. Some was perhaps due to lack of new competition from GM, whose mid-size designs were now five years old. GM had intended to introduce new models for '72, but delays forced a one-year postponement. Even then, Torino sales were hardly affected, and they remained strong through the "energy crisis" of late 1973 and '74.

Torino's redesign was predictably applied to this year's Ranchero, with the same hulky new shape on the 118-inch wagon wheelbase. Somewhat curiously billed now as "The Pickup Car," the erstwhile "intermediate" Ranchero was almost back to its original late-Fifties size, stretching a grand 216 inches long overall and a massive 79.7 inches wide. Some of these increases went into a slightly roomier cargo box with maximum length/width/height dimensions of 78.4 × 53.4 × 16.7 inches. Eliminating the base model left the Ranchero 500 as the least costly offering. GT and duded-up Squire continued as before. All three wore the Gran Torino passenger-car face, as well as the same racy 60-degree windshields, severely curved side glass, and radically tucked lower-body sheetmetal.

Sloganeers billed 1972's fully revamped personal-luxury Ford as "More Thunderbird Than Ever." They weren't kidding. In fact, the T-Bird was a close relative of this year's new Continental Mark IV, sharing basic body structure, a new perimeter chassis, and even one engine. There was also "more" to its price, now almost $5300 basic.

This largest T-Bird yet resulted from a series of decisions made shortly after Lee Iacocca took over the president's chair at Ford's "Glass House" World Headquarters. The main ones were more conservative styling, dumping the slow-selling sedan, and enlarging the two-door to share even more Mark tooling. The last would spread production costs over higher volume than either model would generate alone, thus improving their overall profitability.

All this came to pass, with the mainstay two-door carrying a 120.4-inch wheelbase, 5.7 inches longer than before

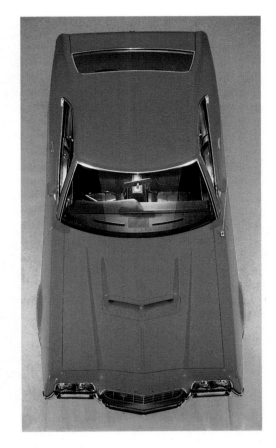

Ford claimed that the Torino's new suspension and chassis provided better handling, but they were really tuned for a softer "big-car" ride. Of course, one could order a firmer suspension for the Gran Torino Sport (above), but it was still a 203.7-inch-long, 3470-pound highway cruiser. A 248-bhp 351 "Cleveland" V-8 was optional for $127. Note the length of the hood relative to the passenger compartment. The $2856 Gran Torino "four-door pillared hardtop" (below) was 207.3 inches long; output reached 102,300 units.

and the same as the new Mark's. Overall length stretched to 216 inches, some four inches less than the Mark IV measure. Though center body sections were identical, Ford stylists played variations on familiar themes at each end of their car: restrained horizontal-bar grille; squared-up front fenders housing the parking lamps; flared wheel arches accented by slim, full-length moldings about half-way up the bodysides; and the now-traditional full-width taillamp treatment. Though it

After the heavy 1971 restyle, Mustang trotted into 1972 virtually unaltered. The biggest change involved the narrowing of engine choices as emissions rules were tightening. The largest V-8 now offered was the 351, which in top form developed 275 horsepower. In an effort perk up falling sales, Ford offered a mid-year "Sprint" option (top) featuring white paint with red and blue accents and a large "USA" rear-fender decal. The luxury-oriented Grandé (above) listed at $2915; output increased slightly to 18,045 units.

looked heavier, the new Bird actually weighed a bit less than its immediate predecessor.

Beneath the larger body was the aforementioned new perimeter chassis. All-coil suspension was retained, but the rear employed new four-link geometry, with the upper links (now made of drawn rather than stamped steel) mounted outboard and splayed inward, assisted by an anti-roll bar. Power front-disc/rear-drum brakes were standard, and there was a new option called "Sure Track," an anti-skid device that acted on the rear wheels to prevent premature lockup in hard

stops. Not many were ordered, but it was highly beneficial—a forerunner of today's more sophisticated anti-lock braking systems—and much less costly than the Bendix all-wheel electronic setup on Chrysler's Imperial. The 429 big-block remained standard power, rated here at 212 bhp SAE net. Lincoln's 430, now 14 years old, was the lone option, packing 212/224 bhp and available only with air conditioning. Both engines were teamed with SelectShift Cruise-O-Matic, of course.

Buyers responded to the new T-Bird with enthusiasm. Model year sales leaped

60 percent above the '71 total to near 58,000—putting Ford's flagship firmly ahead of the Buick Riviera, Oldsmobile Toronado, and Cadillac Eldorado. Road testers found little to get excited about, but the package would prove good enough to last five full years, the longest of any T-Bird generation to date. Though the Middle East oil embargo would cripple sales of most all big cars in 1974-75, Thunderbird maintained a solid lead over the Riv and Toro.

At the small end of the car line, a new Pinto wagon trotted forth in April. It was identical with the two- and three-door sedans ahead of the rear wheels, but had 10 extra inches aft for cargo space, which was pretty good. Appropriately, the optional 2.0-liter four was standard, delivering 86 net bhp versus the measly 54 of this year's 1.6-liter sedan and Runabout. As per Ford tradition, the Pinto wagon could be ordered with plain sides or as a woody-look Squire, the latter earning the nickname "Country Squirt" in some quarters. A string of running detail changes begun in 1971 continued for all Pintos this year. Included were an eight-inch deeper rear window for the Runabout hatchback, standard carpeting on the two-door, and newly optional vinyl roof and Accent exterior moldings. All this had the desired effect as sales improved by about 130,000 units, reaching 480,000 for the model year.

Described as "virtually unchanged," Ford's compact Maverick saw the spring arrival of a new Luxury Decor Option (LDO) for both body styles, with copper-color vinyl top and bodyside moldings, matching wheel covers, whitewall tires, and low-back bucket seats with reclining backrests. In spite of that, volume slipped by about 17,000 units to just under 255,000 for the model year.

Because they'd been heavily revamped for '71, the big Fords stayed pretty much the same this year. Appearance was altered slightly with simpler grilles bisected by a new front-bumper cross-piece, and rear bumpers were extended up to the trunk sill on all models (save wagons, of course). The main new option was an electric sliding sunroof for the wide-quarter hardtop coupes. Base power remained the 240 "Big Six" (downrated to 110 bhp net) and the 140-bhp 302 V-8. Options comprised a two-barrel 351, a lone 172-bhp 400, and an easy-going 208-bhp big-block 429.

There's nothing to do with a one-year-old design but live with it, and that's what Ford did with the '72 Mustang. The main news concerned powerplants, down to five with cancellation of the 429. Ironically, the big-block had been one reason for the '71 model's size increase. Though still running a standard 302, Mach 1 was now the hottest of the herd; the Boss 351 was no more, although the 351 V-8 was still optional with up to 275 horses. Convertibles—all 6401 of them—gained a standard power top mechanism. The dis-

The Sprint option could be ordered on the '72 Mustang convertible (top) as well as other models. But ragtop sales continued to flounder, although they actually picked up 280 units to 6401. With production lines humming, '72 Pinto output jumped 127,000 to 479,775; the new wagon added 101,483 units. The two-door sedan (above), now $1960, actually lost over 107,000 units—buyers wanted the more versatile Runabout and wagon.

heartening sales trend continued as production sank to just under 125,000, a 20-percent decline and Mustang's lowest yearly total to date.

Attempting to perk things up, Ford offered the midyear Sprint Decor Option for hardtops and SportsRoof fastbacks. Features included white paint with red accent striping, broad blue hood stripes and rocker panel paint, and stars-and-stripes shields on rear fenders. A complimentary color scheme was used inside. "Control and balance make it a beautiful experience," said the ads, quite a claim for a mere cosmetics package. Perhaps they referred to the "Magnum 500" road wheels shod with 60-series raised-white-letter tires that were frequently found on Sprints.

Henry Ford II and design chief Gene Bordinat had once said they'd never

change the Continental Mark III. But no design lasts forever, and by 1972 it was time for an update, which they decided to call Mark IV. This wasn't a return to the annual model change that had seen three "Marks" in a row back in 1958-60. Like the companion T-Bird, the Mark IV would be around for five years—and not much altered in any of them.

The design assignment was handed to Wes Dahlberg, with the Cadillac Eldorado his ever-present target. Beat the Eldo, he was told—any way you can. Work began in 1969, when Eldorado rode a 120-inch wheelbase; Dahlberg chose a 120.4-inch spread, aiming for more back seat room rather than outdistancing Cadillac. But 1971 brought a second-generation Eldo on a whopping 126.3-inch span, so the Mark still trailed, though the designers were able to give it a more spa-

cious interior—and a more substantial profile than previous Marks. The IV also had a slightly wider track, giving it a small handling edge over the III, if not the bloated Eldo.

Dahlberg wasn't allowed to change the Mark's big square grille, but he was able to make it more prominent by scooping out the front bumper so that it looked, and was, taller. Equally apparent were the more abrupt rear-fender kick-up and broader roof sails relieved by oval "opera windows." The latter, a Bordinat idea probably inspired by the "porthole"

Ford's mid-year Sprint Decor Option (left) was not a Mustang exclusive. It was also promoted for the Pinto Runabout and two-door Maverick. In addition to the red, white, and blue exterior paint and USA decal, the package included dual white racing mirrors, color-keyed seats and carpets, and white sidewall tires with color-keyed hubcaps and trim rings. Mustang also listed an upgraded Sprint option with mag-type wheels, F60-15 raised-white-letter tires, and competition suspension. The '72 Maverick four-door sedan (below) started at $2195; 73,686 were produced.

T-Birds, may have been a gimmick, but they proved just as popular as they had back in 1956 and soon became a Mark IV trademark—as well as *de rigueur* all over Detroit. They also served the practical purpose of improving over-the-shoulder vision. And they were timely, as Cadillac had oblong ones on the '72 Eldorado, which had been styled after the Mark III and looked more like a Lincoln than ever.

As expected, the Mark IV chassis was basically the same as the new Thunderbird's, engineered for a smoother ride and improved handling. Detail niceties included intermittent windshield wipers and—from your friends in Washington—steel beams within the doors to resist intrusion from side impacts. The Mark IV proved as big a hit as the '72 T-Bird, with production zooming to near 49,000 units for the model year, close to double the '71 figure—and 9000 ahead of the Eldo. Among them was the 100,000th Mark produced since 1939.

Enthusiasts still rightly judged the sprightly imported Capri as the most interesting car at Lincoln-Mercury dealers. This year's Euro-Mustang offered a third engine option and it was a goodie: a 120-bhp 2.6-liter (156-cid) overhead-valve V-6 from Ford Cologne. With that, Capri finally had performance to match its looks. *Road & Track* magazine recorded a brisk 10.4 seconds from 0-60 mph. Even better, the engine came with tach and full engine instrumentation, plus larger 185-13 radial tires, all for a base list of $2821 P.O.E.—America's lowest priced V-6. Simultaneously, the little 1.6-liter four was phased out in favor of the 2.0 as standard.

The V-6 Capri was a standout in the growing "supercoupe" ranks that now included GM's German-built Opel 1900 Rallye and a Japanese newcomer, the Toyota Celica. It may have seemed odd to find such a spirited enthusiast's car sharing showroom space with the big Mark IV, but dealers didn't complain because their cash registers jingled. The engine would prove to be a winner, too, evolving into larger-displacement versions that would power a very different kind of Ford Bronco and Ranger pickup in the late-Eighties and early-Nineties.

Even more interesting than Capri, if less accessible price-wise, was the sleek, mid-engine DeTomaso Pantera from Italy, which L-M had begun selling in earnest during 1971 (after a splashy March 1970 debut at the New York Auto Show). Though intended as simply a rebodied version of Alejandro DeTomaso's earlier Ford-powered Mangusta, the Pantera—Italian for "Panther"—carried an all-new pressed-steel unit structure (which has since caused a lot of pain for restorers). The extra tooling expense was justified by high anticipated U.S. demand; indeed, DeTomaso had geared up to build Panteras by the thousands. Vignale in Turin supplied the bodies, with the DeTomaso plant in Modena handling final assembly. As with the Mangusta, styling

Just as the '72 Torino grew bigger, so did the new Thunderbird, although in the T-Bird's case weight didn't change much. Wheelbase, however, was extended some 5.7 inches to 120.4—exactly the same as that of the new Lincoln Continental Mark IV. That was no accident, as the Mark and the Bird shared the same bodyshell, altered front and rear for brand identity. With the four-door gone, only a hardtop coupe was offered. It started at $5293 ($2 less than the base '71), and output soared 60 percent to 57,814 units.

was entrusted to Ghia, specifically American Tom Tjaarda. The result was more practical than the Mangusta yet just as sleek despite no change to overall length or wheelbase (168 and 99 inches, respectively).

Chassis design was classic Italian supercar: double wishbones and coil springs all-round plus rear radius rods and front and rear anti-roll bars. Disc brakes were located at all four corners. Weight distribution was much more favorable than the Mangusta's, with a 58-percent rear bias. Still, unequal-size tires were retained: 185-section fore, 215-section aft. Dearborn's desire for easy servicing and high reliability dictated plenty of volume components throughout. Pantera's powerplant was thus the high-output version of the familiar 351 Cleveland V-8, mated to a five-speed ZF transaxle. Net horsepower was initially 310 in U.S. form and 330 for European models. Emasculating

emissions controls would bring the former down to 250 bhp by 1973.

Though hardly spacious, the Pantera was at least roomier than the Mangusta. Reflecting Ford input, detail engineering was more thorough and professional, equipment more complete. Even air conditioning was included, unusual for a low-volume Latin but a necessity for the U.S. market. Practicality also dictated more conventional body construction, with a single engine lid, hinged at the cockpit end, instead of the Mangusta's flamboyant gullwing panels.

Though not exactly cheap at its $10,000 base price, the Pantera was a bona fide bargain for a limited-production Italian exotic. Here was all the panache of a Ferrari or Maserati for far less money, plus a rugged, well-known Ford V-8 that could be serviced almost anywhere. Panteras even carried Ford's normal new-car warranty.

four-speed manual gearbox with floorshift. A ladder-type box-section chassis featured American-style double A-arm/coil-spring front suspension and a semifloating live rear axle on progressive-rate, six-leaf semi-elliptic springs. Overall length measured 172 inches, width 63 inches, and height 61.6 inches. The cargo bed covered an area of 74.5×62.2 inches. Payload was 1400 pounds.

That looked small next to "real" pickups—some truckers said *too* small. Nevertheless, the Courier was another sign of the times: the growing Japanese presence in the U.S. car and truck market. Still, its frisky nature, rugged construction, car-like maneuverability, and sub-$2000 price translated into a good many extra sales that Ford would have otherwise missed. In fact, modest though it was for a first effort by the new Dearborn-Tokyo alliance, the Courier was successful enough to suggest that there would be more Mazdas in Ford's future.

Though not major, changes in the rest of the '72 truck line were well considered. Starting at the bottom, the little 4×4 Bronco received standard bucket seats with pleated vinyl upholstery and several new options including 6.50-16 tires. At midyear, the Bronco wagon got the Ranger treatment, a new, specially tailored package option featuring Ginger, Blue, or Avocado paint with white accents on hood and lower body, plus matte-silver grille, deluxe bright-finish wheelcovers, and a swing-away outside spare-tire carrier with a white cover. Inside were cut-pile carpeting front and rear, cloth seat inserts, woodgrain door-panel accents, and a deluxe steering wheel. It was all so nice you hated to risk getting it dirty by going off road. But then, even in those days, a lot of four-wheel-drive buyers seldom if ever ventured off the concrete path.

Econolines now came with a sliding right-side cargo door, standard on the passenger Club Wagons, a no-cost option on the plain-panel commercial units. GVW ratings got their usual slight increases, and power brakes appeared on the options list. Another new option was the "Northland Special Package," an equipment group to ease winter driving in cold climes. Included were engine-block heater, heavy-duty battery and alternator, severe-use antifreeze, and Traction-Lok limited-slip differential. Returning from mid-1971 was the Econoline Camper Special, essentially a cab/chassis ready-made for Class C motorhome conversions. It came only on the 123.5-inch-

A good thing too, because the Pantera was something less than a dream come true. Its Italian style and fine handling were undeniable, but so were a cramped cockpit, peculiar driving position, and indifferent workmanship. Worse, complaints about engine overheating and excessive cabin heat surfaced early, and performance wasn't all it should have been in U.S. form. European models, unfettered by "detox" gear, could beat 160 mph, but American models weren't nearly as fast. Then too, that simple Yankee iron was hardly a bragging point when everyone knew that *real* exotics had all-aluminum engines with overhead cams.

Ultimately, though, the Pantera would be done in by yet another new federal safety standard born this very year of 1972. Among provisions of the new Motor Vehicle Information and Cost Savings Act was a requirement for "crash bumpers" able to withstand five-mph shunts without damage. These would be mandatory at the front of all 1973 models, and at both front and rear from 1974 on.

But the Pantera had been designed with a curious disregard for U.S. regulations existing or proposed, so by 1974 it would be saddled with an ugly black-rubber nose guard and bigger back bumpers as stopgaps. However, the still-stricter

rules anticipated for 1975 would require a major redesign, including a new powertrain. Ford bean-counters deemed that too costly for the car's modest sales (rendered even more modest by the autumn 1973 gas crisis), thus spelling the end of U.S. Pantera imports after 1974. L-M said U.S. Pantera sales totaled 6091, but some thought that figure was exaggerated; at least one source says it was only 5629.

Ford's Truck Operations unit was renamed Truck and Recreation Product Operations this year, yet another sign of the times. Here, too, an import was news. Announced on March 17 was a small pickup reviving the Courier name from Ford-sedan delivery days, the first fruit of Dearborn's association with Toyo Kogyo of Japan. Essentially a badge-engineered version of TK's B-Series Mazda 1800 pickup, the Courier gave Ford dealers a belated weapon against similar offerings from Toyota and Nissan, both of which had enjoyed an ever-healthier U.S. trade in small pickups since the mid-Sixties.

A conventional design on a trim 104.3-inch wheelbase, the Courier arrived with a cross-hatch grille like that of Ford's domestic F-Series, but was pure Mazda elsewhere. Power came from an iron-block, aluminum-head overhead-cam four displacing 1.8 liters (110 cid), which drove the rear wheels through a

Late in 1972 Ford debuted a cab-forward show truck it called the Explorer (above). It featured a mid-mounted engine (note the side vents), carpeted cargo box floor and tailgate, and a fancy interior with high-back bucket seats. As before, the Custom was the mid-line Econoline Club Wagon (right). For 1972, prices started at $3647 and 6608 were called for.

wheelbase E-300 chassis and included the 302 V-8, Cruise-O-Matic, power steering and brakes, and heavy-duty tires and shocks.

This year's F-Series pickups sported a modestly modified split grille with four squares per side instead of six. The 240 six was dropped as base F-100/250/350 power in favor of the bigger 300, and three-speed-plus-overdrive manual transmission was no longer cataloged for F-100s. New options included the Northland Special Package as on Econolines, plus power drum brakes for 4×4s. Bucket seats disappeared from the accessories chart.

New to the medium- and heavy-duty ranks were a 186-inch-wheelbase F-600 chassis and a 206-inch version of the low-cabover C-Series 700/750 and 7000. There was also a wider choice of diesels in Louisville 9000s, and optional Cruise-O-Matic was extended to F-600s. March brought two additions to the Louisville Line in reply to competitors' moves. These were the LT-880 and LNT-880, lower-priced gas-engine tandems with higher horsepower. Both employed a modified "475" version of the 477 Super-Duty V-8 with 220 bhp instead of 213,

giving them higher maximum hauling capacity than their 800-Series linemates. Rounding out major revisions among Ford's biggest trucks were three new Owner-Operator Packages for W-Series high-cabovers—groups of specially selected comfort, convenience, and cosmetic features aimed at independent long-haul truckers.

As noted, 1972 was another splendid year for Ford trucks. Including Club Wagons, combined U.S.-Canadian production for the calendar 12 months was 987,394 units, of which the Walkerville, Ontario plant contributed 167,461. Comparable

1971 production wasn't available, but that year's combined factory sales of 782,523 units gives a rough idea of Ford's increased 1972 volume.

A noteworthy event in Ford's corporate history came on May 22 this year when chairman Henry Ford II and architect John Portman announced a new Ford-financed building project intended to spur the revitalization of what had become a derelict downtown Detroit. That project was destined to become the largest privately financed development in history. Today it stands as the multi-tower complex called Renaissance Center.

1 9 7 3

Recalling Golden Anniversary 1953, new-design F-Series trucks and minimally changed passenger cars highlighted this, Ford Motor Company's 70th year. The reason was another round of federal safety and emissions standards. The trucks needed updating to meet them—and to fend off competitors. This, together with stepped-up efforts in passenger-car compliance, had stretched Dearborn's engineering resources to the point that there was little left for anything really new in cars.

But, of course, new Fords were on the way. A more rational, fully revamped Mustang was getting its finishing touches for what would be a smashing 1974 debut, and the following year would bring an equally successful new upscale compact as an erstwhile replacement for Maverick. Still, the heavy hand of Washington would preclude much product innovation in the mid- to late Seventies as Ford Division, and most everyone else in Detroit, scrambled to keep pace with the regulatory onslaught. As if that weren't enough, a heretofore little-known cartel of oil-producing countries was about to deal a body blow to America's economy with vast consequences, not only for the U.S. auto industry, but the nation's way of life. With the OPEC oil embargo that began late this year, America would never be quite the same again.

Sales-wise, 1973 was a mixed year for Ford Division. Despite an 80,000-unit rise in calendar-year car registrations, the make's market share dropped below 19 percent for the first time in recent memory. Ford Motor Company as a whole declined to 23.5 percent of the total car market, its lowest penetration since 1952 and a far cry from its 30.83-percent postwar high achieved in 1954. On a model-year basis, Ford Division again topped two-million cars for the third straight year and eclipsed its record 1972 volume by more than 100,000 units, reaching nearly 2.4 million. But Chevrolet tacked on about 150,000 cars to maintain a substantial edge of close to 230,000.

On the truck side, Ford again went over the million mark for the calendar year (this time by 48,500 units), but so did Chevy, largely on the strength of its most extensively changed commercial vehicles since 1960. Interestingly, 1973 proved something of a seller's market for heavy and extra-heavy trucks, with operators rushing to buy to avoid a federal rule that was about to mandate anti-skid systems with air brakes. As a result, big-truck makers found themselves short of diesel engines, heavy-duty axles, and other components, all of which limited production relative to demand and, true to the old law, put a premium on prices.

This year's revamped F-Series conventionals weren't totally new in appearance or specifications, as most engines and some body and chassis components were carried over. But cabs *were* different for the first time since 1967: longer and thus roomier. They were also simpler in construction to take advantage of new automated stamping equipment, with one-piece inner and outer body panels. This also applied to the Styleside pickup box, resulting in tougher "double-wall" construction that prevented dents made by cargo shifting inside from showing up on the outside. Wheelbases were upped two inches (to 117) on most models to accommodate the rangier cabs. Accompanying this on the volume-leading F-100 and F-250 4×2s was a new wide-rail frame with broader rear track and a chassis-mounted gas tank, which replaced the former in-cab reservoir. Additionally, all F-100s, 250s, and 350s received standard front-disc power brakes.

But it was hard to guess at all this from '73 cab styling, which remained typically Ford and looked more like a facelift than all-new. A split eggcrate grille was still on hand, but it now held more and smaller "crates." Parking lamps on light-duty models moved back above the headlights into a narrow full-width slot that pulled the usual block-letter nameplate down from the hood, which was flatter now. A keen eye might discern a slightly lower beltline and cowl, as well as a concave instead of convex bodyside "character" line. The taller, brawnier F-Series mediums (500/600/700/750 and diesel-powered equivalents) wore a big crosshatch grille and still displayed "FORD" on their hoods.

Other F-Series changes included a new nine-foot F-350 Flareside on a unique 140-inch wheelbase. Designed for the growing RV (recreational vehicle) trade and thus dubbed "Super Camper Special," it came with a 360 V-8, Cruise-O-Matic, and custom-tailored chassis components. Light-duty Crew Cabs now rode a 150.3-inch chassis regardless of two- or four-wheel drive, and offered a new "short" 6¾-foot Styleside box. A handy box cover—what we'd now call a

Now in the third and final year of its design cycle, the '73 Mustang received only a few minor changes. Among them were color-keyed molded urethane bumpers for all models, a revised grille with a crosshatch pattern and vertically placed parking lamps, new exterior colors, and optional forged aluminum wheels and steel-belted radial tires. The Mach 1 (right), which listed at $3088, came with the 302 V-8 standard. That engine was rated at 136 SAE net bhp, but many buyers opted for one of the two 351 V-8s. Mach 1 standard equipment included a competition suspension and the choice of two hood designs, one with twin NACA air ducts. The '73 model was destined to be the last of the "big" Mustangs.

After watching demand for the Mustang convertible decline from over 100,000 in 1965 to just 6401 for 1972, production took a healthy jump to 11,853 units for 1973. But there were a couple of reasons for that. First, Ford dropped the full-size LTD ragtop for '73, leaving Ford fans a choice of only Mustang or Cougar soft tops. But more importantly, Ford announced ahead of time that there would be no convertibles from Ford Motor Company after 1973, so those who wanted one rushed in to get theirs while they could. The '73 seen here carries a number of options, including upgraded wheels and tires, as well as a tasteful bodyside stripe.

"bed cap" or camper shell—was newly optional for eight-foot Stylesides, and light-duty 4×4s could be ordered with integral air conditioning, Cruise-O-Matic, and power steering for the first time. Another first was availability of the Ranger trim package on Flaresides as well as F-Series stake and platform models. Midyear brought a truck version of the big Lincoln 460 V-8 as a new option for automatic 4×2 F-250s, delivering 239 net horsepower. Arriving simultaneously was a new 188-inch-wheelbase chassis available as an F-6000, 700/7000, and 750. All

F-Series, lights and mediums alike, now featured "Zincrometal," outer body panels galvanized on their inner surfaces to resist rust.

Though the revamped F-Series hogged most of the '73 limelight, worthwhile changes occurred elsewhere in the Ford truck fleet. Starting at the bottom, the little imported Courier pickup was treated to several new options: air conditioning, Philco AM pushbutton radio, full wheel covers, 6 × 9-inch mini-western door mirrors, and three-speed automatic transmission. The last was designed and

supplied by JATCO, short for Japan Automatic Transmission Company, a separate Ford/Toyo Kogyo venture that also built automatics for some Mazda passenger cars. Also new for Courier was an extra-cost Dress-Up Package comprising bright exterior moldings in the usual places, plus front bumper guards and vinyl-insert bodyside rub strips. At midyear, Ford tried fooling more of the people some of the time by substituting "F-O-R-D" for Courier identification on hood and tailgate.

One step up, the go-anywhere Bronco sport-utility moved from the 170 six to the 200-cubic-incher as base power and lost its pickup model, leaving only the full-top wagon. Otherwise, it coasted into 1973 with upgraded trim and reshuffled equipment. The 300-cid six replaced the 240 as standard power for E-300s, and a "dualie" option—twin rear wheels and tires per side, plus vented *rear* disc brakes—arrived for the E-300 cab/chassis late in the year.

Another latecomer was a W-Series high-cabover restyled *a la* the Louisville Line, with the same sort of big, six-sided eggcrate grille, plus a newly woodgrained instrument panel. Added at the same time were 152- and 164-inch wheelbases for the big diesel-powered WT-9000 chassis. The W-Series' successful Owner-Operator Packages were extended to the Louisvilles at midyear, with similar flash and features. All medium- and heavy-truck gas engines adopted evaporative emissions systems per federal dictate, and there were minor adjustments among the

big rigs in both gas- and diesel-engine availability.

Ford took an abortive stab at the RV market this year with the American Road Camper. Named after the street that runs by the company's "Glass House" world headquarters in Dearborn, it was a slide-in fiberglass unit stretching 11.5 feet long. A premium price limited sales, however, and the unit was abruptly dropped after minuscule production. Another 1973 announcement, a large, self-contained motorhome, didn't even get that far. Production constraints delayed introduction to year's end, just in time for the OPEC oil embargo that made big motorhomes virtually unsalable due to their piggish fuel thirst. Thus, as one historian put it, Ford's motorhome had "the dubi-

ous honor of being the domestic...industry's first victim of the Energy Crisis."

The most visible of the federal requirements affecting cars this year was the heavier, bulkier front bumpers used by most manufacturers to meet the new five-mph front-impact protection rule. In most cases this necessitated recalibrating

The Mustang convertible (above) listed at $3102 for 1973; it would be a decade before Mustang would offer a ragtop again. Maverick saw few changes for 1973, but output posted at 14-percent gain to 291,675. One reason was the LDO: Luxury Decor Option (below). It gave Maverick a touch of class by providing reclining independent front seats, deep-cut pile carpeting, white sidewall radial tires, color-keyed hubcaps, vinyl roof, and vinyl-insert bodyside moldings.

suspensions to compensate for the extra weight up front—not to mention hard styling work to make the new battering rams look acceptable.

One of the less successful of such grafts appeared on this year's Torino and Ranchero, bringing shallower grilles and reshaped front fenders to all models. Lesser Torinos retained a full-width grille treatment, while Grans and Rancheros continued with a central "mouth" (now rendered a wide rectangle) and separate headlights. A new Brougham hardtop and sedan arrived to top the Gran Torino series, offering standard cloth and "leatherlike" vinyl upholstery, pseudo-wood interior appliques, electric clock, and other amenities. Engines were detuned, but availability was unchanged. Like other Detroit cars this year, all mid-size Fords, Rancheros included, carried inside hood releases as a new anti-theft measure, plus flame-retardant upholstery in line with a government-specified

"burn rate" of four inches per minute. Radial tires were a new option for some models. Rancheros benefitted from enlarged rear brakes and wider optional tires.

A below-the-belt reskin made this year's full-size Fords appear more substantial and "important." All wore flatter, more muted noses and deeper front bumpers that increased overall length by about three inches. LTDs sported three-element grilles filled with little rectangles; Galaxie 500 and entry-level Custom 500s bore a full-width ensemble. Body-side creaselines were toned down, wheel-arches became a bit rounder, taillamps were set above conventional square-rigged rear bumpers, and trunklids were dipped down in the center. Though not immediately apparent, greenhouses were also restructured, gaining deeper windows. The LTD convertible, Ford's sole full-size ragtop, was axed in anticipation of a federal rollover standard. The base

Custom sedan and wagon also vanished, leaving the model count at 16.

Big-Ford engines stayed the same except for necessary detuning and the addition of a four-barrel, 460-cid Lincoln V-8 as the new top option. The last was advantageous because of its extra torque, not horsepower (a rated 202 bhp versus 201 for the 429), a growing necessity with escalating curb weights. Indeed, this year's lightest big Ford, the Custom 500 sedan, flattened the scales at a none-too-svelte 4059 pounds, while the three-seat Country Squire wagon was up to over 4600, a gain of some 250 pounds just since 1971. Inside, the "front room" curved instrument panel gave way to a more conventional dash with radio and climate controls on the driver's right. New options included a factory-fitted alarm system (reflecting yet another depressing sign of the times), power "mini-vent" front windows on four-doors, and steel-belted radial tires. In a year when

rival makes also had little new, the big Fords picked up a surprising 40,000 or so additional sales, reaching close to 858,000.

Thunderbird was facelifted with a busier eggcrate grille flanked by head-lamps in square chrome nacelles. Another styling fillip was small parallelogram "opera" windows, a new $80 option that also required a vinyl top. Buyers responded to this more glittery package in record numbers, and production soared to over 87,000 units, the third highest total in T-Bird history after 1960 and '64. Base prices jumped substantially to a bit over $6400, and it didn't take much to run that up to $7500 or more.

As noted, Ford was ready to launch a new Mustang, a car more faithful to the spirit of the beloved 1965 original. Typically, the real push for a total redesign came from Lee Iacocca. "I've said it a hundred times and I'll say it again: The Mustang market never left us, we left it," he

would remark later. "We kept the 460 out of it, but we had all the other engines in it." Design vice-president Eugene Bordinat agreed: "We started out with a secretary car and all of a sudden we had a behemoth."

The Mustang to which Bordinat referred remained its hefty self for this final year. Surprisingly, perhaps, the '73s sold a bit better than the '72s. The convertible scored the largest percentage increase—up a resounding 100 percent to nearly 12,000 units—but only because Ford had announced that the body style would not return for '74. Though the '73 Mustang wouldn't be Ford's "last convertible," it would be the make's final factory-built ragtop for the next decade.

Mustang fared better than most '73 Detroiters in front bumpers, which stuck out only a little more than in 1971-72 and thus didn't look too bad. This particular "bumper system" comprised an I-beam mounting bar inside a box-section brack-

et attached to two longitudinal rubber blocks that gave way on contact, then bounced back to their original position. As before, an optional color-keyed rubber cover was available to clean up appearance even more.

Front bumper aside, the '73 Mustang saw little visual change from 1971-72. Mach 1 nose styling was still optionally available on other models in an exterior Decor Group, where the horizontal "sport" parking lamps were now turned vertically, a small spotter's point. Prices, which had been cut the previous year to spark sales, were little changed. The base six-cylinder hardtop listed at $2760, while the V-8 convertible was the most expensive at $3189. The Mach 1, still with a standard two-barrel 302 now rated at 136 net bhp, sold for $3088.

Mechanical mods were few. Bigger brakes were fitted, as were larger calipers for cars with non-power discs, and radial tires were a new option. So, too, was a

Torino, which had been all-new for '72, received a revised front end for '73, but not because Ford had wanted it that way. The reason was the new five-mph bumper standard, which resulted in an unattractive and overly heavy-looking bumper riding below a more rectangularly shaped grille. The Gran Torino formal hardtop (left) retailed for $2921, or $3071 as a Brougham. Together they tallied 138,962 units built. The $3154 Gran Torino Sport SportsRoof (below) offered a "performance look" with color-keyed racing mirrors and raised-white-letter tires. It also shows off the rear bumper pad and "unique taillamp treatment."

"dual ram induction system," a special hood with twin air scoops, matte black or silver paint, decals, and twist-type hood locks, available with the two-barrel 351 option. A two-tone hood with the locks and dummy scoops was also offered. Mustang was now the only Ford offering a High-Output four-barrel 351 V-8. As was true throughout the corporate line, drivetrain choices were thinning due to the high cost of certifying each engine/ transmission/ratio combination for emissions compliance under the Environmental Protection Agency's mandatory 50,000-mile durability test.

Speaking of which, Mustang tailpipe

The '73 Thunderbird (above) saw its sticker price skyrocket $1144 to $6437, but that didn't stop demand from increasing nearly 30,000 units to 87,269. Even Pinto buyers happily optioned up the $2144 Runabout (below) with goodies like the Sports Accent Option and forged aluminum wheels. With 217,763 built, the most popular '73 Pinto was the $2343 wagon (bottom right).

pollutants were now handled by crankcase ventilation and exhaust-gas recirculation. The latter routed gases from the exhaust manifold through a vacuum valve into the carburetor, where they were diluted by the incoming fuel/air mixture. This permitted leaner carburetor settings for lower emissions. The influence of federal requirements was evident elsewhere, too. For example, Mustang's dash got extra padding and was now bereft of sharp knobs and other projections that might cause unnecessary injury in a crash.

Mustang was now nine years old, but the original marketing ploy of offering a wide range of options was still important. The '73, Ford said, was "designed to be designed by you." And it was. The optional vinyl top, now in a choice of six colors, covered the whole roof on hardtops and the front three-quarters on fastbacks. Also on the list were forged aluminum wheels, "metallic glow" paint, and decorative side striping. An electric rear-

window defroster was available for hardtops and SportsRoofs.

Pinto sauntered on with the requisite beefier front bumper, backed by a reinforced structure to better absorb impact loads. Surprisingly, this added only about 40 pounds and 1.5 inches in length. Standard tires were upgraded to A78-13 bias-plys, and air-conditioned cars got an extra pair of dash vents. New options included AM/FM stereo radio, forged-aluminum road wheels, and a handling package. Model-year volume breezed past the half-million mark as Pinto continued outselling the rival Chevy Vega by a comfortable margin. The wagon accounted for nearly 40 percent.

Maverick's main improvement was 35-percent greater lining area for the all-drum brakes, which had been roundly criticized for lack of stopping power. The standard 170-cid six was replaced by the 200-cid unit, which was switched from four to seven main bearings for smoother running and gained six horsepower. All

models now wore the richer-looking Grabber/LDO grille, and wheelarch and greenhouse moldings became standard along with full carpeting and nicer cabin trim. New options included a "halo" vinyl roof for two-doors, AM/FM stereo, and forged-aluminum wheels. Overall length increased by four inches, all of it in the front bumper.

The "energy crisis" that began in October of this year resulted from Middle-East nations, led by the Organization of Petroleum Exporting Countries cartel (OPEC), turning off their oil spigots to the West in partial response to America's continuing support of Israel. Besides altering the daily lives of all Americans more dramatically than any event since the great Depression, the embargo prompted the Nixon Administration and Congress to reduce the national speed limit to 55 mph. At the time this was supposedly just a "temporary" fuel-conservation measure, but it would persist for a dozen years despite being widely ignored—and the advent of an oil *glut* by the mid-Eighties. Which only proves, perhaps, that like buildings, there's nothing so permanent as a "temporary" regulation.

Though the energy crisis would put a big, if temporary, dent in big-car sales, Lincoln-Mercury Division, where big cars were traditional, was better able to weather this storm than most rival producers. The Maverick-clone Mercury Comet, rocking along at about 80,000 units per year, gave it a timely contender in the high-volume compact field, and those buyers attracted to the weighty Mercury Marquis and Lincoln Continental could well afford 80-cent-a-gallon gas. Cougar, which had been on the sales skids since '68, finally showed an upturn for '73, as production rose from 1972's all-time low of just under 54,000 units to nearly 61,000. There were even a few "last convertibles": 1284 standards, 3165 XR-7s. Of course, Capri was now L-M's *real* ponycar—and still selling briskly at $3175 for the 2.0-liter four-cylinder version or $3470 with 2.6 V-6. It, too, wore a front "battering ram," plus a nicely restyled dash with standard full gauges regardless of engine. So despite the difficulties that lay ahead, L-M Division wouldn't have a really bad sales year until 1980.

Ford had been attuned to the growing leisure market for years, so it's not surprising that the firm developed the F-350 Super Camper Special pickup (top), here a '73. It was specifically designed to handle heavy campers with ease, and even received its own front fender badging. Bronco (center) made news for '73 by offering automatic transmission and power steering for the first time. "Primarily a personal transportation and recreational vehicle," Ford noted, "Bronco with its standard four-wheel drive is a popular choice for the outdoor-minded." The Econoline Van, meanwhile, was described as "mainly a work vehicle." Prices started at $2738 for the cargo van.

345

1 9 7 4

Nobody who lived through the winter of 1973-74 will likely forget that time when gasoline, always assumed to be almost as plentiful as water, suddenly became a much more expensive commodity—and, on occasion, a black-market one. Drivers got up at dawn to jostle for position in gas lines that stretched for blocks as behemoth cars bred three to five years before queued for sips at the life-giving pumps. Some owners even resorted to carrying a spare set of license plates in places where gas was rationed by odd/even numbers. Locking gas caps sold like crazy as protection against fuel thieves with syphons.

Still, the Middle East oil embargo and resulting "Energy Crisis" didn't start clobbering sales until about the middle of model year '74. And since we're mainly recounting model years here, it must be said that this was a pretty good one for the industry as a whole and Ford Division in particular. Ford car production was down by a substantial 170,000 units or so, to just shy of 2.1 million units, but Chevrolet dropped a like amount, so little was changed between the perennial front-running duo. Trucks, however, were a bright spot, with Ford reclaiming the calendar-year sales lead despite reduced domestic volume of 886,708 units. Over at sister L-M Division, Lincoln returned to

its '72 volume, which was hardly bad, and though Mercury also went down substantially, the 1974 total was still one of its best-ever years.

The problem, of course, was that a six-million-car year wasn't the boom it had been in the Fifties. Detroit was now geared for 10 million units annually, and moguls muttered when sales didn't match. They also grumbled when profits failed to reach expectations, and Ford had plenty of reason to grumble about a 58-percent drop in corporate earnings in 1974. Most of that reflected an equally important consequence of the oil embargo: skyrocketing manufacturing costs brought on by higher energy and materials prices.

Almost lost in the fuel panic and surrounding hubbub were the latest federal mandates. The main ones called for rear bumpers able to ward off five-mph shunts with no damage to either bumper or surrounding sheetmetal, and something called the "starter interlock." The latter was a praiseworthy but ill-conceived "passive safety" device that prevented the engine from being started until the driver's seatbelt was fastened. But it proved such a nuisance to so many people that it was scratched from the lawbooks before the year was out.

That was small consolation for automakers whose unit costs were burdened by higher energy prices on top of the growing expense of meeting Washington's dictates. It was a frustrating situation—so much so that Ford president Lee Iacocca proposed a five-year moratorium on new federal regulations. Without such relief, he told the Newspaper Advertising Bureau in November 1974, "A Pinto will

no longer be a Pinto." By his reckoning, pending rules for 1975-78 would turn that $2000, 2000-pound car into a $5000, 3000-pound car getting 3-4 fewer miles per gallon. For $820 less than a government-spec '78 Pinto, Iacocca said Ford could a deliver one that would weigh 426 pounds less and get one-third better fuel economy, yet provide "almost the same public health and safety benefits." He also declared that on an annual basis a five-year regulatory freeze would save $9 billion in consumer spending, 20 billion gallons of gas, and two million tons in mate-

Design plans for the Mustang II were well along when this December 1971 styling study (right) was drawn up by designer Dick Nesbitt. Long before the energy crisis of late 1973-1974 it had been decided that the new Mustang would be smaller and lighter, more in keeping with Ford of Europe's mini-Mustang, the Capri. What emerged was a pair of coupes, notchback and fastback, riding a 96.2-inch wheelbase and weighing 2700-2800 pounds. The fastback (below) listed at $3328. The interior was planned to be upmarket for the car's price, as this mock-up (left) shows.

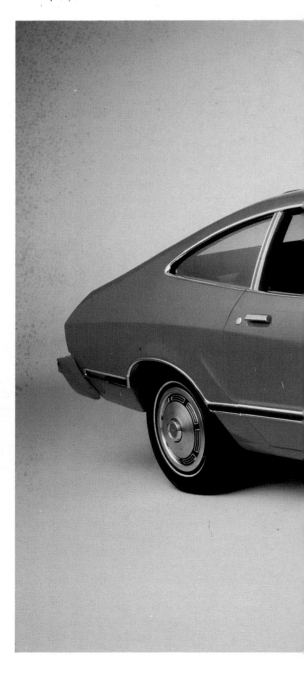

rials. It would also free up $5 billion for industry research and development toward meeting post-'78 regulations.

But Washington wasn't buying this proposal, perhaps because it smacked not a little of putting foxes in chicken coops. And in fact, legislators were about to complicate Detroit's dilemma even more by enacting a new set of rules suggested by the energy crisis: fuel-economy standards. They wouldn't take effect for a few years yet, but that, too, was scant consolation for a motor industry that felt increasingly besieged from all sides.

It was thus more than a little ironic that Ford Division's main car news for 1974 was the smaller, lighter Mustang II, a return to something like the original ponycar concept. That it arrived almost simultaneously with the energy crisis was mere coincidence, of course, as it had been in the works long before. Still, the fortuitous timing undoubtedly contributed to strong sales: close to 386,000 for the model year, a figure within 10 percent of the original Mustang's 12-month production record of nearly 419,000.

That car's "father" was the driving force behind this new Mustang. But while Lee Iacocca had only guessed the first time, he knew *in advance* that Mustang II would hit it big: "When I look at the foreign-car market and see that one in five is a sporty car, I know something's happening." By 1972, small 2+2 coupes like the Opel Manta from GM Germany, Japan's new Toyota Celica, and L-M Division's own imported Capri were running at around 300,000 annual sales, and 1974 projections put them at over 400,000. Mustang II's mission was to capture a big slice of this sizeable new "mini-pony-car" pie.

Once again, Dearborn's army of stylists and engineers worked from parameters clearly defined by Iacocca: sporty appearance, a wheelbase of 96-100 inches, standard four-speed gearbox, four-cylinder or small six-cylinder engine. Most important, the Mustang "must be luxurious—upholstered in quality materials and carefully built...a 'little jewel.'" What Iacocca got was the familiar longhood/short-deck styling themes reinterpreted on a reduced scale—smaller than the original. Against the 1971-73 generation, Mustang II was 20 inches shorter, four inches narrower, an inch

lower, 400-500 pounds lighter, and nearly 15 inches shorter between wheel centers. The real target was the sporty import coupes Iacocca alluded to. The tape measure told the story:

Dimension (in.)	1965 Mustang	1974 Mustang II	1974 Toyota Celica
Wheelbase:	108.0	96.2	95.5
Length:	181.6	175.0	163.9
Width:	70.2	68.2	63.0
Height:	51.0	49.9	51.6

Also recalling the original Mustang was another intramural design competition that Iacocca staged. This time the contestants were the divisional Ford and Lincoln-Mercury staffs, Advanced Design under Don DeLaRossa, the corporate Interior Studio, and the house of Ghia, the renowned Italian coachbuilder

recently acquired by Dearborn. The choice came down to five clay models, a pillared notchback hardtop and four fastbacks, that managers reviewed in November 1971. The one selected as the basis for production styling—and surprisingly little altered—was a fastback from the L-M group under Al Mueller. Like Joe Oros back in 1962, Mueller gave his proposal eye-catching paint—persimmon, no less—to increase his team's chances.

Iacocca had decided that "the convertible is dead and can be forgotten" (though he'd later think otherwise at Chrysler Corporation). This left the traditional hardtop and fastback. There were plain and fancy versions of each, the latter being the Ghia notchback (replacing Grandé) and the Mach 1, which along with the standard fastback gained a European-style lift-up rear hatch "door," a first

for Mustang and another boost to American acceptance of hatchbacks.

The notchback, incidentally, almost didn't make it. The one such proposal at the executive review, designed by DeLaRossa's troops and called "Anaheim," had not gone over well at consumer clinics earlier in 1971. But Iacocca, suspecting that the researchers had missed something, decided to give it one last shot, at San Francisco in February 1972. This time the reaction was positive, so it was decided to offer a "trunked" version of the already-approved fastback, this with barely 16 months left before production startup. "It seems we go through that with every Mustang program," said Jack Telnack, who would later replace Bordinat as Ford design chief. "We always start with the fastback...Then we find out the surveys still say 50/50 [preference] and we have to add the notchback." Ford also explored a two-seat fastback in February 1972 (via a full-scale tape drawing). It looked nice, but was never seriously in contention.

Interior design was somewhat less involved. It was chiefly the work of L. David Ash, who decided to give his interior mockup the feel of a real automobile by making it far more realistic than was customary in the design business. It even had exterior sheetmetal and all four wheels attached. "It was a time-consuming thing to build," Ash said, "but it served its purpose very well. We didn't have to go through an elaborate series of meetings to determine everything. It was all approved right here. We were on a crash basis to get it done, and it was very enthusiastically received...."

Chevrolet had been making hay with its personal-luxury (but popularly-priced) Monte Carlo since 1970, and in 1973 had sold nearly 300,000 of them. Ford didn't have a direct competitor to counter it as the Thunderbird fell into a much higher price bracket. Finally, in mid-1974 Ford debuted its reply, the Gran Torino Elite (top row). As the name implied, it was based closely on the Gran Torino, as well as the repackaged Mercury Cougar. Its calling card listed formal styling, a Thunderbird-inspired grille, twin opera windows ("Twindows"), stand-up hood ornament, vinyl roof, and a posh interior (left) liberally splashed with simulated wood. Priced at $4437, it proved attractive to 96,604 luxury conscious buyers during its short first model year.

Ash later confessed that he was at least partly inspired by the likes of Jaguar, Rolls-Royce, and Mercedes. "We put everything in that we could conceive of that connotes restrained elegance, plus the get-up-and-go that says Mustang—something of a fire breather.... It's a kind of a mini T-Bird."

Unlike the massive, heavily sculptured twin-cowl dashboards of 1969-73, the Mustang II panel was dominated by a simple large oblong shape directly ahead of the driver. This put all controls close at hand, yet still had room for all necessary warning lights and instruments. Surprisingly, the latter included a standard tachometer, temperature gauge, and ammeter. Seats were initially covered in pleated cloth, vinyl, or optional leather—very plush. They had no rake adjustment, sad to say, but were definitely more comfortable than previous Mustang seats. Rear legroom was sparse because the II was seen as being used primarily by one or two adults, who'd sit in front. Backseat room would be sufficient only for a

couple of small children or for an adult passenger to be comfortable on short hops.

At announcement time, some observers suggested the Mustang II was just a sportier Pinto (which was more or less how it started). Sure enough, a good many components were shared, and even the wheelbases were nearly the same: 96.2 inches for the Mustang versus Pinto's 94.2. But the latter was actually upgraded for '74 to take advantage of some parts and features designed for Mustang II.

For example, both models employed unit construction and the same front suspension—independent with unequal-length upper and lower arms and coil springs. For the Mustang, however, the lower arms attached to a rubber-mounted subframe; on the Pinto they bolted directly to the main structure. By carrying the rear of the engine/transmission assembly, the subframe reduced driveline vibration to the Mustang II's passenger compartment. It also contrib-

The Gran Torino wagon (bottom left) was up to a hulking 4209-pound curb weight for '74, 335 pounds more than the similar '72 model. Most of the increase resulted from government mandated safety standards, particularly for stronger bumpers. And listing at $4017, the price had skyrocketed a whopping $921 in two years. Still, 29,866 people bought one. Ford claimed that the Gran Torino Brougham two-door hardtop took on "a more elegant look for '74 with new front and rear bumpers, a bright grille, hood ornament, deluxe wheel covers, and new taillights." Selling at $3975, it saw output reach 26,402 units.

uted to more precise steering and a smoother ride than Pinto's. Watchful company cost accountants could justify this more expensive mounting arrangement because Mustang II was intended to sell for more than Pinto.

Both cars also used the same rack-and-pinion steering mechanism, but the Mustang's was mounted differently, again to minimize shock, and could be power-assisted at extra cost (Pinto's couldn't). At the rear, the Mustang's leaf

351

The major visual difference on the '74 Maverick was a big rear bumper that looked too heavy for the car and a slotted energy-absorbing front bumper. Models with the vinyl roof got Maverick nameplates on the C-pillars and the four-door seen here has the vinyl-insert side moldings. The four-door started at $2824, up $590 since the body style had first bowed for 1971. The 84-bhp 200-cubic-inch six was still standard, but the 91-bhp 250 could be had for $77, while the 140-bhp 302 V-8 cost $177 extra.

formance and thermal efficiency. Supplied only with dual exhausts, the V-6 was optional for any Mustang II save the Mach 1 hatchback, where it was standard. Like early 2.0-liter Pinto fours, it was imported from Ford's West German subsidiary in Cologne.

Mustang II's standard four-speed gearbox was basically the four-speed unit from the British Ford Cortina as used in the Pinto, albeit strengthened to handle the Mustang's more powerful engines. Brakes were a combination of 9.3-inch front discs and 9 × 1.75-inch rear drums with vacuum assist.

Predictably, "cooking" Mustang IIs and the top-line Ghia notchback exhibited typically "American" ride and handling traits. The Mach 1 was both more capable and entertaining with its standard V-6, radial tires, and optional competition suspension. No Mustang II had overwhelming acceleration. The car was heavy for its size (curb weight was 2650-2900 pounds), so a V-6 with four-speed would do 0-60 mph in a lackluster 13-14 seconds and reach only about 100 mph, a far cry from the big-block V-8 days.

As if to prepare buyers for this reduced performance, Ford redesigned the trademark running-horse emblem for the Mustang II, a less muscular steed that seemed to be trotting instead of galloping. The symbolism went largely unnoticed, but not the car itself, of course, as that smashing production total attests. Icing the acceptance cake, Mustang II was honored as *Motor Trend* magazine's 1974 "Car of the Year."

Mustang II would not see significant change over what would turn out to be a five-year production run. The four-cylinder engine, Ghia, and Mach 1 would always be cataloged, and Ford continued to offer plenty of options for all models. Aside from air conditioning and a variety of radios and tape players, the initial '74 roster included a vinyl top, sunroof, and forged aluminum wheels.

For once, Mercury had opted out of cloning a new Ford, odd considering that L-M's proposal was the one chosen as the basis for Mustang II. Ford Design Center photos show that some consideration was given to a Mustang II-based replacement for the Capri (and bearing that name). But the import was selling too well in 1971-72, and Mercury marketers likely wanted a more direct competitor for GM's personal-luxury middleweights, the popular Pontiac Grand Prix and Chevrolet Monte Carlo. The obvious strategy was to upgrade Cougar. They did, and it paid off.

As for the Capri itself, it continued doing good business in 1974. Its main attraction this year was the 2.8-liter V-6 developed for Mustang II, here rated at 119 bhp. But the Capri was becoming expensive—now up to $3566 in base form, $3807 with V-6—thanks to inflation that started to gallop in response to the fuel

springs were two inches longer than Pinto's, and its shock absorbers were staggered, as in previous high-performance Mustangs. Spring rates were computer-calculated to match the equipment, weight, and body style of each car. The Ghia notchback, for example, came with very soft settings, while the optional competition suspension had the stiffest springs, along with a thicker front anti-roll bar, a rear bar, and Gabriel adjustable shock absorbers.

As mentioned, the Mustang II concept gave no thought to a V-8, a first in Mustang history. Initial engine choices were limited to a 2.3-liter (140-cubic-inch) single-overhead-cam inline four and a 2.8-liter (171-cid) enlargement of the Capri's overhead-valve V-6. The four, sometimes called the "Lima" engine after the Ohio city where its factory was located, was the first American-built engine based on metric dimensions. That wasn't surprising. Originally designed for some of Ford's larger European cars, it

was actually a bored-and-stroked version of the 2.0-liter Pinto unit. A novel feature was its "monolithic engine timing." After each engine was assembled, an electronic device hooked to a computer was connected to two engine sensors, an indicator point at the rear of the crankshaft and an electrical terminal between the distributor and coil. The computer compared readings from each sensor, then set timing automatically via distributor adjustment. The computer's high degree of precision made this technique very useful for meeting increasingly tough emissions standards.

The V-6 also had a European counterpart, and used the same camshaft, valvetrain, pushrods, and distributor. It was, in fact, the same engine available in U.S. Capris from 1972. However, it too was bored and stroked for Mustang II duty, with capacity increasing from 2.6 liters (155 cid) to 2.8 (171 cid). At the same time, Ford switched it from siamesed to separate exhaust ports for improved per-

scare, plus currency fluctuations that were beginning to price German cars right out of the U.S. market.

Apart from those already mentioned, changes in this year's Pinto were minor. Stronger roof rails and underbody crossbars strengthened its unit structure. They added weight, of course, which together with tightening emissions controls rendered the original 1.6-liter engine too weak to provide decent performance, so the 2.0-liter four became standard.

This year's big Fords were mainly carryovers. LTDs received new fine-check grille inserts and a standup hood ornament, along with standard steel-belted radial tires. Solid-state ignition was now fitted to all optional V-8s, but the big 429 engine was no longer listed. Electronic ignition, also used on 429s where still offered, was another important technical improvement in that it extended tune-up intervals, though it was dictated more by the need to meet stiffening emission standards (via more precise timing control). The mid-size Torinos were also little changed. All models got vertical bars within the '73 grille frame, and the parking lights at the outboard ends shifted from horizontal to larger, better-integrated vertical units. Rear fender skirts were a new option for Gran Torinos, and hardtop coupes could be ordered with Thunderbird-style rear opera windows.

Mid-year brought an interesting line expansion called the Gran Torino Elite, a "Thunderbird-inspired" pillard coupe on the slightly beefier chassis of the Cougar XR-7, which had parted company as a Mustang variation after 1973. The Elite was, in fact, Ford's Cougar counterpart and was intended to steal sales from Chevy's popular Monte Carlo. Body structure, dimensions, and interior appointments were basically as for Torino, with the ubiquitous two-barrel 351 V-8 standard. Styling hallmarks included an aggressive eggcrate grille, a matching central hood bulge forming vestigial Thirties-style "catwalks" with the front fenders, dual (instead of quad) headlamps in molded square nacelles inboard of fender-mounted parking lamps, wide body moldings, and two slim opera windows per side instead of one. Elite captured 96,604 sales in this short debut season to take over as Ford's most popular mid-size model by far.

This year's Ranchero threesome naturally wore the new Torino face as well as rearranged minor trim. Among new Ranchero options were the big 460 V-8 to replace the 429 as the top engine, low-back bucket seats, a new full-width "Flight" bench seat, automatic-temperature-control heating/air conditioning system, tilt steering column with extra-cost Cruise-O-Matic, power windows, cruise control (except with the base 302 V-8), anti-theft alarm, and Brougham Decor Group with the same basic content

Like just about all American cars during the period, Thunderbird was having a weight problem in the mid-Seventies, escalating from 4373 pounds in 1972 to 4825 in 1974. Accordingly, T-Bird tossed out its standard 429 V-8 in favor of the Lincoln 460 that had been optional since 1972. In its 1974 guise, it was rated at 220 horsepower. Base price was now $7330, up from $5293 in 1972. About the only styling change for '74 was segmented taillamps incorporating a large, central backup lamp with a stylized Bird logo.

as like-named Torinos.

Thunderbird likewise was little altered. A new styling fillip was segmented taillamps incorporating a large, central backup lamp with stylized Bird logo. The 460 V-8, now with solid-state ignition and a rated 220 net bhp, became standard, as did vinyl roof, opera windows, manual air conditioning, power windows, and tinted glass. Alas, the fuel shortage put a crimp in sales, with output crumbling to about 58,500 for the model year.

Two of this year's new Thunderbird options would later show up on less costly Dearborn cars. One was "Autolamp," which used a photocell receptive to changes in ambient light levels to switch the headlamps on or off as needed. It also incorporated a variable delay timer that extinguished the lights a few seconds after switching off the ignition, thus lighting the way for occupants from car to doorstep. Also new was the "moonroof," a tinted glass panel that retracted electrically, a descendant of the Fifties

"bubbletop" idea.

Predictably, the gas crunch benefited sales of the economy-oriented Maverick compact, so output rose by about 10,000 units to 301,000. The '74 models were substantially the same as the '73s, identifiable mainly by their deep-section rear bumpers.

Ford's big truck news this year was called "SuperCab," a response to the Dodge Club Cab of 1973. The idea was the same: a conventional two-door pickup with extra sheetmetal grafted on behind to make room for an extra-cost fold-down auxiliary bench seat or an optional pair of inward-facing flip-up jump seats. But Ford went Dodge one better—or rather, four inches better, adding 22 inches to the existing F-Series structure to provide 44 cubic feet of in-cab cargo space.

Initial SuperCab offerings were all Stylesides: F-100 and 250 with either 6¾- or eight-foot box, and an eight-foot F-350. Wheelbases were lengthened to suit:

138.8 inches with the short box, 155 with the long. Frames and floorpans were stiffened to match, and rear-quarter sheetmetal was, of course, unique, with little rear side windows that could, as an option, be flipped out. Naturally, the same four trim choices were listed as for what were now called the "Regular Cabs." This year's top-line Ranger XLT package became even lusher with the addition of door map pockets, "biscuit-pattern" upholstery, vinyl-insert bodyside moldings, and a few extra pieces of miscellaneous trim.

But styling changes were otherwise few on Ford's light-duty '74 trucks. One reason was new emissions standards that forced a lot of engine swapping and retuning. Some of this was prompted by the special stricter requirements of the California market. As a result, the 300-cid I-6 was reinstated as an F-100 option and was the base engine for California-bound E-100/E-200 Econolines and Club Wagons, and all 300 sixes as well as 400 and 460 V-8s sold in the Golden State were equipped with solid-state ignition. Similarly, all '74 Rancheros carried a base 302 V-8 through March 31, after which the 250 six was substituted for 49-state sale. A running change prompted by performance rather than emissions was the switch from two- to four-barrel carburetion on 390 V-8s in F-250/350s. Another new development was the arrival of a full-time transfer case for 4WD F-100/250s produced from February 4.

Expanding this year's group of heavy conventionals was the F-880, a lower-cost, higher-power version of the F-700. Like its "880" counterparts in the Louisville Line, it carried the "475" rendition of the 477-cid gas V-8, plus higher-capacity axles and wedge-type air brakes. Other changes among the big rigs included another shuffle of diesel-engine choices among the largest Louisvilles, a new 236-inch-wheelbase LT-8000, and a stripped LN-7000 Louisville chassis offered on 136- and 220-inch wheelbases for installation of large, integral van bodies.

This year's Econoline was a virtual '73 carryover apart from the aforementioned engine adjustments and first-time availability of the Camper Special's "dualie" option on the commercial E-300 delivery van and cab/chassis. The winsome Bronco was treated to only detail trim and equipment changes, including a lighted automatic-transmission quadrant. However, the 200 six, Cruise-O-Matic, and 4.11 rear axle were no longer available in California, where a special emissions package was required for the 302 V-8, the only other engine available. Bronco was still generating respectable sales despite a now nine-year-old design and competition from newer truck-based sport/utilities at Chevy/GMC and Dodge/Plymouth. Ford evidently saw no need to rush out a replacement, for the next-generation Bronco wouldn't appear for another four years.

The Bronco (top) bucked its way into 1974 looking and acting as before. The only model offered was the Wagon, and at a base price of $4182 it came with the 84-horse 200 six. For about an extra $150, the 302 V-8 was available, and for a few extra bucks one could add the Ranger package, as shown. Bronco production settled in at 18,786 units for the model year. The Econoline (center) could be had as a Custom Super Van. Custom was for the deluxe trim, such as the full-disc hubcaps, Super referred to the stretched 123.5-inch wheelbase. The F-250 Supercab pickup (bottom) sold for $4473, $909 more than the regular F-250.

1 9 7 5

Thunderbird marked its 20th birthday in a busy model year that also introduced a new "deluxe compact" nameplate, a significant third-generation Econoline series, and a spate of lesser changes elsewhere. The entire U.S. auto industry was still in a sales slump resulting from the Middle East oil embargo. Ford Division's market share reflected this, dropping more than two points for the calendar year to slightly under 18 percent despite the broadest range of models, sizes, and prices since the mid-Sixties—and in spite of cash rebates, a new Detroit ploy to jump-start sales of slow-movers.

Ford production naturally suffered as well. In cars the division fell 610,000 units, ending the model year just shy of 1,570,000. Again, Chevrolet dropped a like amount from a higher starting point and thus maintained its previous margin over Ford with total volume of nearly 1,756,000. Ford's calendar-year truck output was the lowest since 1971, skidding to 692,200 commercial units and another 34,639 Econoline Club Wagons

(still counted as passenger models by most statisticians). The one bright spot in this gloomy picture was that the oil squeeze had ended shortly before the '75 model year began. That gave hope that sales would soon pick up—which they did, of course, but the wait was agonizing. Buyers had lately shown increasing preference for well-equipped, more luxurious, smaller cars, and the 1973-74 gas panic only accelerated their desire. Ford's response was the Granada, trumpeted as the "car designed for the times." Actually, it had been designed to replace Ford's Maverick. The original plan called for a plusher, slightly larger compact of more formal appearance using essentially the same chassis and running gear. But with sales consistently strong, Ford felt it couldn't afford to drop the old compact. Accordingly, the plan changed: Maverick would continue, while its intended successor would be an addition to the line, occupying a size and price niche between Maverick and the mid-size Torinos.

Though its 109.9-inch wheelbase was shared with the Maverick four-door, Granada emerged 10 inches longer, an inch wider, and several hundred pounds heavier. Suspension was also shared and typical Detroit, but Granada was blessed with standard front-disc brakes, more body and suspension bushings, and softer springs and shocks, the last in the interest of the hallowed "big car" ride. There were

no powertrain surprises. Base engine was Maverick's standard 200-cubic-inch six, and options were the same 250-cid six and 302 V-8, plus a two-barrel 351. Three-speed manual transmission was standard, Cruise-O-Matic optional, and floorshift available for both.

Granada also offered two- and four-door body styles like Maverick, but that's where the similarity ended. Where the Maverick looked American, Granada struggled to be European. Styling, supervised by design vice-president Eugene Bordinat, was an unabashed imitation of certain upper-class imports. Mercedes-Benz, in particular, had every reason to be flattered, and Ford advertising hammered away at the size and styling similarities with M-B's junior "New Generation" sedans. TV commercials even showed passers by mistaking a Granada for a Mercedes. The four-door was unquestionably more handsome than the

Lee Iacocca was happy to pose with the new '75 Ford Granada (below), another car which he had greatly influenced. Initially, this new car was to replace the Maverick, but with the fuel crisis a reality it seemed wiser to keep the old compact and make the Granada an addition to the line. Actually, this worked quite well since the Granada was larger than the Maverick, so it slotted nicely between Maverick and Torino. Only two body styles were offered, two- and four-door sedans, both in regular and Ghia trim.

two-door, which was afflicted with opera windows that looked out of place with the Mercedes-like rectangular grille and similarly boxy body. The interior could have come from Lincoln. While a few European touches were available on the costlier Ghia twosome—individual front seats with reclining backrests, grab handles, map pockets, and the like—instrumentation was minimal and dashboards were awash in "test tube" wood.

Enthusiasts were disappointed by Granada's handling and performance. *Road & Track* reported that "the car doesn't handle badly; it corners quite flat . . . and on the skidpad it got around only slightly slower than the vaunted Brand M [Mercedes]. . . . But Ford's power steering still has little road feel . . . and we found ourselves too concerned with just staying on course. . . . The live axle, not particularly well controlled since it's on simple leaf springs, is quite susceptible to bumps and loses traction easily." With 302 V-8, automatic, and 3.00:1 axle ratio, *R&T*'s tester ran 0-60 mph in a respectable 12 seconds but returned a not-so-respectable 12.5 mpg in normal driving. Still, the editors praised the Granada's brakes, driving position, and quietness, as well as its more intelligent design. "If we had expected it to be a surrogate Mercedes . . . we'd be disappointed," *R&T* concluded. "But if we look at the moderate price tag [around $3700] and think of the Granada as a reasonable-size interpretation of the traditional American car with a little inspiration from Europe, there's no problem liking it."

A good many buyers liked Granada—nearly 303,000, in fact. Again, Ford had read the market correctly. What's more, Granada's strong initial acceptance showed clearly that the way to future sales success was upmarket, not down.

Other Fords changed but mildly for 1975. Special "MPG" Pintos and Mustang IIs arrived at mid-year with that new emissions clean-up device, the catalytic converter. Both models would vanish after this short run, though not the "cat con" itself. By obviating the need for much of the add-on emissions hardware of past years, it allowed engines to be retuned for greater efficiency, thus boosting fuel economy—which hadn't been that spectacular of late in Ford's smallest cars. The 2.3-liter "Lima" four was now standard Pinto power, while the 302 V-8 became optional for automatic-equipped Mustang IIs, answering cries for more go with 122 horsepower. V-8 cooling requirements dictated larger grille eggcrates, a change applied to all Mustang IIs this year regardless of engine.

Since the Mustang V-8 displaced about 5.0 liters and Chevrolet's Monza 2+2 (based on its subcompact Vega) offered a 4.3-liter (262-cid) V-8, comparisons were inevitable. *Road & Track* clearly preferred the Monza. And despite the subjective judgments involved, they were probably right. Monza was brand-new

for '75, a fresh, modern design that seemed smoother and more integrated than the Mustang II. And its comfort, ride, handling, and fuel economy were all judged to be better than the Ford's. *R&T* summed up the feelings of many by saying the Mustang II's styling was "humpy and bumpy, and—in its interior—downright garish" and lacking "ergonomic refinement"—hardly the "little jewel" laMonza for acceleration by a healthy margin, as one would expect with more displacement, but it also used more gas. The Ford's only advantage seemed to be in braking. Here are *R&T*'s test results for the 1975 models.

	Mustang II	Monza 2+2
V-8 cid/bhp/rpm:	302/122/3600	262/110/3600
0-to-60 mph, sec:	10.5	13.4
¼-mile, (speed/sec):	77.0/17.9	72.5/19.5
top speed, mph:	106	103
mpg:	13.0	17.0

Other new Mustang II options included a $454 flip-up glass moonroof for the already posh Ghia, as well as a new Silver Luxury Package giving that model cranberry-color crushed-velour upholstery, silver paint, vinyl top, and a stand-up hood ornament. At the same time, the rear-quarter glass on all Ghias was shortened up to form faddish "opera" windows. Newly available throughout the line were handsome forged aluminum wheels and an extended-range (17-gallon) fuel tank. The latter betrayed the fact that even the smallest of Fords in this period were comparatively thirsty.

Mustang II sales fell over 50 percent from 1974, but would hold steady at about 190,000 a year through the end of the line in 1978. If not exactly torrid, this was certainly a lot more encouraging—not to mention profitable—than the tepid pace of 1971-73.

Along with Pinto, the compact Maverick soldiered on with steel-belted radial tires and solid-state ignition as new standard features. "F-O-R-D" appeared in block letters on trunklid and hood, a proper glovebox was added to Grabber and the LDO package, and a heavy-duty suspension option was a new—and overdue—extra for the Grabber. Maverick sales fell way off, plunging from just over 301,000 of the '74s to 162,842 for '75. But that wasn't as bad as it looked, especially given the difficult market and a near six-year-old design that had seen little interim change. Some would-be Maverick buyers undoubtedly wound up in Granadas instead, and import competition, especially from Japan, was tougher than ever.

Torino was virtually untouched save catalytic converters on all engines. Accompanying this was a special fuel-filler neck sized for the small-diameter pump nozzle that had been mandated to pre-

vent using anything but unleaded gas in converter-equipped cars.

The Gran Torino Elite sailed into its sophomore year virtually unchanged, but it saw production rise to more than 123,000 units, making it easily the best selling Ford mid-sizer for the second straight year. Listing at $4767, it also ranked as one of the most expensive Torinos. At the other end of the line, Ford boasted that even base Torinos offered automatic transmission, power front-disc brakes, power steering, V-8, and steel-belted radials for "less than $4000"—which was true, though only the standard sedan and hardtop coupe carried base stickers below that magic figure. Everything else was comfortably above $4000, though no higher than $5000. But

soaring inflation was making buyers a lot more price- and value-conscious, so this year's volume Torino series was the basic Gran group. Demand for the fancy Broughams withered to very low levels: for example, a mere 4849 hardtop coupes and just 5126 Sport hardtops. Excluding

The Granada carried many Ford styling cues of the mid-Seventies, such as formal Mercedes-style grille and taillights, formal lines, and—yes—stand-up hood ornament and, on the two-door, opera windows. Many judged the four-door version more attractive. The regular two-door (below) started at $3756, and 100,810 were built for '75. Maverick, meanwhile, lost sales to Granada, but the two-door sedan (right) had a base price of $3025 and 90,695 were produced.

As it turned out, the more fuel efficient Mustang II had arrived just in time for the fuel crisis, so sales were good for '74. For its second year, there were few changes, although the 302 V-8 was made an option (with automatic only), as was a $454 power moonroof on notchbacks. Prices were up: $4188 for the Mach 1 (above), $3938 for the Ghia coupe (right). Production was down: 188,575 total, 21,062 Mach 1s, 52,320 Ghias.

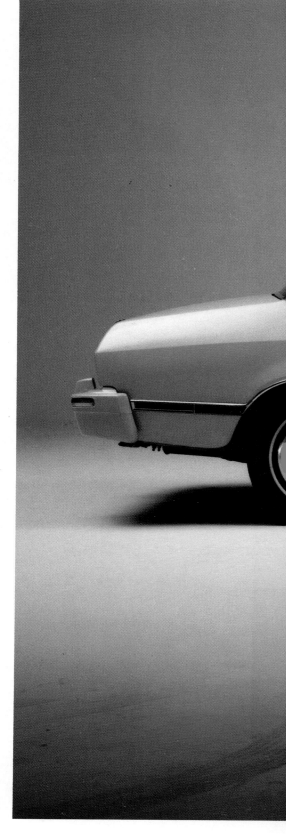

the Elite, Torino output dropped by more than 150,000 units to just shy of 178,000.

As ever, most Torino changes also showed up in the Ranchero, but the car-pickups now caught up with their passenger sisters in certain options, offering power door locks and a Security Lock Group (inside hood release and key-locks for gas cap and spare tire) for the first time. Also new on the list, and for Torinos as well, was "Fuel Sentry," really a manifold-pressure gauge with a dial segmented into red "performance" and green "economy" zones as an aid to more economical driving. The idea was to exercise care with your throttle foot so as to keep the needle in the green sector as much as possible. Ford presumably intended that straying into the red would make you feel downright guilty—anti-social at least.

The big Fords were given a modest restyle, with flatter and more rectangular grilles, raised and planed rear decks, and slim vertical windows cut into B-pillars of two-door "hardtops." Series hierarchy changed, with the new LTD Landau (identified by hidden headlamps) at the top, followed by LTD Brougham, plain LTD, and a Custom 500 sedan and Ranch Wagon. Landau and Brougham were confined to pillared sedan and two-door hardtop. The plain LTD offered these plus two- and three-seat wagons. As ever, the premium wagon was the Country Squire, now trimmed to Landau standards and bearing the same hidden-headlamp front. Some observers noted that the once-familiar Galaxie name was missing from the big-Ford line, consigned to history after 15 years.

Marking 20 years of Thunderbirds were two new luxury option packages for the otherwise unchanged cruiser. One was done in silver, the other copper, both

color-keyed to a fare-thee-well. Though not many people knew it, four-wheel disc brakes had been a T-Bird option since '72, and were now included with the extra-cost Sure-Track anti-lock system. Sales sank to 43,000, down about 16,000 from 1974.

Over at Lincoln-Mercury, sales of the sporty Capri were suspended this year after leftover '74s were disposed of. But the division wasn't abandoning its "Sexy European," merely clearing the decks for something better: the Capri II, which would arrive very late in the model year as an early-'76 entry (and is thus covered under that heading).

Though nobody could know it in 1975, the new third-generation Econoline would be a significant introduction for Ford owing to a very long production run. In fact, Ford would still be building it 15 years later. It was certainly a well-considered vehicle, inspired as much by Chevy's G-Series vans of 1971 as Ford's desire for a bigger, brawnier, and more adaptable Econoline.

Like the second-generation design, the idea behind this new Econoline was pushing the engine further forward for improved serviceability, increased front-seat space, and less noise. The result was a traditional van that looked like it had collided with a conventional-cab pickup. Econoline's hood was still stubby, to be sure, but it was definitely longer. A beveled front edge led it down to a big new square eggcrate grille.

This new configuration naturally led to much longer overhangs and wheelbases, the latter stretched some 18 inches to 124 inches for "short" models and to 138 for "longs," and an even longer 158-inch span was available for parcel delivery and cab/chassis applications. Steering and suspension geometry were revised ac-

cordingly, and power front-disc brakes were standard equipment for the first time, but the big news was body-on-frame construction, a world first for a van. This plus the usual rubber body mounts and the more forward engine location made for a quieter, smoother-riding vehicle, a big reason why Detroit luxury cars in these years still retained body-on-frame construction. And with new options like integrated air conditioning, cruise control, AM/FM stereo, and

tinted "Privacy Glass," it seemed as if these Econolines aimed to be the most luxurious vans anywhere.

As before, Econoline offerings comprised commercial and Club Wagon passenger models, but chassis designations were revised to match F-Series numbers. The E-100 continued, but the E-200 became an E-150, E-250 replaced E-300, and there was a new E-350 chassis designed for gross-vehicle-weight ratings above 10,000 pounds. Other models also boast-

ed higher GVWs: E-100, 5700-6000 pounds; E-150, 6010-6300; and E-250, 6300-8750. Club Wagons were now roomy enough to seat up to eight on the short-wheelbase, 12 on the longer chassis. They also offered a new extra-cost gimmick: "Captain's Chairs." Another van innovation, these were individual swiveling seats mounted on pedestals and supplied with dual fold-down armrests. Available for all models was an auxiliary fuel tank to bolster the regular 24.6-gal-

lon unit.

That last option was well-advised, because the new Econolines had larger engines to match their extra weight and they weren't exactly fuel misers. The 351 Windsor V-8 was now the base engine, and options ran to the big 460 for E-250/350. But neither this nor the much-higher gas prices seemed to deter buyers, who simply loved the cushier, more refined new Econolines. A slow production startup limited sales this first year, but

Opposite page: This '75 Mustang II Ghia (top) has the optional 302 V-8, as noted by front fender badges, as well as the power moonroof. It also sports '75½ trim: no stand-up hood ornament and new hubcaps. The '75 full-size Ford lineup lost the Galaxie and Galaxie 500 models, leaving two Custom 500s and 10 LTDs. The LTD two-door "hardtop" (bottom) cost $4753 and 47,432 were called for. This page: A Copper Luxury Group, which carried the color theme throughout the car, was an option on the $7701 T-Bird (top left). Production fell to 42,685 units. Pinto output was down to 223,763 units for '75; the Runabout (top right) listed at $2984. The $4837 Gran Torino Brougham four-door (center left) was almost ignored—only 5929 were ordered. Likewise, the $4407 Ranchero Squire (center right) found just 1549 customers. Two more models from the '75 truck line (bottom): Econoline Cutaway Chassis (left), with 8750-11,000 pound GVW; Custom Club Wagon (right), $4446 and up.

deliveries would pick up steam from here on.

Federal emissions standards now dictated catalytic converters and thus costlier unleaded fuel for gas-powered trucks below 6000-pound GVWs. Recognizing that some buyers wouldn't go for this, Ford added new F-150 pickups, SuperCab and Regular, with a nominal 6050-pound rating that eliminated the need for a "cat con" and permitted using cheaper leaded regular (which also applied to the new E-150 Econoline, incidentally). Otherwise, this year's light-duty F-Series saw few changes, though a new SuperCab version of the cab/chassis was added.

Other additions to the '75 truck line comprised a rangy 260.5-inch F-Series chassis, 186-inch-wheelbase versions of

the F-Series and Louisville 600/700/750, a four-barrel "389" derivative of the existing 391 medium-duty V-8, and "Extra-Duty" versions of this and other FT-Series gas engines (330 and 361, all with uprated cooling system and low-friction pistons). There were more engine and transmission shuffles among diesel-powered big rigs; the Bronco received electronic ignition, a numerically lower 3:50:1 "economy" axle ratio, and newly optional engine-block heater and cold-weather Northland Special package. Anti-skid air brakes were now mandatory for big rigs and all the appropriate Fords had them. But this was an expensive requirement disliked by both manufacturers and buyers, and Chrysler used it as an excuse to abandon its heavy trucks, whose sales had been fast-withering anyway.

1 9 7 6

America's motor industry continued its halting sales recovery from the oil-embargo days of 1973-75, but this year of the nation's Bicentennial was a mixed one for Dearborn. Ford Division's market share dropped yet again, and the company's penetration slipped below 23 percent. The latter looked bad against GM and Chrysler, both of which moved up from 1975. Highland Park closed the year at 13 percent, GM at just over 47 percent, not far from the postwar GM highs of the mid-Fifties. Despite recent attention, the big Fords ran a poor fifth in the annual sales race, trailing the second-place full-size Chevrolet by 94,205 units. And Ford truck sales were stymied by short supplies of the popular new Econolines, leaving Chevy to finish first in that race for the second year in a row.

But there were bright spots for Ford Division. Mustang II, for instance, was the third best-seller among domestic subcompacts with 187,567 built, bested by Chevy's new-for-'76 Chevette, and then by less than 400 units. And Pinto, despite

its six-year-old design, was still hanging in there in first with a production run of 290,132 units. Granada quickly captured the top spot among compacts with output nudging 450,000 cars, leading a redesigned Chevy Nova and Chrysler's new Dodge Aspen and Plymouth Volaré by very comfortable margins. Most of the changes in this year's passenger Fords involved the smaller models. In further pursuit of sport—or what was left of it—new Stallion trim packages arrived for Mustang II fastbacks and two-door Pintos and Mavericks. Content differed depending on application, but all involved silver body paint set off with lots of contrasting black on hoods, grilles, and greenhouse, plus bold front-fender decals emblazoned with a fiery steed.

More functional, if slightly outrageous, was another new option group for three-door Mustang IIs. Called Cobra II and priced at $312 this year, it was intended to evoke thoughts of the late, great Shelby-Mustangs. Features comprised sports steering wheel, remote-control door mirrors, brushed-aluminum appliques on dash and door panels, plus a black grille, styled steel wheels with trim rings, radial tires, flip-out rear quarter windows with louvered covers, front air dam, rear spoiler, and simulated hood air scoop. Requisite model identification and/ or badges appeared on rocker panels, grille, tail, and front fenders. The '76s were all done in white with blue tape

stripes (applied to rockers and on the hood, rooftop, and tail), but other combinations were added beginning with the '77s. It was flashy, but a far cry from genuine Shelby-Mustangs. Incidentally, the package could be ordered on the Mach 1, which created the amusing official model designation Mustang II Mach 1 Cobra II.

There was one other equipment change involving the '76 edition of Ford's compact ponycar. The Ghia notchback's optional moonroof was newly available for any Mustang II and with a choice of silver or brown tint.

Pinto got a minor freshening via a close-checked grille housing square parking lamps, and a no-frills Pony two-door appeared to battle budget imports with a $2895 base price. Options expanded with the addition of a half-vinyl roof for sedans and pseudo-wood Squire bodyside

The '76 Mustang IIs, even with their various trim options, could hardly be told from the 1974-75 models. The fastback (below), now priced at $3781, doubled in popularity to 62,312 units even though total Mustang II production held steady at 187,567 units. This one has the exterior sport dress-up package and the newly available plaid upholstery. Opposite page: The base coupe (top) stickered at $3525, and was the popular choice for '76 as 78,508 were requested. This one has the exterior accent group. Ford showed a T-top version of the Mustang II (bottom) at some 1976 auto shows—it became a production option for 1977.

appliques for the Runabout. The aging Maverick also got a new grille, a split horizontal-bar affair, and front-disc brakes became standard at last. The highly successful Granada continued with no appearance changes, but a new Luxury Decor Option spiffed up the Ghia four-door with two-tone black/tan exterior and lacy-spoke aluminum wheels plus color-keyed tan interior with crushed-velour upholstery. The base Granada two-door could be newly dressed in a "Sports Sedan" outfit comprising special paint,

Although no muscle car, the '76 Mustang II Cobra II (left and below) certainly looked the part, and when ordered with the 302 V-8 was fast for its day (the V-6 was standard). The Cobra II package added $325 to the 2+2's base price of $3781, while the V-8 added another $250 or so. The '76 Pinto (top right) was easily identified by its new eggcrate grille. Prices started at $2895 for the stripped Pony MPG; the Runabout sold for $3200. New this year was the Squire Runabout (bottom right): $3505 as an MPG, $3952 with V-6.

color-keyed road wheels, pinstripes, floorshift, and leather-rim steering wheel. Other new options included a power moonroof and, interestingly, all-disc power brakes. Headlamp dimmer switches were newly combined with turn-signal stalks on Granada and Mustang II.

The mid-size Torino and Elite as well as the derivative Ranchero car-pickup were practically unchanged. The Elite, however, was now listed as a separate, one-model series and saw output jump to 146,475 units. The Gran Torino Sport hardtop disappeared, but Elite filled the gap by offering bucket seats and console with floorshift as new options. Steel-belted radial tires were now standard for Ranchero 500 and Squire, a power bench seat and a manual split bench were added to Ranchero's options roster, and an automatic parking brake release was now included with the optional Convenience Group for all intermediate Fords. Where needed, engines were retuned and ex-

haust-gas recirculation systems revised to meet emissions standards.

There were no appreciable changes to the big LTDs for 1976, but optional four-wheel power disc brakes showed up here too, along with a half-vinyl top for two-doors. Big Ford output totaled slightly over 400,000. Thunderbird's only alteration was another round of trim and paint packages: Creme and Gold, Bordeaux (as in wine), and Lipstick (a bright red). Besides coordinated colors, each included half-vinyl top, thicker carpeting, special upholstery, and body accent stripes. T-Bird sales recovered somewhat to nearly 53,000 for the model year as the curtain rang down on the big seventh generation.

Company chairman Henry Ford II was apparently unconcerned about the fast-growing competition from small Japanese imports. "People really want big cars," he said. "Give them the option and they'll go for big ones every time." With that attitude at the top, Dearborn's ad-

vance-design department understandably felt no pressure to rush out smaller intermediate and full-size cars in the wake of the energy crisis. Contrary to popular belief, Ford had a few such projects in the works, but the prevailing opinion—or was it a hope?—seemed to be that it would be big-car business as usual just as soon as buyers got used to higher gas prices. Of course, HF II hadn't reckoned on a challenge to Detroit's "bigger is better" tradition—least of all by that bastion of bigness, GM. But it hit like a bomb for '77, rattling the "Glass House" like nothing since the Edsel.

A more enlightened attitude was evident in this year's new Capri II, an updated version of the appealing Euro-Mustang at Lincoln-Mercury dealers. Wheelbase stayed the same, but overall length was stretched by seven inches (to 174.8), most of it in rear overhang to accommodate a roomier luggage compartment accessible via a lift-up hatch. With its attendant structural reinforcements,

the new body configuration swelled curb weight to near 2600 pounds, but performance remained respectable despite minor horsepower losses to emissions tuning. Sensibly, the four was discontinued, leaving the 2.8-liter V-6 as the standard and only engine.

Styling was cleaned up by simplifying the grille and erasing the fussy bodyside character lines, but familiar Capri "cues" persisted: elliptical rear side win-

Since there was so little new for '76, Ford (like other automakers) tried to push its lower-line cars with eye-catching paint-and-stripe packages, in this case the Stallion option, which sold for about $300. Offered on Pinto, Maverick, and Mustang II, it featured silver and black paint, with the darker color covering rocker panels, hood, rear panel, and roof (except Pinto). Huge stallion decals adorned the front fenders. Also included were styled steel wheels and raised-white-letter tires, "competition" suspension, and dual racing mirrors.

dows, domed hood, close-coupled proportions. Base, luxury Ghia, and sporty "S" models were now listed, the last available with a striking black-and-gold color scheme (later called "Le Cat Black") reminiscent of the treatment used on the contemporary John Player/Lotus Grand Prix racers. Interiors continued with front buckets, console-mount shift, and well-arranged, fully instrumented dash, with a newly available fold-down back seat for extra practicality.

Unfortunately, a strengthening deutsch mark lifted Capri II into an altogether different price class from the spot its predecessor had occupied—up to Granada territory, in fact: around $4100 this year, escalating to near $4600 for the '77 Ghia. Capri was still a fine enthusiast's coupe, but fewer buyers saw much reason to prefer it over the mechanically similar Mustang II, not to mention a few Japanese sportsters that cost considerably less. Predictably, then, Capri II would

wither rapidly through the little-changed 1977-78 models, after which it was ousted from the L-M stable by a ponycar of a different color. However, an evolution would continue in Europe (as the Capri III) all the way through 1986, a remarkably long production run that testified to the durable popularity of Capri's basic design.

HF II notwithstanding, Ford had given brief consideration to a smaller van in the early Seventies. Developed under the codename "Carousel," it reflected the view of company president Lee Iacocca and product-planning chief Hal Sperlich that a stylish van of more manageable proportions than the big third-generation Econoline could appeal to a wide range of buyers—everyone from traditional station-wagon customers to the growing number of young light-truck enthusiasts to RV users and custom-van fans.

The planned switch from unit to

body-on-frame construction for the 1975 Econoline, developed as the "Nantucket" project and virtually locked up by 1972, made a downsized derivative both appealing and feasible from the cost and manufacturing standpoints. Indeed, as designer Dick Nesbitt related in the April 1988 issue of *Collectible Automobile*, "...[T]he top-secret Carousel project called for the utilization of as many Nantucket structural and floorpan sheetmetal parts as possible, a factor that would help assure a final production okay from Henry Ford. However, the exterior sheetmetal panels, windshield, window areas, and interior trim were to be all-new and decidedly automotive in styling character. The primary dimensional difference between the Carousel and Nantucket could be seen in the 2.5-inch lower roofline used by the former. This reduction was critical to achieve the 'garagable van' orientation demanded by Product Planning."

Ford's Design Staff went to work, and Nesbitt came up with one of the themes that was selected to be mocked up as a full-size clay for management review. It was a trim, clean-looking package with a short, sloped hood (Iacocca had insisted on a front "crush zone" for safety) and a roofline strongly reminiscent of the handsome 1955-57 Chevrolet Nomad/Pontiac Safari, with the same wide, slant-back B-pillars and thin C- and D-posts. Along the same lines, Nesbitt was "able to get...rear wraparound side windows accepted by Body Engineering, along with a retractable, self-cleaning electric tailgate window." Product Planning ordered up Squire-like fake-wood side panelling as an option for a top-line model. Meanwhile, says Nesbitt, "the truck interior studio developed an innovative series of seating proposals. One, for example, arranged the rear-seat area into a 'U' shape... with the bottom of the U wrapping around the back area of the two front captain's chairs, creating a lounge effect."

With a hearty endorsement from Iacocca, a Carousel engineering mule was built and the final design, largely that of Nesbitt, was passed on for management approval at an early-1973 meeting in Boca Raton, Florida. HF II was enthusiastic, and the Carousel was approved for production, "with Job #1 scheduled to coincide with the launch of the all-new 1975 Econoline," according to Nesbitt. But then came the Energy Crisis that sent corporate profits plunging. Management, suddenly afflicted with a bad case of cold feet, decided to postpone some new forward programs while abandoning others entirely. The Carousel, unfortunately, was in the latter category, and that was too bad. In a few years, a summarily dismissed Lee Iacocca would take the garagable van concept from Dearborn to Chrysler Corporation, where it would be transformed into that firm's biggest success of the Eighties, the front-drive Dodge Caravan/Plymouth Voyager.

Ford may have been shortsighted in

Ford aimed the '76 Stallion package directly at the "youth market," which was very much on the minds of Big Three marketing types at the time. In addition to the features mentioned on page 366, blackout grilles, window surrounds, and windshield wipers were included, as were accent pinstripes, and the Mustang II also sported black bumpers. The cost of the package was $329 on the Maverick (top), $283 on the Pinto (center), and only $72 on the Mustang II (bottom). Other trim options, such as exterior decor and luxury interior packages, chased different market segments, and were often successful in attracting customers.

giving up on that "better idea," but its 1976 truck line provided ample evidence that Iacocca was again thinking young. Leading a plethora of new sporty models was the Econoline Cruising Van, a short-wheelbase E-150 panel wearing bright multi-tone paint, roof luggage rack, mag-type wheel covers, white-letter blackwall tires, and a small dark-tinted porthole high up on each rear quarter panel. Bright exterior trim was borrowed from the plush Chateau Club Wagons, while the interior was decked out with full car-peting and front captain's chairs in color-keyed velour. Dual center-opening right-

side cargo doors were standard. Priced at $2095 over the base E-150, the Cruising Van was essentially a ready-made "sin bin" inspired by the uniquely customized jobs popular with "vannies," but aimed at those who didn't want to bother building their own. It proved highly popular, enough to inspire a pint-sized rendition on the Pinto wagon for 1977.

Also appealing to the youth market this year were two new F-Series offer-ings. One was a revived F-100 Flareside, a model that had been dropped after 1972. A "shorty" pickup of the type then popu-lar among the California surf set, it again

After peddling 219,976 Torino Elites for 1974½ and '75, the Elite (above) became its own one-model series for '76. Listing at $4879, it attracted 146,475 buyers, its best year yet. And it would remain that—Ford had plans to reposition the T-Bird in a lower price slot for '77, which would make the Elite redundant after 1976. Meanwhile, the "precision-size" Granada (below), entered its sophomore year basically unchanged, although trim and options were shuffled around. Ford boasted about Granada's Mercedes-like styling, saying that "its looks and lines remind you of the Mercedes 280 and Cadillac Seville."

carried the narrow 6½-foot cargo box, with initial units sporting 40-degree flared siderails that harked back to 1953! Conventional flat rails were then substi-tuted from spring '76. At that point, Ford introduced a Pinstripe Accent Package as a new option for any Flareside—black, white, or gold tape in multiple rectangles for hood, front fenders, and doors, and as outlining around wheel openings, rear fenders, and box sides. The little Bronco got a sporty appearance package of its own: a Special Decor Group comprising black grille, extra exterior chrome, and jazzy tape striping wrapped over the cowl and around to the upper bodysides.

Of course, there were more sober changes among Ford's light duty '76ers. Front-disc brakes were standardized for all F-Series 4×4s, which now included short- and long-wheelbase F-150 models.

Bronco also got standard front discs as well as larger, self-adjusting rear drum brakes and tighter body sealing. Econolines could be newly ordered with a Convenience Group comprising intermittent or "interval" windshield wipers and other amenities, similar to the F-Series package. The light-duty F-Series grille and exterior trim were revised for the first time since 1972. Also new for pickups was an optional Visibility Group (extra courtesy lights inside) and an expanded Protection Package (door edge guards and front-bumper guards and rubstrips). Colors and GVWs got their perennial revisions throughout the line, a short-chassis E-150 Club Wagon bowed as a passenger counterpart to the Cruising Van, and a 360 V-8 was now standard on the 4WD F-100 (optional on 4×4 F-150s, which carried a 300-cubic-inch I-6).

Not to be overlooked was the little Japanese-made Courier pickup, which received its first substantial changes since being launched four years before. The main ones were a three-inch-longer cab, new grille and exterior trim, extra seat travel (to accommodate longer-legged Occidentals), and a fuel tank enlarged to 12.5 gallons. There were new options, too: five-speed overdrive manual gearbox as an alternative to the standard four-speed, AM/FM radio, Convenience/Decor and Cold Weather Packages, and a "soft-ride" suspension. The last answered com-

plaints of stiff going in earlier models with reduced spring/shock calibrations, but it also reduced Courier's GVW from 4005 to 3490 pounds. For all the improvements, though, sales eased as a weakening dollar and a strengthening yen began lifting prices out of the bargain-basement class.

Changes among Ford's '76 medium and heavy trucks were minor except for two. One was the advent of three new "economy" diesels—one each from Caterpillar, Cummins, and Detroit Diesel—for most 9000-Series models. The other was the introduction of the LTL-9000, a long-nose Louisville conventional with tandem axles and diesel power—Ford's ulti-

Although the Ford Elite (above) shared its rear sheetmetal with the Torino, it was differentiated by what looked like full-width three-section taillights. The center section actually hid the fuel-filler cap. Note the ornate brightwork. The "Twindows" opera windows were an Elite feature during the car's short life span. The press release for the '76 Torino noted that "Ford's Gran Torino two-door hardtop [below] remains basically unchanged for 1976 except for improvements to fuel economy and new optional equipment, which includes bucket seats with console, automatic parking brake release, an electric decklid release, and a space saver spare tire." This model retailed at $4461 for 1976 and enjoyed a production run of 23,939 units.

The $7790 '76 Thunderbird (top row) featured three new colorful luxury groups: Creme and Gold, Bordeaux, and Lipstick. Other new options were a power lumbar seat and AM/FM quadrasonic eight-track tape player. The vinyl roof was standard. The $4752 LTD four-door sedan (center left) was the best seller among the big Fords: 108,168 units. Likewise, the four-door (center right) dominated Maverick sales: 79,076. The '76 Ford pickup could be ordered as a Custom F-150 Flareside with the "shortie" 6½-foot box (above), with or without pinstripes. It could also be ordered as an F-100 in top-line Ranger XLT trim (above right).

mate long-haul tractor. Buyers had a choice of no fewer than seven different proprietary powerplants and five wheelbases (174, 186, 204, 222, and 246 inches). Standard equipment was extensive, running to air conditioning, "Air-Ride" driver's seat, dual 100-gallon fuel tanks, dual-cam air brakes with Kelsey-Hayes anti-skid control, and many items of the existing Owner-Operator Packages. Like similar

"linehaulers" from other makers, the LTL-9000 could be equipped with an extended "sleeper cab" featuring built-in berths for driver and co-pilot behind the "front office."

Running a major corporation is very hard work, but Henry Ford II was beginning to show more than the usual signs of executive stress. In March 1975 he'd been arrested near Santa Barbara, California, for driving under the influence. That would have been sensational enough for a captain of the motor industry. But HF II also had a passenger aboard: model Kathleen DuRoss (whom he would marry in late 1980). Again, tattle-tale tabloids had a field day at the expense of Ford's chairman, but Detroit newspapers now asked questions, too, not only about his driving habits, but also about his relationship with Ms. DuRoss. Never one to suffer unfavorable publicity if he could help it, HF II quickly settled the drunk-driving charge while waving aside reporters with what he said was a long-time personal

motto: "Never complain, never explain." Writer Victor Lasky took that gruff dismissal as the title for a 1981 biography of Ford, which he wrote without much help from its subject.

HF II again made headlines in 1976 when he was hospitalized following an attack of angina (severe heart pains). Maybe the furor over the Santa Barbara incident had gotten to him. Perhaps the early-warning sign of heart trouble merely reflected the mounting aggravations felt by most every Detroit executive in these years. Whatever the reason, Henry took the hint and began changing his ways, giving up smoking (something his late grandfather probably never knew about) and beginning a modest, but steady, exercise program, partly to keep his weight in line.

Did that mean Ford cars and trucks were about to slim down too? As it turned out, yes, though it was only coincidental and wouldn't begin in earnest for several more years.

1 9 7 7

A new slogan waved on Dearborn's flagpole this year: "When America needs a better idea, Ford puts it on wheels." Many thought that more apt for General Motors, which shunned conventional wisdom and stunned the industry with an attention-grabbing "better idea" of its own: smaller big cars. From Chevrolet Caprice to Cadillac De Ville, the General's full-size fleet shed excess inches and hundreds of pounds to become trimmer, lighter, and more sparing of fuel while losing little if anything in the way of interior space.

Coming so soon after the Energy Crisis, these "downsized" cars, as the press was quick to label them, seemed a shrewd move, especially since they sold even better than the outsized models they replaced. But the fact was that GM had planned this well before the OPEC embargo, feeling its largest cars had become *too* large. If the introductions seemed clairvoyant, it was only by dint of fortuitous timing, much like Mustang II's announcement on the eve of the oil embargo itself.

Ford Division did a little downsizing of its own for 1977, albeit by means of altered sheetmetal and different nameplates rather than all-new designs. Attempting to shore up its relatively weak position in the increasingly important mid-size field, Ford evolved the Torino into the LTD II, styled somewhat like the previous Elite but with crisper front and rear sheetmetal. The Elite itself was cancelled, replaced as Ford's "premium" intermediate by a much cheaper Thunderbird on the same platform. (Likewise, Mercury junked its mid-size Montegos for a full range of Cougars, with a T-Bird-like XR-7 coupe topping the line.) For all the name switching and appearance alterations, these "new" cars were essentially the old ones underneath, retaining body-on-frame construction, the same suspension, and most running gear. Someone in Dearborn had evidently been thinking of the Edsel, for this was nothing more than an attempt to improve sales via more popular names. Fortunately for all involved, it worked.

Described as "a sporty new trim-size line in the LTD tradition," the LTD II carried an Elite-type nose comprising a pointed, fine-checked rectangular grille and—something new—rectangular headlamps, stacked in pairs. Turn signals in square-edged front fenders furthered the visual link with the big LTD—and

Lincoln. Rear fenders were also sharpened to carry slim vertical taillights, another styling fillip from Dearborn's luxury liners. Overall, LTD II was straighter and starchier than Torino, but the close similarities in bodyside contours and greenhouse treatment were there for all to see. Thunderbird got its own eggcrate frontispiece flanked by flip-up doors concealing the headlamps, plus a "basket handle" roof with wrapover chrome bands defining body-color B-posts. The latter contained tiny "coach" windows, trailed by large rear quarter panes and slim C-pillars as on two-door LTD IIs.

Continuing Torino's nine-model line of wagons and pillared hardtops and sedans, the LTD II offered base "S," standard, and Brougham series covering a $4528-$5435 price spread. There was only one T-Bird initially, but the Town Landau name was resurrected in January for a second version with an even longer

Mustang was due to trot into 1977 wearing the same sheetmetal it was born with in 1974, which brought up the question of what should be done to differentiate the '77 from earlier models. One suggestion was a revised Stallion package. This proposal, dubbed Stallion II (as noted just above the rocker panels), placed the stallion head on the hood and had a more subdued paint scheme than the '76 edition. For whatever reason, it never made it to production.

list of comfort and convenience features. Respective base list prices there were $5063 and $7990. The 302 V-8 was standard for federal versions of both LTD II and T-Bird; Californians got the optional 49-state 351 at no charge. SelectShift Cruise-O-Matic was now the one and only transmission, and the largest available engine was the corporate 400 V-8 in two- or four-barrel form.

Ad types worked overtime to convince buyers that smaller really was better. "A new look...a new size...a new price...but unmistakably Thunderbird," they boasted of Ford's eighth-generation personal car, a fair description. Its family-oriented sisters were claimed to offer the big "LTD's kind of quality and luxury in a sportier, trimmer car that's priced and handles like a mid-size car"—which makes one wonder what Torinos had been all about in the first place.

"What happened," explained long-time T-Bird designer Bill Boyer, "was a basic marketing decision, but also a move made necessary by CAFE." Boyer refers to the forthcoming Corporate Average Fuel Economy mandates of the Energy Policy and Conservation Act that Congress passed in 1975. "We had to score a certain fuel mileage average [beginning with model year 1978], and that couldn't be done—or would have been much more difficult to do—by continuing to share the Continental [Mark] body, even though the Mark received a major down-

sizing itself [for 1977]. None of us, though, had any idea of what would happen when we started selling the down-sized Bird....I don't think anyone truly realized the magnitude of the Thunderbird name. Between the smaller size, lower price and that...name, sales just skyrocketed."

Which was just as well, because the LTD II failed to match Torino's '76 sales performance, slipping from sixth to seventh among intermediates. The new T-Bird, however, moved right into fifth spot, outselling the entire LTD II line by some 80,000 units—more than 318,000 in all. The magic name Boyer refers to was obviously a big help, but so were dramatically lower prices: down some $2700 for the base Bird compared with its '76 counterpart. So Henry Ford II had been only half-right: Buyers *would* choose small over big—*if* they felt they were getting a better deal.

Of course, some buyers *didn't* think smaller big cars such a good idea, so Ford's adwriters were just as quick to play up this year's mostly unchanged LTD as "the full-size car that kept its size." The message, of course, was that rival GM products hadn't and thus lagged in comfort, quietness, and ride smoothness. Ford, on the other hand, could claim "road-hugging weight" and the greater safety that implied. Auto writers rightfully took Ford to task for promoting poundage in an age of soaring fuel prices

Early '77 Mustang IIs wore the same Cobra II package as in '76, although colors other than white with blue stripes were available. For $535, the buyer got a racy package, complete with a venomous-looking snake, lower panel racing stripes, twin wide stripes over the hood/roof/deck, black grille with Cobra emblem, styled steel wheels, louvered rear quarter windows, and more.

and a growing national reliance on imported crude, and the notion still draws the occasional barb today. What's often overlooked is the fact that many buyers bought Ford's advertising argument—and big LTDs. Indeed, sales moved up by about 24,000 units for '77. Then again, all big cars scored increases this year as memories of the Energy Crisis dimmed, and Chevrolet, Buick, and Oldsmobile scored healthy gains with their trimmer '77s to remain ahead of the big Ford.

A good many folks had judged the Granada a pretty good deal and had put their money where their minds were. Ford's luxury compact was also largely unchanged for this, its third season, though there were several new options. The most notable ones were a new four-speed overdrive manual transmission (basically the old three-speed with a high-geared fourth ratio tacked on), four-way manual driver's seat (up/down as well as the usual fore/aft), leather upholstery for Ghia four-doors, and big-car features like illuminated entry system, heating/air conditioning with automatic temperature

Granada bowed for '77 with its usual four-model lineup. The top-line two-door was the Ghia (top), which this year stickered at $4452. Output of this model came to 34,166 units, down from 46,786 in '76, but this was in line with overall Granada production which dipped from 448,784 units in '76 to 390,579. Top dog of the shrinking full-size Ford line (down from 13 to 11 models) was the LTD Landau. The four-door pillared hardtop (center) listed at $5742, and was selected by 65,030 buyers. Maverick output slipped for '77, from 139,687 to 98,506 units, hardly surprising as it was now in its last year. The $3322 two-door sedan (bottom) found 40,086 customers.

control (a fancy term for thermostat), and front cornering lamps.

Meanwhile, the old-soldier Maverick returned one last time with fewer options and no styling or mechanical changes, and output down to just under 100,000 units. Pinto returned, meanwhile, with another front-end redo plus larger taillamps on both sedan and Runabout. The new sloped-back "soft" nose had taller headlamp buckets and a narrower chrome grille flanked by twin vertical parking lamps. A new Runabout option was a frameless all-glass hatch providing a different look outside and a better view from inside. Other first-time extras: bronze-tint flip-up sunroof, four-way manual driver's seat, and a Sports Rallye Package comprising tachometer, extra engine gauges, sport steering wheel, and front anti-sway bar.

Also new was the Cruising Wagon, a youth-oriented version of the regular Pinto wagon inspired by the new-for-'76 Econoline Cruising Van. Technically a package option, it was easily identified by a standard front spoiler, styled wheels, and blanked-off rear quarters containing glass portholes. Included as well were all the Sports Rallye features plus a fully carpeted rear deck and interior sidewalls, the latter an appeal to the van set. All Pintos now wore front bumpers made of aluminum instead of steel, which together with a lighter energy-absorbing system reduced total weight by about 80 pounds. For all this, Pinto waned in popularity, with sales falling nearly 90,000 units to 202,543 units.

Despite a 34,000-unit drop in production to 153,173, Mustang II handily outpaced Chevy's less sporting, less expensive Chevette by nearly 20,000 units. Much of this came on the strength of new options, among them a T-bar roof with lift-off glass panels for hatchbacks; a tilt-up/take-out glass sunroof for hardtops; two-tone paint; and a color-keyed Sports Appearance Group for the Ghia. The last was offered only with black or tan paint and included many color-keyed components, including console, three-spoke sports steering wheel, cast aluminum wheels with chamois-color spokes, and a decklid adorned with simulated holddown straps and bright non-functioning buckles. Wheel choices expanded to include "lacy spoke" aluminum rims in chrome or with white-painted spokes and red trim rings. Replacing the Stallion option was a Rallye Appearance Package comprising black paint with subtle gold accents. The pretentious Cobra II package was revised late in the season, picking up tri-color tape striping and black side window and backlight louvers.

Still available for V-6 and V-8 Mustang IIs was the useful Rallye Package, priced at $160-$400 depending on model. This grouped the optional competition suspension with Traction-Lok limited-slip differential, an "extra-cooling package," and dual exhausts with chrome tips. Buyers also got larger raised-white-letter

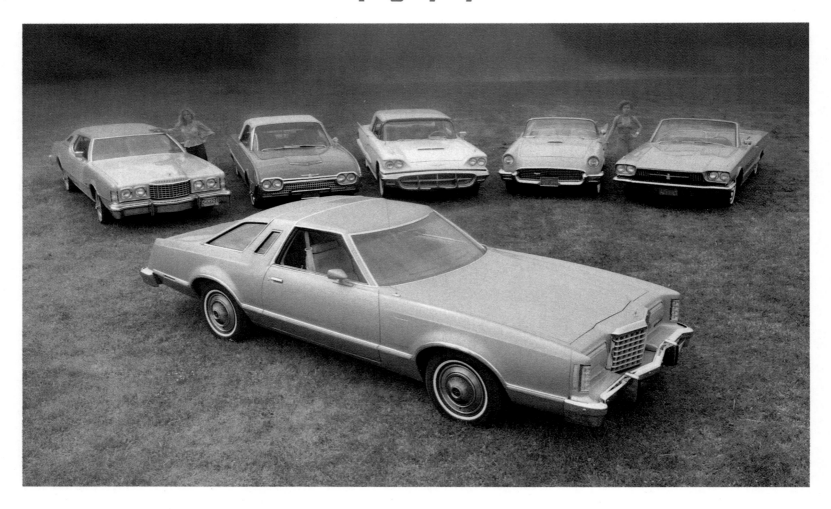

With Corporate Average Fuel Economy (CAFE) rules taking hold in 1978, Ford clearly had to downsize the heavy and thirsty Thunderbird. Further, though the Elite had sold well, it had not burst the Chevy Monte Carlo's bubble. Thus, for '77 the Elite was dropped—or, one could say, facelifted into the new Bird, seen posing here with earlier editions. Wheelbase was down by 5.4 inches, weight by 900 pounds, and price by $2700. Output skyrocketed to a record 318,140 units.

tires, color-keyed remote-adjustable door mirrors, leather-rim steering wheel and quartz digital clock.

Mustang II may have been a smaller, less potent ponycar, but it still hewed to Mustang tradition with numerous options, both packages and individual items, all reasonably priced. Among those not already mentioned: anti-theft alarm system (about $75), electric rear-window defroster ($60-$75), flip-out rear quarter windows for fastbacks ($30), fold-down rear seat for notchbacks (around $60; standard on fastbacks), center console ($65), several sound systems (including a new AM/FM radio with cassette player), and the usual power assists. The competition suspension by itself added only $25-$60.

Engine outputs fluctuated a good deal on most cars of the Seventies and Mustang II was not immune. This year's 2.3-liter four was rated at 92 bhp, the extra-cost 2.8-liter V-6 at only 93, and the 302 V-8 at 139, all SAE net.

Bill Boyer's reference to a "down-

sized" 1977 Lincoln Mark deserves a bit of explaining, for at first glance the new Mark V seemed little different from the superseded Mark IV. After all, wheelbase was unchanged, styling was similar, and the big 460 was still available—and more powerful. But a closer look revealed a crisper, lighter appearance. And appearances weren't deceiving—curb weight was down some 500 pounds. The Mark V also boasted 21 percent more trunk space—which seems like a large gain only because the IV had so little. Engineers paid attention to economy by specifying the corporate 400 V-8 as standard. The old-standby 460 continued as a 49-state option, but it couldn't meet California emissions standards. Despite a base price hiked $330—to a towering $11,396—the Mark V recorded a smart sales gain, up from a little more than 56,000 for the final Mark IV to just over 80,000. Alas, that would prove to be its peak, which must have worried the Ford official who predicted that the model would "run five years unchanged."

If imitation is the sincerest form of flattery, Lincoln paid Cadillac a big compliment with this year's new Versailles, the first addition to the Lincoln line in years and only the make's second attempt at a more compact luxury car (after the 1961-63 Continental). Still, this hastily contrived reply to Cadillac's remarkably successful 1975-76 Seville was little more than a gussied-up Granada. It naturally carried a Continental-style square grille, standup hood ornament, and humped

trunklid, plus gobs of standard equipment. The last was necessary because, again aping Cadillac, Lincoln priced Versailles at the top of the line: $11,500 base list, costlier than even the new Mark V.

But while Cadillac somehow managed to get away with marketing Seville on this "less for more" basis, traditional Lincoln buyers looked askance at Versailles—perhaps because it inevitably sat cheek-to-jowl in L-M showrooms with the Granada-twin Mercury Monarch. Delivering at near $13,000, the Versailles at least competed on price with Seville, which had also been evolved from a rather ordinary car, the compact Chevrolet Nova. But somehow, Bill Mitchell's styling came off better on an uprated Chevy than Gene Bordinat's did on an uprated Ford, perhaps because the former was more cleverly—and more extensively—disguised. The Seville was a melting pot of new ideas, whereas the Versailles was a catch-all for every Continental styling cliché of the past 20 years, yet was still quite obviously a Granada in drag.

You can fool some of the people some of the time, but few were fooled by Versailles, which would go down as Lincoln's biggest marketing mistake during this era. Model-year '77 production ended at just 15,434 units, a third of Seville's total.

Though Ford's overseas products are generally outside the scope of this book, brief mention must be made of the Fiesta, a perky new subcompact arriving at both Ford and Lincoln-Mercury dealers in midsummer as an early-1978 entry. Like

Capri, Fiesta was a joint effort of Dearborn's German and British subsidiaries operating as Ford Europe, with a little styling input from Ghia in Italy. Work got underway in 1970, and the final design was basically locked-in by 1973 (as project "Bobcat," the name used Stateside for Mercury's version of the Pinto).

In many ways, the Fiesta was Ford's best "captive import" yet. A clean-lined two-door hatchback on a 90-inch wheelbase, it offered surprising interior room thanks to a space-saving front-wheel-drive layout with transversely mounted engine and "end-on" four-speed manual gearbox in the manner of the pioneering British Austin/Morris Mini. European Fiestas offered a variety of four-cylinder powerplants as small as 1.0-liter (about 60 cubic inches), but the German-built U.S. version used the British 1.6-liter (98-cid) overhead-valve "Kent" engine familiar from the imported Cortina and early Pintos. Emissions tuning limited horsepower to just 66 SAE net, but it was enough to move the 1800-pound Fiesta from 0 to 60 mph in a brisk 11.5 seconds, according to *Road & Track*. Base, sporty "S," and mini-luxury Ghia models were offered at prices from $3450—costlier than the lowliest Pinto but cheaper than Chevy's aging rival Chevette.

And somehow, the Fiesta contrived to be uncommonly good fun for an "econobox": crisp, nimble, and willing. This goes a long way to explaining why world sales started high—over 118,000 in Europe for the first six months alone—

and would remain so through the end of this first-generation design in 1989. *R&T* called Fiesta a "bright idea" that should enjoy "a long, happy, and successful life in the American market." Happy and successful the Fiesta would be, but not that long-lived here, being phased out after 1980 in favor of a slightly larger car designed in Dearborn along very similar lines. But more about that later.

Ford's Truck and Recreation Products Operations had at least three reasons to celebrate in 1977. The first came on July 27, which marked the 60th anniversary of Ford's formal entry into the truck business with the humble little one-ton Model TT of 1917. Things had certainly changed in six decades, as evidenced by a vast '77 lineup running the gamut from compact Courier pickups to mighty diesel-powered Louisville linehaulers. A more immediate cause for joy came at year's end when Ford tallied a new record for domestic calendar-year truck sales: 1,214,622 units. What's more, the F-Series pickup had become America's single best-selling vehicle. Who would have thought that a "mere" truck could outsell a passenger car? But then, the world had changed a lot, too.

Change was again the order of the model year among Ford's light-duty trucks. After years of faithful service, the venerable Fifties-era FE-Series V-8s were replaced in F-Series and Econolines by new truck versions of the corporate 351 and 400 passenger-car engines. Despite two-barrel carburetors and modest 8.0:1

compression, both offered more power and torque than even their four-barrel '76 counterparts, plus better fuel economy. Depending on application, the 351 delivered 161-165 net bhp, the 400 between 167 and 177. Respective torque outputs were 265-282 and 302-326 at 2000-2200 rpm. Though slight to be sure, the improved gas mileage was timely, as federal economy standards would soon apply to light trucks as well as to cars.

Several new package options were added with a beady eye on the fast-growing ranks of younger truck buyers. Prime among these was the Free Wheeling Package for F-Series Stylesides. This was an evolution of the previous year's Flareside Pinstripe Accent group (which continued), bolstered by multi-color "rainbow" bodyside stripes and black-finish bumpers, grille, and front "push bar." The last was also available separately, as were forged-aluminum wheels shod with raised-white-letter tires. Inside, Free Wheeling Fs wore Ranger-style upholstery and special trim on dash and door panels.

Ford played a name shuffling game for 1977 by moderately facelifting the Torino and renaming it LTD II. The ploy worked—output increased 20 percent to 232,324 units. The hardtop (top) sold for $4785 and garnered 57,449 orders. Ford said the Ranchero GT (center) was "fancy truckin'." New for '77 were an argent and black cross-hatch grille and vertically stacked quad headlights. The 302 V-8 was standard (351 in California). With 12,462 built, the $4984 GT was the best selling Ranchero. The $4618 500 found 9453 buyers; the $4971 woody-look Squire only 1126. The F-150 Ranger pickup (bottom) was really the $4561 Styleside with the Ranger package, which boasted more exterior brightwork and an upmarket interior.

Rainbow stripes were also featured on a second version of the Econoline Cruising Van for '77, and there was a separate Free Wheeling group newly available for shorty E-100/150s. The latter made for a kind of cut-rate Cruising Van, comprising RWL tires on forged-aluminum wheels; black grille, bumpers, rocker panels, and door mirrors; full-length headliner; woodgrain vinyl on interior sidewalls; and full carpeting—plus the distinctive rear porthole windows, of course.

A third Free Wheeling package was developed for this year's imported Courier pickup, which now featured revised lower-body sheetmetal, a handsome new "geometric" grille, and a longer 107-inch wheelbase. New options included the Pinto/Mustang II 2.3-liter engine, XLT-level trim *a la* F-Series, and a long-bed base-trim model with seven-foot cargo box as a running mate to the standard six-footer. The rapid sales growth of Toyota, Nissan, and Honda had caused faint anti-Japanese rumblings in more patriotically minded quarters, so Ford was pleased to state that U.S. companies now supplied some 80 Courier components, most notably the pickup box and newly available "Lima" four, as well as lesser items like radios, carpeting, upholstery, and tires.

Though there were no earthshaking changes in the rest of the light-duty line, F-Series pickups received more extensive anti-corrosion measures, while cruise control, electric rear-window defroster, monaural AM/FM radio, and spare-tire lock were welcome new options for both Regular and SuperCab models. A much-ballyhooed April announcement was a "low-profile" replacement for the F-250 4×4, with reduced overall height and step-up but greater ground clearance, plus a tighter turning circle. *Off-Road* magazine thought enough of this to name it "Four-Wheel-Drive Truck of the Year." Overlooked, but perhaps little mourned, was the fact that the 4×4 F-100 was now missing from the catalog.

The little Bronco was still around, but virtually unchanged for '77. The same could not be said for Ranchero, which switched to the new LTD II frontal styling by the simple means of adopting the same new cowl-forward sheetmetal. The passenger cars' mechanical revisions were also applied, but there was little change otherwise. However, the sporty Ranchero GT became a touch sportier by acquiring standard rear-pillar "strobe" stripes and full instrumentation including tachometer, the latter borrowed from the new T-Bird and optional on LTD IIs. A Flight bench seat and luxury steering wheel were also standard now—and not what enthusiasts expected in the only Ford still wearing the hallowed GT label. But then, this *was* a truck.

Model paring occurred in the medium and heavy ranks, which was perhaps overdue. The P-350/400 parcel vans and chassis, which had been virtually unchanged over 27 years, were retired in favor of stripped Econoline chassis designed for installation of proprietary van bodies: a 138-inch 250, and a 350 with either 138- or 158-inch wheelbase. F-500 models merged with F-600s. A similar move consolidated 700-series chassis with 800s in the F-Series, low-cabover C-Series and LN Louisville lines, where all the high-power "880" models were dropped as well. The resulting new 800 family was powered by the 389 Extra-Duty V-8 as standard and offered the 475 powerplant at extra cost. Elsewhere among mediums and heavies, it was the usual story of minor revisions to axles, transmissions, gear ratios, and weight ratings. For once, though, diesel-engine availability was unchanged from the year previous.

By now, Ford Motor Company was well along with plans for a big 75th Anniversary bash in 1978. Congress sent an early birthday present in August 1977 as it granted all Detroit producers a one-year reprieve from the more stringent '78 pollution standards, which gave the green light to new-model production just days before it was scheduled to begin. Significant for the near future was the September 8 election of Donald E. Petersen, vice-president in charge of Diversified Products, to the board of directors.

Ford had resisted the prospect of mandatory airbag passive restraints more than GM or Chrysler, but had come to fully embrace the concept by now. The firm had even agreed at the end of 1976 to build 140,000 airbag-equipped compacts for government testing during model years 1980-81. But the offer was rendered token in 1977 when the Carter Administration mandated passive restraints beginning with 1982 models. Even then, the airbag battle still ranged, and the edict wouldn't actually take effect until 1987.

There was another cloud on Ford's horizon this year: a July memo from Clarence Ditlow, executive director of the Ralph Nader-founded Center for Auto Safety (CAS), requesting that the National Highway Traffic Safety Administration (NHTSA) investigate whether Ford automatic transmissions could sometimes "jump" out of Park, occasionally with fatal results. Ditlow was responding to a report by one Constance Bartholomew of Falls Church, Virginia. In the fall of 1976 she was loading grocery bags into her idling '73 Lincoln when the car suddenly lurched backward, apparently of its own accord, knocking her down and running over one leg before plowing into some nearby cars. Bartholomew said the transmission was firmly in Park. After complaints to Ford and NHTSA went unanswered, she discovered CAS. Ditlow took it from there. In November, NHTSA director Joan Claybrook, who was just as consumer-minded, issued an advisory statement about the problem and asked for incident reports from owners of Ford Motor

The '77 four-wheel-drive Bronco (top) rode a 92-inch wheelbase, weighed in at 3490 pounds, and had a base sticker price of $5260. Standard features included front disc brakes, solid state ignition, and Mono-Beam front suspension. GVW ratings ranged from 4400-4900 pounds. The Bronco seen here has the optional Special Decor Group that added a black-out grille, tape stripes, big hubcaps, and bright trim around the windows. Just as Pinto had its Cruising Wagon, the Econoline boasted a Cruising Van. Based on the E-150 van with Chateau-level trim, it too sported a porthole toward the rear. The C-8000 tilt cab tractor (bottom) listed an optional 18,500 pound single-speed rear axle. Another extra was an automatic transmission.

The COE linehauler CLT-9000 tractor (right) was diesel powered. This model measured 110 inches from bumper to end of cab (BBC) and was equipped with a double-bed sleeper cab. Announced late in the summer of 1977 for October sales, this all-new and more aerodynamic 9000 series heavy should be considered a 1978 model. The LTL-9000 linehauler (below) came in wheelbases of 174, 186, 204, 222, and 246 inches. The diesel engines were supplied by Cummins, Caterpillar, and Detroit Diesel in a variety of guises.

Company cars with automatic transmissions.

Tellingly, Ford had been aware of this problem as early as 1970, tracing it through customer comments back to 1968 models. However, most company engineers concluded that the fault was improper transmission engagement by owners and not a flaw in the transmission itself. But NHTSA's advisory elicited a torrent of jumping incidents, Claybrook soon amassing 777 reports involving 259 injuries and 23 deaths. The story became page-one news in June 1978 when NHTSA made a "preliminary defect" ruling in the case, the last step before a mandatory recall in a government safety investigation. Besides more damaging publicity and the likelihood of a massive recall, Ford now faced the equally strong prospect of legal action from both government and thousands of owners.

After dragging on for a few years, this sad situation finally came to a head on the last day of 1980, a year when all Detroit was on the skids and Ford was closer to the financial brink than most people realized. By this time, the scope of the alleged jumping problem had widened to encompass no fewer than 26-million domestic Ford-built cars and trucks. With that, according to then Transportation Secretary Neil Goldschmidt, it would take months just to mail out recall notices, while even a minor modification to the involved transmissions would tie up every service bay at all 6700 Ford and Lincoln-Mercury dealers for more than a year—and that assumed that the problem was solvable with a simple fix.

Given Detroit's mounting troubles of the time and the fact that Ronald Reagan had just been elected President partly on a pro-business stance, the outcome was perhaps predictable. In essence, Ford "copped a plea," agreeing to mail dashboard warning stickers to some 23 million owners. There would be no government-ordered recall.

Though the matter might have ended with that announcement of December 31, 1980, it didn't. The settlement incensed consumers and their advocates like Ditlow and Claybrook (the latter went to work for CAS after leaving the Carter Administration NHTSA), and they kept the issue alive. Ford would be haunted by it into the 1990s.

Ironically, a later CAS spot check showed that only seven percent of the af-

fected owners bothered to affix the dashboard stickers, while the *Wall Street Journal* reported in April 1988 that Ford never sent out more than two million stickers. Information about legal action is spotty, but that same *Journal* report stated that some 1000 suits had been brought against Ford by 1980; of the 27 cases in which juries returned a verdict, Ford won 22. In a study of 200 jumping transmission suits, CAS determined that Ford had paid an average $175,000 in settlements or jury awards, about $35 million for those cases. But the total cost to Ford has surely been much higher. The exact figure is still known only to Ford, and Ford's not saying. The cost in human suffering is probably incalculable.

Time does not necessarily heal all wounds, but time is increasingly on

Ford's side in one important respect. By one estimate, nearly all the vehicles with alleged jumping transmissions will have been junked by 1993 or '94. Still, the memories will linger on. How ironic that the one Detroit producer to actively promote automotive safety in the Fifties would be behind the two most celebrated and tragic safety cases of the Seventies: jumping transmissions and "exploding" Pintos (which prompted a separate spate of lawsuits in which Ford was also mostly vindicated). Both did much to establish "product liability" as a bona fide principle in U.S. law—the idea that companies have a public obligation to ensure the safety of the goods and services they sell. It's too bad that such a positive end had to come by such negative means, but that's the way life works sometimes.

1 9 7 8

ast, present, and future seemed to coalesce for Ford Motor Company in this, its 75th-anniversary year. A limited-edition Diamond Jubilee Ford Thunderbird and Lincoln Mark V arrived to honor the past. Also looking back was a revamped Transportation Section at the Henry Ford Museum, the first stage in a thorough renovation for the entire 254-acre Edison Institute, including Greenfield Village.

For the present, all Detroit was obligated to meet the government's new Corporate Average Fuel Economy re-

quirements taking effect this model year. The result of post-Energy Crisis legislation (the Energy Policy and Conservation Act of 1975), it mandated specific miles-per-gallon targets for all cars and light trucks sold in the U.S. EPA-rated fuel economy had to average so many miles per gallon for a given year—initially 18 mpg for cars, rising progressively to 27.5 mpg by 1985. Light trucks were subject to somewhat lower targets in a separate program that would begin with model-year '79. Companies whose "fleet average" fell below the specified figure would be fined a set number of dollars for each 0.1-mpg deviation—multiplied by total sales for that model year. Obviously, failure to comply could be very costly indeed. However, the law also provided that manufacturers who exceeded a given year's target would earn credits that could be either carried forward or carried back to avoid or reduce penalties for non-

compliance in another year.

It was all highly political, of course, not to mention controversial and more than a little complicated. And CAFE would be rendered even more political in the early-Eighties by an unexpected fuel glut and a new President intent on reducing government regulations as an aid to business. Nevertheless, CAFE achieved its intended effect of spurring Detroit to develop smaller, lighter, thriftier cars

The first sign that Ford was serious about downsizing its automotive fleet was the 1978 Fairmont, which was the first car built off the all-new "Fox" platform. A goodly number of other Ford products would spring from the Fox over the next few years. The Fairmont was Ford's compact, riding a trim 105.5-inch wheelbase and weighing as little as 2590 pounds, about 300 less than the now-departed Maverick. Four models were initially offered: two-and four-door sedans, four-door wagon, Squire wagon. A Futura coupe came along at mid-year.

At $4428, the Squire wagon was the most expensive model among the new Fairmonts, and also the heaviest at 2748 pounds. Though it looked quite blocky because it was designed to have about as much interior room as most mid-size cars, the Fairmont was the first Ford product to receive serious aerodynamic study. It also used lightweight materials where possible.

(and trucks) in most every size/price category:

Dearborn's first direct response to CAFE appeared this year in the form of a new compact nostalgically advertised as "The Ford in your future." The words were prophetic. In its engineering and much of its hardware, the Fairmont would be the literal foundation for a new Dearborn design dynasty.

Fairmont and Mercury's near-identical Zephyr originated in the "Fox" program, initiated in the early-Seventies to develop an eventual replacement for the Ford Maverick/Mercury Comet. Significantly, it was started at about the time of the first Energy Crisis, so efficiency became the overriding concern. "The initial objective," said one company press release, "was an overall body design that would enhance performance and fuel economy through minimized weight [plus] aerodynamic refinements. Once these goals were achieved, the challenge was to design an efficient interior package that would make optimum use of available space." Though certain existing components like engines, transmissions, and suspension pieces might be used, the plan was to combine "the economy and maneuverability of a compact with the interior roominess and comfort of a mid-sized car."

The Fox broke fresh engineering ground for Dearborn in several areas. For example, it was the firm's first car de-

signed with the aid of computers as well as three-dimensional scale models and full-size prototypes. Through the use of mathematical models like the so-called "finite analysis" technique, engineers could "pinpoint where the car's structure may require additional strength, or where it can be lightened without decreasing strength or durability." Now called computer-assisted design (CAD), it would prove a great time- and money-saver and, beginning with Fairmont, would figure in the development of all future Dearborn products.

Additionally, the Fox project—more than any previous Ford program—made greater use of lightweight materials like aluminum, high-strength steel, and reinforced plastics, again to save weight in the interest of better fuel economy. And despite its conservative, boxy appearance, the Fairmont was Dearborn's first car shaped with an eye to aerodynamics to reduce fuel-wasting air drag as much as possible. Both ⅜-scale models and late full-size prototypes spent more than 320 hours in wind-tunnel testing. Ford noted that "although almost imperceptible, [the resulting] minor [styling] refinements were responsible for an approximate 13-percent reduction in drag from the first clay models to the finished vehicle."

What finally emerged was thoroughly modern and a definite advance on Maverick. There were now three body styles: two- and four-door sedans and—something sorely needed—a practical five-door wagon. The last was offered in plain-side and fancy wood-look Squire versions. Sedans came in one basic but well-equipped trim level, and could be made more luxurious via an optional Ghia package. This comprised a little more chrome outside, a lot plusher trim inside, and the requisite Ghia logos

throughout. Enthusiasts gravitated toward the ES Option (a.k.a. ESO). The initials ostensibly stood for "European Sedan," but the package was pretty straightforward: black exterior accents, special color-keyed interior, and uprated suspension. Midyear brought a snazzy coupe with a roofline in the then-current T-Bird style. Called Futura, reviving a name from Falcon days, it was initially quite popular, reflecting renewed interest in sporty domestic compacts. It, too, could be equipped as a Ghia, but not as an ES.

Riding a 105.5-inch wheelbase, the Fairmont measured 4.5 inches shorter between wheel centers than the Maverick four-door, yet interiors were roomier in every dimension. Space-saving features helped, like thinner front seatbacks and doors. So did the pleasingly simple styling with a lower beltline, higher roof, and much greater glass area, all of which contributed to improved outward vision and a feeling of greater spaciousness. Sedan trunk room increased by a healthy three cubic feet. The logically organized dashboard boasted European-style steering-column stalk controls for headlamp dimmer and windshield wipers and washer. In overall appearance and packaging, the Fairmont was "close to European middleweights," as Ford put it, cars like the Audi 100-LS and Volvo 240. In fact, *Car and Driver* magazine *did* call the Fairmont "an American Volvo."

In chassis design, Fairmont was, again, conventional but contemporary. Up front was a modified MacPherson-strut suspension with coil springs mounted on lower A-arms instead of encircling the struts. This, said Ford, meant less noise and harshness, and also saved some weight. In addition, it afforded better handling and opened up some extra underhood space for easier servicing. A

front stabilizer or anti-roll bar was standard. Replacing Maverick's recirculating-ball steering was the more precise rack-and-pinion setup favored in Europe. Variable-ratio power assist was available at extra cost, a new item shared with several other Ford models this year. At the rear, antiquated leaf springs gave way to coils, and four links tied down the live axle more securely. The springs and the two lower links were mounted outboard and behind the axle, which Ford said minimized axle tramp and side-to-side shake and also improved ride control. Brakes were the now-expected front discs and rear drums. Chassis upgrades with the ES Option were the usual fare: firmer shocks all-round, stiffer rear springs, a thicker front stabilizer bar, a new rear bar, and wider wheels and tires.

With its light but strong construction, the Fairmont weighed up to 300 pounds less than a '77 Maverick. This allowed the use of smaller engines for better fuel economy with little, if any, performance penalty. Standard power was thus the 2.3-liter overhead-cam "Lima" four from Pinto/Mustang II, the first four ever seen in a postwar Ford compact. Optional were the familiar 3.3-liter (200-cid) six and small-block 302 V-8. The latter required optional three-speed automatic transmission, as did the six in California

and high-altitude areas. Otherwise, the buyer got a four-speed manual with floorshift.

The Fairmont (along with the Zephyr) was greeted with almost unqualified praise. In *Auto Test 1978*, CONSUMER GUIDE® declared it "head and shoulders above the General Motors and Chrysler compacts. It is efficient . . . [and] has more room for passengers than any of its com-

Now entering its fourth year, the Granada was treated to rectangular headlights and a revised grille. The taillights and rear panel were freshened up as well. The $4685 Ghia two-door (top) sported "Twindows." The new $4962 ESS (above) was an attempt at a "European Sports Sedan." Some of the features included a heavy-duty suspension, FR78-14 SRB radials, dual sport mirrors, leather-wrapped steering wheel, reclining bucket seats, and unique ESS blackout trim and badges.

petitors, just as smooth a ride, superior handling, and the look of a more modern car. The improvement over the Maverick...is substantial." CG's six-cylinder/automatic test car returned an average 21 mpg (versus EPA ratings of 19 city/26 highway). With an awkward, stalk-mounted horn button and unsupportive seats the only gripes, CG rated it the "Best Buy" in its class. So did a good many buyers. Fairmont captured the top spot in compact sales for model-year '78 with over 312,000 deliveries, easily surpassing all rivals. Zephyr tallied another 152,000. As a final "vote of confidence," the readers of Car and Driver, mainly enthusiasts not inclined to notice family models, voted Fairmont the most significant new car of the year in the magazine's annual poll. Ford Division's other '78s were overshadowed by the Fairmont and its great success, the reason being that not much had changed. The mid-size LTD II was left alone except for the cancellation of wagons (probably in deference to the new Fairmont line), and saw production of just over 170,000 units. And because a successor was on the way, the full-size LTD stood pat, but still managed to capture nearly 310,000 buyers.

The little Pinto also soldiered on with few differences, the most notable being a standard "bucket-look" rear seat cushion and newly optional variable-ratio power steering. Production eased back by 14,000 units to 189,000, with at least some sales being siphoned off by the Fairmont. After all, why buy a Pinto two-door sedan for $3336 when a roomier, more comfortable four-cylinder Fairmont cost only $250 more?

Granada received a modest update for 1978 via a new grille and single rectangular headlamps, the latter shared with Fairmont. It was also upgraded to the 250-cid six as standard, but in the quest for fuel economy the optional 351 V-8 disappeared. New to the options list were a CB radio and AM/FM/cassette stereo, along with an ESS (European Sports Sedan) package for base models. The last featured black exterior trim, hood and rear-deck paint stripes, color-keyed racing mirrors, a deluxe bucket-seat interior, and heavy-duty suspension. Meanwhile, the opera windows on two-doors strutted a vertical chrome rib,

transforming them into "Twindows." Granada output tumbled some 140,000 units to just under 250,000. No doubt the Fairmont was having a strong effect here.

The Mustang II, now in its fifth and final season, held steady, but did trot out some new options. Packing every racy styling touch a kid could want was something called the King Cobra package. Like the Cobra II, which continued, this was available only for the fastback, but was much gaudier. A stylized snake decal adorned the hood, while tape stripes appeared everywhere: roof, rear deck, rocker panels, A-pillars, around the wheel wells, and on the front air dam. "King Cobra" was written in large letters on each door, the air dam, and on the standard decklid spoiler. Black-out paint adorned the grille, window moldings, headlamp bezels, and wiper arms, while a brushed-aluminum instrument-panel applique completed the cosmetics. Unlike the Cobra II, the King Cobra also included some functional features, namely the 302 V-8, power steering, Rallye Package, and Goodrich 70-series T/A radial tires. Given all that bold advertising, this was the least Ford could do, and it's probably true that the King Cobra's 17-second quarter-mile time was high performance by 1978 standards.

Though up $500 for '78, the Thunderbird (above left) topped the 318,140-unit production record set in 1977. The new record: 352,751. The LTD II didn't do nearly as well, probably because the two-door coupe (above) sold for $5112 and $5448 (Brougham) compared to T-Bird's $5498 base price. The LTD total—all models—was 170,544. The '78 Pinto (below) carried on with 1977's nose job; prices ranged from $3139 to $4343.

Shared by all '78 Mustang IIs were a new electronic voltage regulator and variable-ratio gearing for the optional power steering (replacing fixed-ratio). Plush "Wilshire" cloth seating became available for the Ghia, while a new Fashion Accessory Package arrived for the standard notchback, bringing front-door map pockets, striped fabric upholstery, lighted vanity mirror, and four-way manual driver's seat, all clearly aimed at women buyers.

Mustang II sales were still holding up: 192,000 for the model year, second only to introductory 1974. They might have been higher, but some '78s were delivered to dealers earlier than usual due to low inventory and registered as '77s.

Yet despite its popularity when new, the Mustang II has few fans today. Its styling has not aged gracefully and, for

enthusiasts, its "less ponycar" character is a depressing reminder of the trials and tribulations that made the mid-Seventies such a dull period for most Detroit cars.

In retrospect, though, the Mustang II is significant for successfully bridging the gap between the last of the traditional Mustangs and the first of an exciting new generation of Ford ponycars. That's no small task for any car, and few have done it better. We can thus be grateful to the Mustang II for preserving the ponycar flame in Dearborn at a time when bean-counters might have easily snuffed it out.

Though mechanically untouched, this year's Thunderbird pushed opulence to new heights with a special Diamond Jubilee Edition, a one-year-only 75th Anniversary commemorative. Base-priced near $10,000—a whopping $4300 above the base coupe—it came with a whole slew of extras, including lush velour upholstery and extra interior woodgraining, plus a very personal touch: your very own monogram on each door and your name on a 22-carat-gold dash plaque. Lesser Birds could be ordered with the inaccurately named Sports Decor Group ($396-$446), with light-tan vinyl roof and spoked road wheels plus matching imitation "luggage straps" for the rear deck, a tacky throwback to the Thirties. No matter, Thunderbirds sold at a torrid pace, posting an all-time production record of 352,751 units for the '78 model year. That was enough to move it up two spots on the mid-size hit parade, to third, trailing only Oldsmobile's Cutlass and the Chevrolet Malibu, both newly downsized this year.

Ford's truck unit had just observed its 60th anniversary, but it celebrated the corporation's 75th with several major new products. Heading the list was a second-generation four-wheel-drive Bronco that aped the rival Chevy Blazer/GMC Jimmy and Dodge Ramcharger/Plymouth Trail Duster by being essentially a short-wheelbase full-size pickup. Interestingly enough, Ford had rejected this very approach for the original Bronco, believing a small off-roader *a la* Jeep CJ was a better sales bet. And it had worked just fine, of course. By the late-Seventies, though, Bronco's competition had shown that it was time for a change.

Changed the Bronco definitely was. Beefier and much bigger, its wheelbase ballooned a foot to 104 inches, overall length to 180.3 inches, width to a massive 79.3 inches, and height to 75.5 inches. Weight swelled accordingly—by close to 1000 pounds—necessitating larger, more powerful engines. All this, of course, seemed quite "fuelish" coming so soon after the Energy Crisis, but the explanation lay in production economics. Sharing the basic F-Series chassis and front sheetmetal made the new Bronco more cost-effective than the old and, said Ford marketers, more saleable.

Naturally, most of the differences between the Bronco and the F-Series

showed up in the body behind the doors. Instead of a square-lined cab with pickup bed aft, the Bronco employed foreshortened rear quarters, slanted B-posts, unique tailgate with power drop-down window, and a removable fiberglass half-top—the same basic elements as its Big Three competitors. Shared with this year's F-Series was a husky new face dominated by a big eggcrate grille mimicking the style of the heavyweight Louisville trucks. It featured flanking recesses holding a pair of newly legalized rectangular sealed-beam headlamps. In-

The little Fiesta (top) came to America in 1978. It was Ford of Europe's minicar, smaller than Pinto and up to date with front-wheel drive. It would last here only until the Escort bowed on the scene. Megastar II (above) was a 1978 concept car featuring aerodynamic lines and an interesting side-window design.

side resided the same handsome new dash found on F-Series, plus somewhat more front legroom than the pickups could provide, owing to the Bronco's longer cabin and commensurately rangier seat tracks. A rear bench seat was

again optional. So were F-Series cab trims: Custom, Ranger, and Ranger XLT.

The base powertrain comprised the truck edition of the corporate 351 V-8 driving the rear wheels through a four-speed manual gearbox with part-time two-speed transfer case. Free-running front hubs remained standard.

Options abounded in the best Ford tradition. Besides cab trims, Bronco buyers could bust their wallets with Cruise-O-Matic, a 400 V-8, full-time transfer case, auto-locking front hubs (which eliminated having to get out of the vehicle when moving into four-wheel drive), cruise control, big raised-white-letter off-road tires, chrome grille and exterior moldings, chrome- or white-painted

The Mustang II galloped into the sunset during 1978, but it would return for '79 as a fully revitalized ponycar. Still, swan song 1978 was a good year as output jumped 26 percent to 192,410 units. And although the Mustang II is generally the least loved among Mustangs, some 1,107,718 were built during its five-year run, a very fine record indeed. Changes for '78 were minor: new color selections, revised interior trim, variable-ratio power steering, and a plastic cooling fan for the V-6. The '78 notchback (above) listed at $3731, and 81,304 were called for. Sending the Mustang II out in a blaze of glory was the wildest version of all: King Cobra (right).

wheels, tinted windshield, dark-tint "privacy glass" for other windows, sliding rear side glass, a bigger fuel tank with skid plate (the normal tank held 25 gallons), tilt steering wheel, heavy-duty handling package, big "Western" door mirrors, padded "GT" rollover bar—the list went on and on. Ford's recent success with Free Wheeling packages naturally prompted one for the new Bronco. It featured black-finish grille, bumpers, and

low-mount door mirrors; tri-color tape stripes running forward from the rear fenders to up and over the roof and back down the other side; and styled road wheels with raised-white-letter tires.

Driving the big new Bronco was like moving from—well, a Jeep CJ to an F-Series pickup. From the much loftier driving position to the broad hood ahead to the massive new instrument panel and meaty controls, this was obviously a much big-

ger, more substantial rig with a vastly larger interior. Yet it required a surprisingly light touch, at least with power steering and brakes, and the short wheelbase made close-quarters maneuvering easier than it looked. There was no question about off-road capability—truck-tough construction and mechanicals took care of that.

Which in the end was probably the best argument for the reconstituted Bronco. After all, the truck-based formula had worked well for Blazer and Jimmy, Ramcharger and Trail Duster, especially on the sales chart. It did the same here. In fact, model-year sales soared by no less than 400 percent! With that, the Bronco now vied with Blazer as America's most popular big sport-utility, yet another perennial Ford/Chevy sales battle that rages to this day.

Bronco wasn't the only newcomer to Ford's 1978 light-duty line. A four-wheel-drive SuperCab pickup was inevitable, and it arrived in F-150 and F-250 form, both on a 155-inch wheelbase. A new Free Wheeling Package "B" was added for F-100/150s, basically the previous group (now called "A") with a "GT" rollover bar bolted to the bed just behind the cab, plus white-painted wheels and a spare-tire lock. All models shared Bronco's new Louisville-inspired front end, with round headlamps retained for Custom-trimmed models. The XLT Luxury Group was renamed Ranger Lariat and was plusher than ever. "Tu-tone" paint, special emblems, and black tailgate applique appeared outside. The interior sported a luxury-trim bench seat, button-tuft headliner, padded door-panel inserts, map pockets, and full carpeting including kick panels.

Light-duty F-Series options proliferated quite a bit for '78. For example, a new handling package for 4×4 150/250s offered a front stabilizer bar, quadruple gas-filled front shock absorbers, heavy-duty rear shocks, and stiffer springs—basically the same setup available for Bronco. Also new to the pickup options list were four-speed overdrive manual transmission, AM radio with built-in digital clock and frequency display, "rainbow" body striping for Stylesides, 40-channel CB radio, chrome grille and rear step bumper, and—shades of LTD—illuminated visor vanity mirror. The F-250 4×4 could be had as a Camper Special for the first time,

and with a new Snow Plow Preparation Package when equipped with optional 4500-pound front axle.

Ford's lightest-duty pickups, the imported Courier and car-based Ranchero, were largely carryovers this year. New colors and minor adjustments to standard and optional equipment were the only changes in both. Courier, however, was now on the same fall introduction schedule as Ford's domestic trucks. Before, its model year had begun early each calendar year.

The Econoline family expanded both literally and figuratively with the return of the SuperVan, the normal 138-inch-wheelbase model with 20 extra inches of rear sheetmetal tacked on, available on all three chassis (150/250/350). The same treatment for Club Wagon passenger models produced the SuperWagon with seating for up to 12. Other E-Series news included availability of the Cruising Van package on the long chassis; a new across-the-board handling option comprising front anti-roll bar and heavy-duty springs and front shocks; standard padded instrument panel; detail exterior trim revisions; and a more efficient torque converter for Cruise-O-Matic. A newly opened assembly plant in Oakville, Ontario, Canada, now boosted Econoline's annual production volume by up to 100,000 units. It had been a key factor in restoring Ford to first place in domestic truck sales for calendar 1977.

Ford's mediums and heavies were little changed for '78 aside from higher GVWs on some models, but there was a whole new group of long-distance line-haulers to replace the square-rigged W-Series. Designated CL, for "Cabover Louisville," it was Ford's most serious challenge yet to premium heavies from the likes of Mack, Freightliner, Ken-

worth, and Peterbilt. It came only as a diesel on a 9000-level chassis, but models spanned no fewer than five single-axle wheelbases and nine tandem lengths, the former tagged CL-9000, the latter CLT-9000. Engine offerings were just as extensive: Model KT and KTA Cummins with up to 600 gross horsepower, four 92-Series Detroit Diesel units from GM, and low-speed economy diesels by Cummins, DD, and Caterpillar. Transmission choices numbered nine: direct-gear and overdrive 9-, 10-, and 13-speed units, all by Fuller. All-up weight ratings ranged from 80,000/82,000 pounds single/tandem up to 138,000 pounds for "turnpike" tandems with certain drivetrains.

Designed for rugged durability, easier servicing, and long-haul comfort, the new CLs boasted the most deluxe big-rig cabs in Ford history. Composed of rust-resistant aluminum-alloy sheet over extruded aluminum structural members, they boasted a huge, slightly curved two-piece tinted windshield, ergonomically designed twin-pod instrument panel made of polypropylene plastic, and extruded door frames with adjustable hinges. Sleeper-cab models came with triple climate-control units, each independently adjustable. The frame was bolted together from separate members of high-strength steel and featured sealed, lube-free front spring pins. Options were extensive and occasionally exotic. Typifying the latter was a separate air suspension for the cab. Comprising shock absorbers, control arms, and self-leveling air springs, it served not only to isolate cab from chassis but to stabilize the cab in both the fore/aft and lateral planes, a boon to driver control on rough roads.

In all, the CL was a mighty—and mighty impressive—package. Unmistakable, too: high and wide, yet allegedly

After trotting along basically unchanged since 1966, the little Bronco was totally new for '78. Following Chevrolet's lead, the new Bronco (top row) was really a shortened pickup, which meant that everything was up: wheelbase by 12 inches, weight by 1000 pounds, and price by $1300. The '78 Ranchero GT (above) listed at $5400 and 12,469 were built. Meanwhile, the 2675-pound imported Courier (above right) started at $3895 and proved quite popular as 70,546 were sold.

quite aerodynamic, and easily spotted by its horizontally split version of the now-familiar six-sided Louisville grille. Owner-Operator CLs bore "9000" numerals between the grille segments plus flanking quad rectangular headlights stacked in pairs. Other models substituted "FORD" block letters and dual round headlamps. Yet for all its deluxe features and modern engineering, the CLs would never win the same degree of customer acceptance as premium rivals from companies who built nothing but big rigs. Operators said the Fords just didn't hold up as well.

If not the most successful of Ford Motor Company's 75 years in business, Diamond Jubilee 1978 was certainly a satisfying one. Ford Division's model-year car production improved by more than 83,000 units, rising from 1.84 million to just over 1.92 million in a year when Chevrolet declined by more than 167,000. Ford was still second, just a closer runner-up. Lincoln-Mercury output was in the

second of three record years in a row, and Mercury volume had never been higher. Icing the birthday cake, Ford retained first place in calendar-year truck sales, helped by increased supplies of the popular Econoline range. But less than a month after the gala 75th Anniversary observance of June 16, Dearborn again found itself in the wrong kind of headlines. The reason was Henry Ford II's abrupt dismissal of Lido Anthony Iacocca, the popular company president whose long career of product innovation and consequent sales success had already become Dearborn legend. Ostensibly he was taking early retirement on October 15, his 54th birthday. But many insiders had already surmised that he was going to be dumped sometime before Henry Ford II was scheduled to retire as chief executive in 1980 and as chairman in 1982.

As usual, the boss himself didn't say much. Publicly he cited Iacocca for "insubordination," but privately he was said to have shown Iacocca the door with a simple "I don't like you." No matter. In removing a strong president, HF II was following a 50-year Ford tradition. His grandfather had fired "Big Bill" Knudsen, and he himself had discharged Ernie Breech and Bill's son, Bunkie Knudsen.

Iacocca wasn't bitter, at least publicly. As he said later, "You just surmise that the Breeches of the world got too big, too soon, and he [Ford] doesn't want strong guys around. You know, he wants to diffuse and bureaucratize the company as he

gets to be 61. I guess that's the only thing I can come up with, because I really don't have a good sound answer myself."

Ironically, and as Iacocca carefully noted, June 1978 had been the biggest single sales month in Ford history, capping a first half that netted the company its largest six-month profit on record. "They probably won't be at this peak again," Iacocca said, "so I guess it's a good time to go."

Thus, after 32 years with Ford, Iacocca was a surprising free agent—though not for long, of course. He was too young, too vigorous to retire, and he yearned for a new challenge. He found it soon enough at Chrysler Corporation. There he signed on as president in November 1978, then as chairman the following year, vowing to pull the industry's perennial number-three out of the financial quagmire in which it had been bogged down too long.

Iacocca's appointment pleased a great many people, especially worried Chrysler stockholders. Observed *Automotive News*: "Any other auto company would be willing to give up three future draft choices to get its hands on that kind of talent." Iacocca, said the editorial, "is a manager, a really professional manager. And he was paid a lot for his services [at Ford]...compensation that reached a million dollars a year, figures that defy understanding by mere mortals. Yet by all standards, he earned every penny.... The job he has done seems to speak for itself."

1 9 7 9

Though few could have predicted it, 1979 would be the last year for "business as usual" in Detroit until the mid-Eighties. The reason was a sudden, unexpected new energy crisis that began this spring with the ouster of the Shah of Iran, triggering America's deepest economic recession in four decades. However, none of this would seriously affect 1979 model-year car sales. The industry as a whole built over a half-million more cars, a figure topped only by record '73, and demand remained healthy. But a big drop was just around the corner, signaled by the continuing steep decline in total truck volume since 1977.

More worrisome for Ford Motor Company was the continuing erosion in its market penetration. Indeed, Ford's slice of the pie hit a postwar low in '79: 20.29 percent. Other Detroit producers fell, too. Only the imports were gaining. Indeed, they grabbed almost five percentage points more than in 1978, finishing at 22.7 percent, with Japanese makes leading the way. The advent of "Energy Crisis II" would only make things worse.

As for the perennial Ford/Chevy production battle, both were down, Chevy by nearly 91,000 cars, Ford by almost 88,000; this despite bright, new, eminently saleable models from both makes. Chevy's big attraction was the Citation X-car, a front-drive compact arriving in spring as an early entry for 1980. Ford countered with a smaller full-size LTD and a new-generation Mustang.

Now minus the Roman numeral II, the new fifth-generation Mustang marked another revolution in the history of Ford's pioneering ponycar. Clean and taut, crisp yet substantial-looking, it combined the best thinking of American and European design: deft surface execution, a simple downswept nose, ample glass area, and a pleasing lack of ornamentation. Those who got close enough to see the familiar running-horse emblem (which now looked more like its original self) must have been impressed. At long last, Ford had created the kind of restrained, efficient, elegant sporty car it set out to build in the first place.

Of course, the '79 inherited some perennial Mustang problems. Handling remained far from perfect, the driving position too low, interior space limited. And workmanship wasn't as solid or thorough as on European and Japanese competitors like the Volkswagen Scirocco and Toyota Celica. But no car can be faultless, especially one selling at such comparatively modest prices. By almost any standard, the '79 Mustang was a most attractive buy.

Although downsizing was the order of the day, the '79 Mustang was bigger inside and out and rode a 4.2-inch-longer 100.4-inch wheelbase. Still, it was a couple hundred pounds lighter. The design team was headed by Jack Telnack (in the center), and the goal was to build a new, more aerodynamic Mustang off the same Fox platform that had spawned the '78 Fairmont/Zephyr.

Like Mustang II and the original Mustang, the '79's final shape was selected from proposals submitted by competing in-house teams: this time the Ford and Lincoln-Mercury production studios, Advanced Design, and Ford's Ghia operation in Italy, which was by this time under Don DeLaRossa. All were given the same design parameters (the so-called "hard points" that include length, width, wheelbase, cowl height, etc.) from which were developed the requisite sketches, clay models, and fiberglass mockups. Quarter-scale clay models were tested for 136 hours in wind tunnels because aerodynamics was becoming increasingly recognized—rediscovered actually, from the lessons of streamlining in the Thirties—as important to improved fuel economy, a new fact of life since 1973-74.

Detroit was still reeling from the first energy crisis when work began on a successor to the Mustang II in mid-1975. The design brief called for using the basic suspension and floorpan of the evolving "Fox" project, which had been initiated in early 1973 to develop "a new corporate worldwide sport/family four/five-passenger sedan." In America, Fox was originally slated to replace both Mustang II and the subcompact Pinto, but it ended up a compact, the Ford Fairmont/Mercury Zephyr twins that took over from the 1970-vintage Maverick/Comet for 1978.

Ford planners said the Fox platform could be shortened somewhat for the new Mustang, and it ultimately was: by 5.1 inches in wheelbase, to 100.4 inches. Mustang II power units—2.3-liter four, 2.8-liter V-6, and 302 V-8—would be retained. As with the original ponycar, curb weight was pegged at a comparatively low 2500 pounds. The interior would be larger than the Mustang II's, but still mainly designed to seat only two adults comfortably, four in a pinch.

Like the original Mustang—but unlike the II—the notchback model was styled first and the fastback developed from it. Of the finished, full-size fiberglass models shown to top management, the one chosen as the basis for production styling came from a team headed by Jack Telnack, then executive director of Ford North American Light Truck and Car Design. Telnack had just returned from Ford Europe, where he'd spearheaded prototype development for the pretty front-drive Fiesta minicar (which was sold Stateside from 1978-80). Four trim levels would initially be offered: standard, Sport Option, Ghia, and Cobra. The last arrived with black-finish greenhouse trim and lower bodysides, color-keyed body moldings, and an optional snake decal for the hood, plus sportier seats and cabin appointments.

Telnack described the fifth-generation design effort for the press in June 1978: "One of the basic themes for this car was 'form follows function'....We wanted to be as aerodynamically correct as possible before getting into the wind tunnel. In the past we have designed cars and then gone into the tunnel mainly for tuning the major surfaces that have been approved....With the Mustang, the designers were thinking about aerody-

namics in the initial sketch stages, which made the tuning job in the tunnel much easier. Consequently, we wound up with the most slippery car ever done in the Ford Motor Company: a drag coefficient of 0.44 for the three-door fastback, 0.46 for the two-door notchback. [Aerodynamics is] probably the most cost-effective way to improve corporate average fuel economy. We know that a 10-percent [reduction] in drag can result in a five-percent improvement in fuel economy at a steady-state 50 mph.... That's really worthwhile stuff for us to go after."

It should be noted that though the drag figures Telnack quoted were good for '78, they'd soon be mediocre. Ford's 1983 Thunderbird, for example, arrived at an altogether more impressive 0.35.

Although seen here as the hatchback (bottom), the '79 Mustang (no more II) was also offered as a coupe, and both were available in top-of-the-line Ghia trim. Prices started at $4494 for the base coupe, while the hatchback was pricier at $4828. An interesting model was the Turbo, which was mated to the 2.3-liter four. Ford was always coy about releasing a horsepower rating, but it was generally placed at 130-140. The Turbo could wear Cobra trappings (left) for an extra $1173, and the Cobra hood decal added another $78.

While that difference may not seem dramatic, it represents a reduction of over 20 percent, and shows just how radically standards can change in a few years.

Key members of Telnack's team included Light-Car Design Manager Fritz Mayhew, pre-production design executive David Rees, and pre-production designer Gary Haas. The shape they evolved was a sort of notchback wedge: very slim up front, with the hood sloped down from a rather high cowl—actually an inch higher than Fairmont/Zephyr's. Telnack said this was to "get a faster sloping hood . . . to pivot the hood over the air cleaner." This dictated special inner front fender aprons and radiator supports instead of Fairmont/Zephyr pieces, but everyone agreed the extra expense was warranted. Increased fuel economy was one reward. Another was racier appearance, as expected in a Mustang. Aerodynamic considerations also prompted a slight lip on the decklid and a small spoiler integrated with the front bumper. A distinctive touch was black-finish vertical slats behind the rear side windows, rather like those of the Mercedes 450SLC. They hindered over-the-shoulder vision, however, one of the new design's less functional aspects.

Body engineering aimed at holding the line on weight in the interest of both fuel economy and performance, which implied maximum use of lightweight materials. Sure enough, plastics, aluminum, and high-strength/low-alloy (HSLA) steel all figured prominently. A significant new plastics technology appeared in color-keyed bumper covers of soft urethane made by the reaction-injection molding (RIM) process. HSLA steel was used for rear suspension arms and the number-three frame crossmember, while aluminum was found in drivetrains and in the bumpers of some models. Thinner but stronger glass saved additional pounds, as did slimmer-section doors. As a result, the lightest 1979 Mustang came in at 2471 pounds; overall, the '79s averaged some 200 pounds lighter than the Mustang II despite being slightly larger in every dimension. In an age of downsizing, this was a notable achievement.

Interior design received equally careful attention. Total volume rose by 14 cubic feet on the notchback and by 16 cubic feet on the hatchback. The thinner doors opened up 3.6 inches of additional shoulder room and an extra two of hiproom in front. Back seat gains measured five and six inches, respectively, and rear legroom stretched an added five inches. Cargo volume expanded by two cubic feet on the notchback and four on the hatchback.

Reflecting Telnack's European experience was standard full instrumentation, which consisted of speedometer, trip odometer, tachometer, temperature gauge, oil pressure gauge, ammeter, and fuel gauge. Included also were two new fingertip stalks for turn signals/headlight

dimmer/horn and wiper/washer. They were shared with Fairmont/Zephyr, as was the basic instrument panel and cowl structure. On the right, a third lever was provided when the extra-cost tilt steering wheel was ordered.

Practical new convenience options ran to interval-sweep wipers and a console complete with a graphic display for "Vehicle Systems Monitoring." The latter was a profile outline of the car on which warning lights were placed to indicate low fuel, low windshield washer fluid, and failed headlights, taillights, or brake lamps. A pushbutton allowed the driver to check that the display itself was working. The console also housed a quartz-crystal digital chronometer that showed time, date, or elapsed time at the touch of a button. Finally, luxury-trim models were given higher-quality materials, and the '79 Ghia was less flashy than its '78 counterpart. Like past Mustangs, the '79 was designed for the broadest possible market appeal. Said Ford Division marketing plans manager Michael Woods: "Not too long ago we did a concept study on positioning the [imported] Capri and brought in imported-car owners, some Capri owners—people who own small specialty cars. We showed them the [new Mustang] and talked to them about strategy. We were pretty gratified that an awful lot of people who were interested in the [imported] Capri felt that we had maintained the Capri theme—the functional styling of the car—and that it was consistent with the original car."

Now the European Capri, especially with V-6, was a very competent touring car. For the new Mustang to match it, specifications would have to be greatly altered. Capri fans would not be satisfied with a plush, short-wheelbase coupe that weighed too much and handled sluggishly. At the same time, Ford didn't want to lose all those thousands of Mustang II buyers. Several levels of suspension capability were thus deemed necessary.

As planned, the basic hardware was Fairmont/Zephyr. The front suspension employed modified MacPherson-strut geometry instead of conventional upper A-arms. Unlike similar setups still found in many European and most Japanese cars, the coil spring did not wrap around the strut but mounted between a lower control arm and the body structure, which eliminated the need for an expensive spring compressor for replacing shocks. A front anti-roll bar would be standard on all models, with diameter varied according to engine.

Rear geometry employed a four-bar link arrangement, also with coil springs—lighter and more compact than the Mustang II's leaf-spring Hotchkiss setup. V-8 models would have a standard rear anti-roll bar. Since this served more for lateral location than controlling sway, the car's roll center was effectively lowered and rear spring rates could be commensurately softer.

Mustang was selected as the Official Pace Car (above) for the running of the 63rd Indy 500 on May 27, 1979. Ford celebrated by building about 6000 replicas that spring. Not only was the Mustang new, so was the full-size Ford. Riding a 114.3-inch wheelbase, the 3527-pound Landau four-door (below) listed at $6811.

Product planners ultimately decided to offer three suspension levels—standard, "handling," and "special"—each designed for and issued with its own set of tires. The basic setup was tuned for conventional bias-plys, the mid-level "handling" package for regular radials. The special suspension was designed around Michelin's recently developed TRX radials, whose unusual 390-mm (15.35-inch) diameter required metric-size forged-aluminum wheels.

Initially available only with 14-inch radials, the "handling" package upgraded the basic chassis with higher spring rates, different shock valving, and stiffer bushings. A rear stabilizer bar was also provided when the 2.8-liter V-6 was ordered. The special suspension provided even better handling, company press releases boasting that it was engineered "to extract maximum performance" from the 190/65R-390 Michelin tires. (Ford had already gained experience with this wheel/tire combination on its European Granada.) This meant specific shock absorber valving, high-rate rear springs, 1.12-inch front stabilizer bar, and a rear bar.

There was no need to change the Mustang II's precise rack-and-pinion steering. Power assist was still optional, and the variable-ratio rack issued for 1978 also returned. Again to save weight,

housings for both the manual and power systems were constructed of die-cast aluminum.

Besides Mustang II engines, the '79 was offered with an intriguing new powerplant: a turbocharged version of the standard 2.3-liter "Lima" four, with a rated 131 SAE net horsepower against only 88 bhp for the unblown unit. Though they're common now, turbos were pretty exotic at the time, let alone on a mass-market American car. With the four-speed gearbox, the blown four was good for a claimed 8.3 seconds in 0-55-mph acceleration (with the "double nickel" national speed limit in force, Detroit wasn't quoting 0-60 times), plus fuel economy in the mid-20s.

Though turbocharging was new to Mustang, it had been around for years—like the similar supercharging method, a bolt-on means of improving volumetric efficiency. The principle is simple. A turbine located in the flow of exhaust gases is connected to an impeller (compressor) near the carburetor. In normal running, the turbine spins too slowly to boost manifold pressure or affect fuel consumption. As the throttle is opened, however, the engine speeds up, which increases the flow of exhaust gases. The increased flow spins the turbine, which speeds up the impeller and increases the density (pressure) of the air/fuel mixture fed to the combustion chambers. The result: more power. To prevent engine damage, maximum boost was limited to

six pounds per square inch by a relief valve that allowed gases to bypass the turbine once that pressure was reached.

Carryover engines weren't neglected. The venerable 302 V-8 gained a new low-restriction exhaust system, more lightweight components, and a ribbed V-belt for the accessory drive. The German-made V-6 was in short supply, so the old 200-cubic-inch inline six was brought back to replace it late in the model year. The V-8 and both sixes came with four-speed gearboxes developed specifically for them—basically the standard three-speed manual with direct-drive third gear (1:1 ratio) and an overdrive gear (0.70:1) tacked on. The four and Turbo four had four-speeds with a direct-drive fourth gear. Final drive ratios were 3.08:1 for automatics, four-speed V-6, and the unblown four-cylinder engine, 2.47:1 with the V-8, and 3.45:1 for all other drivetrain combinations. The automatic, by the way, was the familiar three-speed Cruise-O-Matic as used in the Mustang II.

Per Mustang tradition, the performance of any particular '79 depended on drivetrain. The V-8 was practically a drag-race engine by late-Seventies standards: 0-60 mph clocked out at about nine seconds. With four-speed, the V-6 was still in the 13-14-second range, while a like-equipped Turbo-four did the trip in about 12-12.5 seconds.

As expected, press reaction also varied with powertrain. Some writers thought the V-8 Mustang was overpow-

ered and out of step with gasoline prices that were on the rise again. Predictably, the intriguing Turbo-four garnered the most "buff book" attention. Said *Road & Track*'s John Dinkel: "The TRX turbo would seem to be an enthusiast's delight. I just hope that the design compromises dictated by costs and the fact that Ford couldn't start with a completely clean sheet of paper don't wreck that dream.... There's no doubt the new Mustang has the potential to be the best sport coupe Ford has ever built, but in some respects [it] is as enigmatic as its predecessor."

Nevertheless, this "whole new breed" of Mustang turned on a lot of buyers, quickly rising to number-three in the compact class (after Fairmont and the Chevy Citation), where it now competed by dint of its larger interior. Overall calendar-year sales surged to 304,000 units, making Mustang the seventh most popular car in the land, a big improvement over the '78 Mustang II's 22nd-place finish. More impressive was the model year production count of 370,000 units. Interestingly, the increase came despite prices hiked some $500-$1000 above those for the final Mustang IIs. The base notchback was up to nearly $4500, the hatchback to just over $4800, and a loaded Ghia could deliver in excess of $5500—more than a mighty Shelby-Mustang had cost 10 years before. But such is the price of progress. Evidently, a good many buyers agreed that the improved '79 Mustang was worth its extra cost.

This year's new downsized Ford LTD (and the companion Mercury Marquis as well) was less successful in its field, which was curious. Developed as the "Panther" project, it was fully a match for GM's smaller full-size cars, especially the Chevrolet Caprice/Impala, which had enjoyed great success since its '77 model year debut. Despite a seven-inch shorter wheelbase, now 114.4 inches, the new LTD offered more claimed passenger and trunk space than its outsize predecessor, plus superior visibility and better fuel economy. Styling was up to date—boxy, but much cleaner—and ride was more competent thanks to a new all-coil suspension with short-arm/long-arm front geometry and a four-link rear end with the shocks mounted ahead of the axle.

With all this, sales should have gone up. They didn't. LTD fell by some 80,000 units for the calendar year, to nearly 246,000, barely enough to beat the full-size Oldsmobile and far behind Caprice/Impala. (Marquis also declined, though by less than 5000 units.) Model year production looked better: 356,000 for '79 versus

Optioned up, the base $4220 Fairmont four-door sedan looked quite luxurious. The four-door, which weighed a modest 2578 pounds, was the best seller in the lineup, captivating 133,813 customers. Total Fairmont sales were down 14 percent to 395,367 units, however, as the U.S. economy entered a severe economic downturn precipitated by the second fuel crisis. The options list added a tilt steering wheel and flip-up sunroof.

227,000 for '78. Even so, price apparently *was* a problem with the new full-size Fords. Base stickers read about $1000 higher than they had on the "road-hugging" '78s, the line now spanning a Lincoln-like range of $6184 (base two-door) to $7155 for the Squire wagon. There was also GM's two-year head start and the sudden economic downturn that brought renewed inflation, soaring interest rates, and skyrocketing gas prices that knocked the entire market for a loop, especially the full-size segment. The LTD would enjoy a sales resurgence, but not before the U.S. industry passed through some of its bleakest years ever.

The popular Ford Fairmont returned for its sophomore year with few changes apart from additional options: tilt steering wheel, cruise control, more compre-

hensive "performance instrumentation" (including tachometer), and remote deck-lid release for sedans. A standard four-speed overdrive manual came with the base four or optional six, and was extended to the V-8, which was previously restricted to automatic. Despite the lack of change and new X-car competition from GM, Fairmont remained the nation's favorite compact, as model-year output jumped some 33,000 units to just over 395,000. Fairmont was helped in 1979 because production lines were up to speed all year, compared with the slower start-up tempo of an all-new model in 1978. Ford's wee one, the Pinto, got what would be its final facelift, with rectangular headlamps flanking a neater, more coherent grille composed of horizontal slats. Standard equipment was upgraded

to encompass power front-disc brakes, electric rear-window defroster, tinted glass, and AM radio. An ESS appearance option arrived with black grille and exterior moldings, and the wagon's extra-cost Cruising Package was extended to the hatchback Runabout. By now, an unsafe fuel tank and filler neck on pre-1977 Pinto sedans had been highly publicized, and Ford would be forced to defend itself in a series of class-action product liability suits arising from several horrendous collision-related fires. But sales weren't affected, at least for now, as Pinto output actually increased by 12,000 units to 199,000 for the model year.

Perhaps because it was now five model-years old, the Granada was promoted as "An American Classic." It was about all the ad agency could do because

styling was untouched, and interiors were revised only in detail. The four-speed overdrive manual gearbox was made available with V-8s, and the extra-cost all-disc brakes disappeared for lack of interest. Production tumbled by 68,000 units to 182,376.

The mid-size Ford LTD II was also little changed, but that was mainly because it would be gone in a year—and because sales languished to slightly less than 50,000. The optional 400 V-8 was discontinued, and front bumper systems were lightened in a futile attempt to improve mileage. A new option highlighted this line's relatively poor economy: a larger 27.5-gallon fuel tank.

Thunderbird was also little altered, but at least it would return for 1980—and in an all-new form to boot. But for '79,

the grille gained a broad criss-cross grid ahead of thin vertical bars, and full-width taillamps gave way to dual units separated by a central backup lamp. As on LTD II, the 400 V-8 disappeared from the options list. The 1978 Diamond Jubilee Edition returned as the Heritage, with the same blanked-off rear roof quarters and full-luxury treatment—and a stiff sticker price of $11,060. Output dropped by nearly 80,000 units to a bit more than 284,000, yet Thunderbird continued to far outpace LTD II, ending up 12th on the overall industry roster.

It should be noted that Lincoln-Mercury ran counter to the general 1979 industry trend, setting its third consecutive sales record: 670,000 Mercurys and 190,000 Lincolns. Mercury's total was helped by a downsized Marquis sharing

the more sensible new LTD design, and continuing demand for the Fairmont-clone Zephyr.

But another lift to Mercury's '79 fortunes was a second-generation Capri, a kissin' cousin of the new Mustang bearing Mercury nameplates (the German-built Capri never had them) just so no one would think this another "sexy European." Not that most people would. Styling was all-American and very similar to Mustang's. Its main distinctions were a blunt grille with horizontal bars, prominent bodyside bulges around the wheel openings (amazingly predictive of the later Porsche 944), and slightly different taillamps with horizontal instead of vertical ribs. One other difference: Capri buyers could have any body style they liked so long as it was a hatchback.

The '79 Thunderbird (left) was in the third and last year of its design cycle. Styling was freshened up with a bolder grille and taillights separated by a central backup light. The coupe started $6328, but the T-top added another $747. Production was down to 284,141 units, but output for the 1977-79 design cycle was a rousing 955,032. For 1979, Pinto (top right) received what would be its last facelift, which centered around a more neatly integrated grille and rectangular headlights. The Runabout listed at $4055, but the Rallye package (which was really a 1980 option) cost $369 extra. The imported '79 Fiesta (above) sported taller front seatbacks in the $4198 base price, which was up from $3680 in 1978.

Ford pickups for 1979 sported standard rectangular headlights. The base F-100 Custom short-box Flareside pickup sold for $5085, but those who wanted the black bumpers and feisty pinstriping had to order the Free Wheeling package (top). The Ranchero was in its last year in 1979, and sales picked up slightly to 25,010 units. The sporty GT (above) listed at $6289.

Naturally, the '79 Capri also shared the new Mustang's chassis, running gear, interior layout, even dashboard. Model selections were similar, too: base, luxury Ghia, and sporty RS, the last an option package with fortified underpinnings and available with the turbocharged engine. The base model listed about $200 upstream of its Mustang sister, but Ghia hatchback prices were within a few dollars of each other. Though Capri would never outsell Mustang (and wouldn't last as long, either), its first-year reception was good at about 110,000 units, 15 percent of which were Ghias.

There was little action on the truck

front this year—no surprise, really, after the big events of 1978. The Ranchero was virtually unchanged because it was destined for the same fate as the LTD II. Besides, there wasn't any need for "pickup-cars" anymore. Truck buyers seeking something "personal" were now opting for sport-utilities, car-like full-size pickups, and handy imported compacts like Ford's own Courier. The Courier itself got a minor freshening via a restyled dash, two additional paint colors, new tritone striping with the optional Free Wheeling Package, and a new Sports Package option that included bucket seats, sports steering wheel, extra gauges, and pseudo-wood dash applique. Courier's base engine was at last upgraded from the original 1.8-liter to a 2.0-liter enlargement of the same Mazda-built four, though this only kept pace with continuing power losses to detuning for emissions and fuel economy reasons. Ford's 2.3-liter "Lima" four remained optional.

Speaking of mileage, corporate average fuel economy standards now applied to light trucks, with initial targets of 17.2 mpg for two-wheel-drive models and 15.8 mpg for four-wheelers. Ford responded by fitting catalytic converters in all F-Series models below 8500 GVW, thus necessitating the use of unleaded fuel. Axle ratios were rejiggered toward the same end. A 4×4 F-350 joined the line, available as both a Regular and SuperCab. Tilt steering wheel was newly available for all models with four-speed manual gearbox, an extra-cost supercooling package arrived for all F-Series engines, and Customs joined other pickups in using rectangular headlamps. Colors and trims got their usual shuffles, including revised stripe treatments for both Styleside and Flareside Free Wheeling Packages. Ford also boasted better pickup paint this year, with three enamel coats instead of the previous two.

This year's encore edition of the successful second-generation Bronco got most of these same changes—and little else. Specific improvements included the tougher F-Series paint, "cat cons" for all engines, and revised colors, trims, and striping.

Econolines followed suit, but also sported a cleaner face with a new eggcrate grille and parking lamps moved up from just above the bumper to just below the headlights, which shifted from round to rectangular. Power door locks joined the options roster, as did tilt wheel for four-speed-manual units. The Cruising Van could be newly ordered with hinged rear side doors as well as the previous single sliding door. The 302 V-8 was now optional on all three Econoline chassis, and axle ratios were numerically lowered across-the-board in a vain quest for higher mileage.

Reflecting the state of the van market was an intriguing new option for Club Wagons, the "Quad Captain's Chair Package." This consisted of a pair of individual front seats with fold-down armrests, plus two more right behind. All four could be swiveled for face-to-face tete-a-tetes between front and rear passengers—with the vehicle at rest, of course. When ordered on long wheelbase vans the package also came with a fold-up snack table for the rear compartment and a back bench seat with slide-forward cushion and reclining backrest that could be used to form a makeshift bed measuring 62 inches wide by 72 inches long. This, the table, and the four swiveling seats were also available separately. Together, they were just the thing for those who liked to travel but hated leaving their living room behind.

The one notable development among this year's big rigs was three new gas V-8s for F-, C-, and L-Series mediums (500s to 800s). Derived from the corporate 400 V-8 passenger-car engine, they comprised a 370 with two- and four-barrel carburetors and a four-barrel 429. All

The '79 Bronco, here a top-line Ranger XLT (above), came with a two-barrel 351 V-8 as standard, although a 400 was available. Four out of five buyers chose Cruise-O-Matic shift, although a four-speed manual was standard. Base price escalated to $7733, weight to 4569 pounds, and production crept up to 75,761 units. The Econoline Super Wagon (right) was the same as the 138-inch-wheelbase Club Wagon, except for the 20-inch stretch behind the rear side windows.

were "truckized" for extra strength and durability with features like sodium-cooled heavy-duty exhaust valves, larger crank journals and thrust bearings, tin-plated aluminum pistons with special rings, and a heavy-duty 11-quart lubrication system with constant-pressure rotary oil pump. Like the 2.3-liter passenger-car four, these burly new truck powerplants were built at Ford's modern engine facility in Lima, Ohio. Also new this year was a mid-range diesel, by Cummins, as an option in the Louisville 8000/9000 chassis.

Another episode in the continuing passive-restraint saga was played out in Washington this year with the Dingell-Broyhill rider to the House Appropriations Bill for fiscal 1980. The amendment, sponsored by two Michigan Representatives with no little interest in auto-industry matters, prohibited the implementation of FMVSS 208—the so-called "airbag rule"—as applied to anything *other* than belt systems. As a result, GM canceled plans to offer airbags on some of its 1981 cars. Ford, meanwhile, dropped plans to offer passive belts on some of *its* 1980-81 models. This stemmed from GM's experience with optional passive belts for the '79 Chevy Chevette, where Dearborn had discerned "a notable lack of demand," as a company spokesman put it. Then again, that might be expected with a costly extra for a subcompact selling mainly on low price.

But all this was about to be overshadowed by a new era of hard times for Detroit and American industry in general. The great recession of 1980 was at hand, leaving little time for squabbling over such relatively trivial matters. Survival was about to become the main order of business, and for some businesses that wasn't going to be easy.

1 9 8 0

This was a year marked by financial crisis and a change in leadership at Ford Motor Company. For the nation as a whole, 1980 was a year of "stagflation," a combination of a stagnant economy and double-digit inflation that clobbered the U.S. auto market beginning in the spring of '79. A second great fuel crisis touched it off, initiated by the Iranian revolution and an oil cut-off at the behest of an America-hating Ayatollah, who promptly went to war with Iraq. Lines reformed at gas stations and fuel prices doubled. Though gas wasn't as hard to come by as in 1973-74, its higher cost intimidated hundreds of thousands of new-car buyers who were already suffering "sticker shock" from soaring, inflation-riddled prices. The market flip-flopped almost overnight, some 40 percent of it switching from full-size cars to compacts. For Detroit, it was the start of a long nightmare.

After its most successful production run in history in 1977-79, the Thunderbird was downsized once again for 1980. Designers Dennis Jameyfield and Kyu Kim (above) discuss the final design sketch of the new car, which emerged looking rather square and formal (below). The car shown has the Exterior Decor group. Weight on base models was reduced from 775-950 pounds.

As if that weren't enough, this year's Corporate Average Fuel Economy mandate for cars was 20 mpg, up one from '79. It would go to 22 mpg for 1981. Worse, the import invasion was now an all-out assault, aided and abetted by "Energy Crisis II," vastly more competitive Japanese models, and growing buyer awareness that "Detroit quality" had become a contradiction in terms. Back in 1974, imports had captured some 1.4 million sales in a total market of about 8.7 million; by 1979 that number was over 2.3 million in a U.S. market that had peaked in '78 and was de-clining to similar volume.

While Chrysler Corporation's cliff-hanger existence grabbed most of the headlines in 1980, Ford Motor Company was in similarly dire straits, albeit less publicized. In fact, Ford would record its biggest one-year loss ever in 1980—a staggering $1.54 billion—which must have made many an old Dearborn hand think back to the late-Forties.

Ford's situation this year prompted thoughts of the Forties in another way: The leadership guard was about to change at a crucial moment. As sched-

uled, Henry Ford II resigned as chairman, though he would remain head of the board's finance committee. Replacing him was Philip Caldwell, who'd been president since Lee Iacocca's firing in 1978. Taking over for Caldwell was new president Donald E. Petersen. The significance of this change was not lost on historians: For the first time in its history, Ford was being led by people whose name was *not* "on the building."

While Iacocca struggled to keep Highland Park from becoming a ghost town, some wondered whether Ford's new management team could prevent the same from happening to Dearborn. Like its Big Three rivals, Ford was saddled with high production costs owing to too many aging, inefficient plants and a surfeit of workers. Another pressure on profits was the high cost of the planned, massive product overhaul begun with the '78 Fairmont/Zephyr, necessary to stay competitive in the Eighties. For the industry as a whole—and Ford in particular—the bottom dropped out of the market at precisely the wrong time.

But Ford's new team would quickly prove up to the challenges they faced—arguably more astute and capable than the new Roger Smith/James McDonald regime that took charge at General Motors in 1980. Petersen, in particular, would be worth his weight in gold. Then 54, he'd held a variety of key marketing and product planning jobs since joining Ford in epochal 1949, his most recent position was as vice-president for Diversified Products (beginning in late 1977, at which time he was also appointed to the board). More importantly for Ford's immediate future, Petersen was a genuine car enthusiast with an almost unerring instinct for what turned on buyers. This contrasts with Iacocca, who's also been termed a "car guy," but is more accurately viewed as a savvy automotive marketer.

Caldwell, just a year older than Petersen and a career finance man in the hallowed Detroit tradition, had joined Ford in 1953 with an MBA degree from the prestigious Harvard of School of Business. It is to his everlasting credit that he would defer to Petersen on most of the important product decisions in the coming decade. Caldwell, meanwhile, concentrated on reducing overhead and streamlining the entire Ford organiza-

tion. In fact, Caldwell and Petersen worked together with a harmoniousness unusual in the auto industry, and this goes a long way to explaining the spectacular success Ford would achieve later in the decade.

Lest we forget, 1980 would also see a significant shakeup at Ford Design with the retirement of vice-president Gene Bordinat after 19 years. The new chief design executive at North American Automotive Operations (NAAO) was Jack Telnack, the driving force behind the pretty little Fiesta at Ford Europe and, most recently, the handsome fifth-generation Mustang. At year's end, Don Kopka returned from a brief stewardship at Ghia in Italy to head the entire Dearborn Design Staff.

Such was the backdrop for FoMoCo's 1980 rollout. And a very different group of cars it was, led by a new Panther-based Lincoln Continental and Mark, and a realigned Ford fleet that revealed the significance of the sensible "Fox" platform in the firm's near-term product plans.

Heading the Ford line was the 25th edition of the Thunderbird, an all-new car built on what was essentially an elongated Fairmont chassis. Compared to the eighth-generation models, the 1980 measured nearly 16 inches shorter overall, 4.5 inches shorter between wheel centers, and slimmer by more than four inches. Unit construction returned for the first time since 1966, and chassis specifications were identical with Fairmont's. Weight came down dramatically from 1977-79—the division said more than 700 pounds—just the ticket for boosting T-Bird mileage, and thus the division's fleet-average fuel economy.

In addition to reduced size and weight, smaller powerplants and higher gearing also played a part in meeting CAFE standards. Thunderbird's base engine was a newly debored derivative of the 302 V-8 displacing 4.2 liters/255 cubic inches, but delivering only 115 net horsepower. This engine also found its way into 1980 Mustangs and Fairmonts. The lone option was the 302 itself, rated here at 131 bhp and newly available with a four-speed automatic transmission having a tall 0.67:1 overdrive top gear for quiet, low-rpm highway cruising. More importantly, numerically lower axle ratios promoted better fuel economy.

Work on the new T-Bird had begun in 1976. The aim was a four-seater of sporty character and more appropriate size that would nevertheless retain such styling hallmarks as wrapped parking lights and prominent B-pillars. As with the '79 Mustang, aerodynamics was a prime consideration, and over 400 hours of wind tunnel testing reduced drag coefficients from 0.58 on the first clay model to 0.48 on the final fiberglass model (versus 0.55 on the production '79). Even so, the styling was more throwback than predictive: blocky and not very well received. Ford no doubt felt this approach crucial for preserving traditional appearance "cues" in the interest of sales, but they just didn't fit the smaller package. Like the unhappy Lincoln Versailles, the 1980 T-Bird was a gilded lily of the kind not at all favored by Petersen and Telnack. It was, in fact, one of the last Dearborn cars designed under Gene Bordinat, whose tastes had lately turned very much toward the ornate.

Fortunately, downsizing gave the latest Bird a more habitable cabin—though as luxurious as ever—and markedly better handling. Said *Car and Driver's* Rich Ceppos: "If the truth be known, the new car does an infinitely better job of carrying four [adults] than the old one did. According to Ford, no interior room was lost up front . . . though rear hiproom is down about five inches. But more important is the increase of 2.8 inches in rear knee clearance. . . . The Thunderbird still floats along as if it were in dreamland. The [overdrive automatic] shifts as smoothly as any conventional automatic. And little if any of the [previous car's] bank-vault quietness was lost. . . . About the only changes in [its] unenthusiastic road manners are positive ones: a welcome increase in steering effort and precision, and a touch of nimbleness that the engineers couldn't filter out. . . . An optional handling package—recalibrated shocks, alloy rims, and the largest Miche-

The 1980 full-size Ford lineup expanded from eight models to 12. Topping the line was the LTD Crown Victoria series, a name borrowed from the mid-Fifties; on the bottom was the "S" series, intended largely for fleets. In between fell the standard LTD, offered in two- and three-seat wagons and two- and four-door sedans. The last (left) weighed 3475 pounds. A 130-bhp 302 V-8 came standard; a 140-bhp 351 was optional.

1980 drivetrain chart was essentially a photocopy of late 1979's. Both fours still teamed with conventional four-speed manual transmission as standard. The six, still rated at a modest 85 bhp (versus 109 for the now-departed V-6), came with the manual four-speed overdrive unit. Cruise-O-Matic remained available across the board.

Though an old-timer by 1980, the straight six was an efficient, easy-to-service engine. It had less horsepower than the superseded German-built V-6, but this was offset by its greater displacement and torque, so "real-world" performance wasn't all that different. There was nothing exotic about its components: seven-main-bearing crankshaft, hydraulic valve lifters, cast-iron block, one-barrel carburetor. But according to Ford's "Cost-of-Ownership" formula, where required maintenance for the first 50,000 miles was averaged according to dealer parts and labor prices, the inline six cost less to operate than the V-6, an important plus for inflation-weary buyers.

Mustang had been around for 15 years in 1980, and it was natural to ask how the latest version compared with the '65 original. Judging by certain "vital statistics," it was tempting to say little had changed:

	1965 Mustang	1980 Mustang
Length (in.):	181.6	179.1
Width (in.):	68.2	69.1
Wheelbase (in.):	108.0	100.4
Weight, 6-cyl (lbs):	2,445	2,516
base six, cid:	200	200
base V-8, cid:	260	255

Despite their similarity in numbers, these were really quite different Mustangs. Though the '80 was about as long as the '65 and had the same amount of front passenger room, it offered more rear seat space despite a 7.6-inch shorter wheelbase. Ford had obviously learned something about space utilization in 15 years. And though the '80 was burdened with a bevy of government-mandated safety features such as reinforced doors and five-mph bumpers, it weighed hardly more than a comparable '65. Apparently, Ford had also learned something about lightweight materials and construction.

There were equally interesting comparisons to be made in the engine department. The 2.3-liter four, of course, was not comparable to any 1965 Mustang en-

lin TRX tires to date, 220/55R-390s—works small wonders."

Despite its better mileage and handier size, the new Bird failed to make the impression Ford marketing types expected. Model year sales dropped by over 40 percent, and T-Bird slipped from 12th to 19th place in the domestic model rankings. The grand total, a bit more than 156,000 units, was split among base, Town Landau, and mid-year Silver Anniversary offerings. The last, replacing the '79 Heritage, was easily identified by its sparkling, Fifties Crown Victoria-type "tiara" roof band and paintwork keyed to gray-and-silver upholstery. Standard powertrain was the 302 teamed with an automatic overdrive transmission.

The small-bore 255 V-8 replaced the 302 option for this year's Mustang. The latest in a long line of Ford small-blocks dating from the original 1962 Fairlane 221, it looked like a quick response to "Energy Crisis II," but it was really prompted by CAFE and had been planned long before. Regardless, it was a definite help, though performance naturally suffered. Styling, on the other hand, changed only in detail. Nobody at Ford was unhappy with the latest Mustang's looks. Neither were customers. But the new Middle East turmoil devastated the 1980 market, and Mustang suffered as much as any Detroiter. Though it remained seventh among domestic models, model year production plunged from 370,000 to around 271,000.

Mustang had been selected as the Pace Car for the 1979 Indianapolis 500, so it was natural that an "Indy Pace Car" replica would appear as a mid-year addition to the line. It did, with about 6000 built, and went on to inspire a more distinctive Cobra package for 1980. This boasted a similar slat grille, more prominent front and rear spoilers than the '79 Cobra, integral fog lamps, non-functioning hood scoop, and the special TRX suspension. Still built around the Turbo-four and offered for the hatchback only, it upped sticker price by $1482 (versus $1173 in '79), but allowed a $114 credit if the V-8

was chosen over the turbo engine. As before, the hood snake decal was a separate option, this year for $88.

Elsewhere, high-back, all-vinyl bucket seats and color-keyed interior and door trim became across-the-board standards, as did more efficient halogen headlights, which replaced the conventional tungsten sealed-beam units. Hatchbacks now came with the Sport Option at no charge, which meant styled sport wheels with trim rings, black rocker panel and window moldings, wide bodyside moldings, striped rub strip extensions, and a sporty steering wheel.

The two Ghia models remained the luxury Mustangs for 1980, boasting color-keyed seatbelts, mirrors, bodyside moldings, and—on hatchbacks—C-pillar trim, plus low-back vinyl bucket seats with headrests, door map pockets, a visor vanity mirror, thicker pile carpeting, deluxe steering wheel, roof-mounted assist handles, and a full complement of interior lights. Leather or cloth-and-vinyl upholstery was available in six different colors.

Options were more numerous than ever. A partial list included the following items: tilt steering wheel, speed control, power door locks, remote trunklid or hatchback release, rear window wiper/washer, flip-up glass sunroof, and a wide assortment of wheels, wheel covers, and audio systems. New to the slate were Recaro reclining front bucket seats, first offered on the '79 Pace Car Replica. With their infinitely variable seatback recliners and adjustable thigh and lumbar supports, Mustang could no longer be accused of lagging behind its European competition in seat comfort.

Other new 1980 options included a roof-mounted luggage carrier, "window shade" cargo-area cover for the hatchback, and accent side tape stripes. An interesting dress-up item for notchbacks was the extra-cost Carriage Roof, a diamond-grain full vinyl covering set off by black window frames and moldings, designed to simulate the top-up appearance of a true convertible.

Save the smaller V-8, Mustang's

gine. The six, however, was exactly the same powerplant offered on the '65 (except the early cars that used the 170-cid unit). The 255 V-8 was derived from the 302 that had evolved from the 289, which itself was enlarged from the original Mustang's 260. Yet both the six and V-8 got better fuel mileage than their 1965 counterparts.

What the comparisons didn't show was the long, long road Mustang had traveled in 15 years. Along the way it had become one of the world's fastest four-place production cars—as well as too large, too unwieldy, and too wasteful. That the lighter, more efficient 1980 Mustang so closely resembled the '65 in size and performance heartened a lot of enthusiasts. Here was proof that Americans could build a nimble, handsome, efficient automobile that could also be quite entertaining over the twisty bits. After 15 years, the original ponycar had come full circle.

Ford gave every indication during 1980 that it was about to get its performance act back together and put it on the road. Mustang would definitely be the star of the show. Hinting at what might lie ahead was a tantalizing "concept car" that toured this season's auto-show circuit: the Mustang IMSA. Powered by a much-modified turbo-four, it hunkered down on massive Pirelli P7 tires nestled beneath outlandishly flared fenders, matched by a deep front air dam, loop rear spoiler, and racy-looking pop-riveted plastic covers over side windows, back panel, and headlights. In name and appearance it strongly suggested that Ford was more than just thinking about a return to competition—and about the International Motor Sports Association (IMSA) GT series in particular.

Then, in September 1980, Ford announced formation of a Special Vehicle Operations department (SVO). Significantly, it was headed by Michael Kranefuss, newly arrived in Dearborn from his post as competition director for Ford Europe. SVO's stated purpose was to "develop a series of limited-production performance cars and develop their image through motorsport." It quickly got down to business with a turbo Mustang to be driven in selected 1981 IMSA GT events by former Porsche pilot Klaus Ludwig. Other Mustangs receiving similar direct factory help were a Trans-Am car for Dennis Mecham and an IMSA Kelly American Challenge racer for Lyn St. James.

As if to signal its return to the track, Ford debuted the McLaren Mustang in late 1980. The work of designers Todd Gerstenberger and Harry Wykes, this was a heavily modified production model with enough built-in potential for easy conversion to racing trim. Looking somewhat like the IMSA show car, the McLaren sported a grille-less nose above a low-riding "skirt" spoiler, functional hood scoops, tweaked suspension (mostly a mixture of heavy-duty off-the-shelf

components), massive fender flares, and premium European BBS alloy wheels wearing broad-shouldered 225/55R-15 Firestone HPR radial tires. Power was again provided by the turbo-four, but fitted with a new variable boost control. This provided a maximum boost range of five to 11 psi, as opposed to the stock engine's fixed five-psi. At 10 psi, rated output was 175 bhp at 2500 rpm, a considerable jump over the stock mill's, which was usually pegged at around 131 bhp (Ford never released official ratings for its turbo-four). A $25,000 price tag and virtual hand construction limited the number of copies to only 250, including the prototype.

Numerous minor changes marked other 1980 Fords, none of which changed appreciably. The aging LTD II (evolved, you'll recall, from the 1972 Torino) was belatedly consigned to history, leaving Granada as the division's sole representative in the mid-size field. Alas, it continued trailing the Chevrolet Malibu/Monte Carlo and Oldsmobile's Cutlass/Cutlass Supreme in sales by a wide margin. In fact, production tumbled 50 percent to just 90,429 units. An all-new Granada for 1981 would help—but not much.

After a 10-year run, the aged subcompact Pinto was now in its final year, though not because of the widely reported fires allegedly caused by an unsafe fuel-tank design on pre-1976 sedans. Rather, it was because Ford had something better on the horizon: a more modern, Fiesta-like replacement with front-wheel drive. Still, the littlest Ford never quite recovered from the safety controversy, and it lost two spots on this year's sales chart as output dipped to 185,000 units. Lost also was its optional 2.8 V-6, this due to scarce supplies from Germany. But there was a vindication of sorts in March of this year when a jury in Winnemac, Indiana, cleared Ford on three counts of reckless homicide. This closely watched product-liability case stemmed from the deaths of three girls whose Pinto had caught fire after being rear-ended by a van. This verdict, however, didn't end consumer efforts for greater corporate accountability in product safety. On the contrary, it only strengthened that movement. Nor, for that matter, did the Pinto decision counter the adverse publicity surrounding charges of "jumping" automatic transmissions in millions of pre-1980 Dearborn vehicles.

On a happier note for Ford's new management team, Fairmont moved up from fifth to third place among compacts, though it, too, received few changes. The two Ghia models were replaced at midyear by a Futura four-door wearing the coupe's bolder cross-hatch grille and spiffier interior, and the 302 was replaced as this line's V-8 option by the small-bore 255, here delivering a rated 117 bhp. Output settled in at 317,015 units.

There was one more Fairmont power choice for 1980. Dearborn had

With 51,630 built, the $7117 LTD four-door sedan (top) was the best selling full-size Ford for 1980. The six-year-old Granada saw production plummet to 90,429 units, less than half the 1979 total. The two-door started at $5541, while the Ghia four-door listed at $6065 (second and third from top). Fairmont held up better in this recession year as buyers were more interested in economy than performance or pizzazz. The Futura coupe attracted 51,878 customers, although the Turbo model shown here (fourth from top) was quite rare. The $5011 four-door (above) was the best seller: 143,188, including the fancier Futura sedan.

taken due note of the slow but steady rise in sports sedan sales during the Seventies, as well as renewed buyer interest in sporty compacts. Fairmont's ES Option had reached out to those who wanted something close to European road manners and appointments without the high European prices. Now Ford went a step further with a surprising new Fairmont option: the turbocharged Lima four.

We say "surprising" because this engine was a very mixed blessing in its earliest form: strong but noisy, and far from smooth. But smaller, lighter cars with

Mustang persisted with the Turbo (above) into 1980, but it still didn't find many takers, reportedly only about four percent of production. And those who preferred V-8s were quick to discover that the 302 had been yanked from the engine lineup in favor of a smaller 255 that developed only 118 horsepower.

smaller engines seemed almost preordained at the time, so that's what Dearborn would offer, even for those that passed as "performance" cars. And to its credit, Ford was trying to make this sow's ear of a turbo engine into more of a silk purse. *Motor Trend's* Chuck Nerpel reported in September '79 that "Ford engineers have been working for improved performance with smaller engines since [the turbocharged] powerplant was made available on the 1979 Mustangs, and they now feel it is ready to graduate...to a family sedan." Enter Fairmont Turbo.

Nerpel described the engineers' efforts as involving "a new intake manifold, carburetor [fuel-injected turbos were still some ways off at Ford] and air cleaner. The turbo unit is now [closer] to the carburetor, and the entire intake system sits up higher on the engine, requiring a bump in the hood for added clearance... an added-on fiberglass pod...." As before, "the turbo unit is of Garrett origin, designed for Ford with manifolding engineered by Ford. Boost pressures are still in the final stages, but between 5.5 and 6 pounds [per square inch] seems to be ideal...." *Road & Track* in November '79 took note of newly rerouted fuel lines and replacement of the previous engine driven cooling fan with an electric one wired to the battery instead of the igni-

tion switch. "It's said that hot soak after shutdown was the principal problem with [the '79] turbo engine, causing fuel percolation and other attendant distresses," *R&T* explained—hence the changes.

Turbocharging was still pretty new in 1980, and this year's Fairmont brochure took pains to explain it: "The turbocharger is basically an air compressor driven by exhaust gases. At your command, it pressurizes atmospheric air to increase the velocity of the fuel/air mixture to the combustion chambers. The result: excellent acceleration." *Motor Trend* proved the claim, clocking a prototype Fairmont Turbo two-door at 13.5 seconds from 0-60 mph despite the automatic transmission that Ford made mandatory, perhaps as more appropriate for a "family sedan."

Nevertheless, Nerpel termed that performance was "pretty impressive, matching today's trend toward economy while striving for some semblance of the performance some drivers still deem necessary for everyday driving." *Road & Track*, which briefly drove that same prototype, uncharacteristically had no qualms about the automatic, saying the engine's "moderate low-end torque blends very well with a torque converter." Over the hills and dales of Ford's Romeo, Michigan, proving grounds, *R&T* judged the Fairmont Turbo "more than adequate. Also, its added sound insulation makes for a less buzzy package than that of Mustang/Capri."

For some reason, Ford never quoted outputs for its turbo four in this period. The generally accepted figure was 140— the magic "1 h.p. per cu. in."—but this early version was surely nearer 130.

Though even that was well up on the normal four's 88 bhp and the optional six's 91 bhp, it was no more than what the two-barrel 302 V-8 delivered. But, as noted, the 302 wasn't available in a 1980 Fairmont. So the turbo-four option seemed the only real choice for performance-minded Fairmont buyers in 1980. Available in any model—even the workhorse wagon—it was reasonably priced at $481, though the required automatic cost an extra $340, bringing its real cost to $821. For comparison, the ES Option cost $378, but a separate and effective "handling suspension" was listed at a mere $44. Either chassis upgrade was a natural (some said necessary) partner for the blown engine.

Speaking of comparisons, MT's Nerpel gleefully recorded that the Fairmont Turbo prototype was discernibly quicker than the magazine's '79 six-cylinder/automatic wagon, which did 0-60 in 15.2 seconds. "If the production 1980 turbo-fours can come anywhere close to the engineering prototypes, this combo should be a winner."

But it wasn't, as CONSUMER GUIDE® virtually predicted in *Auto 1980*: "Ford's rationale for offering the turbocharged four [in the Fairmont] is difficult to figure out. Undoubtedly, the engine will appeal to sports-car buffs who'd rather have a Mustang but need the room of a full six-passenger sedan...but [this engine has been] a disappointment to many experts who expected more performance and refinement. There's also the question of whether the typical Fairmont buyer will be ready to accept the complexity of the turbocharger....So although [this engine] will add a touch of glamour to the

1980 Fairmont line, it may not be as popular as in the Mustang."

Nowhere near, as it turned out, despite being plastered all over the brochures. Installations totaled just 1158, a mere 0.4 percent or so of total 1980 Fairmont production, versus some five-percent turbos among this year's Mustangs (roughly 13,500 out of 271,000). Hindsight shows the reason why: As ever, Ford compact buyers wanted the known simplicity and dauntless reliability of workaday power-plants, not some exotic, potentially troublesome pseudo-European engine. Exit the Fairmont Turbo, never to be seen again. However, the turbo engine itself *would* be seen again, but that's a story for the next chapter.

Advertising again compared the big Ford LTD with Rolls-Royce for ride and quietness. The one significant mechanical change was the availability in most areas of the new four-speed overdrive automatic with the standard 302 and optional 351 V-8s. A fleet-market "S" sedan and wagon joined the lineup, but less than 20,000 were ordered. The premium Landau series was rechristened LTD Crown Victoria, reviving a mid-Fifties name, but less than 50,000 were called for. Total full-size Ford sales for 1980 were a disaster; output plummeted more than 200,000 units, leaving the big Ford in 16th place among domestic nameplates.

On paper, Lincoln appeared fairly well prepared for the second energy crisis as it unveiled both a downsized Continental and a new Mark, the VI. More alike than ever, each line nonetheless retained its traditional appearance "cues," but not the big-block V-8s. Instead, they carried a standard 302 with a newly developed

throttle-body electronic fuel injection system. Output was a lowly 129 horse-power, but the familiar, now optional 351 had scarcely more muscle, a rated 140 bhp. It was all for the sake of CAFE, of course. The new corporate OD automatic also aided efficiency.

Underneath was the body-on-frame "Panther" platform of the '79 LTD/Marquis, with the same wheelbase for the Mark VI coupe and a three-inch-longer 117.3-inch span for other models. Compared to their immediate predecessors, the '80s were some 10 inches shorter in wheelbase and about 800 pounds lighter, yet almost as roomy thanks to their taller, boxier bodies. They also handled better on the Panther's all-coil suspension, and refinement benefited from retuned body mounts and suspension bushings, plus standard high-pressure radial tires.

Thus Lincoln had come full circle—and back to its old image problem of the Fifties: too much like a Mercury, let alone a Ford. History-wise observers would have realized that the 1958-60 experience proved the inappropriateness of Mark sedans, yet here was a four-door Mark VI virtually identical with the Continental sedan. The main differences were hidden headlamps (Continentals reverted to exposed lamps, albeit rectangular, horizontal quads), fancier trim, and the expected opera windows and humped trunklid. Both Marks were available in base and upmarket "Signature Series" guise. The standard Continental coupe and sedan were slightly detrimmed but still very expensive at $13,250 and $13,650, respectively, about $3000 below base Mark VIs.

Nevertheless, time would prove the wisdom of this basic Lincoln design,

which would surprise most everyone by enduring through decade's end as one of Detroit's most popular and profitable products. For now, though, everyone was hurting, L-M Division more than most. Mercury's model-year production plunged a hefty 48 percent below its '79 level, Lincoln's a whopping 60 percent. Unhappily, things wouldn't get better right away.

The same would be true in trucks despite a brighter look for this year's Bronco and light-duty F-Series pickups. The result of a $700-million "truck program for the 1980s," both sported new wind tunnel tested front sheetmetal that was claimed to reduce air drag and thus "horsepower requirements," which presumably translated into more economical open-road cruising. Flaresides complemented this more aggressive front with more muscular-looking rear fenders, now made of fiberglass to resist corrosion. All pickups featured more easily removed tailgates (presumably to facilitate camper shell installation) and a bit more glass area (up nine percent on Regulars, 13 percent on SuperCabs).

Other shared changes included a new maintenance-free battery, new-design instrument panel of molded Lexan plastic with international gauge/control markings (already adopted for most Ford cars), newly optional "Sports" (full) in-

Although the Mustang hardly changed for 1980, the Cobra (top) received a mild facelift front and rear. The $1482 package included the "boy racer" exterior graphics plus hood scoop, tuned exhaust, black sport mirrors, engine-turned dash panel, tach, heavy-duty suspension, 190/65R × 390 TRX tires on forged aluminum wheels, and the Turbo four. The 255 V-8 was a $144 delete option. Fiberglass fenders, new Free Wheeling packages, and "wind tunnel tested aerodynamic styling" were found on the '80 Flareside pickup (above).

strumentation including tachometer, upgraded factory sound systems, and a convenient new resume-speed feature for the optional cruise control. Broncos and Styleside pickups took on wrapped taillights that obviated the need for separate side markers, anti-corrosion measures were more extensive across the board, and colors and trim received the usual shuffling.

Bolstering F-Series model choices for 1980 was a 350 Styleside with dual rear wheels, a first for Ford. Powerteams expanded for both F-Series and Bronco. The base 49-state engine was now the tried-and-true 300-cid six, or 4.9-liter in newly fashionable metric terminology. The equally familiar 5.0-liter/302 V-8 was standard in California and available elsewhere. Also optional for both was the 5.8-liter/351. A 6.6-liter/400 V-8 was the top power option for four-wheel-drive F-

250s and all F-350s.

But the big light-duty news was Twin I-Beam front suspension for all 4×4s, including Bronco—the first-ever independent front suspension on a four-wheeler. Ford boasted spending $50 million on it as well as nearly 4000 hours in lab tests and nearly a million miles on the road. This may explain why the company took out a patent on the design. Touted as "a major engineering breakthrough," it not only reduced weight but improved ride and handling by removing 50-150 pounds in unsprung weight from the front wheels compared to the previous monobeam front axle with tube-encased driveshaft.

Simplicity was a hallmark: two stamped lateral arms of high-strength steel on a central pivot, a differential carrier integral with the left arm, and exposed halfshafts running through uni-

versal joints. The right shaft was splined to an intermediate slip joint that allowed a slight amount of shaft compliance for turning. As before, Bronco and F-150 used front coil springs; F-250/350 retained semi-elliptic leaf springs. All the Twin I-Beam 4×4s came with an integral skidplate to protect the diff, a not inconsiderable benefit. Two additional benefits accrued to Bronco: slight gains in wheelbase and front track, which now measured 104.7 and 65.1 inches, respectively.

The successful Econolines and their Club Wagon passenger equivalents weren't drastically altered for 1980, as most changes involved only detail trim, color, and equipment revisions. However, engine choices now duplicated the new F-Series lineup, including the 400 V-8 option. P-metric radial tires were standardized for E-100/150, and a new "Comfort Ride" suspension with softer spring and shock calibrations became optionally available for E-250s.

Even less change attended the little Courier pickup—just a new Exterior Decor Group option with additional bright moldings. As before, buyers could choose the basic 107-inch-wheelbase model with a six-foot cargo box, or a seven-footer on a 113-inch span. Both chassis were also offered in cab-only form for vocational body mounting. Though its Japanese heritage was still plain to anyone who saw a Courier parked next to Mazda's own B1800, Ford continued talking as though the little hauler was truly its own. One of this year's press blurbs, for example, proclaimed Courier "another tough truck from Ford"—technically correct, though not wholly accurate in fact.

Design revisions in light-duty F-Series offerings hadn't always shown up in their heavier counterparts, but this year they did as Ford unveiled its first fully redesigned medium conventionals in four decades. Though general cab appearance was broadly similar to that of the new Bronco and F-Series pickups, the new F-600/700/800 stood apart with their own big, Louisville-style eggcrate grille, flanked by new square headlamps recessed in bulging fenders with rounded corners. But one couldn't say "front-end sheetmetal" anymore, because the grille surround and fenders switched from steel to fiberglass and the grille to ABS plastic, all for less weight and freedom from rust.

Elsewhere, simplification for improved strength and durability was the order of the day. Among numerous new features were all-welded construction with one-piece windshield header, a single roof inner panel, a welded-on heat/vent plenum chamber that doubled as cowl reinforcement, sturdier box-section floor members, and stronger roof pillars and door hinges. Anti-corrosion measures were extensive, including the use of galvanized steel for some body panels, zinc-coated metal for doors and cowl sides, and the dipping of hinges, joints, and similar smaller parts in aluminized wax or a chromate-zinc solution.

Underneath was an equally new frame with straight siderails to facilitate vocational-body installation. Depending on body and GVW, siderail torsional rigidity was 36,500, 50,000, or 100,000 pounds per square inch. Other chassis improvements included longer front springs, new rubber bushings for rear-spring eyes, wider front track, a new standard power steering system located for easier servicing, and a more reliable split-circuit brake system with new hydraulic booster (replacing vacuum). Powerteam choices comprised the trio of gas V-8s introduced for '79—two- and four-barrel 370s and four-pot 429—plus a new 8.2-liter Ford-built diesel V-8 (about 500 cid) available in turbocharged and normally aspirated form. Respective gas-engine ratings: 174, 204, and 234 net bhp. For the diesel: 165 and 205 gross bhp. All engines teamed with manual or four-speed automatic transmissions, the latter providing better economy in light of the continuing sales growth for self-shift mediums.

Inside, Ford managed to find a little extra leg room despite shortening the front-bumper-to-back-of-cab dimension (BBC) by five inches in the interest of easier maneuvering. Further enhancing comfort in the new mediums were upgraded seats, a redesigned instrument panel from the Bronco/pickup, and a spiffy new "high-level Custom" trim option.

With so much new to show, Ford did quite well in a total truck market that skidded nearly 29 percent in just one year, plunging from about 3.47 million units to just under 2.48 million. In fact, Ford was the only maker to increase its share of the light-truck market, tacking on 11 percentage points to end with 43.5 percent of that pie. Chevy remained a distant second in light trucks at about 33.6 percent despite selling close to 42,000 El Camino car-pickups, a vehicle Ford had now abandoned. Equally gratifying to Dearborn marketers, Ford led Chevy in individual light-truck lines from pickups and sport-utilities through passenger and commercial vans.

But the effect of new fuel shortages and soaring fuel prices was undeniable, and Ford suffered along with other truckmakers in 1980. Its total calendar-year registrations, including mediums and heavies, nosedived from 1.12-million units to just over 784,000, good for 31.7 percent of the total truck market. Chevy fell a like amount in volume but lost more in market share, surrendering about 1.5 percentage points versus Ford's 0.70-point loss. Even so, a loss is a loss no matter how small, and losses were something Dearborn could ill afford. Unhappily for Ford accountants and stockholders alike, things here weren't going to turn around for some time, either.

Topping the Pinto's final lineup was the '80 Squire station wagon (top). It stickered at $5320, but only 39,159 wagons were built that year, including the Pony and the regular model. During the Pinto's decade-long lifetime, an impressive total of 3,150,309 units were built. Ford boasted that its medium-duty F-Series trucks, shown here in a tractor/trailer combination (center), were adaptable to virtually any specialized body application. They had, Ford said, an "I-want-to-work" appearance highlighted by "swept-back fenders and a new front end, made of corrosion-free fiberglass." The LTD Country Squire (above) had price tags of $7463 (two-seat) and $7609 (three-seat), but production totaled a disappointing 11,718 units, down from 37,955 the year before. Total big Ford output skidded to just 141,562 units for the model year.

1 9 8 1

After a dismal 1980, Ford Motor Company endured a 1981 that in most respects was just as grim. The firm posted another huge loss—$1.06 billion, not quite as bad as the previous year's deficit but gruesome enough—and working capital had shriveled to a razor-thin $237 million. It would have been worse had continuing profits from Ford Europe not partly offset these staggering setbacks in America.

There was more bad news on the production front. For the model year, Ford Division dropped to less than a million cars for the first time since 1958, and was almost passed by Oldsmobile. Mercury sold a bit better, avoiding the massive factory layoffs of most other makes, but Lincoln took another plunge, ending below 70,000.

The deep recession continued to dampen car sales generally and American-built models in particular. With inflation pushing prices ever higher and car-loan interest rates soaring to unbelievable levels, many Americans could no longer afford new cars—or at least to buy them as often as they once did. Dearborn's share of this shrinking market was itself shrinking,

hitting an all-time low of 16.5 percent at the end of 1980. Worse, the general slump came at a time when the firm could least afford it. Ford had committed to a multi-billion-dollar program that would overhaul its entire product line by mid-decade, and the sudden sales drop only accelerated the drain on the company's capital reserves.

Of course, American Motors, Chrysler, and General Motors were hurting, too, plagued like Ford by higher production costs and inferior workmanship compared to increasingly popular Japanese makes. But Detroit now actually had a friend in Washington, the newly elected Reagan Administration, which provided partial relief this year by "jawboning"

The Escort represented a complete re-think at Ford Motor Company about how to build small cars. It rode a 94.2-inch wheelbase, virtually the same as the Pinto it replaced, and weighed about 2000 pounds, a svelte 400 pounds less. The hatchback SS (above) was the sportiest model in the line. It listed at $6139. The luxury GLX (below) cost an additional $343.

Japan's Ministry of International Trade and Industry (MITI) into agreeing to a temporary limit on car exports to the U.S. The idea behind this Voluntary Restraint Agreement (VRA) was to give Detroit producers time to bring out new fuel-efficient models of their own as well as to improve workmanship and modernize manufacturing systems, all of which

would presumably "level" the competitive playing field. As it was, Japanese automakers reportedly enjoyed a unit cost advantage of some $1500, yet Japan's formidable tariff and regulatory barriers all but precluded U.S. companies from competing in that market.

Those rankling issues, not to mention the burgeoning unemployment in Motown as the recession deepened, made for one very hot political potato that had to be addressed. Nevertheless, the VRA represented a stunning turnaround for a President long known as an advocate of traditional free-enterprise economics and a *laissez-faire* attitude toward business. Detroit lobbyists surely earned their pay with the VRA. Still, there were critics on both sides who said that perhaps the real issue was not how Japanese producers had become more competitive but why Detroit had fallen behind.

But the U.S. industry was not without competitive products. As proof, Dearborn unveiled two highly significant ones this year: the Ford Escort and the near-identical Mercury Lynx, the all-new "world car" replacement for the Pinto/Bobcat. Like Chrysler's similar Dodge Omni/Plymouth Horizon of 1978, these new subcompacts were a big departure from usual domestic practice: front-wheel drive, all-independent suspension, overhead-cam four-cylinder engine of advanced specification, and a truly international package size. As Dearborn's first direct challenger to a hoard of small imports—mainly Japanese models—Escort/Lynx was commercially crucial. It was also something of a symbol: a measure of the U.S. industry's ability to fight back against the strongest overseas onslaught ever.

Escort/Lynx was the end product of the "Erika" project that originated in 1972 when a powertrain development team within the Dearborn Engineering and Research Staff began exploring engine designs for the much smaller cars that might be needed in the Eighties. Meanwhile, Ford of Europe had embarked on a new front-wheel-drive car to replace rear-drive designs in the British and German lineups. This became the Fiesta, which bowed in the fall of 1976 and was also sold in America through 1980. It was such a success that European executives decided to offer a slightly larger car of similar design as the next step up the range. This idea dovetailed neatly with U.S. plans for a smaller successor to Pinto/Bobcat. By mid-1977, the two efforts had been brought together and the "world car" was born.

Complicated but sensible, the Erika project envisioned a single basic package designed for high-volume production so as to realize cost savings through economies of scale but tailored to suit buyer preferences in each market. Components would be a mixture of local and imported, again to cut costs. Early on, it was decided that Erika's engine would be developed

and engineered in Europe but built on both sides of the Atlantic, while manual transaxles and other running gear would come from Japanese affiliate Toyo Kogyo (Mazda). Because American demand would be higher, the optional automatic transmission would be developed in Dearborn. Body design would be a joint effort facilitated by computer hookups and frequent on-site personnel exchange.

Erika's heart was a clean-sheet overhead-cam four dubbed "CVH" for Compound Valve Hemispherical, a reference to its valve and head layout. It had long been engineering gospel that, for a variety of reasons, a hemispherical (or halfdome) combustion-chamber shape was the best for both efficiency and performance, and that spark plugs are best placed as close to the chamber center as possible. The CVH design reflected this thinking by having valve stems slanted at 45 degrees, which in turn allowed relatively larger valve faces, plus separate cam lobes for both intakes and exhausts and crossflow breathing. Two displacements were planned, 1.3 and 1.6 liters, but only the latter was ultimately built in the U.S. The CVH also featured a machined aluminum cylinder head, and a block made of reliable cast iron.

To save space up front, the compact engine was mounted transversely in the now almost-universal manner of small front-drive cars. The standard four-speed manual transaxle was a wide-ratio unit with a slightly overdriven top gear. The new automatic transaxle (ATX) featured what was called a "splitter" gearset within the torque converter. This apportioned torque between the converter and a direct mechanical drive to the halfshafts, thus reducing frictional losses

from converter rotation for better fuel efficiency.

Dimensionally, Erika was to match the outgoing rear-drive Escort, the next-to-smallest model in Ford's European line, but would be narrower and slightly shorter than the U.S. Pinto. A three-door hatchback sedan would be offered everywhere. Americans would also get a five-door wagon, while Europeans could choose from a five-door sedan and three-door wagon as well. Styling was a separate, though coordinated, effort. Partly because of U.S. safety requirements, the American Escort wasn't as smooth as its overseas cousin, though Dearborn touted its sedan's 0.40 drag coefficient—quite good for a short, boxy car all things considered. An aerodynamic aid common to all sedans was a tiny back bustle (called a "decklid kicker") that helped lower drag and rear-end lift by minimizing turbulence.

The U.S. Escort emerged on a 94.2-inch wheelbase, virtually the same as the Pinto's, and also used rack-and-pinion steering. Everything else was different. Front suspension featured MacPherson struts instead of A-arms, with lower control arms, anti-roll bar and, of course, coil springs. The rear was fully independent—much more modern

Compared to the Pinto it replaced, the Escort featured front- rather than rear-wheel drive and four-wheel independent suspension in place of ox-cart rear leaf springs. Overall length was down by seven inches (15 for wagons), but higher seating and greater glass area made for a more comfortable cabin. Priced from $5731 to $6788, the wagon (below) came in five guises: base, L, GL, GLX, and SS. Production for '81 totaled 128,173 wagons, plus 192,554 hatchbacks.

The Escort GLX hatchback (above) retailed for $6467, making it the most expensive three-door model offered in 1981. New for '81 was the Granada, based now on the Fairmont's Fox platform and riding its 105.5-inch wheelbase. However, it was a bit longer and heavier and had more formal styling. The top-of-the-line GLX four-door sedan (above right) listed at $7148.

than Pinto's leaf-sprung live axle—comprising one-piece forged spindles mounted laterally, pivoted inboard on the rear crossmember and acting on vertical shock/struts. Coil springs were positioned between the arms and longitudinal chassis beams above. A tie rod ran from the hub carrier on each lateral arm to a forward mounting point. In all, it was an elegant, low-cost IRS arrangement, and gave Ford a class exclusive among domestics, not to mention many imports. As in later Pintos, the standard front brakes would be discs, with drums continuing at the rear. Naturally, extra-cost power assist would be available for both brakes and steering.

Though three inches narrower outside, the "world car" was much roomier than the Pinto inside, thanks to thinner, space-saving doors and the more compact new drivetrain. In overall length, the Escort three-door was some seven inches shorter than the Pinto Runabout, the wagon a full 15 inches trimmer than its predecessor. Escort was also several hundred pounds lighter, had higher seats, and much more cargo space and glass area. In all, the Escort was not only a genuine import-fighter but America's most sophisticated subcompact.

The Escort was greeted with enthusiasm, if not always the highest praise. CONSUMER GUIDE® magazine's initial test car ran 0-60 mph in 15.4 seconds with four-speed—nothing to get excited about—and returned a creditable 25.5 mpg in demanding city/suburban driving. CG thought it a great advance over Pinto, but concluded that against foreign rivals it "sadly lags behind in ride and handling control, interior design, and workmanship. Still, Ford's billion-dollar baby has a lot of potential. All it needs is detail refinement to stand up fully to the best in its class. Then, it would be a 'world car' in the true sense of the term."

Ford evidently took such comments to heart, because running changes were instituted almost as soon as sales began. By the end of the model year, the Escort (and Lynx) had become more pleasant, better-riding, and smoother-running. And such "fine tuning" would continue all the way through the end of this design as a 1990 model. Considering the gloomy national economy and the depressed car market, Escort sold exceedingly well in its debut season. More than 60,000 were retailed between October and the end of December 1980. The model-year '81 total came to over 320,000, making it the second most popular car in the country (after Chevrolet's Chevette). Lynx, as expected, did about half as well—near 112,000—though that was far above its predecessor's best. Competitive prices helped—as little as $5158 for the basic three-door Escort—as did a choice of five trim levels. Escort offerings comprised standard, L, GL, luxury GLX, and sporty SS. Chevy took issue with the last, so Ford would substitute the old-faithful GT initials after this one year.

Pushed out of the limelight by Escort was a new Ford Granada. Actually, the '81 version of Ford's erstwhile intermediate was less new than it appeared, for it was essentially a restyled Fairmont—two- or four-door sedan—with softer chassis settings and plusher interior trim. Still, a reconstituted Fairmont wasn't a bad thing to be. The '81 Granada weighed some 350-400 pounds less than the 1975-80 models, offered more room inside, a better control layout, more precise steering, greater maneuverability, and somewhat better ride control. Fuel economy was also improved even if performance wasn't. While this bit of badge engineering made economic sense for Ford, the Fairmont remained a better buy in the opinion of CONSUMER GUIDE® magazine's editors. Nevertheless, model-year volume rose by some 30,000 units, to more than 121,000, spread among L, mid-range GL, and plush GLX models.

Mustang's extracurricular muscle-flexing during 1980 was too late to affect the '81 models, which were little changed visually or mechanically. Reclining backrests were added to the standard bucket seats, interior trim was upgraded in ap-

pearance and completeness, and the options list lengthened with the addition of power door windows and a T-bar roof with twin lift-off glass panels. The 2.3-liter turbo-four was now limited to manual transmission only.

A five-speed overdrive manual gearbox had been announced as an option for both Mustang fours in mid-1980, and it was more widely available for '81. This pulled a shorter 3.45:1 final drive (versus the four-speeder's 3.08:1) for better off-the-line snap. The overdrive fifth was geared at 0.82:1 for economical highway cruising. It was just what the base Mustang needed.

Except for one thing—in adding the extra gear, Ford goofed. As CONSUMER GUIDE® noted at the time: "Our biggest objections to the five-speed are its linkage—stiff, yet vague—and its shift pattern. As with the four-speed, first through fourth are in the usual H-pattern. But fifth is awkwardly located at the bottom of the dogleg to the right of and opposite fourth, instead of up and to the right.... Why Ford did it this way is a mystery, but it makes getting into or out of fifth real work. Our guess is that the engineers wanted to prevent inexperienced drivers from accidentally engaging overdrive and needlessly lugging the engine, as well as to prevent confusion with the often-used third. If so, they've succeeded admirably."

Ford apparently felt most drivers would want to downshift from fifth directly to third, bypassing fourth. At least that's what one transmission engineer told us. A more logical reason was that putting fifth over and up would have entailed excessively long arm reach. The factory's "official" explanation was that the U-shaped shift motion would better emphasize the economy benefits of the overdrive fifth gear. Whatever the reason, it just didn't work.

But even this annoyance would soon be forgotten. Performance was about to make a comeback in embattled Detroit, and Mustang would lead the charge. Meanwhile, production fell back drastically for '81: down one third to 182,552, a loss of nearly 89,000 units from 1980. And output would go lower still before making a surprising recovery.

Ford's other '81 models saw few changes apart from engine availability. The 4.2-liter/255-cubic-inch V-8 took over as standard in the full-size LTD, the 302 moving to the options column. The 351 Windsor, now in its last year, returned as the top option, rated at 145 bhp. The standard three-speed automatic transmission was phased out in favor of the four-speed overdrive unit introduced as a 1980 option. There were almost no alterations to appearance or equipment availability.

The compact Fairmont returned with no styling modifications either, but the lineup expanded with the addition of a Futura station wagon. The 4.2 replaced the 5.0 V-8 at the top of the engine chart, and the turbo-four option disappeared with the wind. New options included a Mustang-style diagnostic graphic display and digital clock with console, plus Michelin TRX wheels/tires and an illuminated entry system *a la* Thunderbird and the full-size Fords.

The Thunderbird itself also continued with little change. Ford had made history at mid-1980 by making the 3.3-liter/200-cid six a $76 credit option, the first time a six had ever been seen in the Bird. Now it was standard, with the 4.2- and 5.0-liter V-8s optional. External identification was provided by removing the below-bumper grille extension, and all models acquired the former extra-cost Exterior Luxury Group trim. In a move paralleling 1978-79, the 1980 Silver Anniversary model returned under the Heritage name but was otherwise the same. Its roof treatment was now applied to the middle Town Landau model, with smaller "coach" rear side windows framed by a wrapover roof band, plus rear-half vinyl top, bodyside striping, and nighttime coach lamps. Alas, model year production dropped by nearly half, to

86,693 units.

In fact, aside from Escort and Granada, Ford Division suffered lower production across the line. Mustang, as noted, dropped severely. The full-size line sank by nearly 10,000, Fairmont by almost 106,000. No wonder advertising began asking, almost plaintively, "Have you driven a Ford, lately?"

It was a reasonable question, because Ford—the company as well as its products—was embarking on a period of historic change. Some of this was prompted by the twin traumas of the recession and

Energy Crisis II, but it also reflected the rapid globalization of the world motor industry—increasing interdependence among vehicle makers despite unprecedented competition. Ford, of course, had been a large multi-national corporation from its earliest days. But starting in the Eighties, it would bring far-flung resources to bear on individual products as never before. The Escort "world car" was just the first of many.

Dearborn also began seeking joint ventures as never before, a necessity given the multi-billion-dollar price tags

As it turned out, the recession underway in 1981 would be hard on all Detroit automakers, and Ford was no exception. Its compact Fairmont, now in its fourth model year, suffered along with all the rest as total production plummeted from 317,105 units for 1980 to 211,300 in '81, a drop of 33 percent. The top-line Futura four-door sedan (top) retailed for at $6361. With output of 104,883 units, the four-doors were the easy favorites, followed by the station wagons, which attracted 86,284 buyers. The big Fords, facing a tough sell in 1981, saw only 9443 LTD Country Squires (above) ordered. List price started at $8640.

Mustang trotted into 1981 with the same models and engine lineup, although an $874 T-top (above) was now available. Coupe prices started at $6171. Only 5327 Mustangs received the 255-cid V-8 this year. The McLaren Mustang (left) featured a grille-less nose, low-riding "skirt" spoiler, functional hood scoops, stiff suspension, widely flared fenders, and a 175-horsepower version of the turbo-four. It sold for $25,000; at that price only about 250 were built.

that now attached to most any new-model development program at most any company—high stakes that left little room for marketing *mis*takes. Of course, Ford knew better than most automakers how easily financial defeat could be snatched from the jaws of product-planning victory, and it's probably true that the company was well served in the Eighties by memories of its painful Edsel experience. Yet, as time would prove, the difficulties of these years would not dampen innovation in Dearborn but encourage it.

For example, Ford had strengthened its ties with Toyo Kogyo in 1979 by buying a full 25-percent stock interest in the Japanese firm. Now, in 1981, Ford ar-

ranged to purchase up to 190,000 diesel passenger-car engines each year from BMW-Steyr Motoren G.m.b.H., which was itself a joint venture pairing Germany's famed Bavarian Motor Works with the Austrian company Steyr-Daimler-Puch. Though little known in the United States, S-D-P had long been a respected diesel-engine builder as well as a leader in four-wheel-drive technology. The engine in question was a new 2.4-liter turbocharged inline six designed by BMW for its own models. It was naturally a response to the equally severe impact of the second energy crisis in Europe that had made diesel cars more popular than ever.

Diesels attracted more American buyers than ever in the fuel panic of the

early Eighties, too. Ford, lacking both the time and the money for devising a passenger-car diesel of its own, wanted the BMW-Steyr engine as a way to get into this market. But by the time the engines were genuinely available, the market was waning rapidly as the oil shortage turned into an oil glut and gasoline not only flowed freely again but at reduced prices. So after building a handful of turbodiesel Continental Mark VII coupes for 1985-86, Ford ended its agreement with the Austrian consortium.

Still, Energy Crisis II would leave an important legacy in prompting the industry to begin work on adapting cheaper, more plentiful fuels for automotive use as alternatives to gasoline. Ford was quicker than most to recognize that the need for such fuels would loom ever larger in the future—if not strictly for conserving precious petroleum, then for helping to reduce the nation's growing air pollution problem via cleaner-burning substitutes.

Dearborn showed two interesting developments along this line in 1981. One was a prototype Alternative Fuels Vehicle (APV), a slick, very aerodynamic Escort-size coupe designed to run on a combination of gasoline and methanol. The other was the late-1981 announcement that a limited run of mid-size Ford Granada and Mercury Cougar sedans would be built with ordinary 2.3-liter "Lima" fours fueled by propane or "LP gas." The conversion was surprisingly simple. Two high-pressure tanks under the trunk floor with a combined 25-gallon capacity fed the gaseous propane to a solenoid-actuated fuel lock that opened when the engine was started. This, in turn, allowed the fuel to flow to a converter-regulator that reduced its pressure, thus changing it to a vapor for combustion. An ordinary one-barrel carburetor mixed this with air in the usual way. The only other change was higher 10:1 compression ratio to take advantage of propane's much higher octane rating: 110 versus 87 for regular unleaded gas.

CONSUMER GUIDE® and *Car and Driver* were among the few magazines to drive a propane Granada. Both agreed that the conversion worked quite well save the fact that no fuel could give decent performance in a heavyish car with such a small engine. But there were three nagging problems. Finding fuel wasn't easy (*CG* used an LP bottling station), and refueling came up a lot more often owing to propane's relatively lower heat energy per unit. Where the gas-four Granada carried an EPA city rating of 21 mpg with automatic, the propane car returned only 15 mpg. Most telling of all, however, was that propane wasn't much cheaper than gasoline—about 90 cents per gallon at the time versus about $1.10 for gasoline—which made Ford's projected fuel savings of $250 a year look a tad optimistic. On the other hand, propane had no additives to leave internal engine deposits the way gasoline does, which promised longer engine life and associated savings in less frequent replacement of items like spark plugs, oil, and filter. Ford calculated the propane system itself would last 200,000 miles, just the thing for high-mileage owners.

But interesting though it was, Ford's propane exercise was ultimately academic. As *C/D* summarized in July 1982, "[even] Ford sees a limited future for propane as an automotive fuel, since it's a by-

Thunderbird prices started at $7551 for 1981, an $1119—or 17.4-percent—increase from 1980. But it should be remembered that double-digit inflation was rampant in the early Eighties. One step above the base T-Bird was the $8689 Town Landau (top), which featured "luxury" wheel covers, an opera window wrapover band, 255 V-8, and more. Topping the line was the ultra-luxurious $11,355 Heritage (second from top). The LTD line was pared from 12 to eight models for 1981 and stickers were up about $600. Priciest of the sedans was the Crown Victoria, which listed at $8251 in two-door form (third from top). It wasn't very popular, however, with only 11,061 built. Buyers preferred the four-door models, such as the $7718 LTD (bottom), of which 35,932 were built.

Price leader among the '81 Granadas was the "L" two-door sedan (top): $6474. Ford boasted that the '81 Bronco (center) was the only full-size 4×4 with independent front suspension and that buyers had the option of buying automatic locking hubs: "No more muddy, frozen or wet feet!" was the sales pitch. Ford touted its pickup as America's best-selling vehicle. For '81, fuel economy ratings were improved, partly because of the new (and optional) 4.2-liter small-block V-8. Shown is the F-150 Ranger (bottom).

product of oil production. Methanol, it says, is a better bet because it can be made from [America's] huge coal reserves. That technology is still pretty costly, though, while propane power is not. Propane is portable, it's easily converted for use in a car, it's cheap and it does the job. At least for some folks. We're not quite ready to break the gasoline habit, however. As prices for good old lead-free keep falling toward a buck a gallon, it looks better and better all the time."

Ford's light-duty trucks certainly looked better than ever, but seldom had there been so few changes between model years. Tightening fuel-economy standards for trucks, now 18.0 mpg for 4×2s and 15.5 for 4×4s, prompted adoption of low-rolling-resistance P-metric tires for F-Series and Bronco, where axle ratios were again rejiggered toward the same end. Also new for those models were brighter halogen headlamps as standard and newly optional power windows, power door locks and, with four-wheel drive, automatic-locking front hubs. The debored 4.2-liter passenger-car V-8 was a new option for the F-100, four-speed overdrive manual transmission was newly offered in Bronco and the 4×4 F-150, and the corporate four-speed overdrive automatic transmission was a new option for 4×2 F-100/150/250s with 302 V-8. There was also one new F-Series offering: a four-wheel-drive F-350 Regular cab/chassis. The one other notable change for Bronco was first-time availability of two Snow Plow Preparation Packages like those already listed for the F-Series.

Elsewhere, the small Courier pickup was once more a virtual rerun, while the Econoline/Club Wagon fleet put most of the emphasis on new color and trim combinations. A new option group for the long E-150 Club Wagon was the whimsically named "King of Clubs." Featured were deluxe upholstery, carpeting, headliner and door trim, plus a pair of front swivel-and-recline captain's chairs and a number of popular individual options including power steering, automatic transmission, tilt steering wheel with "Fingertip Speed Control," dual electric remote-control door mirrors, extra engine gauges, tinted rear "Privacy Glass," power door locks, and whitewall tires. The previous Captain's Chair Package option continued as before.

Changes were just as sparse up among the mediums and heavies. The long-running 900 tandem model in the low-cabover C-Series was dropped, and there were the usual adjustments to proprietary diesel-engine availability and GVWs throughout the ranks, but that was about it.

Despite the lack of change, Ford notched a fractional percentage gain in a total truck market that declined in calendar-year registrations by over 291,000 units. The year-end totals showed Ford with 31.9 percent versus a virtually unchanged 29.8 percent for Chevy. Things went more Chevy's way in light-duty calendar-year production. Though both makes recorded higher volume, Chevy rose some 56,000 units against Ford's 52,000, and market shares changed accordingly, Ford losing 0.77 percent to close at 42.7 percent, though that was still way ahead of Chevy's 34.46 percent, up 0.88 from the previous year.

Fending off bad publicity had come to be a full-time job for Ford publicists, and this year they had to contend with two more negative events. Pinto fire cases raged on in the courts despite the 1980 pro-Ford verdict in Winnemac, Indiana. In June of 1981, the California Court of Appeals ruled against Ford by upholding a $6.3-million settlement awarded in a 1978 suit to Robert Grimshaw, who'd been burned over 90 percent of his body in one such accident.

The following month brought release of *Never Complain, Never Explain*, the much-ballyhooed life story of Henry Ford II by professional chronicler Victor Lasky. The publishers predictably hyped both author and subject to the hilt. Lasky was billed as "America's most feared biographer" while HF II was painted as a "rich little rich boy" with "all the money, all the women, all the power a man could want—any man but him, that is."

At least the stomachs of Dearborn PR types got some relief with this one. Trade weekly *Automotive News* termed Lasky a "hatchet man through earlier works on Jimmy Carter, Watergate, Robert Kennedy and John F. Kennedy." *AN* judged the book itself a "potboiler" comprising "some threads of fact and pieces of history woven together with wide bands of pure gossip and hearsay. [Lasky] could be nominated for cut-and-paste artist of the year; he could have a best-seller on his hands because he does tell a good story; he could [also] be the object of a lawsuit."

Included in *AN*'s review were comments from David L. Lewis, professor of business history at the University of Michigan and a contributor to an earlier Ford work by the editors of the book you are holding. "The elder Ford was described as a train with 28 tracks," Lewis told *AN*'s Jenny L. King. "And you'd never know which one he'd be traveling when he got to you. Perhaps Henry II is the same. He is as you perceive him. I have interviewed him at length myself," Lewis went on. "He treated me wonderfully well. He was gracious, charming and affable." Though Lewis surmised that biographer Lasky had never spoken with his subject face-to-face, he predicted that *Never Complain, Never Explain* "will spawn a dozen new books about Mr. Ford."

Lewis was both right and wrong. More books on HF II were indeed on the way. They wouldn't number a dozen, but there would be enough over the next few years to keep Ford's image-makers racing for the bicarbonate.

Ford's big trucks didn't change much for '81, but that didn't stop the 9000 cement mixer unit (top) from getting the job done. The F-800 was a versatile workhorse, fitted here with an Omaha Standard stake platform (center). "The top-of-the-line Econoline for 1981," said the PR blurb, "features a luxurious King of Clubs Wagon outfitted for sophisticated group parties or stylish family vacation travel" (bottom).

1 9 8 2

Dearborn ponycar performance, a surprise two-seater, and a new compact pickup helped carry Dearborn through the year in which the deep recession that had been going on since 1979 finally bottomed out. The U.S. auto industry as a whole suffered its lowest annual sales in 20 years, and Ford was not immune. The company's share of this diminished market held at just under 16.5 percent, but production was down across all car lines, off by more than 230,000 units in all. And there was another sizeable financial loss, this time $658 million—not as bad as the red ink of the previous two years but hardly encouraging, either. Ford's cumulative losses since 1980 now totaled a

staggering $3.26 billion.

But there were bright spots. Industrywide truck registrations rebounded to over 2.4 million for the calendar year, up almost 245,000 from 1981, and though bowing to Chevy as the leader in that category, Ford was still ahead in light-truck production, if only by some 10,000 units. Escort, voted 1981's "Most Significant New Domestic Car" in the annual *Car and Driver* readers' poll, shot to the top of the sales charts, ousting Chevy's antiquated Chevette by close to 75,000 units. Among compacts, Mustang remained a solid fourth, and Fairmont was right behind in fifth place despite a now five-year-old design. Unfortunately, Granada was well down among mid-sizers, Thunderbird fell even further behind, and the full-size Ford continued trailing the big Oldsmobile, Chevrolet, and Buick.

Enthusiasts cheered the newly fortified 302 V-8 that arrived this year as an across-the-board option for Mustang (and Mercury's Capri). The most potent Ford small-block in a decade, it was labelled HO, again for "high output," leaving

no doubt about its mission. Even better, it formed the heart of a reborn Mustang GT, heralded in steamy magazine ads with the headline "The Boss is Back!"

It certainly was, packing a muscular 157 horsepower and 240 pounds/feet torque which peaked at a low 2400 rpm. Features contributing to the new HO engine's higher output were a special camshaft adapted from a marine version of the long-running V-8, as well as a larger two-barrel carb, a bigger and smoother exhaust system, and low-restriction twin-inlet air cleaner. Teamed exclusively with four-speed overdrive manual transmission, this revitalized small-block made for the fastest Mustang in years. Claimed 0-60-mph acceleration was below eight seconds, but some magazines reported times closer to *seven*.

The GT looked much like the Cobra package it replaced, save for the merciful lack of the gaudy snake decal on the hood. It came only as a hatchback with the top-grade TRX suspension, which meant stiffer front and rear anti-roll bars, the grippy 185-section Michelin radial tires

412

on specially sized metric alloy rims, and recalibrated springs, bushings, and shocks. Also on hand were front airdam with integral foglamps, rear lip spoiler, black-finish trim inside and out, console, luxury seat and door-panel coverings, and other goodies—all for a reasonable introductory price of $8308. The hot HO engine was available for other '82 Mustangs at $402 with the TRX suspension or $452 without. GTs undoubtedly accounted for the bulk of installations. Incidentally, the tame 4.2 V-8, now in its final year for Mustang, was available in GTs as a $57 credit option, though few buyers were likely penny-wise and performance-foolish this way.

HO apart, the '82 Mustangs offered little to get excited about. Model nomenclature was revised, with L, GL, and GLX hatchbacks and notchbacks arrayed below the GT in ascending order of price and luxury. Standard equipment for these models now included a larger gas tank (up from 12.5 to 15.4 gallons, also true for GTs), wider wheels and tires, and a remote-control lefthand door mirror.

After compiling a poor reliability record, the turbo-four was withdrawn, though it would return in a considerably altered state in about a year. Other drivetrains stood pat save the optional 4.2 V-8, whose "mandatory option" SelectShift automatic transmission got a lockup torque-converter clutch, a device that would be increasingly popular in coming years. The more powerful new Mustang GT (and its Capri RS stablemate) signalled a performance revival in Detroit after a dull decade in which all U.S. automakers had learned to cope with government safety, emissions, and fuel economy mandates. Of course, Ford wasn't alone in swinging back to excitement. At midyear, GM rolled out a totally restyled and somewhat smaller third-generation Chevrolet Camaro and Pontiac Firebird. Yet despite this new competition and the continuing market slump, Mustang fared fairly well for a four-year-old design. Model-year production totaled about 130,500 against some 179,000 of the all-new Camaros and 116,000 Firebirds.

With its 5.0-liter V-8, tuned chassis, and race-inspired styling touches, the Mustang GT was quickly matched with the Camaro Z-28 and Firebird Trans Am in "buff book" comparison tests. While the GM cars won points for their superior handling and arguably more modern design, the Mustang was judged more practical for everyday use. And it was discernibly quicker. *Car and Driver* reported 0-60-mph times of 8.1 seconds for the GT against 8.6 for the injected V-8 Camaro with automatic and a comparatively sluggish 10.6 seconds for the carbureted V-8

Trans Am with four-speed. Writing in the magazine's August 1982 issue, technical editor Don Sherman noted that "...in terms of sheer visceral appeal, [the Mustang] is right up there with the Porsche [928]"—high praise indeed.

Not all was sweetness and light, though. In testing the GT's Capri sister ship, CONSUMER GUIDE® magazine found the power rack-and-pinion steering irritatingly vague, overly light, and lacking in feel. Wet-weather traction was a problem, partly because there was so much torque on tap. *CA* wasn't able to fully evaluate handling because the test coincided with one of the coldest weeks in Chicago's history, making conditions far from ideal. Even so, it was possible to light the back tires easily in brisk takeoffs, accompanied by occasional rear-end jitter that made the *CG* staff wonder what would happen in hard cornering on bumpy surfaces. *C/D*'s Sherman echoed these concerns: "In left-hand sweepers, the gas pedal acts as a power-oversteer switch.... That smooth two-step unfortunately turns into a jitterbug in right-hand bends, where power hop conspires to make life difficult."

Despite such faults, Ford's latterday performance ponycar had much to recommend it. *CG* judged its interior not only more practical than Camaro/Firebird's, but roomier as well. Though all three cars were hatchbacks, Ford somehow managed to provide a good deal more usable luggage space than GM. *CG* also liked Dearborn's manual gearbox for its agreeably lighter shift action (and more comfortably placed shifter) com-

The Excort-based EXP sport coupe went on sale in April 1981 as an '82 model. It was billed as "...the first two-passenger Ford in a quarter century...a fuel-efficient sport coupe with handling characteristics and styling designed to please driving enthusiasts. Although the EXP's size and sporty appearance are reminiscent of the classic two-passenger Thunderbird, Ford's newest model has a combination of high-technology features unheard of in the Fifties." Options included a flip-up sunroof and leather or shearling-and-leather seating surfaces.

Although the two-passenger EXP rode the same 94.2-inch wheelbase as the Escort, it weighed about 200 pounds more. And at $7387 it was priced nearly $700 higher than the sportiest Escort, the GT. Initially, it was powered by the 70-bhp CVH four, which made for slow going, but the 80-hp version of the 1600-cc four became available a bit later. The standard equipment level was praiseworthy, but the styling—especially the "frog-eye" headlights—was frequently criticized.

pared to the truck-like Camaro/Firebird linkage. The *CG* staff was divided on driving position, however, some preferring the snug, low-slung stance of the GM cars to the more upright "vintage" openness of the Ford products. Yet most agreed the Mustang/Capri was a far better compromise for those who had to contend with the daily drudgery of stop-and-go traffic, where the manual-shift Camaro/Firebird was tiring to drive for any length of time. Although there was still work to be done, the extra dose of performance pizzazz was a heartening sign to Mustang fans everywhere.

Pizzazz of a different sort arrived in Dearborn's first production two-seater since the '57 Thunderbird. In the tradition of two best-selling Fords of the past—Maverick and the original Mustang—the new EXP and a Mercury derivative called LN7 were announced about six months ahead of their actual model year, in early 1981. Both were sporty coupes based on the Escort/Lynx platform, planned around a more rakish body with reworked interior dimensions. In other words, they were to the "world cars" what the original Mustang had been to the Falcon.

EXP/LN7 (the designations signified nothing) shared the 94.2-inch Escort/Lynx wheelbase, as well as suspension, running gear, and instrument panel. They measured about 6.5 inches longer overall, nearly three inches narrower, and more than two inches lower. Styling drew sharp love/hate reactions. There was hatchback convenience, as on Escort/Lynx, but EXP wore a notchback lid that sharply limited trunk space, while LN7 was saddled with a large (and heavy) "bubble-back" rear window. Both bore large wrapped taillamps, prominently lipped wheelarches, and wide bodyside moldings about a third of the way up from the rockers. "Faces" were dominated by single rectangular headlamps in large nacelles faired into the hood and front fenders. They flanked a sloped center section running down to a grille composed of two wide, narrow intakes on EXP, 10 small slots on LN7. The overall effect was certainly different, though there were those who said the styling vaguely recalled an Escort with adenoid trouble. Others said the EXP/LN7 had a "frog-eye" look somewhat akin to—but not as "cute" as—the original Austin-Healey Sprite.

Underneath, EXP/LN7 differed from Escort/Lynx in using stiffer springs and shock valving for flatter cornering response. Initially offered for the coupes, and later extended to the sportier sedans, was an optional suspension designed around Michelin's premium TRX tires in a new-to-America P165/70R-365 size. This setup comprised harder pivot bushings for front and rear lateral control arms, harder rear tie-rod bushings, stiffer shock valving all-around, higher-rate front springs, larger-diameter front anti-roll bar, and variable-rate (instead of constant-rate) rear springs. With either suspension, power steering came with higher-effort valving for more precise control and better road feel than on Escort/Lynx.

The coupes also carried more standard equipment than the sedans, in keeping with their higher list prices: $7387 for the basic EXP against $5518 for the least expensive Escort. Included were power brakes, electric rear-window defroster, full carpeting, tachometer and extra engine gauges, electric hatch release, digital clock, and a handy roller-blind shade to hide cargo from prying eyes.

Early road tests found a lot to like in the new little sportsters—except performance. The reason was that the sedans' 70-bhp CVH four had to pull about 200 extra pounds. Additional sound insulation and the extra comfort/convenience features accounted for some of the difference, but most of it was in the extra body bracing needed to support the heavy hatchback.

Ford recognized the problem and, as an interim step, made a shorter 4.05:1 final drive ratio a no-cost option with manual gearbox at the start of the formal 1982 model year. Testing an LN7 so equipped (the Mercury got more press play than EXP, probably because of its more radical shape), *Road & Track* recorded a 0-60-mph time of 15.0 seconds, about a second longer than the lighter sedan. CONSUMER GUIDE® clocked a lackluster 15.8 seconds for a similarly equipped LN7, and an even slower time of nearly 18 seconds for an automatic-equipped EXP.

Embarrassed by such reports, Ford offered a close-ratio gearset with 3.59:1 final drive that accomplished much the same thing as the wide-ratio box with 4.05 gearing. Then, in March 1982, came a high-output CVH engine developing 80 bhp at 5800 rpm, a 14-percent increase. The extra horses resulted from higher compression (upped from 8.7:1 to 9.0:1), larger air-cleaner intake, free-flow muffler and twin-branch exhaust manifold, higher-lift camshaft, and larger carburetor venturis. But this knocked only about a second off acceleration times—and magnified the noisy gruffness inherent in the "world car" engine.

As for roadability, most reviewers found the EXP/LN7 quite capable with the TRX package. Quantitatively, *R&T* ranked it up with such nimble handlers as the VW Scirocco. Qualitatively, the story was different. Nobody liked the power steering—too insensitive and overassisted—or the ride—an unhappy combination of overly stiff springs and overly soft shocks. CONSUMER GUIDE® judged the ride harsh, choppy, and irritating, but found the car fun to drive on smooth, twisty roads. And compensating for the Milquetoast performance was very good mileage: a genuine 28 mpg in *CG*'s test versus the government's 27-mpg city estimate.

Ford has often been accused of relying too heavily on market research ever since the Edsel debacle. This may have been the biggest problem with the new two-seaters. EXP/LN7 clearly aimed at a new sort of buyer: young, mainly single people seeking something sporty, personal, and fun for errand-running or the occasional cross-country trip with a favorite companion. What they got was an

economy coupe with somewhat dubious styling, indifferent workmanship, and no back seat (a promised rear jump-seat option never materialized). This was hardly a formula for success, so despite an extra-long model year, EXP managed only a bit more than 98,000 units. The LN7 did even worse, just over 35,000 units, and would be gone after 1983.

At least Ford was still trying to give people something they couldn't get elsewhere. Of course, Dearborn designers had never forgotten the magical two-seat Thunderbirds of 1955-57, and there might have been a new "little Bird" had it not been for the '79 recession and consequent difficulties at Ford's North American operations. Predictably, it would have been a cut-down version of the ninth-generation Fairmont-based design of 1980. Historian Richard M. Langworth, another contributor to the present volume, unearthed sketches for it in researching his 1980 book *Personal Luxury: The Thunderbird Story*. What's more, "a full-size model existed...as late as the spring of 1979."

Langworth says this was done "just for the fun of it, for the sake of fond memories...after the four-passenger car was locked up for production. In appearance it was a 1980 Thunderbird from the cowl forward and the rear window back. The difference was in between. Cut out of the wheelbase were 8.4 inches; the front seat was met by a carpeted package shelf that extended back to a not-distant rear window. The rear roof quarter contained genuine 1957-style portholes—they could have come off a production '57.

Frosted into the porthole glass was the legend 'Collector's Edition' and '1/2000.'"

Intriguingly, some outsiders suggested to Langworth that a two-seat Bird would have been tried for 1980 had Lee Iacocca remained in Dearborn. However, Langworth also reported that Ford insiders didn't think so, believing that "even Iacocca would have hesitated before committing funds for what is, after all, the sake of tradition. Iacocca's Thunderbird contribution was toward the body-sharing, high-selling models we have right now...." And, no doubt, the EXP.

Yet that new two-seater and the blocky ninth-generation Bird had not exactly been roaring sales successes, the more difficult early-Eighties market notwithstanding. Had Ford lost its marketing touch? Not at all. As veteran T-Bird designer Bill Boyer told Langworth: "You have to bear in mind the market in which [Fords] are sold. Ford dealers are volume dealers. They aren't too interested in luxury or prestige cars, and for this reason the four-door Birds of 1967-71 were quite a problem. It's a completely different orientation. Ford dealers aspire to what they have now—a [Thunderbird] marque image with high sales potential. This is the course we've taken. We're still trying to make the Thunderbird the most advanced car in the line, yet acceptable as a personal-luxury car." In retrospect, it's easy to see that Boyer was being quite prophetic. A very different and far more exciting T-Bird was on the way, a significant car for Ford's immediate future that would all but obliterate memories of the unfortunate ninth-generation Bird,

In addition to the EXP, which was at first marketed separately, the Escort lineup expanded for 1982 with the addition of a five-door hatchback (forefront), which was available in base, L, LX, and GLX guises at prices ranging from $5668 to $7302. It enjoyed a production run of 130,473 units, compared to 165,660 three-doors, 88,999 wagons, and 98,256 EXPs.

which saw output drop to just 45,142 units in its last year.

The rest of Ford's 1982 automotive story mainly involved refinements for improved fuel economy. A new engine was part of the plan—Dearborn's first domestic V-6. At 3.8 liters/232 cubic inches, this new "Essex" engine was about the same size as the successful Buick V-6 that had appeared in 1975 and was now a workhorse throughout the GM line. Ford's unit was far lighter, however—a mere four pounds heavier than the 2.3 "Lima" four, in fact—thanks to the use of weight-saving aluminum for cylinder heads, front cover/accessory drive, and intake manifold. With bore and stroke dimensions of 3.87×3.44 inches, initial outputs came in at 112 net horsepower at 4000 rpm and peak torque of 175 lbs/ft at 2600 rpm. An important powerplant for Ford's future, it was offered this year as Granada's top power option, a step-up choice for Thunderbird, and as the new standard engine for the basic F-100 pickup.

As expected, Escort added five-door sedans for 1982, but made few other changes. Identifying all models front and rear were blue oval emblems bearing old Henry's famous signature script. It was

Ads in 1982 blared out, "The Boss is Back!" And it was, except that Ford called it the Mustang GT. What was back was the 5.0-liter (302-cid) V-8, now in HO form with 157 horses and 240 pounds/feet torque. With its free-flowing exhaust and four-speed stick, the GT hatchback could thunder from 0-60 mph in under eight seconds—all for a modest base sticker price of $8308.

the first time the insignia had appeared on Ford exteriors since the late Forties, and it was adopted throughout the '82 line (including Bronco and light-duty F-Series pickups). Escort's five series returned minus the base and sporty SS wagons, but the new five-doors in stan-

dard, L, GL, and GLX trim lifted the model count from 10 to 12. Standard equipment upgrades included wider radial tires, power front-disc brakes for wagons, larger-diameter exhaust system and, with air conditioning, an accelerator switch that interrupted the A/C drive at full throttle, thus providing maximum performance.

Ford's middleweights also changed little this year, although all Fairmonts were now called Futura. The two-door sedan body style departed early and the wagon was restyled and transferred to the Granada line. The latter was offered as a base L, step-up GL and, as in its Fair-

mont iteration, as a high-zoot Squire with woody-look side trim. Reshaped fuel tanks in Fairmont and Granada sedans permitted the center of the trunk floor to be dropped slightly for extra cargo space. Gas caps with plastic tethers to prevent loss during fillups were new to these models as well as other '82 Fords. Fairmont's most powerful engine was now the 200-cid six, still in production after some two decades, though it was down now to just 87 net bhp. A new option for the Granada wagon was a rear window that could be flipped up for loading or unloading small items without having to open the entire liftgate. The new 3.8 V-6

416

Ford showed this "1982" Mustang convertible (right) at the Chicago Auto Show in February 1982, saying that it would debut "in limited quantity late this summer." In reality, the ragtop didn't appear until '83. "Representing Ford Motor Company's active reentry into domestic motorsports competition," said Ford, "the turbocharged Mustang GT is leaving its mark on its challengers. The Mustang GT, powered by a modified 1.7-liter four-cylinder Ford engine which produces 560 horsepower at 9,000 rpm, has breathed new life into the U.S. racing scene by winning both the Brainerd and Sears Point IMSA races in 1981." Advanced technology and aerodynamics were touted.

took over from the 4.2-liter V-8 as the top Granada engine.

Still seeking better fuel economy, Ford added a lockup torque-converter clutch to its three-speed automatic for six-cylinder Fairmonts, Granadas, and Thunderbirds, the same device found in this year's 4.2-liter Mustangs. Unlike GM's similar system, however, this one was effective in all forward ratios, not just top gear. The lockup clutch provided direct mechanical drive from crankshaft to propshaft, thus eliminating the inherent torque-converter slip that eats up fuel. It was one of many subtle extremes Detroit engineers were turning to in the face of tightening corporate average fuel economy targets. This year's mandate was 24 mpg. A practical demonstration of Ford's work in automotive electronics appeared in a new option for Thunderbird and LTD, which were otherwise virtual reruns. The '81 T-Bird had offered an optional electronic instrument cluster with digital speedometer and bar-graph readouts for fuel level and coolant temperature. This year's new "Tripminder" was the next logical step. A sophisticated quartz clock linked with the trip odometer, it kept tabs on fuel flow, vehicle speed, and real or elapsed time, from which it could calculate such information as instantaneous or average miles per gallon, fuel used, average trip speed, trip mileage, and journey time.

We should not forget that Lincoln finally fielded a "proper" luxury compact in this year's new Continental sedan. Taking over for the unfortunate Versailles, which had been canned after 1980, it boasted an impressive array of no-cost standards as well as "bustleback" styling *a la* Cadillac's successful, second-generation Seville of 1980. Ford denied any copying, but there's reason to wonder given Detroit's usual three-year new-model development time. Underneath was the stretched 108.5-inch-wheelbase Fox platform used for the Thunderbird (and Mercury Cougar XR-7). That meant the same suspension, of course, but spring/shock rates differed, and Lincoln claimed two firsts in the Continental's standard gas-pressurized shock absorbers and self-sealing radial tires. Hydraulically assisted four-wheel disc brakes and the four-speed overdrive automatic completed the basic specs. Standard power was the venerable 302 V-8, here in 130-

bhp carburetor form. The 112-bhp 3.8 V-6 was a credit option, but few were ordered and it was soon dropped.

There was only one body style, but Lincoln offered it in lush Signature Series and Givenchy "designer" editions that cost a cool $3000 more than the base model—up to $24,800. That was a lot, but everything was included: cruise control, variable-ratio power steering, air, electronic instrumentation, and a complicated travel computer with alpha-numeric "message center." Options ran to a garage door opener, power moonroof, wire-spoke wheel covers, and oversize fuel tank. Weighing in at 3600 pounds, the Continental was altogether the most efficient package Lincoln had sold in eons. And at near 24,000 copies, it sold respectably well considering the bleak economic times.

Efficiency was also still the name of

the game in light-duty trucks, hence the dandy new Ford pickup that arrived in March bearing the well-known Ranger badge, borrowed from the F-Series line. Though technically a 1983 offering, it's discussed here because of interim changes that distinguish the formal '83s from the early "1982½" models.

The choice of name was deliberate. Ford wanted everyone to know that the "new-size" Ranger had little to do with the small Japanese-made Courier and everything in common with the big F-Series—"engineered and manufactured by the [same] people who have made Ford the number-one-selling truck line in North America," as one press release was careful to note. It even looked like a scaled-down F-100, offered only as a Styleside with choice of seven-foot cargo box on a 108-inch wheelbase or an eight-footer on a 114-inch span. But "new-size"

really meant "compact," as the tape measure proved:

	Ranger "long"	Courier "long"	F-100 "short"
Wheelbase (in.):	113.9	112.8	116.8
Overall length (in.):	187.6	189.4	192.1
Overall width (in.):	66.9	63.0	77.2
Overall height (in.):	64.0	61.5	69.3
Bed length (in.):	85.0	86.0	81.0
Max. bed width (in.):	54.3	61.4	70.0
Min. bed width (in.):	40.4	38.6	50.8
Bed depth (in.):	16.5	16.0	19.5
Curb weight (lbs):	2550	2215	3181
Maximum payload (lbs):	1605	1400	1435-1630

No matter. A lot of people liked the idea of compact pickups, but not the idea of their purchase dollars flying off to Japan. The market was certainly worth going after: over half a million total sales in 1981 alone, by Ford's reckoning. GM had done a little reckoning of its own, so the Ranger had domestic competition right from the start in this year's new Chevy S-10 and GMC's nearly identical S-15. GM won this particular race, building over 209,500 S-models for calendar '82, but the Ranger was hardly disgraced at better than 159,000—a rollicking 54 percent of this year's F-Series volume.

Predictably, the Ranger was every inch a Ford in design, engineering, and construction: all-welded double-wall cargo box, Twin-I-Beam front suspension with coil springs, leaf-sprung live rear axle, standard front-disc/rear-drum brakes, recirculating-ball steering with optional power assist. Of course, GM's new compacts matched these features, and went Ranger one better with a 2.8-liter V-6 as an extra-cost alternative to a standard 2.5-liter four. Ranger offered only the same two four-cylinder engines as Courier, with the 49-state-option 2.3 "Lima" unit standard in California. Common to both were solid-state "DuraSpark" ignition, efficient viscous-clutch fan—and a strangling one-barrel carburetor. Even so, Ranger carried a higher maximum payload than the V-6s from GM, though one had to order the optional upgrade package with heavy-duty springs and rear axle as well as larger tires and power steering and brakes (base payload was 1210 pounds).

Other extras were as numerous as for the F-Series: Traction-Lok limited-slip differential, SelectShift automatic in lieu

The Mazda-built Courier was in its last year in the Ford truck lineup in 1982 as Ford had its own "better idea," the domestically built Ranger compact pickup. Still, 66,155 Couriers were sold for '82, this one (top) with the seven-foot cargo box. This F-100 Styleside pickup (center) wears the XL trim option. Prices started at $6713. The F-150, here in XLT trim (bottom), was the "heavy-duty" half-tonner. New for '82 were a 3.8-liter V-6, standard in the F-100, and an optional SelectShift with locking torque converter for both the V-6 and 4.2-liter V-8. Ford also crowed about having the best-selling truck line in America.

The Fairmont-based Granada was a flash in the pan: here in 1981, gone after '82. It garnered 121,341 orders the first year, and did about the same for '82 as 120,323 were built. Eight models were offered for '82, up two, both of them wagons (which Fairmont had droppped): a $7983 GL and an $8399 GLX. This GLX sports the $282 Squire woody package. The 200 six was standard for wagons; V-8s were no longer offered. Granada was replaced by the mid-size LTD for '83.

of the standard four-speed overdrive manual, air conditioning, intermittent wipers, "Tu-Tone" paint, fancy wheels, whitewall tires, "Western" door mirrors, AM/FM and AM/FM/cassette stereos, tilt steering wheel, reclining bucket seats, extra engine gauges, and a handy two-piece sliding rear window. Trim levels numbered four: base, XL, XLT, and sporty XLS. The last featured a four-spoke sport steering wheel like that on the new EXP, bucket seats with jazzy striped upholstery, black instead of chrome bumpers and grille, two-color bodyside tape stripes, and a charcoal finish on roof, hood, and around the door windows. Prices were competitive: $6203 for the basic "shorty" and $6354 for the longbed model, about dead-level with the new GM compacts and a bit lower than most imports, which were somewhat better-equipped in standard form.

CONSUMER GUIDE® judged the Ranger a worthy competitor in more ways than just price. Its test 2.3-liter XLS automatic was hardly a fireball, but easily kept pace with a V-6 S-10 Chevy. Moreover, the Ford was quieter, smoother-riding, and obviously better-built, with a tight, sturdy feel no rival could match. Observed economy wasn't so hot at 18 mpg, though perhaps not all that surprising for just 79 horses and 124 lbs/ft torque. CG also found the power steering too light and the cab too tight for long-legged types, and was disappointed that the cargo box was no bigger than those on most imports despite Ranger's higher payload ratings. Overall, though, CG very much liked this new in-between Ford. As if to confirm CG's judgment, the Ranger would become America's best-selling compact truck, foreign or domestic, by 1987.

With Ranger getting most of the '82 marketing emphasis, other Ford trucks were little changed. The new 3.8-liter corporate V-6 became the new standard powerplant for F-100s, except for those sold in California and high-altitude areas, where the old 4.9-liter/300-cid straight six was continued. Ordering SelectShift with either V-6 or the 4.2 V-8 brought the same new locking torque-converter clutch found in Ford passenger cars. Still another economy move was a new F-100

FS model, the initials denoting "Fuel Saver." EPA-rated at 22 mpg city, it came only as a short-wheelbase 4×2 Styleside with the 4.9 six, four-speed manual transmission, high 2.47:1 rear axle, and a limited selection of mostly lightweight options. Camber adjustment was added to Twin-I-Beam on F-100s and 150s, and electric remote-control door mirrors joined the options list along with new cast-aluminum and deluxe styled-steel wheels. The advent of Ranger required new names for Bronco and F-Series trim levels, so these were now base, XL, XLT Lariat, and XLS. The last was roughly comparable to the Ranger XLS, with plenty of black accents outside and sportier trimmings inside.

Other models changed even less. The Courier was a virtual rerun save for a newly standard AM radio. It even missed out on the new 2.2-liter diesel-four available this year in its Mazda B-Series counterpart—a significant omission all things considered. But in retrospect, this was just a sign that the Courier would not be back for '83. Mazda would continue with its version, but Ford no longer needed an imported compact pickup now that the Ranger was around. As for Bronco and the Econoline/Club Wagon, they got only detail trim and color revisions. Mediums and heavies also saw no appreciable change.

1 9 8 3

Saleswise, 1983 was a mixed year for Dearborn. While every domestic nameplate save Chevrolet and Pontiac saw higher output, Ford was swamped by a surging Oldsmobile, whose full-size models constituted the year's best-selling car line. As Olds also had the most popular intermediate series, the Cutlass, it slashed into second place, making this the first year since 1905 that Ford did *not* finish in the top two in U.S. production. In fact, Ford ended '83 at number-four, behind Buick, despite building nearly 35,000 more cars for the model year. Ford, however, *did* hang on to the number-two spot in sales, due in good part to the large number of Escorts and Tempos produced in Canada for sale in the U.S.

But it wasn't all bad. Mercury rallied to near 1981 sales levels, Lincoln racked up its first 100,000-unit model year since

'79, and the Ford Escort remained king of the subcompacts, garnering 142,000 more sales than Chevy's ancient Chevette, its nearest rival. There was also strong support from the truck side. Ford returned to the top spot in both light-duty truck production and total calendar-year registrations, earning respective market shares of 41.6 and 31.65 percent to Chevy's 39.7 and 30.4 percent. Only the compact Ranger's results were disappointing, as it still trailed Chevy's S-10.

The U.S. motor industry had been through some very rough times of late—and they weren't over despite signs of a general economic recovery as the '83 model year began. Some critics suggested that the events of the early Eighties, the result of a complex set of forces, had forever changed the way American cars were designed and manufactured. They were right. Not widely appreciated at the time was the fact that Ford was in the vanguard of what would be an industry-wide renaissance.

All very fitting as Ford Motor Com-

pany observed its 80th year in business. Especially since something else was staging a comeback in Dearborn: "Total Performance." Though knocked out of second, Ford Division fielded one of its most exciting lineups in years, with an unusual number of new or heavily revised models, plus a new emphasis on fun combined with practical high technology. Nowhere was there a better expression of Detroit's new way of doing business—or its determination to survive in the face of unprecedented foreign competition and an economic crisis of historic proportions.

A perfect example of the new order was this year's dramatically restyled Thunderbird. Though mechanically and structurally similar to the 1980-82 models, this 10th-generation design signaled a complete break with established Ford styling philosophy. Familiar fripperies once used to imply luxury and status—half-vinyl tops, stand-up grilles, opera windows, and all the rest—were consigned to history. Henceforth, aerodynamic considerations would make Dear-

born design "functional" and "organic"— a new aesthetic that relied on form for attractiveness instead of tacked-on glitz.

Design development for the '83 Thunderbird and companion Mercury Cougar involved more than 500 hours of wind-tunnel tests with ⅜-scale and full-size clay models beginning in early 1979, and eventually led to more than 850 changes. The result was sleek—even daring—and far more distinctive than the square-cut Chrysler Cordoba/Dodge Mirada and more contemporary than midsize GM coupes like the Olds Cutlass and Buick Regal, which had received a socalled "aerodynamic" facelift for '81.

As before, Thunderbird/Cougar shared roughly the same sheetmetal, but contours were rounded now, decoration minimal. In plan (overhead) view their bodies tapered markedly toward the front to minimize frontal area, a key factor in reducing air drag. The same reason prompted a much "faster" new 60-degree windshield angle, the steepest slope ever seen on a Dearborn production car. The

main difference was in rear rooflines. Cougar went "formal," with a near-vertical backlight and upswept rear side window line. Thunderbird sported a more rounded backlight and a smoother window-to-deck transition. Wind-tunnel results favored the Ford, which registered an impressive 0.35 drag coefficient at the Lockheed facility in Georgia. The Mercury's 0.40 Cd didn't look so hot by comparison, but that didn't bother the product planners. Let Cougar appeal to traditional mid-size coupe buyers; Thunderbird would be aimed at trendier types.

Curiously, a rival aero-engineer claimed the notchback Cougar was more slippery than the slantback Bird: "We put both of them through our new wind tunnel," he told the editors at the GM Tech Center in 1983. "There was a definite advantage for the Cougar—less turbulence aft." He then coined an interesting term for Ford Motor Company's new fling with slippery shapes: "perceived aerodynamics."

More familiar fare lurked beneath

the new styling. Unit construction continued on what Ford now called the "Sshell," one of several spinoffs from the rear-drive "Fox" platform, but the '83 was detectably smaller than the previous T-Bird/Cougar. Notable were a 4.4-inch cut in wheelbase, now 104.0 inches, a 2.8-inch chop in overall length (to 197.6 inches), and 3.0 inches less width (to 71.1). Overall proportions were much the same, but rear overhang was trimmed, which meant about three cubic feet of trunk space in exchange for a slightly tighter turning circle. Despite the shrink-

Just as the 1980-82 Thunderbird had been based on Ford's versatile "Fox" platform, so too was the '83. Not that one could tell by looking at it, for the new Bird was a bit trimmer in most dimensions—riding a 4.4-inch-shorter 104-inch wheelbase—and far sportier looking than before. Enthusiasts rejoiced over the $11,790 Turbo Coupe (bottom left), a serious road car powered by a 142-bhp turbo four (bottom right) mated to a five-speed stick. Inside, the driver sat on contoured Lear-Siegler bucket seats (below).

Aside from the Turbo Coupe, there were two other '83 T-Birds: a $9197 base model, here with extra-cost styled wheels, and the luxury-laden $12,228 Heritage, which boasted unique quarter windows and coach lamps. Ford advertised the '83 as "Conceived for today with an eye on tomorrow," and the public agreed as output shot up from 45,142 units to 121,999.

age, interior space was about equal to 1980-82 except for 1.2 inches less rear legroom.

Predictably, the latest T-Bird/Cougar chassis retained all-coil suspension with modified MacPherson-strut geometry and anti-roll bar in front and a four-link live-axle in back, plus standard rack-and-pinion power steering and power front-disc/rear-drum brakes. One new wrinkle was standard nitrogen-pressurized shock absorbers as introduced on the '82 Continental sedan, claimed to improve handling response with no penalty in ride comfort.

Bird buyers found a few surprises on the '83 model and engine charts. The Town Landau was dropped for an equally well-equipped base model starting at $9197. Heritage returned as the most expensive offering, with standard amenities like power windows, tinted glass, electronic instrumentation, velour upholstery, and illuminated keyless entry system included on its $12,228 base sticker. The standard powertrain for this pair was the 3.8-liter "Essex" V-6, down two horsepower to 110 net bhp, teamed with three-speed SelectShift automatic. Optional was the revived 302 V-8, newly revamped with "central" throttle-body-type electronic fuel injection that yielded 130 bhp, the same as when last available

in 1981 and 10 bhp more than the discontinued 4.2 V-8. In the T-Bird, it teamed only with the corporate overdrive automatic, which could be had at extra cost with the V-6.

But the real excitement was the mid-year Turbo Coupe, the sportiest T-Bird since the original mid-Fifties two-seaters and the first ever powered by a four-cylinder engine. With specially uprated chassis, mandatory five-speed manual transmission, and multi-adjustable bucket seats, it made even jaded enthusiasts take notice.

The Turbo Coupe engine was actually a reengineered version of the blown 2.3-liter overhead-cam "Lima" four last offered on the '81 Mustang/Capri. Mechanical changes involved junking the carburetor for Bosch multiport electronic injection and positioning the turbocharger upstream of the induction system to "blow through" it rather than "draw down" from it. Ford's latest electronic engine control system, EEC-IV, governed injector timing, idle speed, wastegate operation, supplementary fuel enrichment, engine idle, and emissions control. Other changes included forged-aluminum pistons, valves made of a special temperature-resistant alloy, lighter flywheel, die-cast aluminum rocker cover, and engine oil cooler. Per usual turbo practice, compression was lowered from 9.0:1 to 8.0:1, and premium-unleaded fuel was recommended for best performance. The result of all this was a healthy 145 bhp at 4600 rpm—better than the magic "1 horsepower per cubic inch" ideal—and 180 pounds/feet torque peaking at a relatively low 3600 rpm.

For the road manners enthusiasts demanded, Ford developed a special han-

dling package for the Turbo Coupe. Optional on other '83 T-Birds, it comprised P205/70HR-14 Goodyear Eagle HR performance radials on distinctive aluminum wheels, plus firmer springs and shocks. Unique to the TC was "Quadra-Trac," an extra pair of rear shock absorbers mounted horizontally to resist axle patter on bumps and tramp in hard acceleration. Complementing this was standard Traction-Lok limited-slip differential with a 3.45:1 rear axle ratio.

Distinguishing Turbo Coupe externally were black-finish headlamp surrounds and greenhouse moldings, and a pair of foglamps in a modest under-bumper front spoiler. Inside were contoured Lear-Siegler bucket seats with sphygmomanometer-type inflatable lumbar support, adjustable thigh support and side bolsters, reclining backrests, and open-mesh head restraints. Unfortunately, the Turbo Coupe dash was shared with lesser Birds and thus wasn't ideal for an enthusiast's machine, though an afterthought tachometer and turbocharger "on-boost" and "overboost" warning lights were provided.

Announced at a base price of $11,790, the Turbo Coupe was roundly applauded by "buff books" and even CONSUMER GUIDE® magazine, though its critics did find a few faults. The main ones were undue high-rpm engine harshness, an irritatingly narrow power band, ill-placed shifter, overassisted power steering, and unhappily incomplete instrumentation. *CG* also wondered about the turbo engine's long-term reliability—and TC sales, as the proven V-8 offered similar performance for less money, albeit at the expense of extra front-end weight that affected handling agility.

But there was no denying Turbo Coupe performance: 0-60 mph in just 9.6 seconds and an honest 23 mpg in demanding city/suburban driving. For a posh, emissions-controlled coupe weighing almost 1.5 tons, the TC represented an amazing balance between performance and economy.

It also proved that Ford's recently adopted corporate ad slogan, "Quality is Job 1," was more than just talk. In fact, Dearborn's newest products were showing a level of workmanship that would have been miraculous just a few years before: tight, rattle-free bodies, properly aligned exterior trim and panels, and interiors neatly finished with good-looking, apparently sturdy materials. Even paint finish, once a literal Detroit blotch, begged comparison with the best. *CG* knew, because by chance its '83 Turbo Coupe test car arrived while it was evaluating a Mercedes-Benz 380SL, and there wasn't that much difference in exterior finish. Considering that the Turbo Coupe sold for about a fourth as much, this was heartening indeed.

Buyers were quick to recognize the excellence of what Ford had wrought, snapping up nearly 122,000 of the '83 Thunderbirds, a sensational 250-percent increase over 1982. The Turbo Coupe ac-

counted for only about 10 percent, but like T-Birds always have, it undoubtedly brought in many prospects who left in one of the tamer versions or another Ford model.

With that rousing sales performance, Dearborn planners breathed a big collective sigh of relief. Though no one outside the company really knew it at the time, the '83 Thunderbird was the testbed for a dramatically different "aerodynamic look" that would characterize most

Escort dropped from five series to four for '83: L, GL, GLX, and GT. The last came only as a $6706 three-door hatchback. As the sportiest Escort, the GT (top) got a multi-port injected version of the 1.6-liter four rated at 88 bhp (mated to a five-speed manual) and an uprated suspension rolling on Michelin TRX tires. The EXP (above), priced from $6426 to $8739, looked pretty much as in '82, but it could be had with all three versions of the 1.6: base 70-bhp, 80-bhp with two-barrel carb, and 88-bhp as on the GT.

The '83 Mustang GT hatchback (top) received a $1020 price increase to $9328, while its 5.0-liter V-8 got a boost from 157 horses to a more satisfying 175. Meanwhile, the Mustang convertible became a reality for '83, Ford's first ponycar ragtop in a decade. It was available as a $13,479 GT, the priciest model in the lineup, or as a $12,467 GLX (above). The latter was powered by the 3.8-liter V-6 rated at 112 bhp.

all the company's cars by decade's end. Had this Bird laid an egg, Ford might have been in real trouble (as much or more as if the Fairmont had bombed five years before).

The decision to break away from the Detroit styling herd came straight from the top floor of the Glass House—namely, chairman Philip Caldwell. But the task

of actually setting the new direction was left to Don Petersen and the NAAO design team under Jack Telnack. As Telnack later recalled for *Motor Trend*: "In 1980, shortly after Petersen was named president, he asked us if we were producing designs we truly liked. I told him we could do better and he said, 'Fine, show me your best stuff.' We showed him the design that became the 1983 Thunderbird." Seldom do managers give designers such enthusiastic cooperation.

But then, seldom has styling bravery produced such pleasing results. Today, most analysts credit Caldwell's decision and the Telnack team's creativity as key factors in the astounding sales success Ford has enjoyed in the years since 1983. *Motor Trend* observed that while initially "There was some resistance in buyerland to [the] new Ford look... the general reaction was quite positive. [Moreover,] the company was ready for a little... high-risk derring-do." Though the 10th-generation T-Bird was undeniably daring for 1983, Ford had been gradually preparing the public for such radical shapes with "concept cars" like the dramatic Probe series of ultra-aerodynamic experiments, the first of which had been seen in 1980. Time and further acquaintance on production models would do the rest.

Of course, not everybody would warm to the new look. Even now, some critics persist in calling it "jellybean styling." If nothing else, Dearborn's new direction was a welcome change in a market increasingly dominated by look-alike cars. As ever, Ford was, as Jim Nance said of Packard back in the Fifties, seeking "a difference to sell."

Differences were certainly apparent in this year's Mustang, which received its first major appearance alterations since 1979, and its first convertible in 10 years. All models wore a newly rounded nose bearing a sloped, slightly vee'd horizontal-bar grille, all of which Ford said was good for a 2.5-percent reduction in aerodynamic drag. Running-horse emblems gave way to blue Ford ovals on grille and rear decks; there were wider, restyled taillights; and of course the usual trim and color shuffles occurred. In all, it was an effective, low-cost makeover.

Special attention was lavished on this year's Mustang GT to achieve greater parity with Camaro/Firebird in the renewed ponycar performance wars. This involved wider-section standard tires, newly optional 220/55-390 Michelin TRX covers, slightly larger rear anti-roll bar, softer rear spring rates, stiffer bushings for the front control arms, and revised shock valving. Higher-effort power

The '83 Mustang GL could be ordered as a $7264 coupe or as a $7439 hatchback (top), which weighed 2788 pounds at the curb. It came with the 90-bhp 2.3-liter four, now with a one-barrel carb, as standard, but many buyers upgraded to the 3.8-liter (232-cid) V-6, which replaced the 200-cid straight six for '83. Standard GL features included black rocker panels, twin upper bodyside pinstripes, a black driver's-side remote exterior mirror, and bright door and window moldings. Inside (center), the GL featured a woodgrain dash, as on the base L model, but exchanged the L's wood-accent four-spoke steering wheel for an all-black sport wheel. The 5.0-liter V-8 (bottom) gained 18 bhp by switching from a two- to a four-barrel carb. It also got a freer-flowing exhaust.

Fairmont entered 1983 little changed, although two price-leader "S" sedans joined the lineup. All models were labeled Futura as in '82. The best seller was the four-door sedan (above), which listed at $6590. Together with the S, the four-doors attracted 69,287 buyers. The sport coupe and the two-door were less successful: 7882 and 3664 units. Fairmont was now in its last year, but it had not only given its Fox platform to many other Ford cars, but on its own it accounted for 1,488,046 units built from 1978-83.

steering was also included, for better high-speed control.

Speaking of speed, the HO V-8 was boosted to 175 bhp via a new four-barrel carb, aluminum intake manifold, high-flow air cleaner, enlarged exhaust passages, and minor valvetrain modifications. Even better, it mated with Borg-Warner's recently introduced T-5 close-ratio five-speed gearbox, the same one used for Camaro/Firebird, which answered complaints about poor gear spacing on the wide-ratio four-speed it replaced. All this plus a shorter final drive (3.27 versus 3.01:1) made for even faster takeoffs.

Further emphasizing Mustang's return to performance, the extra-cost 4.2-liter V-8 was dropped and the 200-cid straight six was replaced as the step-up power option by the new lightweight overhead-valve Essex V-6. With two-barrel carburetor, the latter delivered a rated 105 bhp (versus the I-6's 88) and 181 lbs/ft torque (against 158). The 2.3-liter "Lima" four, still standard for all Mus-

tangs save GT, gained a more efficient one-barrel carb (replacing a two-barrel), plus longer-reach spark plugs for fast-burn combustion, a move aimed at reducing emissions while improving warmup and part-throttle engine response. Curiously, these changes boosted alleged horsepower by five, to 93 bhp, though the rating would fall back to 88 for '84. Newly standard for all manual-shift Mustangs was a Volkswagen-like upshift indicator light. Reflecting the fuel jitters of 1979-80, this was an economy aid that signalled the driver when to shift to the next higher gear, based on the fact that an engine is usually most fuel-efficient at relatively low revs on wide throttle openings. It was useful, if hardly in the free-spirited tradition of the original ponycar.

Other Mustang alterations for '83 included a standard roller-blind cargo cover for hatchbacks, easier-to-read gauge markings, and less interior brightwork. A new Sport seat option with mesh-insert headrests replaced the extra-cost Recaro buckets, which hadn't sold well. Reflecting its new concern with aerodynamics, Ford also deleted the hatchback's liftgate louvers and the notchback's Carriage Roof from the options list.

But the most glamorous development by far was the return of the Mustang convertible, initially available only in top-line GLX trim. Ever since the last ragtop Mustang of 1973, a number of aftermarket companies had done good business in snipping the tops from Mustang

notchbacks (and other cars as well) to satisfy a small but steady demand for top-down motoring. Ford decided to get in on this action itself.

Like the new Buick Riviera and Chrysler LeBaron ragtops that arrived at about the same time, the reborn drop-top Mustang was an out-of-house conversion, a notchback coupe modified and trimmed (including top installation) by independent contractor Cars & Concepts of Brighton, Michigan. Like the Riv—but unlike the LeBaron—the Mustang had roll-down rear side windows and a tempered-glass rear window. It was available with any drivetrain save the four-cylinder/automatic combination. As the first open-air ponycar in a decade, it added another dash of excitement to an already impressive Mustang lineup.

That lineup expanded at mid-season with a ragtop GT and a new Turbo GT hatchback and convertible, the latter pair powered by the newly reengineered version of the hyperaspirated 2.3-liter Lima four developed for the T-Bird Turbo Coupe. Though this engine delivered only 5 bhp more than the previous turbo, it was better in most every way: smoother, quieter, more tractable, and somewhat more reliable.

Aside from slightly different nameplates, the Turbo GTs were visual twins to their V-8 counterparts. Blackout trim, beefy Eagle GT performance radials, aluminum wheels, Sport bucket seats, the usual businesslike Mustang gauge cluster and five-speed manual gearbox were standard for both, and the V-8 GT suspension was retuned to match the lighter turbo-four. Packing the same horsepower Chevy advertised for its base Z-28, the Turbo GT could run 0-60 mph in well under 10 seconds and the standing quarter-mile in about 16 seconds while returning a creditable 25 mpg overall. But the T-Bird TC could match all those numbers, and the fortified 5.0-liter Mustang could now fly to 60 in near six seconds flat.

So though it seemed to offer the best of both worlds, this improved turbo Mustang proved no more popular than its 1979-81 predecessor. Aside from the fact that it couldn't be had with automatic or air conditioning—a severe drawback for many buyers—it cost $386 *more* than a comparably equipped V-8 GT. Yet it was slower, and with a peakier, less torquey engine it had to be driven that much harder. Ford said a late introduction and restricted availability limited Turbo GT sales. And indeed, only 483 of the '83s were called for. But the real damper was best expressed by that time-worn Detroit adage, "There's no substitute for cubic inches"—not even high technology.

And neither this, the facelift, the hotter V-8, nor the reborn convertible improved Mustang sales, which dropped another 10,000 units for the model year to 120,873—a new Mustang low. Convertibles accounted for 23,438 of these units. Things would get better soon enough, though—for 1984, in fact, when the market recovery got underway in earnest.

Among 1983 Escorts was a newly revised GT three-door that more closely approximated the handling, performance, and appearance of the sportiest European Escort, the XR3. Included were port electronic fuel injection (EFI) for the 1.6 "CVH" four, plus a new five-speed overdrive manual transaxle pulling a shorter 3.73:1 final drive. Suspension was specifically tuned for standard Michelin TRX tires, and there were new appearance touches including front and rear spoilers, front fog lamps, and "spats" around the wheel openings. Featured inside were standard full instrumentation with special graphics, floor console, and new Sport bucket seats with cloth upholstery and mesh-type headrests. It was a zippy little package, and attractively priced at $7339.

The new five-speed and EFI engine were optional for other Escorts as well as EXP. The port-injected CVH delivered 88 bhp at 5400 rpm compared to 80 bhp for the HO version, which was still available, and only 72 for the base mill. Other changes included upshift indicator light with manual transmissions, larger fuel tank, standard all-season radial tires, and a fourth speed for the heater fan. Base Escorts were dropped. A locking fuel-filler flap with inside release was a new standard for all but L models.

Recalling 1977, Ford applied the LTD

badge to a second model line this year. Replacing the slow-selling Granada as the division's mid-size contender, this was essentially a reskinned Fairmont sedan and wagon wearing a sloped rectangular grille, aero-look lower-body sheetmetal and, on the sedan, a slantback six-window greenhouse and modestly lipped trunklid. There were no major mechanical changes for this latest version of the Fox except for gas-pressurized front struts and rear shock absorbers and availability of the corporate four-speed OD automatic. Engine choices comprised standard Lima four and optional straight and V-angle sixes, plus a propane-fuel version of the four, offered on a very limited basis for this one final year. Model choices were few: just a well-equipped base sedan and wagon plus a fancier Brougham sedan spanning a narrow $7777-$8577 price range. That looked quite a bit downstream of this year's full-size Fords, the cheapest of which listed at $9130, but the difference wasn't as great as in earlier years due to the debilitating effects of inflation on the purchasing power of the once-strong dollar.

Though it wasn't all that different from Fairmont or the last Granada, this "little LTD" (we can be grateful they didn't call it "LTD III") had a design role to play that was every bit as critical as the new T-Bird's. *Car and Driver* aptly termed it a "transition car, a piece that hints of the new direction in car design in which Ford hopes to take us." Jack Telnack was more specific, telling the magazine that this smaller LTD was a "first step... a very natural evolution of the shape that buyers in that category are coming from. It's not a radical departure [like] the Thunderbird. We didn't want to reach so far that they wouldn't understand the car." Quite logical, that. Besides, there'd plenty of "reach" in due course.

To avoid confusion with the little LTDs, the big-Ford line was renamed LTD Crown Victoria. Fleet-trim "S" four-door sedan and wagon continued, as did the standard two- and four-door sedans, plain-sided wagon, and woody-look Country Squire. A more open eggcrate grille appeared, and drivetrain choices

The Fairmont Futura sport coupe (top) was base priced at $6666 for 1983. A new Fairmont offshoot was the mid-size LTD, offered as "L" or Brougham four-door sedans or an $8577 wagon (second from top), of which 43,945 were built. All full-size Fords now became LTD Crown Victorias. The Country Squire listed at $10,253, while the four-door sedan carried a base sticker price of $10,094 (third and fourth from top).

were reduced to the new fuel-injected 5.0-liter V-8 with overdrive automatic. Otherwise, all was as before, except that production dipped about 15,000 units to a lowly 113,616.

Fairmont was absolutely as before, mainly because of a scheduled phase-out after a half-year production run, which totaled some 80,800 units. The reason? A smaller, front-drive compact was replacing it in March: the new Tempo. Because

Aerodynamics were becoming important even for trucks in the Eighties, as this Ranger in the Lockheed Georgia wind tunnel suggests (left). Corporate Average Fuel Economy (CAFE) regulations were the reason, as they applied to light-duty trucks, too. Ford debuted a four-wheel-drive version of the Ranger pickup for '83 (below). It featured a two-speed part-time transfer case and a 2700-pound rear axle, plus Twin-Traction-Beam front suspension, 2.3-liter four-cylinder engine, and manual four-speed gearbox.

ly new spirit, as they definitely did, it only reflected the spirit of president Don Petersen. In '82, Petersen furthered his reputation as a true "car guy" and gave enthusiasts reason to hope for even more exciting Fords in the future by signing up for a high-performance driving course at the Bob Bondurant School in Northern California. It was a signal act given the conservative, aloof image of most Detroit executives, though the fact that Bondurant's pupils usually tooled around in tuned Mustangs may have had something to do with Petersen's interest. At any rate, as *Motor Trend* later recounted, "He had so much fun testing a specially prepared Mustang on the Sears Point race track and finding out first-hand what his company's products could do, he decided the experience would be good for employees...." Accordingly, Petersen invited Bondurant instructors to the Dearborn Proving Grounds in September 1983, where 32 engineers and product planners took the course—with 175-bhp Mustang GTs as "trainers."

Frankly, it's difficult to imagine GM's Roger Smith—or even Chrysler's Lee Iacocca—ordering the troops to tear around a race track in their hottest cars, let alone strapping on helmets themselves. But under Caldwell and Petersen, Ford was taking a decidedly different attitude about many things, styling and performance most obviously, but also about *esprit de corps* and the very nature of the company's mission. As *Motor Trend* correctly observed, the Bondurant experience demonstrated "to each employee the company's attitude toward its products with more conviction than any memo, handbook, or speech ever could. You can't spend a couple days bashing apexes—at company expense—and not come away thinking performance, durability and, most of all, fun."

It's also hard not to come away from such a good time without a heightened sense of enthusiasm and loyalty. Of all the Big Three makers, only Ford seemed to realize the inherent connection between the quality of its products and the level of employee morale. That the company still encourages its executives to take the Bondurant course is but one small example. Perhaps Ford had learned from the Japanese that a happy company produces happy products, which in turn make for happy customers. This, too, has been a major factor in Dearborn's remarkable Eighties success.

that one's officially a 1984 model, it's covered under that heading.

Ford's mixed sales fortunes of 1983 were mostly due to shortfalls among the family cars. Escort, though still doing well, was no longer the nation's top-selling model line, as noted. EXP continued going nowhere, down to less than 20,000 units, perhaps because it was neither family nor sporty car. Fairmont dropped by almost 47,000 units, and the big Ford slipped slightly. The one bright spot apart from the new T-Bird's spectacular success was the little LTD, which notched over 35,000 more sales than the '82 Granada.

It's worth noting that Mercury's 1983 Capri received a modified grille, a new "bubbleback hatch" *a la* LN7 (and as aesthetically questionable), and Mustang's latest HO V-8 option. But Capri was denied the new Mustang convertible, perhaps for greater brand distinction, but a telling omission nonetheless. In fact, Mercury was beginning to act as though it were ashamed of its Mustang-clone, and half-hearted promotion only aggravated the lack of meaningful change. Thus, while Mustang production would

steadily improve after 1983, Capri's would worsen, dropping from its 1980 level of nearly 80,000 units to only some 18,500 by 1985 (versus over 156,000 Mustangs). At that level, Capri was too costly to sustain, and it would vanish after 1986.

Of course, Mercury's main focus for '83 was a sleek new T-Bird-based Cougar. It's already been described, except to point out that it had no Turbo Coupe equivalent. What it *did* have was a different styling feel and image, Dearborn having rediscovered the sales value of emphasizing make identity via styling—if not model and mechanical variations.

As sales of certain GM cars were proving, people still had definite ideas about what various makes stood for, and they didn't take kindly to Cadillacs that looked like Oldsmobiles that looked like Pontiacs that looked like Chevys. Perhaps because of the Edsel fiasco, Dearborn had learned this lesson sooner and was starting to make more distinctions between the Ford and Mercury versions of a shared design. The '83 Cougar was one of the first Mercs to go "back to the future" this way. If some '83 Fords showed a live-

The Club Wagon (above) continued into 1983 basically unchanged. It came in two wheelbases, 124 and 138 inches, resulting in overall lengths of 186.8 and 206.8 inches. Five series were offered—E-100, E-150, E-150 Super Wagon, E-250, E-350—but the E-100 would disappear after 1983. The pride of Ford's truck fleet were the Louisville 9000 line haulers (above right).

Things were a lot more prosaic on Ford's '83 truck scene, where newly available diesel power was the big event for Ranger, F-Series, and Econoline/Club Wagon. Unlike GM, Ford had not rushed to diesel-engine cars and light-duty trucks in the wake of the first energy crisis—a good thing, in retrospect, given the poor service record of GM's 350 diesel V-8. But the advent of CAFE followed by Energy Crisis II made compression-ignition engines desirable, and 1983 was the year Ford finally caught up with its rival, at least in trucks.

There were actually two new oil-burners, both naturally aspirated: a Mazda-built 2.2-liter (135-cubic-inch) in-line four for Ranger, and Dearborn's own new 6.9-liter V-8 (about 421 cid) for the F- and E-Series. The latter was advertised as a "true-truck diesel," likely to convey the notion that the "smoker" 6.2-liter Chevy/GMC V-8 wasn't. In any case, Ford claimed 160-162 bhp or 19 percent more power, plus 307-314 lbs/ft torque. To get it, you had to order a pickup or van with the 250 or 350 chassis and a GVW of 8500 pounds or higher. For CAFE reasons, the 6.9 was offered only with manual transmission in pickups, but only with automatic in vans. The Ranger's new diesel-four, which delivered just 59 horses and only 90 lbs/ft, teamed exclusively with the standard four-speed manual.

More exciting was the arrival of four-wheel-drive Rangers, regular and longbed models powered by the gasoline-fueled 2.3 Lima four that remained optional for 4×2s (as an alternative to the ex-Courier 2.0-liter Mazda engine). Front suspension was an evolution of that on two-wheel-drive models. Called "Twin-Traction Beam," it boasted adjustable camber and permanently lubed ball joints. The transfer case was the usual

two-speed part-time affair with manual-lock front hubs, but auto-locking hubs were available at extra cost. A newly optional five-speed overdrive manual transmission gave all gas-engine Rangers improved performance and slightly better highway fuel economy. Mileage concerns also prompted some axle-ratio juggling for certain drivetrains.

Other new Ranger options for '83 comprised a handling package, "fingertip" cruise control with steering-wheel-mounted buttons, Snow Plow Special and heavy-duty front suspension packages for 4×4s, overhead console with digital clock and map light, and a floor console with a storage bin and Mustang-type graphic warning-light display. Last but not least was a new 4×2 Ranger cab/chassis for commercial applications.

Model and powertrain choices changed considerably in the senior-pickup and Econoline/Club Wagon lines. The latter's optional four-barrel 460 V-8 was now extended to the F-Series in the same over-8500-pound GVW class, and the corporate four-speed overdrive automatic replaced the previous three-speeder for the 300-cid six and 302 V-8 in F-100/150 4×2s and sub-8500 GVW Econolines and Club Wagons. The small-block V-8 was mildly modified for improved running, and the 255 and 400 V-8s were scratched from F-Series offerings. Model-wise, a plus-8500 E-250 SuperWagon arrived and the E-100 Club Wagon and 150 SuperWagon departed. The F-Series exchanged a short-wheelbase 250 Super Cab for new F-350 Styleside Crew Cabs, both two- and four-wheel drive versions boasting four doors and seating for six. Both E- and F-Series got the usual trim and equipment shuffles, with higher-grade standard upholstery and more luxurious extra-cost choices that included "leather-look" vinyl for XL and XLT E-Series. Most non-radial tire options were gone by now, as were eight-track tape players and the F-Series' Free Wheeling packages (the last effectively replaced by XLS trim options). The F-Series' XLT Lariat option became simply XLT, and an easier-to-use digital clock with stopwatch was optional for most of these pickups and vans.

By contrast, the burly Bronco saw far fewer changes. Included were revised dashboard graphics per this year's F-Series, assorted new colors and upholstery materials, deletion of the "Lariat" name on the XLT trim package, and an extra-cost 302 V-8 with the latest E/F-Series modifications. Ford was evidently getting a handle on its truck emissions problems, because the 300 six was again available for California-bound Broncos and with optional automatic in the other 49 states. Expanding standard equipment for the big "sport-ute" were a flip-fold rear bench seat and ammeter and oil-pressure gauges. New options included the aforementioned clock/stopwatch and bright-finish swing-out door mirrors in either low-mount "Western" style or the larger RV type with A-bracket mounting.

Ford's large trucks returned with no major changes save a trio of new Caterpillar diesel options for F-Series mediums: one turbocharged and two normally aspirated units delivering 175 to 225 bhp. Also on the books for these models was an economy-oriented 8.2-liter diesel V-8 dubbed the "Fuel Pincher." Most F-Series front axles and some rear axles were heavier and thus rated for higher payloads—on the top FT-800 tandem, up to 46,000 and 50,000 pounds, respectively.

Ford's 1983 press kit took pains to note that the booming light-truck market was increasingly dominated by younger, better-educated urban buyers seeking a more "personal" vehicle, in many cases as an alternative to a car. Then came this word: "Ford will spend about $2 billion by the [mid-Eighties] to retain U.S. truck sales leadership, much of it to reach these buyers. Expenditures for smaller trucks—expected to account for as much as half of all light-truck sales by 1985—are key to that goal, and Ranger and Bronco II are the first two building blocks in that program."

Bronco II? Yup, Ford was readying a downsized sport-utility that promised a whole new kind of fun. Detroit was certainly ready for some fun after all the upheavals and traumas of 1980-82. Fortunately, things were starting to look up at last, and all of Motown would soon be whistling "Happy Days are Here Again."

1 9 8 4

The title year of George Orwell's apocalyptic novel came and went without incident. Well, not quite, at least as far as the motor industry was concerned. Total U.S. car sales, domestic and import, had risen from just under 8 million in 1982 to a little more than 9 million in '83. This year they went above 10 million for the first time since 1979.

Ford Motor Company's share, as measured by calendar-year registrations, went up as well, tacking on more than two points to end at 19.26 percent, again the highest in five years. GM still held about 44.5 percent of the market, and Chrysler had settled in at just under 10 percent (up from barely seven percent in pivotal 1980). Imports were down to slightly less than 25 percent after reaching an all-time high of over 29.5 percent in 1982, but this would only be a temporary plateau.

Profits reflected the continuing market recovery, and Ford posted a dandy 1984 result: a new one-year record of $2.91 billion. It was great news for Ford workers, whose individual profit-sharing checks, having shriveled to just $400 two years before, ballooned to a more gratifying $2000.

The truck market was also bouncing back, and Ford again led in total calendar-year registrations (though it finished second to International in heavy trucks). The race with Chevy was close, Ford managing 28.7 percent of the domestic total with 1,162,001 units, versus Chevy's 26.9 percent and slightly more than a million registrations. There was greater disparity in domestic light-truck production. Ford built close to 1.28 million units, good for 42.2 percent of that pie, versus fewer than 969,000 and 32.3 percent for Chevy. Even better for Dearborn's truck folks, their compact Ranger pickup beat Chevy's S-10 in model-year production for the first time.

Ford was far less dominant on the car side, claiming only two of this year's top-10 domestic sellers: the subcompact Escort, in second spot, and the new front-drive Tempo compact, number seven. The remaining eight were all GM products. And though Ford enjoyed higher production in both the U.S. and Canada, the competitors sales were also up. More worrisome, perhaps, was the fact of the more than 1.8 million cars built by Ford U.S. for the model year, close to 1.2 million came from Ford Division. One could almost hear the ghost of Jack Reith laughing through the corridors of the Glass House.

Nevertheless, Dearborn had much

to be proud of in 1984. Again jumping the gun on a busy model year, Ford announced its first '84 models in May 1983: the aforementioned Tempo and its near-twin, the Mercury Topaz. As the replacements for the successful Fairmont/Zephyr, these were important cars: the company's first front-drive entries in the high-volume, family-compact market then dominated by GM's X-car quartet (Buick Skylark, Chevrolet Citation, et al) and Chrysler's popular Dodge Aries/Plymouth Reliant K-cars. Their mission was simple if difficult: win back sales lost to these front-drive competitors while further polishing Ford's image as a builder of modern, high-technology cars with advanced aerodynamic styling.

Tempo emerged as one of the few recent American cars that honestly deserved the overworked "all-new" moniker. Ford also took great pains to point out that it was *not* simply a puffed-up Escort. It stemmed from the "Topaz" project that had been initiated in late 1979 to develop a larger running mate for Escort, incorporating some of the same design principles, but not necessarily the same hardware. Unlike the Erika program, Topaz was strictly an American effort. The goal was to maximize the packaging benefits of front-wheel drive to provide a Fairmont-size interior within a smaller, lighter envelope. That implied a purpose-designed engine, as Escort's 1.6-liter four was simply too small. Body design would reflect all that Ford had learned about aerodynamics, not just for distinctive appearance, but also for enhanced fuel economy and reduced wind noise. Of course, the company would hedge its marketing bets by effectively continuing the Fairmont in plusher, restyled form as the little LTD.

For initial design considerations, Dearborn engineers again went to the wind tunnel, spending more than 450 hours on scale and full-size clay models that led to more than 950 separate design changes. Interestingly, this work started a full year before Topaz got management's formal go-ahead, and continued until quite late in the game, March 1981. Tests with production-approved prototypes followed in 1982. Only coupe and sedan body styles were devised, both notchbacks to separate the compacts from Escort/Lynx. A wagon was deemed unnecessary, strange considering the popularity of Chrysler's K-wagons. Evidently, product planners felt their Erika and Fox wagons catered adequately to those seeking small haulers.

Styling was definitely from Dearborn's new "jellybean" school: chunky and rounded, with a shortish, sloped nose and abbreviated bustle tail. At least it differed from the boxy GM and Chrysler compacts. A 60-degree windshield slope, as on the latest T-Bird, helped cheat the wind, while drip rails were hidden in "aircraft-style" door openings cut into the roof. Tempo and Topaz rooflines differed

markedly. The four-door Tempo had the "six-light" styling (three side windows) so favored in Europe. The Topaz sedan used solid, more formal-looking rear roof quarters. Both coupes had rather thick A- and C-posts, like the sedans, but their long rear side windows gave them an altogether sportier look. Grilles differed too: narrowish body-color slats on Tempo, a broader black-finish ensemble for Topaz. It was further evidence of Dearborn's return to more distinct Ford/Mercury identities.

The wind tunnel work paid off. Tempo's drag coefficient came in at 0.36 for coupe and 0.37 for sedan. Significantly, the vaunted big Mercedes-Benz S-class also claimed 0.36. Since achieving a low Cd is much more difficult on a shorter car, the Tempo design was even more

The Tempo bowed in May 1983 as an '84. It was Ford's new front-drive entry into the compact field—and it was all *new: body, chassis, engine, and of course the "jellybean" aero styling. Six models were offered in three series: L, GL, and GLX. The top-line GLX four-door sedan (below) listed at $7621, while the mid-range GL two-door coupe (right) cost $7159. During the long model year, output reached 402,214.*

430

efficient than the cold numbers suggested.

Dimensionally, Tempo fell about midway between Escort and Fairmont. Its 99.9-inch wheelbase and 176.2-inch overall length were 5.5 and a whopping 20 inches less than corresponding Fairmont dimensions, and the new front-driver was a significant 400 pounds lighter. All this put it quite close to Chrysler's 99.6-inch-wheelbase K-cars. Compared to GM's X-bodies, Tempo offered similar interior space despite a four-inch-shorter wheelbase.

Chassis specs were bang up to date. Front suspension featured MacPherson struts with coaxial coil springs (as on Escort), a standard anti-roll bar, and Escort/Lynx rack-and-pinion steering. However, instead of using beam rear axles like its competitors, Tempo/Topaz boasted fully independent "Quadrilink" geometry. It was similar to Escort's but used twin, thin lateral arms either side of the hub carrier instead of a single arm pivoted at the center. The carriers, in turn, acted on vertical shock/strut units, again with coaxial coil springs, and connected to tie-rods running forward to the chassis rails. Brakes were front-disc/rear-drum with standard power assist, while the tires were a new all-season radial design, size P175/80R-13.

Under the hood was the first of a promised family of "fast burn" powerplants. Though roughly the same size as the 2.3-liter overhead-cam "Lima" four, this was actually a reengineered version of Ford's early-Sixties 200-cid overhead-valve six. It even had the same 3.68-inch bore, though a longer 3.30-inch stroke—and, of course, two fewer cylinders.

Called 2300 HSC—for "High Swirl Combustion"—this semi-new powerplant featured wedge-shaped combustion chambers with shrouds around the intake valves to speed up ("swirl") the incoming mixture for faster, more complete burning. Ford claimed this promoted lower emissions and provided more torque at low rpm, the latter a key consideration in handling the optional automatic transmission that most buyers were expected to order. Engine ancillaries were carefully placed to keep the entire package as compact as possible. Intake manifold, water pump, and front cover were made of aluminum to save weight. With a two-barrel carburetor and a fairly

high 9.0:1 compression ratio, the HSC arrived with 85 horsepower at 4400 rpm and 125 pounds/feet torque peaking at a low 2400 rpm.

Initially, Tempo's standard transaxle was either a wide-ratio four-speed overdrive manual or a closer-ratio five-speed. The former was part of a special Escort-style Fuel Saver package but wasn't available with air conditioning, so most manual-transaxle (MTX) cars had the five-speed. As with Escort, both gearboxes were supplied by Japanese affiliate Toyo Kogyo (Mazda). Optional at extra-cost was an American-made three-speed automatic (ATX) similar to Escort's.

At the start of the formal model year, a 2.0-liter four-cylinder diesel, also from Mazda, became optionally available on five-speed Tempos. Ford stressed that this wasn't simply a converted gas engine but had been designed *as* a diesel—no doubt to assure buyers that it wasn't another pile of trouble like GM's 350 diesel V-8. Features included belt-driven overhead camshaft, aluminum cylinder head, altitude-compensated fuel-injection pump, swirl-type combustion chambers, and precisely "square" bore and stroke dimensions of 3.39 × 3.39 inches. Besides the now-customary quick-start glow plugs, this diesel had an "after glow" device that kept the plugs lit even after the engine was running to burn off excess hydrocarbons and particulates visible as white smoke, a nod to environmentalists. Ford had long since mastered the art of merchandising-with-options but, except for the basic L versions, Tempo was quite well-equipped. The upper-level GL and GLX models boasted such niceties as full carpeting, padded door panels with armrests, intermittent wipers, sound insulation package and individual front seats with reclining backrests. Still, options were extensive, per Ford tradition: electronic radios, extra gauges, Fingertip Speed Control, air conditioning, power windows, and tilt steering wheel. (Topaz came in just two trim levels and was marketed a bit differently).

With its handy size, good looks, and five-speed gearbox, the Tempo two-door was a relatively sporting coupe. Ford lent credence to that notion with an optional TR Handling Package comprising special Michelin tires on metric-size cast-aluminum wheels, plus uprated steering and suitably recalibrated suspension. But while this did wonders for transient response, it didn't make for an enthusiast's car. Even with five-speed, CONSUMER GUIDE® magazine's test two-door needed some 14 seconds in the 0-60-mph dash—adequate, but hardly exciting.

Car and Driver, whose similar test Tempo was slightly quicker at 13.2 seconds, had a more pointed assessment: "Despite its styling, the Tempo is no import-fighter; it will not strike fear into the hearts of Honda and Audi. Aimed instead at the traditional American compact-sedan buyer, the Tempo performs its duties at an affordable price [$6936 base for the low-line L coupe, ranging up to $7621 for the GLX four-door] and demands little adjustment from lifelong domestic-car owners. Its rivals at GM and Chrysler do the same, but Ford is gambling that Americans are growing tired of nondescript alphabet cars. If Ford is right, the Tempo's distinctive styling may be enough to overcome the competition's three-year lead."

As it turned out, Ford *was* right—very right. As noted, the Tempo finished seventh in domestic-model calendar-year sales, garnering a healthy 256,532 orders (including some '85 models, of course). But helped by an extra-long sales season, overall *model*-year *production* was considerably higher: 402,214, second only to the 462,612 units of Chevy's top-selling subcompact Cavalier.

If even the sportiest Tempo wasn't all that exciting, several other '84 Fords definitely were. Easily the most striking of this year's performance models was the long-rumored Mustang SVO, the first of the promised hot limited-editions from Dearborn's new Special Vehicle Operations section under Michael Kranefuss.

The '84 Mustang SVO (opposite page) was a noble idea gone awry. Bowing as the most sophisticated Mustang ever, it featured a 175-bhp turbocharged 2.3-liter four, which was intercooled and electronically controlled to vary boost pressure up to 14 psi. Included also were a host of chassis upgrades, special interior, and unique styling that embraced a "biplane" rear spoiler. The trouble was that the SVO listed at $15,596, fully $6010 more than a Mustang GT hatchback, which was just about as fast. Only 4508 were built for '84. The 20th Anniversary Mustang (right) was called the GT-350, and Carroll Shelby protested!

The Thunderbird lineup expanded from three to four models for '84 as the $12,661 Elan replaced Heritage and a pricey $14,471 Fila joined the ranks. The base Bird stickered at $9633, while the Turbo Coupe (above) sold for $12,330, up $540 from '83. Horsepower of the TC's turbo four was rated at 140, down two, but this year it could be teamed with automatic transmission. The instrument panel (left) featured an analog speedometer and tach, plus a turbo boost gauge.

Based on the Turbo GT hatchback, the SVO boasted a lengthy list of modifications that read like a hop-up artist's wishbook. Notable mods included an air-to-air intercooler for the turbocharger and the first-ever use of electronic control to vary turbo boost pressure—which ranged up to 14 psi, said to be the highest of any turbo engine then in production. These and other changes produced a claimed 20-percent gain in horsepower over the '83 turbo—up to a remarkable 175 bhp at 4500 rpm—and 10-percent more torque—210 lbs/ft at 3000.

Also included in SVO's mechanical exotica were a cockpit selector switch that "tuned" the engine's electronics to the grade of fuel being used, and special dampers to resist driveline rocking or "rubberbanding" under full power. Putting that power to the ground was a five-speed manual gearbox with special Hurst linkage, and a standard Traction-Lok limited-slip differential with 3.45:1 final drive.

SVO chassis revisions were equally thorough. In place of the stock 9.0-inch-diameter rear drum brakes were beefy 11.25-inch discs working in concert with front rotors enlarged from 10.06 to 10.92 inches. Tires were V-rated high-speed European Goodyear NCT radials on fat, 16 × 7-inch cast-aluminum wheels. Rubber was later switched to P225/50VR-16 Goodyear Eagle GT50s with unidirectional "gatorback" tread (as used on the mostly new '84 Corvette). Spring rates and bushings were stiffened, premium Koni ad-

justable shocks replaced the stock dampers, the front anti-roll bar was thickened from 0.94 to 1.20 inches, and a rear bar was added along with an extra inch of front wheel travel. Mustang's stock rack-and-pinion power steering was changed from variable-ratio to fast constant-ratio gearing, but retained high-effort valving for optimum road feel.

Setting SVO apart from lesser Mustangs were a distinctive "biplane" rear spoiler made of polycarbonate plastic, a unique grille-less nose (engine air entered from below the bumper and through a small slot above, making this a "bottom breather"), a large hood scoop to feed the intercooler, and dual square headlamps instead of the normal Mustang's smaller quads. A deep front air dam incorporated standard foglamps, and small "spats" or fairings at the leading edges of the rear wheel openings helped smooth airflow around the fat tires.

Inside were such driver-oriented accoutrements as left footrest, brake and accelerator pedals put closer together for easier heel/toe shifting, 8000-rpm tachometer, turbo-boost gauge, and multi-adjustable seats like those in the T-Bird Turbo Coupe. Other standard features included electric rear-window defroster, tinted glass, AM/FM stereo radio with

speaker/amplifier system, leather-rim tilt steering wheel, and center console. Only a few factory options were listed: air, power windows, cassette player, flip-up glass sunroof, and leather upholstery.

The SVO was perhaps the closest thing to a European-style GT yet seen from America. It was certainly the best-balanced high-performance Mustang in a long time. Handling was near neutral, cornering flat and undramatic, steering direct and properly assisted, braking swift and sure. Performance was exhilarating: 0-60 mph in about 7.5 seconds, the quarter-mile in just under 16 seconds at near 90 mph, top speed approaching 135—real dragstrip stuff. "Buff books" applauded this sophisticated screamer, but buyers didn't. At over $16,000 out the door, the SVO was expensive next to the V-8 GT, which delivered similar style and sizzle for a whopping $6000 less. As a result, Ford retailed fewer than 4000 SVOs for the model year, though it had capacity to build 15,000 per annum.

Between them, SVO and the V-8 Mustangs killed off the Turbo GT after model-year '84 and a not-so-grand total of 3000 hatchbacks and about 600 convertibles (including '83 units). All early-'84 GTs, both V-8 and Turbo, were virtual '83 reruns save the new split rear seatback applied to most Mustang hatchbacks, and substitution of solid front headrests for the previous open type. Several welcome running changes occurred effective with December 1983 production: closer accelerator/brake pedal (as in the SVO), staggered rear shocks for reduced axle tramp in hard takeoffs, foglights integrated with the front spoiler, and restyled rear spoiler.

Trouble was, gasoline had not only become plentiful again but was selling at prices that were actually *dropping* in some places, and many folks just couldn't resist the urge to splurge on a good old-fashioned V-8. This illustrated a peculiar irony of the Eighties: the renewed popularity of relatively large-displacement engines at a time when automakers were discouraged from selling them by government fuel-economy regulations, which were suddenly out of synch with market forces and an unexpected worldwide oil glut. (One reason for the latter: Washington had been stockpiling crude since the mid-Seventies.) Too bad, because the Turbo GT was an honest attempt at reconciling performance with economy, a worthy goal in any age and certain to remain one of the touchstones of our long-term automotive future.

Mustang's other changes for '84 were comparatively minor. A base-trim hatchback joined the existing two-door notchback, and GL and GLX equipment were combined into a single LX trim level available in all three body styles. In line with a widening industry trend, all manual-shift Mustangs received a starter interlock that prevented accidental lurching should the driver attempt to start the car in gear.

This year also brought a second Mustang V-8, a 302 with throttle-body electronic fuel injection (TBI) and 10 fewer horses than the carbureted HO unit (165 versus 175). It was reserved for non-GTs with automatic transmission, which itself now came in two forms: the familiar three-speed gearbox, and Ford's corporate four-speed unit, whose overdrive top gear allowed use of a shorter (numerically higher) final-drive ratio (3.27:1 versus 2.73:1) with no ill effects on mileage. TBI was also applied to the "Essex" V-6 option, lifting it to 120 bhp and 205 lbs/ft torque; here, three-speed SelectShift was now the only choice.

The original ponycar reached the ripe old age of 20 this year—time really *does* fly when you're having fun—and Ford ran off 5000 copies of a special edition to mark the occasion. Reviving the famed GT-350 designation from Shelby days, it was officially a trim option for the convertible and hatchback, distinguished by "Shelby White" paint set off by maroon rocker-panel stripes but otherwise little different from the normal GT. It was a nice remembrance, but the legal department forgot to clear the name with Mr. Shelby, who claimed he owned "GT-350" and had been promised that Ford wouldn't use it again without his okay. Carroll, by now working again with his old friend Lee Iacocca at Chrysler, may have been thinking of using it for one of the hot Dodges he was building at his small-scale production facility in Southern California. In any case, he was miffed enough to hit Ford with a copyright infringement suit. Sometimes, it just doesn't pay to be sentimental.

Mustang sales seemed a pretty good barometer of the general market and the economy as a whole, bottoming out for 1983 before moving upwards again. The

After a meager 19,697 copies for '83, EXP entered 1984 with a smaller three-model lineup. The $9942 Turbo Coupe (left) boasted a 120-bhp 1.6-liter four. The Ford Probe series of show cars probed the frontiers of aerodynamics, here the 1984 Probe IV (bottom left). The $8680 '84 Escort GT (right) started the year with an 84-horse four, but later in the year the EXP's turbo four was offered. Topping the wagon lineup was the $7939 GL (bottom right). A 52-bhp two-liter diesel joined the '84 engine lineup.

total this year was 141,580 (including 17,600 convertibles), and it would go above 156,000 for 1985. By contrast, Camaro/Firebird sales, though initially much higher, began trending down, and by 1987 would be below those of Ford's veteran ponycar.

Which is quite remarkable when you remember that the Mustang was an older, boxier design with a less sophisticated chassis and somewhat lower handling/roadholding limits. Yet these apparent minuses were actually pluses. Many buyers preferred Mustang's more traditional on-road behavior, and earlier amortization of tooling costs allowed Ford to keep prices somewhat lower than GM could, even though the end of a decade-long inflationary spiral was now helping both companies in that regard. But Ford also seemed to build its cars better each year—GM didn't—and kept improving them faster, too.

Manual-shift EXPs and Escorts also received the clutch/starter interlock, but the hot tip among this year's smallest Fords was a new blown edition of the 1.6-liter CVH four. Like its 2.3-liter brother, this featured a blow-through turbo system and electronic multipoint fuel injection. Also included were high-lift cam (from the HO 1.6), high-flow air cleaner, EEC-IV electronic engine controls, and a turbo wastegate integral with a new bifurcated low-restriction exhaust manifold. At its maximum boost of eight psi, the little puffer spun out 120 bhp and 120 lbs/ft torque.

This engine was the heart of a new turbo package option for the two-seat EXP, and was extended to the three-door Escort GT at midyear to create a Turbo GT. Included for both models was an uprated chassis boasting Koni shocks, higher-rate front springs, P185/65R-365 Michelin TRX tires on newly styled cast-aluminum wheels, and front ride height lowered 0.75-inch (to reduce halfshaft angles and thus "torque-steer" in hard acceleration, a common problem in higher-power front-drive cars). Completing the package were five-speed MTX (automatic was *verboten*), front air dam, "teatray" rear spoiler, and black lower-bodyside paint with "Turbo" lettering.

Mercury cancelled its LN7 this year due to slow sales, but EXP picked up its taillamps and "bubbleback" hatch. The normally aspirated HO 1.6 returned from '83 as the new base engine. Other changes included a redesigned instrument panel, fold-down center armrest, and overhead console with map light and electronic digital clock/stopwatch. Electronic radios, graphic equalizer, and tilt steering wheel arrived as options. With all this, Ford was effectively reintroducing its odd little coupe after suspending production in '83 (at just 2250 units; LN7 saw but 699). To some extent, it worked, as model-year volume jumped to 23,016. But the new Turbo was crude-running, rough-riding, and not very attractive against sporty import coupes, most of them 2+2s that admittedly cost more.

Escort suffered no such problems, recording a smart production gain to close at more than 372,000 units. All models received EXP's redesigned dash and many of its new options. Also newly available was Tempo's Mazda-made 2.0-liter diesel four, again limited to five-speed manual. Replacing the three top-line GLX models were an LX five-door sedan and wagon with standard fuel-injected engine, TR suspension package, black-finish exterior trim, luxury cloth upholstery, floor console, overhead console, and tachometer. On all models, rear seatbacks got a two-stage folding mechanism to replace the former flop-down arrangement, thus providing a flatter cargo deck, plus standard split backrests except on the basic L models. Power door locks, tilt steering wheel, and electronically tuned radios joined the options list.

Though only a year old, the smooth 10th-generation Thunderbird boasted several embellishments for 1984, including a Tempo-style "A-frame" steering wheel with hub-mounted horn hooter (except on Turbo Coupe) and amber instead of clear parking-lamp lenses. Powerteam revisions comprised port electronic injection for the base Essex V-6 (thus eliminating carbureted Birds), availability of three-speed automatic with that engine nationwide, and optional automatic—though only a three-speed—for the Turbo Coupe. The top-trim Heritage was renamed Elan, and a new Fila "designer" model—named for and conjured up with the Italian sportswear maker—arrived with white-over-dark-charcoal paint set off by red and blue pinstripes. Exclusive to the Turbo Coupe were a new viscous-clutch radiator fan and oil-temperature warning switch.

The full-size Crown Victorias—standard and detrimmed "S" sedans and wagons plus Country Squire—returned virtually unchanged. Big-car sales were on a general rebound as buyers took advantage of declining fuel prices to grab what they feared would be Detroit's last biggies. Unlike GM, Ford saw no reason to change its full-size cars as long as they continued selling, having mostly written off their tooling costs. And sell they did, model-year volume jumping from 113,600 to near 173,500. Every one represented almost pure profit—and a handsome one at that—which delighted cash-

437

The '84 Bronco II listed at $9998 and came with a 115-bhp V-6. The XLS package added three-color tape striping, spats around the wheelwells, black-out trim everywhere, sport wheels, and deluxe interior fittings.

starved dealers no end.

Having enjoyed a good first-year reception, the mid-size LTD returned with more of the same, and saw more production—nearly 214,000 units. The faithful 200-cid six was retired after more than 20 years, leaving just a standard Lima four and optional 3.8 V-6 in its new fuel-injected form. Amber parking-light lenses and hub-mount horn buttons were featured here, too, along with newly standardized power steering for all models. A return to the bad old styling days was a standard (previously optional) cloth roof cover for the upscale Brougham sedan, with blind sail panels and a smaller "frenched" backlight. To get the Brougham without this, you ordered the regular sedan with the Interior Luxury Group (also available for the wagon). Another throwback was still available, too: imitation wire wheel covers.

A far more interesting LTD came along at midseason, the LX. Ford president Don Petersen got the idea for it from the Bob Bondurant high-performance driving school, which had adapted Mustang GT components to an LTD sedan that Petersen and other Ford executives had seen at the school. Featured in the production model were a 165-bhp 302 V-8, fortified suspension, Traction-Lok axle with 3.27:1 final drive, and P205/70R-14 Goodyear Eagle GT tires. Transmission was limited to a four-speed automatic, but tachometer, shift console, blackout exterior, and a plush bucket-seat interior were all included for a modest base price of $11,098. The LTD LX was a timely response to the growing hoard of domestic sports sedans like the Dodge 600ES

Turbo and Pontiac 6000 STE. A rapid one, too: 0-60 mph in an easy nine seconds, 16.8 seconds at 81.3 mph in the standing quarter-mile. Alas, it went nowhere with the public, and production would stop after model year '85 and just 3260 copies.

Overall, though, Ford Division had reason to be pleased with its 1984 performance. At 1.19 million units, it outstripped all of Chrysler Corporation in model-year production and pushed aside a faltering Buick to take third place in the industry. Escort remained the division's outright volume champ, but Tempo made an impressive debut, as noted, and Thunderbird rose to better than 170,500 units, a gain of some 48,000. Lincoln-Mercury was also up, notching close to 633,000 units (up from 461,000) on the strength of good gains by Cougar, the mid-size Marquis (a twin to the small LTD), Continental, and Lincoln Town Car, not to mention Topaz (some 129,250). Lynx, Capri, and Grand Marquis were down, but not by much.

Sharing the divisional limelight with Topaz was the long-awaited new Continental Mark VII. Built on the Continental sedan's 108.6-inch wheelbase but sharing the latest T-Bird bodyshell, it left the 1980-vintage Town Car as Lincoln's sole old-time biggie. Styling borrowed much from T-Bird/Cougar but differed in details, such as a squat but clearly recognizable Mark grille and the obligatory trunklid spare-tire hump. Bodysides were sculptured, with prominent full wheel cut-outs imparting an aggressive, road-hungry stance.

Mark VII arrived in base, plus Bill Blass and Versace designer editions, but the real surprise was the LSC (Luxury Sport Coupe). The last was audaciously targeted at the likes of the $55,000 Mercedes-Benz 500SEC—and was a much stronger rival than some Europhiles liked to admit. Though not as sophisticated as the vaunted M-B, it was very close not

only in workmanship—a surprise in itself—but roadability. Best of all, it sold for less than half as much: $23,706.

Motor noters were quick to paint the LSC as the "hot rod Lincoln" of pop-song fame, though few Lincoln or even Mercedes owners ever drove anywhere near their cars' limits. Still, Mark VII had the capable Thunderbird/Cougar suspension, augmented by new electronically controlled Goodyear air springs with automatic leveling (shared with this year's Continental). In standard form this made for substantial body lean and howling tires through even moderately fast corners, but the firmer LSC setup provided noticeably improved grip, quicker response, less lean, and great stability.

The LSC cost $2000 more than the base Mark VII but added a performance axle ratio, leather-covered console/steering wheel/gearshift knob, leather seat trim, dark charcoal lower-bodyside paint, and the all-important handling suspension. Alas, power was provided by the same mildly tuned 302 V-8, with throttle-body electronic injection and 140 bhp. However, more muscle was coming. Belatedly chasing the oil-burner market, Lincoln now offered the 2.4-liter (149-cid) turbodiesel-six that Ford had contracted to buy from the Austrian BMW-Steyr consortium, offering it in what was basically an LSC without the badges. But as V-8s were back in vogue—and diesels were out—the option would be withdrawn after only a few thousand installations.

Overall, the Mark VII was a fine development by any standard, and helped Lincoln to its third-highest model-year output in history. Significantly, that amounted to 54 percent of this year's Cadillac volume, Lincoln's best showing against its perennial foe in many a year. But most of that came from the big Town Car, which rolled on as a four-door sedan in three versions, each one still a glitzmobile with plenty of appeal to traditional-minded buyers, of which there were nearly 94,000 this year.

Mercury enjoyed another fine season, tallying close to half a million '84 sales. Among its notable newcomers was a revived Cougar XR-7, a cousin to the T-Bird Turbo Coupe. The Capri was waning, and its RS Turbo model would be abruptly cancelled at the same time as its Mustang counterpart.

Ford's big truck news this year was the snappy little Bronco II, which had actually bowed in March 1983—another "early riser." A smaller, thriftier, more agile four-wheel-drive sport-utility in the image of the first 1966 Bronco, it derived from the compact Ranger in the same way its big brother had been spun off the full-size F-Series pickup back in '78. This meant Ranger chassis specs and shared front sheetmetal combined with a shortened wheelbase—a handy 94 inches—and a unique body aft of the cowl. Against the big Bronco, the new II was 10.7 inches

shorter between wheel centers and a whopping 19.2 inches trimmer overall. It also stood some five inches lower and a good half-ton lighter. One other difference concerned the rear roof: fixed on Bronco II instead of removable as on the big Bronco.

Arriving with Bronco II was a revived 2.8-liter overhead-valve V-6, basically the same German-made unit available in the Seventies in the Pinto, Mustang II, and the imported Capri sports coupe. Also offered as a new Ranger option for '84, it was the standard and only power source for Bronco II. Ford went out of its way to emphasize that this V-6 had been considerably reengineered for truck use, doubtless to quell worries about reliability, which hadn't been a strong suit of the original passenger-car version. Though it still inhaled through a two-barrel carb, the modified V-6 was Ford's first truck engine to employ the firm's fourth-generation EEC-IV electronic engine controls, which was promoted as a plus for both reliability and smoothness.

Ford also promoted this engine as having more power and torque than Chevy's similar 2.8 V-6—about 115 bhp and 180 lbs/ft. As in 4×4 Rangers, it teamed in Bronco IIs with a standard four-speed manual, or optional five-speed overdrive manual or three-speed automatic. Also on hand were standard power steering and brakes and the same two-speed transfer case with manual-locking front hubs. Auto-locking hubs cost extra.

Other Bronco II features—both no-charge and extra-cost—predictably followed Ranger's, including the same selection of base, luxury XLT, and sporty XLS trim levels. Reclining front bucket seats in "knitted" vinyl, flip-fold rear bench seat and full carpeting were included in a base sticker price just two bucks shy of $10,000. Beyond that, you were on your own. Among the option choices: dark-tint "privacy" glass; pivoting front-door vent windows; a tilt-out feature for the high-arched rear side windows; exterior spare tire on a handy swing-out carrier (necessary for hauling bulky loads inside, as the spare ate up a lot of room there); chassis skid plates; heavy-duty shocks and battery; Snow Plow Prep package;

4050-pound towing package; and expected items like air, cruise, limited-slip differential, and stereo sound.

In all, Ford's "brand new kick" looked set to take the market by storm. The press certainly seemed to like it. *Car and Driver's* Pat Bedard termed the II "a sprightly bite-size Bronco . . . [a] first cousin to a car in the way it behaves, and like a sports car that goads you into driving it." *Four Wheeler* magazine predicted the baby Bronco wouldn't "take a back seat to any other rig on the road." But it didn't quite work out that way on the sales chart. Chevy hatched a baby Blazer from its S-10 pickup at the same time, and it outsold the Bronco II for the combined 1983-84 calendar years 248,360 to 161,225. Still, that was hardly a bad showing, and Ford added to Bronco II's appeal at the start of the formal '84 model year with several new options, including front captain's chairs, flip-or-remove rear side windows, flip-up glass sunroof, rear-window wiper and electric defroster, ski rack, and a lush special-edition trim package created in conjunction with the Eddie Bauer outdoor-clothing/equipment stores.

The Ranger received a few updates besides the interim V-6 option. Five-speed manual transmission became available with the 2.2-liter diesel, and a heavy-duty V-6 chassis/cab platform was added. Common to all models were clutch/starter interlock and, per federal decree, a "key-in-ignition" warning buzzer (both also found on Bronco II), plus the usual trim and equipment shuffle.

Extra power was the main highlight for this year's F-Series, big Bronco, and E-Series Econoline/Club Wagon. All now offered a new high-output version of the optional 5.8-liter/351-cid V-8. Massaged with four-barrel carb, wilder camshaft, bigger air cleaner, and low-restriction dual-exhaust system, the venerable Windsor churned out 210 bhp at 4000 rpm and 304 lbs/ft torque at 2800 rpm. Availability was confined to sub-8500-pound GVW models with automatic. So equipped, they were claimed to be the most potent such trucks around. Also found in Ford's larger light-duty trucks were the new clutch/starter interlock (with manual transmission), ignition-key buzzer, and standard parking-brake warning light.

Otherwise, there was little substantive change. The big Bronco was a virtual holdover save minor trim and option revisions, and the 100 designation disappeared from both F- and E-Series, these low-end models being combined with the step-up 150s to form new a F-150 and E-150. Pickup partisans must have been saddened by the loss of the trusty F-100 even though many of them had long been buying 150s.

Also common to this year's F- and E-Series was EEC-IV electronic engine controls for the 300 six, California 302 V-8, and the two-barrel 351 in models under 8500 pounds GVW. Added for the big pickups was an easier-shifting four-speed overdrive manual transmission, rear springs revised for a smoother ride on most F-250/350s, and a switch from semi- to full-floating rear axles on some 250/350s. Taken away were the 3.8-liter V-6 option, F-100 Fuel Saver, and sub-8500-pound GVW F-250 SuperCab. Making up for the last was the addition of a heavy-duty (over-8500 GVW) 4WD F-250 SuperCab. The big 460 gas V-8 and 6.9-liter diesel were now restricted to E/F-350s and heavy-duty E/F-250s, offered with non-overdrive four-speed manual or three-speed automatic transmission. Manual-shift Econolines and Club Wagons exchanged mechanical clutch actuation for hydraulic.

It's worth noting that F-Series payload ratings now ranged from 1395 pounds for the basic 2WD Regular Cab F-150 Styleside to 5680 pounds for the 4×2 Regular Cab F-350 Styleside and 6960 pounds for the 350 cab/chassis. Corresponding GVWs ran from 4800 to 10,000/11,000 pounds. SuperCabs had been wearing silly rear-side window appliques for the past couple of years, and these continued for '84, a throwback to the "Twindows" on late-Seventies Granada two-doors that made the truck look downright "dandified." Some traditions die hard.

1 9 8 5

After a long dry spell, Detroit was awash in money again, with most all companies earning record profits and—controversially—paying record executive bonuses. Though Japan's self-imposed quotas on U.S. car exports were still in effect, the market was tougher than ever and import sales reached a new calendar-year high of over 2.8 million units, up almost 400,000 from 1984, itself a record. Included were over 200,000 domestically built Japanese Honda Accords, Nissan Sentras, and Chevrolet Novas—the last a Toyota Corolla clone produced by New

United Motor Manufacturing, Inc. (NUMMI), the historic GM-Toyota joint venture in Fremont, California.

The advent of such Oriental "transplant" operations only added to a worsening production capacity surplus in the U.S., the impact of which has yet to be fully felt, even at this writing. Meanwhile, domestic makers strengthened their established ties with Japanese companies (if you can't beat 'em . . .) while "outsourcing" more key components "offshore"—necessary to cut production costs in an increasingly price-competitive market. Understandably, this was not at all popular with the unions.

Like its Big Three rivals, Ford Motor Company already had a Japanese affiliate in Mazda, and the relationship ripened this year as plans were laid for future joint models. Prime among these was a Mazda-designed sporty coupe to replace the Mustang, and an Escort successor

based on the next generation of Mazda's front-drive 323 subcompact. Old Henry wouldn't have believed it.

Still, Dearborn was prospering in the general recovery. Worldwide 1985 sales came to a healthy $52.77 billion, good for $2.52 billion in earnings and $1200 profit-sharing checks for U.S. Ford employees. Dearborn's share of U.S. car registrations slipped a bit, easing from 19.3 to 18.8 percent for the calendar year. Chrysler was up slightly, but General Motors fell to just over 42 percent, its lowest share since 1975. GM would go lower still, while Ford would soon shoot above its usual 20 percent.

Incidentally, calendar-year sales and registration figures are being cited here more often than in earlier chapters because they become more meaningful given the aforementioned "transplants" and the fact that many American-brand car and truck sales encompassed units

built both in the U.S. and Canada. Of course, model-year production figures will be cited where appropriate.

Truck demand continued booming right along with car sales. Calendar-year registrations for all classes set a new record: nearly 4.68-million units, up some 650,000 from 1984. Chevrolet took a slight lead over Ford with 1,256,964 registrations versus 1,245,805, and Ford again trailed International in heavy trucks, though that gap closed to fewer than 3000 units compared with better than 6600 in '84. Ford scored higher calendar-year truck sales of close to 1.28 million units, but Chevy did even better with just over 1.3 million. What's interesting here is that Chevy was phasing out of heavy trucks now, leaving those to sister division GMC. So, in that race, at least, Ford was a winner, selling 15,087 big rigs to GMC's 10,856.

A significant changing of the Glass House guard took place on February 1 when Philip Caldwell stepped down as FoMoCo chairman. Don Petersen replaced him—to absolutely no one's surprise. Company veteran Harold "Red" Poling took over for Petersen as president, a post later renamed vice-chairman.

Equally significant for Dearborn's future were its two major product introductions of 1985. One was the bold new front-drive Taurus and Sable family cars, which were previewed throughout the year but wouldn't go on sale until late December as 1986 models. For that reason, they're covered in the next section. Ford's other newcomer, the Aerostar minivan, was also an '86 but went on sale in the summer of '85, so it's covered here.

Ford had one other newcomer, though it wouldn't prove anywhere near as significant. This was the Merkur XR4Ti, a German-built, Americanized version of the Sierra XR4i, hotshot of

Ford Europe's mid-size family-car line. People were slow to recognize the marque name, which was pronounced "mare-COOR"—German for "Mercury." But Dearborn definitely intended that they should, for this was the first in a promised fleet of upmarket Teutonic Fords that would be brought over to duke it out with junior Audis and BMWs, the Saab 900, and similar cars in the lucrative, so-called "yuppie" market. Merkur was, in fact, a new franchise intended exclusively for Lincoln-Mercury, and some 800 of the division's dealers signed up for it.

Though close to Tempo/Topaz in overall size, XR4Ti rode a longer, 102.7-inch wheelbase and was motivated by its rear wheels—not the fronts. Only one model was offered, a sporty three-door hatchback sedan bearing yet another interpretation of the new "jellybean" corporate look, this one created under Ford

The LTD Crown Victoria sailed into 1985 with only minor changes: new colors, gas-filled shock absorbers, horn moved from stalk back to steering wheel, flash-to-pass control, and a diagnostic monitor on EEC-IV electronic engine controls. As before, buyers overwhelmingly preferred the four-door sedan, some 154,612 of them this year. The standard model (left) retailed for $11,627, although the $10,609 "S" four-door, intended mainly for fleets, was still available. So, too, was the two-door sedan, which listed at the same $11,627 as the four-door. It sold poorly, however, as only 13,673 were ordered for '85.

The 1985½ Mustang SVO (top) sported aero headlamps, and the turbo-four was tweaked another 30 horsepower to 205. Even so, only 1954 '85 SVOs were sold. The price tag of the '85 Mustang GT convertible (above) was $13,585, and it boasted 210 bhp. The 1985½ Escort (above right) received aero headlamps.

Europe design chief Uwe Bahnsen. An all-coil suspension with gas-pressurized shocks employed modified MacPherson struts, lower control arms, and anti-roll bar in front; the rear relied on BMW style semi-trailing arms. Power rack-and-pinion steering and assisted disc/drum

brakes were standard, as expected. But instead of the German XR4i's 2.8-liter V-6, the XR4Ti ran with the blown, port-injected 2.3-liter four from the Thunderbird Turbo Coupe (hence the "T" in the model name). Reworked to produce the same 175 horsepower as in the Mustang

SVO (but without the need of an inter-cooler), it mated to a five-speed overdrive manual transmission or optional three-speed automatic.

With a curb weight of just over 2900 pounds, the XR4Ti carried only about 16 pounds for each net horsepower, which meant 0-60 mph in under nine seconds—with manual, that is. Automatic cars had 30 fewer horses and 180 instead of 200 pounds/feet torque, which didn't exactly make them underpowered, though the deficits were noticeable. Despite marked body roll in tight turns, the XR4Ti exhibited balanced, agile handling—quick to the helm and somewhat less twitchy than a small Bimmer, though damp surfaces demanded right-foot restraint to avoid kicking in the blower at the wrong moment, thus spinning the wheels and going into a tail slide. The styling drew mixed reviews, especially the SVO-style "biplane" backlight spoiler, but most everyone acknowledged the first-rate workmanship, good ride, and well planned "driving environment."

Base-priced near $16,400 and boasting an impressive list of standard equipment, the XR4Ti looked to give Lincoln-Mercury a strong competitor for established Eurosedans, which was the whole idea, of course. Why, it was even made in Germany just like Audi, BMW, and Mercedes, a fact proclaimed on Merkur badges with the legend "Ford Werke Koln" (Cologne). Alas, buyers wanted automatic and leather upholstery more often than L-M expected, and early short supplies of these options put such a damper on sales that Ford was later forced to deny that it was planning to dump the entire Merkur program. L-M tried to perk up interest by putting the cars into various rental fleets, which seemed to help, but sales would continue to remain far below expectations.

This year's domestic Fords were, by and large, simply more of the same good things people had liked in 1984, with considered—if not earthshaking—improvements. Starting with the least changed, the mid-size LTD exchanged its fine-mesh grille insert for an eggcrate affair bearing a blue Ford oval in dead center (instead of on the grille header). Sedan taillights were modestly reworked, and minor trim changes were made throughout. The standard all-season radial tires grew a size larger to 195/75R-14s, and the base 2.3-liter "Lima" four was a little punchier and thriftier thanks to low-friction piston rings and higher compression ratio that yielded 88 horsepower and 122 lbs/ft torque. Model year output declined by about 8000 units to 205,526, but it didn't matter as the LTD would only last till 1986. Something far different and much better would soon be at hand.

Equally minor changes attended the big LTD Crown Victoria: standard gas-pressure shocks, ignition diagnostics added to EEC IV engine controls (shared with mid-sizers), and the usual trim/color

The '85 EXP's fuel-injected 1.6 was still rated at 80 bhp and 88 lbs/ft torque, but the 120-bhp turbo-four was still listed. While styling didn't change, the price of the Turbo Coupe (top) went up $55 to $9997. Total '85 EXP output was 26,462 units. The mid-size LTD continued with the same four models as since 1964½. The slow-selling LX Euro-sedan would quickly be axed, however, as LTD buyers chose the regular four-door and $9262 Brougham (above) instead. Together the two sedans enjoyed a production run of 162,884 units.

shuffles and upgraded sound systems. Arriving as a late-season option was an electronic rear self-leveling suspension that made use of air shocks. Production continued upward, reaching near 185,500, a gain of some 12,000. Whoever said that traditional American big cars were doomed obviously hadn't talked with buyers.

The popular compact Tempo re-

turned with throttle-body electronic fuel injection for its standard 2.3-liter HSC overhead-valve four, which was duly re-rated to 86 bhp, while a new 100-bhp high-output version, again with TBI, became an option. Other changes ran to a more convenient shift pattern for the now-standard five-speed manual transaxle (Reverse moved from a dogleg at the upper left of the H-pattern to the lower

The Thunderbird Turbo Coupe (opposite) charged into 1985 with the same 140-bhp turbo-four, now with water-cooled bearings for increased reliability, plus a revised grille insert and full-width wraparound taillights. The price tag now read $13,365, up $1035 over '84. Thirtieth anniversaries don't happen every year, so Ford trotted out a few thousand Anniversary Edition Birds (above), basically the Elan painted Medium Regatta Blue, fitted with a color-keyed interior and, of course, appropriate badging (left).

right), a larger 15.2-gallon fuel tank, newly-designed dash, and more no-cost extras. Among the last were tilt steering wheel and power steering and door locks added on the top-line GLX models. A new option for mid-range GL coupes and sedans was a Sports Performance Group, a faint gesture to the enthusiast set offering uprated suspension, 14-inch wheels and tires (versus 13s), more "buckety" front seats, and special trim. Despite class competition that remained intense, Tempo moved up from seventh to sixth in domestic-model calendar-year sales, tacking on close to 25,000 orders for a total of 281,144. Model-year production was stronger, too: a smashing 339,087.

Like its linemates, Mustang offered uncommonly fine value this year. Prices ranged from just $6885 for the basic LX notchback to $13,585 for the top-line GT convertible and $14,521 for the slow-selling SVO. Though quite a bit above 1979 levels in raw dollars, those figures were mighty competitive, especially once a strengthening yen began escalating prices on four-cylinder Japanese sports coupes that couldn't match the V-8 Mustang in performance or charisma.

Both those qualities were further enhanced for '85. Low-friction roller tappets and a new high-performance camshaft lifted the carbureted HO V-8 to 210 bhp, an impressive 35-bhp increase. Similar changes brought the throttle-body-injected 302, still restricted to automatic,

to 180 bhp. As before, the HO was available only with five-speed manual, which came in for revised internal ratios and a more precise linkage. Rounding out GT improvements were beefier P225/60VR-15 "Gatorback" tires on seven-inch-wide cast-aluminum wheels, both borrowed from the SVO, plus gas-pressurized front shock absorbers and an extra pair of rear shocks as a further aid in controlling axle tramp under hard acceleration which Ford called "quadra-shock".

Elsewhere, the cheap L versions were cancelled and remaining models acquired an SVO-style front-end cap with integral air dam and a simple air slot above the bumper. The SVO itself returned at midyear with square flush-mount or "composite" headlights, newly allowed by the government (and pioneered by Ford among domestics with the '84 Continental Mark VII). A change in intercooler type from water-to-air to air-to-air helped add an impressive 30 bhp to the turbo-four, now rated at 205 bhp. The latter was also applied to a short-lived revival of the Turbo GT, which vanished again after minuscule sales. Its vastly more popular V-8 brother continued to trade points with Camaro/Firebird in magazine showdown tests. In all, Mustang watched output increase some 15,000 units for the model year, to 156,514, and found better than 19,000 more buyers for the calendar year.

There were no major mechanical

Tempo continued with its six-model lineup for 1985. Surprisingly, there were no wagons, just the coupe and sedan in L, GL, and GLX trim. Tempo's 2300 HSC engine received throttle-body fuel injection for '85, which nudged horsepower up two, to 86, but a new high-output unit with revised cylinder head and intake manifold bumped that to 100. This engine became part of a $900 Sport GL package for the $7160 GL (top). The option also included P185/70R-14 tires mounted on seven-spoke aluminum wheels, upgraded suspension, dual remote mirrors, sporty seating, and a tell-tale blue exterior stripe. The GLX four-door (above) cost $8302.

changes for the svelte Thunderbird. However, the Turbo Coupe became a bit more reliable and convenient via new water-cooled turbo bearings that did away with the usual cooling-off "coast-down" period before shutting off. All Bird engines were also easier to get to thanks to a newly counterbalanced hood that did away with the clumsy old prop rod. Among the precious few styling changes were a revised grille insert and full-width wraparound taillamps. Inside, the TC now carried a complete set of analog gauges in a reworked instrument panel shared with other Birds, whose standard instrumentation combined analog fuel and temperature dials with a vacuum-fluorescent digital speedometer. A new all-electronic display with bar-graph readouts for fuel and engine functions was optionally available except on the TC. Other first-time Bird extras included an audio-system graphic equalizer and power front-seat recliners. Standard tires were upped one size across the board (to 225/60VR-15s on TC, 205/70R-14s elsewhere). Model-year production fell, though not drastically, losing 18,682 units to 151,851. Sales during the model year period, however, came in at a more satisfying 169,770.

Included in the totals were a few

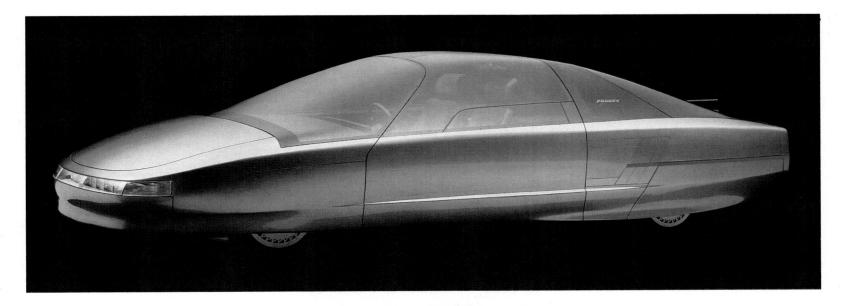

thousand examples of a 30th Anniversary Thunderbird issued to commemorate three decades of personal-luxury Fords. It was depressingly stock for a limited-edition birthday special: really just the Elan model with Medium Regatta Blue clearcoat metallic paint, color-keyed interior, special wheels, and the requisite badges. Most were motivated by 302 V-8s working through overdrive automatic. Technically a package option, the 30th seemed a poor way to celebrate a car that had always been captivating—and sometimes exciting. But if Bird lovers were disappointed, they had only to wait until 1989.

The subcompact Escort and EXP sporty coupe were carryovers until mid-model year, when they received a needed freshening up that included tidier grilles and flush headlamps. At the same time, the Turbo CVH option was dropped and the base and HO 1.6-liter fours gave way to a 1.9-liter enlargement offering 86 bhp with two-barrel carburetor or 108 bhp with port fuel injection. The only other alteration was a rearranged five-speed shift pattern with more conveniently sited Reverse, as on Mustang. These updates evidently sparked interest. Escort model-year volume jumped by nearly 34,600 units, reaching just over 407,000

in all, including better than 186,000 of the improved 1985½s. EXP went up too, though not as much, as production rose some 3500 units to 26,462 for the model year—still pretty small potatoes.

At the top of the Dearborn heap, the winning Continental sedan and Continental Mark VII coupes saw only minor trim changes for '85. And curiously, they no longer wore Lincoln nameplates. The big Town Car was unchanged in most respects save one: a reworked rump with rounded corners, matched by smoother front fenders. Evidently, even this blocky barge wasn't immune from the aero-fever raging throughout the Dearborn Design Center. The Mark VII LSC became more of a "hot rod Lincoln" with a more powerful 302 V-8, basically the '84 Mustang unit with throttle-body injection and new tubular exhaust headers, but tuned for a milder 180 bhp.

But Lincoln's most significant mechanical news was the arrival of anti-lock brakes as standard equipment for all V-8 Designer Series Continentals and Mark VIIs and models sold in five Pacific states. Jointly developed with the Alfred Teves company in Germany, it employed a microcomputer that modulated line pressure in response to signals of imminent lockup from any of three wheel-mounted

Ford continued to pursue better aerodynamics for its passenger cars via extensive wind tunnel tests, and the experimental Probe series was another end to that means. The Probe IV seen earlier was followed by the even-more-striking Probe V, which had a thermoplastic skin, skirted wheels, and a transversely mounted mid-engine layout. Its drag coefficient was just 0.137—less than that of an F-15 fighter plane.

sensors, thus providing rapid "cadence" braking to keep the wheels rolling so as to avoid a skid. It was a first for the American industry, and an important safety feature that would soon be picked up for other Dearborn cars—and by rival companies.

Unhappily, Mark VII production dropped by about a third, sinking to 18,355 units for the model year. This surely must have bothered Dearborn product planners, committed as they were to "aero styling" up and down the line—which may partly explain the extraordinary decision to preview the vital new Ford Taurus and Mercury Sable a full six months before their scheduled sale date, a story that unfolds in the next section.

Ford's awkwardly named Truck and Recreational Products Operations section had been given a daunting task: A "minivan" to answer the Dodge Caravan/Plymouth Voyager that Chrysler was selling as fast as it could build them. Now the notion of a compact box on wheels was hardly new when those Highland Park twins bowed for 1984. Volkswagen's rear-engine Type 2 Van/Bus had been around in various forms since the early Fifties, and Chevy's first Corvan of 1961 was essentially an Americanized rendition of the same good idea. So, too, for that matter, were Ford's original Econoline/Club Wagon and the Dodge A-Series, albeit with a conventional front-engine/rear-drive format on both. But as with so many Detroit cars, all these replies grew larger and heavier, to the point that VW again found itself alone peddling compact vans by the mid-Seventies. This market gap, with its high potential sales, was obvious to anyone who cared to look—as indeed Ford had with the "Carousel" project that almost made it for 1975 along with the third-generation Econoline. But it was left to a desperate, and thus gutsier-than-usual, Chrysler Corporation to reinvent the concept by creating what amounted to a high-built station wagon on the front-drive K-car platform. The result seemed the best of all worlds, offering car-like comfort, convenience, and driving ease combined with van-like versatility and more cargo space than a conventional station wagon. Caravan/Voyager took off immediately, prompting Toyota to bring in a curious little 88-inch-wheelbase "mid/front-engine" job from its Japanese home-market line—and sending GM and Ford racing to develop their own minivans.

But not necessarily to rush them out. Thanks to the Japanese invasion, American buyers now demanded superior workmanship even in brand-new vehicle designs; anything less could stymie sales and damage a manufacturer's reputation for years to come. This partly explains why Ford's new Aerostar arrived in the summer of '85 rather than the fall of 1984 as originally planned. "Quality is Job 1," Ford had been saying, so there was no point in introducing the Aerostar—or any other new product for that matter—until it was completely "right."

Quality the Aerostar had, but its "more minivan" concept made it somewhat less appealing than the Chrysler twins. Like GM with its new-for-'85 Chevy Astro/GMC Safari, Ford assumed that buyers really wanted a minivan that was more truck than car, a scaled-down version of the traditional big Detroit van, with rear drive and suitable engines to provide greater towing capability than the front-drive Chrysler models. This is what Ford delivered, and somewhat more. At 174.9 inches overall, the Aerostar was actually an inch shorter than Caravan/Voyager, but its 119-inch wheelbase was the longest of any minivan: seven inches greater than on Chrysler's vans, eight inches longer than GM's versions, and a whopping 27 inches

Henry Ford II savored many triumphs during his four decades of running Ford Motor Company, but saving the creaking colossus in the late '40s was the major one.

rangier than the Toyota Van's. Aerostar also had the dubious honor of being the porkiest of this lot at 3500 pounds base curb weight, a good quarter-ton heavier than its Big Three rivals. Unlike the big Econoline, Aerostar used unit construction, but the rest of the engineering package was resolutely conventional: power rack-and-pinion steering, power disc/drum brakes, and all-coil suspension with upper and lower controls arms at each end.

None of this was necessarily bad. The long wheelbase made for uncommon people and cargo space and a better ride, and the windowed Wagon models offered seating for up to seven via a standard pair of front buckets, a middle two-passenger bench, and an optional full-width three-person rear bench. A maximum payload of 2000 pounds and rated towing capacity of up to 5000 pounds were both well up on competitors' specs. But that was with the optional 2.8-liter V-6, here rated at only 115 bhp and 150 lbs/ft of torque—way too weak to provide decent go with even modest loads, let alone heavy ones. Performance suffered even further with the four-speed overdrive automatic, an optional alternative to the standard five-speed manual. And the base engine was the corporate 2.3-liter four-cylinder, which was not only weaker, but rough and noiser still.

Aerostar styling was, perhaps, unfortunate. There was nothing wrong from the cowl back: smooth and rounded in Ford's new mold, with a trace of the aborted Carousel in the raked-forward side-window leading edges on Wagons (the commercial Van versions had this in painted metal). Like other minivans, there were two conventional front doors, a sliding right-side door, lift-up tailgate,

and a vestigial hood so that the engine could mostly live ahead of the front compartment and thus not intrude too much. Trouble was, Ford sloped the hood at about the same angle as the windshield, creating an almost unbroken line that may have been good for aerodynamics but made for strange aesthetics—a sort of "anteater" snout that proved quite controversial. Chrysler and GM, meanwhile, used a more orthodox hood-to-windshield "break" that was more pleasing to most eyes. Aerostar's styling and a surprisingly low driving position made for tricky parking and forward visibility that wasn't as good as it looked from the outside.

Chrysler's Lee Iacocca looked at his new minivan competitors, then rushed out ads chortling, "Even when we showed them how, they didn't get the message." But the Aerostar was hardly a loser. It offered big-van extras like separate rear air conditioner, car-like amenities such as trip computer, and nifty new options like a rear-compartment audio console with headphone jacks for the kids. There was also a new marketing twist: "Rapid-Spec Packages," popular options grouped together and sold at lower prices than if ordered individually, this to take advantage of production "economies of scale."

Overall, though, the Aerostar was neither fish nor fowl. As CONSUMER GUIDE® concluded in *Auto Test '86:* "Ford has tried to hit two markets...the passenger-wagon market, where Chrysler has done so well, and the small-van market, where the Chevrolet Astro is a good choice because of its brawn and trailer-towing ability. Aerostar has landed somewhere between these two types of vehicles without really scoring a direct hit on either rival."

Sales and production reflected this compromise character. Against better than a quarter-million Chryslers and some 130,000 GM minivans, Ford sold only 30,324 Aerostars in calendar '85, though this was due partly to a late introduction. The 1986 figure would be a healthier 150,000, but rivals also improved, suggesting that Aerostar had indeed fallen between two stools. Dearborn would later admit as much by signing an agreement with Nissan to develop a new front-drive minivan for sale under both nameplates, with the FoMoCo version to be sold through Mercury dealers.

Ford's other light-duty trucks evidenced the same considered changes found in this year's passenger cars, some matching competitors' moves. Ranger and Bronco II offered a new 2.3-liter turbocharged four-cylinder diesel engine with ultra-fast glow plugs said to eliminate waiting time before cold starts. This was not a "dieselized" Lima unit but a purpose-designed engine with different bore/stroke dimensions (3.59 × 3.54 inches). Rated outputs were 89 bhp and 134 lbs/ft torque. Ranger's base 2.3 gaso-

line four, which *was* the Lima unit, switched from carburetion to electronic port injection. Outputs stayed about the same, but drivability and fuel efficiency both improved.

Elsewhere, the four-speed manual was dropped as the standard Ranger/Bronco II transmission in favor of the previously optional five-speed. The automatic option for 2.8 V-6 models remained the corporate four-speed overdrive unit, now with an electronically controlled torque-converter clutch that reduced the irritating "hunting" between third and fourth gears on upgrades. Features and trim got the usual adjustments, with Bronco II receiving tinted glass, transfer-case skidplate, trip odometer, ammeter, and oil-pressure gauge as standard equipment. Dark-tint "privacy glass" was added to the sport-ute's Eddie Bauer package, a Power Convenience Group (door locks and windows) expanded Ranger options, and all the compacts featured a more convenient single-key lock system and lower bodysides coated with chip-resistant urethane.

Highlighting this year's big Bronco and F-Series pickups was a 302 V-8 fortified with port fuel injection, higher 9.0:1 compression, and low-restriction exhaust system, all of which lifted bhp to 190—a 24-percent increase—and torque to 285 lbs/ft. It was included in a new Eddie Bauer package option for the big Bronco featuring the outdoor outfitter's trademark blue/cream color scheme as well as standard air conditioning, tilt steering wheel, cruise control, and front captain's chairs. Expanding standard equipment on this year's full-size sport-utility were high-output heater, front anti-roll bar, dual horns, intermittent wipers, and larger standard tires, the last still low-rolling-resistance all-season radials but in a new P235/75R-15XL size.

A raft of additional changes marked this year's F-Series, starting with three new F-350s: a 4×2 Crew Cab with "dualie" rear wheels, a 4WD cab/chassis version of same on a 137-inch wheelbase, and a non-"dualie" 4×2 cab/chassis on a 161-inch span. The HO 351 option was extended to over-8500-pound GVW models, the 6.9-liter diesel V-8 to Crew Cabs, and breathing improvements upped horsepower by some 15 percent on the big 460 gas V-8. Power steering was now standard for the base 2WD 150, overdrive automatic was a new option on 5.0-liter 4×4s, and the Lariat name was reinstated for an upgraded XLT trim package.

This year's E-Series vans, Econolines, and Club Wagons also offered the tuned 460 gas V-8 and wider availability of the HO 351, plus an optional Power Convenience Group *a la* Ranger and standard power steering for E-150s (thus making it line-wide). Club Wagons were treated to standard XL trim and intermittent wipers and tinted glass, though base prices were hiked upward to suit, and their XLT package option gained a few convenience features. Asbestos-free rear brake linings were adopted for E-250/350 (as well as corresponding F-pickups), along with low-roll-resistance tires. A high-output heater was used across the board. Several low-demand options were dropped, while many of the more popular options were newly offered in value-priced packages as on the Aerostar.

In all, Ford had another good truck year in 1985 despite losing the overall sales race to Chevy. Sales for the calendar 12 months were up throughout the line save Club Wagons, which lost a negligible 600 or so units. Ranger added better than 26,000 to finish at over 247,000, and Bronco II went up nearly 7000 to end at near 105,000. Even the big Bronco was selling better: up by close to 5000 units from calendar '84. And lest we forget, Ford's full-size F-Series remained far and away the nation's top-selling model line, car or truck, this year garnering over 562,000 orders. For perspective, that represented some 83 percent of this year's total Lincoln-Mercury volume.

Whatever the miscues and setbacks of 1985, Ford was confident about 1986. There were certainly sound reasons for that, but even the most optimistic Dearborners couldn't have imagined what lay ahead. After a long *long* time, Ford Motor Company was about to become what it had been in old Henry's prime: Detroit's undisputed number one.

1 9 8 6

T his was a banner year for Detroit in general and Ford Motor Company in particular. Total calendar-year car registrations and combined domestic/import sales reached their highest levels since record 1973: 11.1- and 11.5-million units, respectively. And both total truck registrations and light-duty truck sales hit new all-time highs for the calendar year: 4.8 and 4.6 million units. But though no one could know it at the time, 1986 would be the industry's last really good selling year until the 1990s.

Well, some might have predicted that if they'd looked at the continuing growth of imports, both cars and trucks. Again based on calendar-year sales, the foreigners that Henry Ford II said he would push back "into the sea" in the Seventies now accounted for three of out every 10 cars sold in the U.S. and one in five light trucks. Again, both were all-time bests. For Detroit, the fact that imports were somehow able to keep gaining share in an expanding market had to be worrisome to say the least. Primarily it meant that their own shares of the total market were shrinking. The one consolation was that a

fair number of those imports were sold by Big Three dealers.

But Detroit was happy to count up record profits anyway. Some of these came from hiking prices in lock step with Japanese makes whose products were being forced upmarket by a steady weakening in the dollar-to-yen exchange rate, aggravated by Voluntary Restraint Agreement quotas. A good many critics blasted the Big Three for taking short-term profits, saying they should take advantage of a growing Japanese disadvantage by holding prices and building

Ford had reason to celebrate in 1986 (above) as the new Taurus (left), seen here with North American executive vice-president Louis R. Ross standing by, copped Motor Trend's "Car of the Year" award. Equally satisfying was that Ford of Europe's new Scorpio (right) was crowned the "European Car of the Year 1986." Robert A. Lutz, then Ford executive vice president and chairman of the board of Ford of Europe, Inc., seems pleased with the honor. The LX was the top-of-the-line Taurus for 1986. Listing at $13,351 in four-door sedan form (below), it rode a 106-inch wheelbase and weighed 3109 pounds.

market share instead.

General Motors and Chrysler got the most heat, especially as both seemed to be on a spending spree, paying another round of unheard-of executive salaries and bonuses while snapping up non-automotive companies left and right, ostensibly as expansionistic hedges against a future downturn in their "core" car/truck business. Ford, meantime, was increasingly pictured as the industry's biggest success of the Eighties, its products and more-efficient-than-ever organization were models for others. Chairman Don Petersen was portrayed as a savvy executive with a Midas touch—a latterday Lee Iacocca.

There was a good deal of truth in this portrait, and the proof was as close as the bottom line. For the first time in 62 years, Ford out-earned GM, posting a record $3.29-billion profit in fiscal 1986 against GM's $2.95 billion, this on only one-third of GM's volume. Even more impressive, Ford's earnings represented a healthy 31-percent increase over 1985 on 19-percent higher worldwide sales of $62.72 billion. Obviously, Dearborn was doing a lot of things right.

Styling was among the most obvious things Ford was doing right, the firm now clearly setting the pace for all Detroit thanks to the revolutionary changes fostered by design chief Jack Telnack and his team. General Motors, the industry's styling arbiter for half a century, didn't seem to care anymore; Chrysler hadn't

been a trendsetter since 1957. Of course, Ford Motor Company had had its share of leading-edge cars in the past: the first and second Continentals, the Lincoln-Zephyrs, the '61 Continental four-doors, the '55 and '58 Thunderbirds, and the original Mustang, to name a few. But never had its lineup been so replete with state-of-the-art styling.

Dearborn advanced the art even further for 1986 with the new Ford Taurus and Mercury Sable, the sleek front-drive replacements for the Fairmont-based LTD/Marquis rear-drivers and among

The '86 Taurus lineup comprised two body styles, sedan and wagon, in four series: L, MT5, GL, and LX. The MT5 was billed as offering a "perfect blend of driving fun and luxury in a world class touring car," and although it came only with a five-speed stick, its 88-bhp 2.5-liter four just didn't have enough punch. The MT5 was predictably a slow seller. Among the "mainstream" Taurus models, almost all ended up with the V-6 and automatic. "There has never been a wagon quite like this one," noted the '86 brochure in hyping the $13,860 LX wagon (above and below). And indeed, the shape at the rear was unique, but it still allowed for an impressive 81-cubic-foot cargo hold.

the most daring American cars in years. The sedans had a drag coefficient of 0.32, one of the best in the world. But while "aerodynamic" cars are often ugly, these were beautiful. There was hardly a bad line or angle anywhere—nor should there have been as development costs for Project Taurus had totaled about three *billion* dollars.

Likewise, Taurus/Sable demonstrated Ford's canny realization that it no longer paid to build "corporate clones" differing mainly in nameplates. Most sheetmetal, for example, was different. Faces were very different, too, Taurus' being simpler, with a body-color insert between flush-fit headlamps. Sable's, on the other hand, was jazzier, with a full-width "light bar" incorporating nighttime running lamps. There were differences aft of the cowl, too. Taurus had the more conventional greenhouse, a Euro-style six-window treatment. Sable's was smooth and glassy, with a backlight artfully wrapped around to conceal the C-pillars. Other distinctions were rear tail-lamps and wheel openings, the latter rounded on Taurus, flat-topped on Sable.

Opposite page: The Escort had been updated for 1985½ with a new aero-look front end and a larger 1.9-liter four, so it marched into '86 unchanged. The GT, still the sporty model (although the closely related EXP would also be updated), sold for $8112 and was separated from other Escorts by its asymmetrical grille, lower body cladding, and front and rear spoilers. It boasted a 108-bhp version of the 1.9 four. This page: The '86 Mustang LX coupe listed at $7189 with the 2.3-liter four, but an extra $1120 endowed it with the GT's 200-bhp V-8 and suspension (top). The GT ragtop (right) cost $14,523.

There were fewer differences between the five-door wagons, the only other body style offered, but they were Detroit's most exotic-looking "estate cars" yet.

Taurus provoked a bit of controversy up front by wearing a blue Ford oval within a larger ellipse, a treatment promptly dubbed the "navel" in some quarters. Prototypes suggest that this was originally to be reserved for the top-line LX, with base L and mid-range GL wearing a small oval over simple horizontal slats. But the latter was abandoned very late in the game, so all models ended up sporting the navel. If you're going to "reach," Ford officials must have figured, you might as well go all the way.

And in most respects, Ford did. Like the Tempo and Topaz earlier, Taurus and Sable were new from the ground up. Nary a screw, molding, or fixture was carried over. Oh, they did have unit con-

struction like their Fox-y predecessors, but wheelbase stretched a tad longer to 106 inches. And the mechanical layout was, of course, entirely different: front drive with transversely mounted engines. All models were initially built with a new 3.0-liter/183-cubic-inch "Vulcan" V-6 teamed with a new-design four-speed overdrive automatic transaxle. An overhead-valve design with classic over-square dimensions (bore and stroke: 3.50 × 3.15 inches), the Vulcan boasted multi-port electronic fuel injection and 9.25:1 compression, good for 140 horsepower and 160 pounds/feet torque, fairly tame outputs indicating a mild level of tuning. Arriving a bit later for the Taurus was a 2.5-liter (153-cid) ohv four, essentially an enlarged version of the HSC Tempo/Topaz unit, available with three-speed automatic or five-speed manual. That manual could only be had in a special MT5 Taurus sedan or wagon, a faint nod at the

Due to poor sales, the pricey Fila was dropped from the T-Bird lineup for '86, leaving three models: standard, Elan, and Turbo Coupe. The $14,143 TC (top) was still the performance model and little changed, but turbo-four was tweaked to 155 bhp when teamed the five-speed manual, 145 with automatic. Ford called it "The ultimate Thunderbird for the driving enthusiast." The $12,554 Elan, meanwhile, was "A most luxurious place to be," and with split bench seats with four-way adjustable headrests and 24-ounce carpeting, plus power everything, it was that (above). Total output was up a bit to 164,965 for the model year.

"sports sedan" crowd offering a little more black trim outside, tachometer and front bucket seats inside, mildly recalibrated suspension—and absolutely nothing in the way of performance or handling to threaten high-end Europeans like BMW or Mercedes.

By contrast, V-6 Taurus/Sables, weighing in at a lithe 3100 pounds, allowed for adequate acceleration. However, quiet highway cruising and excellent directional stability were strong suits. The four-cylinder/automatic job

was mainly for fleet duty, and *very* much slower.

Ford put great effort into Taurus/Sable chassis development, and it showed. All models employed MacPherson struts, lower control arms, and coil springs for the front suspension, plus power rack-and-pinion steering and assisted front-disc/rear-drum brakes. Rear suspension was also independent, still unusual for a Detroiter—and with different geometry for each body style. Sedans rode on MacPherson strut/coils plus twin parallel arms. Wagons had the coils between double wishbones, an arrangement deemed more suitable for the heavier loads they might carry, and used shorter shock towers to maximize cargo space. Regardless of body type, ride was compliant thanks to ample wheel travel and well-judged spring/shock rates, body lean modest even in hard corners.

High-tech styling, front drive, all-independent suspension. It sounded like the makings of a premium European sports sedan. Yet Taurus (and Sable) was actually a high-volume family car competing against the conservative likes of the square-lined Chevy Celebrity and other GM A-bodies at a starting price of just under $10,000. The sophisticated styling was a bold departure for this market, especially after the innocuous LTD, and Ford knew it. To give middle-of-the-road buyers time to adjust to the striking aero looks, management decided to unveil Taurus/Sable at the Chicago Auto Show in February 1985—some 10 months before the scheduled on-sale date of December 26. At the same time, pre-production cars went out to major magazines for preliminary assessment.

Ford's product people needn't have worried. Helped by glowing press reports, Taurus and Sable were hot sellers from day one, and the two plants building them, Atlanta and Chicago, went on overtime to meet the demand. Taurus zoomed to the number-six sales spot among domestic cars, attracting 267,506 buyers by the end of 1986. (Sable, as expected, did half as well: 101,023 units for the same period, finishing 34th among 82 domestic models.) The styling was definitely a plus. By coincidence, Ford's new intermediates bore more than a passing resemblance to the futuristic Audi 5000, already embraced by trendy, upwardly mobile types as *the* status car of the day. Though the Taurus/Sable had a distinctive shape, the pair was undoubtedly viewed as a sort of bargain-basement Audi, offering the same "with it" looks and similar roadability for thousands less. As such, it seemed too good to be true. Yet the Taurus was no mirage: solidly built, understated, refined, well equipped, and priced right.

But not perfect, of course. CONSUMER GUIDE® judged it a "fine effort in ergonomics, styling and especially handling/roadholding for a family car," but found the suspension "too stiff" on cratered city streets, the V-6 lacking "the spirit Ford has promised. But those are rough edges we hope to see corrected. Taurus is well made, enjoyable to drive and very competent." *Car and Driver* found a few literal rough edges in the workmanship department, but termed Taurus "an outstanding car" with "all the comfort and utility that one expects in a larger cruiser. And for the person who enjoys driving, American sedans don't come any better.... The Taurus doesn't quite have the assembly quality or the careful detail design of the best European cars, but are the small differences worth several thousand dollars? [We] think not. Furthermore, we suspect Ford will do its best to smooth out the Taurus's few rough edges.... Then the only remaining problem will be to convince the skeptics that one of the world's finest sedans is a Ford."

More than a few GM folks must have been worried by Taurus/Sable and the public's enthusiastic response; if they weren't, then GM was in more trouble than it appeared. Here was solid proof that America could still produce world-class automobiles—about the best news from Detroit since the Model T put the nation on wheels. Further evidence came from CONSUMER GUIDE®, which rated Taurus a "Best Buy" and one of 1986's "50 Best New Cars," while *Motor*

After being off the market for the better part of a year, a rejuvenated 1986½ EXP emerged having traded its ungainly "frog-eye" face for a smooth aero-look front end. Now officially an Escort EXP, it came in two flavors: Luxury Coupe and Sport Coupe. The former boasted a long list of standard equipment for the $8235 base price, with the emphasis on a luxury-oriented interior. It utilized the 88-bhp 1.9-liter four. The $7186 Sport Coupe (top and center) chased the boy-racer crowd with the 108-bhp 1.9 HO, firmer suspension, meatier tires, and "sport performance" bucket seats. Meanwhile, the $12,562 LTD Crown Victoria (bottom) had its 5.0-liter V-8 upgraded via the adoption of sequential multi-port fuel injection.

Trend named it domestic "Car of the Year."

At the opposite end of the conceptual spectrum, Ford's big Crown Victoria (and Mercury's Grand Marquis) continued to fill the residual need for Sixties-style land yachts, necessary for a certain conservative buyer group that remained significant. The main change on this year's models involved a thoroughly overhauled version of the venerable 302 V-8, with multiport electronic injection (replacing throttle-body), new-design fast-burn combustion chambers, higher 8.9:1 compression, roller tappets, low-friction piston rings, and viscous-clutch radiator fan. The resulting output gains were modest, up to 150 bhp and a sizeable 270 lbs/ft peak torque. The one other change of note was making the former Interior Luxury Group option into a new four-model LX series: two- and four-door sedans, plain-side wagon, and woody-look Country Squire.

For all that, Crown Vic model-year production plunged by more than 40,000 units, finishing at just over 124,000. The

For 1986, the Tempo traded its triple-slot grille and single rectangular headlights for a twin-slot front with aero-style halogen headlamps, and also sported a new full-width taillight treatment. The model lineup, pared down to four, consisted of GL and GX. The $7358 GL coupe (above) was enhanced with the $934 Sport GL option, while the GL four-door sedan (left), which was far more popular, listed at $7508. Output came in at 69,101 coupes and 208,570 sedans.

loss partly reflected higher prices, with minimums now up to $12,505-$13,612, though some sales were doubtless lost to Taurus.

Tempo lost some of its initial clumsiness via a new slat grille and flush-mount "aero" headlamps, plus revised bumpers and taillamps. Detail updates comprised inch-larger 14-inch wheels and tires, optional 15-inch roadwear with the extra-cost Sport package, relocated switchgear (including a retrograde, dash-mount wiper/washer control), single-key lock system, and miscellaneous trim/equipment alterations. Model offerings thinned with cancellation of the cheap Ls,

and the top GLX group was renamed LX. Tempo remained the fifth-best seller among domestic cars, but model-year output skidded almost 19 percent, ending just short of 278,000.

Escort returned unchanged from its "1985½" makeover, though single-key locks were adopted. There was also a new price/economy leader called Pony, a no-frills three-door reviving a name from Pinto days and budget-priced at $6052 to take on low-end imports. The reborn GT three-door still carried P195/60HR-15 tires on six-inch-wide aluminum wheels, fortified suspension with rear stabilizer bar and larger front bar, plus a unique

sporty asymmetric grille, fore/aft spoilers, and rocker-panel skirts, all in body color. EXP got this same treatment save a Tempo-style nose with slat grille. The little two-seater enjoyed slightly better model-year volume, rising 4500 units to near 31,000. Escort maintained its position as Detroit's number-two seller but attracted 18,500 fewer buyers for the calendar year despite higher model-year production of 430,053, up some 27,000 from '85.

Back at the horsepower war, Mustang shed its old carbureted and TBI V-8s in favor of a single new 200-bhp small-block with sequential port electronic fuel injection, available with either five-speed manual or four-speed automatic. The rear axle was strengthened to handle peak torque that now stood at a mighty 285 lbs/ft, and viscous (fluid-filled) engine mounts, introduced on the SVO the previous year, were adopted for both V-8 and V-6 models. Ford's continuing attention to practicality was evident in a longer anti-corrosion warranty, increased use of sound-deadening material, and the more convenient single-key lock system.

The inevitable annual price increases were still evident, too, but fairly modest. For '86, the notchback Mustang LX was up to $7295, the GT convertible to $14,420. The SVO was still around—and costlier at $15,272—but its days were numbered. With sales that had always been far below even Ford's modest projections, the SVO was just too unprofitable to sustain, and it would not return for '87. Model-year 1984-86 production was 4508, 1954, and 3382—9844 in all, barely half the available production capacity for one year. For Mustang as a whole, model-year production jumped to 224,410, remarkable considering the relative lack of change. Alas, this would be the decade high for Ford's ponycar, for reasons that will be clear a bit later on.

Thunderbird fared somewhat better volume-wise, increasing to 163,965 units, a gain of nearly 12,000. It, too, was largely a rerun, but V-8 efficiency and driveability improved a bit with adoption of the same 150-bhp port-injected 302 used in this year's Crown Victoria. Standard tires again went up one size, to 205/70R-14, but the trendy Fila was axed, and a sliding power moonroof gave buyers a new reason to spend $726 extra.

Over at L-M Division, the Mark VII (and Continental sedan) returned to wearing Lincoln badges (why they vanished for '85 remains a mystery). More significant was standardization of the previously optional Ford/Teves anti-lock braking system. The optional turbodiesel-six disappeared virtually unnoticed, and the 150-bhp V-8 was now the one and only engine for all Mark models save LSC. But the "hot rod Lincoln" wasn't ignored, picking up the port-injected, 200-bhp Mustang GT V-8, plus a new analog gauge cluster where other models had electronics. The latter was obviously a hasty afterthought, but in the old days Ford wouldn't have even bothered with such a small improvement on a marginal seller like this. Clearly, the Glass House was still populated by genuine enthusiasts who appreciated the fact that there's more to running a car company than just the bottom line. Much like the hallowed Continental Mark II of the Fifties, the LSC was a labor of love, a goodwill ambassador whose main mission was to cast an aura of class over the rest of the Lincoln line. In that—and as a satisfying road car—it was superb.

The Ranger received the most changes of this year's light-duty Ford trucks, and they helped the compact pickups to a new calendar-year sales high of close to 269,500 units, some 20,000 better than combined 1986 Chevy S-10/GMC S-15 volume. The two big items of interest were new SuperCab models, two- and four-wheel-drives with a nomi-

nal six-foot cargo box on a 125-inch wheelbase, and a V-6 engine so fully reengineered that only the flywheel and fan were carried over from the previous 2.8-liter version. Naturally, the V-6 also resided in this year's Bronco II.

Also making news on 4×4 Rangers as well as Bronco II was optional "Touch Drive." Not to be confused with the old "Teletouch Drive" of Edsel days, this was a two-speed transfer case with electronic controls that allowed shifting between two- and four-wheel drive at the touch of a button. Like Jeep's similar "Selec-Trac," this one required auto-locking front hubs, so Ford included them. But Touch Drive wasn't exactly a full "shift-on-the-fly" system like Jeep claimed for Selec-Trac, because Ford recommended that you stop and back up a few yards when returning to the two-wheel mode, a

Show cars—or concept cars as the automakers preferred to call them—made a comeback during the '80s, and Ford churned out its share. One that made the rounds in 1986 was the Ghia Vignale, a wagon sporting a raised roof section behind the front seat. The upper "windshield" was reminiscent of the '64 Olds Vista Cruiser wagon. Another show car was the Cobra 230 ME, a racy-looking coupe with an amidships-mounted engine, roof spoiler, and a single windshield wiper.

minor limitation that would later prompt a heated Ford/Chevy advertising battle.

Space precludes listing all the changes in this year's newly revamped V-6, but the major ones will suffice. Still supplied by Ford Germany, the previous 2.8 unit was upped to 2.9 liters/177 cubic inches via a 0.05-inch-longer stroke, now 2.83 inches, and multiport fuel injection replaced the carburetor. Other changes

Ford's compact van, the Aerostar, hit the streets in the late summer of 1985 as an '86 model. Although competing against Chrysler's front-drive minivans, Aerostar had rear-wheel drive (like Chevy's Astro) and rode a 6.9-inch-longer 118.9-inch wheelbase. And at 3500 pounds, it was 600 pounds heavier. Prices started at $9064 for the passenger version with the 2.3-liter four. A 115-bhp 2.8-liter V-6 was optional.

inclusions were power brakes, full gauges, power steering, and heavy-duty shocks for 4×4s, and skid plates for V-6 4×4s.

Ranger's XL and XLT package options also remained much as before, but the revamped sporty XLS emerged as the STX. It combined similar black exterior accents with the new V-6 and a luxury interior featuring cloth upholstery, tachometer, and leather-rim steering wheel. Ford had test-marketed the STX in Hawaii and five mainland Pacific states during 1985, where it accounted for 12 percent of Ranger sales, a successful showing that prompted the division to offer it nationwide for '86. Like their F-Series counterparts, Ranger SuperCabs could be ordered with a pair of inward-facing flip-up jump seats. Also available were flip-out rear side windows and a handy roller-blind cargo cover to forestall thievery of items left inside.

Besides sharing relevant features with 4×4 Rangers, this year's Bronco II added a dual-note horn, heavy-duty battery, and low-engine-oil warning light to its standard-equipment roster, as well as a tachometer with the XLT and Eddie Bauer packages. Gas-charged dampers replaced conventional units with the heavy-duty shock option, a spare-tire cover was included with the extra-cost swing-away carrier, and the optional flip/takeout rear windows were no longer available, replaced by fixed "privacy glass."

But the big news was the advent of a two-wheel-drive Bronco II. As other makers were discovering, a good many buyers wanted the look and driving feel of a sport-utility but didn't really need all-wheel traction, hence this rear-drive-only model. In a blinding bit of deduction, Ford said it would find its strongest appeal in the Sunbelt areas of Southern California, Texas, and the Southeast. Division publicists also noted that the Bauer option was increasingly popular on Bronco II, attracting "many new metropolitan-area and younger buyers, particularly those in the 'YUMP' (Young Upwardly Mobile Professionals) demographic group." Someone in Dearborn had evidently missed the term "yuppie." Incidentally, the 4×2 Bronco II listed for about $1400 less than the 4×4, but was otherwise identical.

Detail improvements were the only news for this year's big Bronco and F-Series pickups. A more powerful 60-amp alternator and single-key lock system were featured on both. Bronco received additional corrosion protection, while the F-Series took on a few minor standard-equipment items such as glovebox lock and, on SuperCabs, the previously optional fold-up rear bench seat. Availability of four-speed overdrive manual transmission was extended to 5.8-liter V-8 models over 8500-pounds GVW and to 5.0-liter F-150s and 4×4 F-150 SuperCabs.

included larger valves, higher 9.0:1 compression, fast-burn combustion chambers, hydraulic instead of solid lifters, improved intake manifolding, more efficient roller-chain camshaft drive, and a lightweight aluminum front cover (replacing cast iron). For all that, output gains were a bit disappointing. Horsepower jumped 25 to 140, but torque improved by only 20 lbs/ft to 170, still not quite enough for good go at maximum payloads. So why all the bother? Slightly better fuel efficiency and greater reliability.

Boasting nearly 17 additional inches behind the seats, the new SuperCab topped a realigned Ranger lineup that

began with a price-leader S, a shorty 4×2 regular cab with the 2.0-liter four (2.3-liter in California and high-altitude areas), five-speed manual transmission, and virtually no options. Standard Rangers comprised 4×2 and 4×4 regulars with short and long beds, as well as the new SuperCabs. These had the 2.3-liter four as standard and offered a choice of manual or optional four-speed automatic, plus all the usual extras including the new 2.9 V-6. Also still listed was the commercial V-6-only Ranger chassis/cab. Trim and equipment were roughly as before, but standard features expanded for all models save the stripped S. Among the new

Among Ford vans, the Aerostar, introduced at mid-'85 as a 1986 model, carried into the new calendar year with no change, then received several updates for "1986½." Prime among these was substitution of the new 3.0-liter Taurus V-6 for the optional 2.8-liter unit. It was big step in the right direction for both performance and hauling ability. Other interim changes included a "mechanical" gauge package to replace the previous vacuum-fluorescent display (which shifted to the options column), standard bodyside protection moldings, and low-oil-level warning light (the latter reflecting Aerostar's poor underhood service access), plus an illuminated-entry feature for the optional Light Group.

This year's Econolines and Club Wagons were upgraded along F-Series/Bronco lines, and options were now merchandised *a la* Aerostar's "Rapid-Spec" formula. All E-Series received standard all-season steel-belted radial tires, the usual minor trim and GVW revisions, an inside hood release, and front-door courtesy-light switches. Additionally, Econolines now came with the Club Wagon's sliding right-side door, the center-opening twin doors becoming a no-cost option. The extra-cost XL package added interval wipers, "premium-vinyl" front bucket seats, and chrome grille, while a heavy-duty service package and a window-van insulation package joined the options roster.

Ford and Jeep were the only domestic makes recording higher light-truck sales for calendar '86, perhaps confirming the view of some analysts that the truck market predicts where the car market will go in six to 12 months. Tougher times certainly seemed to lay ahead, judging by Ford's individual model-line results. Econoline was some 1700 units short of its '85 sales level, Club Wagons were off 4200 to 27,374 units, Bronco dipped nearly 2700 to just under 50,000, and its kid brother was down nearly 2000 units to a bit over 103,000. Most ominously, the full-size F-Series pickup, still America's best-selling vehicle, lost over 17,500 sales. The only gains came from Aerostar, which had nowhere to go but up, and the Ranger, which attracted nearly 22,500 more buyers to finish near 269,500.

Still, there was no sign of immediate sales trouble. Indeed, Ford Division was poised to win another moral victory over archrival Chevrolet, and Ford Motor Company as a whole had never been in better shape.

Testimony for that appeared this year with the October release of *The Reckoning*, a new book by David Halberstam, America's premier analyst of American business. It was the lengthy tale of one automaker on the rise, Nissan of Japan, and one on the decline, Ford of Dearborn. Funny thing was, these were stories of the Seventies, not the Eighties. At the time of pressing, the book was outdated—and the fortunes of its subjects

The Aerostar (top) was available as a cargo van as well as a passenger wagon. As a hauler, it could easily be uprated to 1600 and 2000 pounds capacity by ticking off the appropriate Payload Package. Note the aerodynamic styling compared to the Econoline van next to it. The '86 full-size pickup (above) carried on as before with F-150, F-250, and F-350 models and with the usual long list of options and packages. Prices started at $8625.

reversed. Now Nissan was being pulled down by dull, stagnant products approved by a management team determined to hold onto previous gains, while Ford was roaring back from near disaster on the strength of bold new initiatives from leaders who didn't fear to take risks—as with the Taurus. An apt symbol of Ford's resurgence came on November 14, when chairman Don Petersen cut the ribbon for a big new assembly plant in Hermosillo, Mexico, erected to build a new Mazda-designed subcompact for 1987, the Mercury Tracer.

Meanwhile, another author had produced still another gossipy chronicle of

the Ford family. This was *Ford: The Men and the Machine*, released in May. British author Robert Lacey claimed exhaustive research, but his work was long on incidents and personalities, short on analysis and product details. Enthusiasts generally judged it more drama than history. Which may explain why its treatment of Henry Ford I was later made into a TV "docudrama" with Cliff Robertson ill-cast as the great man himself. Ford publicists groaned, but the Lacey book sold well in both hardcover and paperback, proving once again that America still wanted to get all the lowdown it could on one of its most royal of families.

1 9 8 7

Overshadowing any of Ford Motor Company's many triumphs this year was a singular tragedy: On September 29, only 25 days after reaching 70 years of age, Henry Ford II died of pneumonia. For his family, and for the company to which he had devoted his life, it was truly the end of an era.

He was widely mourned, of course. What else for the man who had revitalized a national institution while himself maturing from apple-cheeked beginner to one of the most accomplished leaders in American business? Perhaps typical of the man, New Orleans' famed Preservation Hall Jazz Band played for his memorial service at Detroit's Cathedral Church of St. Paul. It was where his grandfather's funeral had taken place 40 years before, a

fact not lost on students of Ford tradition.

Friends, and even a few foes, came to pay their respects. GM chairman Roger Smith attended. So did Semon E. "Bunkie" Knudsen, whom HF II had dismissed as Ford president back in 1969. Another one-time Ford president, Lee Iacocca, was conspicuously absent, but Chrysler Motors was represented by two of its many other former Ford employees, chairman Gerald Greenwald and vice-chairman Ben Bidwell. From the Ford corporate family came recently retired chairman Philip Caldwell, current chairman Donald E. Petersen, vice-chairman Harold "Red" Poling, and many other leaders from Ford's past, including Arjay Miller and J. Edward Lundy, two of the original "Whiz Kids" whom HF II had had the good sense to hire way back when. Even Japanese affiliate Mazda sent an ambassador in its president, Kenichi Yamamoto.

As HF II had eulogized both his father and grandfather, so now was he publicly remembered by his own son and heir apparent, Edsel B. Ford II. "They said that daddy's name was on the building, but it

was more than that," young Edsel told the assembly. "He dominated the company, but the company dominated him, too. His first duty was to the tradition of the family and the company that bears the family name." Brother William Clay Ford, now the sole surviving grandson of the company founder, delivered an address that also touched on tradition. "Today we celebrate the public man," he said. "The name on the building represents all of us."

Car lovers remembered "Henry the Deuce" as the man who "saved a company for enthusiasts," as *AutoWeek* headlined his obituary. It was typical of "buff book" tributes. "His star moment," said the magazine, "came in the 1960s when, though reluctant to break the non-racing pact among U.S. automakers...he took Ford Motor Company racing—first in NASCAR and USAC...[then] to Le Mans. The Ford GTs, from the first GT40 through the Mk IV, remain the high-water mark of American automakers' entries in European road-racing events." *Road & Track* observed how incredible it seemed "that one company could have competed successfully in so many forms

Although it kept the same chassis, the Thunderbird was completely reskinned for 1987. It looked even more aerodynamic than before, and it wore two different faces. The $16,805 Turbo Coupe (above and top right) sported a thrust-forward grille-less beak nestled between aero headlights. However, the $15,383 LX (right) featured a more traditional shiny grille. The TC concentrated on performance, so its 2.3-liter turbo-four was intercooled to boost horsepower to 190 (150 with automatic), and it also got anti-lock brakes and electronic Automatic Ride Control. The LX, on the other hand, boasted an exceptionally luxurious interior.

of racing simultaneously. While it is true that Henry was not personally involved in any of these...activities, he was the boss and could easily have squelched all of it as so much money-wasting—something his penny-pinching grandfather would surely have done. But he didn't, and thereby enriched beyond measure the lives of [those] to whom the sweet shriek of a racing engine is the music of the spheres."

AutoWeek also pointed to "the cars developed under his watch: The '55 Thunderbird, the '64 Mustang and its European cousin the Capri, the Lincoln Continental Mark II and the current Mark VII, the Fiesta and the cars sold here under the Merkur banner, among others. Yes, there was the Edsel and the Pinto, and Henry II kept Dearborn out of the early-'70s rush to smaller cars until it was almost too late and killed an idea [the Carousel] that later became Chrysler's minivans.... But consider, too, that he took the firm public in 1956, and retired while his son Edsel...was getting the kind of training in the business [that] Henry II never had. He thus assured that leader-

The heavily facelifted '87 Mustang emerged with the most aggressive-looking GT yet (top). It faced the world without a grille, and sliced through the wind more easily because of its new aero-style headlights. Meanwhile, the LX convertible (above) listed at $12,840, and came with the 90-bhp 2.3-liter four as standard, and there was no longer the 120-bhp V-6 to step up to as it had been dropped for '87. Note the LX grille bar with the blue-and-white Ford oval.

ship could be held outside the family—even if by less colorful men than the one the *Detroit Free Press* called 'The Last Tycoon'—and that any Ford who does assume the helm will be prepared for it.

"Despite much-publicized divorces and womanizing," *AutoWeek* concluded, "Ford was a family man in the sense that he cared deeply for his relatives and children and fiercely supported them. Carroll

Shelby, who was involved in the race programs and with whom Edsel lived for a while, recalls Henry II calling regularly with concern for his son. At the same time, he made Ford Motor a modern corporation that may always acknowledge its family heritage...but responds to the larger world as well. That may be his greatest legacy."

His successors had built well on the

foundation he laid. Unlike his grandfather, whose passing came amidst great turmoil for Ford Motor Company, HF II lived to see a string of stupendous accomplishments that represented not only the peak of the Caldwell/Petersen years but the company's entire postwar history. For one thing, Dearborn posted record profits in 1987: $4.63 billion, up a colossal 41 percent from 1986. And for the second straight year, FoMoCo outearned General Motors. Even better, operating costs had been trimmed $5 billion since 1979 (to an estimated $65 billion), individual worker productivity had increased six percent annually since 1980, and the firm's share of total new-car registrations was back above 20 percent for the first time since '79, this even as GM fell below 40 percent for the first time in anyone's memory. Dearborn's profit-sharing checks this year totaled $370 million—$2100 for each U.S. employee.

There was more good news. The revamped 1987 Thunderbird was selected "Car of the Year" by *Motor Trend*, which named chairman Don Petersen "Man of the Year." In October, Petersen was also voted the nation's most effective business leader in a survey of 206 corporate chiefs conducted by *Fortune* magazine, garnering 25 percent of their votes, five more than Chrysler's Iacocca. And according to *Ward's Automotive Reports*, the mid-size Taurus was the country's best-selling car in 1987, outranking Ford's own Escort as well as the Chevy Celebrity and Honda Accord.

Nineteen eighty-seven was also a year of "passages" for Ford Design. On June 1, Don Kopka retired as worldwide design chief at age 60. His replacement, as expected, was 50-year-old Jack Telnack. Taking over for Telnack at North American Automotive Operations was Fred C. "Fritz" Mayhew, previously NAAO's director of small-car styling. Sadly, this special family had to contend with a death of its own, the passing of former corporate design chief Eugene Bordinat in August at age 67.

On a happier note, Ford Motor Company's 1987 fleet elegantly disproved the hoary old myth that Detroit builds the cars it wants to build and forces them down buyers' throats. The wide, traffic-choked avenues of Southern Michigan are hardly the best places for evaluat-

ing—or enjoying—a Taurus or T-Bird, but that environment alone didn't spawn such cars. Ford people had been out driving the twisty lanes of New England, the high-speed byways of the West, the desert wastes of Nevada, the mountain routes of West Virginia—and it showed. Perhaps more than at any time in their history, Ford, Mercury, and Lincoln were delivering precisely the kind of products Americans wanted. Having seized the design initiative among U.S. producers, Dearborn now targeted engineering leadership: specifically, by extending its use of anti-lock brakes and pioneering four-wheel drive among high-volume cars. The latter arrived for '87 in the form of a new "All-Wheel-Drive" option for Tempo (and Mercury's Topaz). A part-time system intended for use in slippery conditions, not on dry pavement or off-road, it teamed with a "High Specific Output" (HSO) version of the existing 2.3-liter HSC four delivering 94 horse-

power. The only transmission offered was a new three-speed automatic with a so-called "fluidically linked" torque converter (FLC) that obviated the need for a lockup torque-converter clutch. Unlike 4×4 trucks, there was no separate transfer case or locking front hubs. Instead, a center differential took care of coupling in rear-wheel drive when required. However, Ford's AWD system incorporated a "shift-on-the-fly" capability for convenience (via a dashboard rocker switch), meaning one could go into or out of 4WD without stopping. Unlike other 4WD cars, this one showed little detectable difference in ride height from its two-wheel-drive sister, and there were no major suspension changes save appropriate spring/shock tuning.

Some of this reflected Ford's European work with the purpose-built, mid-engine RS 200 rally car and the high-performance Sierra XR 4×4 and 4WD Scorpio. But, coming as it did in the family

For 1987, the two-passenger Escort EXP came as a Luxury Coupe or a Sport Coupe (left), the latter running with the 115-bhp 1.9-liter four. Although 1.5 inches longer than the four-seater Escort, its 31.5-cubic-foot cargo area was six cubic feet smaller. A new AWD (All-Wheel-Drive) series joined the '87 Tempo lineup, offered as a $9984 coupe or a $10,138 sedan (bottom). AWD was a part-time system intended for use in adverse conditions, not on dry pavement or off-road, and was backed up by the higher-output 94-bhp 2.3-liter four.

four-wheel disc brakes with electronic anti-lock control, 225/60VR-16 unidirectional tires, and a first-for-Ford variable-rate shock-absorber system called Automatic Ride Control. Air conditioning and tinted glass became standard for all '87 Birds, and the four-speed overdrive automatic took over entirely for the less efficient three-speeder. The market cooled down a bit from torrid 1986, so T-Bird model-year production fell by almost 35,900 units, ending at a still-respectable 128,135.

Had Ford followed conventional Detroit wisdom, the fifth-generation Mustang would have been replaced by 1987, if not sooner. Though still popular heading into its ninth model year and a vivid performer in GT guise, the basic '79 design was looking dated next to the newer Chevy Camaro/Pontiac Firebird—let alone some sporty Japanese coupes that were newer still. But Ford was now a very *un*conventional car company, and it was performance value-for-money rather than styling that had sustained Mustang sales since 1982. Of course, that wouldn't have happened without the advent of vastly reduced inflation, lower interest rates, higher employment, rising personal income, and the steep drop in gas prices resulting from a worldwide oil glut, all of which contributed to a big upsurge in hot-car demand. At the same time, a whole new generation that hadn't been around for the original Mustang phenomenon was reaching car-buying age, and they craved sporty performance every bit as much as their "baby boomer" parents still did.

Trouble was, the Mustang was now a car of Ford's past, not its future, a throwback selling partly on nostalgia—hardly in keeping with the high-tech image Ford sought to portray via aero styling and other advances. Ford also knew as well as anyone that no design—no matter how popular or successfully updated—can last forever, and planners had been worrying about what might happen to Mustang sales should the market suddenly reverse itself again, not to mention the new sporty cars competitors were conjuring up.

These and other considerations formed the backdrop for work toward a sixth-generation Mustang that began in 1982. Given the economic conditions of the day, the predictable consensus was that this ponycar for the Nineties would need to be smaller and lighter than the

market, the All-Wheel-Drive Tempo represented not only a price breakthrough—base list was just under $10,000—but the first domestic challenge to a growing number of 4WD European and Japanese cars. It also indicated that Ford still wasn't afraid to try something different, especially if it upstaged General Motors or Chrysler.

GM, in fact, paid Ford a compliment by offering anti-lock brakes on some of its upmarket front-drive cars during 1986, albeit on a limited basis. Not to be outdone, Dearborn also brought this significant feature to a lower price bracket by extending its Teves system to this year's Thunderbird Turbo Coupe as standard equipment—and throwing in rear-disc brakes for good measure.

Proving it wasn't resting on its styling laurels either, Ford issued a reskinned T-Bird (and Mercury Cougar) and a heavily facelifted Mustang. The former retained its trend-setting aero silhouette, but looked even slicker. Glass areas were larger—though not the actual window openings, which remained a bit small—and both headlamps and side glass were newly flush-mounted to further improve "airflow management." The rear end was

also cleaned up and the front freshened, and the Turbo Coupe now wore twin functional hood scoops and a unique grille-less nose bearing a big Bird emblem. Other models displayed a rather gaudy chrome eggcrate between the headlamps.

T-Bird model choices went from three to four again as the mid-range Elan departed and two new offerings arrived: luxury LX and the Sport. The latter combined the worthy 302 V-8 with a TC-style chassis, interior, and exterior, but was otherwise equipped like the standard car. Base-priced just over $15,000, it cost some $1800 less than the Turbo Coupe, which made it a terrific performance buy—perhaps second only to the Mustang GT.

There were also plenty of mechanical and equipment improvements. The Turbo Coupe received the intercooled Mustang SVO powerplant, albeit slightly detuned in the interest of durability and refinement to "only" 190 bhp and 240 pounds/feet torque. But that was with standard five-speed manual. Ordering the optional automatic gave somewhat less: 150 bhp and 200 lbs/ft. More encouraging were the TC's newly standard

existing model—something like the old Mustang II or European Capri—with a shape obviously born in the wind tunnel, front-wheel drive for maximum space inside, and a new range of high-efficiency, overhead-cam four-cylinder engines to replace the low-tech ironmongery of the traditional V-8.

But just a year into this program, Ford decided to start over and collaborate with Japanese partner Mazda, whose small-car expertise was at least equal, if not superior, to Ford's own. Mazda was then laying plans for the successor to its first front-drive 626 series of compacts, which included a sporty coupe. Dearborn figured it might save money and end up with a better new Mustang by getting in on this project. The result would be two cars, each with its own styling and separate dealer network, but sharing basic chassis, running gear, and some inner structure. Making the idea even more attractive was Mazda's decision to build cars at a new plant in Flat Rock, Michigan (not far from Ford's historic River Rouge operations), and to make part of its output available to Ford.

It seemed a marriage made in heaven. Ford would get a new Mustang for a fraction of the cost of developing one from scratch on its own, while building it for Ford would make Flat Rock economically feasible for Mazda. And lest anyone forget, Mazda—like other Japanese makers—really *needed* to build cars in America, not least because a worsening yen/dollar relationship was threatening to price its wares right out of the market. A U.S. production base would also foster a "good citizen" image, necessary to help ward off a Congress that had lately been threatening protectionist legislation amid hysterical reports of Japanese "dumping."

What Ford hadn't counted on was a storm of protest from Mustang loyalists once word of this project leaked out. A new Mustang was a good thing to be sure, maybe even overdue. But *Japanese* engineering? Unthinkable! After all, no

car was more all-American than Mustang. So how dare Ford put the name Mustang on a restyled import? And besides, while front-wheel drive might be okay for little econoboxes, everyone knew that *real* performance cars put power to the pavement with their *back* tires.

Though the decision was made almost at the 11th hour, Ford took heed and decided to release the once-and-future "Mazda Mustang" as the 1988 Probe, named after Dearborn's recent series of aerodynamic show cars. Meantime, die-hard Mustangers got a rejuvenated version of their "real" ponycar, which Dearborn could well afford since profits had become embarrassingly large.

The result arrived for '87 as the most fully overhauled Mustang since 1979. The SVO was consigned to the great slow-sellers' parking lot in the sky (as was Mercury's Capri), but other models returned: LX notchback and LX and GT hatchbacks and convertibles. The familiar fifth-generation shape was still clearly recognizable, but smoother than ever, dominated by a neater nose bearing flush headlamps inboard of large, wraparound directional/side-marker lamps. Rear side glass on closed models was pulled out to surrounding sheetmetal surfaces, taillamps were restyled, and most exterior brightwork was finished in black. Besides a more contemporary appearance, the sheetmetal reshaping made for more competitive drag coefficients: down to a claimed 0.40 for the notchback, 0.42 for convertibles, and 0.36 for the LX hatchback. The three-door GT tested out at a slightly blockier at 0.38.

As before, GTs looked quite different than LXs. The latter were more restrained, announced by a shallow "slot" grille with a horizontal bar bearing a small Ford oval—a sort of smaller rendition of the Taurus "navel." Below it rode a body-color bumper with integral spoiler. Wide black rub strips flanking the license-plate holder curved around to the front

For 1987, Taurus retained its eight-model lineup. At the top was the LX series, here (top) the $14,613 sedan, which came with the 140-bhp 3.0-liter V-6 and four-speed overdrive automatic as standard. Total Taurus output rose to a healthy 374,763 units. Other '87 Fords included the $15,213 Taurus LX wagon (second from top); the $15,454 LTD Crown Victoria four-door, here with the $665 Brougham Roof Treatment (third from top); and the $14,507 LTD Country Squire (above).

wheelarches, then carried back as lower-body protection moldings to a color-keyed rear bumper. GTs seemed rather brash by comparison, with heavily sculptured rocker-panel "skirts" that looked like the adds-on they were, plus low-riding faux scoops ahead of the front and rear wheels, a prominent faired-in spoiler on the hatchback, and multi-slotted "cheese grater" taillamps. At least the grille-less front was properly aggressive,

The '87 Aerostar, base priced at $10,682, marched into 1987 with the 3.0-liter V-6 standard (the 2.3-liter four remained standard for the cargo van). It mated to a five-speed manual or a four-speed overdrive automatic. New options were electric remote-control mirrors and special seats that converted into a bed.

with air entering via a wide "mouth" in a forward-jutting airdam flanked by round foglamps. So that no one would miss it, big "Mustang GT" lettering was molded into the rocker extensions and rear bumper cover. Instrument panels are among the costliest components to change in any car, so the fact that the '87 Mustangs sported a new one was taken as a sign that the fifth generation would hang on for a few more years. The design, bearing a strong likeness to the latest 626 dash, could almost have come from Mazda. The right side was cut away on top to form a useful package shelf and give a sense of greater interior spaciousness. On the driver's side was an upright pod with a pair of rocker switches on each side covering lights, hazard flasher, and rear-window defroster. Wipers and indicators were left to steering-column stalks. Cruise-control buttons were still conveniently placed in the steering-wheel spokes. Dropping down from dash center was a broad console housing large rotary controls for the climate system. A quartet of large, square vents marched across the dash rail. Modernization was also evident in new-design armrests, door panels, and seat adjusters.

Mustang's most noteworthy mechanical alterations for '87 involved the venerable small-block V-8—no surprise, as it was now way ahead of the 2.3-liter four in customer preference. Improved induction, including a return to freer-breathing pre-1986 cylinder heads, added

25 horses to bring the total to 225, thus matching output of the top Camaro/Firebird V-8, the larger 5.7-liter Corvette unit. Torque was up too, to a mighty 300 lbs/ft. The 302 remained standard for GTs, which also received larger-diameter front disc brakes (10.9 versus 10.1 inches) and recalibrated front suspension.

As for the four, it finally shed the old one-barrel carburetor for multiport electronic fuel injection, but was hardly any more potent at 90 bhp and 130 lbs/ft. However, it now came with a standard five-speed manual or optional four-speed automatic overdrive transmission—versus the previous four-speed stick and three-speed slushbox—which helped maximize what performance it could muster. The big surprise was that the 3.8-liter V-6 option was gone, leaving a huge power/performance gap between the four and V-8. The obvious conclusion, as CONSUMER GUIDE® noted in *Auto 1987*, was that "Ford clearly plans on selling mostly V-8-powered Mustangs this year."

Ford did, only a lot of those were sold in LX trim, an $1885 package that included the GT's chassis and rolling stock. In fact, demand for 5.0-liter LXs proved so strong that Ford actually ran short of engines during the year, telling buyers that if they wanted a V-8 Mustang, it would have to be a GT. There were reasons for this rather odd situation. For some buyers, the facelifted GT was either ugly, outlandish, or both, which must have dismayed Jack Telnack. Others simply preferred the quieter-looking LX because it was less likely to be noticed by the law.

Regardless, the newly fortified small-block provided blistering performance reminiscent of the so-called "good old days": 0-60 mph now took slightly less

than six seconds. This illustrated that technology was now allowing Ford (and others) to achieve what had once been possible only by adding cubic inches. For example, to get around 225 net horsepower in, say, a 1972 Mustang, it took an optional 351 V-8, which came in three versions spanning 168 to 275 net bhp. Yet the '87 small-block was more fuel-efficient and ran smoother cold, demanded less maintenance, and was likely more reliable to boot.

While the price of progress is often high, Mustang remained an exception. As CONSUMER GUIDE® noted in 1987: "Though far from perfect—or perfected—the Mustang GT is put together well enough and offers a ton of go for your dough. Despite a full option load—air, premium sound system, cruise control, and power windows, door locks and mirrors—our test [hatchback] came to $14,352, which is an exceptional value when IROC-Z Camaros, Toyota Supras, and Nissan 300ZXs can go for $5000 more." To paraphrase the old adage, the more some things change, the more others stay the same.

But change doesn't guarantee success, and Mustang saw substantially lower output for '87 despite its extensive progress—over 65,000 units lower. Still, 159,000 was quite good all things considered (the previous year's production spurt stemmed in part from rush buying in advance of revised tax laws that took effect with the start of calendar '87). And though costly, the facelift would be amortized over the next few years.

Refinement was the word for Ford's other '87 cars. The big Crown Victorias, still little changed from the first downsized LTDs of nine years before, gained standard air conditioning, tinted glass, and electronic digital clock, but little else. They were still selling well, 125,761 for the model year, and model-year production was up by nearly 5000 units.

As noted, Ford's hot-selling mid-size Taurus became the nation's top-seller this year according to *Ward's*, though *Automotive News* had it second behind Escort. No matter—Ford built a lot more for the model year: 374,763 in all, an increase of nearly 138,500. Of course, Taurus was only a year old in 1987, and its design looked advanced enough to continue successfully for the next several years with little if any change required. But Ford knew it couldn't let this one languish, and had planned some useful improvements for '88. For now, the one significant change was a switch from three to four speeds for the optional automatic in four-cylinder models, which weren't selling at anywhere near the rate of V-6s. Still available were the sporty four-pot/five-speed MT5 sedan and wagon, "Eurocars" in every way except for decidedly sluggish performance.

Among the smaller Fords, the unhappy EXP was still hanging around, but it attracted some 5000 fewer buyers this

year and only 25,888 were built. It had actually been resurrected—again—for "1986½," this time as part of a rejiggered Escort line that now encompassed base Pony and sporty GT three-door sedans plus GL (nee LX) three-door, five-door, and wagon. Weeding out the last carburetors from its engine lineup, Ford switched Escort's base 1.9-liter four to throttle-body electronic fuel injection, which yielded four more horses—up to 90 bhp in all—and a similarly small gain in torque to 106 lbs/ft. EXP and GT retained their port-injected 1.9, now with 115 bhp and 120 lbs/ft. Still available, if seldom ordered, was the 2.0-liter Mazda diesel-four, again rated at just 58 bhp. It hardly mattered, though, as diesel demand was now all but non-existent throughout the industry: down to a mere 16,600 smokers, less than 0.3-percent of the more than seven million U.S. cars sold this calendar year.

Escort was down too, with model-year production falling by over 55,000 units to just shy of 375,000 (not counting EXP). To a large degree, the aging design of Ford's subcompact was less to blame than the general market pullback which reduced total domestic calendar-year sales by 13.8 percent and industrywide model-year production by close to 9.4 percent. Even import sales were down, albeit by less than 3 percent.

Tempo managed about 5000 additional sales despite virtually no changes other than the aforementioned All-Wheel-Drive option, whose new fluidically linked converter was adopted for front-drive models as well. However, the government had finally gotten its act together on passive restraints, and there was a new mandate that affected both

Ford's Italian Ghia operation tried its hand at designing a compact van in 1987, the HFX Aerostar XLT (top), and it was seen at many auto shows. Looking like an Aerostar in a conservative business suit, it featured a sharply raked front windshield and hood similar to the production model, but overall it looked squarer. The interior (right) was up to the minute with all of the digital/computer goodies one could hope for. Note the pushbuttons for controlling the transmission just below the central air vents.

Tempo and Escort. This called for each manufacturer to install these devices—airbags, passive seatbelts, or whatever—on 10 percent of its 1987 production. Ford had offered an optional driver-side airbag for '86 Tempos (and Topazes), albeit on a limited basis. Only about 100 were ordered by private customers, and only a few thousand made it into fleet cars, including those of the insurance companies who lobbied so hard for airbags. For its part, Ford promised to promote them more heavily for '87.

Because of this new government regulation, Escort (as well as Mercury's Lynx) was tapped for this year's 10-percent solution, so it got motorized front shoulder belts that automatically pivoted around occupants on closing the doors. Full protection, however, still required fastening a good old-fashioned manual lap belt. The previous year had brought another new government-required safety feature, the central high-mount stoplamp (CHMSL). Ford continued to satisfy this rule for '87, typically with a lot more elegance than some rivals.

Though the Erika/Escort project had gone down somewhat different paths on each side of the Atlantic, "world cars" were still very much in Ford's future, as

shown by a trio of mid-1987 introductions. In May, West Coast Ford dealers began selling a car even smaller than Escort. Called Festiva, it was a petite three-door sedan with tall and boxy "phone booth" styling on a 90.4-inch wheelbase. Significantly, it was a Mazda design, sold by the Japanese company in other markets under its own brand as the 121. Perhaps more significant in light of Detroit's growing cost/profit squeeze, the Festiva was built in South Korea, a country with much lower labor rates than either the U.S. or Japan. Assembly was carried out by Kia Motors, in which both Ford and Mazda both had a financial interest.

Measuring just 140.4 inches long, the Festiva drove its front wheels via a carbureted 1.3-liter four with 58 bhp. The base L model came with a four-speed manual transaxle, while the better-equipped LX version got a five-speed. Styling, though rectilinear, was recognizably Ford, with aero headlamps and slat-type grille, rounded corners, and smooth, wraparound bumpers. Chassis engineering was typical Japanese small car: all-coil, all-independent MacPherson-strut suspension; disc/drum brakes; rack-and-pinion steering. Power steering wasn't offered, nor genuinely needed,

With the popularity of sport/utility vehicles exploding, the late Eighties saw a good many concept vehicles specifically designed to tie in with Americans' "play time." The Bronco DM-1 was just such a vehicle, a small, stylized (egg-shaped, if you will) 4×4 that people would hopefully like to be seen in at the beach, in the desert, or at a ski lodge. Compared to a good many show cars, this one looked like it could have fairly easily been put into production.

but many buyers surely missed an optional automatic transmission.

But then, Festiva was only an "entry-level" car, Ford Division's answer to low-price minis—as in minimal—cars like the three-cylinder (that's right) Japanese-built Chevy Sprint. As such, it seemed right on the money. Though far from the ultimate in performance, roadability, or quietness, Festiva offered high mileage, a decent ride, and room enough for four adults to sit in fair comfort, with a little room for belongings behind. Trim and equipment weren't lavish, but all the essentials were there. The nicer LX even had a tachometer, trip odometer, and intermittent wipers, and both models could be ordered with air conditioning, stereo sound, rear wiper/washer, backlight defroster, and aluminum wheels. Perhaps the best things about the Festiva were its perky personality and modest prices: under $5800 for the L, less than $6900 for the LX. With that, it shaped up as an attractive second or third car for the family as well as an appealing first car for younger buyers. Unfortunately for Ford Division, only 26,750 buyers were convinced enough to buy a Festiva in calendar '87. Considering its limited distribution, that wasn't a bad showing, but it wasn't as good as the marketing mavens had hoped.

The same could be said for another spring newcomer, the Tracer, replacement for the languishing Escort-clone Lynx at Mercury. Essentially a restyled version of Mazda's second-series front-drive 323, it offered a choice of three- and five-door sedan and five-door wagon in one semi-upmarket trim level at prices starting around $7900. Though minutely longer than the 323 in wheelbase and overall length, Tracer ran with the same 1.6-liter overhead-cam four with port fuel injection and 82 bhp, mated to a five-speed manual or three-speed automatic transaxle. Chassis specs were the same, too—much like Festiva's, in fact. Appearance was pleasingly chunky and refresh-

ingly quite distinct from the 323's, basically the same as that of the Australian Ford Laser, which had gone on sale in Canada shortly before. Perhaps the most significant thing about the Tracer was that it was built at Ford's highly automated new Hermosillo, Mexico, plant—which underlined the growing importance of "third world" countries in determining the winners and losers in the increasingly high-stakes auto game of the late Eighties.

Also bowing at L-M dealers in May was a second Merkur, the German-built Scorpio five-door sedan. Initially priced at $23,000, it was essentially a federalized version of the like-named overseas Ford voted Europe's 1986 "Car of the Year." Like the Sierra-based XR4Ti, it was a rear-drive design with "jellybean" styling, though it looked smoother and more attractive to most eyes. Also like the smaller Merkur, the Scorpio was comparable in size to an existing U.S. product, in this case the Taurus/Sable, next to which it only looked different, not necessarily better. Wheelbase measured three inches longer at 108.7 inches, but less overhang at each end made Scorpio about 4.5 inches shorter overall (186.4 inches). Power was supplied by the redesigned 2.9-liter ohv V-6 introduced to the U.S. in the '86 Ranger/Bronco II, albeit with slightly different rated output: 144 bhp and 162 lbs/ft torque. The usual five-speed manual and extra-cost four-speed automatic gearboxes were listed, but the self-shifter would be all but unavailable.

Despite a planned 1986 debut, which was put back several times for unexplained reasons, the Scorpio added some extra spice to an increasingly impressive L-M lineup. But it wouldn't add many sales, and in retrospect perhaps that's not too surprising. Though fully equipped and expensive-looking next to the Sables with which it shared showroom floor space, its generally similar appearance must have been confusing to a good many buyers.

Worse, devotees of premium European sports sedans weren't usual patrons of L-M dealers, and those who actually drove a Scorpio found several shortcomings. Though improved, the Cologne V-6 wasn't up to the 3230-pound curb weight, so the Scorpio was no threat to the likes of BMW for performance and refinement. Handling was fine, as were the standard all-disc anti-lock brakes. Interior room was a definite plus, especially in the back seat—even against Taurus/Sable. So was hatchback versatility for the relatively few who cared about practical things. But what mattered more to upscale types was brand prestige. "Merkur" was hard to pronounce, and the badges on nose and tail still bore the name Ford, even if in a German context. But in the end, bungled, half-hearted promotion all but doomed the entire Merkur franchise.

As a result, neither Scorpio nor XR4Ti would ever generate anywhere near the sales projected for them, and L-M would drop both models after 1989 and few interim changes. For calendar years 1987-89, respectively, Scorpio attracted 5178, 9516, and 4748 sales—19,442 in all, less than a fifth of Sable's volume for 1987 alone. The capable XR4Ti made a good start with calendar '86 sales of 14,315, but it then tailed off rapidly to 9123, 5745, and 4017—33,200 in all, barely a third of Topaz sales for 1987 alone. In all, the Merkur experience was a big embarrassment for Dearborn, but it would play a role in a surprising drama that unfolded in the closing months of 1989.

Dearborn fared far better on the truck front in 1987. The total market saw but a slim 1.4-percent gain in calendar-year sales, but Ford extended its lead over runner-up Chevy from 133,843 to 261,760 units, including mediums and heavies. Respective year-end totals: 1,453,205 for Ford, which went up from '86; 1,191,445 for Chevy, which dropped. Chrysler pushed out more minivans this year and offered a new mid-size pickup, the Dodge Dakota, but nevertheless managed only about half of Ford's volume.

Much of Ford's success was due to the numerous upgrades made throughout the light-truck line. Most extensively changed were the big Bronco and F-Series pickups, which got their own version of the corporate "aero look." This translated into more rounded front sheetmetal, new flush-fit headlamps (with replaceable halogen bulbs) wrapped around into the parking/side-marker lamps, and a new grille and front bumper, the latter with a small integral "lip" spoiler. Rear ends were also rounded off a bit, and fenders were reshaped on Flaresides and "dualies." Inside was a more modern-looking dash, complemented by suitably reworked minor appointments and generally higher-grade furnishings for all trim levels. Despite Ford's claims, the exterior facelift likely had little effect in the wind tunnel, as these remained high, blocky vehicles, but it did impart a fresh look at a time when GM was readying its first all-new full-size pickups in more than a decade.

The main mechanical highlight for this year's F-Series and big Bronco was praiseworthy indeed: standard electronic anti-lock rear brakes on all models. Ford was also ridding itself of carbureted truck engines, so multiport electronic fuel injection was applied to the veteran 4.9-liter/300-cid straight six that remained standard power for both these lines. It combined with a revised cylinder head boasting "fast burn" combustion chambers for better economy.

Among other significant improvements were standard twin-tube gas-pressure shock absorbers across the board, incorporation of front camber and caster adjustment for all 4WDs save F-350s, increased use of one- and two-sided galvanized sheetmetal in F-Series models, and first-time availability of shift-on-the-fly "Touch Drive" for the big Bronco. Numerous detail refinements were aimed at improved reliability, such as the adoption of a one-belt serpentine accessory drive for the 300 six. A manual four-speed overdrive transmission replaced the previous non-overdrive unit as standard with the big 460 gas V-8 and 6.9-liter diesel. Axle-ratio choices were simplified, a see-through brake master cylinder was adopted, windshield-washer and radiator-overflow tanks were enlarged, trim and options were shuffled—the list went on and on. Last but not least, the Custom name returned to denote standard cab trim. Ford's compact Ranger pickups and Bronco II sport-utility also received the new rear anti-lock brakes as standard, as well as more galvanized body panels. Also on hand were the single-key lock system previously applied to larger trucks, plus minor trim and equipment revisions. Included in the latter were standard gas-pressure shocks for all 4×2s, standard full engine gauges for the price-leading Ranger S, a new intake manifold and non-feedback carburetor for that model's 2.0-liter four, cancellation of Ranger cab/chassis offerings, and the familiar XL initials to denote base cab trim on Ranger and Bronco II alike.

This year's Econolines and Club Wagons got most of the same changes described for Bronco/F-Series, but the rear anti-lock brakes were a sad exception. The big vans needed them just as much. Aerostar's main news was adoption of the 3.0-liter Taurus/Sable V-6 as standard power for passenger Wagons. This was another curious move, as the cargo Vans could certainly have benefitted from this, too. As it was, they continued with the underpowered 2.3-liter four as standard and offered the "Vulcan" V-6 optionally. The former 2.8-liter V-6 was dropped. There were a few other new options: center-opening dual rear doors for Vans in lieu of a liftgate, dual remote-electric door mirrors and, for Wagons with the third-seat option, an arrangement that turned the middle and rearmost seats into a makeshift bed. As before, Aerostar commercials carried a basic 1200-pound payload rating, with option packages lifting that to 1600 or 2040 pounds. Maximum towing capacity was 5000 pounds for Vans, 4900 for Wagons.

In all, Ford had reason to be pleased with its 1987 truck sales. The F-Series and big Bronco held steady, Bronco II gained better than 17,000 to close near 121,000, the F-Series did 11,000 units more to go over 550,000 again, and the Ranger attracted an impressive 35,000 extra sales to break the 300,000 barrier for the first time. Chrysler still led all players in minivan sales by a wide margin, but Ford bested both Chevy and GMC in that category, as well as in big vans and, of course, full-size pickups, the F-Series remaining America's single most popular vehicle.

Ford Division's calendar-year car sales weren't shabby, either. Though fractionally down on the 1986 tally at 1,389,886, they were strong enough to best a faltering Chevy by nearly 26,700 cars. Ford was even further ahead in combined car/truck sales, which at 2.85-million units bested Chevrolet by 160,000.

AutoWeek noted that this was the first time the division had managed that feat since 1956, though, as we've seen, Ford had edged Chevy in model-year car production several times since. The figures were in some dispute anyway, and *AutoWeek* reported that General Motors quickly made "pointed references to its worldwide leadership in automotive sales" to steal some of Ford's thunder. But *AW* also observed that GM held "a clean 20 percent share of the world car market, a proportion not even Ford Motor Company as whole can threaten as yet. [But] Ford is doing well in Europe, too . . . easily outpacing GM's German Opel and British Vauxhall subsidiaries."

So for all the talk at HF II's passing, tradition had little place in the fast-changing late Eighties, as the "Japanization" of America and Ford's own accomplishments were proving so pointedly. Yet, as the automobile prepared to enter its second century, many were moved to observe that Ford Motor Company had not only been a giant for most of the first one, but had become the American automaker best prepared for the new challenges that surely lay ahead. In that, at least, Henry Ford II could rest in peace.

Ford's light-duty trucks for 1987 included the full-size Bronco (top), which could be had with a 300-cid six, 302 V-8, or 351 V-8 (150, 185, and 190 bhp). Prices started at $14,166. The E-250 Super Van (second from top) featured a 20-inch stretch at the rear. This 4×4 Ranger regular cab (third from top) started out at $10,124, but the STX equipment and Sport Appearance Group upped that considerably. The full-size '87 pickups received aero-look styling, a new instrument cluster, and anti-lock rear brakes. Shown are the F-150 XL Styleside (fourth from top) and the F-150 XLT Lariat SuperCab Styleside (above).

1 9 8 8

The world paused in 1988 to honor the automobile on the occasion of its centenary—a hundred years since Germany's Gottlieb Daimler and Karl Benz built the first true cars in the modern sense. To say that a lot had happened in that century, both to the automobile and the world at large, was not only obvious but an understatement.

Yet looking back from 1988, the vast changes of those 100 years seemed no more momentous than the events of just the past 10. A second fuel crisis and a deep national recession had been followed, ironically enough, by a fuel glut and a strong economic recovery. Ford—and Chrysler as well—had come back from the brink of oblivion, and all Detroit went from worrisome losses to unprecedented profits in a market that again flip-flopped almost overnight.

But not all history runs in cycles, and a good many aspects of the auto business had changed forever, at least in the U.S. Twenty years of government safety, emissions, and fuel-economy regulations had put a permanent end to the sloppy, drunkardly, outsize cars Americans had known in the Sixties and Seventies. The mid-size car of that era had become the full-size car of the new one, intermediates had shrunk to the size of Detroit's first postwar compacts, and the industry was turning out more subcompacts than anyone would have dreamed of two decades before. The V-6, meanwhile, replaced the inline six as Detroit's in-between engine, but the most ubiquitous powerplant was again a four-cylinder, something that hadn't been true since the Twenties. What few U.S. V-8s still existed were descended from what we'd called "small-blocks" in the muscle-car era; in the brave new world of the Eighties they were considered "big" engines. For all that, cars like Ford's latest Mustang GT and Thunderbird Turbo Coupe had proved that performance and

Mustang trotted into 1988 with only a minor updating. In fact, the only difference the PR types could hype was an upgraded 540-amp battery for the LX. That model still came with the 2.3-liter (140-cubic-inch) four as standard, but the next jump power-wise was the 225-bhp 5.0-liter V-8, which left quite a gap in between. There were the usual two V-8-powered GTs this year, but the LX series embraced three models: $8726 notchback coupe (above), $9221 hatch (right), and $13,702 convertible (top left). Still available for those who preferred the more laid-back styling of the LX was the $1885 "5.0-Liter PFI V-8 Package," which bought the V-8 and upgraded suspension and tires, as on the soft top and hatch shown.

excitement still had their place—that regulation, however irksome, didn't have to mean dull.

Something else had changed, too. Imports, once a here-today-gone-tomorrow sales threat, had become a permanent part of the American scene—replacing in a sense the independent U.S. automakers of the "good old days." This despite Detroit's best efforts to "drive them back into the sea," as HF II promised in the early Seventies. Not only were foreign makers now building cars and trucks on hallowed American soil, but in fast-growing numbers.

Volkswagen of Germany had been the first to establish a U.S. manufacturing outpost—and the first to fail. Renault of France tried nosing its way into the American market by buying American Motors, but it failed too, thus paving the way for Chrysler to take over AMC in 1987 and, in the process, save the all-American Jeep from extinction. The Japanese, however, were succeeding handsomely as "American" manufacturers, perhaps even beyond their own expectations. Already in business were Nissan in Tennessee, Honda in Ohio, and Toyota as GM's partner in California (and later on its own in Kentucky). Now Mitsubishi was about to join in via a collaborative venture with Chrysler in central Illinois, and Mazda had set up shop with Ford in Flat Rock, Michigan—practically in Dearborn's backyard. About to come on stream were Subaru and Isuzu in Indiana, while Suzuki and the Korean automaker Hyundai were about to establish beachheads in Canada.

Such was the state of the U.S. industry in the automobile's hundredth year, which also marked the 85th anniversary of Ford Motor Company. In the main, it was a happy time for Detroit in general and Ford in particular, the national economy having more or less ignored Wall Street's unprecedented 508-point loss of "Black Monday," October 19, 1987. U.S. car production rose by nearly 4.9 percent, to 7.13-million units, and domestic calendar-year car sales edged up 6.25 percent while imports eased by some 2.5 percent. On the truck side, domestic light-truck production climbed some 12.2 percent, and total calendar-year truck sales broke the five-million barrier for the first time.

Ford Motor Company did exceedingly well in this still-buoyant market. Its share of total new-car registrations rose to 21.58 percent, the highest since 1979, while GM sank again, to just barely above 36 percent. Escort finished first in domestic calendar-year sales, while Taurus was a solid third, trailing Chevy's new Corsica/Beretta compacts. Tempo, meanwhile, ran a strong fifth, outpacing Chevy's subcompact Cavalier. In trucks, Ford posted gains to beat all rivals in both light-duty sales and overall, capturing 30.7 percent of the light-truck market to Chevy's 27.8 and Chrysler's 15.9. Dearborn was also stronger than ever in combined car/light-duty truck sales, capturing 24.3 percent of this year's slightly higher 15.6-million-unit total, versus 35.6 percent for GM and 14.3 percent for Chrysler.

All this predictably benefited Ford's bank account. Dearborn outearned GM for the third straight year, and with a record $5.3 billion to boot. Profit-sharing checks totaled $636 million this year—fully $3700 per employee—believed to be the largest such payout ever made by a U.S. company.

CONSUMER GUIDE® also celebrated a birthday in 1988, its 20th. It's interesting note that among *CG's* 50 Best New Car selections for the year, no fewer than seven came from Ford Motor Company. The big LTD Crown Victoria remained a fine choice in a conventional full-size car; the Mustang GT was again tops in bang-for-the-buck performance; and the Ford Taurus/Mercury Sable duo

Sheetmetal-wise, the first-generation Escort received its second—and last—updating for 1988½. All in all, it was quite remarkable that Ford could keep the Escort a top seller for an entire decade with so few visible changes, and relatively modest ones in both 1985½ and '88½, at that. The latest facelift centered mainly at the back, where more rounded lines and new taillights could be seen. Bumpers were also smoothed out and better integrated. The GT (opposite page) remained the sporty version, now $9093 and with an open rectangle above the bumper and eggcrate "grille" below. Other models were the $6747 Pony (three-door only), and three LXs (replacing GL): $7127 three-door hatch (top left), $7457 five-door hatch (top right), and the $8058 wagon (right).

was unquestionably the outstanding buy among mid-size domestics. The classy Mark VII LSC repeated as a "Best Buy" among premium coupes, and there was a new Lincoln on the list: the posh second-generation Continental sedan, based on the Taurus. *CG* even recommended the slow-selling Merkur Scorpio as an underrated alternative to other premium European sedans.

Such accolades and continuing high sales naturally kept Ford very much in the news. Everywhere, it seemed, the company was trumpeted as a remarkable comeback success and thus a timely symbol of America's ability to compete on equal terms with foreign rivals—something that seemed *decreasingly* true of General Motors. As ever, Ford chairman Don Petersen got special attention not only as a savvy, enthusiastic, product-wise executive, but one with a plan.

Indeed, Ford had plowed back much of its enormous profits since 1985 into new products and more efficient manufacturing. It had also been sensible in recent corporate acquisitions, unlike GM or Chrysler, whose takeovers seemed like just so much mindless spending. Of course, Ford had plenty of cash to burn, but analysts agreed that Petersen and company spent well: for example, $1.3

billion for 80 percent of Hertz Rent-a-Car; $493 million for First Nationwide Bank of California, the country's fourth largest savings and loan; $425 million for the military-research firm BDM International, this as an adjunct to Ford Aerospace. In short, Ford was a company that could seem to do no wrong in the late Eighties. The only question was, how long could this continue?

The answer seemed to be a fair stretch, at least if Ford Division's 1988 offerings were anything to go by. Starting at the top, the Crown Victoria line was purged of its two-door body style and all the fleet-market S models. The remaining standard and luxury LX four-door sedans and wagons received an "aero" facelift, the first major restyling for the big "Panther" cars since their 1979 debut. As facelifts go, this one was modest: just new bumpers, sedan trunklid, a more rounded front, and big Oldsmobile-style taillights. Some might have expected more after 10 years, but the decision had already been made to give the Crown Vic (and companion Mercury Marquis) a complete reskin for the early Nineties, so this makeover was just a holding action. And really, that's all that was needed. A lot of buyers still craved big, Detroit-style luxury, and the fact that far fewer such

The Thunderbird received a few timely updates for 1988, including multi-point fuel injection and a balancer shaft for the V-6, which was standard in the base coupe and LX. Horsepower increased from 120 to 140 and torque from 201 to 215 lbs/ft. The V-8-powered Sport, meanwhile, received dual exhausts and new interior appointments. The Turbo Coupe (above) carried on as before, listing this year at $17,250, an increase of $445. Production for the model year increased nearly 20,000 units to 147,243.

cars were now available only worked in the Crown Vic's favor.

So did another mild upgrading in standard equipment: P215/70R-15 whitewall tires, intermittent wipers, trip odometer, Autolamp headlight on/off/ delay system, low fuel and oil-level warning lights, front-door map pockets, and remote right-door mirror. Also new to the big Ford was the Rapid-Spec marketing scheme that grouped popular options into special value-priced packages. Taurus was still probably stealing a few sales, but the Crown Vic didn't lose too many this calendar year—a bit less than 4000— and was still quite profitable at about

114,000 units (not to mention another 114,000 Grand Marquis and 122,000 big Lincolns built off the same basic chassis).

Though it dropped a spot on the sales chart, Taurus kept charging like a bull in a china shop. Model-year production rose by almost 13,000 units to over 387,500; calendar-year sales followed suit, climbing almost 30,000 to near 375,000 units. The car itself charged better on the road, too, thanks to the first-time availability of the corporate 3.8-liter V-6, newly reengineered for front-wheel drive. Teamed exclusively with four-speed overdrive automatic, it was just what the Taurus needed. Though rated at the same 140 horsepower as the familiar 3.0-liter "Vulcan," which continued, the revised 3.8 "Essex" delivered one-third more torque—215 pounds/feet total—and at lower revs (2200 versus 3000 rpm). Result? Markedly better off-the-line go— 9.5 seconds 0-60 mph in CONSUMER GUIDE®'s test—plus stronger pulling power in any situation. Best of all, gas mileage wasn't sacrificed, though that remained a bit disappointing at 18.5 mpg overall in "real world" day-to-day driving.

The one problem with the 3.8 was that it wasn't available on the sporty MT5 or base L sedans.

Otherwise, Taurus changed only in detail for '88. The MT5 wagon was dropped for lack of interest; optional leather upholstery was extended to mid-range GLs, the MT5 sedan, and LX wagon; and standard equipment on base L models was expanded to embrace tinted glass, electric remote-control door mirrors, trip odometer, electronic-tune stereo radio, and a split front bench seat with reclining backrests. Styling wasn't changed, but it hardly needed to be.

CONSUMER GUIDE® noted at the time that Taurus sales had been strong partly because of the cash rebates and low-interest financing schemes Ford was using to attract customers. Dearborn wasn't alone in this, of course. Chrysler is generally credited with starting rebates in the early Eighties (actually Chrysler started the first round in the inflation-ridden mid-Seventies), an incentive that others were bound to follow—or else. Low-rate new-car loans made through automakers' financing arms were a sales aid devised as an alternative to rebates, though they were just as costly. In fact, these and other incentives had become so entrenched by 1988 that buyers wouldn't buy without them. Yet they added greatly to a manufacturer's overhead—in Ford's case, an estimated $800-$1200 per car—thus partly negating the higher prices levied during the mid-decade boom market. Incentives amounted to nothing more than taking away with one hand and giving back with the other, and they would soon haunt not only Detroit but even some Japanese makers who'd be forced to resort to them, too.

Ford's compact Tempo became a lot prettier for '88 with a top-to-bottom re-skin that made the four-door sedans look like baby Tauruses. Accompanying their all-new body panels were a tidier two-slot grille, flush-mount "aero" headlights wrapped around into combined parking/side-marker lamps, new bumpers and taillamps, and a lighter-appearing greenhouse (achieved as on the '87 T-Bird by overlapping glass and artful use of black paint). Tempo two-doors got the smoother front end, too, but a different back bumper and taillamps. Inside was a new Mazda-like dash with standard coolant-temperature gauge, pushbutton heat/vent controls and rotary knobs for wipers and fan speed. Passive restraints were required on 25-percent of each manufacturer's 1988-model production, and Tempo helped Ford comply with standard Escort-style motorized front shoulder belts. But Ford hadn't given up on airbag-equipped Tempos, so the inflatable restraint returned as a $751 option. With it, the motorized belts were replaced by conventional three-point lap/shoulder harnesses.

A welcome mechanical improvement brought port fuel injection to both the regular and HSO versions of Tempo's 2.3-liter ohv four. The former gained 12 extra horses, but a nominal four lbs/ft more torque—98 bhp and 124 lbs/ft in all. The high-output unit added six and 12, respectively, for totals of 100 bhp and 130 lbs/ft. The lineup changed, too. The All-Wheel-Drive option became a distinct four-door model (no more AWD two-doors), the top-line LX was also now four-door only, and the mid-range Sport GL twosome was retitled GLS, although it still carried the HSO engine as standard, as did the AWD.

All these changes had the desired effect. Though quite a way down from Chevy's hot-selling Corsica/Beretta, Tempo garnered about 65,000 additional calendar-year sales to finish at better than 285,000. Though still a rather uninspired compact by late-Eighties standards, it did offer fine value—and that's exactly what most buyers in this category cared about.

Thunderbird flew on with its handsome 1987 facelift and the same model group of V-6 base and LX, V-8 Sport, and four-cylinder Turbo Coupe. But here,

The LTD Crown Victoria lost its two-door sedan for 1988, but it hardly mattered as it hadn't sold well anyway. The remaining four-doors and wagons (six models in all) received a new hood, grille, and bumpers, and the sedans also sported a new decklid and Oldsmobile-style taillights. The top-line LX Country Squire (top) stickered at $16,643. The Tempo was reskinned for '88, emerging looking more like a Taurus—no bad thing. The LX four-door sedan (above) weighed in at 2626 pounds and retailed for $9737.

too, the Essex V-6 was heavily revised, gaining 20 horsepower—for a total of 140—via multiport fuel injection, plus greater smoothness from a new "balancer" shaft mounted in the vee between cylinder banks to help quell secondary vibrations. Dual exhaust was newly standard for the V-8, though the rated output of 155 bhp was unchanged for this version of Ford's one-time "small-block." A standard analog gauge cluster (replacing electronic) and multi-adjustable "articulated" front seats like those in the Turbo

Coupe helped the Sport better live up to its name. The TC itself was essentially untouched. Though overall T-Bird sales eased by 15,000 units, slipping to just under 118,000 for the calendar 12 months, model-year production jumped some 19,000 units to 147,000.

Down among the smallest Fords, the Korean-built Festiva, which had bowed for '88 in May '87, was untouched for the balance of this model year, though it was now available nationwide. This "domestic-sponsored" import, as *Automotive News*

Taurus, Ford's best selling car in 1987, added an optional 3.8-liter V-6 for 1988. Previously used only in Ford's rear-drive cars, it was revised for front-drive use (and would also be used in the Mercury Sable and the new Lincoln Continental). Rated at the same 140-bhp as the 3.0-liter V-6, it developed 215 lbs/ft torque, 55 more than the 3.0. Rear-seat shoulder belts were added in mid-year. The top-line LX four-door (above) had a base sticker price of $15,295.

rather quaintly described it, saw calendar-year sales rise from 24,400 units to 67,500.

The Escort/EXP looked about the same, too, but only until midyear. At that point, Ford introduced a subtly facelifted Escort that looked more than ever like its slick European cousin. Despite extensive changes, the overall result was neater rather than dramatically smoother lines: new front fenders, taillamps, bodyside moldings, rear-quarter panels, and 14-inch wheels and tires on all models (the last replacing 13-inchers). Also new were overlapping glass/pillars on hatchbacks and, for the GT, a new grille, rear spoiler, and a 15-inch wheel/tire package (ousting 14-inchers). A shame the still-awkward EXP (which had been officially labeled an Escort since 1986½) wasn't similarly beautified, but continuing slow sales had prompted division marketers to reduce it to just a single model, inappropriately named Luxury Coupe, and even that would be gone with the end of the model year—and hardly missed.

Whether "early" or "late" '88, Escort model choices and mechanical specs stayed the same save the "half-year" inclusion of standard gas-pressure shocks across the board and the return of the LX

designation to replace GL on the volume-leading models. As before, the stripper Pony came as a three-door only. Calendar-year sales eased by some 5500 units but, as noted, Escort was America's most popular 1988 car, garnering 387,815 orders.

Mustang lost fewer than 2600 sales, which wasn't too bad considering that it was virtually unchanged. In fact, this year's sole alteration was a higher-capacity standard battery for LXs. Then too, Mustang now had to share the sporty-car spotlight with its erstwhile replacement, the swoopy new Probe. Whether this car was American or Japanese depended entirely on one's point of view. Strictly speaking, it was American, built at the new Flat Rock, Michigan, plant—which was admittedly owned by Mazda—and blessed with Dearborn styling inside and out. "Blessed" because the Probe was a mechanical cousin to Mazda's own new MX-6 sport coupe, but far more striking. Indeed, Mazda designers had taken to calling Ford's version "the pretty one" during the joint Probe/MX-6 development program, high praise indeed.

As noted (see *1987*), that effort began in 1982 with a Ford project designated SN-8 (for "sporty car, North America"). The goal was a smaller, thriftier new Mustang based on the Tempo/Topaz platform, but Dearborn managers weren't satisfied with the mechanical package—though they liked the styling, which would survive to production with little change. Thus, they turned to Mazda for engineering help.

The result was a basic chassis and drivetrain shared with Mazda's evolving

MX-6, but with a recalibrated suspension to give the Probe a more distinctly "Ford feel." The suspension itself was fairly straightforward: front coil-spring/struts on single control arms, plus anti-roll bar; an independent rear with a pair of coil/struts located by one trailing link and two lateral links per side (what Mazda called "Twin Trapezoidal Link" geometry), and another anti-roll bar. Steering was assisted rack-and-pinion, which Ford also rejiggered a bit. Brakes were the expected power front discs and rear drums except on the sporty GTs, where rear discs were standard.

Mazda also supplied the Probe/MX-6 engine, a new aluminum-head/iron-block inline four of 2.2 liters (133 cubic inches) with electronic multiport fuel injection and a belt-driven single overhead camshaft operating three valves per cylinder (two intakes, one exhaust). There were two versions: a normally aspirated unit with 110 bhp and 130 lbs/ft peak torque for the base GL and mid-range LX Probes, and an intercooled turbocharged edition with 145 bhp and a strong 190 lbs/ft for the enthusiast-oriented GT. MX-6 offered a similar lineup: normally aspirated DX and step-up LX, hyperaspirated GT Turbo. Whether Ford or Mazda, the standard transaxle was a manual five-speed, with a four-speed automatic optional for non-turbo models. Further distinguishing the GT from other Probes were an air slot above the front bumper, a spoiler at the base of the hatchback's rear window (MX-6s were notchbacks only), and plastic lower-body "cladding" *a la* Taurus LX. Firmer suspension with 15-inch alloy wheels and driver-variable shock damping was also included, and an

For 1988, the Aerostar saw only minor changes, the major one being that a new $6233 Eddie Bauer option now topped the line. This left the XLT (right) as the mid-level choice, with its two packages listing at $3437 and $4821. Base price was $11,165. The mini Festiva (below), which bowed in May 1987 on the West Coast, went nationwide during 1988. Riding a 90.2-inch wheelbase, it was powered by a 58-bhp 1.3-liter four and sold for $5765 as an L, $6868 as an LX.

anti-lock braking system (ABS) was an exclusive GT option.

With its higher performance, the GT naturally got the most "Probe-ing" from jaded journalists who'd perhaps tired of the Mustang. Styling was almost universally praised. *Car and Driver* judged that Ford's designers had "done a remarkable job. The Probe looks nothing like the conservative MX-6. It doesn't even look Japanese...distinctive and instantly likable. And like the series of aerodynamic show cars for which it's named, the Probe presents a clean face to the wind. The relatively unadorned GL and LX versions boast a drag coefficient of 0.30. The GT, with its wider tires [195/60VR-15s versus 185/70SR-14s on other models] and additional air intake is only slightly less efficient [at] 0.32."

Writers also liked the cozy 2+2 Probe cockpit, especially the well-arranged dash whose instrument pod moved with the standard tilt steering wheel on LX and GT. It was a feature found on only one other car, Porsche's super-pricey 928.

As for Probe performance, the GT, at least, felt far removed from any MX-6— more like a Mustang, in fact, though that was really no surprise. *C/D* termed the GT suspension "tightly snubbed. [It] reports every variation in road surface directly to the driver. This isn't much of a problem over smooth pavement, because a switch on the console allows you to dial in the amount of shock-absorber control you want. [But] the GT rides hard over potholes and sharp-edged bumps...no matter how soft the shocks are set. In exchange, [it's] precise and responsive on winding roads. And its speed-sensitive variable-assist power steering provides sharp on-center feel and reassuring feedback as cornering forces increase."

On that subject, *C/D* found maximum lateral acceleration was an impressive 0.81g. That might have seemed even more impressive were it not for an undue amount of torque-steer in hard acceleration—the unwanted pulling that typically affects high-power front-drive cars. And the Probe GT left no doubt about its power in a straight line. *Car and Driver* clocked its late prototype at a near-sensational 6.7 seconds 0-60 mph and at 15.2 seconds/91 mph in the standing quarter-mile. "Those times," said the magazine, "are about a half-second slower than the Mustang GT's and quicker than the 5.0-liter Camaro/Firebird's.... Even more amazing, the Probe GT doesn't *feel* too different from [those] V-8-powered cars....

It doesn't produce the same deep, throaty exhaust rumble and isn't as smooth, but it's every bit as eager to run. Boost builds quickly in the turbo-four; although shifting the gearbox is a joy, you can get plenty of thrust without winding the engine out."

CONSUMER GUIDE® reached many of the same conclusions, though its full-production GT wasn't quite as quick. Still, it was hardly slow at an observed 7.95 seconds 0-60 mph. By contrast, an automatic LX *CG* tried needed 11.7 seconds for the same dash. In all, *CG* judged the Probe a welcome newcomer to the sporty-coupe ranks: stylish, reasonably practical for its ilk, spirited, capable, and fun. Buyers apparently agreed; they snapped up nearly 78,000 for the Probe's abbreviated debut calendar year that began in May.

Because of its size and general performance, the Probe may have evoked a

few memories of the original ponycar, but Ford had surely been wise in deciding not to call it a Mustang. It was just too "foreign" in appearance and basic driving feel to pass as an American-style ponycar, new-wave or otherwise. But then, as program manager Barry Johnson told *Automotive News*: "We knew we were going to make a radical change dictated by what the market was doing. It couldn't be a Mustang II. It had to be a good car [his words, not ours]. It had to perform, it had to handle, it had to have feature and option content to sell against the [Toyota] Celica or [Honda] Prelude."

It also had to have high quality, of course, and in that, Ford succeeded handsomely, for the Probe was well built right from the start. As other transplants were showing, American workers could build cars as well as their cohorts in Japan or Europe—maybe even better. All they needed was a fair chance, which meant a

477

A new Mazda-built five-speed manual transmission and an XL Sport model (above) were the major changes for the 1988 Bronco II, which was available with two- or four-wheel drive ($11,866 and $13,316). The two XLT packages added either $888 or $1796 to the tab.

modern factory, sane work rules, a cooperative attitude from management, and a product designed to go together in a simple, logical, orderly way.

By now, Ford had shown another kind of wisdom in deciding to base its future domestic small cars—anything below Tempo-size—on future Mazda designs, with the Japanese company handling the bulk of the basic engineering work. Such sharing was not only of mutual economic benefit, but likely to mean better products than Ford might have done itself. Of course, this would hardly sit well with the jingoistic, America-first diehards who wouldn't be caught dead in a car of Japanese origin—even one built in the U.S.—with a domestic nameplate and with plenty of "American" design input. But they're the only ones who seemed bothered. If the Probe was to be the wave of the future—and *CG* thought so (which kind of put a different light on its name)—then small-car buyers have a lot to look forward to, at least at Ford dealerships.

Detail refinements were the order of this year for Ford's light-duty trucks. Highlighting developments for the compact Ranger pickups and Bronco II sport-utility was a new standard five-speed overdrive manual transmission. Supplied by Mazda, it offered easier shift action and, unusually, a fully synchronized reverse gear. Intermittent wipers were adopted for XL models on up, and driver's seats on Bronco IIs and Ranger SuperCabs adopted a tip-and-slide-forward feature, as already used on the passen-

ger's seat, for easier rear entry/exit from the left side. "Deep-dish" cast-aluminum wheels and electric remote-control door mirrors joined the options sheet. Additional Ranger revisions included new "S Plus" cab trim, a little more deluxe than the basic S below it (but less than the Custom above it), plus vibration-absorbing hydroelastic mounts with the 2.0-liter S/S Plus four-cylinder engine, and standard tinted glass (except S/S Plus). Bronco II was newly offered as an XL Sport, essentially the base XL model with more black trim outside and a bit nicer furnishings inside.

Ford shed the last of its truck carburetors by substituting multiport fuel injection on the 5.8-liter V-8 in the big Bronco, F-Series pickups, and full-size Econolines and Club Wagons, as well as on the E/F-Series 7.5-liter/460 gas V-8. Additionally, the 351 Windsor adopted a single-belt serpentine accessory drive and was again available in California. E- and F-Series also offered a new 7.3-liter enlargement of the 6.9 diesel V-8 to replace that unit in all its applications. All three lines received a more reliable, integrated alternator/voltage regulator and exchanged their four-speed manual gearboxes for five-speeders, again with synchronized Reverse and reduced shift effort. Trim and equipment were slightly upgraded for Bronco XLT, E-Series XL and XLT, and F-Series XLT Lariat. The first now included tilt wheel with cruise control; the last, intermittent wipers.

Changes exclusive to the F-Series involved higher GVW ratings on 2WD 150/ 250 and 4×4 250 Regular Cabs; new "dualie" versions of the 2WD 150 and 4WD 350 chassis/cabs; a new dualie 4×2 350 SuperCab; and, surprisingly, cancellation of all the once-popular Flareside models. Big Broncos now wore a standard transfer-case skid plate and chrome grille

and headlamp bezels, and offered a revised front-suspension option under the Heavy-Duty name.

Most welcome among the improvements on this year's Aerostars was adoption of the 3.0-liter, 140-bhp Taurus V-6 as standard for cargo Vans as well as passenger Wagons, thus belatedly putting out to pasture the underpowered 2.3-liter four. This also upped the Van's standard payload capacity from its relatively anemic 1200 pounds to a brawnier 1615. All Aerostars, Vans and Wagons alike, now came with a high-capacity battery, heavy-duty cooling system, and P215/70R14 tires (two sizes wider than before). XLT Wagons also added standard air, tilt wheel/cruise control, rear wiper/defroster, and seven-passenger seating package, and the Power Convenience Group option for Wagons was expanded to include electric-remote door mirrors. Ford had made hay with extra-cost Eddie Bauer packages on Bronco and Bronco II, so there was now one for Aerostar. This consisted of a seven-seat Wagon with the "convert-a-bed" feature, unique cloth interior trim, separate rear heater/air conditioner, exterior luggage rack, and blue/chestnut color scheme throughout.

Nineteen eighty-eight was another fine truck year for Ford Division. Chrysler was still unassailable in minivan sales and Chevy/GMC remained ahead in compact sport-utilities, but Ford led in most other model categories and, of course, in overall volume: better than 1.5 million units, a figure once considered excellent for cars, let alone trucks. Chevrolet closed the overall sales gap somewhat by moving about 1.35 million units, but that still trailed Ford by a wide margin.

As noted, Ford had become perhaps the most newsworthy outfit in Detroit, its continuing product, sales, and financial successes prompting intense, close coverage of most everything that went on at the Glass House. It was thus no surprise that reporters descended on Dearborn in January 1988 to cover the announcement of two notable additions to the firm's board of directors: Edsel B. Ford II, son of the late Henry Ford II, and his cousin William Clay Ford, Jr., son of HF II's sole surviving brother. Coming so soon after the death of the fabled HF II, the appointment of these fourth-generation Fords signalled in no uncertain terms that despite the great accomplishments of Petersen, Phil Caldwell, and other "outsiders," the founding family would continue to play a major role in running their firm.

The appointments were not without merit despite the youthfulness of the appointees. Edsel, then about to turn 40, had joined the company as a product analyst in 1974 after graduating from Babson College. After four years in domestic sales, he was named managing director at Ford Australia, then returned home for a brief stint at the Harvard Business School before moving to Ford Division as manager of market planning. Next came a tour in product planning at Lincoln-Mercury, followed by a promotion to that division's general sales manager in the summer of 1987. "Billy," as Edsel's 30-year-old cousin was known, started out in product planning in 1979 and served on the team for the crucial launch of the Escort/Lynx for 1981. Following a stint as sales manager for the New York zone, he went overseas to head up commercial vehicle marketing for Ford Europe, then left in September 1987 to become chairman and general manager of Ford's small subsidiary in Switzerland.

With all that, Billy and Edsel looked to be driving toward the top echelons of Ford management with the speed of a Mustang GT. Indeed, HF II, before his death, had let it be known that he wanted both young men to replace him on the board. William Clay, Sr. seemed satisfied once that happened. As he told *Fortune* magazine a year later: "There are three of us [Fords] on the board [now]. I don't see the need for any more."

Yet despite the cousins' growing managerial experience, the lack of any overt rivalry between them, and their modest, unassuming public attitude about themselves and their current place in the Ford organization, their increasing public visibility together with speculation about their ultimate destinies couldn't help but rankle Don Petersen. "I'm not a caretaker for anybody," he told *Fortune* in that same January 1989 article. "I admire the fact that [Edsel and Billy] are trying very hard to go as far as they can. But being a Ford does not give them a leg up. The principle we must operate on is that selection to top management is based solely on merit."

Industry watchers agreed. So, apparently, did the two young Fords. As Edsel told Bob Irvin of *Automotive News* back in 1978: "I am doing my best to live up to my family and the company and the people who work for it. The most important thing in my life is to gain the respect of people within the ranks of the corporation. You can't succeed without people on your side. It's my goal . . . it's one thing my father has done." Unfortunately, he managed to irritate Petersen even more with this comment to *Fortune*: "I've made it clear on one or two occasions to [him] that it does seem a bit odd to me that there are three classes of directors: inside, outside and Billy and me." But then, the two young men were the first Ford board members to be appointed without any specific committee responsibilities.

That remark led to a public tiff between Petersen and young Edsel that both tried to smooth over. Edsel told the *Wall Street Journal* a few days after the *Fortune* article appeared that it was basically correct, but not "where it says the fourth generation are at odds with not only Don Petersen but with William Clay Ford [Sr.]. . . . The conflict . . . does not exist." As to his charge that he and his cousin

were "second-class" board members, Edsel told the *Journal* that he'd since talked to Petersen and that they were "going to have a continuing dialogue." For his part, Petersen termed the company's relationship with the cousins as "in transition . . . and that is a matter of plowing new ground. . . . So we're having a lot of discussions about it in a very informal way."

That seemed to end the row, but some weren't so sure. "Ford managers have now seen 10 years of remarkably peaceful executive transition," the *Journal* concluded. "During that time, Ford has set earnings and sales records—some say because it hasn't been distracted by internecine squabbles. But 'you're [now] going to start hearing whispers, rumors of a palace revolt,' said one long-time Ford manager. . . . Speculation about why [Edsel] has publicly expressed his dissatisfaction is rampant among employees. 'Has he tried to get more power, more jobs and they've turned him down and now he's groping?' wondered one. One source close to [Edsel] said that is part of his motivation. Without being specific, he said Mr. Ford has tried several times to gain more power, but 'Don Petersen has shut him down.'"

Nevertheless, much more will doubtless be heard from both Edsel and William Clay, Jr., in the years ahead. But as *Automotive News* editorialized in January 1988, their continued push for positions of real authority will not be easy. "[For now,] they will maintain their current jobs and, as such, work a half-dozen rungs from the top. Thus, as employees, they will be working for people who they, as directors, have to make important managerial review and career decisions about. Yet the Fords' treat-me-like-anyone-else professional attitude should allow them to play both roles with grace and humility. In short, their elevation [to the board] makes Ford both a better and stronger company—and a better and stronger family." There are many in Dearborn who hope that will indeed be the case.

You could have your trucks just about any way you wanted from Ford in 1988. Models ranged from compact to the largest line haulers sold in America. Among the light-duty offerings were the Bronco, here an XLT (top), which came with a 4.9-liter six with 150 horsepower at 3400 rpm and 170 pounds/feet torque at 2000 rpm. Power steering and brakes were standard, as was a five-speed manual transmission. The compact Ranger received the same new five-speed manual as Bronco II plus newly standard tinted glass, intermittent wipers, and a black rear step bumper (except S and S Plus). The V-6 was standard on the STX, here a 4×4 (second from top). Among the full-size F-Series trucks, multi-port fuel injection was made standard on the 5.8- and 7.5-liter V-8s, upping horsepower to 210 and 320. Base engine was the 4.9-liter 150-bhp six. Shown are the F-150 XLT Lariat (third from top) and the F-350 XLT Lariat "dualie" (above), which boasted a 5270-pound payload.

1989

The brief public spat between Edsel B. Ford II and top Dearborn managers was only a prelude to a very busy and historically significant year for Ford Motor Company. Actually, 1989 couldn't help but be significant. For one thing, there was a new man in the White House, former Vice-President George Bush, and he was talking much tougher emissions, fuel-economy, and safety standards, a real shock for Detroit after eight years of "benign neglect" from the Reagan Administration. Suddenly the industry faced the return of the 27.5-mpg CAFE target that had been rolled back to 26 mpg for 1986, then eased up to 26.5 for 1989. In view for the Nineties were drastically lower emissions levels and required car-type safety equipment for light trucks, a conserted push toward alternate fueled vehicles, and Congress seemed ready to mandate a 40-mpg car CAFE for the year 2000.

In the midst of all this, the market contracted after three years of force-feeding by incentives. Total calendar-year sales dipped six percent, to 14.8-million units—however, still an excellent year. Cars fell 6.8 percent to just under 9.88 million; light trucks lost 4.4 percent to drop below the five-million mark again. Imports were not immune from the

downturn, slipping 8.8 percent, but this was scant consolation to Detroit bean-counters. Calendar-year production at "transplant" operations went above a million units for the first time, and Big Three earnings went way down. Ford's profits slid 28 percent to $3.8 billion, aggravated by a dismal fourth quarter in which the firm logged its first red ink for North American operations since 1982. GM and Chrysler fared no better, recording respective calendar-year losses of 13 percent (to $4.2 billion) and close to 60 percent (down to $359 million).

Dearborn's earnings would have been higher, if still below its '88 figure, had it not been for taxes on the historic sale of its Rouge Steel operations. And Ford could find comfort in other statistics. Take market shares, where the firm captured 22.2 percent of calendar-year car sales, up 0.6 percent, and 24.6 percent of model-year car/light-truck sales, up 0.5 percent. Though such gains don't sound like much, each 0.1-percent gain represented a lot of money for the company, its workers, and its dealers—not to mention continuing strength against archrival GM, which again fell in calendar-year car sales, this time losing a bit more than one percent to end at just under 35 percent, its worst postwar performance ever.

There were other bright spots for Dearborn. Besides fractionally higher model-year sales for both car divisions, Ford maintained truck-sales supremacy over Chevrolet even though both makes notched higher volume. Still, incentives and higher prices had stolen some sales from 1989 and given them to 1988. Reflecting this was the growing number of

Big Three plant closings throughout the year, both permanent shutdowns and temporary ones for "inventory adjustment." And while Ford's big F-Series pickup remained the nation's best-selling vehicle, a strong December surge enabled the Honda Accord to oust Ford's Escort as America's best-selling car for the calendar 12 months—the first time a foreign model had ever done that. Though some sources put Escort first in model-year sales, Detroit was mightily dispirited by Honda's achievement, especially as American-made Accords accounted for fully 61 percent of the Japanese firm's total U.S. sales.

This ambiguous market situation underscored the importance of several key shifts in the Dearborn executive ranks during 1989. The first came in March with the retirement of 64-year-old vice-chairman William Clay Ford, Sr., effective April 1. Though he would remain on the board and its executive and finance committees, his departure left the firm without a Ford family member in top management for the first time ever. Announced simultaneously was the appointment of his son, William, Jr., then chief of Ford Switzerland, to head engineering and manufacturing for the do-

The redesigned '89 Thunderbird retained its rear-drive layout, but got an all-new body that was 3.4 inches shorter, 1.6 inches wider, and almost an inch lower than its predecessor. Meanwhile, the wheelbase was stretched nine inches to 113, resulting in a roomier interior. Topping the line was the $19,823 Super Coupe (below), which ran with a supercharged V-6 that cranked out 210 bhp and 315 lbs/ft torque.

mestic truck operations units beginning July 1.

Not two months later, both Billy and his cousin Edsel were named to the executive and finance committees, thus negating Edsel's charge that the fourth-generation youngsters had been "second-class" board members since first being appointed without committee assignments 16 months before. Interestingly, this announcement coincided with an annual stockholders meeting that was one of the shortest (under two hours) and most sparsely attended (only 560 showed up) in the firm's history.

Next up was a promotion for the fast-rising Edsel, from L-M Division general sales manager to executive director of the worldwide corporate marketing staff as of July 1. *Automotive News* noted that this put Edsel in "Ford's third tier of management, below the chief executive and a step shy of the vice-president. At age 40, he [is] the youngest member among a group of nearly 40 executives at that level." Though some wondered whether this didn't further limit a man who seemed destined to lead the company and would thus need more than marketing experience, most agreed that Edsel would benefit from having responsibilities on a global scale.

But the big news came in November, when Donald E. Petersen announced his early retirement, effective March 1, 1990. His energy level had declined, the 63-year-old chairman said, and after 10 years at the top it was time to "repot" himself by changing jobs (in line with the thinking of a one-time dean of the Stanford University graduate business school). Though Petersen's immediate personal plans were unclear, his resignation caused no panic, the line of succession having long been laid out. His teammate, 64-year-old Vice-Chairman Harold A. "Red" Poling, would become chairman, and Philip E. Benton, Jr., would move up to Poling's old job from president of Ford's automotive group. Benton, in turn, would be replaced by Allan D. Gilmour, executive vice-president of corporate staffs. Ironically, Petersen had again been honored for his executive acumen only the previous July, being named "American Manager of the Year" by the National Management Association.

If industry-watchers were a bit surprised by Petersen's early retirement, they weren't dismayed. Trade weekly *Automotive News* editorialized that the timing of it made "such good sense: It paves the way for a smooth transition of power throughout the 1990s. Petersen has been a prime mover behind Ford's [recent] success, and he is leaving the job to a capable, long-time teammate—Harold Poling. The early retirement will give Poling—who wasn't expected to get a chance—up to three years to leave his mark as chairman. The Poling years will give finance man Allan Gilmour time to gain more experience with worldwide car and truck

Announcing the Super Coupe (top) was a "Thunderbird SC" designation on the rear bumper. Standard equipment included a handling suspension, four-wheel disc brakes, ABS, articulated sport seats, lower bodyside cladding, and fog lights. The mid-range T-Bird LX (above) listed at $16,817. It came with a 140-bhp version of the 3.8-liter V-6, power driver's seat, power locks, cruise control, and power mirrors.

operations. If Gilmour succeeds Poling as anticipated, he will come to the job arguably as the most-rounded, best-prepared chief executive in Ford history—at 58 years of age. Ford family members must feel comfortable in that knowledge.... Edsel and Billy are clearly on their way up through the management ranks. The current transition seems to insure that they will be able to develop and expand their responsibilities at a reasonable pace."

But things weren't going to be easy for the Poling regime or any that followed. As *AN* continued: "The North American market is saturated with too many products from too many producers, and that means vicious competition. Ford must find ways to stem rising product development costs, to shorten product development cycles and to retain market share despite that competition. Ford must also capitalize on its advantages in Europe, and execute product replace-

ments for successful models like Taurus/ Sable." *AN* might have added that Ford—and the rest of Detroit—would have to figure out how to do all this while satisfying the strict new government mandates that looked increasingly certain, not to mention turning out cars and trucks that people would prefer over Japanese competitors.

Ford Division's '89 lineup gave evidence that the firm still recognized the crucial importance of good products. The biggest event by far was a completely new Thunderbird, the 11th-generation "personal" Ford. Spawned along the same lines and chassis of the T-Bird, was its sister, the Mercury Cougar. Named project MN12 (for "mid-size, North America"), it was even smoother than the winning 1983-88 design, and slightly lower and wider. Yet it measured nearly 3.5-inches shorter overall, while riding a wheelbase stretched 8.8 inches to 113 inches, which placed the wheels closer to the corners of

The basically unchanged '89 Mustang GT was powered by a five-liter V-8 that punched out 225 bhp at 4200 rpm and 300 lbs/ft torque at 3200 rpm. The GT hatchback (above) stickered at $13,272. Standard equipment included heavy duty suspension, Traction-Lok rear axle, 225/60VR-15 tires on alloy wheels, driver's foot rest, remote hatch release, and power windows and locks.

the car. Overall appearance reminded many of BMW's classic Six-Series coupe, but it managed to be distinctively Ford—proving, perhaps, that the first "aero" Bird and the equally neat Taurus weren't flukes after all.

Surprisingly, both the V-8 and turbo-four engines were gone, replaced by a brace of reworked 232 "Essex" V-6s. The familiar 140-horsepower unit returned with sequential multiport fuel injection (SFI) for the base and luxury LX models, teamed only with automatic. The Sport was gone, too, as was the Turbo Coupe, but that was okay because there was a *very* hot newcomer called the SC. The initials allegedly denoted "Super Coupe," which was an apt name, for the SC's powerplant was a supercharged and intercooled SFI V-6 packing 210 bhp and a substantial 315 pounds/feet torque (100 lbs/ft more than the normal unit). Predictably, it mated with a standard five-speed manual; the automatic came at extra cost. Engine-driven superchargers were a 1930's idea that has lately been revived on several European and Japanese cars, and their well-known advantages over the exhaust-driven turbocharger were just as evident in the SC—mainly smoother, more progressive power delivery at a slight sacrifice in noise and efficiency.

Chassis engineering was equally new. Though the front suspension retained MacPherson-style coil-over-shock units, geometry now comprised an A-arm at the top of each strut and a trans-

verse arm at its base, then connecting to a long, sickle-shaped member integral with the hub carrier. Rear suspension was fully independent—a first for Thunderbird—and quite compact, with a variable-rate coil spring sandwiched between an upper lateral link and a wide H-shaped lower member. Vertical shocks rode ahead of the hub carriers. Steering remained power rack-and-pinion, but with a new speed-sensitive variable-assist feature as standard. This delivered maximum boost for easy parking and low-speed maneuvering, while progressively decreasing it with rising road speed to afford better steering feel and control. Base and LX carried front-disc/rear-drum power brakes, but the SC's standard all-disc system with Teves anti-lock control was optional for the first time on these "cooking" models. The SC also came with a more sophisticated version of the Turbo Coupe's electronically variable shock damping.

Inside was a logical, very European instrument panel with digital/graphic or analog instruments, the latter standard on SC. Maintaining tradition was a functional center console on all models. Seats were arguably the best in T-Bird history. And thanks partly to the longer wheelbase, rear legroom received a welcome increase.

There was only one problem: weight. The '89 T-Birds were anywhere from 300 to 500 pounds heavier than comparably equipped '88s. Even so, the SC delivered terrific go, its prodigious torque helping it do 0-60 mph in 7.8 seconds with automatic, according to CONSUMER GUIDE®, and 7.1 with manual, as clocked by *Car and Driver*. Even better, a supercharger boosts most all the time, so the SC had none of the irritating throttle lag that so plagued the Turbo Coupe—just smooth, abundant power instantly

available at the touch of the right foot. Alas, 140 horses just weren't enough for the normally aspirated slushbox-only models, which ambled through the same test in a lackluster 10.4 seconds by CONSUMER GUIDE® magazine's stopwatch.

Surprising, perhaps, given the extra poundage, Bird tire sizes were unchanged from '88. The SC thus rode on the same 225/60VR-16 rubber as the last Turbo Coupe, yet generated slightly higher cornering power of 0.82 g (versus 0.80), according to *Car and Driver*. "Better still," said that magazine, was "this big bruiser's balance. When you wind in toward the apex, the nose and tail bite as one. Neither end twitches or threatens. Experts will find that on those rare occasions when they can push to the absolute limit of adhesion . . . the SC is remarkably neutral. When the grip is all used up, the tail steps out ever so gingerly. . . ."

Yet, the curious thing about the SC, as *C/D* reported, was that "it's better at going fast than it is at going slow. We think it ought to be the other way around, because a lot of the enjoyment an enthusiast derives from his car comes from the way it drives at normal speeds. . . . Here the Super Coupe is a day late and a dollar short. The tactile sensations coming through your fingers and the seat of your pants are undistinguished. The T-Bird's shifter, steering and switchgear lack the jewel-like feel you find in Benzes, Bimmers and the better Japanese brands."

Ride drew mixed reviews. "Buff books" generally thought it too soft, while CONSUMER GUIDE® judged it just fine for all-round driving. There were no quibbles about workmanship from any quarter. All the new Birds had a Teutonic tightness and solidity that almost made one overlook certain tacky details like cheap-looking dash appliqués—cross-hatched metal on SCs, too-obvious

fake wood elsewhere.

But there was a reason for these seeming contradictions: Despite being Dearborn's first specialty car with its own platform, the MN12 missed both its weight and cost targets—so much so that the project manager was dismissed following an internal audit. That didn't prevent *Motor Trend* from naming the SC its 1989 domestic "Car of the Year," but it did leave room for improvements. "The big stuff is already handled," *Car and Driver* observed. "The rest is small-change refinement. If Ford can cast aside its cost-cutter Mustang mentality long enough to massage the Super Coupe to its full potential, the automotive pantheon awaits. Until then, *we'll* wait."

Some buyers must have waited, too, perhaps put off by higher prices ranging from $14,612 for the base Bird to $19,283 for the SC. The latter didn't look at all bad for a car that could run with a BMW yet cost less than half as much, but T-Bird sales had long since depended on bread-and-butter models, not sporty performers like the SC. In any case, T-Bird model-year production fell by more than 32,300 units to 114,868 (due partly to a slow production start up), its lowest since 1982. Curiously, calendar-year sales, which naturally included some 1990 models, went up by about 3000 units to near 121,000.

That may prove to be Thunderbird's new "natural" volume level, but there was no question that the personal-luxury Ford was in the best shape it had been in for a long time. Its Eighties metamorphosis from flash cruiser to tasteful tourer was gradual but dramatic, and continuing strong sales after 1983 suggested that many people hadn't forgotten the special character of the classic little Birds and the early four-seaters. How wonderful that Ford hadn't forgotten either. As the T-

Bird approached its 35th birthday, it was again a car to fire the imagination and stir the soul.

Soul-stirring was still an apt description for the Mustang and its one-time replacement, the Japanese-American Probe. The latter had bowed in advance of the model year and was untouched for the balance of it. Mustang changed scarcely more as the fifth-generation design headed into its 11th model year. In belated recognition of customer styling preferences, Ford made the LX V-8 package option a distinct model trio called "LX 5.0L Sport," and threw in the GT's multi-adjustable sports seats. The only other change of consequence was standardizing the optional power windows and Power Lock Group for the two convertibles.

But wasn't 1989 the 25th anniversary of Mustang's introduction? Technically yes, but the year passed without a commemorative special. Though one had been rumored through most of '88, Ford said it wouldn't arrive until 1990. The reason was that by Ford's calendar, that would be the proper year, the division always having regarded the first Mustang as a '65 model, not a "1964½" as some enthusiasts would have it.

Speculation ran wild as to what this Silver Anniversary Mustang might be. The rumor mill first spoke of a GT with extra-heavy-duty suspension and a 351 truck V-8 hopped up with twin turbochargers to an alleged 400 bhp, a package engineered by factory-contract race-car builder Jack Roush. But though this idea went as far as one developmental prototype, it was doomed by high costs relative to the planned production of only 2000 units. A better bet seemed to be a 302 GT with an extra 35-50 bhp via tuned intake runners and tweaked engine electronics, plus the usual suspension upgrades, some

Those who craved the Mustang GT's performance— but not the aggressive looks—could order the LX 5.0L Sport. If power didn't matter, buyers could opt for the $14,140 LX convertible (above). It trotted along with a 2.3-liter four that developed 90 bhp and 130 lbs/ft torque, but that engine had to struggle to overcome the 3200-pound weight. The GT's interior featured articulated sport seats.

different bolt-on body pieces for styling distinction, and possibly four-wheel disc brakes left over from the SVO. More exotic possibilities were also whispered, including the T-Bird SC's supercharged V-6 or possibly a new double-overhead-cam 32-valve V-8, the latter stemming from Ford's new "modular" engine program for the Nineties.

Alas, the 25th-birthday Mustang turned out to be pretty tame when it finally appeared halfway through the 1990 model year. But enthusiasts had no cause to grumble. Not only was the Mustang itself still around, it was much the same car it had been in the beginning. In fact, it's remarkable that Mustang emerged from the Eighties in the fine fettle it did. Chevy's Camaro and Pontiac's Firebird had also survived, but they mostly languished in both the sales and design departments as Mustang improved on those counts. Perhaps it only goes to show what happens when you've got enthusiasts making the key product decisions.

In any case, Mustang finished 1989 with slightly lower calendar-year sales and model-year production: respectively, 161,148 (down about 9000) and 209,769 (off by only some 1500). Even so, Mustang seemed certain to have a place in Ford's future. Indeed, the rumor mill confirmed in late '89 that work had already started toward a sixth-generation Mustang—a true all-American ponycar, this time, not a trans-Pacific hybrid like the

The front-drive Probe, introduced in May 1988 as an '89 model, was originally intended to replace the Mustang. But Mustangers wanted a rear-drive all-American ponycar, so the Probe became an addition to the line. It came in three flavors: base GL, LX, and top-line GT (above and below). Priced at $14,077, the 2720-pound GT came with a turbocharged 145-bhp 2.2-liter four. The Mazda-built Probe's drivetrain was similar to the MX-6.

Probe—cheering news indeed to Mustang lovers everywhere.

With one exception, developments for Ford's other '89 passenger cars weren't that interesting. The sole change for the big LTD Crown Victoria was replacement of the low-oil warning light with a new government-required "check engine" telltale. By this time, both Crown Vic and Mercury's Grand Marquis were being built solely in Canada, and they bucked the wavering market with higher model-year production. The Ford ended at just over 134,000 units, nearly 9000 better than its '88 run, while the Merc,

oddly enough, did even better—nearly 139,000 units, up almost 18,000.

The subcompact battle had become a bloody one indeed, thanks to the fiercest competition and greatest price-sensitivity of any market sector. Escort suffered more than most rivals, perhaps because it was less changed than most. In fact, the '89 line was a complete rerun from "1988½" save cancellation of the unhappy, slow-selling two-seat EXP coupe. Sales and production both tumbled. The former fell by over 54,000 units to just over 335,500 for the calendar year. More telling, perhaps, model-year volume plunged by almost 59,000, ending a bit above 363,000 units. Yet even that was creditable for what was now a nine-year-old package. And there was little reason for worry anyway. A new Mazda-based '91 Escort was slated to bow in April 1990 though, curiously, the existing model was slated to continue alongside it for a time.

Ford had trouble moving the little

Festiva this year, selling fewer than 200 more for the calendar 12 months—69,328 in all. One big problem was the low price that had been Festiva's main reason for being. At just under $5700 for the basic L model, Festiva competed not so much with other low-end imports like the Hyundai Excel, another Korean-built price-leader, but with two- and three-year-old used cars, mostly domestic compacts and intermediates that appealed to buyers who still equated size with value. But that was the subcompact market in 1989, and Festiva suffered along with Escort, the Excel, and most other small cars.

The Festiva was also likely hurt by lack of change. Optional three-speed automatic transmission arrived, and with the bonus of multiport fuel injection, which lifted the little 1.3-liter four from 58 to 63 bhp. Stickshift cars, however, stuck with an archaic carburetor. The only other change was a new in-between "L Plus" model with standard electric rear-window defroster and AM/FM stereo

priced $673 above the base L and $729 less than the much better-equipped LX. All things considered, Festiva did well to maintain its previous volume.

Lack of change also hampered the compact Tempo, which lost close to 24,500 units in model-year volume (to just under 289,000) and nearly 57,000 in U.S. calendar-year sales (to about 228,500). Technical changes were limited to standard gas-pressure shocks for the base GLs and a larger battery and new "check engine" warning light for all models. A front-center armrest was added to the mid-range GLS offerings, and GLS four-doors got the previously optional Sport Appearance Group—mainly lower-body plastic "cladding" *a la* Taurus.

The mid-size Ford was now the division's volume-leading car line, eclipsing Escort despite losing more than 26,500 calendar-year sales to finish at just over 348,000. Taurus' model-year production rose, though not much, with almost 7700 additional units lifting the total above 395,000. Why the discrepancy? Because Ford, like other Detroit makers, had overbuilt a little, trying to keep factories open by using incentives to prop up demand. But this only worked for a little while. By year's end, the Taurus was being "incentivized" as much as some slow sellers to move an ominously growing backlog of unsold cars.

Taurus also evidenced little change for '89: just minor alterations to grille, headlamps, taillamps, and interior door panels. Ford gave up on the oddball MT5 sedan, but nobody mourned because something much better took its place as the sporting Taurus. It went by the title SHO, which denoted a "Super High-Output" V-6 packing 220 bhp, teamed exclusively with a new five-speed Mazda-supplied manual transaxle. The result was the best-ever American attempt at a genuine Eurostyle sports sedan.

Designed in conjunction with Yamaha and nicknamed "Shogun" by Ford engineers partly because of that, the exotic new SHO V-6 boasted twin overhead camshafts and four valves per cylinder, but the same 3.0-liter displacement as the tame overhead-valve Vulcan V-6. It even used the same bore spacings, 89 × 83-mm bore and stroke (3.50 × 3.27 inches), cast-iron block construction (albeit fortified), and 60-degree cylinder-bank angle. Otherwise, it was completely different. The new heads, Yamaha's principal contribution, featured pent-roof combustion chambers, enlarged valves, and centrally sited platinum-tipped sparkplugs good for 60,000 miles. A single belt, driven off the front of the crankshaft, actuated the intake cams in both heads; each exhaust cam was chain-driven from the rear of its adjacent intake cam.

More unusual still was a two-stage induction system comprising a pair of linked plenum chambers, one per cylinder bank, from which ran 12 intake runners—three short and three long per side.

The Splash was a concept car that made the rounds of the 1989 auto shows. As the name implies, it was intended as a fun car for leisure-time activities such as a day at the beach. What better way to be noticed there than in a monochromatic blue beach buggy with bold pink lettering and pink trimmed tires? Features included a rear hatch, built-in roll bar, sharply raked windshield, wild styling, sport wheels, and a blue and black interior. Of course, the Splash was never seriously intended for production.

The former fed the cylinders directly, the latter the cylinders on the opposite side. The engine inhaled only through the long tracts below 4000 rpm; above that, a butterfly valve opened the short ones for full breathing. An ignition cutout limited revs to 7300, allegedly to keep the accessory drive intact, though the engine was said to run safely all day at 8500-plus. Other features contributing to durability included forged-steel crank and conrods, strengthened main-bearing supports, full water-jacketing, extra-large cooling passages, and a water-filled oil cooler. A specific version of Ford's EEC-IV electronic engine control system regulated six sequentially activated dual-port fuel injectors and a three-coil distributorless ignition system.

Because this impressive-looking powerhouse mounted transversely like other Taurus engines, the SHO was treated to equal-length halfshafts to minimize front-drive torque-steer in hard takeoffs. The all-coil, all-strut Taurus suspension was beefed up, but not drastically: larger rear anti-roll bar, firmer shock valving, high-rate bushings, and P215/65R-15 Goodyear Eagle GT+4 all-season performance radials. A sensible step was rear disc brakes to replace the standard-issue drums. Helped by the Shogun engine's formidable extra pull, the SHO exhibited safe but spirited cornering allied to a firm but comfortable ride.

Performance was well-nigh sensational. Banzai standing-starts were spectacular tire-smoking affairs that netted CONSUMER GUIDE® testers an average 7.3 seconds 0-60 mph, making this Taurus almost a second quicker than BMW's latest manual-shift 535i. Even better, the Shogun proved a very elastic

engine that pulled well from low revs and with gusto in the middle-rpm range, so there was little need for constant cog-swapping in stop-and-go grinds.

When not charging like *el toro*, the SHO could cruise at 60 mph in fifth with but 2200 rpm on the tach and a quiet 68-69 decibels on the sound meter. Fast touring was its forte, and the interior helped the driver enjoy that. Alas, the cabin was mostly stock Taurus, but it did include multi-adjustable sport front seats, crisp analog instrumentation, and a full front-center console with convenient storage nooks. In contrast with its fresh ergonomics the foot-operated parking brake was retained from the tame Tauruses, and it seemed woefully out of place here. The same held true for the metal trim on dash and doors; it looked like something off a cheap boom-box.

But overall, Ford's new BMW-basher was mighty impressive, and with a reasonable $19,739 base price, it should have sold like gangbusters. But it didn't—model-year production came to only about 12,000 units, about half of what was expected. There were two basic problems. One was styling that was understated to a fault. Against the hundreds of thousands of ordinary Tauruses running the streets, the SHO differed only in having a small slot beneath the up-front "navel" and an equally modest aero treatment along the rocker panels and below each bumper. The result was a bull in sheep's clothing that *AutoWeek* observed did "little to trumpet its status or let passers-by know the driver ... is a cut above the garden-variety Taurus owner." No doubt the bean-counters wanted to minimize costs on a limited-production job, but that seemed just penny-pinching foolishness after all the money they lav-

New to Ford's hot-selling line of front-drive family cars for '89 was the Taurus SHO (above right). Available only as a four-door sedan, it was powered by a "Super-High Output" 3.0-liter V-6 developed and built in Japan by Yamaha. The 220-horsepower V-6 boasted dual overhead cams and four valves per cylinder. Ford put its 0-60-mph acceleration time at about eight seconds and its top speed at around 140 miles per hour. Exclusive to the SHO was a special handling suspension and the first four-wheel disc brake system available on any Taurus. The only transmission offered was a Mazda-built five-speed manual. Ford had planned to build at least 20,000 SHOs, but sales came in only slightly better than half that. The LX series consisted of a $15,282 four-door sedan (top) and a $16,524 wagon (above).

ished on Yamaha for the primo engine.

The SHO's other big problem was its lack of an automatic option. Americans tend to prefer self-shift transmissions even in their sportiest cars, and the deficit was compounded here by a mandatory manual that was none too pleasant. Ford said the normal Taurus' four-speed automatic wasn't strong enough for the revvy SHO engine's 200 lbs/ft torque, which was 15 less than that of the 3.8 V-6 but peaked 1000 rpm higher (at 4800 rpm). "Our big problem," as one engineer confessed to *AutoWeek*, "is finding a torque converter with a 4200-rpm stall speed. The units we have now just won't meet

durability requirements when tweaked to give the performance that buyers demand. And the units that meet the durability requirements don't offer the performance we need.... The SHO produces its power so far up the rev range [peak power came at 6000 rpm] the torque converters cook themselves when we try to get acceptable performance out of them."

As for the manual, it was precise enough but needed a heavy hand, thanks to apparently slow synchro action (admittedly not unexpected in a high-performance machine). We say "slow" because of a warning tag that made one think twice about backing up. It said the driver *must* completely declutch and put the lever in Neutral, "wait a minimum of three seconds before attempting to shift into reverse gear," then push far right and pull back. Get it wrong and "a grinding noise may occur." If an unlucky driver missed Reverse, he was implored not to let the clutch out, but rather to return the stick to Neutral, and then "momentarily release the clutch pedal from the floor," and, finally, to try again. The actual procedure was neither as lengthy or perilous as this all sounded—just clumsy.

Yet despite such flaws, the Taurus SHO was a thoroughly well-developed and satisfying package, as exciting and welcome as the Thunderbird Super Coupe. More important, perhaps, it proved that America—or at least Ford—could build a high-quality, high-performance sedan able to stand comparison with Europe's best.

Ranger and Bronco II received the most attention among Ford's 1989 light-duty trucks, a handsome facelift making the compact pickups and sport-utility look a lot like their big brothers. It was all done in Dearborn's rounded "aero" idiom, with new hood, fenders, grille, and integrated headlamps/turn signals wrapped around into the front side-marker lights. Inside was yet another new dashboard, also like that on the full-sizers but also very Mazda-like with its cutaway dash-top tray on the right. Other shared changes were moving the automatic transmission lever from the floor to the steering column and wider standard tires (205/75R-15SL) with quieter-running tread.

Specific improvements for Bronco II included a power-steering valve modified for better feel, incorporation of front-axle camber adjustment, and a new no-cost AM/FM stereo radio with digital clock. Standard rear anti-lock brakes were a big step forward for Ranger, but so was cancellation of the weak 2.0-liter base engine. Standard power for most models was now an improved version of the familiar 2.3-liter four, with a revised head incorporating twin sparkplugs on each cylinder. Ford said this was mainly to benefit mileage and emissions, but it also upped horsepower by 10 to an even 100. As before, 4×4 SuperCabs and the sporty STX regular came with the 140-bhp 2.9-liter V-6 that remained optional elsewhere.

Ranger "models" were now marketed more as package options, and there were more choices for '89 as the S and S Plus groups were available in longbed form for the first time. A more interesting newcomer was the GT. Offered only on the short-bed 4×2, this $3533 package bolstered STX features with front and rear bumper covers and car-like rocker-panel extensions done in body-color plastic, plus front foglamps. Among the usual trim and equipment adjustments throughout the Ranger line were half-

The '89 Taurus SHO was sticker priced at $19,739, fully $4457 more than the LX four-door, and a whopping $7961 more than the base L four-door. Visually, the SHO featured relatively modest ground-effects, including a front air dam with fog lamps (top). The SHO's V-6 (above) developed its 220 horsepower quite high up in the rev range: 6000 rpm. Torque was an even 200 pounds/feet at 4800 rpm. Although the engine was praised, some road testers complained that the gearbox needed refinement.

The '89 Aerostar was available with a 15.4-inch stretch behind the rear wheels. Also new was the grille and front bumper. Base priced at $11,567, the Aerostar could also be had with a $6503 Eddie Bauer package (top). At $6372, L Plus (second from top) was the mid-range Festiva for '89. The Tempo LX (third from top) came only as a $10,156 four-door sedan, while the LTD Crown Victoria lineup consisted of six models, among them the $16,767 LX four-door sedan (above).

inch wider standard wheels for 4×4s (now 6.0 versus 5.5 inches), underbody spare-tire mount (thus freeing up some extra cargo-box space), newly optional "sport cloth" bucket seats and remote-electric door mirrors, and a larger, 17-gallon fuel tank.

By now, the Ranger had evolved into a highly pleasing and competitive little workhorse, and CONSUMER GUIDE® had lots of praise for it in a special 1989 buyers guide: "Overall, this is one of the best small trucks available, offering a range of models designed for everything from light hauling to off-road sorties. In addition, Ranger has competitive base prices, attractive discounts with its 'preferred equipment packages,' and Ford's 6-year/60,000 mile powertrain warranty. Put this one first on your shopping list." A lot of people did just that, and Ranger again came in first in calendar-year sales among compact pickups. There were fewer buyers around, but Ranger maintained a sizable lead over Chevy's S-10 with more than 284,000 orders versus some 229,000.

The Bronco II was less competitive in its field, though CONSUMER GUIDE® had good things to say about it, too. Though it compromised more in ride comfort and cabin space than some rivals, CG applauded the standard rear anti-lock brakes and liked the interior furnishings, the V-6 engine, the optional Touch Drive 4×4 system and—most of all—pricing. "A nicely furnished XL or XL Sport with Touch Drive can still be thousands less than a similar vehicle from Jeep, GM, Nissan, or Toyota."

Unfortunately for Ford, another consumer magazine was less kind to the Bronco II, branding its emergency handling "poor" in a rather odd track test. Shortly before, that same publication had all but wiped out demand for the tiny Japanese-built Suzuki Samurai in declaring its handling "not acceptable"—which was tantamount to "unsafe." But Ford countered the charge against Bronco II even more aggressively than Suzuki had against its sport-ute, going so far as to hire an independent firm to duplicate the magazine's test. The results supported Ford's contention that the Bronco II was at least as safe as other vehicles of its ilk.

This, plus a hard and fast "get out the facts" dealer campaign, resulted in sales of just under 109,000 units, down a sizable 16,000 from calendar '88, though the loss could have been much worse.

Ford's Aerostar enjoyed its best sales year yet with 188,000-plus, up some 3400 on 1988. That was enough to again outdistance Chevy's Astro and, for the first time, even the Plymouth Voyager. The big news here was availability of extended-body Vans and Wagons with an extra 15.4 inches of rear sheetmetal adding 28 cubic feet in cargo volume. It was the old "SuperWagon" idea, of course, and hinted that Ford's compact van was about to go the way of the original Econoline, though not immediately. Mechanical changes were nil, but all Aerostars received a minor front-end redo and a larger 21-gallon fuel tank (up from 17). Almost inevitably, Ford trotted out a new option package. Called XL Sport Wagon, it was basically an appearance treatment for passenger Aerostars comprising lower-body cladding and monochromatic—"single color" in plain English—paint.

Changes among this year's full-size Ford trucks were minimal. The big Bronco returned with a higher-capacity standard cooling system its only improvement, while a new electronically controlled four-speed automatic replaced three-speed on selected heavy-duty E-and F-Series models. The F-Series also saw detail trim and equipment adjustments, including standard tinted glass on Regular cabs, plus three new "Super Duty" stripped chassis with dualie rear wheels and a 16,000-pound GVW. The latter comprised a 158-inch-wheelbase platform with the 7.3-liter diesel V-8 and a five-speed manual, and 178- and 208-inch motorhome chassis with the 460 gas V-8 and four-speed automatic.

Unprecedented foreign competition and hazy near-term market prospects prompted Chrysler to embark on a billion-dollar cost-cutting program during 1989. Ford announced a similar effort of its own in mid-December, partly in response to cost overruns not only on the MN12 program but a forthcoming replacement for Bronco II and the new '91-model "CT20" Ford Escort (and Mercury Tracer). But Dearborn kept spending, too, setting aside $97 million to expand its research labs in anticipation of much tougher government safety and emissions standards. Ford was also still working on alternative power sources. This year it unveiled the EXT-II, an Aerostar converted to electric operation that culminated a seven-year, $20-million development program. Alas, this vehicle's capabilities weren't all that impressive. Top speed came in at just 65 mph, and it could only go 100 miles on a charge.

A big chunk of Ford's swollen cash reserves went toward expanding its growing financial-services operation. The firm had already purchased seven savings-and-loans in 1988 via First Nationwide Financial Corporation. In March 1989 Dearborn bought into Meritor Credit Corporation, then followed in August by paying $14 billion to Paramount Communications to acquire The Associates, the nation's third-largest independent loan company. If this seemed to echo old Henry's opening his own Detroit bank in the early Thirties, there was no Depression-era altruism to these purchases. As Wall Street auto analyst Maryann Keller later observed: "Detroit thinks of finance as secure, because even in poor years for car sales, the credit companies—Ford Credit, GMAC [and] Chrysler Credit—[are] always profitable." In short, Ford was again hedging its bets against another likely downturn in the car and truck business.

How, then, would one explain Dearborn's much-publicized purchase of Britain's Jaguar at year's end? The answer had to do partly with corporate pride and partly with the failure of the U.S. Merkur experiment. Ford had been trying for several years to acquire a prestigious European automaker in hopes of competing at the very top of the market both in Europe and the U.S., something its own European luxury models like the Scorpio had been unable to do. There were some definite "bargain" companies waiting to be snapped up, but Ford lost out in Italy when shaky Alfa Romeo preferred to go with Fiat, and talks with Saab of Sweden ultimately fell through. Meanwhile, Chrysler acquired a piece of Italy's Maserati, and General Motors bought out England's Lotus in 1987. Ford responded by acquiring another tiny British producer of high-performance sports cars, Aston Martin.

Jaguar looked equally ripe for a takeover. After being as close to oblivion as Chrysler or Ford in 1980, the firm had made a remarkable comeback, only to lose momentum by decade's end as sales in the critical U.S. market tailed off. The British government had taken Jaguar under its protective wing for a time, then released it back into the public sector in 1984. Now, five years later, the firm's prospects weren't nearly so bright. But Jaguar was still a shining jewel that dazzled both GM and Ford with its possibilities as the crown for their respective corporate lines. The result was a sort of undeclared "bidding war" between the two giant American multinationals.

The battle began in earnest during the summer of '89. Despite all its recent purchases, Ford was still loaded with money from several years of record profits, so it purchased 10.4 percent of outstanding Jaguar stock with the announced intention of buying the rest. GM, with Jaguar's blessing, promised to take a similar stake, ostensibly to ensure Jaguar's independence but more likely just to block its archrival. Ford promptly upped its ante to 13.2 percent. Finally, on November 2, Jaguar reversed its public opposition and acquiesced to a Ford buy-

out. Significantly, this came only a day after the British government announced an early end to its so-called "golden share" policy that had precluded individual stakes in Jaguar of more than 15 percent before 1991. Just like that, it was over, and without a shot being fired. The final purchase price: $2.56 billion.

That worked out to about twice the per-share price for Jaguar stock, which some critics took as a tacit admission that Ford couldn't build a "Jaguar" of its own. They were probably right. Noting the $2-billion design bill for the upcoming new Escort, analyst Keller wondered: "If Ford is spending that much on a small car, imagine what it would cost them to develop their own line of European luxury cars. They could never do it as cheaply as the Japanese. So...maybe $2.5 billion isn't such a bad price for them to pay for Jaguar." GM evidently didn't think so, one reason it withdrew from the bidding.

Regardless, bringing Jaguar into the "Ford Family of Fine Cars" was great news for the many fans of the fabled British marque. As with Aston Martin, Ford promised to maintain Jaguar as a separate entity under its own management while supplying cash and expertise for modernizing plant and product to make the firm more efficient, competitive, and thus profitable. Specifically, the takeover assured the future for Jaguar's long-rumored "F-Type" sports car, whose development was already ahead of schedule. Ditto the oft-delayed long-wheelbase and V-12 versions of the new-generation XJ6 sedan. Ford money would also spur a twin-turbo six-cylinder "SuperJag" in the image of the show-stopping XJ220, a recent mid-engine experimental, and should speed the arrival of XJ80, a smaller-than-XJ6 sports sedan to rival the BMW Five-Series and Mercedes 300-class, among others. As Jaguar's first compact four-door since the late Sixties, the XJ80 could boost annual production at Browns Lane from 50,000 units to 100,000-plus by the mid-Nineties.

The '89 Bronco II (top) sported revised front end styling that made it look more like the big Bronco. New were the fenders, hood, grille, aero-headlights, and front bumper. Prices started at $11,707. Like the Bronco II, the Ranger pickup (center) was restyled to look more like its full-size brothers. Although prices started at $7693 ($11,525 for four-wheel-drive models), the STX package added $2084 or $1678. The '89 Club Wagon, here in XLT trim (bottom), boasted a new electronically controlled four-speed overdrive automatic transmission for certain models.

The one thorn in this rosy picture was the admittedly remote possibility of Ford's coffers running dry, not unthinkable given a prolonged U.S. sales slump. Indeed, the more difficult U.S. market was already affecting earnings at Ford, GM, and especially Chrysler. Jaguar might thus be the last major acquisition by an American automaker for some time. But we shouldn't borrow trouble. Ford's financial strength and technical resources are precisely what Jaguar has needed to be a serious player in the high-stakes luxury-car game, and the prospect of more and better Jaguars is a happy thought indeed.

Model-year 1990 is still in progress as this is being written, so its sales and production stories must await a future edition of this book. However, Ford Division's 1990 cars and trucks, and even a few '91s announced early in calendar 1990, can be described here, as can the state of Ford Motor Company as it enters a new decade fraught with problems.

Some say a problem is merely an opportunity waiting to be exploited, something Ford became very good at in the Eighties. Yet for all its success in that decade, Dearborn faced several lingering problems that could undermine maintaining that success into the Nineties. Among the most critical was a woefully long new-product cycle: up to 10 years for certain vital, high-volume products like Tempo/Topaz and Taurus/Sable, versus four years for most Japanese competitors. Rising development costs were another thorny issue. These factors put the squeeze on profitability every bit as much as the industry's continuing reliance on expensive sales incentives. A group of mostly aging powertrains didn't bode well for the stiffer new emissions and

fuel-economy rules that loomed ahead, much less for keeping up with the competition. And by Ford's own standards, quality—though far better than it was—still wasn't as good as it needed to be for the toughest U.S. market ever.

Fortunately, the new management team under Harold A. "Red" Poling seemed acutely aware of these weaknes-

Hitting the 1990 auto show circuit was the Ford Ghia Via (below), billed as a "four-seat sports car for the year 2000." It boasted excellent aerodynamics, fiber-optic front lights, and a removable Targa-type roof with photosensitive glass. And like some other contemporary concept cars, it featured a "cabin-forward" layout for a roomier passenger compartment. The interior (above) used a twin-cockpit theme.

ses. Only days before taking over from Don Petersen as Ford chairman on March 1, 1990, Poling told *Automotive News*: "The memories of the early 1980s are indelibly seared in my mind. I'll never forget them. Just as we began the last decade with serious obstacles to overcome, the next decade promises to offer its own difficulties. . . . I believe these may well be greater than before, but I also believe that we are better prepared to face them."

Many analysts agreed, for the Poling regime also inherited several major strengths that Ford didn't possess a decade before. Prime among them were a shrinking but still sizeable corporate cash kitty of more than $5.7 billion, the nation's top-selling trucks (Ranger and F-Series), a design staff of proven ability, strong overseas operations, a work force of appropriate size, and modernized factories with the highest utilization rate in Detroit (102 percent, as opposed to GM and Chrysler, both of which still had too much production capacity relative to sales). Alas, the answer to the question of whether Ford can use these pluses to offset its minuses must also await a future edition of this book.

Meanwhile, it might be useful to review Ford Division's 1990 lineup, as well the early '91s. As noted, the latter included an all-new Escort, which meant that the familiar first-generation design was on the way out. But not entirely, as it continued to be built for the time being at Ford's Metuchen, New Jersey, plant even

as the first '91s rolled off the Wayne, Michigan, assembly line. There was predictably little change in the '90s, the main one being standard shoulder belts for outboard rear passengers.

Still chasing higher volume, the little Festiva was spruced up with a revised grille bearing a Taurus-like "navel," plus new taillamps, larger front-seat cushions, and reshuffled interior trim. Federal requirements now dictated that all new cars have passive restraints, either airbags or self-buckling belts, as well as those outboard rear lap/shoulder harnesses. Festiva complied, using motorized webbing up front. Additionally, the five-speed manual transaxle once reserved for the top-line LX became standard across the board, as did the 63-horsepower port-injected engine formerly tied to the automatic option on LX and L Plus. Those models now offered extra-cost power steering for the first time—a good move for low-speed maneuvering ease—and a hatch-window wiper/washer was newly available for L and L Plus. Prices took a sizeable jump of about $700, so stickers now read $6319 for the base L, $7111 for L Plus, and $7750 for LX. That had been Escort territory only a few years before, but it was a sign of the times.

The compact Tempo also got the required outboard rear shoulder belts as well as standard floormats and trunk and footwell courtesy lights. The relative lack of change for a second straight year might have implied that a new Tempo

was on the way, and that was exactly the case. But it was still a bit distant: not scheduled until model-year '92, some said, though others reported it would be a 1994 offering.

Taurus, too, entered 1990 little changed, but a driver's airbag in a newly standard tilt steering wheel prompted a reworked dashboard with slightly different minor controls and new cup and coin holders. More praiseworthy was the arrival of four-wheel anti-lock brakes as an option for sedans. Though especially welcome on the hot-rod SHO, it's a shame the anti-lock feature was not offered on the wagons as well. Other new extras comprised a compact-disc player and, for the standard analog gauge cluster, a tachometer—except on SHO, where it remained standard. Also available were vacuum-fluorescent digital/graphic instruments, again SHO excepted.

Also new for Taurus was its first police package option, designed to make Ford's slick mid-size sedan "a patrol vehicle offering excellent maneuverability and fuel economy, plus all the inherent advantages of front-wheel drive." The result was a little brother to the big police-

The Ghia Via was unusual for a "sports car" in that it was a four-door model. Featured were an exceptionally steeply raked roof front and rear, short overhangs at both ends, low-nose/high-tail styling, high-mounted full-width taillights beneath a large rear spoiler, and aggressive-looking wheels.

equipped Crown Victorias so popular with highway patrol departments across the land. Features included a tuned 3.8-liter V-6, four-speed overdrive automatic transaxle, low-restriction "quasi-dual" exhaust system, all-disc brakes with semi-metallic pads, high-capacity engine and transmission cooling, numerous structural and component upgrades, and two vertical banks of discreet air slots flanking the front navel. Even more than the SHO, this was a Taurus you'd best move over for if you saw one coming up fast in your rearview mirror. The LTD Crown Victoria rolled into its 12th season

on the the original 1979 "Panther" platform with an unusual number of changes for this evergreen rear-drive biggie. Besides standard driver's airbag and the new mandatory outboard rear shoulder belts, the big Ford was treated to a more modern-looking dash with a larger glovebox, revised graphics, independently closeable air vents and, for the first time, a coolant-temperature gauge. Bumpers switched from steel to lighter aluminum as a fuel-economy aid (tiny though it was), front seat tracks now extended a full nine inches, and tilt wheel, power windows, and power door mirrors shifted

from optional to standard equipment. Pivoting front vent windows and the "Tripminder" computer vanished from the accessories folder.

Saving the best for last brings up the three sportiest 1990 Fords. Thunderbird ended up being the least changed, no surprise since it had been all-new for '89 (and had arrived with motorized front belts). For 1990, there were only two new option packages to talk about: a Power Equipment Group (electric door locks, driver's seat, and remote fuel-filler and decklid releases) and a Luxury Group (cruise control, tilt steering wheel, power

mirrors, and extra courtesy lights).

Actually, there was another model, because Ford remembered that the T-Bird's 35th birthday fell in 1990. It therefore ran off 5000 commemorative specials based on the hard-charging supercharged Super Coupe. Alas, like the 30th-birthday Bird of 1985, this was pretty tame for a limited edition: just black over "titanium" (dark gray) paint with blue accent striping, plus black road wheels and the usual custom badges. Then again, maybe the 35th didn't really need more than this. After all, it was based on the much more powerful and exciting Thun-

derbird SC.

Like the Crown Vic, the fifth-generation Mustang turned 12 years old in 1990. It met passive-restraint rules with a driver's airbag, but somehow Ford wasn't able to make this compatible with a tilt steering wheel, so that option vanished. Perhaps as compensation, door map pockets were added to all models and LXs got the useful left-foot "dead pedal" previously limited to GTs. New extras were confined to clearcoat paint, a Power Equipment Group similar to the T-Bird's, and leather trim for LX 5.0L hatchbacks and GT coupe and convertible.

As for the long-awaited Silver Anniversary Mustang, Ford finally came up with one, showing it first at the Chicago Auto Show in February 1990. But it was a non-event after all the rumors of 1988-89—just a V-8 LX convertible with emerald-green clearcoat metallic paint, white top, white hide-trimmed interior, and the GT's 15-inch aluminum wheels. Also on hand were color-matched door mirrors, bodyside moldings, and front and rear bumpers. Announced production was a mere 3800 units, beginning in January. Curiously, Ford now backtracked and acknowledged that Mustang had celebrated

America's best selling car in model year 1989 headed into 1990 with few changes because an all-new '91 Escort was scheduled for introduction on April 26, 1990. The '90 received rear shoulder belts as standard and the optional polycast wheels had a slightly different appearance, while the premium sound system and heavy-duty alternator were available only as part of the LX and GT Special Value Packages. Model offerings included the $9804 GT (left), $7806 LX three-door hatchback and $8136 LX five-door (top right), and the $8737 LX five-door wagon (above). Not shown is the price leader, the $7402 Pony three-door hatch.

its 25th anniversary in 1989—which makes one wonder why they ignored it that year, not to mention waiting until year 26 to release this special.

There was no such monkey business for the sophomore edition of the erstwhile mini-Mustang, the Japanese/American Probe. Focusing on the mid-range LX model, Ford substituted the 3.0-liter Taurus V-6 for the previous 2.2-liter Mazda four and threw in all-disc brakes. Though even this fortified LX wouldn't threaten the turbocharged GT for straightline acceleration, the bigger, torquier standard engine made it much stronger in mid-range passing sprints and pleasantly more relaxed on the highway. Even after all these years, there was still no substitute for cubic—er, centimeters. The base

GL retained its normally aspirated 2.2 and the GT its blown version of same, but the latter was newly available with optional automatic transaxle.

Identifying all 1990 Probes were revised taillamps and prominent new under-bumper grilles done in body color—a fine mesh on GL and LX, a more aggressive eggcrate with integral foglamps on GT. Rounding out Probe chang-

es were first-time availability of leather seat trim, new standard cloth upholstery selections, and a padded-rim "soft-feel" steering wheel as a new no-cost LX feature.

In contrast to mostly detail refinements on the car side, Ford's 1990 light-truck line boasted several major engineering developments. Chief among these was a larger 4.0-liter V-6 engine for

Opposite page: Mustang galloped into 1990 with a driver's side airbag and rear shoulder belts, but without a tilt steering column and console armrest. The V-8-powered GT series topped the line, listing at $13,986 as a hatchback (top). The base LXs were powered by a 2.3-liter four, which developed 88 bhp. One step up was the LX 5.0L, available in all three body styles. In hatchback form (bottom) it listed at $13,007. This page: The convertible LX 5.0L (top) carried a base price of $18,183. Meanwhile, Ford's Korean-built minicar, the Festiva, received new standard equipment: five-speed manual shift, port fuel-injection, and first-time availability of power steering. The top-line LX (right) started at $7750.

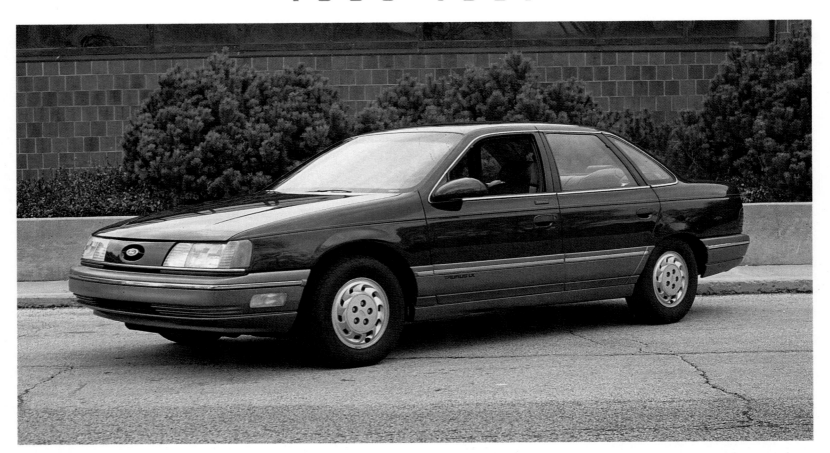

Ford's intermediate Taurus gained a driver's-side airbag for 1990, plus a new instrument panel and extra cost anti-lock brakes for sedans. The LX series could be had with speed-sensitive power steering, while a compact-disc player was a new option. The $21,633 SHO (above), Ford's hot-rod Taurus, ran with a 220-bhp 3.0-liter V-6 (with dual-overhead cams and 24 valves) mated to a five-speed manual. SHO also boasted dual exhausts, handling suspension, and later, standard anti-lock brakes. The $16,180 LX sedan (top left), which was more luxury oriented, came with the 140-bhp 3.0 V-6 as standard, although a 3.8 V-6 was optional. The Taurus wagon (left) came in L, GL, and LX trim, at prices ranging from $14,272 to $17,771.

the compact Ranger pickups and Aerostar minivans. At first glance, it appeared to be simply a bored-and-stroked 2.9, enlarged from 3.66 × 2.83 inches to 3.95 × 3.32 inches. But the 4.0 incorporated so many other changes that it was, for all intents and purposes, brand-new. Key differences included raised deck height, a pan rail opened up to accommodate a stiffer oil pan, low-friction roller valve lifters, one-belt serpentine accessory drive, and "Tri-Pack" distributorless ignition. The last, similar to the system on the Taurus SHO engine, comprised two sets of three integrated coils, one per cylinder bank, with each coil firing a separate spark plug. Other technical highlights included low-friction pistons, revised manifolding, slightly larger intake valves, smaller exhaust valves, and revised EEC-IV electronics for controlling multiport fuel injection, idle speed, spark timing, exhaust-gas recirculation, and other vital functions.

On the same 9.0:1 compression, the 4.0-liter produced 155 horsepower and 220 pounds/feet torque, respective gains over the 2.9 of 11 and 30 percent. That made it the most powerful engine ever offered in a compact Ford truck, though the division was only keeping pace with the 4.3-liter V-6 option in Chevy's S-10

models. Handling the 4.0-liter's extra oomph was an upgraded four-speed automatic transmission that was effectively a "mandatory option" in Ranger and Aerostar. The beefier drivetrain lifted the pickups' rated towing capacity by a healthy 1300 pounds to 6300 pounds.

Initially, the new V-6/automatic combo was optional only for Ranger STX and XLT 4×4s and two-wheel-drive extended Aerostars, but it also came standard with this year's new full-time four-wheel-drive option on the Aerostar. The last, of course, was a first for Ford's minivan. Timely, too, as the Chevy Astro/GMC Safari twins also offered this feature for 1990.

Ford called the Aerostar's system "E-4WD," with "E" denoting "electronic." It was permanently engaged and thus always functioned without the need to shift a transfer case or even touch a button. In brief, E-4WD employed a central transfer case with epicyclic gears and chain drive to spin the front and rear driveshafts, whose rates of rotation were constantly monitored by a separate electronic module—really a minicomputer. Under normal conditions, engine torque was split ⅓ front and ⅔ rear. In slippery going, the computer would interpret any rotational difference between the drive-

All new for '89, the mid-size rear-drive Thunderbird winged its way into 1990 with few changes while looking forward to the return of V-8 power for '91. The $17,283 mid-level LX (top) came with a standard 140-horsepower 3.8-liter V-6, but this was partly offset by the Bird's 3600-pound curb weight. Little change was evident in the 1990 Tempo other than newly standard footwell and trunk lights, floormats, and restyled polycast wheels. Rear-seat shoulder belts were scheduled to be added during the model run. The All-Wheel-Drive sedan was still available, priced now at $11,331, but among the front-drive models the LX series reigned supreme. The four-door sedan (above) carried a $10,605 sticker.

shafts as wheel spin, and responded by engaging an electromagnetic clutch in the transfer case that changed the torque split to 50/50, thus improving traction. In practice, clutch engagement was "cycled" fairly rapidly to avoid unwanted wheel locking, a feature that made E-4WD compatible with the anti-lock rear brakes adopted as standard equipment for all 1990 Aerostars.

E-4WD itself, designed in conjunction with Dana Corporation, was said to be compatible with existing 2WD Aerostar components, which offered the

claimed advantages of simpler production and thus likely higher reliability over other 4WD systems. Durability was also touted. Dana supplied both the transfer case and front drive axles from factories whose quality-control procedures had been set up with Ford's input. Not too many years before, the notion of a vehicle maker working so closely with one of its suppliers would have been hooted down as "collusion." But the Japanese had proved the wisdom of it, and Ford had been quicker than most in Detroit to take heed. Incidentally, E-4WD wasn't cheap:

The Mazda-built Ford Probe listed three engines for 1990: 110-bhp 2.2-liter four, 145-bhp turbocharged 2.2 four, and a 140-bhp 3.0-liter V-6 (from Taurus). The first was standard on the $11,470 GL, the second on the $14,726 GT (left), the third on the $13,006 LX (above). The last was also treated to four-wheel disc brakes, with ABS optional. Meanwhile, the GT could now be ordered with an automatic transmission.

a $2200 option for both standard and extended Aerostars, which now carried base list prices of $12,469 and $13,216, respectively. But it wasn't a bad deal, either, since it included the larger V-6.

These developments and the equally laudable rear anti-lock brakes were the only real news for the 1990 Aerostar. Ranger, however, received a number of additional changes. Among the highlights were cancellation of the GT and 4×2 STX models, a 20-gallon fuel tank for SuperCabs (Regulars stayed at 17 gallons), the usual trim shuffles, and an in-

teresting High-Strength Composite (HSC) cargo-box option for S Plus 4×4s. The last looked just like the regular six-foot steel box, but was made of reaction-injection-molded plastic, with the inner walls made of a high-tech polycarbonate. It's an intriguing development, one that could spread to other pickups, though that naturally depends on customer acceptance.

Ford's full-size light trucks changed only in detail for 1990, though some of their small improvements were noteworthy. For example, an electronically

controlled overdrive automatic replaced the previous mechanical unit in F-Series, E-Series, and big Broncos with 4.9-liter six and 5.8-liter V-8, while Econolines and Club Wagons finally got standard rear anti-lock brakes and, on 250/350s, gas-pressurized shocks. Auto-lock front hubs became standard on F-150 4×4s, and Touch Drive was a new option for same with the 5.0-liter V-8. All the full-sizers now grouped a few related individual options into packages, EEC-IV engine electronics were modified so service technicians could call up diagnostic data on malfunctions, and a 178-inch-wheelbase stripped chassis was added to the F-Super Duty commercial line.

There hadn't been much recent change among Ford's medium and heavy trucks, but 1990 brought a significant newcomer. "AeroMax 8000" was its name, and that said it all. Essentially, it was a redesigned version of the big diesel-powered Louisville conventional tractor

The LTD Crown Victoria received a driver's-side airbag and rear shoulder belts for 1990. It also sported a new instrument panel (left) featuring revised graphics, a coolant temperature gauge, and a larger glovebox. The full bench seat was retired in favor of a split bench with folding armrests and reclining backrests. The six-model Crown Vic lineup included three wagons, two of them woody-look Country Squires. The LX wagon (above), which did without the fake wood, was powered by a 150-bhp 5.0-liter V-8.

with every trick Ford designers could think of to cheat the wind for better over-the-road fuel economy. Large cabtop spoilers to smooth airflow over the semitrailer weren't new, of course, but AeroMax's was specially sculpted to be among the most effective. Though the big six-sided Louisville grille still graced the snout, front-end contours were rounded, aided by new flush-mount headlamps, a deep-section under-bumper airdam and—shades of the Fifties—a one-piece wraparound windshield. Less weight also helped mileage, and the AeroMax weighed some 2500 pounds less than a like-equipped L-Line.

AeroMax had actually bowed back in 1987 as a 9000 model with a set-back front axle. This year's new 8000 gave Ford a more competitive entry in what had come to be called the "Baby 8" class—short-haul rigs of up to 75,000-pounds

gross combined weight (tractor plus trailer with maximum load). Wheelbases ranged from 143 to 239 inches. Common to all chassis was a 7.8-liter turbodiesel V-8 with air-to-air aftercooler and horsepower ratings of 210 to 270. Alas, the cost of greater fuel efficiency came high, in this case anywhere from $17,000 to $20,000 over a comparable L-Line. But the AeroMax was yet another example of how functional styling could change the shape of even the biggest and brawniest vehicles.

There wasn't much to say about the little Bronco II for 1990 because it bowed as a virtual rerun—and the last of its kind. For 1991, Ford's compact sport-utility would give way to the brand-new Explorer, a name snitched from the F-Series line. It was chosen partly to get away from the time-worn practice of using Roman numerals and partly in hopes that the public would forget the recent bad publicity surrounding the Bronco II.

Even without its new name, the Explorer offered many reasons to forget the Bronco II altogether. For starters, it boasted smoother and more modern styling. More aerodynamic, too, with flush windshield and side glass and car-like "limousine doors" cut up into the roof, which also eased entry/exit. The result was a 0.43 drag coefficient—pretty good for what was still a tall, boxy little vehicle.

But Explorer wasn't quite as little as

Bronco II. The familiar two-door strode a 102.1-inch wheelbase, 6.1-inches longer than before, and stretched 12.5-inches longer at 174.4 inches overall. Width increased by 2.2 inches, to 70.8, but height came down an inch or so, to 68.3 inches on the 4×4 and 67.3 inches with 2WD. Even better was the advent of a four-door model, something that might have helped Bronco II against competitive offerings like the Jeep Cherokee and Wagoneer, whose four-door versions had regularly outsold their two-door companions. The Explorer four-door rode a rangy 111.9-inch wheelbase and measured 184.3 inches long, which made it one of the most accommodating sport-utilities in both passenger and cargo space.

Ford proudly declared that the Explorer was designed more for car-like civility and quiet performance than strict off-road ruggedness. As other makers had found, sport-utilities rarely left the beaten path, and the market was showing a fast-growing preference for comfort, convenience, and even luxury features. For many buyers, in fact, the sport-ute had become as much a substitute for the traditional station wagon as the minivan.

Explorer catered to the market accordingly. All models came with the new 4.0-liter Ranger/Aerostar V-6, and with a choice of manual or automatic transmission, plus power steering, power brakes with rear anti-lock control, and easy-rid-

Optional full-time four-wheel drive (E-4WD), a larger available engine, and standard anti-lock rear brakes highlighted the changes to the rear-drive Aerostar for 1990. The E-4WD setup sent one-third of the power to the front wheels, two-thirds to the rear, but this changed automatically to 50-50 when wheelspin was detected. The new 4.0-liter V-6 was standard with E-4WD, optional on the extended-length 2WD van. Prices started at $12,469 for 2WD, $14,669 for AWD. The stretched Aerostars came at a $747 premium.

ing all-season P225/70 passenger-car radial tires abetted by gas-pressure shocks. Touch Drive was standard on 4×4s, but a manual system was available at reduced cost. Body-on-frame construction allowed passengers to be better isolated from noise, vibration, and harshness. Suspension was much like Bronco II's, with Ford's Twin-I-Beam (2WD) or Twin-Traction-Beam (4WD) geometry in front. However, spring/shock rates were somewhat softer, again in the interest of ride comfort.

Interiors were lush, upholstered in handsome cloth (or optional leather) and rather lavish for this sort of rig. Standard accoutrements included full engine gauges (including tach), a forced-air heating/air conditioning system, AM/FM stereo radio, and a 60/40 split rear seat that folded up to provide a flat cargo deck almost five-feet long on two-doors and

over six feet on four-doors. There was a choice of trim levels, of course: base XL, top-line Eddie Bauer, and mid-range XL Sport two-door and XLT four-door.

Though it hasn't gone on sale as of this writing, the Explorer should at least keep Ford in the thick of the fierce sport-utility wars and may even improve the division's market share. *Four Wheeler* magazine found enough to like that it jumped the gun and named Explorer, a '91 model, its 1990 "Four Wheeler of the Year"—surely some kind of first. Not that it wasn't deserving. The Explorer is decently peppy with either transmission, very stable-feeling (discernibly more so than Bronco II), surprisingly quiet, roomy, and—here's that word again—comfortable. Prices should be competitive, and Ford will most certainly work hard to insure high quality from "Job 1." If this is the kind of Ford in our future, Dearborn should make it to the millennium in fine style.

Another interesting thing about the Explorer was that Mazda would be selling the two-door version under its own badge as the Navajo—proof that today's Detroit-Tokyo linkups *can* cut both ways. It marked the first time a Japanese maker had sold a U.S.-designed vehicle under its own banner, though it wasn't the first time Mazda had sold a product with the blue Ford oval. In Japan, its import-oriented "Autorama" dealer network had been selling various Australian Fords for some years, and about 7500 Probes had been exported from Flat Rock for sale through that channel in 1988. The latter wasn't much compensation for America's huge trade deficit with Japan, but it answered in part those critics who felt U.S. companies couldn't turn out products with sufficient appeal and quality to compete in that most protected of world marketplaces.

The fruits of a far more significant Ford/Mazda collaboration arrived along with the Explorer in the spring of 1990. It was, of course, the new second-series U.S. Escort, successor to one of Detroit's perennial best-sellers of the Eighties. It was, perhaps, long overdue given the fact that Japanese rivals like Mazda's 323 had gone through several design generations since the original '81 Escort. But that

Opposite page: Ford's compact sport-utility was largely carried over for 1990 because a replacement called Explorer stood in the wings to take over for Bronco II in the spring of 1990 as a '91 model. Until then, Bronco II (top) continued with its three-door body style, 94-inch wheelbase, and 2.9-liter V-6. Prices started at $13,001. Like some Aerostars, the Ranger could be fitted with the 155-bhp 4.0-liter V-6, but at first only on the XLT and STX (bottom) 4×4s. This page: The Econoline and Club Wagon (top) finally got anti-lock rear brakes for 1990, and F-250/350s now rode on gas pressurized shocks. Meanwhile, the big Bronco (bottom) received an electronically controlled overdrive automatic for the 4.9-liter six and 5.8 V-8, this in place of the previous mechanical unit.

basic car had been such a success through periodic updates that Ford was understandably reluctant to let go of it until absolutely necessary—and then only with a good deal of trepidation.

While the new Escort's ultimate success remains to be seen, Ford should have little cause for worry. Once again its army of designers, engineers, and product planners took a Mazda platform—in this case the third-generation front-drive 323/Protege of 1989—and gave it their own special touches. Like the Probe, the new Escort looked nothing like a conservative Mazda sibling; rather, it was distinctively Dearborn and, to many eyes, more attractive than the 323. In fact, it wasn't hard to see a lot of Taurus here, surely no bad thing. It even sported an up-front "navel." Yet the new car still remains true to its Escort lineage.

There was, in fact, quite a bit of the old Escort in the new one. The same three body styles persisted—two- and four-door hatchbacks with vestigial "decklets," plus a five-door wagon. So did model choices: LX sedans and wagon and price-leader Pony and sporty GT two-doors.

Although little changed in package size or weight, and general profiles were still recognizably Escort, the much smoother new styling brought the expected reduction in aerodynamic drag, now 0.35 versus the previous 0.39. Overall length grew 0.6-inch on sedans and 0.9-inch on the wagon, yet the wheelbase measured a useful 4.2 inches longer, now 98.4 inches. There was more claimed front headroom despite a fractional reduction in overall height, and shoulder room spread an extra 1.5 inches despite only a 0.5-inch gain in overall width. Curb weights came in slightly higher, around 100 pounds or so, some of that because of a separate Taurus-style front subframe to better isolate powertrain noise, vibration, and harshness.

Of course, the same basic mechanical layout was used: transverse four-cylinder engine driving the front wheels through either manual five-speed or optional four-speed automatic transaxle, both overdrive units as before. Steering remained rack-and-pinion with optional power assist; brakes were vacuum-boosted front discs and rear drums except on the GT, which was treated to standard rear discs. All-coil strut suspension also continued, although with different geometry. Front springs were offset from the struts, and a single control arm handled strut location in conjunction with an anti-roll bar (0.87-inch on GT, 0.75-inch

on other models). Mazda's Twin Trapezoidal Link design was featured in back, again with a standard stabilizer bar (0.87-inch GT, 0.79-inch elsewhere).

Motive power mixed new with old. All '91 Escorts save GT retained the Ford-built 1.9-liter single-overhead-cam engine derived from the original 1.6 CVH unit. However, a new wrinkle in sequential port-electronic fuel injection swapped two horsepower for four extra lbs/ft torque compared to the 1990 engine, making for new outputs of 88 bhp and 108 lbs/ft. More exciting was the GT's Mazda-built 1.8-liter four with twin overhead camshafts (driven by belt), four valves per cylinder, and port-electronic injection. Basically the same engine used in Mazda's speedy Protege LX sedan, it delivered 127 bhp at a high 6500 rpm and 114 lbs/ft torque at 4500 rpm. Axle ratios were naturally tailored for each model's mission in life, ranging from a long-striding 3.41:1 for the economy-minded five-speed Pony to a performance-oriented 4.10:1 on the five-speed GT.

Dominating the '91 Escort interior was a handsome new low-profile dashboard, which combined with the new bodies' greater glass area for greatly improved outward vision. Not surprisingly, the panel blended Ford and Mazda thinking with a little Europe thrown in, evidenced in features like a backlit analog gauge cluster, a quartet of large air vents,

Ford's full-size light-duty trucks changed little for 1990, although the F-150 (above) saw its EEC-IV engine electronics modified so service technicians could call up diagnostic data on malfunctions. The multi-hued Surf (opposite, top) was a '90 show vehicle based on the new compact Explorer, but decked out as an all-for-fun leisure 4×4 to make getting to the beach almost as much fun as being there. It sported a cutaway roof, auxiliary roof and grille lights, and swing-out speakers for music while sunbathing. Ford also worked up a 1990 F-150 concept pickup (opposite, bottom) whose twin blue stripes encircled the front end.

and central climate and audio controls. Base equipment was complete, though not lavish, and Ford naturally listed a full range of options: air, cruise control, tilt steering wheel, power door locks for four-doors and wagons, even a power moonroof for LX hatchbacks. The GT again came with its own unique asymmetric grille, plus body-color bumpers, prominent hatchlid spoiler, and performance tires (P185/60HR-15 Goodyear Eagle GT+4s) on sporty alloy wheels.

Ford Division chief Tom Wagner said the new Escort "is much more than a new car. It represents an entirely new way of doing business." Indeed, the '91 was arguably more a "world car" than the original '81, though the parts of the automotive world it drew from were quite different. It was certainly a big financial gamble. Ford spent $2 billion on the CT20 pro-

While the model lineup of the '91 Escort was the same as in '90, the car itself was totally new. Developed with Mazda, and based on its 323/Protege, the styling came from Ford, as did the Pony/LX engine. However, the GT (both cars) used a dohc 16-valve 1800-cc Mazda unit. Horsepower was 127, torque 114 lbs/ft. The GT could now be ordered with automatic shift, a first.

gram that sired the '91 Escort and its similarly revised Mercury sister, the Tracer (which was already being built off the old 323 platform). Ford spent $600 million alone for retooling the Wayne, Michigan, Escort assembly plant. The styling bill is unknown, though no doubt considerable, but it appeared to be money well spent.

As Car and Driver observed, the new Escort and Tracer "look surprisingly different not only from Mazda's 323/Protege but from each other as well." The Tracer, still Mexican-built, emerged as a baby Sable, much as the new Escort looked like a junior Taurus. Unlike the Escort, the Tracer was offered only in wagon and four-door notchback form.

Two other new products from Dearborn's luxury division deserve mention. One, the totally reskinned 1990 Lincoln Town Car, was essentially the square-lined 1980 design with newly rounded "aero" outer body panels that managed to preserve the basic look of this traditional rear-drive luxury car. At the same time, Ford dialed in a touch more chassis control via new speed-sensitive power steering, computer-controlled rear air springs, and optional four-wheel anti-lock brakes. None of this turned the Town Car into a Mustang—or even a Mark VII LSC—but it was a pleasing, well-judged update of a still-popular "classic." *Motor Trend* was moved to give this Lincoln its 1990 "Car of the Year" award, which may say more about that magazine than the Town Car. And lest anyone forget, 1990 marked a half-century of Continentals. L-M celebrated by issuing a 50th Anniversary version of the fine Taurus-based Continental sedan. It was another lightly touched paint-and-plaques job, though its special "geometric" spoked road wheels were an appropriately sporty touch.

Speaking of sporty brings up L-M's other newcomer, the 1991 Mercury Capri. In some ways this car was more a throwback to the lumpy EXP/LN7 than the two-seat T-Bird. It certainly wasn't anything like the recently deceased Mustang-based model or the earlier imported Capris. In fact, it was another Mazda spinoff: a front-drive, 2+2 convertible built on the second-generation 323 chassis. In this market niche, at least, Ford and Mazda had gone separate ways, Mazda with the winsome rear-drive Miata that bowed in early 1989 and wowed everyone with nostalgic Sixties-style looks allied to Eighties-style competence.

The impetus for this latest Capri was a Ghia-designed 1982 showmobile called Barchetta, whose generally chunky flavor survived through to production despite some interim fiddling by Giorgio Giugiaro's Ital Design. Riding a tidy 94.5-inch wheelbase, the Capri ended up being slightly larger and heavier than Miata, measuring 166 inches long and averaging 2350 pounds at the curb. Both used 1.6-liter four-cylinder engines, but the Capri came with a choice of two, both somewhat different from Miata's. The base Capri carried an 82-bhp single-cam unit, while the higher-performance XR-2 packed a 134-bhp turbocharged version of same, with twincam heads and four valves per cylinder. Capri also departed from Miata in offering a four-speed automatic transmission as an alternative to the standard five-speed stick, and in its "+2" carrying capacity. In reality, though, that back "seat" was really little more than a package shelf—hard and not very comfortable even for kids or dogs. Performance was slightly down on Miata's, with early road tests showing 0-60-mph times as 11.5 and 8.9 seconds for the base and XR-2 models, respectively, versus the

The '91 Escort LX series consisted of three models: $8247 three-door hatchback (top), $8674 five-door hatch (center), and $9259 five-door wagon (bottom). LXs (and the Pony) utilized the Ford-built 1.9-liter four, which was newly updated with new sequential multi-point fuel injection and an electronic ignition system that eliminated the distributor. Horsepower was now rated at 88 at 4400 rpm and torque at 108 lbs/ft at 3800 rpm. All '91 Escorts rode a 98.4-inch wheelbase, 4.2 inches longer than before, and also measured about an inch longer overall. Curb weight, meanwhile, came in at a modest 2321-2446 pounds.

The '91 Explorer debuted in the spring of 1990 as a replacement for the Bronco II. Unlike the latter, it was offered as a five-door model as well as a three-door. It was larger, too, with a 111.9-inch wheelbase (102.1 on the three-door) and an overall length of 194.3 inches (174.4), and it was 450-650 pounds heavier.

Mazda's 8.5. Capri's suspension was more economy car than sports car, too, but it served up a very good ride/handling compromise, if not quite as satisfying as Miata's.

Mercury might have stolen a march on Mazda had it not been for production delays—mostly to tighten up workmanship—at Ford Australia, which had been tapped to build Capris not only for the U.S., but other world markets as well. Indeed, the car had made its public debut at the 1988 Chicago Auto Show, but wouldn't go on sale for another two years.

How it will fare is another question that can't be answered at this writing, but there's probably more than enough room for Capri to succeed even in today's more-crowded-than-ever U.S. market. It certainly debuted dressed for success.

Among numerous standard features were power steering and brakes, power windows, tinted glass, power-remote mirrors, electronic AM/FM stereo radio, and three-speed intermittent wipers. Besides turbo go and a suitably stiffer chassis, the XR-2 added air conditioning, foglamps, aluminum wheels, cruise control, cassette player, and blower boost gauge. A lift-off hardtop was optional. If nothing else, the Capri was another heartening sign that fun cars still have a big place in Dearborn—and always will have. But it'll take much more for Ford to prosper in the years ahead, as the company itself knows all too well. Judging by what is known of its near-term product plans, Ford's chances for continued success look pretty good. Herewith, a few details.

Scheduled for '91 are light facelifts for Mustang and Tempo/Topaz, as well as

the return of available 302 V-8 power for base and LX Thunderbirds and all Mercury Cougars. Next comes a Town Car-style aero reskin for the 1992 Crown Victoria and Mercury Grand Marquis, which bow early in calendar '91 with the same general new low-drag look but different details—notably a Jaguar-like "six-light" roofline on the Crown Vic versus the Marquis' conventional four-window (and more formal) treatment. Intriguingly, both these rejuvenated Panthers will reportedly use more non-U.S. components so they can be counted as "imports"—and thus not count against Ford's domestic corporate average fuel economy numbers. This point is quite curious in that it is the direct opposite of what GM is doing to meet CAFE restrictions. GM is adding more domestic parts to its captive imports in an effort to get them reclassified as domestics. Who's right? Only time will tell.

A bit further out is a new Lincoln Mark VIII derived from the latest MN12 T-Bird/Cougar, with the usual styling distinctions, of course. A shortened version of this platform may also be the foundation for the next-generation Mustang, which should appear by the mid-Nineties. Due at about the same time are replacements for Taurus/Sable and Tempo/Topaz, though both may be needed well before. In the meantime, an all-new F-Series pickup and, presumably, a revamped big Bronco are due in 1991-92.

Also likely is a much-discussed new Ford minivan by mid-decade, and possibly two. One is the VX54, being developed in conjunction with Nissan. It's to be built by Ford at Avon Lake, Ohio, for sale by the L-M Division under a Mercury badge, and intended for Nissan dealers as well. Said to be a little larger and more luxurious than Aerostar, VX54 will likely be powered by a revamped version of Nissan's current 3.0-liter truck V-6, which will be supplied by the Japanese firm's Smyrna, Tennessee, transplant factory. Also in view is WIN88, a front-drive design to be derived from the next-generation Taurus as the replacement for Aerostar at Ford dealers, probably sometime in 1992. Less is known about this project, but it's doubtful that Dearborn will go ahead with it if GM proves unsuccessful in marketing both rear- and front-drive minivans (Astro/Safari and the new-for-'90 Chevy APV/Pontiac Trans Sport/Olds Silhouette). Definitely in the works is a fourth-generation full-size Econoline/Club Wagon, known internally as VN58. It, too, is slated for 1992 and will surely be more aerodynamic than the current, boxy 1975-vintage design.

Some intriguing engineering developments also lie ahead. Ford has lately experimented with Taurus bodyshells made entirely of glass-reinforced plastic, which may become a weight-reducing necessity given the much-stiffer fuel-economy mandates that seem likely to be enacted. Then there's the much-discussed "modu-

Due to its greater heft than Bronco II, the Explorer came with a standard 4.0-liter V-6, which developed 155 bhp and 220 lbs/ft torque. Prices started at $13,820 for an XL three-door 4×2 and escalated to $21,315 for an Eddie Bauer five-door 4×4. Ford expected 70 percent of sales to go to the five-door.

lar" powerplant: a family of V-engines spanning four, six, and eight cylinders and displacements of 2.0 to 4.0 liters. They will share a basic design to facilitate production on common tools in the interest of reducing costs. The first of these, a 4.0-liter V-8, is whispered to be for the 1991 Town Car, though other applications should follow in short order.

Ford has also been looking at two-stroke engines, as have GM, Chrysler, and several Japanese makers including Mazda. Indeed, Ford was among the first to take note of the so-called "orbital" two-stroke developed by Ralph Sarich, and—along with GM—concluded a licensing agreement with Australia's Orbital Engine Company, the current generally acknowledged leader in two-stroke technology. Advances in engine electronics over the past decade are one reason for the renewed widespread interest in two-strokes, not least because their traditional advantages of less weight, greater simplicity, and more efficient operation over four-stroke engines make them look appealing against the prospect of tighter fuel-economy standards (though not against more stringent emissions limits). While it's unclear just what role two-strokes may play in the future, there's a wide variety of approaches being tried—everything from cheap, simple inline "triples" and V-6s, which Ford is said to favor, to complex, multivalve super-charged units, which, not surprisingly,

are favored by the Japanese.

Equally uncertain are prospects for the all-wheel-drive Thunderbird that Ford had been developing with help from none other than Porsche of Germany. Several prototypes were built in 1988-89 and reportedly worked well, but the program has ostensibly been killed due to questions of profitability, plus weight and fuel consumption that looked excessive in light of forthcoming regulations. Interestingly, though, one of the AWD Bird prototypes was not returned to Porsche, as Ford decided to keep it for additional cold-weather testing. Does this mean the program still has a chance? Could be. As world history so graphically reminds us of late, most anything is possible.

Change, of course, is the one thing that can be depended upon—other than death and taxes, that is. Undeniably, the

automotive world is a far different place in 1990 than it was in 1980, just as Ford was a far different company. It's a safe bet that both will see equally profound changes—some good, some not so good—in the last decade of the Twentieth Century.

But it also seems safe to say that the firm old Henry built will not only survive, but thrive, in the years leading up to its historic centennial in 2003. The recent past has taught all of American industry some very hard and painful lessons, but Ford seems to be the one Detroit outfit most likely to remember them, and thus profit by them. In the end, that's perhaps the closest one can come to a guarantee that not only will there be more books about Ford Motor Company in the future, but more Ford Motor Company history for them to cover.

INDEX